THIRD EDITION

The Business of Fashion

DESIGNING, MANUFACTURING, AND MARKETING

THIRD EDITION

The Business of Fashion

DESIGNING, MANUFACTURING, AND MARKETING

Leslie Davis Burns
Nancy O. Bryant

OREGON STATE UNIVERSITY

Fairchild Publications, Inc.

New York

Director of Sales and Acquisitions: Dana Meltzer-Berkowitz
Executive Editor: Olga T. Kontzias
Acquisitions Editor: Joseph Miranda
Senior Associate Acquisitions Editor: Jaclyn Bergeron
Senior Development Editor: Jennifer Crane
Art Director: Adam B. Bohannon
Production Manager: Ginger Hillman
Associate Production Editor: Jessica Rozler
Photo Researcher: Erin Fitzsimmons
Assistant Editor: Blake Royer
Cover Design: Adam B. Bohannon
Cover Art: Photodisc

Developed and Produced by Focus Strategic Communications, Inc.
Project Manager: Adrianna Edwards
Development Editors: Linda Aspen-Baxter, Adrianna Edwards
Copy Editors: Linda Aspen-Baxter, Linda Szostak
Proofreaders: Linda Szostak, Susan McNish
Index: Ron Edwards
Art Director: Adrianna Edwards
Interior Design: Kyle Gell
Interior Layout: Valentino Sanna
Photo Research and Permissions: Elizabeth Kelly

Library of Congress Catalog Card Number: 2007931387

ISBN: 978-1-56367-570-6

GST R 133004424

Printed in the United States of America

CH07, TP13

Contents

Extended Contents

Preface

Since the publication of the second edition of *The Business of Fashion: Designing, Manufacturing, and Marketing*, the textile, apparel, accessories, home fashions, and retailing industries have continued to undergo tremendous change. Quick Response strategies have evolved into supply chain management, product lifecycle management, and fast fashion; Web-based business-to-business and business-to-consumer communications and commerce have grown; mass customization is being used in a variety of applications; trade agreements continue to affect sourcing options; and retailing venues continue to expand. As such, the third edition of this book attempts to capture the dynamics of the fashion industry by emphasizing the technological changes, organizational changes, and changes in the global dimensions of its various components.

The Business of Fashion focuses on the organization and operation of the U.S. fashion industry—how fashion apparel and accessories and home fashions are designed, manufactured, marketed, and distributed—within the global economy. As we investigate this ever-changing industry, it is important to set current strategies within their historical context. Thus, Chapter 1 begins with a history of the U.S. textile and apparel industry—from its inception in the late 1700s to the development and implementation of Quick Response, supply chain management strategies, and fast fashion. Once this historical context is set, we turn to current organizational structures and forms of competition among companies within the fashion industry. Chapter 2 discusses types of company ownership within the fashion business, including sole proprietorships, partnerships, and corporations. Because of the prevalence of licensing, licensing contracts and the advantages and disadvantages of licensing are discussed. Marketing channels within the industry (i.e., direct, limited, and extended), as well as marketing channel integration, are outlined and explained. The chapter ends with an overview of the laws affecting the textile, apparel, and home fashions industries, including laws protecting inventions and designs and laws related to business practices.

Chapter 3 outlines the organization and operation of the U.S. textile industry —that is, the designing, manufacturing, and marketing of fabrics used in the production of apparel and home fashions. We follow textile production from color forecasting and fiber processing through the marketing of seasonal lines of fabrics. Recent developments and issues within the industry, including textile trade, supply chain management strategies, technological advancements, and environmental issues, provide a basis for our understanding of future trends in the textile industry.

Chapter 4 focuses on the general classifications and organizational structures of apparel companies that produce men's, women's, and children's apparel. Comparisons between ready-to-wear and couture, and among types of producers, classifications of apparel brand names, and price zones, reinforce an appreciation of the complexities of the apparel industry. The major divisions within apparel organizations are introduced (research and merchandising, design and product development, operations, sales/marketing, advertising/sales promotion, and finance and information technology). Trade associations and trade publications also are introduced in this chapter.

Chapter 5 begins a four-chapter sequence on the creation and marketing of fashion apparel. This sequence follows an apparel line/collection through the various stages of research, design development and style selection, and marketing. Chapter 5 focuses on the various forms of research conducted prior to the development of the line/collection: consumer research, product research, market analysis, and fashion research. The chapter explains the importance of accurately profiling the company's target customer. Chapter 6 highlights the design stage—design inspiration, designing for the market niche, planning the line, designing sketches, and writing garment specification sheets. The creation of an apparel line continues in Chapter 7, which discusses design development and style selection, including the development of first patterns, sewing of prototypes, initial cost estimates, and selection of styles for the final line. This chapter also describes product development for two growing segments of the industry: private-label and store brand merchandise. The discussion concludes at the stage when the final line is marketed to retail buyers. Chapter 8 describes locations of and roles played by marts and trade shows in facilitating the marketing of apparel and home fashions. Next, it discusses how merchandise is sold through corporate selling and sales representatives. The chapter ends with an overview of marketing strategies used by apparel and home fashions companies in the distribution and promotion of their lines. Throughout this sequence of events in the creation and marketing of apparel and home fashions lines, the chapters highlight new technological developments, including product lifecycle management, business-to-business Web-based communications, global perspectives, and organizational changes within the industry.

Chapter 9 begins a four-chapter sequence on the production and distribution of apparel and home fashions. Preproduction processes, including determining production orders, factoring, ordering production fabrics, pattern finalization, pattern grading, making the production marker, and production cutting, are described. Chapter 10 outlines the sourcing options for apparel and home fashions production, and the criteria used by companies in making sourcing decisions. Issues surrounding domestic and foreign production of apparel and home fashions, such as sweatshops and human rights, are also discussed. Chapter 11 explores the various methods by which apparel is produced, focusing on new technological advancements in these methods. Manufacturing environments, including mass production, short-cycle production, and mass customization, are explained. Next, production sewing systems and technological developments in production equipment are described. The chapter ends with a summary of product finishing and the creation of floor-ready merchandise. Once produced, the merchandise is distributed, often through distribution centers, to retailers. Chapter 12 summarizes distribution strategies and processes used by apparel and home fashions companies. A description of the various types of store and nonstore retailers ends this chapter. Quick Response, product lifecycle management, and supply chain management strategies are also highlighted throughout this discussion of production and distribution.

Our focus turns to accessories and home fashions in Chapters 13 and 14. A strong relationship exists between these industries and the textile and apparel industries. Thus, an overview of the organization and operation of the primary accessories industries is included in Chapter 13. Chapter 14 introduces the various facets of the home fashions industry, with specific focus on the use of textiles in the production of home fashions such as sheets, towels, and draperies.

In introducing students to this dynamic, multifaceted business, the book incorporates real-world examples from its component industries. Near the end of Chapters 10, 11, and 12, Success Stories provide real-life examples of information that is presented in each of these chapters.

Career profiles are also included near the end of each chapter to give readers a sampling of the many career opportunities throughout the fashion industry. Other end-of-chapter features that help students prepare for their own entry into the fashion business include chapter summaries, lists of key terms, discussion questions, and references.

Many people have assisted with the development of this book, and we would like to thank them for their time, effort, and support. Leslie Burns would like to thank her students, former students, and colleagues at Oregon State University, who shared their ideas and resources in the development of the book. Leslie particularly appreciates her coauthor, Nancy Bryant, who brought extensive technical expertise and knowledge of the apparel industry to this work and was a true collaborator throughout the writing process.

Nancy Bryant would like to express her appreciation first to her coauthor, Leslie Burns, whose initial concept and direction for this book brought it into existence. Her knowledge of marketing and merchandising provided the text with the breadth necessary to reflect the industry as it operates now and as it will operate in the future. Her leadership through the publication process was invaluable. Nancy would also like to thank her former students for their continual sharing of information about the apparel industry. Many other professional contacts in the apparel industry also most willingly shared their expertise. The support of her colleagues at Oregon State University is deeply appreciated.

We wish to thank the following readers and reviewers on the first two editions of the book: Ardis Koester, Cheryl Jordan, Carol Caughey, and Elaine Pedersen, Oregon State University; and Pamela Ulrich, Auburn University. Readers selected by the publisher were also very helpful. They include Cindi Baker, Berkeley College; Martha Baker, University of Massachusetts-Amherst; Mary Boni, Kwantlen University College; and Robert L. Woods, Berkeley College. We owe our deepest appreciation to Jennifer Crane at Fairchild Publications and to Adrianna Edwards, Elizabeth Kelly, and the other members of the team at Focus Strategic Communications for their invaluable assistance with this book. Thank you!

Leslie Davis Burns
Nancy O. Bryant
Oregon State University

PART 1

Organization of the U.S. Textile, Apparel, and Home Fashions Industries

CHAPTER 1

From Spinning Machine to Fast Fashion

In this chapter, you will learn the following:

- the technological developments in the textile and apparel industries
- the history of the transition of the apparel industry from a craft industry to a factory-based industry
- the historical basis for the emergence of the Quick Response philosophy
- the forms of interindustry cooperation and technologies needed for the success of Quick Response strategies, including supply chain management
- characteristics of current trends affecting the textile apparel industries, including globalization and fast fashion

*T*he U.S. textile and apparel industries consist of large and small companies that design, produce, and market fibers, textiles, apparel, and home fashions products for consumers in the United States as well as around the world. These industries are among the largest and most productive in the world. Textile and apparel companies can be found in every state, employing one and a quarter million people. When apparel and home fashions distribution through retailers is included, these industries contribute to the economy of virtually every community in the nation. How did it all begin? How did these industries develop and grow into the dynamic industries they are today? To fully understand the modern textile, apparel, and home fashions industries, a brief review of how they began, grew, and changed over the past 200-plus years is important.

1789–1890: Mechanization of Spinning, Weaving, and Sewing

For thousands of years, the spinning and weaving of fabrics were labor-intensive hand processes. Then, in England, in the mid-1700s, the spinning of yarn and weaving of cloth began to be mechanized. At that time, England's cotton and wool textile industries were the most technologically developed in the western world. In response to a growing demand for textiles both in England and abroad, a series of advances in the spinning and weaving of fabrics by English inventors brought the British industry to world prominence. These inventions included the following:

- the flying shuttle loom invented by John Kay in 1733
- the spinning machine or "jenny" invented by James Hargreaves in 1764
- the water-powered spinning machine invented by Sir Richard Arkwright in 1769
- the mechanized **power loom** invented by Reverend Edmund Cartwright in 1785–1787

In addition, the process for printing fabrics was also being mechanized. England was protective of its technological developments, and severe penalties existed for attempting to take blueprints and/or machines or their parts out of the country. Even the mechanics themselves were restricted from leaving the country.

At the time, the textile factory system in England was not only one of the most productive, but also one of the most dehumanizing and unhealthy for the workers subjected to it. England's labor reform movement in the mid-1800s was a call for reform in the textile industry (Yafa, 2005).

In the United States, a fledgling cotton industry was taking root, but America lacked England's advanced technology for spinning and weaving cotton fibers. Then, in 1789, Samuel Slater, a skilled mechanic, brought English textile technology to the United States by memorizing the blueprints of the Arkwright water-powered spinning machine. Farmers were permitted to leave England, so he declared himself a farmer and came to the United States. He settled in New England where a ready supply of water existed. Hired by Moses Brown, a merchant, Slater set up a **spinning mill** similar to the one shown in Figure 1.1. Who would have thought that this small spinning mill in Pawtucket, Rhode Island, would prove that cotton yarn could be spun profitably in the United States? This mill, which opened in 1791, sparked the textile industry in the United States. Within a few years, spinning mills had sprung up all over New England. By the mid-1800s, towns such as Waltham, Lowell, Lawrence, and New Bedford, Massachusetts, and Biddeford, Maine, became centers of the newly emerging textile industry. A reliance on British inventions still existed;

Figure 1.1 Early spinning mills, as introduced by Samuel Slater, included carding, drawing, roving, and spinning.

any technological changes were based on reproducing and improving textile machinery used in England.

Although the spinning process was becoming mechanized, the weaving process continued to be contracted out to individual handweavers. In 1813, Francis Cabot Lowell originated a functional power loom. He set the stage for **vertical integration** within the industry; his factory was the first in the United States to perform mechanically all processes from spinning yarn to producing finished cloth under one roof. As early as 1817, power looms were being installed in textile mills all over New England. Despite the technological developments in weaving, the contracting out of the weaving process to handweavers for complex fabrics continued until the late 1800s.

The mechanization of spinning and weaving made these processes so much faster that fiber producers were pressured to supply a greater amount of cotton and wool. However, cotton growers in the South were limited by the time needed to handpick seeds from cotton. In 1794, Eli Whitney patented the **cotton gin** (*gin* for *engine*), which could clean as much cotton in one day as 50 men (see Figure 1.2). As a result of this invention, the cotton growers soon were able to supply New England's spinning and weaving mills with the needed amount of fiber.

To be closer to this very important source of cotton, manufacturers built textile mills in the southern states. The northeast continued to be a primary producer of wool fabrics. By 1847, more people were employed in textile mills than in any other industry in the United States. Unfortunately, the squalor of the textile factory towns in England was also found in textile factory towns in the northeastern and southeastern United States. It took many years for unions and labor reforms to improve the pay and factory working conditions for those in the textile industry. In the meantime, consumer demand for cotton increased, and, by the late 1890s, three-quarters of the clothing in Europe and the United States was made from cotton (Yafa, 2005).

Figure 1.2 The Whitney Cotton Gin, constructed by Eli Whitney, increased the speed of the cotton-cleaning process.

The **ready-to-wear (RTW)** industry had its beginnings in the early eighteenth century. To meet the demand for ready-made clothing, tailors would make less expensive clothes from scrap material left over from sewing custom-made suits. Sailors, miners, and slaves were the primary target market for these early ready-made clothes, which were cut in "slop shops" and sewn by women at home. The term *slops* later became a standard term for cheap, ready-made clothing.

In the early nineteenth century, the demand for ready-to-wear clothing grew. The expanding number of middle-class consumers wanted good-quality apparel but did not want to pay the high prices associated with custom-made clothing. However, it was not until the sewing process of apparel production became mechanized that ready-to-wear apparel became available to the majority of consumers. **Sewing machine** inventions by Walter Hunt (1832), Elias Howe (1845), and Isaac Singer (1846) made it possible for apparel to be produced by machine, thereby speeding the process by which it could be made. From 1842 to 1895, 7,339 patents for sewing machines and accessories were issued in the United States. The advertisement in Figure 1.3 shows how competitive the business had become. The sewing machine allowed relatively unskilled immigrant workers to sew garments in their homes. In addition, sewing factories were established, with some of the first men's clothing factories appearing as early as 1831. In fact, Singer's sewing machine, patented in 1851, was designed for factory use.

In the United States, men's RTW developed first. Children's RTW followed, with boys' apparel developing before girls' apparel. The last to develop was women's RTW apparel. Men's RTW developed first because men's **size standards** existed for apparel producers to use. The development of men's wear size standards and their use in sewing uniforms during the Civil War allowed further advances in the industry. The term *size standards* refers to the proportional increase or decrease in garment measurements for each size produced. Patterns could be made for a range of men's sizes. Thus, multiple sizes could be cut and sewn using mass-production methods. In addition, in the late nineteenth century, the styling of men's apparel was less complicated than that of women's apparel.

By 1860, a variety of ready-made men's clothing was available. Indeed, between 1822 and 1860, the ready-to-wear segment of the men's wear tailoring industry grew larger than the custom-made segment. Because of this increased demand, the number of sewing factories also grew.

A number of other advances contributed to the growth of the industry at this time. During the late 1800s, motorized cutting knives and pressing equipment were developed. **Mass production** of apparel was also facilitated by the invention

Figure 1.3 Sewing machine inventions provided increased speed in the production of apparel.

of paper patterns. Ebenezer Butterick started a pattern business in 1863; James McCall started a similar one in 1870. Thus, by the end of the nineteenth century, mechanization of the textile and apparel production processes resulted in a growing number of companies.

With the availability of ready-made clothing, distribution outlets to consumers in cities increased. Brooks Brothers, the first men's apparel store, opened in New York City in 1818 and catered primarily to sailors and working-class men who could not afford custom-tailored clothing. The mid-1800s saw the development of dry goods stores in cities, which later became department stores:

- In New York City's Greenwich Village, Lord & Taylor opened in 1826; in 1903, it was moved to Fifth Avenue.

- In Haverhill, Massachusetts, Macy's Wholesale and Retail Dry Goods House (see Figure 1.4, left) opened in 1857.
- In Chicago, Marshall Field's opened in 1852, and Carson Pirie Scott & Co. opened in 1854.
- In Philadelphia, John Wanamaker and Co. opened in 1869.

Although these stores initially offered a limited range of products, by the end of the Civil War, the range of merchandise expanded and included apparel.

To those consumers unable to shop in the cities, illustrated catalogs offered a wide variety of goods by the latter part of the nineteenth century. With the expansion of the U.S. postal service due to the introduction of parcel post in 1913, the continued development of railroads, and the introduction of rural free delivery (RFD) in 1893, a growing mail-order business for ready-made clothing was created by such companies as Montgomery Ward (established in 1872) and Sears, Roebuck & Co. (established in 1886). Table 1.1 summarizes these supply and demand needs for the emergence and growth of the textile and apparel industries in the United States.

Figure 1.4 Distribution of ready-to-wear apparel and accessories was facilitated by retail stores such as R.H. Macy's Dry Goods in New York City (left) and Rike's Department Store in Dayton, Ohio (right).

Supply and Demand Needs for the Emergence and Growth of Textile and Apparel Industries in the United States

SUPPLY

The need for plenty of fabric that could be produced quickly and the means to sew it quickly was achieved by the following:

- spinning machine (1764)
- power loom (1785–87)
- cotton gin (1794)
- sewing machine (1832, 1845, 1846)

The need for a ready supply of labor was achieved by immigrant workers who

- began production sewing in their homes
- were employed by sewing factories

DEMAND

The need for customers and consumer demand for mass-produced apparel was achieved by the following:

- sailors, miners, and slaves who needed cheap, ready-made clothing (slops)
- an expanding number of middle-class consumers who wanted good-quality apparel at "reasonable" prices

The need for a distribution system for mass-produced apparel and accessories was achieved by the following:

- mail-order catalogs
- general stores in rural areas
- department stores (mid-1800s) in cities

1890–1950: Growth of the Ready-to-Wear Industry

Although most men's apparel was available ready-made by the mid-nineteenth century, the women's RTW industry did not expand until the late nineteenth century (see Figures 1.5, 1.6, and 1.7). The first types of RTW apparel produced for women were outerwear capes, cloaks, and coats. Because these garments fit more loosely than fashionable dresses, sizing was not a critical problem. Manufactured corsets, petticoats, and other underwear items were also accepted by consumers, perhaps because these clothing items were hidden from public view. By the beginning of the twentieth century, RTW skirts and shirtwaists

Figure 1.5 The popularity of separates for women, epitomized by the "Gibson girl," led to a growth in RTW production.

(blouses) were offered for sale. The popularity of the shirtwaist, made fashionable by Charles Dana Gibson's "Gibson girl," shifted women's apparel production away from a craft industry to a factory-based industry. It was the shirtwaist and the popularity of *separates*—that is, coat, blouse (shirtwaist), and skirt worn by young working women in the cities—that provided the basis for the development of the women's RTW industry.

The production of RTW apparel was labor intensive. A ready supply of immigrant workers spurred the growth of the mass production of apparel. By 1900, approximately 500 shops in New York City were producing shirtwaists. The contracting system of production grew in popularity, as it was estimated that a $50 investment was all that was necessary to start a business with a few workers and a bundle of cut garments obtained from a manufacturer or wholesaler. Production was divided into two segments:

1. a large number of sewing operations located in the homes of immigrants producing lower-priced garments

2. a relatively small number of large, modern sewing factories engaged in the production of better-quality garments

These sewing factories, primarily on the Lower East Side of New York City, were notorious for their poor working conditions. The term *sweatshop* originally referred to the system of contractors and subcontractors whereby work was "sweated off." Later, the term became associated with the long hours, unclean and unsafe working conditions, and low pay of contract sewing factories, as well as with the dismal conditions of *home factories*, where contract workers sewed clothing.

Figure 1.6 By the 1890s, most men's apparel and some women's apparel were available as RTW.

In an effort to improve working conditions for the employees in the industry, most of whom were young immigrant women, the **International Ladies' Garment Workers' Union (ILGWU)** was formed in 1900 at a convention in New York City. The tragic fire in the Triangle Shirtwaist Co. factory on March 25, 1911, in which 146 young women died, brought public attention to the horrid working conditions and increased support for the ILGWU. (It is now part of the Union of Needletrades, Industrial, and Textile Employees, UNITE.)

In the 1920s, the women's fashion industry in New York moved from the Lower East Side to Seventh Avenue. This area of midtown Manhattan became known as New York's *garment district,* and it has remained the hub of women's fashions. The manufacturing of men's wear was less centralized, with Chicago, Baltimore, and New York emerging as manufacturing centers.

At the beginning of the twentieth century, the majority of RTW clothing was made from cotton and wool. Silk fabric, imported from France and Italy, was highly desired for its luxurious qualities. However, it was very expensive, and

Figure 1.7 Boys' apparel was also available as RTW by the 1890s.

the supply was limited. Therefore, when synthetic substitutes for natural fibers were initially explored, "artificial silk" (rayon, made from wood pulp) was the first to be developed and patented in the United States. The first American rayon plant was opened in 1910. Synthetic dyestuffs for textile dyeing were developed and available by the beginning of the twentieth century.

Other inventions made during this time became staples in the RTW industry. An invention called the *locker* was demonstrated at the Chicago World's Fair in 1893. Named the *zipper* in 1926, it was to have a major impact on the apparel industry. First used to fasten boots, the zipper was not generally used in fashion apparel until the 1930s.

Fashion magazines, such as *Vogue*, were first published in 1892. These magazines provided consumers with up-to-date fashion information and helped spur the desire for new fashions. Between 1910 and 1920, a variety of communication channels helped unite the fledgling RTW industry. Trade publications, such as the *Daily Trade Record* (men's wear), established in 1892, and *Women's Wear Daily*, established in 1910, provided a great impetus to the RTW industry.

Another step in the developmental progress of the RTW industry was the result of wartime manufacturing. World War I spurred the need for the manufacture of military uniforms, and, in turn, helped streamline apparel production methods. Also important to the U.S. textile and apparel industries was the closing of French and British fashion houses during the war, which allowed American fashion to develop from 1914 to 1918.

Although most items of women's clothing were available ready-made by the early 1900s, growth in the garment industry came about with the simplification of garment styles in the 1920s (see Figure 1.8). Who knows which came first? The simpler styles may have spurred the growth of the industry, but industry methods also affected the styles of apparel that could be produced for, and thus adopted by, consumers. By the 1920s, mass-produced clothing was available to the majority of individuals. The era of inexpensive fashion had begun. New styles and variety became more valued than costly one-of-a-kind apparel by the majority of consumers. Retail stores increased their inventory ratio of moderately priced clothing in proportion to more expensive goods.

Figure 1.8 The loose-fitting styles of the 1920s were ideal for mass production.

A new development in retailing during this decade was the country's first outdoor shopping mall. The Country Club Plaza was built in 1922 in Kansas City, Kansas. It remains a gem among shopping malls, with its Spanish-style architecture and fountains reminiscent of Seville, Spain.

The boyish chemise-style dresses of the 1920s were easy to manufacture because there were few contours to shape and fit. This loose, boxy style also fit a wider variety of figures than did previous styles. However, this style was not favored by the textile manufacturers because it utilized approximately one-third less yardage per garment than the styles of the previous decade. With the growing popularity of movies, movie stars began to influence the fashion preferences of consumers. Fashion news also became available over a new invention—the radio. Fortunately for textile manufacturers, the women's garment styles of the 1930s used more fabric than those of the 1920s.

New York City remained the center of the women's fashion industry, and Seventh Avenue was becoming synonymous with women's fashion. By 1923, New York City was producing nearly 80 percent of U.S. women's apparel in the city's growing garment district. Also during the 1920s, specialized sewing machines were developed, such as overlockers (sergers) and power-driven cutting equipment.

As mass communications expanded in the 1920s, so did the flow of fashion information. France dominated the fashion scene, where a new generation of high-fashion designers, including Patou, Chanel, Vionnet, and Schiaparelli, was rising. Covering the fashion shows in Paris and bringing this news to American consumers was a huge undertaking. In 1926, more than 100 reporters covered the Paris couture openings for newspapers and magazines.

When the stock market crashed in 1929, it devastated all aspects of the American economy. Repercussions were felt in Paris, as retail stores and private clients canceled orders overnight. The Great Depression of the 1930s, which resulted from the 1929 stock market crash, caused a severe blow to the textile and apparel industries. These and other industries did not recover until the start of World War II. In 1929, it was estimated that New York had 3,500 dress companies; by 1933, there were only 2,300.

However, the 1930s brought about the development of the first "synthetic" fibers synthesized entirely from chemicals. Because most manufactured fibers were developed as substitutes for natural fibers, their properties were intended to emulate those of silk, wool, and cotton. Nylon, the first synthetic fiber, was conceptualized by E. I. du Pont de Nemours and Company in 1928, successfully synthesized in 1935, marketed in 1938, and introduced in nylon stockings in 1939. However, nylon production for consumer use was interrupted by

World War II, so that its widespread use for consumer products did not come until after the war.

It also became more common for manufacturers to contract and subcontract some of the sewing operations. Some contractors specialized in specific processes, such as fabric pleating. For example, the manufacturer would ship the needed quantity of yard goods to the contractor for pleating. The contractor would return the pleated goods to the apparel manufacturer. Then the manufacturer would proceed with cutting and sewing operations.

During the 1930s, a number of large dress and sportswear companies emerged and grew in New York. In addition, the sportswear industry in California and other western states began to expand. The California sportswear industry actually began in the 1850s, when Levi Strauss & Co. began production of work trousers. It was not until the 1930s that sportswear made by other companies, such as White Stag, Jantzen, Cole of California, Pendleton Woolen Mills, and Catalina, became popular. The sportswear trend was further legitimized by American designers, such as Claire McCardell and Vera Maxwell. These designers introduced informal, casual "designer" clothing in the late 1930s.

A number of fashion magazines also debuted in the 1930s, each catering to a particular segment of consumers. *Mademoiselle*, established in 1935, and *Glamour*, first published in 1939 as *Glamour of Hollywood*, catered to fashionable college coeds and young working women. *Esquire*, first published in 1933, was designed to enlighten men about the world of fashion and elegance. Movies of the era also served as a source of fashion information for consumers, and movie stars became the fashion leaders of the day (see Figure 1.9).

Figure 1.9 The 1930s brought a growth in the sportswear industry and the influence of California (particularly Hollywood) on fashion.

Brand names of manufacturers gained strong consumer recognition during the 1930s. One of the first to gain national recognition was the Arrow shirt. Launched in 1905, the Arrow shirt advertising campaign continued for many years. The ads featured color fashion illustrations of a very sophisticated male, wearing an Arrow shirt, engaged in a variety of activities suitable to a man of taste and leisure. These ads remain classic examples of lifestyle advertising.

By the 1930s, the college student and young working woman were clearly identified as target customers for the fashion industry; special markets included junior and large-size customers. Size standards were widely adopted by the industry after the U.S. Department of Agriculture published size measurements in 1941. The demand for good-quality RTW was strong, and fashion news spread quickly.

A number of changes in the 1940s had profound influences on the U.S. apparel industry. Although World War II devastated the fashion industry in France, Paris emerged once again after the war as a prominent player in the international fashion industry. However, the war did allow American designers such as Claire McCardell to become well known among consumers. The United States became known as the sportswear capital, and it held on to this title even after the Paris fashion houses reopened.

The U.S. fashion industry founded several organizations during the 1930s and 1940s to strengthen and promote the industry. These organizations included The Fashion Group International, the New York Couture Group, and the California Fashion Creators. The Coty American Fashion Critics Award was founded in 1942 to recognize outstanding American fashion designers.

By the 1940s, the production of ready-to-wear clothing was located primarily in modern factories. Because of rising costs in New York City, factories had been built in New Jersey, Connecticut, and upstate New York. Apparel manufacturing factories also were springing up in other parts of the country. The apparel industry in California, centered in Los Angeles, emerged as the hub for the growing active and casual sportswear industry in the West. Dallas, Texas, also gained prominence in apparel manufacturing.

1950–1980: Diversification and Incorporation

The 1950s saw not only a general growth in consumer demand for apparel, but also a shift in the product mix demanded by consumers. Because of lifestyle changes, casual clothing and sportswear were an expanding segment of the fashion industry. In fact, between 1947 and 1961, wholesale shipments of casual apparel and sportswear increased approximately 160 percent. During the same period, suit sales decreased by approximately 40 percent.

Teenage fashion developed as a special category during the 1950s (see Figure 1.10). It reached its peak during the youth explosion of the 1960s, when "mass fashion" became affordable to the majority of the population. In 1965, half the U.S. population was under 25, and teenagers spent $3.5 million annually on apparel.

Spurred by increased orders from the military in the early 1950s, the textile industry also grew. In 1950, Burlington ranked as the largest Fortune 500 textile manufacturer, with annual sales just over $1 billion.

Developed in the 1940s, acrylic and polyester were available to the U.S. market by the early 1950s. Triacetate was introduced in 1954, and it provided a less heat-sensitive alternative to acetate, a previously developed synthetic fiber. The use of synthetic fibers in apparel provided consumers with easy-care, wrinkle-free, and "drip-dry" clothing that freed them from the high demands of caring for cotton and woolen clothing. These new fibers provided lower-cost and

Figure 1.10 Ozzie and Harriet Nelson, with sons David and Ricky. Spurred by the popularity of television and pop music, teenage fashion became a separate category in the 1950s.

lighter-weight alternatives. Textile mills developed new texturizing processes that made possible such innovations as stretch yarn. Nylon stretch socks became available in 1952. Later in the decade, nylon stretch pants became a fashion sensation.

In the 1960s, synthetic fibers began to overtake natural fibers in popularity. Apparel designers, such as Pierre Cardin, experimented with space-age materials. Plastic was used extensively, and heat-fusing techniques were developed. The natural fiber industry fought back with strong organizations such as the Cotton Council and the International Wool Secretariat. Eventually, natural fibers would again gain public favor, but not until after the 1970s—the decade of America's love affair with polyester.

After World War II came Christian Dior's New Look, and consumer attention turned again to Paris. During the 1950s and 1960s, Parisian haute couture continued to set fashion trends worldwide. However, increased productivity in mass-produced clothing made it possible for designer fashions to be copied and reproduced at a fraction of the cost of haute couture (see Figure 1.11). During this period, ready-to-wear fashions became the standard worldwide, and "Chanel" suits, which were less expensive copies of the originals, were available to everyone. Since the 1970s, haute couture has been overshadowed by mass-market apparel. In fact, currently all haute couture designers also create ready-to-wear collections.

One of the most apparent changes in the apparel industry during the late 1950s and throughout the 1960s was the increase in large, publicly owned apparel corporations. In 1959, only 22 public apparel companies existed, but, by the end of the 1960s, more than 100 apparel companies had become public corporations. Some companies that "went public" early on were Jonathan Logan, Bobbie Brooks, and Leslie Fay.

Because of the growth of suburbia in the United States, fewer people lived in cities, and consumers wanted shopping outlets closer to their new homes. Thus,

Figure 1.11 Mass-produced apparel, such as the clothing worn by these UCLA students in 1958, copied the couture designers of the time.

the shopping mall emerged. In 1956, Southdale Center, the first enclosed shopping mall, was built in a suburb of Minneapolis. During the 1960s, shopping malls appeared in virtually every suburb. Typically, regional or national department stores served as anchors.

During the 1960s and 1970s, American designer names saw increased prominence. Although American designers were first promoted by the Lord & Taylor department store in New York in the 1930s, it was not until the late 1960s that stores such as Saks Fifth Avenue featured specific American designers. Aware of the broad appeal of their names, designers such as Halston and Bill Blass ventured into licensing their names for a variety of products.

However, rising labor costs in the United States led to increased prices for consumers. In an attempt to keep costs down, retailers explored the idea of low overhead, self-service, and high-volume stores for apparel and other products. The strategy was successful, and retailers such as Kmart (see Figure 1.12), Target, Wal-Mart, and Woolco, known as *discounters*, flourished. In addition, as labor costs continued to rise, companies searched for a cheaper workforce. Their search began within the United States, particularly in the Southeast.

Figure 1.12   Discount retailers such as Kmart grew out of the attempt to keep merchandise costs down for consumers.

Then, it was expanded outside the United States, particularly in Hong Kong and Southeast Asia. Textile technology, once the domain of American companies, was increasingly imported from abroad. In 1967, for the first time in its history, the United States ran a trade deficit in textile machinery.

The 1970s saw the beginning of trends in which companies became vertically integrated, and large, publicly owned conglomerates bought apparel companies. For example, during this time, General Mills acquired Izod, David Crystal, and Monet jewelers; Consolidated Foods purchased Hanes hosiery and Aris gloves; and Gulf & Western bought Kayser-Roth.

Technological advances in the textile industry included a new generation of photographic printing and dyeing processes. Computer technology entered the textile and apparel manufacturing areas. The popularity of polyester double knit and denim fabrics sparked sales in the textile industry. However, increased competition from textile companies outside the United States cut into profits, and textile imports rose 581 percent between 1961 and 1976.

1980–Present: Quick Response to Fast Fashion

In the 1970s and early 1980s, the U.S. textile and apparel industries saw a decline in consumer demand for their products and an increase in labor, energy, and materials costs. Consumer demands for lower prices, quality merchandise, and better service were reflected in business strategies. During the 1980s, several of the largest department store groups were leveraged by management or as part of aquisitions and takeovers. Among the largest of these deals were the following:

- May Department Stores' acquisition of Associated Dry Goods in 1986
- Robert Campeau's purchase of Allied Stores in 1986 and Federated in 1988
- Macy's purchase of Bullock's and I. Magnin in 1988

Store acquisitions continued through the 1990s and early 2000s:

- Federated Department Stores acquired Macy's in 1994 and Broadway Stores in 1995.
- Profitt purchased Saks Fifth Avenue and smaller regional stores in 1998.
- In 2005, Federated Department Stores acquired May Department Stores and realigned the retailers under eight divisions: one Bloomingdales and seven Macy's divisions. With this acquisition, retailers such as Abraham & Straus, Bon Marché, Burdines, Filene's, L.S. Ayres, Marshall Field's, Meier & Frank, and Robinsons-May were converted to the Macy's moniker.

However, not all retailers were able to adapt to the changing retailing environment. By the late 1990s, many well-known retailers were out of business, including B. Altman & Co., Bonwit Teller, Gimbels, E. J. Korvette, I. Magnin, Peck & Peck, and The Broadway. At the same time, stores such as Nordstrom, The Limited, Gap, Target, and Wal-Mart were thriving.

The 1980s and 1990s also saw an increase in vertical integration among manufacturing and retailers. Vertical integration is a business strategy whereby companies control several steps of the design, production, marketing, and/or distribution of products. Strategies included the following:

- manufacturers (e.g., Nike, Tommy Hilfiger, Liz Claiborne) opening or expanding retail store operations
- department and specialty stores entering into partnerships with manufacturers and contractors to produce private-label merchandise for their stores
- retail stores (e.g., The Limited, Gap, Banana Republic, Old Navy, Victoria's Secret, Eddie Bauer) adopting a *store brand* concept, whereby the store offers only merchandise with the store name as its brand

With the introduction of e-commerce in the mid-1990s, many companies began experimenting with online business. At this time, the idea of multichannel retailing meant that a bricks-and-mortar store might also have a seasonal catalog. A number of issues needed to be resolved before online retailing would become readily accepted. Retailers struggled with the relationships between bricks-and-mortar stores and online extensions. Both retailers and consumers were skeptical about the security of ordering merchandise online. For example, in 1998, Liz Claiborne launched its Web site lizclaiborne.com as an information/branding Web site only. They relaunched the site in 2000 as an e-commerce destination. By the beginning of the twenty-first century, online retailing became an important component of many retailers' multichannel approach.

During the early 1980s, certain segments of the industry were affected by the continued growth of textile and apparel imports. Companies such as Liz Claiborne, founded in 1976, and Nike, Inc. founded in 1972, were producing apparel worldwide in order to obtain the best labor price for production. Concern about rising labor costs in the United States and the continued surge of imports led industry executives to join forces in examining ways to improve the productivity of the U.S. textile and apparel industries. Analyses indicated that apparel manufacturers and retailers were working with a 66-week (1¼-year) cycle to go from raw fiber to a garment on the retail selling floor. It was estimated that for 55 weeks (83 percent of this cycle), products were in inventory.

Thus, products were actually being processed for only 11 weeks (*Quick Response*, 1988). Industry executives recognized that this represented a huge inefficiency.

In 1984–1985, the Crafted with Pride in U.S.A. Council engaged Kurt Salmon Associates, textile and apparel industry analysts, to analyze industry inefficiencies. This project developed the idea of **Quick Response (QR)** to describe a philosophy that promoted potential ways to increase efficiencies.

The following year, the Crafted with Pride in U.S.A. Council sponsored pilot projects linking fabric producers, apparel manufacturers, and retailers to determine if QR was feasible, and to identify obstacles and difficulties in implementing QR strategies. Results from these pilot projects, in terms of increases in sales, *stock turnover* (the number of times during a specific period that the average inventory on hand has been sold), and *return on investment* (relationship between company profits and investment in capital items), were positive.

A few mass merchants and department stores, as well as top name-branded manufacturers, ventured to implement new technologies (Hasty, 1994). Because investments in technology led to higher productivity, companies found that their investments paid off quickly. Pioneers in QR included textile companies such as Milliken and Burlington; apparel manufacturers such as Haggar, Levi Strauss, and Arrow; and retailers such as Dillard's, JCPenney, and Belk, among others.

What Is Quick Response?

The phrase *Quick Response* is an umbrella term used to identify various management systems and business strategies in the textile and apparel industries that reduce the time between fiber production and sale to the ultimate consumer. Specific definitions of QR vary, depending on the industry division:

- For textile producers, QR focuses on connections among fiber producers, fabric producers, and apparel manufacturers.
- For apparel manufacturers, QR focuses on increased use of technology and connections among fabric producers, apparel producers, and retailers.

The Quick Response Leadership Committee of the American Apparel Manufacturing Association (AAMA, 1995) defines Quick Response as follows:

> A comprehensive business strategy to continually meet changing requirements of a competitive marketplace which promotes responsiveness to consumer demand, encourages business partnerships, makes effective use of resources, and shortens the business cycle throughout the chain from raw materials to the consumer.

In general, these strategies include the following:

- increasing the speed of design and production through the use of computers
- increasing the efficiency with which companies communicate and conduct business with one another
- reducing the amount of time goods are in warehouses or in transit
- decreasing the amount of time needed to replenish stock on the retail floor

Quick Response is a change from the *push system* of the past, in which supply-side strategies were used to push the products produced on the consumer. In contrast, QR is a *pull system* of demand-side strategies that are based on the flow of timely and accurate information about consumers' wants and needs from consumers to the manufacturers.

Quick Response strategies are implemented at all stages of the textile and apparel manufacturing and distribution processes, generally referred to as the **marketing channel** or **marketing pipeline**, from fiber production to retail sale to the ultimate consumer. As such, QR strategies will be discussed throughout this text. Business strategies that fall under the QR umbrella include the following:

- use of computer-aided design and manufacturing systems
- use of the most efficient fabric and apparel production systems
- use of UPC bar codes on merchandise and shipping cartons
- receiving and sharing of product information
- sending of orders and other forms electronically

In other words, any business strategy that improves accuracy and/or quality and reduces the amount of time used in the production and distribution of fabric and apparel can be considered part of QR.

It soon became apparent that the key barrier in the implementation of QR was the use of a variety of computer systems by manufacturers and retailers and the lack of standards within the industry. Thus, in the mid-1980s, interindustry councils were formed to establish voluntary communications standards. Once these standards were instituted and adopted, companies that had embraced QR saw growth in sales and market share. By the late 1990s, virtually all successful firms had implemented some QR strategies. Even though the phrase *Quick Response* is used in conjunction with the slogans *Made in U.S.A.* and *Crafted with Pride in U.S.A.*, QR strategies have also been adopted by overseas apparel manufacturers, especially those manufacturers that work with large retailers in the United States (Douglas-David, 1989).

Industry Cooperation and Partnerships

For Quick Response strategies to be successful, cooperation among the various components of the textile, apparel, and retailing industries is essential (see Figure 1.13). A level of trust also must exist between companies for many of the strategies to be effective. For example, with QR, because fabric is inspected for flaws at the mill, apparel producers do not have to reinspect it at the apparel plant. However, the apparel producers must trust that the fabric producers have adequately inspected the fabric. A number of partnerships were formalized to focus on ways in which companies within the various industries could best cooperate to increase productivity. These partnerships included **Textile/Clothing Technology Corporation ([TC]²)**, industry linkage councils, the Crafted with Pride in U.S.A. Council, and the American Textile Partnership.

TEXTILE/CLOTHING TECHNOLOGY CORPORATION

In the late 1970s, Harvard professors John T. Dunlop and Frederick H. Abernathy assessed the productivity of the U.S. apparel industry within the global economy. They argued that new approaches were needed to reduce labor

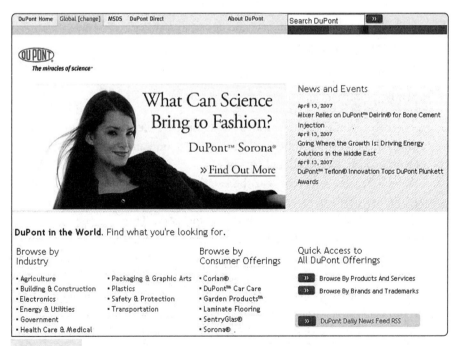

Figure 1.13   The Internet and World Wide Web are being used to enhance communications among companies in the textile, apparel, and retailing industries.

costs if the apparel industry was to maintain its market share. This study led to a two-day conference of industry, union, government, and university representatives to plan a joint research and development program. This 1979 conference led to much industry speculation about the viability of a joint research and development program.

In 1980, the Tailored Clothing Technology Corporation ([TC]^2) was established by the Amalgamated Clothing and Textile Workers Union (ACTWU), three men's suits manufacturers (Hartmarx, Palm Beach, and Greif), and the men's wear division of fabric producer Burlington Industries (Kazis, 1989). In 1985, the name was changed to the Textile/Clothing Technology Corporation to better reflect its broader focus (see Figure 1.14, left). Currently, [TC]^2 remains a nonprofit consortium of over 200 textile, apparel, retail, labor, and government organizations with the mission of being the "provider of solutions for the sewn products and related soft goods industries specializing in technology development and supply chain improvement" ([TC]^2, 2006).

Since its beginning, [TC]^2 has focused on developing, testing, and teaching advanced apparel technology that could contribute to the reduction of direct labor costs involved in the production of apparel made in the United States. Initially, its work focused on automating the men's tailored clothing industry, but the group's current work is much broader in nature and represents needs throughout the entire fiber-textile-apparel industry. The work of [TC]^2 includes 3D body scanning (see Figure 1.14, right), sizing, and inkdrop printing.

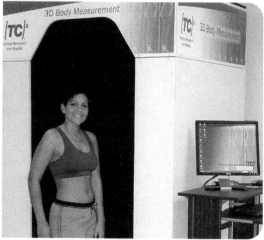

Figure 1.14 Established in 1980, [TC]^2 (left) conducts research and development for the apparel industry. An example of the technology provided by [TC]^2 is 3D body scanning (right).

One of the biggest challenges for [TC]^2 was to gain the support of small and midsize apparel companies through technology transfer. Therefore, in 1988, a "teaching factory," the National Apparel Technology Center, was opened. Located in Cary, North Carolina, the objectives of the center are to demonstrate, educate, and carry out short-term development of state-of-the-art equipment for apparel production. These objectives are carried out through teaching facilities/factories, educational services, computer simulation services for companies, and research and development projects (e.g., body scanning, knitwear automation, and digital printing).

INTERINDUSTRY LINKAGE COUNCILS

In the mid-1980s, a number of councils were formed to develop and encourage the use of voluntary standards to facilitate faster, more accurate information flow between producers and suppliers (see Figure 1.15). The **Voluntary Interindustry Communications Standards (VICS) Committee** was formed in 1986 by a group of industry executives who wanted to "take a global leadership role in the ongoing improvement of the flow of product and information about the product throughout the entire supply chain in the retail industry" (VICS Mission Statement). Their initial efforts focused on the following:

- gaining agreement among retailers and producers on the use of the Universal Product Code (UPC) system (bar codes) to identify products and to acquire accurate information on consumers' purchases on an individual stock-keeping unit (SKU) basis
- encouraging the creation of common item-identification standards for yarn and fabric products used in the production of consumer apparel and textile items
- gaining agreement on a single set of communication formats and electronic data interchange (EDI)
- encouraging the development of equipment to record and make available to producers information concerning consumer purchases of these products

VICS was very successful in meeting these objectives. In 1987, the UPC-A bar code was recommended for branded general merchandise, including apparel. This voluntary standard was later endorsed by the National Retail Merchants Association (now called the National Retail Federation) and the International Mass Retailer Association. Shipping container marking (SCM) standards were also established. These marking standards support the flow of merchandise through distribution centers.

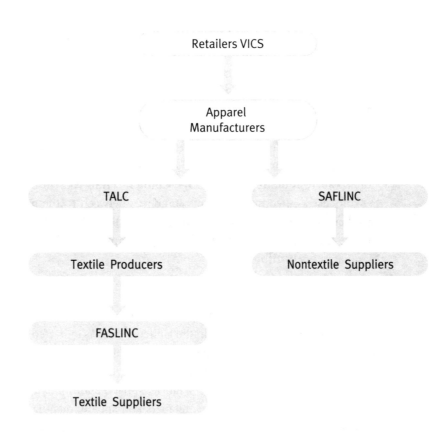

This flowchart depicts the role of interindustry linkage councils in the Quick Response chain.

In terms of EDI, a retail-specific version of the ANSI X.12 standard was published and made available through the Uniform Code Council. This standard was developed by the American National Standards Institute (ANSI), a national voluntary organization of companies and individuals who develop standardized business practices. The retail-specific version of the ANSI X.12 standard focuses on electronic transmission of data for business transactions, such as purchase orders and invoices.

Once these standards were put in place, the VICS committee focused on conducting cost/benefit analyses of using VICS for UPC marking, EDI, and shipping container marking. Under a new name, the **Voluntary Interindustry Commerce Standards (VICS) Association**, this organization has published reports on recommended floor-ready merchandise standards and recommended technologies for Internet commerce.

The **Textile/Apparel Linkage Council (TALC)** and **Sundries and Apparel Findings Linkage Council (SAFLINC)** were originally formed in 1986 and 1987, respectively, to establish voluntary EDI standards between apparel manufacturers and their suppliers. Since that time, the councils have completed and published all of the required standards. In 1992, they merged to form TALC/SAFLINC, and in 1994, they were integrated into the Quick Response Committee of the American Apparel Manufacturers Association (now part of the American Apparel and Footwear Association).

The **Fabric and Suppliers Linkage Council (FASLINC)**, also organized in 1987, focused on communications standards between textile manufacturers and their suppliers. After completing its goals, FASLINC disbanded in 1991, leaving the implementation of future programs to the American Textile Manufacturers Institute.

CRAFTED WITH PRIDE IN U.S.A. COUNCIL

The **Crafted with Pride in U.S.A. Council** is a "one-industry" approach to marketing textiles and apparel made in the United States. As indicated in its mission statement, "The Crafted with Pride in U.S.A. Council, Inc. is a committed force of U.S. cotton growers and shippers, labor organizations, fabric distributors and manufacturers of man-made fibers, fabric, apparel and home fashions whose mission is to convince consumers, retailers and apparel manufacturers of the value of purchasing and promoting U.S.-made products" (Crafted with Pride in U.S.A. mission statement). From its conception in 1984, the Crafted with Pride in U.S.A. Council has played an important role in coordinating unified efforts among the various segments of the industry to communicate to consumers that "buying American" matters for them and for the U.S. economy. This has been accomplished by the use of TV spots, magazine supplements, syndicated columns and newsletters, labels and hangtags, in-store displays, and other promotions (see Figure 1.16).

Figure 1.16 Crafted with Pride in U.S.A. logo

AMERICAN TEXTILE PARTNERSHIP

During the 1990s, a number of other partnership groups were formed to build cooperative efforts. The American Textile Partnership (AMTEX) strives to "enhance the competitiveness of the U.S. Textile

Industry, from fibers through fabricated products and retail, by implementing technologies developed in collaborative R&D programs that link the scientific and engineering resources of government, universities, and industry" (AMTEX Mission Statement). AMTEX links Department of Energy laboratories operated by the U.S. government with nonprofit technical organizations such as [TC]². AMTEX projects include Demand Activated Manufacturing Automation (DAMA), Computer-Aided Fabric Evaluation (CAFE), and Textile Resource Conservation (TReC).

Beyond QR: Supply Chain Management and RFID

By the late 1990s, QR strategies had been adopted by large and small companies alike. By this time, three types of apparel companies made up the supply chain for soft goods (Parnell, 1998):

- companies that performed almost all of their own manufacturing, from yarn or fabric to finished garments or other textile products

- companies that had a particular niche within the industry, performing specific manufacturing operations such as manufacturing yarns or fabrics, finishing fabrics, or performing sewing operations

- companies that were involved in the design, marketing, and distribution of apparel but contracted sewing operations to other companies, either domestically or in other countries

For each type of company, QR highlighted the importance of and need for additional partnerships among companies throughout the soft goods pipeline. With advances in information technology, the ways companies design, manufacture, and distribute soft goods were affected. This philosophy of sharing and coordinating information across all segments of the soft goods industry was termed **supply chain management (SCM)**. Supply chain management comprises the "collection of actions required to coordinate and manage all activities necessary to bring a product to market, including procuring raw materials, producing goods, transporting and distributing those goods, and managing the selling process" (Abend, 1998, p. 48).

Similar to QR, the goals of SCM are to reduce inventory, shorten the time for raw material to become a finished product in the hands of a consumer, and provide better service to the consumer. Collaboration, trust, and dependability are the cornerstones to making both the QR and the SCM processes effective. However, some analysts view SCM as what enables the QR philosophy to be successful. SCM goes beyond QR in that SCM companies share forecasting, point-of-sale data, inventory information, and information about unforeseen changes in supply or demand for materials or products.

By 2002, large companies, such as VF Corporation, invested in the information technology infrastructure to make SCM a reality. As **business-to-business (B2B)** Web-based technologies emerged, both smaller and larger companies have implemented effective supply chain management strategies for information sharing. Through the use of password-protected Web sites, businesses can share information and conduct business transactions effectively and efficiently.

As supply chain management strategies brought increased efficiencies to companies, new technologies continued to provide companies with tools for communication and integration. One such tool was **Radio Frequency Identification (RFID)** (see Figure 1.17). RFID is sometimes referred to as the next generation bar code as its primary functions are to increase supply chain management through the tagging of containers, pallets, and individual items so that they can be accurately tracked as they move through the supply chain. However, unlike bar codes, RFID tags do not rely on line-of-sight readability. In fact, multiple RFID tags can be read simultaneously; they have memory and, therefore, can store and update data, and they provide fully automated data collection. Large

Figure 1.17 RFID tags are now used by many large retailers and suppliers to increase supply chain management.

global retailers, such as Wal-Mart and Target, have pushed the adoption of RFID by requiring all their suppliers to apply RFID tags to pallets and cases.

Although RFID tags are significant in increasing efficiencies along the supply chain, concerns have been raised about item-level tagging. For example, because RFID tags are always "on," are there privacy issues when tags are placed on individual items? In 2005, Mitsukoshi, a Japanese department store, successfully piloted the use of RFID tags on selected shoes. In 2006, Marks & Spencer, a U.K. retailer, launched a trial of using RFID tags on certain individual apparel items to improve its inventory management. RFID tags are also being used as a means to identify authentic products from counterfeit products. However, for most suppliers and retailers, item-level RFID tagging remains too expensive and does not yet provide significant economic advantages over the use of bar codes.

Globalization and Fast Fashion

Although the textile, apparel, home fashions, and retailing industries have been an integral part of the process of **globalization** for decades, the end of the twentieth century and the beginning of the twenty-first century brought increased attention to how the industries would adapt to and reflect the evolving global economy. Globalization is a process whereby the economies of nation states become integrated. Trade among countries for fibers, fabrics, apparel, home fashions, and the machinery needed to produce textiles and apparel has contributed to globalization. From its inception, the textile and apparel industries have offered countries opportunities for increased employment and economic growth. Regulation of international trade has evolved over the centuries, with countries setting up trade incentives and barriers as mechanisms for improving their economies or protecting domestic industries.

In 1995, the World Trade Organization (WTO) was created as a vehicle by which member countries (150 as of 2007) would decide on the rules of trade with an overall goal of enhancing international trade. It was decided that many of the barriers to trading textiles and apparel would be removed over a 10-year period (1995–2004). Thus, countries such as the United States that protected their domestic production of textiles and apparel through the use of quotas (numerical limits on imports) and tariffs (taxes on imports) would be required to lower or eliminate these barriers to trade. These new rules have resulted in countries redefining their roles in order to maximize their competitive advantages:

- Countries such as the United States and France are focusing primarily on design and marketing.

- Countries such as China and India are focusing primarily on production.
- Other countries are exploring the appropriate niches for their expertise and infrastructure. For example, Japan and Taiwan are producers of high-tech textiles.

As the twentieth century came to a close, reflections of the industries 100 years earlier were seen. The same inhumane conditions of the early textile factory towns in England and the United States were found again in factories around the world. In 1996, President Clinton created the Apparel Industry Partnership to create a standardized code of conduct for apparel companies. Over the past decade, numerous companies have implemented codes of conduct, and they routinely monitor factories. These topics will be discussed in greater detail in Chapter 10.

Within this context of globalization and supply chain management, international companies have expanded their capabilities of vertical integration across countries. At the same time, consumers are demanding high-quality and fashion-forward products at reasonable prices. Creating this ultra-fast supply chain that focuses on consumer demand is known as **fast fashion**. One of the most successful fast-fashion companies is Zara (see Figure 1.18), a vertical

Figure 1.18   Zara is an example of a successful fast-fashion company.

retailer headquartered in Spain with over 800 stores in 60 countries. Its success is dependent upon the following:

- vertical integration (controlling many stages of the supply chain)
- making design and production decisions based on consumer demand
- offering consumers limited quantities of multiple styles of merchandise
- having the ability to produce merchandise in weeks instead of months

Indeed, Zara can design and produce a garment and distribute it to a retailer in just 15 days. Swedish company H&M, and U.S. companies such as Bebe, Forever 21, and Charlotte Russe, are also implementing fast-fashion philosophies.

Fast fashion relies on constant communication among all elements of a company's supply chain—from customers to store personnel, from store managers to designers and merchandisers, from designers to buyers and sourcing agents, from buyers to contractors, from contractors to warehouse managers and distributors. Although not all companies will be able to or even want to focus on all elements of fast fashion, aspects such as producing merchandise closer to the purchase by the ultimate customer are being copied by large and small companies worldwide.

Table 1.2   A Brief History of the U.S. Textile, Apparel, and Retailing Industries

1789–1890: Mechanization of Spinning, Weaving, and Sewing

1791	Samuel Slater, who came to the United States in 1788, opens the first U.S. spinning mill.
1793	Hannah Slater, Samuel's wife, invents the 2-ply cotton sewing thread.
1794	Eli Whitney's cotton gin is patented.
1818	Brooks Brothers opens in New York City.
1853	Levi Strauss joins the family business founded by his brother-in-law, David Stern, which will come to be known as Levi Strauss & Co.

Mid-1800s to late 1890s: Dry goods stores (forerunners of today's department stores) are opened:

1826—Lord & Taylor
1841—Jordan Marsh
1842—Gimbels
1849—Famous-Barr
1852—Marshall Field's
1854—Carson Pirie Scott & Co.
1857—R.H. Macy & Co.

Table 1.2 A Brief History of the U.S. Textile, Apparel, and Retailing Industries *(continued)*

	1862—Stewart's
	1867—Rich's
	1869—John Wanamaker and Co.
	1872—Bloomingdale Brothers, Inc.
	1898—Burdines
1854	The first U.S. trade association, Hampden County Cotton Manufacturers Association, starts in Hampden County, Massachusetts.
1860	Census data on the women's clothing industry indicated 96 manufacturers producing apparel worth $2,261,546 annually.
1865	William Carter begins knitting cardigan jackets in the kitchen of his house in Needham Heights, Massachusetts. The William Carter Co. will grow to be one of the nation's largest children's underwear companies.

1890–1950: Growth of the Ready-to-Wear Industry

1892	American *Vogue* magazine begins publication.
1892	*Daily Trade Record*, the trade newspaper for the RTW men's wear industry, begins publication; became *Daily News Record* in 1916.
1900	The International Ladies' Garment Workers' Union (ILGWU) is founded.
1901	Walin & Nordstrom Shoe Store opens in downtown Seattle.
1902	James Cash Penney, age 26, opens a dry goods and clothing store in Kemmerer, Wyoming. Opening day receipts totaled $466.59.
1904	New York seamstress Lena Bryant introduces ready-to-wear maternity wear. Her company, named Lane Bryant, becomes the first large-size ready-to-wear producer.
1907	Herbert Marcus, Sr., his sister Carrie, and brother-in-law, A.L. Neiman, start Neiman Marcus department store in Dallas.
1908	Filene's opens its "automatic bargain basement" in Boston. Merchandise in the upstairs store is automatically marked down 25 percent every week for three weeks, then sent to the basement. This practice marks the beginnings of the off-price store.
1909	In November, 20,000 New York shirtwaist makers stage the largest strike by American women to that time.
1910	*Women's Wear Daily*, trade newspaper for the women's wear industry, begins publication.
1911	146 garment workers die in a fire at the Triangle Shirtwaist Co. factory in New York's garment district. The tragedy stimulates a movement to end sweatshop conditions.
1914	The Amalgamated Clothing Workers of America Union is formed as the primary union for the men's wear industry.
1920	Membership in the ILGWU grows to 200,000.
1922	Country Club Plaza, the country's first outdoor shopping mall, opens in Kansas City, Kansas.

A Brief History of the U.S. Textile, Apparel, and Retailing Industries *(continued)*

1923	Pushed by the growing demand among women for ready-to-wear clothing, New York leads the growing industry, manufacturing 80 percent of all women's apparel.
1925	The first Sears Roebuck & Co. store opens in Chicago.
1926	J. M. Haggar starts his own men's wear company in Dallas, Texas, using assembly lines to manufacture men's trousers.
1927	The average price for women's full-fashioned silk stockings is $11.50 per dozen; by 1933 the price plummets to a low of $5.10 per dozen.
1928	Sanford Cluett develops a process to compress fabric under tension to reduce shrinkage, and the "Sanforized" trademark is licensed to cotton finishers.
1932	Sales at Sears, Roebuck & Co. retail stores surpass catalog sales.
1934	Membership in the ILGWU grows to 217,000.
1939	Textile Workers Union is founded.
1939	Nylon stockings are introduced.
1941	Congress fixes Thanksgiving, which previously had been a floating holiday in November, at the fourth Thursday in November. Fred Lazarus Jr. is credited with the idea as a way to expand the Christmas shopping season.
1941	Employment in the textile industry peaks at approximately 1.4 million.
1944	The Fashion Institute of Technology is founded to support New York's fashion industry.
1947	Leslie Fay is established—and becomes one of the largest women's apparel companies.
1949	Bloomingdale's opens its first branch store in Fresh Meadows, New York.

1950–1980: Diversification and Incorporation

1951	Employment in the apparel and knitwear industries in New York City peaks at 380,000.
1952	Stiletto heels are introduced by Christian Dior.
1952	Orlon® acrylic is introduced; by 1956, over 70 million Orlon sweaters are sold.
1955	Mary Quant opens her boutique, Bazaar, in London.
1956	Southdale Center, the first enclosed shopping mall, is built in a Minneapolis suburb to serve shoppers.
1957	*Gentlemen's Quarterly* is first published and distributed through men's wear stores.
1957	Christian Dior dies, and Yves Saint Laurent takes over as head designer of the House of Dior.
1958	Supp-hose, a 100 percent nylon stocking designed for women suffering from leg fatigue, is patented by the Chester H. Roth Co.
1958–59	To the benefit of intimate apparel, hosiery, and swimwear companies, DuPont introduces its first spandex fiber.
1960	Hanes-Millis Sales Corp. becomes the first national sock manufacturer to distribute its products through wholesalers.
1960	The first Bobbin Show takes place in Columbia, South Carolina, with 12 exhibitors.

Table 1.2   A Brief History of the U.S. Textile, Apparel, and Retailing Industries *(continued)*

1960	American Apparel Manufacturers Association (AAMA) is founded.
1964	John Weitz becomes the first American designer to put his name on a men's wear collection.
1967	Pierre Cardin and Bill Blass boutiques open in Bonwit Teller's New York store.
1968	Calvin Klein Ltd. is established.
1968	Polo Ralph Lauren is created.
1968	Minimum wage is increased to $1.60 per hour.
1969	The Gap opens in San Francisco, selling records, cassettes, and Levi's. The store drew its name from the "generation gap."
1970	L'eggs Products introduces egg-shaped packaging and self-service distribution for hosiery.
1970	First introduced in Europe, hot pants are a short-lived fad in America.
1971	Diane Von Furstenberg introduces her jersey wrap dress, which is an immediate success.
1972	The Care Labeling of Textile Wearing Apparel and Certain Piece Goods Act goes into effect.
1973	No nonsense hosiery is first distributed by Kayser Roth.
1975	Giorgio Armani Co. is founded, and Armani launches his first men's wear line.
1975	Geoffrey Beene becomes the first American designer to show his collections during fashion openings in Milan, Italy.
1975	John T. Malloy's *Dress for Success* is published.
1976	Liz Claiborne, Inc. is created and later grows to be the largest U.S. women's apparel company.
1976	The nation's first major warehouse retailer, Price Club, opens in San Diego.
1976	The Amalgamated Clothing Workers of America Union merges with the Textile Workers of America and the United Shoe Workers of America unions to form the Amalgamated Clothing and Textile Workers Union (ACTWU).
1977	Ralph Lauren designs the costumes for the movie *Annie Hall*.
1978	Calvin Klein introduces his first men's wear collection.

1980–Present: Quick Response to Fast Fashion

1980	[TC]² begins operation to research and demonstrate new computer technology in the textile and apparel industries.
1984	Donna Karan New York is founded by Donna Karan and her husband Stephan Weiss.
1984	Crafted With Pride in U.S.A. Council is formed.
1986	The Voluntary Interindustry Communications Standards (VICS) Committee is formed.
1986	May Department Stores acquires Associated Dry Goods.
1987	Christian Lacroix opens a new couture house in Paris.
1990	Tom Ford joins Gucci and becomes creative director in 1994; he later becomes creative director for YSL.
1991	Donna Karan launches her men's wear line.
1992	Levi Strauss & Co. establishes a code of conduct for contractors worldwide.

A Brief History of the U.S. Textile, Apparel, and Retailing Industries *(continued)*

1994	The North American Free Trade Agreement (NAFTA) goes into effect.
1994	Federated Department Stores acquires Macy's.
1995	The two primary labor unions in the textile and apparel industries—the Amalgamated Clothing and Textile Workers Union and the International Ladies Garment Workers Union— merge to become the Union of Needletrades, Industrial and Textile Employees (UNITE).
1995	Federated Department Stores acquires Broadway Stores.
1996	President Clinton creates the Apparel Industry Partnership to develop a plan to eliminate sweatshops.
1997	Designer superstar Gianni Versace is murdered.
1998	[TC]² makes a 3D body measurement system commercially available.
1998	Liz Claiborne, Inc. launches lizclaiborne.com as a branding/information Web site. It is relaunched in 2000 as an e-commerce Web site.
2000–06	Liz Claiborne expands to 40 brands, with $4.85 billion in sales; acquisitions include Monet (2000), Mexx (2001), Ellen Tracy (2002), Juicy Couture (2003), Enyce (2003), and Mac & Jac (2006).
2002	José Mariá Castellano Rios, CEO of Inditex/Zara, is named International Retailer of the Year by the National Retail Federation.
2003	Target launches its exclusive licensing agreement with Isaac Mizrahi.
2004	Tom Ford leaves Gucci and YSL to start his own line of luxury men's wear.
2005	Quotas on textiles and apparel imported from World Trade Organization (WTO) members are phased out.
2005	Federated Department Stores acquires May Department Stores, realigning stores into eight operating divisions: one Bloomingdale's and seven Macy's.
2007	Kohl's launches its exclusive licensing agreement with Vera Wang, introducing Very Vera by Vera Wang.
2007	Federated Department Stores changes its name to Macy's, Inc.

Summary

Since their beginnings in the Industrial Revolution of the eighteenth and nineteenth centuries, the textile and apparel industries have maintained an important place in the American economy. Spurred by mechanization of spinning, weaving, and sewing processes, the textile and apparel industries moved from craft industries to factory-based industries. Immigrants provided the necessary labor force for these growing industries.

By the 1920s, ready-made apparel was available to most consumers. Two types of apparel production were developed—modern, large factories, and small contractors who sewed piecework at home. The textile and apparel industries emerged from the Great Depression of the 1930s with the need to address growing and changing demands from consumers. Technological advancements in synthetic fibers provided a new source of materials for apparel. However, it was not until after World War II that these easy-care fibers hit the American market.

The 1950s saw growth and expansion of apparel companies, many becoming large, publicly owned corporations. This growth continued through the 1960s. However, as labor costs in the United States increased and consumer demand for lower-cost clothing also increased, companies began moving production outside the United States.

As imports of textiles and apparel surged, the American industry examined how it could increase productivity and global competitiveness. The result of this analysis was the development of the Quick Response system, an industry-wide program made up of a number of strategies to shorten the production time from raw fiber to the sale of a finished product to the ultimate consumer. Quick Response strategies are seen in all segments of the textile, apparel, and retailing industries. Interindustry cooperation through joint research ventures, [TC]², interindustry linkage councils, the Crafted with Pride in U.S.A. Council, and the American Textile Partnership increased the effectiveness of Quick Response strategies.

Enhanced information technology has allowed for increased partnerships throughout the soft goods pipeline. Supply chain management (SCM) encompasses these information-sharing processes to improve the efficiency and effectiveness of the textile and apparel industries. RFID tagging has evolved as an important tool for companies wanting to increase their efficiencies in SCM.

Since the beginning of the twenty-first century, the textile and apparel industries have been adapting to new rules associated with international trade and consumer demand for high-quality, fashionable, and reasonably priced goods. Philosophies such as fast fashion will tap the industries' capabilities for effective integration and communication. The textile and apparel industries will continue to be integral industries for globalization and economic growth.

Key Terms

business-to-business (B2B)

cotton gin

Crafted with Pride in U.S.A. Council

Fabric and Suppliers Linkage
    Council (FASLINC)

fast fashion

globalization

International Ladies' Garment
    Workers' Union (ILGWU)

marketing channel

marketing pipeline

mass production

power loom

Quick Response (QR)

Radio Frequency Identification
    (RFID)

ready-to-wear (RTW)

sewing machine

size standards

spinning mill

Sundries and Apparel Findings
    Linkage Council (SAFLINC)

supply chain management (SCM)

Textile/Apparel Linkage Council
    (TALC)

Textile/Clothing Technology
    Corporation ([TC]²)

vertical integration

Voluntary Interindustry Commerce
    Standards (VICS) Association

Voluntary Interindustry
    Communications Standards
    (VICS) Committee

Discussion Questions

1. What technological developments were imperative for the development and growth of the textile and apparel industries in the United States and globally?

2. Look in a historic costume book, and select a fashion from at least 15 years ago. What social and technological developments were necessary for the production and distribution of the fashion?

3. In your own words, define *Quick Response*. Why would a textile or apparel manufacturer want to adopt QR strategies? What technological developments have led to supply chain management?

4. What are the disadvantages and advantages of fast fashion for textile, apparel, and home fashions companies? What are the advantages and disadvantages of fast fashion for consumers?

References

Abend, Jules. (1995, October). Textiles making all the right moves. *Bobbin*, pp. 40–45.

Abend, Jules. (1998, May). SCM is putting a buzz in industry ears. *Bobbin*, pp. 48–54.

American Apparel Manufacturing Association. (1995, January). *Quick Response Handout* [online]. Available: http://www.tc2.com/qrlc/qrhand.htm [December 6, 1995].

American Textile Manufacturers Institute. (1978). *Textiles: Our First Great Industry.* Charlotte, NC: Author.

Bedell, Thomas. (1994, March). Innocents lost: The great Triangle fire. *Destination Discovery*, pp. 24–31.

Bicentennial of U.S. Textiles. (1990, October). *Textile World.*

Brill, Eileen B. (1985). From immigrants to imports. In *WWD/75 Years in Fashion, 1910–1985.* Supplement to *Women's Wear Daily*, pp. 10–14. New York: Fairchild Publications.

Butenhoff, Peter. (1999, May). Future perfect: Will past tensions dissolve with SCM? *Apparel Industry Magazine,* pp. SCM-2–SCM-4.

Davis-Meyers, Mary L. (1992). The development of American menswear pattern drafting technology, 1822 to 1860. *Clothing and Textiles Research Journal*, 10 (3), pp. 12–20.

Douglas-David, Lynn. (1989, October). EDI: Fiction or reality? *Bobbin*, pp. 86–90.

Ewing, Elizabeth. (1992). *History of Twentieth Century Fashion* (3rd ed.). Lanham, MD: Barnes & Noble Books.

Ferdows, Kasra, Lewis, Michael A., and Machuca, Jose A.D. (2004). Rapid-Fire Fulfillment. *Harvard Business Review*, Vol. 82, No. 11.

Fortess, Fred. (1988, May). Squaring off with the competition. *Bobbin*, pp. 104–110.

Fraser, Steven. (1983). Combined and uneven development in the men's clothing industry. *Business History Review*, 57, pp. 522–547.

Hasty, Susan E. (Ed.). (1994, March). *The Quick Response Handbook.* Supplement to *Apparel Industry Magazine.*

Hohanty, Gail F. (1990). From craft to industry: Textile production in the United States. *Material History Bulletin*, 31, pp. 23–31.

Hosiery and Underwear. (1976, July). Issue devoted to the history of hosiery and underwear. NY: Harcourt Brace Jovanovich.

Kazis, Richard. (1989, August/September). Rags to riches? *Technology Review*, pp. 42–53.

Kidwell, Claudia B., and Christman, Margaret C. (1974). *Suiting Everyone: The Democratization of Clothing in America.* Washington, DC: Smithsonian Institution.

Kramer, William M., and Stern, Norton B. (1987). Levi Strauss: The man behind the myth. *Western States Jewish Historical Quarterly*, 19 (3), pp. 257–263.

Melinkoff, Ellen. (1984). *What We Wore.* New York: Quill.

Parnell, Clay. (1998, June). Supply chain management in the soft goods industry. *Apparel Industry Magazine*, pp. 60–61.

Quick Response: America's Competitive Advantage [slide set program guide]. (1988). Washington, DC: American Textile Manufacturer's Institute.

Richards, Florence S. (1951). *The Ready-to-Wear Industry* 1900–1950. New York: Fairchild Publications.

Smarr, Susan L. (1988, December). [TC]^2's call to action. *Bobbin*, pp. 127–135.

Steele, Valerie. (1988). *Paris Fashion: A Cultural History.* New York: Oxford University Press.

Stegemeyer, Anne. (1996). *Who's Who in Fashion* (3rd ed.). New York: Fairchild Publications.

Symbol Technologies, Inc. (2006). *Synchronize Your Supply Chain with RFID.* Holtsville, New York: Author.

[TC]^2 Turning Research into Reality (2006). [TC]^2 Home Page [online]. Available: http://www.tc2.com [September 12, 2006].

Yafa, Stephen. (2005). *Big Cotton.* New York: Viking/Penguin Books.

CHAPTER 2

Business and Legal Framework of Textile, Apparel, and Home Fashions Companies

In this chapter, you will learn the following:

- the ways in which a business can be owned and operated—sole proprietorships, partnerships, and corporations

- terminology related to business organization

- the ways in which businesses within the textile, apparel, home fashions, and retailing industries compete

- the definition of licensing and how textile, apparel, and home fashions companies use licensing agreements

- the primary marketing channels used by textile, apparel, and home fashions companies

- the federal laws that can affect textile, apparel, and home fashions companies

extile, apparel, and home fashions companies come in all sizes and types. Some are large corporations that employ thousands of people; others are small companies with one or two employees. Regardless of size and organizational structure, every company in the textile and apparel pipeline is in business to make a profit by providing consumers with the products and services they desire and need. Because many people planning careers in the textile, apparel, and home fashions industries hope to own their own businesses someday, an understanding of the variety of business organizations among companies is an important starting point for our further examination of the operation of these companies. In addition, information about business organizations is important for planning careers and assessing companies in terms of employment and advancement opportunities. Depending on their objectives, needs, and size, textile, apparel, and home fashions companies can be owned and organized in a number of ways. The three most common legal forms of business ownership are sole proprietorships, partnerships, and corporations. The three types of business ownership are compared in Table 2.1. Each form of business can be found among textile, apparel, and home fashions companies.

Sole Proprietorships

The **sole proprietorship** is a very common form of business ownership in which an individual, the "sole proprietor," owns the business and its property. Indeed, from a legal perspective, the sole proprietor or owner is indistinguishable from the company itself. The sole proprietor typically runs the overall day-to-day operations of the company but may have employees to help with specific aspects of the business. Employees may be full-time, part-time, or hired to conduct certain tasks. Any profit from the business is considered personal income of the sole proprietor and taxed accordingly; the owner is personally liable for any debt the business may incur.

ADVANTAGES OF SOLE PROPRIETORSHIPS

This type of business ownership has a number of advantages. For one thing, only a few business licenses are needed. For example, in Los Angeles, the following licenses are needed to open an apparel manufacturing business:

Table 2.1   Comparisons among Sole Proprietorships, Partnerships, and Corporations

Business Organization Form	Sole Proprietorship	Partnership	Corporation
Ease of formation	Easy to form Business licenses required	Easy to form Business licenses required Written contract advisable	Difficult to form Charter required Registration with the SEC required for publicly held corporations
Operational strategies	Owner also runs the business	Partners can bring range of expertise to running the business	Board hires individuals with specific expertise to run the business
Liability	Unlimited personal liability	Unlimited personal liability for each partner	Limited liability; stockholders not personally liable for corporate debt
Tax considerations	Sole proprietor's income taxed as personal income	Partners' income taxed as personal income	Double taxation (corporation's income taxed, and dividends taxed as personal income)
Potential for employee advancement	Limited, depending upon size of company	Some incentive for employees to become partners	Employees can move up through the ranks
Examples	Small companies Freelance designer Independent sales representative	Small- or medium-size companies Designer and marketer who join forces to form an apparel company	Large companies May be private or publicly held (e.g., Celanese Corporation, Liz Claiborne, VF Corporation, Macy's Inc.) Some may be multinational

- City of Los Angeles business license
- garment license
- resale license
- public health license
- federal employer identification number (if there are employees)
- state employer identification number (if there are employees)
- registration number (for labeling purposes, in lieu of putting the company name on labels)

Sole proprietorships are also easy to dissolve. When the sole proprietor decides to stop doing business, the sole proprietorship is essentially ended. Another advantage of a sole proprietorship is the control and flexibility given the sole proprietor, who often finds personal satisfaction in being the boss and making the decisions regarding the direction the business will take. This personal satisfaction is the characteristic of this form of business ownership that individuals most often desire.

DISADVANTAGES OF SOLE PROPRIETORSHIPS

This type of business ownership also has a number of disadvantages. The biggest disadvantage is that sole proprietors are personally liable for any business debts. This means that if the business owes money, creditors can take all business and personal assets (such as the owner's home) to pay the debts of the business. This **unlimited liability** is one of the largest risks a sole proprietor takes in starting the business.

Another disadvantage of sole proprietorships is that because there are no partners, the sole proprietor needs to have expertise in all areas of running the business. For example, an apparel designer who wants to start his or her own business must do the following:

- Handle the design aspect of the business.
- Work with fabric suppliers, contractors, and retailers.
- Deal with accounting.
- Manage personnel.
- Market the product.

The difficulty in running all aspects of the business is often overwhelming for new sole proprietors. In some cases, sole proprietors will hire employees who have expertise in specific areas in which the owner is not expert. For example, a designer may hire an accountant to manage the financial aspects of the business.

In a sole proprietorship, raising capital (funds or resources) for business initiation or expansion can be difficult. Capital needed to start or expand the business may be obtained in the following ways:

- by tapping the owner's personal funds

- by purchasing goods and services on credit

- by the sole proprietor personally borrowing money from banks, friends, family members, or other investors

A well-written business plan is essential for a sole proprietor to garner funds from banks and other investors. As with other forms of business ownership, sole proprietorships must keep books of account for federal, state, and municipal income tax and other regulatory purposes. Profits are taxed as personal income.

EXAMPLES OF SOLE PROPRIETORSHIPS

Sole proprietorships tend to be small companies, the resources and complexities of which can be handled by one owner. Individuals may start companies as sole proprietorships and then, as the company grows, change the form of ownership to a partnership or corporation. Examples of sole proprietorships within textile, apparel, and home fashions industries might include the following:

- a freelance textile or apparel designer who sells his or her work to larger textile or apparel companies

- an independent sales representative who sells apparel lines to retailers

- an apparel retailer who owns a small specialty store

The Bureau of Labor Statistics estimates that more than one out of every four fashion designers are self-employed (U.S. Department of Labor, 2006).

Partnerships

There are times when two or more people want to join forces in owning a business. In these cases, a **partnership** may be formed. According to the Uniform Partnership Act (UPA), a partnership is an "association of two or more persons to carry on as co-owners of a business for profit." A partnership may be formed between two individuals or among three or more individuals through written contracts called *articles of partnership*. Although contracts will vary, they typically include the following:

the partnership's name

the partners' and officers' names

the intentions or purposes of the partnership

the amount and form of contributions (e.g., money and real estate) from each partner

the length of the partnership

procedures to add and eliminate partners

the way profit or losses will be divided among the partners

the degree of management authority each partner will have

the designation of which partners, if any, are entitled to salaries

how partnership affairs will be handled if a partner dies or is disabled

Profits are shared among the partners, known as **general partners**, according to the conditions laid out in the partnership contract. Profit from a partnership is taxed as part of each partner's personal income. Similar to sole proprietors, partners have unlimited liability. This means that, together, they are liable for the entire debt of the partnership as outlined in the partnership contract. Dissolution of a partnership can result from the following:

a partner's withdrawal

the entry of new partners

a partner's death

a partner's bankruptcy

a partner's incapacity or misconduct

the goals of the business becoming obsolete

LIMITED PARTNERSHIPS

Sometimes individuals want to join or invest in a partnership, but they do not want to have the unlimited liability for partnership debt that may be larger than their investment. This can be achieved through a **limited partnership**. In this type of partnership, a limited partner has **limited liability**; that is, he or she is liable only for the amount of capital that he or she invested in the business.

Any profits are shared according to the conditions of the limited partnership contract. Establishing limited partnerships can be an attractive way for general partners to raise capital to initiate or expand their business. Typically, the limited partner does not take an active role in managing the business, which is handled by the general partners.

ADVANTAGES OF PARTNERSHIPS

Partnerships have some advantages over sole proprietorships. Similar to sole proprietorships, partnerships are relatively easy to establish; the same business licenses are required to start a partnership as a sole proprietorship. Unlike sole proprietorships, where only one person owns the business, partners can pool their range of expertise and resources to run the company. For example, one partner in an apparel company may have expertise in design, and another partner may have expertise in business and accounting.

Raising capital for partnerships is also somewhat easier than for sole proprietors because the resources of more than one person can be tapped, and the combined resources of partners can be used as collateral when borrowing money. Through the use of limited partnerships, resources can also be raised for business initiation or expansion. As with sole proprietorships, a quality business plan is needed for partnerships to secure funding from investors.

Another advantage of partnerships over sole proprietorships is that advancement opportunities for employees are greater: employees may be given the opportunity to become partners in the business. This can be a valuable incentive when recruiting and hiring employees.

DISADVANTAGES OF PARTNERSHIPS

Partnerships also have a number of disadvantages. As with sole proprietorships, the primary disadvantage of partnerships is liability exposure. This means that each partner is personally liable for any debt of the partnership, regardless of which partner was responsible for incurring the debt. In addition to books of account, the UPA also requires that partnerships keep minutes of meetings and business records.

Another disadvantage of a partnership is the potential for disagreement among partners in running the business or setting the future direction of the business. Partnerships often dissolve because of such disagreements. As with sole proprietorships, a partnership is dependent on its owners, and dissolution is presumed when a partner leaves the partnership. Although ease of dissolution of a partnership can be viewed as an advantage, it can also lead to a lack of continuity in the business operations.

EXAMPLES OF PARTNERSHIPS

Partnerships are typically small to medium-size companies that require a combination of specialized skills to be successful. For example, two or more individuals may start an apparel company, each bringing unique skills (e.g., design, marketing, operations, and so on) to the business. A number of large apparel manufacturers, such as Calvin Klein, Esprit de Corp., and Liz Claiborne, started as partnerships.

- Calvin Klein borrowed money from his friend Barry Schwartz to start his design company, and the two remained partners in the business until it was sold to Phillips-Van Heusen in 2002.

- In the 1960s and 1970s, Doug Tompkins, Susie Tompkins, and Jane Tise owned an apparel company called Plain Jane. In 1979, the Tompkins bought out Tise and renamed the company Esprit de Corp. Since the Tompkins divorced in the early 1990s, Susie Tompkins runs Esprit, now a private corporation.

- Elisabeth "Liz" Claiborne started her business in 1976 with her husband, Arthur Ortenberg, and a manufacturing expert, Leonard Boxer, as partners. Later, Jerome Chazen joined as a partner. Within a year, the company was making a profit, and in 1981, it became a publicly traded corporation.

Corporations

The **corporation** is the most complex form of business ownership because corporations are considered legal entities that exist regardless of who owns them. Corporations are created through the filing of **articles of incorporation** (sometimes referred to as articles of organization or articles of association) with the state or federal government. General requirements of articles of incorporation include the following:

- name of corporation
- purpose and power of the corporation
- time frame or period of existence
- authorized number of shares/owners
- types of shares
- other conditions of operation

Typically, corporations are designated by the words *Corporation*, *Corp.*, or *Inc.* Although assets owned by the corporation, such as buildings or equipment, are tangible, the corporation itself is considered intangible.

Unlike a sole proprietorship or partnership, ownership of a corporation is held by **stockholders** (or *shareholders*), who own shares of stock in the corporation. Each share of stock represents a percentage of the company, so that if someone owns 50 percent of the stock in a company, he or she owns 50 percent of the company. Stockholders in a corporation are liable only for the amount they paid for their stock. Thus, if the company fails, stockholders are not liable for the corporation's debts beyond their investments in the company's stock.

The **board of directors** of the corporation is elected by the stockholders. Each stockholder has a percentage of votes in electing the board that reflects the percentage of stock he or she owns. The board of directors is the chief governing body of the corporation. It plans the direction the company will take and sets policy for the corporation. The board also hires the officers of the corporation (e.g., the president, chief executive officer, chief financial officer, and so on), who run the business. Stockholders may participate in the management of the business, but many stockholders in corporations have very little or no participation in day-to-day operations.

Profit is paid out to stockholders in the form of **dividends**, which are taxed as personal income. Stockholders may also receive dividends in the form of additional stock in the company. Figure 2.1 shows some examples of corporations in the textile, apparel, and home fashions industries.

Figure 2.1 These logos represent examples of corporations in the textile, apparel, and home fashions industries.

C Corporations and S Corporations

The most common type of corporation is the **C corporation**, or **regular corporation**. This type of corporation distributes profits to shareholders through dividends. Therefore, earnings of the corporation are taxed twice— once at the corporate level, and again at the individual level. This is known as **double taxation**. For small domestic corporations with a limited number of domestic individual shareholders, **S corporations** are becoming more common. S corporations are given special status by the Internal Revenue Service whereby earnings are taxed only at the individual level, thus eliminating double taxation.

Publicly Traded and Privately Held Corporations

Differences between publicly traded and privately held corporations are primarily in terms of the ownership and transferability of shares of stock. In **publicly traded corporations**, (or **publicly held corporations**), at least some of the shares of stock are owned by the general public. Publicly traded corporations usually have a large number of stockholders who buy and sell their stock on the public market, either through an exchange (New York Stock Exchange, American Stock Exchange, or National Association of Securities Dealers Automatic Quotation System [NASDAQ]), or through brokers "over the counter." Publicly traded corporations must submit financial information to the Securities and Exchange Commission (SEC), which regulates the securities markets. Table 2.2 lists selected publicly traded corporations in the textile and home fashions industries. Table 2.3 lists selected publicly traded corporations in the apparel industry.

Table 2.2 Examples of U.S. Publicly Held Fiber and Textile Corporations

Celanese Corporation	INVISTA
Collins and Aikman	Paxar
Culp, Inc.	Quaker Fabric
Delta Woodside Industries, Inc.	The Dixie Group
DuPont	Unifi, Inc.
Hanesbrands, Inc.	Wellman, Inc.
International Textile Group	

Table 2.3   Examples of U.S. Publicly Held Apparel Corporations

adidas Group	Liz Claiborne, Inc.
Angelica Corporation	Nike, Inc.
Carter's, Inc.	Oxford Industries, Inc.
Coach, Inc.	Phillips-Van Heusen Corporation
Columbia Sportswear Company	Polo Ralph Lauren Corporation
Guess?, Inc.	Tarrant Apparel Group
Hanesbrands, Inc.	The Timberland Company
Hartmarx Corporation	Under Armour, Inc.
Jones Apparel Group, Inc.	VF Corporation
Kellwood Company	Warnaco Group, Inc.
Kenneth Cole Productions, Inc.	

Privately held corporations (also called **private corporations, closely held corporations**, or **close corporations**) are those in which the shares are owned by a small number of individuals; that is, the stock is not available in public markets and has not been issued for public purchase. Typically, the stockholders of a private corporation are highly involved in the operations of the company. Vera Wang Bridal House, L.L.Bean, Patagonia, Pendleton Woolen Mills, Belk, Inc., and Retail Brand Alliance, Inc. (owners of Brooks Brothers, Carolee Designs, and Adrienne Vittadini) are examples of private corporations in the apparel and retailing industries.

Multinational corporations are either private or publicly traded corporations that operate in several countries. In today's global economy—with increased world production and trade of apparel, accessories, and home fashions—multinational corporations have grown in number and importance. Multinational corporations can be set up in the following ways:

- In horizontally integrated corporations, operations throughout the world are involved in producing the same or similar products.
- In vertically integrated corporations, operations throughout the world are involved in specific aspects of the production across the supply chain.
- Diversified corporations include some aspects of both horizontal and vertical integration.

Examples of multinational corporations include Nike, Inc. and Wal-Mart.

Limited Liability Companies

Authorized in 1977 and expanded in 1988, **Limited Liability Companies (LLC)** provide business owners with tax advantages (as with partnerships) along with limited liability (as with corporations). These companies are owned by a few members who all participate in management of the company.

Although LLCs are more complex to form than partnerships, they are easier to form than corporations. Examples include the following:

- small companies, such as PFW Productions, LLC, the production company for Portland (Oregon) Fashion Week

- large companies, such as the following:
  - 7 for All Mankind, a high-end denim manufacturer headquartered in Los Angeles that was founded in 2000 as an LLC
  - American Apparel, LLC, one the largest vertically integrated knitwear companies in the United States, also headquartered in Los Angeles

ADVANTAGES OF CORPORATIONS

Corporations have a number of advantages over other forms of business ownership. The main advantage of incorporation is the limited liability of the owners (stockholders). If the corporation fails, creditors cannot seize the personal assets of the stockholders to pay the corporate debt. This is the primary reason why two or more individuals may decide to create a private corporation rather than a partnership when beginning a business.

Another advantage corporations have is the flexibility and ease with which ownership can be transferred. Unlike a sole proprietorship or partnership, a corporation does not cease to exist if one of its owners withdraws or dies. Shares are simply transferred to heirs or sold. In most cases, stockholders are free to sell their stock at any time. Because of this ease of transferring ownership, corporations seldom dissolve because of ownership issues.

Unlike the management of a sole proprietorship or partnership, management of a corporation is not dependent on ownership. The management group runs the day-to-day operations of the company regardless of who owns the business that day. This allows the board of directors to hire the best-qualified individuals to manage the specialized areas of the company.

In addition, in large corporations, there is great potential for employee advancement within the organization. Employees may work in specialized areas of the company and advance through the ranks. Such potential for advancement can serve as an incentive for employees.

For publicly traded corporations, the act of "going public," or becoming a publicly traded corporation, can be a benefit to businesses in raising capital to expand or diversify. When a corporation goes public, investors buy shares of stock based upon how well they believe the company will perform in the future. These investments can then be used to expand or improve the company.

DISADVANTAGES OF CORPORATIONS

With all of these advantages, why are not all businesses corporations? Despite the apparent advantages, a number of disadvantages exist. It is much more complicated to establish a corporation than a sole proprietorship or partnership. As previously noted, a corporation is organized around a legal charter or articles of incorporation that outline its scope and activity. Because of this, legal fees and other costs involved in incorporation are higher than for other forms of business ownership. This is especially true if a company wants to become a publicly traded corporation, or "go public" through the selling of shares to public investors. It is estimated that the costs of an initial public offering (IPO) can be up to 25 percent of the company's equity (the difference between the company's assets and its liabilities).

The corporation's articles of incorporation also restrict the type of business performed by the corporation. In other words, the board of directors or officers of a publicly traded apparel company cannot shift from producing apparel to producing automobiles without filing new articles of incorporation.

Corporations are organized under the laws of specific states, and each state has statutes that govern corporations. There are also federal laws (i.e., Securities Act of 1933, Securities Exchange Act of 1934) that regulate publicly held corporations in the issuing and selling of their shares of stock. Other federal laws that govern businesses, including corporations, are described later in this chapter.

Another disadvantage to corporations are corporate taxes. Because they are legal entities, corporations are taxed on their income at a tax rate higher than that on personal income. In addition, for C corporations, dividends paid to stockholders are considered personal income, and, therefore, they are subject to personal income tax.

Corporations are often large companies that can have thousands of employees. Because of this, employees sometimes view corporations as impersonal and bureaucratic. In addition, unlike other forms of business ownership, owners of corporations, especially publicly traded corporations, might not be involved in the day-to-day operations of the business. Employees who are not stockholders are not likely to have the same commitment to the corporation as owners of sole proprietorships or partnerships may have.

Despite these disadvantages, the limited liability associated with corporations and ease of transferring ownership make them very attractive for investors who want to own part of specific companies. Thus, privately held and publicly traded corporations are the most powerful forms of business in the textile and apparel industries. In fact, some categories within the industry, such as intimate apparel, are dominated by large corporations. Within the intimate apparel category, corporations control most of the production and distribution:

- Maidenform, Inc., with brands including Maidenform, Flexees, and Lilyette

- Warnaco Group, with brands including Axcelerate, Calvin Klein underwear, Warner's, Olga, BoDY Nancy Ganz, and Lejaby

- Hanesbrands, Inc., with brands including Playtex, Bali, L'eggs, Just My Size, Barely There, and Wonderbra

- Kayser-Roth Corporation, with brands including No nonsense, Hue, Calvin Klein hosiery, and Burlington hosiery

- Fruit of the Loom, Inc., with brands including Vanity Fair, Vassarette, Lily of France, Bestform, and Curvation

Terms Associated with Company Expansion and Diversification

As one reads trade and consumer literature about companies' organizations and operations, one comes across a number of terms (e.g., *merger, consolidation, takeover,* and *conglomerate*) related to the company's organization. In order to interpret the literature, it is important to have a basic understanding of these terms.

A **merger** is the blending of one company into another company. If company A and company B merge, the result will be a larger company A, which will assume ownership of company B's assets and liability for all of company B's debts. For example, in 2006, Tommy Hilfiger Corporation was acquired through a merger agreement by Apex Partners, whose other investments include Tommy Bahama, Charlotte Russe, and Spyder Active Sports. This agreement resulted in taking the Tommy Hilfiger Corporation private.

A **consolidation** is the combining of two companies, with the result being a new company. If company A and company B consolidate, the result is company C.

A **takeover** results when one company or individual gains control of another company by buying a large enough portion of its shares. For example, in 2005, a German company, adidas Group, completed a takeover of its North

American-based rival Reebok. Takeovers can be either mergers or consolidations; *friendly,* in that the company that is taken over agrees to the association; or *hostile,* in that the company that is taken over does not agree to the association. Being informed about possible mergers and consolidations within the industry is important for management-level textile and apparel executives in their strategic decision making.

Conglomerates are diversified companies (typically corporations) that are involved with significantly different lines of business. The biggest advantage for conglomerates is their ability to realign assets among companies to increase efficiencies, support expansions, and minimize the impact of losses. For example, LVMH Group is a conglomerate including companies focusing on wine and spirits (e.g., Moët and Chandon champagne), fashion leather goods (e.g., Louis Vuitton), perfumes and cosmetics (e.g., Dior cosmetics), watches and jewelry (e.g., TAG Heuer SA), and retailing (e.g., DFS Galleria).

Forms of Competition

The goal of every sole proprietorship, partnership, and corporation in the textile, apparel, and home fashions industries is to provide products or services that are desired by the ultimate consumer. However, many companies are vying for the consumer's dollar. Thus, companies, whether they are sole proprietorships, partnerships, or corporations, compete with one another. Companies that successfully compete will make a profit that will either be reinvested in the company or paid to the company's owners or stockholders.

Competitive Strategies

Companies compete in a number of ways that, in part, determine their business strategies. Companies typically compete on any of the following bases:

- the *price* of the merchandise to the retailer or consumer
- the *quality* of the design, fabrics, and construction
- the *innovation*—how unique or fashionable the merchandise is
- *services* offered to the retailer or consumer
- a combination of these factors

For example, one company that produces children's wear may have lower prices than its competition; another may provide better-quality merchandise; another may produce children's wear that is more innovative; and still another may provide consumers with catalogs or other services. Thus, a company's business practices are based on competitive strategies.

For example, Hanna Andersson, a children's apparel manufacturer and multichannel retailer headquartered in Portland, Oregon, is known for its socially responsible business practices (see Figure 2.2). As their mission statement states:

> We market clothes to enhance the lives of our customers through quality, functionality, durability, and design. We keep a commitment to the values of respect, integrity and responsibility in all we do.

As part of this corporate philosophy, the Hanna Helps Program gives grants to schools and nonprofit organizations that focus on children. In 1994, it began the "Cash for Kids" Program in which the company gives $100 checks each year

Figure 2.2 Children's sleepwear is part of the line of clothing created by Hanna Andersson. One of Hanna Andersson's competitive strategies is to focus on the quality, functionality, durability, and design of their clothing lines.

to the school-age children of Hanna Andersson employees. The children present the checks to the school principal, and they help to decide how the funds should be used. Donations are made to programs that support home-schooled children, as well as to schools of children mentored by Hanna Andersson employees. Such corporate practices are one way Hanna Andersson separates itself from its competition and appeals to the company's customers.

Competitive Situations or Market Forms

Within American society, five primary competitive situations or market forms exist:

1. monopoly
2. oligopoly
3. oligopsony
4. pure or perfect competition
5. monopolistic competition

In a **monopoly**, one company typically dominates the market and, thus, can price its goods and/or services at whatever level it wishes. Because a monopoly essentially eliminates or drastically reduces competition, federal laws prohibit companies from buying out their competition and, in effect, becoming a monopoly. Only essential services, such as utilities, can legally operate as monopolies in today's market, and the prices they charge are heavily regulated by the government.

In an **oligopoly**, a few companies dominate and essentially have control of the market, thereby making it very difficult for other companies to enter. The dominant companies compete among themselves through product and service differentiation and advertising. Although oligopolies are not illegal, it is illegal for the dominant companies to set artificial prices among themselves. In many ways, the athletic shoe industry can be considered an oligopoly because it is dominated by a few companies (e.g., Nike, adidas Group including Reebok, and New Balance). Thus, the companies have some control over the price they charge for their goods.

Oligopsony exists when there is a small number of buyers for goods and services offered by a large number of sellers. This type of competition is most often found in agricultural products (e.g., cocoa) whereby numerous growers sell to a limited number of buyers worldwide.

In **pure competition**, or **perfect competition**, there are many producers and consumers of similar products, so price is determined by market demand. The market for agricultural commodities, such as cotton or wool, is the closest to pure competition that can be found in the textile and apparel industries. In these cases, the price for the product—raw cotton or wool—is determined by supply and demand of the commodity. For example, supply and demand for cotton are estimated two years in advance. Cotton supplies can be affected by weather conditions, production yield, trade negotiations, legislation, and other factors that impact how many bales of cotton are produced. When supplies are high and demand stable or low, prices of cotton can decrease. When supplies are low and demand high, prices of cotton can increase.

The most common form of competition in the textile, apparel, and home fashions industries is **monopolistic competition**, in which many companies compete in terms of product type, but the specific products of any one company are perceived as unique by consumers. For example, many companies produce denim jeans, including Levi Strauss & Co., Lee, Wrangler, Guess?, 7 for All Mankind, Marc by Marc Jacobs, Liz Claiborne, Gap, Old Navy, and Calvin Klein. However, through product differentiation, advertising, distribution strategy, and pricing, each company has created a unique image. By creating this unique image in consumers' minds, each has, in some respect, a monopoly in terms of its specific product and, therefore, has some control over price. A consumer who wants only 7 for All Mankind jeans and seeks out that particular brand may be willing to pay a premium for that brand.

Within monopolistic competition, each company must create a perceived difference between its product and the competition's products. This can be achieved in the following ways:

The product is differentiated by design characteristics.

The company uses advertising to create public awareness of its brand name or trademark (see Figure 2.3).

The company buys the use of a well-established brand name, trademark, or other image through licensing programs.

A retailer creates **private-label brand** or **store brand** merchandise that is unique to its store or catalog. Examples of private-label brands are Arizona (JCPenney), Classiques Entier and Halogen (Nordstrom), and Charter Club and INC International (Macy's). Examples of store brands are Abercrombie and Fitch, Gap, Eddie Bauer, and L.L.Bean.

ELLEN TRACY

Apparel companies strive to create unique images to gain competitive advantage.

A manufacturer may expand its services to consumers, as when it opens retail stores (e.g., Polo Ralph Lauren, Liz Claiborne, Tommy Hilfiger) or offers goods through catalogs, Web sites, and other nonstore venues.

In these ways, consumers associate a company's goods with a particular unique image.

Licensing

One of the methods used by textile and apparel companies to create a perceived difference in their product is **licensing**. Because of the widespread use of licensing within the textile, apparel, and home fashions industries, an understanding of the role it plays in textile and apparel production is important. Licensing is the selling by the owner (*licensor*) of the right to use a particular name, image, or design to another party (*licensee*), typically a manufacturer, for payment of royalties. The licensee buys the right to use the name, image, or design, referred to as the *property,* on merchandise to add value to the merchandise. Licensing has grown dramatically as companies recognize the value of established brand names, characters, and **brand extensions**. Examples of licensed products include the following:

eyewear produced by CXD with the Hugo Boss brand label

hosiery manufactured by Kayser-Roth Corporation under the brand name Calvin Klein hosiery

sportswear manufactured by VF Corporation with the San Francisco 49ers football team logo on the front

infant and toddler apparel produced by Franco Apparel under the brands Starter Baby, Starter Kids, Eddie Bauer, New Balance, and with professional and college sports team logos

decorative pillows and throw rugs manufactured by WestPoint Stevens with the Harley-Davidson logo sheets and pillowcases manufactured by WestPoint Stevens under the Lauren Ralph Lauren label

Some companies are entirely licensed (e.g., J. G. Hook, Hang Ten) in that all of their products are licensed; other companies license certain product lines (e.g., Vera Wang fragrance, Donna Karan sunglasses, Polo by Ralph Lauren boys' wear).

Types of Licensed Names, Images, and Designs

The types of names, images, and designs that are licensed vary widely, although the majority fall into the following categories:

Character and entertainment licensing: Such images as cartoon characters, movie or television characters, and fictional characters are often licensed to appear on a range of merchandise, from sleepwear to backpacks to sheets and towels. Examples include the following:
– Disney characters; Peanuts or South Park cartoon characters
– Barbie dolls
– Star Wars characters
– likenesses of Spiderman or Superman

In recent years, licensed merchandise relating to movies and movie characters has been extremely popular, particularly for infant and children's clothing and other children's merchandise.

Corporate licensing: The licensing of brand names and trademarks of corporations such as IBM, Harley-Davidson, or Coca-Cola is also common. This type of brand extension licensing extends a brand that is well known in a particular product area to a different product area. Examples include Porsche sunglasses, Coca-Cola stuffed toy polar bears, Pillsbury Doughboy potholders, and Harley-Davidson armchairs.

Designer name licensing: Designers, including Pierre Cardin, Chanel, Yves Saint Laurent, Ralph Lauren, Calvin Klein, Donna Karan, and many others, license their names as brand names for products including scarfs, jewelry, fragrances, cosmetics, home fashions, and shoes.

Celebrity name licensing: Celebrities also license their names to create immediately recognized brands of merchandise. Examples include the following:
– Elizabeth Taylor, Jennifer Lopez, and Sarah Jessica Parker (see Figure 2.4), who have licensed their names and images to perfumes
– Jessica Simpson, who sold the use of her name to Tarrant Apparel Group for a line of sportswear

Figure 2.4 Celebrity name licensing adds immediate image and recognition to the product.

– Eminem, who partnered with Nike on a collection of footwear
– Kathy Ireland's collection of home furniture that bears her name

Exclusive licensing for a retailer: In recent years, retailers have teamed up with celebrities and designers to create merchandise sold exclusively at a particular retailer, creating a unique form of private-label merchandise. Examples include the following:
– Jaclyn Smith and Martha Stewart, who have licensed their names to Kmart for apparel and home fashions, respectively
– Kathie Lee Gifford, who has licensed her name to Wal-Mart for lines of apparel
– Vera Wang's Very Vera exclusive brand for Kohl's
– Isaac Mizrahi, who has an exclusive licensing agreement with Target

Nostalgia licensing: Manufacturers license the names and images of legends, such as Marilyn Monroe, James Dean, and Babe Ruth, as well as old-time movies and radio and TV shows, such as *The Lone Ranger, Superman,* and *King Kong.*

Sports and collegiate licensing: Professional sports team and university logos are licensed to appear on sport-related merchandise, such as sweatshirts with the Green Bay Packers logo, jackets with the Boston Red Sox logo, and caps with the Oregon State University logo.

Event and festival licensing: The names or logos of such events as the Kentucky Derby, the Indianapolis 500, Wimbledon, and the Masters golf tournament are also licensed for use on products.

Art licensing: Manufacturers license great works of art to be reproduced on their merchandise.

The success of licensing depends on consumers' desire for goods with a perceived difference based on brand name, trademark, or image. The diversity of types of licensed goods attests to its effectiveness in creating a favorable perceived difference in the eyes of consumers.

The Development of Licensed Products

A well-established image-oriented property is a must for the success of any licensed product. When such a property exists, the development of licensed products based on it involves a number of steps. The stages of development of licensed products are as follows (Altchuler, 1988):

1. The image or design, commonly referred to as the property, is created. For example, the red, white, and blue logo of Tommy Hilfiger is created.

2. Consumers are exposed to the property through the media. The Tommy Hilfiger name and trademark are used in advertising, hangtags, publications, and so on.

3. The property is marketed by the licensor to build name or image recognition. Tommy Hilfiger builds a reputation among consumers for trendy fashion, quality, and value. The name and trademark are associated with these characteristics in consumers' minds.

4. Merchandise with the property added is produced by a variety of manufacturers. Tommy Hilfiger licenses the name and trademark to several manufacturers of apparel, accessories, and fragrances.

5. Merchandise is distributed by retailers. Retailers who have been successful with Tommy Hilfiger sportswear will also want to carry licensed Tommy Hilfiger merchandise, such as accessories and fragrances.

6. Merchandise is demanded by consumers. Consumers identify with the Tommy Hilfiger name and perceive the licensed products as having an added

value because the Tommy Hilfiger name and trademark are attached to the merchandise.

The Licensing Contract

The terms of the agreement between the licensee and licensor are outlined in a contract. Typically, a licensing agreement will include the following elements:

- *Time limit:* For many licensed products, timing is everything. For example, the contract for the image of a currently popular movie character may be for a shorter time than for a classic designer name.

- *Royalty payment:* Typically, royalties of 7 to 14 percent of the wholesale price of the goods sold are paid by the licensee to the licensor.

- *Image:* Contract clauses specify how the image will appear, giving the licensor control over graphics, colors, and other design details. For example, Ocean Pacific (OP) controls the design of all graphics on its licensed merchandise.

- *Marketing and distribution:* Licensors often want to control the consistency of the marketing of their licensed merchandise. Also, many designers do not want their licensed merchandise distributed through discount or off-price retailers, and they put clauses in their contracts to prevent it.

- *Quality:* Clauses about the materials and manufacture of merchandise and the submission of samples of merchandise for approval by the licensor give the licensor control over the quality of the product.

- *Advances:* Contract clauses set the amount of the advance money that will be paid up front and then deducted from the royalty payments.

- *Guarantees:* Contracts often guarantee that a minimum dollar amount will be paid to the licensee, even if royalties fall below this amount.

- *Notification of agreements to customs department:* If goods are being manufactured offshore, or outside the United States, this notification is needed so the goods will clear customs and not be confiscated as counterfeit goods. Contract clauses assure licensees that the licensor will provide notification if it is needed.

Advantages of Licensing

Licensing agreements have a number of advantages for both the licensee and licensor. For the licensee, the value added to the merchandise by a licensed name, image, or design comes in many interrelated forms. The licensee gets automatic brand identification (see Figure 2.4 on page 62). For example, a children's T-shirt with a picture of Captain Jack Sparrow, from the 2006 movie *Pirates of the Caribbean: Dead Man's Chest*, received automatic recognition from children and parent-consumers.

In many instances, the licensed product is trusted for qualities that stem from the licensor. For example, a designer name attached to a handbag adds fashion credibility to the handbag. For manufacturers, a licensed product can also be a marketing shortcut for launching new products. For example, by purchasing the rights to a designer or celebrity name, a fragrance company can launch a new fragrance with immediate brand name recognition.

The licensor also gains from licensing agreements. Licensing allows for brand extension into other categories of merchandise without revealing to consumers that the licensor is not manufacturing the merchandise. Such arrangements allow companies to expand their product lines by taking advantage of the manufacturing and distribution expertise and facilities of other companies.

For example, when Nike decided to expand its product line into women's swimwear, rather than spending the resources to develop the expertise in this area, it licensed its name to Jantzen, one of the world's largest women's swimwear manufacturers. By such an agreement, Nike was able to take advantage of the expertise at Jantzen, and Jantzen had the opportunity to expand its business by producing a new line of women's swimwear for a new target market.

As another example of this cooperation between corporations in licensing, Hartmarx, a well-known and well-respected producer of men's tailored clothing, is one of Tommy Hilfiger's licensees, handling all tailored clothing and slacks for Tommy Hilfiger. Hilfiger controls the design, distribution, and visual presentation of the products, and Hartmarx handles the production.

Designer–manufacturer licensing collaborations are common in intimate apparel and legwear, as shown in the following examples:

- Tommy Hilfiger Corporation has a licensing agreement with Fruit of the Loom's Bestform division, which produces and distributes intimate apparel with the Hilfiger label.

- Hanesbrands, Inc. licenses legwear under the Donna Karan and DKNY labels.

- Warnaco Group produces Calvin Klein women's underwear.

For well-established names or images, licensing arrangements can also be very lucrative. It is estimated that designers such as Calvin Klein and Ralph Lauren make millions of dollars each year in royalties from licensed merchandise.

Disadvantages of Licensing

There are also a number of disadvantages for the licensor and licensee. For the licensor, overuse of licensing arrangements may result in a saturation of the property in the marketplace. This can lead to consumers who do not perceive a distinct image with the property. For example, with hundreds of licensing agreements, Pierre Cardin's name can be seen on everything from luggage to cookware to children's apparel. Because of this, in recent years, the name has lost some of its prestige.

When a licensed product sells well, the licensor must rely on the licensee's ability to react by producing goods quickly. Depending on the licensing contract, licensors also risk a loss of control over quality or distribution of licensed merchandise. To assure consistent quality, the licensor must provide constant monitoring of production quality by inspecting samples or production facilities.

A tragic example of the risk involved with losing control of a licensed name is that of the designer Halston. In the 1960s and 1970s, Halston became a well-known designer of expensive apparel worn by celebrities. In 1973, Halston sold the exclusive rights to his name to Norton Simon Industries (NSI). In 1982, NSI asked Halston to design a line of affordable mass-merchandised clothing for JCPenney. The introduction of this line resulted in high-end retailers dropping his designer-priced collection. Although Halston received some royalties until his death in 1990, he never regained control over the use of the Halston name, which changed ownership six times during the 1980s. The Halston name continues to gain prestige with new management.

More recently, in 2004, Tommy Hilfiger purchased the trademarks of Karl Lagerfeld (i.e., Lagerfeld Collection and Lagerfeld). By 2006, however, Tommy Hilfiger completed a restructuring plan that closed the Karl Lagerfeld New York office; the future of the label is in question.

The major disadvantage of licensing for the licensee is the risk associated with predicting the popularity of the licensed name or image. Timing is extremely important for the success of many licensed products, and licensees must be experts in understanding and predicting consumer demand. Sometimes, however, the license does not turn out as anticipated. This often happens when big-budget movies flop.

Licensees also incur the expense of controlling channels of distribution and trying to prevent the counterfeiting of the licensed goods. They are also responsible for additional costs related to the manufacture of the licensed products, according to the licensor's rules and regulations. For example, many licensors have rules governing where a product may be manufactured, which may make producing more expensive than it otherwise might be (Henricks, 1998).

However, despite these disadvantages, licensing will continue to be an important business strategy for many companies.

In addition to understanding the different forms of business ownership and competitive strategies of companies in the textile and apparel industries, it is important to differentiate among the various marketing channels within the industry. Marketing channels are routes that products follow to get to the ultimate user. They consist of businesses that perform manufacturing, wholesaling, and retailing functions in order to get merchandise to the consumer. Marketing channels have several structural systems, including the following (see also Table 2.4):

- direct marketing channel
- limited marketing channel
- extended marketing channel

With the **direct marketing channel**, apparel manufacturers sell directly to consumers. For example, consumers may purchase goods directly from the manufacturer through catalogs or over the Internet. Although some apparel products are available to consumers through this channel, consumers do not have the resources to deal directly with manufacturers for all of their apparel purchases, nor do manufacturers have the resources to deal directly with individual consumers. Therefore, consumers must rely on retailers to search for and screen manufacturers and products for them.

Marketing Channels

Direct Marketing Channel

Manufacturer ⟶ Consumer

Limited Marketing Channel

Manufacturer ⟶ Retailer ⟶ Consumer

Extended Marketing Channels

Manufacturer ⟶ Wholesaler ⟶ Retailer ⟶ Consumer

Manufacturer ⟶ Wholesaler ⟶ Jobber ⟶ Retailer ⟶ Consumer

In a **limited marketing channel**, retailers survey the various manufacturers and select (i.e., buy) merchandise that they believe their customers will want. Retailers also serve as gatekeepers by narrowing the choices for consumers and providing them with access (through retail outlets) to the merchandise, thus performing an important service to consumers. Retailers may also arrange for the production of specific goods (private-label merchandise) that they then make available to their customers. In some cases, apparel manufacturers sell merchandise through their own retail stores (e.g., Ralph Lauren, Nike, Guess?, Juicy Couture, Diesel). Because of the use of a retail store in the process, this form of distribution is considered a limited marketing channel rather than a direct marketing channel, even though the product is sold by the manufacturer. The limited marketing channel is the most typical marketing channel for apparel and home fashions products.

Extended marketing channels involve one of the following:

Wholesalers acquire products from manufacturers and make them readily available to buyers, usually retailers.

Intermediaries buy products from wholesalers at special rates and make them available to retailers. Intermediaries are sometimes referred to as jobbers in this segment of the industry.

Extended marketing channels are used in the distribution of many basic items, such as T-shirts, underwear, and hosiery. For example, a company may produce white T-shirt "blanks" and sell them to wholesalers. The wholesalers will sell the T-shirts to manufacturers that will have designs screen printed on the shirts, using a textile converter for the screen printing process. The shirts are then sold to retailers. However, because of the increased time involved, this type of marketing channel is seldom used for fashion goods that companies want to get to the consumer as quickly as possible.

Marketing Channel Integration

Marketing channel integration is the process of connecting the various levels of the marketing channel so that they work together to provide the right products to consumers in the right quantities, in the right place, and at the right time. Integration can be created through conventional marketing channels or through vertical marketing channels.

Conventional marketing channels consist of independent companies that separately perform the designing, manufacturing, and retailing functions. For example, FUBU International, a Queens-based apparel company, designs and markets merchandise. Partner companies produce and distribute the merchandise through store and nonstore venues. **Vertical marketing channels** (also called vertical integration) consist of companies that work as a united group to design, produce, market, and distribute merchandise. Examples of vertical marketing channels include the following:

- An apparel manufacturer sells merchandise only through its own (or franchised) retail stores.

- A textile producer also manufactures and distributes finished textile products (e.g., hosiery, sheets, towels) to retail stores.

- Private-label (e.g., JCPenney's Arizona brand, Nordstrom's Caslon and Pure Stuff brands) and store brand merchandise (e.g., Crate and Barrel, The Limited, Gap, Old Navy) is produced specifically for a retailer.

In some cases, manufacturers will sell their merchandise through their own stores as well as through other retailers. This distribution strategy is known as **dual distribution**. Many manufacturers, such as Tommy Hilfiger, Liz Claiborne, Ralph Lauren, Pendleton, and Nike, distribute merchandise through both their own bricks-and-mortar stores and through other bricks-and-mortar retailers. Thus, they are engaged in dual distribution.

A growing distribution strategy for companies is a **multichannel distribution** approach. In multichannel distribution, companies offer merchandise through varying retail venues: bricks-and-mortar stores, catalogs, and/or Web sites. For example, J. Jill offers merchandise through bricks-and-mortar stores, catalogs, and a Web site. Multichannel retailing will be discussed more in Chapter 12.

A marketing channel connects the companies in it in several streams, including ones for **physical flow**, **ownership flow** (or **title flow**), **information flow**, **payment flow**, and **promotion flow**. Each stream relates to specific functions that companies perform throughout the marketing channel.

Physical flow: This is the tracking of merchandise from the manufacturer to the retailer or ultimate consumer. It includes warehousing (or storing), handling, and transporting merchandise so that it is available to consumers at the right time, at the right place, and in the right quantity.

Ownership flow or *title flow:* This is the transfer of ownership or title from one company to the next. For example, does the retailer own the merchandise when it leaves the manufacturer's distribution center or when the retailer actually receives the merchandise? The point at which the title is transferred is negotiated between the manufacturer and retailer.

- *Information flow:* This is communication among companies within the marketing channel pipeline. Increased information flow between manufacturers and retailers has resulted from many Quick Response and supply chain management strategies.

- *Payment flow:* This is the transfer of monies among companies as payment for merchandise or services rendered. This includes both the methods used for payment and to whom payments are made.

- *Promotion flow:* This is the flow of communications designed to promote the merchandise either to other companies (*trade promotions*) or to consumers (*consumer promotions*) in order to influence sales.

Laws Affecting the Textile and Apparel Industries

This section briefly reviews a number of federal laws and international treaties that affect the textile, apparel, and home fashions industries. Obviously, not all of these laws will affect all companies, but it is important to note the variety of areas that are covered by federal laws and international treaties—everything from protecting personal property to protecting consumers to protecting fair trade. In addition to these federal laws, a number of state and municipal laws may apply to companies. Professionals in the industries must be aware of and abide by these laws, the details of which can be found in federal, state, and municipal government documents.

Laws Protecting Textile, Apparel, and Home Fashions Inventions and Designs

Many companies in the textile, apparel, and home fashions industries are involved in creating, inventing, or designing new processes and products. Laws related to patents, trademarks, and copyrights were established to protect such inventions and creations.

Laws protecting original garment designs vary from one country to another. Unlike designs created in European countries, in the United States, apparel designs, in and of themselves, are not protected. The United States has generally held a philosophy that laws protecting industrial design (including apparel) would impede design innovation. Inventions, textile print designs, and logos are protected under patent, trademark, and copyright laws, respectively; however, apparel designs are not protected by U.S. law. Some believe this lack of design protection in the United States inhibits apparel design innovation in the United States and has resulted in many U.S. designers working instead in Europe (Keyder, 1999).

The laws in Europe do provide more design protection than do current U.S. laws. As noted by Virginia Brown Keyder (1999), an attorney who specializes in design law:

> European design law, though widely divergent in terms of detail at the national level, continues to afford stronger protection to the designer and is fast becoming harmonized across Europe. In addition, EU [European Union] design law is increasingly being used as a model of legal reform throughout the world.

An example of how a designer in France used French laws to protect his work occurred in 1994 when French designer Yves Saint Laurent took Ralph Lauren to court in a dispute over the copying of a tuxedo dress ("Tuxedo Junction," 1994).

PATENTS

According to the U.S. Patent and Trademark Office, a **patent** grants property rights to an inventor, which includes "the right to exclude others from making, using, offering for sale, or selling the invention in the United States or importing the invention into the United States." A patent allows the inventor or producer the exclusive right to use, make, or sell a product for a period of 20 years. From a legal perspective, products must be new inventions or technological advancements in product design. In the textile, apparel, and home fashions industries, patents can be acquired for technological advancements in textile processing, apparel production, or in products themselves.

For example, Nike acquired a patent (#5,396,675) for a "method of manufacturing a midsole for a shoe and construction therefore." Patents cannot be acquired for garment designs per se. If someone else uses a patented product or process, the owner of the patent has the right to sue the party for patent infringement. For example, in 2007, Reebok sued Nike for patent infringement. Reebok claimed that Nike's flexible sole athletic shoes infringed on Reebok's patent for "collapsible shoe" technology.

TRADEMARKS AND SERVICEMARKS

A **trademark** or trade name is a "word, phrase, symbol, or design, or a combination of words, phrases, symbols, or designs, that identifies and distinguishes the source of the goods of one party from those of others" (U.S. Patent and Trademark Office). **Servicemarks** are similar to trademarks but refer to identifications for services rather than for products. The Lanham Act (Federal Trademark Act) provides for federal registration and protection of trademarks. Although any company can claim rights to a trademark or servicemark by using the TM or SM designators, trademarks can be registered through the U.S. Patent and Trademark Office for a period of 10 years and can be renewed as long as the trademark remains in use. Once it has been registered, the ® symbol is used, and others cannot use the trademark without permission. If they do, they can be sued for **trademark infringement**. Trademark and patent searches are conducted by attorneys who specialize in ensuring that a trademark, trade name, patent, or business name is available for use.

Trademarks and trade names may not be generic terms such as *wonderful* or *exciting*, or, in the apparel industry, such generic terms as *trouser* or *dress*. In the early 1990s, Fruit of the Loom claimed to have ownership of the word *fruit* and sued another company for trademark infringement for using the word *fruit* as a trademark on apparel goods. Fruit of the Loom did not win the case. In 2006, Pendleton Woolen Mills filed a trademark infringement suit against Kmart Corporation for a line of flannel sheets sold at Kmart stores with packaging that indicated "Pendleton flannel sheet set" and featured an Indian trade blanket design similar to designs used by Pendleton Woolen Mills. Pendleton did not have a licensing agreement with Kmart or the company that manufactured the sheets and had not authorized the use of the Pendleton name.

In the textile, apparel, and home fashions industries, registered trademarks and trade names are widespread and include the following:

- trade names of manufactured fibers used for apparel and home fashions (e.g., Dacron polyester, Lycra spandex)
- trade names of natural fiber associations and companies (e.g., Cotton Incorporated's cotton symbol, Wool Company's Woolmark symbol)
- apparel and home fashions manufacturers' trade names (e.g., Levi's Dockers, WestPoint Steven's Vellux)
- trademarks of apparel and footwear manufacturers (e.g., Nike's swoosh, the stitching on the back pocket of Levi's jeans)

Well-known and well-respected trade names and trademarks take years to establish through concentrated efforts in designing goods that meet the needs of consumers, quality control, and advertising. Consumers become confident that goods with a well-known trade name or trademark will meet certain standards in terms of quality and/or image. Thus, they desire these goods. Figure 2.5 shows some well-known trademarks and trade names.

Trade names and trademarks provide immediate consumer recognition of products.

Consumers' desire for apparel with well-known and visible trade names and trademarks has led to numerous trademark infringements and a proliferation of **counterfeit goods** (goods bearing unauthorized registered trade names or trademarks). Typically, counterfeit goods are of much lower quality than the authentic merchandise and are sold at a fraction of the genuine merchandise's price. Counterfeiters exploit consumer awareness and trust of a brand image by producing low-quality merchandise, and they do not pay royalties to the companies that may have spent millions creating that awareness and trust.

To establish trademark infringement in court, the plaintiff must prove the following:

1. Its trademark has achieved a secondary meaning (that is, the consumer associates the trademark with the company or product).

2. The trademark is nonfunctional (that is, the trademark is ornamental or does not contribute to the function of the product).

3. There is likelihood of confusion by the consumer for "famous" trademarks or the trademark has been weakened by the association with the infringing product.

The International Anti-Counterfeiting Coalition estimates that more than $600 billion worth of counterfeit goods are sold every year to knowing or unknowing consumers. The Trademark Counterfeiting Act of 1984 created criminal sanctions against the domestic manufacture of counterfeit goods. Retailers who knowingly sell counterfeit goods can also be criminally liable (see Figure 2.6). Companies also discourage trademark infringement by doing the following:

monitoring the production of their goods

using fabric codes and coded labels (see Figure 2.7) to distinguish authentic goods from imitations

Figure 2.6   Trademark infringement—the unauthorized use of a registered trademark—is illegal.

working with the U.S. Customs and Border Protection to stop the flow of imported counterfeit goods into the United States. In 2004, 68 percent (in dollar value) of the counterfeit goods seized by the U.S. Customs and Border Protection originated in either China or Hong Kong.

Recently, **trade dress** infringement has been tested in the courts with mixed rulings. Trade dress is

a subset of trademark law, only instead of protecting the identifying words or logos, the law of trade dress protects the overall look or image of a product itself or the packaging of a product, provided that the overall look or combination of features has come to identify the manufacturer of the product. (Welt, 1999, p. 88)

FAKE MERCHANDISE

No CAPS - MEMBER LOGO

RIPPED TAG

POORLY RENDERED LOGOS/COLORS

NO NBA HOLOGRAM ATTACHED

NO LICENSEE IDENTIFICATION

AUTHENTIC ITEMS

CAPS - MEMBER LOGOS

NBA HOLOGRAM ATTACHED

LICENSEE IDENTIFICATION

Figure 2.7 Companies often use special sewn-in labels, hangtags, and logos on authentic licensed goods.

Classic examples of trade dress are the distinctive shape of a Coca-Cola bottle and the turquoise packaging of merchandise purchased at Tiffany & Co.

Although it is more difficult to prove trade dress infringement than trademark infringement, and courts generally do not want to interfere with competition, companies do win trade dress lawsuits. For example, Columbia Sportswear Company settled a trade dress infringement against the Orvis Company, which agreed to remove from its product line a pullover windbreaker that Columbia described as a "substantial copy" of Columbia's Gizzmo parka. Recently, jewelry manufacturer Denny Wong Designs won a trade dress lawsuit against Po Sun Hon jewelry company. Rulings indicated that Hon had illegally copied Wong's registered Tropical Memories Plumeria flower jewelry. In this case, it was ruled that the consumer was confused by the copied merchandise.

COPYRIGHTS

Copyrights protect a number of written, pictorial, and performed works, including literature, music, films, television shows, artworks, dramatic works, and advertisements. Under the Copyright Act of 1976 (amended in 1988, 1998, 2005), the copyright holder has the exclusive right to use, perform, or reproduce the material for life of the author plus 70 years or for 95 years for works of corporate authorship (e.g., Disney characters). All works published before 1923 are considered to be in the public domain. Under the *fair use* doctrine, works protected by copyright can be used on a limited basis for educational or research purposes. Reproduction of material protected by copyright without permission is considered infringement.

In the U.S. textile, apparel, and home fashions industries, although garment or product style is not protected by copyright, original textile prints and graphic designs are protected, even when incorporated into a garment or home fashions item (see Figure 2.8). In order to be able to collect damages when a copyright is infringed, the copyright must be registered with the Copyright Office of the U.S. Library of Congress. A textile designer may also put a copyright notice (©) in the selvage of the fabric, although this notice is not necessary (Hughes, 1991). A designer owns the copyright unless the designer is a salaried employee of a company; then the copyright is held by the employer. Any unauthorized reproduction of the textile print or design protected by copyright is considered copyright infringement, and once the copyright is registered, the copyright holder can take the infringer to court. Examples of copyright infringement in the textile industry include the following:

- dishonest textile converters who buy apparel or home fashions at retail in order to copy the textile print

- unscrupulous apparel or home fashions manufacturers that work with one converter to develop new prints, and then take the samples to another converter to have them reproduced more cheaply

Figure 2.8 In the U.S. textile, apparel, and home fashions industries, original textile prints are protected by copyright.

fraudulent retailers that copy textile prints for use in their private-label merchandise (Ellis, 1995)

U.S. copyrights are partially protected in the international market under the Berne Convention, an international treaty designed to help fight infringement across national borders.

Federal Laws Related to Business Practices and International Trade

Many federal laws relate to how a company must run its business, including requirements concerning fair competition, international trade, environmental practices, consumer protection, and employment practices.

FAIR COMPETITION

A number of federal laws have been established to assure fair competition. Table 2.5 reviews the primary laws that prohibit monopolies and unfair or deceptive practices in interstate commerce. Any textile and apparel company that distributes products or services across state lines is governed by these laws. These laws are all administered by the Federal Trade Commission (FTC).

INTERNATIONAL TRADE

Federal regulations and international treaties also exist concerning the international trade of products, including textiles, apparel, and home fashions (see Table 2.6). The primary objective of these laws and treaties is to establish fair trade among countries. Because of shifts in international relations, these laws and treaties are reviewed and amended regularly. Any textile, apparel, or home fashions company that imports goods into or exports goods from the United States is affected by these laws and treaties. In the United States, trade policy is set by the executive branch of the government and carried out by the U.S. Trade Representative. The implementation and administration of trade laws are conducted by several departments, including the following:

- The Export Trade Act is administered by the Federal Trade Commission.

- The Department of Commerce oversees the Committee for the Implementation of Textile Agreements (CITA) and the Office of Textiles (OTEXA).

- The U.S. Customs and Border Protection oversees the physical control of imports and the collection of tariffs (taxes on imports), and prevents counterfeit goods from entering the country.

Table 2.5 Federal Laws Related to Competition

- Sherman Antitrust Act (1890): outlawed monopolies and attempts to form monopolies.
- Clayton Act (1914): amended the Sherman Antitrust Act by
  - forbidding a seller from discriminating in price between and among different purchases of the same commodity
  - outlawing exclusive dealing and tie-in arrangements
  - forbidding corporate asset or stock mergers where the effect may be to create a monopoly
  - forbidding persons from serving on boards of directors of competing corporations
- Federal Trade Commission Act (1914): declared unlawful unfair methods of competition in or affecting commerce and unfair or deceptive acts or practices in interstate commerce. The FTC's Bureau of Competition investigates potential law violations and serves as a resource for policy makers regarding competition (http://www.ftc.gov).
- Robinson-Patman Act (1936): amended the Clayton Act by preventing large firms from exerting excessive economic power to drive out small competitors in local markets.
- Cellar-Kefauver Act (1950): made it illegal to create a monopoly by eliminating competition through company mergers and acquisitions.
- Wheeler-Lea Act (1938): amended the Federal Trade Commission Act by allowing the FTC to stop unfair competition, even if a competitor is not shown to be harmed by a business practice when a consumer is injured by deceptive acts or practices.

Table 2.6 Laws, Agreements, and Organizations Related to International Trade Practices

- General Agreement on Tariffs and Trade (GATT, 1947): a multinational agreement regarding global trade policies. In international trade of textiles and apparel, GATT allowed for the use of tariffs (taxes on imports) to protect domestic industries and for quantitative limits (quotas) on certain textile and apparel merchandise entering the United States from specified countries during a specified period of time.
- Multifiber Arrangement (MFA I: 1947–1977, MFA II: 1977–1981, MFA III: 1981–1986, MFA IV: 1986–1991, extensions to MFA IV: 1991, 1992, 1993): a general framework for international textile trade that operated under the authority of GATT and allowed for the establishment of bilateral agreements between trading partners. The MFA was phased out in 2005 when international trade for textile, apparel, and home fashions industries came under the jurisdiction of the World Trade Organization.

Laws, Agreements, and Organizations Related to International Trade Practices *(continued)*

World Trade Organization (WTO, 1995): the World Trade Organization (WTO) Agreement on Textiles and Clothing (ATC) provided for the reduction and phasing out of quotas on textiles and apparel imported from WTO member countries in three stages between 1995 and 2005. The ATC was approved as part of the Uruguay Round Agreements Act by the U.S. Congress in December 1994 and went into effect on January 1, 1995. In 2007, the WTO had 150 member countries. Most quotas had been phased out for member countries.

Trade Act of 2000: implemented the African Growth and Opportunity Act and the U.S.–Caribbean Basin Trade Partnership.

Trade Act of 2002: modified the Caribbean Basin Economic Recovery Act and the African Growth and Opportunity Act; implemented the Andean Trade Promotion and Drug Eradication Act.

Tax Relief Act of 2006: authorized trade relations with Vietnam, implemented the Haitian Hemispheric Opportunity Through Partnership Encouragement Act, implemented the African Investment Incentive Act, and Andean Trade Preferences Extension Act.

U.S. Free Trade Agreements and implementation dates:
- North American Free Trade Agreement (NAFTA, 1994): United States, Canada, and Mexico
- Central America–Dominican Republic–United States Free Trade Agreement (CAFTA-DR, 2005): Costa Rica, El Salvador, Guatemala, Honduras, Nicaragua, the Dominican Republic, and the United States
- U.S.–Australia (2005)
- U.S.–Bahrain (2006)
- U.S.–Chile (2004)
- U.S.–Columbia (2006)
- U.S.–Israel (1985)
- U.S.–Jordan (2001)
- U.S.–Morocco (2006)
- U.S.–Singapore (2004)

ENVIRONMENTAL PRACTICES

Federal environmental laws regulate business practices related to environmental pollution. The goal of these laws is to protect the environment from toxic pollutants. In the fashion industries, these laws particularly affect chemical companies that manufacture fibers. These companies' processes often produce or require the use of toxic substances, and their factories may emit toxic substances considered pollutants. Table 2.7 lists the primary environmental laws. These laws are administered by the Environmental Protection Agency (EPA).

Table 2.7 Federal Laws Related to Practices to Protect the Environment

- National Environmental Policy Act of 1969: established the national charter for the protection of the environment.
- Clean Air Act (1970): controls air pollution through air quality standards to protect public health.
- Endangered Species Act (1973): provides for the conservation of threatened or endangered plants and animals and the habitats in which the are found.
- Resource Conservation and Recovery Act of 1976: controls the management of solid waste products and encourages resource conservation and recovery.
- Toxic Substances Control Act (1976): allows regulation of the manufacturing, use, and disposal of toxic substances.
- Clean Water Act (1977): controls water pollution by keeping pollutants out of lakes, rivers, and streams.
- Pollution Prevention Act (1990): focused on reducing pollution through cost-effective changes in production, operations, and use of raw materials.

CONSUMER PROTECTION

Beginning in the 1930s and 1940s, a number of laws were enacted to protect the health and safety of consumers (see Table 2.8). Over the years since then, many additional protections have been added. These laws require companies to label truthfully the fiber content and care procedures of products and prohibit companies from selling flammable products. They are administered by either the Federal Trade Commission or the Consumer Product Safety Commission.

EMPLOYMENT PRACTICES

To assure fair hiring and employment practices among companies, a number of laws have been enacted to regulate child labor and homework (piecework contracted to individuals who do the work in their homes) and to prohibit discrimination based on such characteristics as race, sex, age, or physical disability. Any company with employees is regulated by these laws (see Table 2.9).

Federal Laws Associated with Practices for Consumer Protection

Wool Products Labeling Act (1939), Fur Products Labeling Act (1952), the Textile Fiber Products Identification Act (1958, effective 1960, last amended 2006): require specified information to be on textile and fur product labels; require the advertising of country of origin in mail-order catalogs and promotional materials. Administered by the FTC.
 – Enforcement Policy Statement on U.S. Origins Claims (1997): provides guidelines for labeling products as Made in the U.S. to be "all or virtually all" made in the U.S.

Flammable Fabrics Act (1953, last amended 1990): regulates the manufacturing of wearing apparel and fabrics (including carpets, rugs, and mattresses) that are so highly flammable as to be dangerous when worn. Sets standards of flammability and test methods. Sets standards for flammability of children's sleepwear. Originally administed by the FTC; administration transferred to the the CPSC in 1972.

Consumer Products Safety Act (1972): established the Consumer Products Safety Commission (CPSC) to reduce or eliminate risk of injury associated with selected consumer products.

Care Labeling of Textile Wearing Apparel and Certain Piece Goods Act (1971, last amended 2000): requires that care labels be affixed to most apparel and be attached to retail piece goods. Administered by the FTC.

Federal Hazardous Substance Act (1960; last amended 1995): addresses issue of choking, ingestion, aspiration of small items by children, and hazards from sharp points and edges on articles intended for use by children by requiring that decorative buttons or other decorative items on children's clothing pass use and abuse testing procedures. Prohibits the use of lead paint on children's articles, including clothing. Administered by the CPSC.

Table 2.9   Federal Laws Related to Employment Practices

Fair Labor Standards Act of 1938 (last amended 2004): guarantees fair employment status by establishing minimum wage standards, child labor restrictions, and other employment regulations.

Equal Pay Act of 1963: amends the Fair Labor Standards Act by requiring employers to provide equal pay to men and women for doing equal work.

Age Discrimination in Employment Act (1967): prohibits an employer from discriminating in hiring or other aspects of employment because of age. Administered by the Equal Employment Opportunity Commission (EEOC).

Table 2.9   Federal Laws Related to Employment Practices *(continued)*

- Occupational Safety and Health Act of 1970 (last amended 2004): created the Occupational Safety and Health Administration (OSHA); assures safe and healthful working conditions for employees by setting general occupational safety and health standards, and requiring that employers prepare and maintain records of occupational injuries and illnesses. Administered by the Department of Labor/OSHA.
- Equal Employment Opportunity Act of 1972: prohibits discrimination by employers in hiring, promotions, discharge, and conditions of employment if such discrimination is based on race, color, religion, sex, or national origin.
- Americans with Disabilities Act (ADA) of 1990: prohibits discrimination against qualified individuals with disabilities in all aspects of employment; prohibits discrimination on the basis of disability by requiring that public accommodations and commercial facilities be designed, constructed, and altered in compliance with accessibility standards. Administered by the Office of the ADA, Department of Justice.
- Family and Medical Leave Act of 1993: grants eligible employees up to a total of 12 work weeks of unpaid leave for one or more family and medical reasons (e.g., birth of a child, care of an immediate family member).
- Immigration and Nationality Act (last amended 2000): establishes conditions for temporary employment in the United States by non-U.S. citizens.
- Trade Adjustment Assistance Reform Act of 2002 (last amended 2006): reauthorized the Trade Adjustment Assistance Program (first established in 1974), which provides aid to workers whose employment is negatively affected by increased imports.

Summary

Depending on the objectives, needs, and size of textile, apparel, and home fashions companies, they are owned as sole proprietorships, partnerships, or corporations. The advantages and disadvantages of each form of business ownership are related to the ease of formation and dissolution (advantage of sole proprietorship and partnership and disadvantage of corporations), the degree of liability that owners have for business debts (advantage of corporations and disadvantage for sole proprietorship and partnerships), and operational strategies (some advantages and disadvantages for each form of ownership).

Each company—whether a sole proprietorship, partnership, or corporation—competes with other companies on the basis of price, quality, innovation, service, or a combination of these factors. Within the textile, apparel, and home fashions industries, the competitive strategies include monopolies, oligopolies (e.g., athletic shoe industry), oligopsonies, pure competition (e.g., textile commodities), and monopolistic competition, the most common of the five. In monopolistic competition, although companies compete in terms of product type (denim jeans), the specific product attributes of any one company (7 for All Mankind jeans) are perceived as different from the product attributes of other companies (Guess? jeans, Calvin Klein jeans).

Companies create this perceived difference through product differentiation, advertising, licensing programs, private-label merchandise, or services offered. In licensing programs, the owner (licensor) of a particular name, image, or design (property) sells the right to use the name, image, or design to another party, typically a manufacturer (licensee), for payment of royalties. For example, Hartmarx pays Tommy Hilfiger royalties for the use of the Tommy Hilfiger name on a line of men's tailored clothing. Tommy Hilfiger controls the design, distribution, and presentation of the products; Hartmarx controls the production. A licensing contract outlines the terms of the licensing agreement. Licensing programs can be advantageous to both licensors and licensees in terms of expanding product lines and exposure. Possible disadvantages include market saturation and problems in timing of the release of the product.

To get merchandise to the consumer, direct, limited, and extended marketing channels are used by businesses that perform manufacturing, wholesaling, and retailing functions. In conventional marketing channels, separate companies perform these functions; in vertical marketing channels, a single company performs multiple functions.

A number of federal laws affect businesses in the textile, apparel, and home fashions industries. Laws related to patents, trademarks, and copyrights protect the identity, inventions, and designs of designers and companies. For example, a textile designer's fabric design is protected by the copyright law so that others cannot legally copy it. Laws have also been established that relate to how companies must run their businesses, including requirements regarding competition, international trade, protecting consumers, protecting the environment, and employment practices.

Individuals who have careers in the apparel, accessories, and home fashions industries may be part of companies that are sole proprietorships, partnerships, or corporations.

Owner, Sole Proprietor
Women's Specialty Store

Position Description
Responsible for all of the purchasing (buying), advertising, supervising of personnel, special events (in-store and community), in-store selling, and visual merchandising.

Typical Tasks and Responsibilities
- Write orders for merchandise.
- Handle special orders.
- Organize and implement store promotions.
- Determine pricing policies.
- Determine policies regarding merchandise returns.
- Handle in-store customer service.
- Oversee ongoing merchandising of the store to create a "fresh" look.
- Hire, train, schedule, and motivate sales associates.

Corporate Executive Officer, Chairman of the Board
Privately Owned Children's Apparel Manufacturer and Retailer

Position Description
Ultimately responsible for everything from financial decisions to store maintenance. Conceive and create all new products sold wholesale by the company. Run the retail stores. Work with all management personnel, including those who report directly to the chairman, along with the 300 company employees. Motivate and supervise employees at all levels. Sell all products to customers at wholesale and retail.

CAREER PROFILES

Typical Tasks and Responsibilities

Set the vision of the organization.

Model the values of the company with regard to professionalism, integrity, and community involvement.

Apply knowledge of the latest trends and ideas in the market to the design and sale of new products.

Oversee the overall management of the organization.

Make sure everyone remembers that the customer is always right.

Key Terms

articles of incorporation	limited partnership
board of directors	marketing channel integration
brand extension	merger
C corporation	monopolistic competition
close corporation	monopoly
closely held corporation	multichannel distribution
conglomerate	multinational corporation
consolidation	oligopoly
conventional marketing channel	oligopsony
copyright	ownership flow
corporation	partnership
counterfeit goods	patent
direct marketing channel	payment flow
dividend	perfect competition
double taxation	physical flow
dual distribution	private corporation
extended marketing channel	private-label brand
general partner	privately held corporation
information flow	promotion flow
licensing	publicly held corporation
limited liability	publicly traded corporation
Limited Liability Company (LLC)	pure competition
limited marketing channel	regular corporation

Key Terms *(continued)*

S corporation	title flow
servicemark	trade dress
sole proprietorship	trademark
stockholder	trademark infringement
store brand	unlimited liability
takeover	vertical marketing channel

Discussion Questions

1. Interview a small-business owner in your community. Find out whether the business is a sole proprietorship, partnership, LLC, or corporation. Ask the owner why this form of business ownership was chosen and what he or she views as the primary advantages and disadvantages to the ownership form. Find out what business licenses were required of the owner to start the company. Compare this information with information others in class received.

2. Suppose you wanted to invest (buy stock) in a publicly traded corporation. Where can you find information about the corporation? Select a publicly traded corporation in the textile, apparel, and home fashions industries, and find information about the company.

3. What are some examples of licensed textile, apparel, and home fashions products that you own? Which category of licensed goods does each fall into? What characteristic of the property or product was appealing to you as a consumer? Why?

4. Currently, textile designs and prints are protected by copyright from illegal copying, but apparel designs (designs of the garment itself) are not protected in the United States. Do you think that apparel designs should also be covered under copyright law? Why or why not? Justify your response.

References

Altchuler, Murray. (1988). Welcome to your share of $13 million an hour! In F. Ash (Ed.) *The International Licensing Directory*, p. 5. East Sussex, England: A4 Publications Ltd.

Alterbaum, James. (1987, January). What to look for in going public. *Apparel Industry Magazine*, pp. 30–31.

American Apparel Manufacturers Association. (1992). *Federal Standards and Regulations for the Apparel Industry.* Arlington, VA: Author.

Bosworth, Mike. (1999, April). Gavels pound on knockoff vendors. *Apparel Industry Magazine*, pp. 86–90.

Cohen, Gordon S. (1995, April). Hartmarx and Hilfiger team up for success. *Bobbin*, pp. 54–62.

Dickerson, Kitty G. (1999). *Textiles and Apparel in the Global Economy* (3rd ed.). Englewood Cliffs, NJ: Prentice-Hall.

Ellis, Kristi. (1995, June 2–8). Imitation has its price. *California Apparel News*, pp. 18, 20.

Fisher, Bruce D., and Jennings, Marianne M. (1991). *Law for Business* (2nd ed.). St. Paul, MN: West Publishing Co.

Gerber, David A. (1984, September 14). Protecting apparel designs: Tough, but there are ways. *California Apparel News*, p. 24.

Henricks, Mark. (1998, June). The licensing explosion. *Apparel Industry Magazine*, pp. 50–57.

Hughes, John. (1991, January 4–10). Getting it in writing. *California Apparel News*, pp. 16–17.

Keyder, Virginia Brown. (November 12, 1999). *Design Law in Europe and the U.S.* Presentation at the Annual Meeting of the International Textile and Apparel Association, Santa Fe, NM.

Office of Textiles and Apparel, U.S. Department of Commerce. (2006). Trade Acts [online]. Available: http://otexa.ita.doc.gov/Trade_Act_2000.htm [August 27, 2006].

Office of Textiles and Apparel, U.S. Department of Commerce. (2006). WTO (World Trade Organization) [online]. Available: http://otexa.doc.gov/wtolink.htm [August 27, 2006].

Tuxedo Junction: YSL, Ralph square off. (1994, April 28). *Women's Wear Daily*, pp. 1, 15.

U.S. Department of Labor (2006). Bureau of Labor Statistics, Occupational Outlook Handbook [online]. Available: http://www.bls.gov/oco/home.htm [August 30, 2006].

Welt, Henry. (1999, April). Trade dress: Another look at the Samara case. *Apparel Industry Magazine*, p. 88.

CHAPTER 3

Structure of the U.S. Textile Industry

In this chapter, you will learn the following:

- the importance of textile knowledge for the successful design, production, and marketing of apparel and home fashions

- terms used in describing textiles and textile manufacturing

- the organization and operation of the textile industry

- procedures followed in the processing and marketing of natural and manufactured fibers, yarns, and fabrics

- current developments in the textile industry, including international trade, supply chain management strategies, and responses to environmental issues

onsider the following scenarios: an apparel designer is starting a new line of apparel, but before she begins, she examines the newest fabrics shown by textile companies in their showrooms; or, a buyer for a home fashions retailer decides to attend a textile trade show in order to become familiar with the newest trends in colors and fabrics. These scenarios highlight the integrated nature of the textile, apparel, home fashions, and retailing industries. As textiles are the foundation of the soft-goods industries, an understanding of the organization and operation of the textile industry is important for all professionals. Therefore, this chapter describes the organization and operation of the U.S. textile industry and the marketing of fibers and fabrics. It also gives an overview of new developments in the field.

What Are Textiles?

Before we review the organization and operation of the U.S. textile industry, let us first reexamine the basic terminology used to describe textiles. This terminology forms the basis for an understanding of the fabrics used in apparel and home fashions. First, what are **textiles**? The term *textile* is used to describe "any product made from fibers" (Joseph, 1988, p. 347). There are four basic components of textile production:

- fiber processing
- yarn spinning
- fabric production or fabrication
- fabric finishing

Fibers comprise the basic unit used in making textile yarns and fabrics. Fibers are classified into **generic families** according to their chemical composition and can be divided into two primary divisions:

- natural fibers
- manufactured (man-made) fibers

Natural fibers include those made from natural protein fibers of animal origin (e.g., wool, cashmere, camel, mohair, angora, and silk) and natural cellulose fibers of plant origin (e.g., cotton, flax, jute, ramie, and sisal). Leather and fur are considered natural-fiber products created from the **pelts, skins,** and **hides** of various animals. Leather and fur are unique textiles in that the fibers are not spun into yarns and then constructed into fabrics. Instead, the pelts are tawned or tanned to create supple and durable "fabrics."

Whereas natural fibers have been used in making textiles for thousands of years, manufactured fibers have been around for about 120 years. In the mid-1800s, scientists became interested in duplicating natural fibers.

- In 1891, "artificial silk," made from a solution of cellulose, was commercially produced in France.
- In 1924, the name of this fiber was changed to rayon.
- In 1939, nylon, the first fiber to be synthesized entirely from chemicals (synthetic), was introduced by E. I. du Pont de Nemours and Company.

Since then, many more manufactured fibers have been developed, including the following:

- cellulose-based fibers (e.g., lyocell, acetate)
- synthetic fibers (e.g., acrylic, aramid, modacrylic, olefin, polyester, and spandex)
- mineral-based fibers (e.g., glass, metallic)

Until the 1930s, fiber production in the United States focused entirely on natural fibers. By the end of the 1940s, natural-fiber production accounted for 85 percent of the nation's textile mill fiber consumption, and manufactured-fiber production accounted for only 15 percent. By 1965, manufactured fibers accounted for more than 42 percent of total fiber consumption by U.S. textile mills. In 2004, 13.5 billion pounds of fibers were consumed by textile mills, with manufactured fibers accounting for 76 percent, cotton accounting for 23 percent, and wool, silk, and flax accounting for 1 percent.

The word **yarns** refers to the collection of fibers or filaments laid or twisted together to form a continuous strand strong enough for use in fabrics. Yarns are classified as **spun yarns** made from shorter staple fibers, or **filament yarns** made from long continuous fibers. Filament yarns can be either plain or textured. The type of yarn selected will affect the performance, tactile qualities, and appearance of the fabric.

Fabric construction or **fabrication** processes include the following methods used to make fabrics:

- from solutions (e.g., films, foam)
- directly from fibers (e.g., felt, nonwoven fabrics)
- from yarns (e.g., braid, knitted fabrics, woven fabrics, and lace)

The fabric construction process used often determines the name of the fabric (e.g., satin, jersey, lace, felt).

Dyeing and finishing the fabric complete the textile production process. **Finishing** refers to "any process that is done to fiber, yarn, or fabric either before or after fabrication to change the *appearance* (what is seen), the *hand* (what is felt), or the *performance* (what the fabric does)" (Kadolph & Langford, 2002, p. 270). **Greige goods** (also referred to as *grey, gray,* or *loom state goods*) are fabrics that have not received finishing treatments, such as bleaching, shearing, brushing, embossing, or dyeing. Once finished, the fabrics are then referred to as **converted goods**, or **finished goods**. Finishes can be classified in the following ways:

- *general* or *functional*
- *mechanical* or *chemical*
- *durable* (permanent) or *renewable* (impermanent)

Both greige goods and finished fabrics are used in a variety of end uses: apparel, home fashions, other sewn products such as sleeping bags and flags, and industrial uses such as liners for highways and hoses.

Organization of the Textile Industry

Overview of the Industry

The textile industry is one of the oldest manufacturing industries in the United States. With its beginnings during the Industrial Revolution, the textile industry has been an important part of the U.S. manufacturing base for over 200 years.

A combined $60 billion (2002) industy, the textile mills and textile product industries employed approximately 416,000 workers in 2004, down from 560,000 in 1999 and a high of 1.3 million employees in 1951. Another 230,000 were employed by cotton producers, 35,000 by manufactured-fiber producers, and 8,000 in textile machinery production. In the United States, the majority of textiles are produced in southeastern states—North Carolina, South Carolina, Virginia, Tennessee, and Georgia—along with California. In 2005, North Carolina, Georgia, and South Carolina accounted for 57 percent of total textile employment. Because of the nature of the industry, most textile companies are large; 87 percent of all apparel and textile workers are employed in companies with 20 or more employees (Bureau of Labor Statistics, 2005, 2006).

Over the past 15 years, the U.S. textile industry has seen a dramatic decline of 60 percent in employment, with 33 percent of the decline in just the past five years. From 1997 to 2007, 425 U.S. textile mills closed, 171 in North Carolina alone. Nearly 157,000 textile workers lost their jobs from 2000 to 2007 (National Council of Textile Organizations, 2007). This decline can be attributed to the following factors:

the loss of trade protection from less expensive imports (particularly those being imported from Asian countries) that came with the phase-out of quotas by WTO members. As can be seen in Table 3.1, many of the largest synthetic fiber companies in the world are either headquartered or have plants located in Asia.

the growth of vertical integration by retailers (e.g., Wal-Mart, Target, JCPenney) and their decision to purchase fabrics closer to where the apparel or home fashions are being produced

increase in the technologies and capabilities of textile industries worldwide

Largest Global Synthetic Fiber Companies

Formosa Plastics Group

Total: 1.38 million tons

Country: Taiwan

Formosa Plastics Group currently produces six types of fibers: polyester, acrylic, nylon, rayon, carbon, and spandex. Formosa has become one of the largest textile and finishing and dyeing producers in Taiwan, producing different kinds of yarn, plain-weave fabric, knitted cloth, and dyed products. FPG is currently expanding its operations by building a polyester plant in China. The $15 billion global enterprise is based in Taiwan, with 72,000 employees.

Reliance Industries Ltd.

Total: 1.29 million tons

Country: India

With revenues of $22.6 billion, Reliance is the world's largest polyester fiber producer. The company purchased Trevira Polyester Fiber in Germany in 2004. Its research and development arm has developed many new products, such as fluorescent shades on polyester fabrics, and water and oil-repellent finishes on Poly Wool and Lycra spandex stretch fabrics and flame-retardant fabrics, among others. Future R&D efforts will be concentrated on waterproof, colorfast fabrics for outdoor applications.

Largest Global Synthetic Fiber Companies *(continued)*

INVISTA

Total: 1.24 million tons
Country: U.S.A.
INVISTA, owned by Koch Industries, is the world's largest producer of nylon and spandex, with plants in the Americas, Europe, and Asia. Though INVISTA slipped from number one to number three this year, the Wichita, Kansas-based company has a manufacturing or marketing presence in every garment-making region worldwide. INVISTA brands include Lycra, Stainmaster, Thermolite, and Coolmax, among others.

Tuntex

Total: 900,000 tons
Country: Taiwan
Tuntex is a polyester manufacturing company with production operations in Thailand and China. Incorporated in July 1987 as a joint venture between a group of Thai shareholders and the Taiwanese Tuntex group, Tuntex manufactures high-quality polyester products (for nonwovens and yarn manufacturing applications) for global and Thai markets. The company also makes polyester chips and various filament yarns for weaving and knitting.

Yizheng Chemical Fiber Co. Ltd.

Total: 855,000 tons
Country: China
Yizheng is part of number 10-ranked Sinopec, but operates with a level of independence, according to PCI Fibres. As a leading producer of polyester fiber, the company recently formed a joint venture with Unifi of the United States to make specialty-textured polyester in China. In September 2005, Yizheng began construction on a multifunctional polyester staple fiber production line. Yizheng has also recently begun devoting itself to the development of differential fibers.

Shaoxing Yuandong

Total: 820,000 tons
Country: China
Having grown from 100,000 tons in 1999 to 820,000 in 2005, Shaoxing Yuandong, with headquarters in China's Zhejiang province, has even more expansion plans, with projected growth to 1.6 million tons by 2007. Three years ago, Frankfurt-based plant engineering contractor Zimmer AG constructed a polyester staple fiber plant for Shaoxing. The plant was designed for a capacity of 300 tons per day.

Table 3.1   Largest Global Synthetic Fiber Companies *(continued)*

7. *Huvis*

Total: 788,000 tons
Country: South Korea
According to PCI Fibres, South Korean synthetic fiber companies have been facing difficulties in competing with China. Huvis, formed in 2000, has reduced its capacity in South Korea and has instead added capacity in China. Now, close to 40 percent of Huvis's capacity is outside South Korea. The polyester business at Huvis is centered on three sectors: filament yarn, chip fiber, and staple fiber. The Seoul-based company has large-scale polyester production factories located in Jeonju, Suwon, and Ulsan in South Korea.

8. Jiangying Sanfangxiang

Total: 710,000 tons
Country: China
Established in 2001, Jiangying Sanfangxiang has two joint ventures and has been growing steadily since obtaining its import and export license in 1993. The company, located in Jiangsu, concentrates on polyester but also specializes in chemical fiber, textiles, and printed and dyed fabrics as well as chemicals.

9. *Far Eastern Textile Ltd.*

Total: 604,000 tons
Country: Taiwan
Founded in 1942 as the Far Eastern Knitting Factory Co. Ltd., Far Eastern is a diverse group that encompasses everything from retail to cement, according to PCI Fibres. The synthetic fiber division has been a leader in the Taiwanese industry and now has facilities in China. In 2002, Far Eastern formed a new joint venture with DuPont U.S.A. The joint venture has acquired DuPont's polyester plant in Suzhou, China, and transformed it to produce fibers for industrial and special applications.

10. Sinopec Corp.

Total: 595,000 tons
Country: China
Sinopec is a vertically integrated energy and chemical company engaging in oil exploration, refining, petrochemicals, synthetic fiber, gas stations, and so on. The company was set up on February 28, 2000, by China Petrochemical Corp. Sinopec is the number one producer and supplier of major petrochemical products (including petrochemical intermediates, synthetic resin, synthetic fiber monomers and polymers, synthetic fiber, and chemical fertilizer).

SOURCE: Hall, C. and Kaiser, E. (2005, December 1). Global Synthetic Leaders. *Women's Wear Daily*, 190 (116), p. 12. Data provided by PCI Fibres from the "World Synthetic Fibres Supply and Demand Report—2005"; 2005 Annual Capacities (excluding polypropylene).

According to the U.S. Department of Commerce, the one area of the U.S. textile industry that has seen growth over the past few years is the carpet and rug industry. In 2004, the United States supplied approximately 45 percent of the world's carpet (Carpet and Rug Institute, 2006). Corporations producing carpets in the United States include Milliken Carpet, The Dixie Group, and Mohawk Industries, Inc. Chapter 14 discusses home fashions in greater detail.

Structure of the Industry

Companies within the textile industry take part in one or more of the four basic components of textile production: fiber processing, yarn spinning, fabric production, and fabric finishing. The structure of the textile industry is illustrated in Figure 3.1. Some companies specialize in certain aspects of textile production, as shown in the following examples:

- **Throwsters** modify filament yarns for specific end uses, such as increasing luster or texture through altering the yarn.
- **Textile mills** concentrate on the fabric construction stage of production (e.g., weaving, knitting, nonwoven fabric, lace).
- Companies that specialize in finishing fabrics are called **textile converters**.
- Finished fabrics are sold to apparel and home fashions manufacturers, retailers that sell fabrics, or jobbers that sell surplus goods.
- Retailers that sell private-label merchandise may also work directly with converters and/or textile mills.

Within the textile industry are a number of large corporations that operate through a **vertically integrated** marketing channel. Each corporation handles all four steps—from processing the fiber to finishing the fabric—within its own organization. Some vertically integrated companies are also involved in the production of end-use products, such as towels, sheets, or hosiery. Vertically integrated companies include companies that produce textile products made from both natural and manufactured fibers. Although vertically integrated companies may process fibers, they might not actually produce their own fibers. For example, a vertically integrated company that produces cotton knit fabrics might not be involved in growing the cotton. Instead, raw cotton might be purchased from cotton growers. Some companies are partially integrated, in that they focus on several steps of production. For example, some knitting operations (e.g., hosiery, sweaters) not only knit, dye, and cut the fabrics, but they also construct the knitted garments to be sold to retailers.

Natural- and Manufactured-Fiber Production and Marketing

Yarn Mills	Throwster	Vertically Integrated Mills
		Yarn Production
Greige Goods Mills		Greige Goods Production
	Dyeing, Printing, and Finishing Contractors	
Converters		Dyeing, Printing, and Finishing
		Consumer Product Finishing
Findings Production	Importers/Exporters Brokers/Wholesalers/Jobbers	

Apparel Production	Home Fashions Production	Industrial Production

Importers/Exporters Apparel and Home Fashions Markets	Wholesale and Supply Services

Over the Counter	Manufacturers' Outlets	Retailers	Industry and Institutions

Consumers

This flowchart depicts the structure of the textile industry.

One of the oldest vertically integrated textile companies in the United States is Pendleton Woolen Mills, headquartered in Portland, Oregon. Pendleton was started by Clarence and Roy Bishop in Pendleton, Oregon, in 1909. Led by a fourth generation of Bishops, the company now manufactures woolen men's wear, women's wear, and blankets; nonwoolen apparel; and over-the-counter fabrics. It is involved with the following:

the selection and processing of wool

the designing and weaving of fabrics

the development of garments

the shipment and sale of garments, over-the-counter piece goods, and blankets

Such vertical integration allows for coordination among all production steps and increased control of quality throughout the production of the textiles and end-use products. For example, Pendleton textile designers work closely with the apparel designers in engineering the plaid fabrics that will work best for pleated skirt designs.

A number of trade publications cater to the textile industry by providing timely information about trends in the industry, new products, company success stories, and technological advancements. Table 3.2 lists selected trade publications in the textile industry.

Selected Trade Publications in the Textile Industry

The Apparel Strategist (www.apparelstrategist.com): published monthly; business journal of the textile and apparel industries; sections include retail sales and store performance, consumer data, international trade in textiles and apparel, wholesale information, financial information, company spotlights, and industry outlooks

DNR (Daily News Record) (www.dnrnews.com): published weekly; news and in-depth features on menswear manufacturing and retailing, apparel, fibers, and fabrics

EmergingTextiles.com (www.emergingtextiles.com): online statistical reports on textiles and apparel trade including prices, country reports, and tariff and quota updates

Fiber Economics Bureau Publications (www.fibersource.com/feb/feb1.htm):
  Fiber Organon (www.fibersource.com/feb/feb3c.htm): published monthly; statistical journal summarizing producer information on the natural and manufactured-fiber markets including monthly production and shipments, quarterly trends and analyses, and trade information

Table 3.2   Selected Trade Publications in the Textile Industry *(continued)*

- *Manufactured Fiber Handbook* (www.fibersource.com/feb/feb3a.htm): the official data source on the U.S. manufactured-fiber industry
- *Manufactured Fiber Review* (www.fibersource.com/feb/feb3b.htm): monthly newsletter review of the latest U.S. data on manufactured fibers

Nonwovens Industry (www.nonwovens-industry.com): published monthly; for manufacturers, converters, distributors, and suppliers of non-woven soft goods; covers manufacturing processes, distribution, and end-use applications of nonwoven textile products

Southern Textile News (www.textilenews.com): published bi-weekly, offers textile news, including trade matters; new advancements in textile equipment; developments in yarn, thread, knits, wovens, nonwovens, cotton, dyeing and finishing, and apparel; updates on mill news

Textile World (www.textileworld.com): published monthly; for textile executives in their dual role as technologists and managers; leading resource for textile news and information; covers technical developments in the textile industry

Women's Wear Daily (WWD) (www.wwd.com): published daily, Monday through Friday (except holidays); covers all aspects of the business of fashion and beauty including textile, apparel, and home fashions designers, manufacturers, marketers, and retailers

End Uses of Textiles

Although apparel and home fashions are the primary end uses for textiles, it is important to note the variety of other goods made from natural and manufactured fibers. End uses for U.S. textiles vary widely, as shown in the following estimates:

- Thirty-six percent of the total pounds of textiles produced in the United States goes into fabrics for men's, women's, and children's apparel and hosiery; over-the-counter retail piece goods; and craft fabric.
- Twenty-five percent goes into floor coverings, such as carpets, rugs, and paddings.
- Twenty-three percent goes into industrial and other products, such as tires, ropes and cordage, tents, belting, bags, shoes and slippers, and medical and surgical supplies.
- Sixteen percent goes into home fashions products, such as drapery and upholstery fabrics; sheets, pillowcases, and mattresses; blankets; bedspreads; tablecloths; and towels.

Fiber Processing
and Yarn Spinning

The development and marketing of natural versus manufactured fibers vary greatly. In general, natural fibers, as part of the larger agricultural industry, are the product of a crop that is grown and harvested or of an animal that is raised. Manufactured fibers, on the other hand, are created by large non-agricultural corporations through research and development efforts.

Natural-Fiber Processing

Of the natural fibers produced in the United States, cotton has the largest production and wool the second largest production. Worldwide, China, the United States, India, and Pakistan are the four largest producers of cotton, accounting for approximately two-thirds of the production (International Cotton Advisory Committee, 2006).

Figure 3.2 Textiles are used for a variety of end-use products, including apparel, hosiery, and home fashions.

Cotton is obtained from the fibers surrounding the seeds of the cotton plant. The plant is grown most satisfactorily in warm climates where irrigation water is available. Cotton is grown in 17 states, with the combined production of Texas (the leading cotton-producing state), Arkansas, Mississippi, Georgia, California, North Carolina, Tennessee, and Louisiana accounting for 85 percent of U.S. production (National Cotton Council of America, 2005). According to the National Cotton Council of America, 64 percent of cotton produced in the United States each year goes into apparel, 28 percent is used for home furnishings, and 8 percent is used for industrial products.

In conventionally grown cotton, synthetic fertilizers, insecticides, herbicides, fungicides, and defoliants are used. The significant amounts of chemical pesticides and fertilizers—as well as water—used in production has led to criticism of the industry. Organic cotton has emerged as an environmentally responsible approach to growing cotton. Rather than using synthetic chemical fertilizers and pesticides, the following organic techniques are used:

- Natural fertilizers, such as manure, are used. These fertilizers biodegrade.

- Fields are weeded by hand, or cover crops are planted to control weeds.

- Crops are rotated for disease control.

- Beneficial insects that consume destructive insects are introduced.

- Once harvested, certified organic cotton is stored without the use of chemical rodenticides and fungicides.

According to the Organic Trade Association, organic cotton is grown in four states—Texas (leading producer), California, New Mexico, and Missouri—and 12 countries around the world. Worldwide, the United States and Turkey are the largest organic cotton producers, followed by India, Peru, Uganda, Tanzania, and Egypt. Although production of organic cotton represents only .03 percent of total worldwide cotton production, an increase in the amount of organic cotton grown is expected with the escalating demand for this product.

As a result of consumer interest, many apparel and home fashions producers and retailers (e.g., Nike, Patagonia) have organic cotton programs, thus increasing the demand for certified organic cotton. The United States Department of Agriculture (USDA) sets standards and certifies cotton (and other organic agricultural products). The USDA Organic Certification is used in advertising end-use products to the consumer. In 1994, Mission Valley Textiles was the first woven apparel and home furnishings fabrics mill in the United States to receive the government's organic fiber processing certification (Rudie, 1994). Since then, numerous companies have adopted organic cotton programs. Organic cotton and naturally colored cotton programs will be discussed later in this chapter.

In traditional cotton production, after the cotton is picked, a cotton gin is used to separate the fiber, called *cotton lint*, from the seeds. (The seeds, a valuable by-product of the cotton industry, are used to produce cattle feed and cottonseed oil.) The cotton lint is then packed into large bales and shipped to yarn and textile mills. The spinning process of cotton yarns is highly automated; cotton fibers are cleaned, carded, combed, and drawn and spun to create yarns. For blended yarns, other fibers, such as polyester, nylon, or wool, are blended with the cotton during the spinning process. Figure 3.3 shows a cotton processing plant.

Wool fibers are derived from the fleece of sheep, goats, alpacas, and llamas. Worldwide, the largest producers of wool are Australia, New Zealand, and the United Kingdom. China and Italy are the world's largest wool buyers. Although wool production occurs in every state and has a long history in the United States, currently it plays a minor role in U.S. textile production.

Cotton fiber production includes multiple steps, from the cotton gin through carding and combing cotton fibers.

Most wool comes from a number of specific breeds of sheep, including Delaine-Merino, Rambouillet, Hampshire, and Suffolk. Some breeds of sheep can graze in areas of the country with extreme climates that are unsuitable for other livestock. Farm flock production (animals raised in a more confined area) is best suited for other breeds of sheep. Because wool growers often produce small amounts of wool, the use of wool co-ops or pools and warehousing operations is common.

The steps in wool processing are as follows:

1. The first step is shearing the sheep. Shearing usually takes place once a year in the spring, just before lambing. Using electric clippers, a skilled shearer can remove the fleece from a sheep in five minutes. Some shearers can shear more than 100 sheep per day. A chemical shearing process is also used on a limited basis.

2. Bags of wool fleece are inspected, graded, and sorted according to the diameter and length of the wool fibers.

3. Fibers are scoured to remove grease (unrefined lanolin) and impurities. The lanolin is separated from the wash water, purified, and used in soaps, creams, cosmetics, and other products.

4. Clean wool fibers from different batches are blended to achieve uniform color and quality.

5. Fibers are carded, a process that straightens the fibers and removes any remaining vegetable matter. Wool to be used in worsted fabrics undergoes a combing process in which the fibers are further straightened.

6. The fibers are drawn and spun into yarns.

Organic wool is produced using organic feed and without the use of synthetic hormones, insecticides, pesticides, and feed additives. In 2005, organic wool was grown in six U.S. states, with over 80 percent of certified organic wool grown in the United States coming from New Mexico, followed by Montana and Maine (Organic Trade Association, 2006).

Wool fabrics are often processed by the same company that processes the fiber. Wool, like other fibers, can be dyed at one of the following stages in the production process:

• immediately after it is washed and blended (*stock dyed* or *vat dyed*)

• after it has been spun into yarns (*yarn dyed*)

• after it has been woven or knitted into fabric (*piece dyed*)

Wool absorbs many different dyes uniformly. Some wool producers market wools that, rather than being dyed, are sorted and sold in natural sheep colors, ranging from cream to a broad spectrum of browns, blacks, and grays.

Mohair comes from the wool of the Angora goat. In the United States, mohair production has steadily decreased over the past 20 years, with production found primarily in Texas, Arizona, and New Mexico. Almost all of the raw mohair fiber produced in the United States is exported for processing, primarily to China. This is because most U.S. textile mills have equipment designed to process cotton and wool—which are much larger industries in the United States than is mohair. Cotton and wool fibers measure two inches or less, whereas mohair fibers are often four to six inches long. Therefore, machinery designed to process cotton and wool cannot be used for mohair. Worldwide, mohair production is found primarily in South Africa, the United States, and Turkey. Worldwide production has also declined as other luxury fibers have gained favor. However, in recent years, products such as specialty carpeting, wall hangings, and upholstery made from mohair and mohair blends have spurred new interest in this luxury fiber.

Cashmere comes from the undercoat wool of the Cashmere or Kashmir goat. Most of the world's cashmere comes from China, Mongolia, and Tibet. China, Italy, and the United Kingdom are the world's largest buyers of cashmere.

Cashmere is considered a luxury fiber because of its cost and is often blended with other, less-expensive, wools. However, demand for cashmere has grown in recent years as high-end designers (e.g., Burberry, Gucci, Armani) have included cashmere products in their collections and consumer desire for the soft fibers has increased.

Leather Production

Leather is obtained from the skins and hides of cattle, goats, and sheep, as well as from a variety of reptiles, fish, and birds. Most skins and hides are a by-product of animals raised primarily for their meat or fiber. Thus, "the leather industry is a bridge between production of the hide, a by-product of the meat industry, and manufacture of basic raw material into nondurable goods, such as shoes and wearing apparel" (Eberspacher, 1993, p. 26). Pelts are categorized according to the following weights:

- The term *skins* refers to pelts weighing 15 pounds or less when shipped to the tannery.
- The term **kips** refers to pelts weighing from 15 to 25 pounds.
- The term *hides* refers to pelts weighing more than 25 pounds.

Animal pelts go through a number of processes that transform them into leather. They are first cleaned to remove hair. Then, they are tanned, colored or dyed, and finished (e.g., glazed, embossed, napped, or buffed).

Tanning is the process used to make skins and hides pliable and water resistant. The tanning process can use a number of agents, including vegetable materials, oils, chemicals, and minerals, or a combination of more than one type of agent. With vegetable tanning, natural tannic acids found in extracts from tree bark are used. Because vegetable tanning is extremely slow and labor intensive, it is seldom used in commercial tanning. Oil tanning uses fish oil (usually codfish) as a tanning agent. Oil tanning is used to make chamois, doe-skin, and buckskin. One of the quickest tanning methods is through the use of chemicals, typically formaldehyde.

Two tanning methods use minerals—alum tanning and chrome tanning. Alum tanning is rarely used today. Chrome tanning, the least expensive and most commonly used method, requires the use of heavy metals and acids, which are toxic. The chrome tanning process also produces acidic waste water with a pH of 4.5 to 5.0 (acidic). Thus, this industry is heavily regulated by the Environmental Protection Agency (EPA) and must meet their waste standards for air, liquid, and solid wastes. This explains why there are few leather tanneries and finishers in the United States (just over 300, with Pennsylvania, Massachusetts, New York, and Wisconsin as the leading employers), and a growth of tanneries in developing countries where labor costs are less and environmental standards are not as strict. However, tanning systems that include recycling chromium have been developed and have allowed U.S. companies to reduce the amount of chromium found in waste.

The few U.S. tanneries remaining are typically small privately held companies. Approximately 7,000 individuals are employed in the U.S. leather and hide tanning and finishing industry with the majority working in production (U.S. Bureau of Labor Statistics, 2005). **Regular tanneries**, the most common type of tannery, buy skins, kips, and hides and sell finished leather. Leather **converters** buy skins, kips, and hides, contract with a tannery to tan them according to specifications, and then sell the finished leather. Most of the U.S. companies tan and finish cattle hides. As costs increase, raw hides are typically being shipped overseas for finishing.

Compared to other textiles, leather production is a relatively slow process. Because of the longer lead time needed in the production from hide to finished product, leather producers often must make styling and color decisions before other textile producers. Therefore, they are keenly involved with trend forecasting and market research. Casual footwear and automobile upholstery account for most of the leather market in the U.S. Leather is also used for such products as apparel (e.g., jackets, coats) and handbags (see Figure 3.4).

Fur Production

Fur fibers are considered luxury products that come from animals valued for their pelts, such as mink, rabbit, beaver, and muskrat. Pelts are the unshorn skins of these and other animals. The United States is the largest consumer market for fur products in the world and the third-largest producer of raw fur.

Figure 3.4   End uses for leather include footwear, apparel, handbags, and other accessories.

Fur is divided into two categories: farm-raised and wild fur. Farm-raised fur is derived from reproducing, rearing, and harvesting domestic fur-bearing animals in captivity. Worldwide, 64 percent of fur farms are found in Northern Europe, and 11 percent are found in North America. Over 85 percent of total fur production is farm raised, with mink comprising 90 percent of farm-raised production and fox comprising 10 percent. Wild fur is derived from the selective and regulated harvesting of surplus fur-bearing animals that are not endangered or threatened species and that do not live in captivity. Fur pelts are sold at fur auctions to fur processors. Major fur auction houses are located in Copenhagen, Frankfurt, Helsinki, Hong Kong, Leipzig, New York, Seattle, St. Petersburg, Toronto, and Vancouver.

The tanning process for fur, known as **tawning**, differs from the tanning of hides for leather. To tan fur pelts, salt, water, alum, soda ash, sawdust, cornstarch, and lanolin are used. Each ingredient is natural and nontoxic, and the tawning process produces neutral waste water with a pH of 7 (neutral—neither acidic nor alkaline). Many furs are also bleached or dyed to improve their natural color or to give them a nonnatural color (e.g., blue, green). Pelts are also glazed to add beauty and luster to the fur.

Fur production and the wearing of fur have been politically charged topics for many years. In the 1970s, efforts of animal rights and other organizations (e.g., World Wildlife Fund, Fur Conservation Institute of America) pushed for the enactment of the Endangered Species Conservation Act of 1973, which protected endangered animal species in 80 countries worldwide. More recently, animal rights groups have organized anti-fur campaigns, creating an intense and widespread debate over the humane treatment of animals used for fur production and environmental claims of the fur industry. The Fur Commission USA (2007) Animal Welfare Committee certifies fur farmers who are committed to humane treatment in all aspects of fur farming, including "attention to nutritional needs; clean, safe and appropriate housing; prompt veterinary care; consideration for the animals' disposition and reproductive needs; and elimination of outside stress." However, even with such assurances, anti-fur activists continue to campaign against the killing of animals for the production of luxury goods.

Manufactured-Fiber Processing

Since the first synthetic fiber (nylon) was introduced in 1939, the demand for synthetics has steadily increased. Synthetic fibers now account for 94 percent of the world's fiber production. Of the manufactured fibers produced, polyester production accounts for 58 percent, olefin (polypropylene) 17 percent, nylon 11 percent, acrylic 8 percent, and cellulosic (e.g., rayon) 6 percent.

In the past 20 years, dramatic shifts in manufactured-fiber production have occurred. In 2002, Asia produced approximately 65 percent of the world's manufactured fibers (up from 30 percent in 1982). North America and Western Europe saw small overall growth in production and declines in share of the world production. In 2002, North America and Western Europe accounted for 14 and 13 percent of world production, respectively. According to the American Fiber Manufacturers Association, the U.S. manufactured-fiber industry employs approximately 30,000 people, primarily in North Carolina, South Carolina, Alabama, Georgia, Virginia, and Tennessee. The most widely produced manufactured fibers in the United States are polyester, nylon, olefin, and acrylic. Because of the high capital investment needed, manufactured-fiber producers are typically owned by or are part of large chemical or plastics companies.

The largest synthetic textile company in the United States is INVISTA, a multinational company and the world's largest producer of nylon and spandex. Originally the textiles and interiors division of DuPont, it was renamed INVISTA in 2004. INVISTA produces and markets fiber brand names such as Lycra spandex and Antron nylon carpet fiber. Table 3.3 lists selected U.S. manufactured-fiber producers. Many of these companies are said to be **horizontally integrated**, in that they produce several fibers or variations of fibers that are at the same stage in the process (i.e., fiber processing). For example, INVISTA produces several types of nylon.

New manufactured fibers are developed through research efforts that take up to five years before the fiber is available on the market. According to the Textile Products Identification Act, when a fiber belonging to a new generic family is invented, the U.S. Federal Trade Commission assigns it a new generic name. Currently, more than 25 generic fibers are recognized by the FTC; see Table 3.4 for a listing of these fibers.

The steps in producing manufactured fibers are as follows:

1. The raw material is converted into a group of related chemical compounds that are treated with intense steam heat, chemicals, and pressure. During this process, which is called *polymerization*, the molecules become long-chain synthetic polymers. The molten resin is then converted into flakes or chips.

2. The flakes or chips are melted and extruded to form filaments. Variations in the appearance of the filaments may be obtained at this stage by changing the shape of the fiber or adding chemicals to modify the fiber characteristics.

Selected Manufactured-Fiber Producers and Fiber Trade Names

American Fibers and Yarns Co.	Impressa Olefin
	Innova Olefin
Celanese Corporation	Celanese Acetate
	Celstar Acetate
DAK Americas	Dacron Plus Polyester
DuPont Performance Materials	Kevlar Aramid
	Nomex Aramid
	Tyvek Olefin
FiberVisions, Inc.	Herculon Olefin
Honeywell Nylon, Inc.	Anso Nylon 6
	Caprolan Nylon 6
	Zeftron Nylon 6
Honeywell International	Spectra Olefin
INVISTA, Inc.	Antron Nylon 6.6
	Cordura Nylon 6.6
	TACTEL Nylon 6.6
	Lycra Spandex
Lenzing Group	TENCEL Lyocell
Nylstar, Inc.	Meryl Nylon
Solutia, Inc.	Acrilan Acrylic
	Duraspun Acrylic
	SEF Modacrylic
	Ultron Nylon 6.6
Sterling Fibers, Inc.	Creslan Acrylic
	Creslite Acrylic
	Cresloft Acrylic
Wellman, Inc.	Wellon Nylon
	Fortrel Polyester
	ComFortrel Polyester
	Ultra Polyester

Table 3.4   Names of Generic Fibers

acetate	olefin (polypropylene)
acrylic	PBI (polybenzimidazole)
anidex	PBO (polyphenylenebenzobisozazole)
aramid	PEN (polyethylene naphthalate)
azlon	PLA (polylactic acid fiber)
elastoester	polyester
glass	rayon
lyocell (subcategory of rayon)	saran
melamine	spandex
metallic	sulfar or PPS (polyphenylene sulfide)
modacrylic	triacetate
nylon	vinal
nytril	vinyon

3. The cold-drawing process winds and stretches the filaments from one rotating wheel to a second faster-rotating one. This straightens the molecules and permanently introduces strength, elasticity, flexibility, and pliability to the yarn.

Manufactured fibers can be modified in terms of shape (cross-section), molecular structure, chemical additives, or spinning procedures to create better-quality or more versatile fibers and yarns. Generic fibers are also combined within a single fiber or yarn to take advantage of specific fiber characteristics. Yarn variations include monofilament and multifilament yarns, stretch yarns, textured yarns, and spun yarns. Companies continue to invest in research to create fiber and yarn innovations to meet consumer demand. Innovations such as microfiber yarns (introduced in 1986) and TENCEL Lyocell (introduced in 1992) have met with favorable consumer response. Many of the same companies in the United States that produce manufactured fibers also produce yarns (e.g., INVISTA, Solutia, and Wellman). In addition, many textile mills focus on producing yarns with natural, manufactured, and blended fibers (e.g., Carolina Mills, Frontier Spinning Mills, Patrick Yarns, Richmond Yarns, Tuscarora Yarns, Unifi, and Waverly Mills).

Natural fibers are considered commodities; they are bought and sold on global markets, with prices based upon market demand. For example, in the mid-1990s, cotton prices soared as consumer demand went up and cotton supplies dwindled because of devastating weather and insect-related crop failures in China (the world's largest producer of cotton) and other major producing countries, such as India and Pakistan. The largest commodity markets for cotton in the United States are Dallas, Houston, Memphis, and New Orleans; for wool, Boston; and for mohair, a warehouse system throughout Texas. These natural fibers are sold to mills for yarn spinning and fabric production. Furs are sold at public auction. In the United States, the largest fur market where furs are auctioned is New York.

Not until the late 1940s and early 1950s, when the popularity of manufactured fibers was growing, were marketing efforts for natural fibers initiated by each **trade association** that represents a specific fiber. These trade associations—such as Cotton Incorporated, the American Wool Council, the Mohair Council of America, and the Cashmere and Camel Hair Manufacturers Institute (CCMI)—are supported by natural-fiber producers and promote the use of the natural fibers through activities such as research, educational programs, and advertising on television and in trade and consumer publications. Through these activities, natural-fiber trade associations have become an important support arm for the apparel and home fashions industries, and strong relationships have developed between the trade associations and the apparel and home fashions companies that use natural fibers.

Founded in 1961, Cotton Incorporated is a research and promotional organization supported by U.S. cotton growers and importers of cotton products. Cotton Incorporated's members receive technical services, color and trend forecasting services, and promotional services. In 2000, Cotton Incorporated opened a new research and development headquarters in Cary, North Carolina. The research facility includes textile testing, product care, and color labs. Cotton Incorporated's Seal of Cotton trademark (see Figure 3.5) is used on hangtags and in advertisements, along with

Figure 3.5 This is Cotton Incorporated's trademark for products made of 100 percent (upland) cotton.

the association's slogan "The Fabric of Our Lives." In recent years, Cotton Incorporated has sponsored collections of new designers during the spring fashion shows in New York City. Cotton Incorporated is also involved in market research, such as its ongoing *Lifestyle Monitor* program designed to "monitor America's attitudes and behaviors toward apparel and home furnishings" (Cotton, Incorporated, 2007). Research results are published as print and Web reports in the *Lifestyle Monitor*. It includes consumer segment profiles, retail patronage profiles, summaries of consumers' attitudes, and forecasts.

Trade associations focusing on wool fall into the following two categories:

- those that focus on wool production (e.g., California Wool Growers Association, Montana Wool Growers Association)
- those that focus on product development, marketing, and education (e.g., American Wool Council and Australian Wool Services Limited)

Established in 1955, the American Wool Council is a division of the American Sheep Industry Association. Its programs are involved in all aspects of wool marketing, from raw wool marketing and product development to registered trademark programs, advertising, and publicity. The American Wool Council has been involved in standardizing quality levels of wool and promoting wool applications with spinners, weavers, knitters, designers, manufacturers, and retailers.

The Woolmark Company was established in 1937 as the International Wool Secretariat (IWS) and is now a subsidiary of Australian Wool Services Limited. The overall goal of The Woolmark Company is to expand the use of wool throughout the world. In 1964, the Woolmark program, with its well-known Woolmark symbol (see Figure 3.6), was created to identify quality products made from new wool. The Woolmark Blend symbol was introduced in 1971 to identify products made from at least 50 percent new wool, and the Wool Blend symbol was introduced in 1999 to identify products containing between 30 and 50 percent new wool. The IWS officially changed its name to The Woolmark Company in 1997, and, in 2001, Australian Wool Services Limited was established, with The Woolmark Company one of its two subsidiaries. Currently, The Woolmark Company licenses the Woolmark symbols across 65 countries. Its services include trend and color forecasting, textile testing, licensing the Woolmark symbols, and global market analyses.

Figure 3.6 The Woolmark, a registered trademark of The Woolmark Company, is used on hangtags and in advertising.

Established in 1966, the Mohair Council of America is "dedicated to promoting the general welfare of the mohair industry" (Mohair Council of America). The council has offices in San Angelo, Texas, and New York City. The council's programs focus on market surveys, research, and development activities, including advertising, workshops, and seminars. Because most of the mohair produced in the United States is exported, the council conducts foreign as well as domestic market research and promotion. The council's trademark in shown in Figure 3.7.

The Cashmere and Camel Hair Manufacturers Institute (CCMI) is an international trade association of producers and manufacturers of camel hair and cashmere fiber, yarn, fabric, and garments. Established in 1984, the goals of the institute are to "promote the use of genuine cashmere and camel hair products and to protect the interests of manufacturers, retailers, and consumers of these products and to maintain the integrity of cashmere and camel hair products through education, information, and industry cooperation" (CCMI, 2006). Other trade associations focusing on natural fibers include the International Linen Promotion Commission, National Cotton Council, and International Silk Association.

Trade associations also play an important part in marketing leather and fur. Associations, such as the Leather Industries of America and the Fur Information Council of America, are involved with promotion, including advertising (see Figure 3.8) and consumer education

Figure 3.7   Registered trademark of the Mohair Council of America

Figure 3.8   Natural fiber trade associations promote the use of natural fibers through advertising.

programs. The mink industry also has a number of breeder associations, such as the Fur Commission USA and the Canada Mink Breeders Association, that are involved in promotion efforts.

The trade associations discussed above concentrate their efforts on specific segments of the natural-fiber industry. The National Council of Textile Organizations (NCTO) has a broader mission, as it represents the entire spectrum of the textile sector, including fiber producers, textile mills, and other textile suppliers. The NCTO is highly involved with lobbying efforts in Washington, D.C., on the behalf of the U.S. textile industry. As its Web site states: "Domestically focused to ensure a prosperous future for the U.S. textile sector and globally driven to utilize the vast resources of our allies to establish a balanced and fair trading environment, NCTO is on the front lines meeting the challenges of the twenty-first century. From fibers to finished products, from machinery manufacturers to power suppliers, NCTO is the voice of the U.S. textile industry" (National Council of Textile Organizations, 2007). Table 3.5 lists selected trade associations in the textile industry.

Table 3.5   Selected Textile Trade Associations

American Association of Textiles Chemists and Colorists (AATCC)
P.O. Box 12215
Research Triangle Park, NC 27709
Tel: (919) 549-8141
Fax: (919) 549-8933
www.aatcc.org

American Fiber Manufacturers Association (AFMA)
1530 Wilson Blvd.
Suite 690
Arlington, VA 22209
Tel: (703) 875-0432
Fax: (703) 875-0907
www.afma.org

American Textile Machinery Association
201 Park Washington Court
Falls Church, VA 22046
Tel: (703) 538-1789
www.atmanet.org

American Wool Council
c/o American Sheep Industry Association
9785 Maroon Circle
Suite 360
Centennial, CO 80112
Tel: (303) 771-3500
Fax: (303) 771-8200
www.sheepusa.org

American Yarn Spinners Association, Inc. (AYSA)
2500 Lowell Road
Gastonia, NC 28053
Tel: (704) 824-3522
Fax: (704) 824-0630
www.textileweb.com/storefronts/aysa.html

Association of Nonwoven Fabrics Industry
1100 Crescent Green, Suite 115
Cary, NC 27518
Tel: (919) 233-1210
Fax: (919) 233-1282
www.inda.org

Selected Textile Trade Associations *(continued)*

Australian Wool Services Limited
The Woolmark Company
1230 Avenue of the Americas, 7th Floor
New York, NY 10020
Tel: (646) 756-2535
Fax: (646) 756-2538
www.woolmark.com

Carpet and Rug Institute
730 College Drive
Dalton, Georgia 30720
Tel: (706) 278-3176
Fax: (706) 278-8835
www.carpet-rug.com

Cashmere and Camel Hair Manufacturers Institute (CCMI)
6 Beacon Street
Suite 1125
Boston, MA 02108
Tel: (617) 542-7481
Fax: (617) 542-2199
www.cashmere.org

Cotton Council International
1521 New Hampshire Avenue NW
Washington, DC 20036
Tel: (202) 745-7805
Fax: (202) 483-4040
www.cottonusa.org

Cotton Incorporated
6399 Weston Parkway
Cary, NC 27513
Tel: (919) 678-2220
Fax: (919) 678-2230
www.cottoninc.com

Fur Information Council of America (FICA)
8424 A Santa Monica Blvd. #860
West Hollywood, CA 90069
Tel: (323) 848-7940
Fax: (323) 848-2931
www.fur.org

Leather Industries of America
3050 K Street, NW
Suite 400
Washington, DC 20007
Tel: (202) 342-8086
Fax: (202) 342-8583
www.leatherusa.com

National Cotton Council of America
1918 N. Parkway
Memphis, TN 38112
Tel: (901) 274-9030
Fax: (901) 725-0510
www.cotton.org

National Council of Textile Organizations
910 17th Street NW, Suite 1020
Washington, DC 20006
Tel: (202) 822-8028
Fax: (202) 822-8029
www.ncto.org

Synthetic Yarn and Fiber Association
PO Box 66
Gastonia, NC 28053
Tel: (704) 824-3522
Fax: (704) 824-0630
www.thesyfa.org

Marketing Manufactured Fibers

Manufactured fibers are most often produced by vertically integrated companies. Prices are set primarily by the cost of developing and producing the fibers. Manufactured fibers are sold either as commodity fibers or brand name fibers.

- *Commodity fibers* are generic manufactured fibers (parent fibers) sold without a brand name attached. For example, a carpet labeled "100 percent" nylon is probably manufactured with commodity nylon fibers.

- Manufactured fibers are also sold under **brand names** (or **trade names**) given to the fibers by manufacturers. Brand names distinguish one fiber from another in the same generic family. Modified manufactured fibers with special characteristics are typically sold under brand names (See Table 3.3 on page 107). Examples include the following:
  - Lycra spandex (INVISTA)
  - TENCEL Lyocell (Lenzing Fibers)
  - Dacron polyester (INVISTA)
  - Fortrel polyester (Wellman, Inc.)
  - Ascend nylon (Solutia, Inc.)
  - Antron nylon carpet fiber (INVISTA)

To establish consumer recognition of brand name fibers, promotion activities focus on the company, the brand name, and the specific qualities of the fiber (see Figure 3.9). Companies spend a great deal of money establishing brand name identification among consumers, and brand name fibers are generally higher in price than commodity fibers. Advertisements also connect brand name fibers with specific end uses. Therefore, cooperative advertising between manufactured fiber companies and apparel and home fashions manufacturers is common.

Licensed brand name programs, or **controlled brand name programs**, set minimum standards of fabric performance for the trademarked fibers. Determined through regular textile testing, these standards are established as a form of quality assurance and relate to a specific end use. The following examples illustrate minimum standards for trademarked fibers:

- The Wear-Dated brand of nylon carpet fibers produced by Solutia, Inc. has minimum standards for wear and soil resistance, stain resistance, color and light fastness, and tuft bind (adhesion to carpet backing).

- The Trevira polyester program (Trevira is a company in the Reliance Group) establishes minimum standards for fabric quality for specific end uses.

- Coolmax is a registered trademark of INVISTA. It certifies high-performance fabrics that include INVISTA and, in some cases, other companies' fibers.

The standards set through these programs can be especially beneficial to apparel and home fashions manufacturers in quality assurance and marketing end-use products.

Fiber producers also design and create **concept garments** to promote their new fibers to textile mills. For example, when Solutia, Inc. has a new product to show textile mills, it will often show the new product in garment form. When creating concept garments, fiber companies will either create fabrics and the garment on their own machinery, or work with a textile mill and manufacturer that will produce small runs of the concept garment. For example, INVISTA shows samples of Coolmax fabrics made into actual performance garments as part of their marketing program.

As with natural fibers, trade associations are also important to the manufactured-fiber industry. The American Fiber Manufacturers Association (AFMA) began in 1933, first as the Rayon Institute, and then as the Man-Made Fiber Producers Association. The current name was adopted in 1988. AFMA members include companies such as the following:

The future of fashion.

Soft. Relaxed. Fashion forward. Micromattique. The premier microfiber.

HAGGAR Black Label

MICROMATTIQUE DUPONT

A finer feel for life

Look for HAGGAR Black Label at fine department stores.

MICROMATTIQUE is a DuPont trademark.

Figure 3.9 Brand name manufactured fibers are advertised to increase name recognition among customers.

- American Fibers and Yarns Company
- INVISTA
- Lenzing Fibers, Inc.
- Solutia, Inc.
- Unifi, Inc.
- Wellman, Inc.

The AFMA focuses on domestic production of synthetic and cellulosic manufactured fibers. Programs include government relations, international trade policy, the environment, technical issues, and education services. AFMA's statistics division, the Fiber Economics Bureau, collects and publishes data on production and trade of manufactured fibers.

Color Forecasting in the Textile Industry

Color is an important criterion used by consumers in the selection of textile products, including apparel and home fashions. Therefore, an understanding of consumers' color preferences is crucial to successfully marketing a particular textile product. Whereas some classic colors remain popular over many years, fashion colors have a shorter fashion lifecycle. Because color is typically applied at the textile production stage, textile companies are often involved in determining which colors are to be used in the end-use products. Through the process of **color forecasting**, color palettes or **color stories** are selected and translated into fabrics produced by a company for a specific fashion season. Color forecasting is also conducted by apparel and home fashions manufacturers (see Chapter 5).

The Color Association of the United States (CAUS) is a nonprofit service organization that has been involved in color forecasting since 1915. More than 700 companies, including fiber producers, textile companies, apparel manufacturers, and home fashions producers, belong to CAUS. A committee of volunteers from these companies determines general color palettes for the coming 18 to 24 months. Twice a year (in March and September), swatch cards (see Figure 3.10) are sent to member companies for their use in determining color palettes for their own products.

The International Colour Authority (ICA) is an international **color forecasting service**. Teams of representatives from member companies and color experts meet biannually to determine general color palettes approximately 22 to 24 months before the products they produce will be available to the consumer. ICA services provide some of the earliest predictions in the industry. Separate palettes are created for men's wear, women's wear, leather, home fashions, and paints. Forecasts are then sent to member companies for their use.

A number of other color forecasting services also sell color forecasts to companies. These forecasts may be

Figure 3.10 Swatch cards from color forecasting services assist textile companies in their color decisions.

specific to a particular target market and product (e.g., women's apparel, children's apparel). Often the services will also include style and fabrication forecasting. *The color box* provides subscribers with four color and design forecasts per year for men's wear, children's wear, and women's wear. Color forecasting services include the following:

Trendstop.com is a highly regarded online global color and trend forecasting service that provides subscribers with current research on a variety of international fashion trends.

Headquartered in Paris, Promostyl is an international color, fabric, and style forecasting service that provides trend analyses for men's, women's, and children's apparel 12 to 18 months ahead of the fashion season.

Peclers Paris also offers color and trend forecasts for fashion, industrial design, and home fashions.

Color forecasts may also be conducted by trade associations for their member companies. For example, Cotton Incorporated provides color forecasting services to its members.

Textile, apparel, and home fashions companies also conduct their own color forecasting, which is more specific to their product and target market than the information provided by color forecasting services. This type of color forecasting is accomplished through the following steps:

reviewing color predictions from color forecasting services

tracking color trends by examining the colors that were the best and worst selling from previous seasons

observing general trends that may affect color preferences of the target market

looking at what colors have been missing from the color palettes in order to select colors that may be viewed as "new"

Textile mills focus on the fabric construction or fabrication stage of textiles. According to North American Industry Classification System (NAICS, 2002) definitions, Sector 313 Textile Mills are companies "that transform a basic fiber (natural or synthetic) into a product, such as yarn or fabric, that is further manufactured into usable items, such as apparel, sheets, towels, and textile bags

Figure 3.11 Fabric production is highly automated. These machines are used at Pendleton Woolen Mills for carding or straightening the tangled wool fibers (top), spinning the wool into yarn (center), and weaving woolen fabric (bottom).

for individual or industrial consumption." The two most common fabric construction methods are weaving and knitting. Except for vertically integrated companies that produce both woven and knitted goods, textile mills typically specialize in the production of one type of fabric. In addition to fabric production, woven textile mills often spin their own yarn (see Figure 3.11), whereas knitters typically purchase their yarn. All textile mills sell greige goods. Greige goods may be used "as is" or bought by converters who finish the goods. In addition to selling greige goods, vertically integrated companies also finish the goods themselves and may produce end-use products, such as home textiles (e.g., sheets and towels).

In 2004, 3.1 billion pounds of cotton (down from 5.2 billion pounds in 1994) and 43 million pounds of wool (down from a high of 153.3 million pounds in 1994) were used by U.S. textile mills. On a much smaller level, specialty fibers, such as mohair and cashmere, are also produced. Almost all linen and silk are imported by U.S. companies. In 2004, 77.7 million pounds of linen and silk were used.

Mills sell staple and/or specialty (novelty) fabrics. Staple fabrics, such as denim or tricot, are produced continually each year with little change in construction or finish. Novelty fabrics have special design features (e.g., surface texture, specialty weave) that are fashion-based and, therefore, change with fashion cycles. Because of this, fashion fabrics require shorter production runs and greater flexibility.

The knitting industry has two main divisions:

- the knitted products industry, which manufactures end-use products, such as T-shirts, hosiery, and sweaters
- the knitted fabrics industry, which manufactures knitted yard goods sold to apparel and home fashions manufacturers and retailers

Textile mills are found throughout the world, with eastern Asian countries (China, Taiwan, Japan) and India accounting for most of the world's textiles. Many multinational companies have textile mills in a variety of countries. For example, headquartered in Greensboro, North Carolina, International Textile Group (ITG) comprises four companies: Cone Denim, Burlington Worldwide Apparel, Burlington House Interior Fabrics, and Carlisle Finishing. ITG has plants in China, India, Vietnam, Mexico, Nicaragua, and Guatemala. Similarly, Springs Global, a subsidiary of Springs Global Participações S.A. and head-quartered in Fort Mill, South Carolina, has operations in Argentina, Brazil, Canada, Mexico, and the United States.

Textile Design

Textile design involves the interrelationships among the following:

- color (e.g., dyeing, printing)
- fabric structure (e.g., woven or knitted fabric)
- finishes (e.g., napping, embossing)

In addition to knowing about color and fabric structure, textile designers must have expertise in computer-aided design or graphics software and an under-standing of the technology used in producing textiles. The use of computer-aided design or graphics software allows the textile designer to experiment with color and fabric construction, and then to print and prepare exact instructions to replicate the fabric design (see Figure 3.12).

Textile designers specialize according to printing method and fabric structure; they may be freelance designers or work for textile design studios, textile mills, or converters. For example, one textile designer may work for a textile mill and specialize in direct roller-printing processes; another may be a freelance designer of graphics for T-shirts and specialize in screen printing processes. The term **textile stylist** is currently used to designate individuals who have expertise in the design and manufacturing of textiles, as well as an understanding of the textile market. The stylist's combination of design, technical, and consumer/business expertise is particularly important in reflecting consumer preferences in the

Figure 3.12 Computer-aided design facilitates the work of textile designers in creating new fabrics.

textiles being designed. Designers and stylists may work directly with apparel and home fashions manufacturers to create special prints, or with retailers to create prints to be used for private-label merchandise.

Textile Converters

Textile converters buy greige goods from mills; have the fabrics dyed, printed, or finished; and then sell the finished fabrics. Textile converters focus on the following:

- aesthetic finishes (e.g., glazing, crinkling)
- performance finishes (e.g., colorfast, stain resistant, water resistant, durable pressed)
- dyeing or printing fabrics

Most U.S. textile converters are headquartered in New York City, with many others located in eastern U.S. states and Los Angeles. Textile converters are experts in color forecasting and understand consumer preferences in fiber content, fabric construction, and various aesthetic and performance fabric finishes.

Often textile converters will contract with dyers, printers, and finishers to create fabrics that they market to apparel and home fashions manufacturers, jobbers, and retailers. Some converters specialize in a certain type of fabric; others may design several types of fabrics. Most converters that print fabrics use rotary printing presses. Digital printing with ink jet printers is becoming more widespread (see Chapter 11). Because the fabric is finished close to the time when consumers will be purchasing the end-use product, converters play an important role in analyzing and responding to changing consumer preferences.

Although most fabric finishing is done by converters, not all finishing operations are handled by them. For example, apparel and home fashions manufacturers and retailers fulfill the converter's functions to some extent when they specify to a textile mill the color they want a fabric dyed. Woolen and worsted wool fabrics are seldom sold through converters, but rather are generally sold finished by mills. In addition, industrial fabrics are typically sold directly from mills because they are made to meet buyer specifications and may require special performance tests. Also, converters are seldom used in the manufacturing of sweaters and other knitwear, which are typically knitted and then constructed into garments by the same company.

Other Fabric Resources

Textile jobbers and fabric retail stores buy and sell fabric without any involvement in producing or finishing the fabric. Textile jobbers buy from textile mills, converters, and large manufacturers, and then sell to smaller manufacturers and retailers. Typically, jobbers will buy mill overruns (fabrics the textile mill produces beyond what was ordered) or discontinued fabric colors or prints. For example, a textile jobber may buy extra or discontinued fabric from a textile mill and sell it to a small apparel manufacturer who does not need a large volume of fabric. Retail fabric stores sell over-the-counter piece goods primarily to home sewers. Fabric stores may purchase their bolt yardage from fabric wholesalers that have purchased large rolls from textile mills.

Textile brokers serve as liaisons between textile sellers and textile buyers. For example, a broker may connect a small textile mill wanting to sell greige goods to a small converter that wants to buy them. Textile brokers differ from jobbers in that brokers never own the fabric.

Textile Testing and Quality Assurance

The textile industry is highly involved in quality assurance programs and **textile testing**. Textile testing involves inspection and measurement of textile characteristics (e.g., strength, flammability, abrasion resistance, colorfastness) throughout the production and finishing of the textile. Standard test methods developed by the American Society for Testing and Materials (ASTM) and the American Association of Textile Chemists and Colorists (AATCC) are used by companies in testing the quality and specific performance requirements of the textile materials they use.

Although the terms **quality control** and **quality assurance** are sometimes used interchangeably, they have different meanings:

- *Quality control* involves inspecting finished textiles to make sure they adhere to specific quality standards as measured by a variety of textile testing methods (see Figure 3.13).

- *Quality assurance* is a broader concept, covering not only the fabric's general functional performance (quality), but also how well it satisfies consumer needs for a specific end use. For example, a textile to be used in children's apparel must not only meet minimum standards of functional performance, but it must also meet specifications such as colorfastness that are important

Figure 3.13 Fabrics are inspected by trained experts to ensure that they meet quality standards.

to the consumer of children's apparel. Whereas a textile mill may test for general functional performance of the fabric, often the apparel or home fashions manufacturer or retailer must determine if the fabric meets the specifications of importance to its consumers. This is why the testing of fabrics is often conducted by the following:

- apparel and home fashions manufacturers (e.g., Nike, Pendleton Woolen Mills, Guess)
- by retailers (e.g., JCPenney, Target) of these goods
- by independent textile testing companies contracted by manufacturers or retailers

Marketing and Distribution of Fabrics

Marketing Seasonal Lines

Fiber producers, textile mills, and converters take part in the marketing of textile fabrics. Most manufactured-fiber producers have showrooms that exhibit fabrics and end-use products made from their fibers. Textile showrooms are located in most major U.S. cities (e.g., Los Angeles, Dallas, Atlanta, Chicago), although New York is the primary market center for textile mills, converters, and textile product manufacturers. Internationally, textile showrooms are prevalent in the major cities of countries with large numbers of textile mills, as well as large marketing headquarters (e.g., Paris, Milan, Taipei, Hong Kong, Shanghai, Tokyo). Showrooms house the fabric samples to be marketed by textile mills or converters to designers and apparel or home fashions manufacturers.

Textile mills and converters market their textile fabrics as Fall/Winter and Spring/Summer seasonal lines. Each fabric line includes a grouping of fabrics with a similar theme or **color story**. It is the responsibility of the merchandising or marketing staff of textile companies to show fabric samples to prospective buyers in their showrooms or at textile trade shows. Samples of Fall/Winter lines of fabrics are shown to prospective fabric buyers in October or November, approximately nine to twelve months before the end-use product (e.g., apparel) hits the stores. Spring/Summer lines of fabrics are shown in March or April. During these shows, apparel and home fashions companies will purchase yardage for their samples. Some large manufacturers may order their end-use fabrics at this time, but most will wait until their own orders from retailers are known. For large accounts, fabric samples can be *confined,* which means that the textile company will not sell the fabric to other end-use companies.

Fabric companies also promote their lines through sites on the Internet and through other online services (see Color Plate 4). Such online marketing of fabrics offers an efficient method for companies to advertise their products to prospective fabric buyers. Online buying and selling of wholesale fabrics/textiles has emerged as a growing segment of the industry. A number of Internet companies focus on connecting fabric/textile sellers with fabric/textile buyers in the apparel industry. This type of business-to-business (B2B) e-commerce benefits fabric/textile sellers by linking them to prospective buyers throughout the world. It also benefits fabric/textile buyers by creating a faster and more efficient process for finding and selecting fabrics for their next lines (Maycumber, 2000).

Textile Trade Shows

Textile **trade shows** exhibit textile mills' newest fabrics for the coming fashion seasons. Typically held twice per year, in spring (March) and fall (October/November), textile trade shows offer visitors a look at general trends in color, textures, prints, and fabrications (see Figure 3.14). For example, a textile trade show held in March 2008 would exhibit Spring/Summer 2009 fabrics. Because every apparel line or collection begins with fabrics, textile shows provide designers and manufacturers with inspirations for their next line or collection. "A designer's creativity is limited by what a fabric can be made to do, so, in a sense, a collection doesn't really start with the [apparel] designer but with the fabric mill" (Schiro, 1995, p. L16). Below is a listing of selected textile trade shows:

Direction, an international textile design show held in New York City, focuses on trendsetting textiles from around the world.

Sourcing at MAGIC, held in Las Vegas in association with MAGIC Marketplace, connects apparel and accessory manufacturers with fabric and trim suppliers from around the world.

Interstoff, managed by Messe Frankfurt, is one of the largest textile trade show organizations in the world. Interstoff includes the following:
- Interstoff Asia (Hong Kong)
- Interstoff Rossija (Moscow)
- Intertextile Beijing
- Intertextile Shanghai
- Source It (Hong Kong)
- Texworld (Paris)

- Texworld India (Mumbai)
- Texworld USA (New York City)
- Yarn Expo

Première Vision, held in Villepinte, near Paris, focuses on high-quality and innovative fabrics. Designers often get inspirations for apparel designs from the textiles shown at Première Vision. Première Vision has expanded worldwide to include the following:

- Première Vision Shanghai
- Première Vision New York
- Première Vision Moscow
- Première Vision Tokyo

Material World New York, sponsored by the American Apparel and Footwear Association, is a growing textile trade show in the United States. Material World Miami Beach was launched in 2000.

Ideacomo, held in Como, Italy (near Milan), was created in 1975 by silk apparel producers near Como. It now focuses on medium- to high-market luxury and innovative fabric collections of member companies.

Figure 3.14 Textile trade shows provide opportunities for textile companies to promote their lines to manufacturers.

L.A. International Textile Show, held at the California Market Center and sponsored by the Textile Association of L.A., is one of the largest textile trade shows in the United States. It focuses on creative domestic and European designer fabric and trim collections and other textile resources.

Taipei Innovative Textile Application Show (TITAS) focuses on high-tech and innovative textiles (primarily from Asian countries) and their applications for a variety of end uses.

Leather producers also use biannual trade shows to market their products. Some of the best known are LE CUIR A PARIS, China International Leather Fair, Moscow International Fur Trade Fair, and Fur and Fashion Frankfurt Fair.

Developments in the Textile Industry
International Trade and Supply Chain Management

As part of a global economy, textiles are traded among countries throughout the world. It is estimated that 200 countries worldwide have textile production industries for domestic use and international trade. Until 1981, the United States exported more textiles than it imported. Since that time, however, a trade deficit has existed. This means that the United States imports more textiles than it exports. Increased productivity in the industry because of capital investments has resulted in an increase of textile exports. According to U.S. Department of Commerce data, textile exports have steadily increased since 1989. In 2005, textile exports reached an all-time high of $12.14 billion. Mexico is the largest market for U.S. textile mill products; Canada is the second largest, Honduras is third, and the Dominican Republic is fourth. These markets for textile mill products have benefited from the North American Free Trade Agreement (NAFTA) among Canada, Mexico, and the United States; and the Central America–Dominican Republic–United States Free Trade Agreement (CAFTA-DR), which provided trade incentives to countries in Central America when using U.S. textiles. Even with this growth in exports, the trade deficit still exists. This is because textile imports have risen steadily over the past 20 years. In 2005, $20.5 billion in textiles (non-apparel) were imported into the United States.

Technological Advances

In order to compete successfully in a global economy, the U.S. textile industry has invested in new technology to increase productivity in textile mills and improve communication among textile mills, their suppliers, and their customers. These investments in technology are part of Quick Response, supply chain management, and product lifecycle management.

As discussed in Chapter 1, *Quick Response* is an umbrella term that refers to any strategy that shortens the time from fiber production to sale to the ultimate consumer. Supply chain management takes QR further by enhancing the communications and partnerships among industry sectors. In the textile industry, Quick Response and supply chain management strategies include computer-aided textile design, computerized knitting machines, and computer-controlled robots (see Figure 3.15). Enhanced communication links between textile companies, their suppliers, and their customers have also contributed to effective supply chain management strategies.

The textile industry has also played an important role in the research, development, and implementation of new strategies to increase productivity and competitiveness. According to the National Council of Textile Organizations, over the past 10 years, the industry has invested more than $30 billion in new plants and equipment, making it one of the most modern and productive textile sectors in the world. Examples of investment in technologically advanced equipment and processes include the following:

- In the woven fabric industry, companies have invested in shuttleless looms (e.g., rapier, projectile, air-jet, and water-jet looms) that have the capability to weave more than twice as many yards per hour as shuttle looms.

- Digital textile printing (see Figure 3.16) has also reshaped the way in which fabric designs are created. Digital textile printing is "the process of creating printable designs for fabric on a computer, which can be sent directly from the computer to fabric printing machinery without the use of screens and color separation" (Campbell & Kim, 1999, p. 113).

Figure 3.15 Computer-controlled robots are used to transport packages in textile mills. Such investments in technology have increased the textile industry's productivity.

Another technological advancement that has affected the textile industry is **nanotechnology**. Nanotechnology is the "manufacturing technology that operates in the range of nanometers, one-billionth of a metre" ("Nanotechnology's new potential," 2006). Nanotechnology applications in textile manufacturing have been used to create faster and more precise textile-processing machinery, and have improved the quality and speed of textile surface coatings/finishes. It is expected that new nanotechnology applications will provide competitive advantages for companies incorporating this technology into the manufacturing processes. Optical fibers with integrated electronics have also been developed, allowing fibers that can sense, process, and store data to be woven into

Figure 3.16   Digital printing allows companies to send fabric designs from computers directly to fabric-printing machinery.

fabric. Initial applications for these **"smart" fibers** and materials include military uniforms, medical devices, protective garments for extreme environments, and performance athletic wear.

Environmental Issues

Demand for environmentally responsible products, once limited to younger consumers and consumers who had a sense of social responsibility, has become mainstream. Companies, including textile producers, are working to improve environmental conditions and to show they are environmentally conscious. They are incorporating environmentally responsible processes (see Figure 3.17), such as the following:

- manufacturing products that include organic or recycled materials
- using less toxic materials, such as low-impact dyes
- using less water in production

Apparel manufacturers are also pressuring textile producers to supply environmentally responsible textiles. Therefore, a number of environmentally responsible textile manufacturing processes have been implemented, including organically grown cotton, cleaner dyeing and finishing processes, and waste reduction (see discussion of organic cotton earlier in this chapter).

Each year, textile companies spend billions of dollars to ensure that their processes are environmentally responsible through efforts in conserving water, energy, and electricity and in recycling products (e.g., paper and plastic) and natural resources (e.g., water and energy). Plants are built or adapted with environmental impact in mind. For example, Malden Mills' (producer of Polartec and Polarfleece fleece fabric) plant in Lawrence, Massachusetts, has built-in environmental systems that reduce water use, reuse heat, and treat wastewater.

Trade associations and other organizations have played an important role in research, implementation, and promotion of environmentally safe processes. For example, the National Council of Textile Organizations lists companies that produce organic, recycled, or environmentally friendly yarns. The Sustainable Style Foundation (SSF), headquartered in Seattle, Washington, "is an international, member-supported nonprofit organization created to provide information, resources, and innovative programs that promote sustainable living and sustainable design" (SSF, 2006). Founded in 2003, SSF provides the most current information about sustainable style to designers, producers, and consumers; promotes sustainable style in the media; and uses "popular culture to influence consumer choices." Each year, SSF presents the Outstanding Sustainable Style Awards in categories including fashion and beauty, designed environments, entertainment, and food and restaurant.

Figure 3.17 EDUN is a socially and environmentally conscious clothing company that seeks to foster sustainable employment in developing nations and to use organic materials in their clothing collections.

A number of "environmentally cleaner" processes have been implemented in the cotton industry. These include naturally colored cotton, organic cotton, "cleaner" dyeing methods, and reduced water use. For example, one cotton producer, Sally Fox, developed naturally colored cotton in various shades of green, brown, and red. Natural colors had been bred out of modern cotton because the colored fibers were too short and weak for automated textile manufacturing. Fox began crossing the longer, stronger white cotton fibers with colored cotton to create Foxfibre cotton, the first naturally colored cotton that could be processed with modern textile equipment (Vreseis, 2007). The natural colors did more than eliminate the need for dyeing the cotton; instead of fading, naturally colored cotton actually deepens in color when washed. In addition, Foxfibre cotton has a silky feel and a wool-like elasticity. Foxfibre, Colour-by-Nature, and Colorganic are all registered trademarks for naturally colored cottons.

Fox is also committed to organic cotton production, in which synthetic chemical fertilizers and pesticides are used minimally or not used at all. Fox is not the only cotton producer interested in organic cotton. According to the Organic Trade Association, sales of organic cotton have been steadily rising over the past five years, with estimates that it will continue to grow 15 percent per year over the next few years. Organic cotton fibers are now used in end-use products, ranging from cotton puffs and ear swabs to sheets and blankets to diapers to fashion apparel.

Companies that have joined the organic cotton movement include the following:

- In 1996, Patagonia (the Ventura, California, manufacturer of sportswear and outdoor clothing), shifted its entire line of cotton apparel to organic cotton fabrics. Although the goods cost slightly more than if regular cotton fabrics were used, its customers have responded positively to the more innovative fabrics.

- Nike currently blends approximately 2.5 percent of organic cotton into their various cotton product lines, with a goal of blending at least 10 percent by 2010. This may not seem like a large percentage of organic cotton. However, 2.5 percent of the cotton used in Nike products represents approximately 3 million pounds of organic cotton.

- Eileen Fisher, American Apparel, Hanna Andersson, Timberland, and REI are just a few companies that offer 100 percent or blended organic cotton apparel.

- DIBB International, Dream Designs, and Coyuchi are just a few companies that offer organic cotton home fashions.

Because the majority of textiles are colored using chemical dyes to create bright, colorfast characteristics, some manufacturers are attempting to lessen the environmental impact of cotton production through the use of "cleaner" dyeing processes, including synthetic "low-impact" dyes, natural dyes, and undyed, unbleached cottons. Natural dyes are extracted from a variety of leaves, barks, flowers, berries, lichens, mushrooms, roots, wood, peels, nutshells, minerals, shellfish, and insects. However, many of these sources do not produce stable dyes for textiles. The most common natural dyes currently used include the following:

- cochineal (red), which is derived from the body of an insect

- osage orange (yellow), which is extracted from the osage orange tree

- madder root (red), which is extracted from the woody root of the madder plant

- indigo (blue), which is extracted from a number of plants

It is estimated, however, that in current production, natural dyes add 10 to 40 percent to the cost of the goods. This is primarily the result of the cost of the dyestuffs themselves, since most natural dye producers are small operations (McManus & Wipplinger, 1994).

A number of manufactured-fiber companies developed more environmentally responsible production processes, including the use of recycling. For example, in 1988, Courtalds Fibres UK developed lyocell, a cellulosic fiber made from harvested wood pulp (and, therefore, a subcategory of rayon) that is processed with recycled nontoxic solvents. In its production, virtually all the dissolving agent is recycled. In addition, waste emissions (air and wastewater) are lower than for other manufactured-fiber production. The resulting fiber is machine washable and is stronger than cotton or wool—as well as having a silkier touch. Currently, the only company manufacturing lyocell in the United States is Lenzing Inc. (headquartered in Austria) under the TENCEL trade name. Fabrics made from 100 percent lyocell or in a variety of blends are used for apparel, accessories, and home fashions.

In addition to lyocell, some companies are making rayon from bamboo fibers. Because of its fast growth rate, renewability, and ability to take in greenhouse gases, the use of bamboo is being promoted by environmentalists. Rayon made from bamboo fibers has a silk-like hand, making it popular for apparel and home fashions. Linda Loudermilk's Luxury eco collection combines fabrics made from bamboo and other renewable plants in high-fashion collections shown on New York City runways.

Polyester staple fibers are also being recycled from plastic soda bottles, which are made of polyethylene teraphthalate, or PET. The process of making recycled polyester fibers includes the following steps:

1. All caps, labels, and bases made of other materials are removed from the bottles.

2. The bottles are sorted by color (clear and green).

3. The bottles are chopped.

4. The pieces are washed and dried.

5. The pieces are heated, purified, and formed into pellets.

6. The purified polyester is extruded as fine fibers that can be spun into thread, yarn, or other materials.

It takes an average of 25 plastic soda bottles to make one garment. Foss Manufacturing LLC produces Fortrel Ecospun®, a polyester that contains 100 percent recycled fiber used by dozens of apparel companies (see Figure 3.18). It is estimated that 2.4 billion bottles are kept out of landfills per year through the manufacturing of Fortrel Ecospun® fibers.

Several companies are also recycling scrap yarns and fabric as a means of reducing the amount of scrap materials ending up in landfill. Recycled scrap denim is being used in a variety of products, including fabrics, pencils, and paper. Milliken Floor Covering promises to recover all carpets returned to them

Figure 3.18   Fortrel Ecospun® is made of 100 percent recycled plastic bottles and is used in a variety of end products.

through renewing the product, donating them to charities, recycling them, or using them in energy cogeneration (an environmentally responsible means of producing power). According to Milliken's Web site, since 1999, the company's carpet manufacturing plants have not sent any waste to landfill.

Summary

The textile industry includes companies that contribute to the four basic stages of textile production: fiber processing, yarn spinning, fabric production or fabrication, and fabric finishing. Some companies specialize in one or more of the production processes; vertically integrated companies handle all four. Both natural and manufactured fibers are processed in the United States.

Natural fibers produced in the United States include cotton, wool, mohair, and other specialty fibers. Leather and fur, also produced in the United States, are considered natural-fiber products. Natural fibers are commodities bought and sold on international markets and are generally promoted by trade associations that focus on specific fibers. These trade associations encourage the use of the various natural fibers through such activities as market research, advertising, and consumer education programs.

Manufactured fibers are typically produced by large vertically integrated companies. They are marketed either as commodity fibers or brand name (trademarked) fibers, such as Lycra spandex fiber or Dacron polyester fiber. Brand name fibers are advertised by companies in order to create consumer awareness and preference for the specific fibers. Trade associations are also involved in promoting manufactured fibers.

Textile companies are often involved in determining the colors to be used in end-use products. Through the process of color forecasting, color palettes are selected and translated into fabrics produced by a company for a specific fashion season. Color forecasts are available from nonprofit service organizations, such as the Color Association of the United States, or from color forecasting services. Companies may also conduct their own color forecasting.

Textile mills focus on fabric production and sell greige goods; some textile mills will finish the fabric as well. Textile design involves the interrelationships among color (e.g., dyeing, printing), fabric structure (e.g., woven, knitted), and finishes (e.g., napping, embossing). Textile converters specialize in fabric finishing. They buy greige goods and finish the fabric according to textile mills', apparel manufacturers', or retailers' specifications. Other fabric resources include textile jobbers, textile brokers, and fabric retail stores. Through quality assurance programs, textile mills, apparel manufacturers, and retailers test textiles according to standards for end-use products. Textile mills and converters market their textile fabrics as Fall/Winter and Spring/Summer seasonal lines in showrooms and at textile trade shows held throughout the world.

In order to compete successfully in a global economy, the U.S. textile industry continues to invest in new technology to increase the productivity of textile mills and improve communication among textile mills, their suppliers, and their customers. These investments in technology are part of Quick Response and supply chain management strategies, designed to shorten the time from fiber to finished product. Nanotechnology and "smart" fibers and materials are paving the way for high-tech fabrics for a variety of specialized end uses.

The textile industry is addressing environmental concerns through manufacturing and by making available to consumers products that include organic or recycled materials, are produced with less-toxic materials such as low-impact dyes, use less water in production, or have incorporated other environmentally responsible processes.

Careers in the textile industry are as varied as the industry itself. Textile chemist, textile designer, textile production supervisor, and textile marketer are just a few of the many careers available in this industry.

Textile Designer
Product Development Department, Publicly Held Retailer

Position Description

Part of a dynamic product development team responsible for creating private-label merchandise for a major publicly held retail corporation. Work with textile mills in designing fabrics to be used in private-label merchandise.

Typical Tasks and Responsibilities

- Create color artwork for prints, stripes, and yarn dyes using CAD.
- Approve lab dips for production use.
- Track lab dip status.
- Prepare presentation boards.
- Travel overseas.

Independent Sales Representative
Fabrics and Trims

Position Description

Show lines of fabrics and trims to designers and merchandisers, send samples, help design products, follow up with vendors to see that goods are delivered through production, negotiate prices, and make presentation books and boards.

Typical Tasks and Responsibilities

- Drive to accounts in several states and Canada—traveling two to three days per week minimum.
- Show lines to designers and merchandisers.
- Pack and unpack sample bags.
- Keep price lists organized.
- Manage the office and finances; purchase supplies and office equipment.
- Work with purchasing agents.
- Write orders, follow-up letters, and price quotes.
- File, update files and materials, and keep the office clean.

Key Terms

brand name
cashmere
color forecasting
color forecasting service
color story
concept garment
controlled brand name program
converted goods
converter
cotton
fabric construction
fabrication
fiber
filament yarn
finished goods
finishing
generic family
greige goods
hide
horizontally integrated
kip
licensed brand name program
mohair

nanotechnology
pelt
quality assurance
quality control
regular tannery
skin
"smart" fiber
spun yarn
tanning
tawning
textile
textile converter
textile jobber
textile mill
textile stylist
textile testing
throwster
trade association
trade name
trade show
vertically integrated
wool
yarn

Discussion Questions

1. What are the advantages and disadvantages to a textile company of being horizontally integrated? Vertically integrated? How are the advantages and disadvantages of each type of integration related to the types of textile companies that are horizontally and vertically integrated?

2. Follow a cotton/polyester blend woven fabric from the fiber production to the marketing of the fabric to apparel manufacturers. What are the primary stages of production and marketing? Give the approximate time frame for this process.

3. What are the differences between the production and marketing of natural fibers and manufactured fibers? Why do these differences exist?

4. What roles do trade associations play in the promotion of natural and manufactured fibers? Give examples of the activities performed by trade associations. Bring in examples of cooperative advertising between trade associations and end-use producers.

5. What are greige goods? Why are converters important in creating the end-use products that can best meet the needs of consumers?

References

Abend, Jules. (1994, November). The green wave swells. *Bobbin*, pp. 92–98.

American Fiber Manufacturers Association (2006). About AFMA [online]. Available: http://www.fibersource.com/afma/afma.htm [July 2, 2007].

American Sheep Industry Association (2006). American Sheep Industry Home Page [online]. Available: http://www.sheepusa.org [September 3, 2006].

American Textile Manufacturers Institute (1999, June). *Textile HiLights*. Washington, DC: Author.

Bamboo Textiles (2006). Bamboo Clothes Home Page [online]. Available: http://www.bambooclothes.com/Merchant2/merchant.mvc [September 15, 2006].

Bonner, Staci. (1997, February). It's not easy being green: Strategies and challenges. *Apparel Industry Magazine*, pp. 52–68.

Bureau of Labor Statistics (2006). U.S. Department of Labor, *Career Guide to Industries, 2006–07 Edition*. Textile, Textile Product, and Apparel Manufacturing [online]. Available: http://www.bls.gov/oco/cg/cgs015.htm [September 3, 2006].

Campbell, J.R. and Kim, Eundeok. (1999, November). Concepts in Digital Textile Printing That Affect the Approach to Textile Design. Proceedings Annual Meeting of the Textile and Apparel Association. Santa Fe, NM, pp. 113–114.

Carpet and Rug Institute (2006). Carpet and Rug Institute Home Page [online]. Available: http://www.carpet-rug.com [September 3, 2006].

Cashmere and Camel Hair Manufacturers Institute (2006). CCMI Home Page [online]. Available: http://www.cashmere.org [September 10, 2006].

Cohen, Allen C. (1989). *Marketing Textiles: From Fiber to Retail*. New York: Fairchild Publications.

Cotton, Incorporated (2007). *Lifestyle Monitor* [online]. Available: http://www.cottoninc.com [April 16, 2007].

Eberspacher, Jinger J. (1993). The declining domestic leather industry: Implications and opportunities. *Clothing and Textiles Research Journal*, 12 (1), pp. 26–30.

Fur Commission USA (2007). Fur farming in North America [online]. Available: http://www.furcommission.com/farming/index.html [April 15, 2007].

Greco, M. (1996, February). Is on-line fabric sourcing next? *Apparel Industry Magazine*, pp. 32–34.

Hollen, Norma, Sadler, Jane, Langford, Anna L., and Kadolph, Sara J. (1988). *Textiles* (6th ed.). New York: Macmillan.

International Cotton Advisory Committee (2006). World Cotton Trade to Remain at Record Levels [online]. Available: http://www.icac.org/cotton_info/publications/press/2006/english.html [May 1, 2006].

IT Strategies (1997, February). Getting a grip on digital printing. [online] Available: http://www.bobbin.com/media/97feb/digital.htm.

Joseph, Marjory L. (1988). *Essentials of Textiles* (4th ed.). New York: Holt, Rinehart and Winston.

Kadolph, Sara J., and Langford, Anna L. (2002). *Textiles* (9th ed.). NY: Fairchild Publications.

Maycumber, S. Gray. (1994, April 26). L.L.Bean to ATMI: Environment key factor. *Women's Wear Daily*, p. 14.

Maycumber, S. Gray. (2000, May 12). Online sourcing/selling: textiles' biggest revolution is coming. *DNR*, pp. 4–5.

McManus, Fred, and Wipplinger, Michele. (1994, February/March). Nature shows her true colors. *Green Alternatives*, pp. 26–31.

McNamara, Michael. (1995, February 9). Cotton Inc. lifestyle monitor to survey consumer attitude. *Women's Wear Daily*, p. 11.

Mohair Council of America (2006). Mohair Council of America Home Page [online]. Available: http://www.mohairusa.com [September 10, 2006].

Musselman, Faye. (1998, March). Clear on the concept. *Apparel Industry Magazine*, pp. 46–50.

Nanotechnology's new potential in apparel machinery (2006, September 8). Just-style.com [online]. Available: http://www.just-style.com [September 8, 2006].

National Cotton Council of America (2005). United States Cotton Production: 2005 Crop Year [online]. Available: http://www.cotton.org/econ/world/detail.cfm [September 15, 2006].

National Council of Textile Organizations (2007). About NCTO [online]. Available: http://www.ncto.org [April 16, 2007].

Nike, Inc. (2006). Organic Cotton: More Is Better [online]. Available: http://www.nike.com/nikebiz/nikebiz.jhtml?page=27&cat=ogcotton&subcat=commitment [September 15, 2006].

North American Industry Classification System (2002). Definitions: 313 Textile Mills [online]. Available: http://www.census.gov/epcd/naics02/def/NDEF313.HTM#N313 [April 16, 2007].

Organic Trade Association (2005). Organic Wool Fact Sheet [online]. Available: http://www.ota.com/organic/environment/wool.html [September 15, 2006].

Patagonia switches to organic cotton. (1995, October). *Bobbin*, p. 24.

Robbins, Jim. (1994, December). Undying devotion. *Destination Discovery*, pp. 18–21.

Rudie, Raye. (1994, February). How green is the future? *Bobbin*, pp. 16–20.

Schiro, Anne-Marie. (1995, May 7). Mills weave trends in fabric of fashion. *The Oregonian*, p. L16.

Scrap denim spun into "Green" jeans. (1995, February). *Apparel Industry Magazine*, p. 16.

Sustainable Style Foundation (2006). About us [online]. Available: http://www.sustainablestyle.org [September 15, 2006].

United States Department of Agriculture (2006). USDA Econmic Research Service. Cotton and Wool Yearbook [online]. Available: http://usda.mannlib.cornell.edu/MannUsda/viewDocumentInfo.do?documentID=1281 [September 3, 2006].

United States Department of Agriculture (2006). USDA National Organic Program [online]. Available: http://www.ams.usda.gov/nop/indexIE.htm [September 3, 2006].

Vreseis, Ltd. (2007). Sally Fox: Innovation in the Field. [online]. Available: http://www.vreseis.com [April 15, 2007].

Yates, Dorian. (1994, February/March). Organic cotton. *Green Alternatives*, pp. 33–36.

CHAPTER 4

Ready-to-Wear:
Company Organization

In this chapter, you will learn the following:

- the difference between the ready-to-wear industry and haute couture
- the various types of ready-to-wear companies
- the organizational structure of apparel companies
- the merchandising philosophies of apparel companies
- the primary trade associations and trade publications in the apparel industry

ommy Hilfiger, Donna Karan International, Russell Athletic, OshKosh B'Gosh, American Apparel LLC, Monet, Polo Ralph Lauren, WestPoint Stevens—all are examples of successful U.S. apparel, accessories, and home fashions companies. Although each of these companies creates merchandise brands recognized by consumers around the world, they vary in the way they are organized and in the way they operate. This chapter focuses on the general organization and operation of companies that produce men's, women's, and children's apparel, accessories, and home fashions. Apparel companies are classified by the categories of apparel products they produce, such as size range, styling, price zone, and type of product (suits, active sportswear), as well as by the age and gender of the target market customer. These classifications, in turn, relate to the organizational structure of the producers and retailers of fashion goods.

Ready-to-Wear: What Does It Mean?

The majority of apparel produced and sold is called *ready-to-wear (RTW)*. As the term implies, the apparel is completely made and ready to be worn (except for finishing details, such as pant hemming in tailored clothing) at the time it is purchased. In England, this merchandise is called *off-the-peg*; in France, it is called *prêt-à-porter*; and in Italy, it is called *moda pronto*. RTW apparel is made in large quantities using mass-manufacturing processes that require little or no hand sewing.

Many apparel companies produce seasonal **lines** or **collections** of merchandise. Lines or collections are groups of styles designed for a particular **fashion season**. The primary difference between a line and a collection is the cost of the merchandise—the term *collection* typically refers to more expensive merchandise. Often name designers will create and offer *collections*; other apparel companies will offer *lines*.

Apparel companies typically produce four to six new collections or lines per year, corresponding to the fashion seasons: Spring, Summer, Fall I, Fall II, Holiday, and Resort or Cruise. These fashion seasons coincide with the times consumers would most likely wear the merchandise, not to when companies design or manufacture the merchandise or when the merchandise is delivered to stores. For example, a company may start to design a Fall season line in September, market the line in March, actually manufacture it from March through April, and deliver the merchandise to the stores in June. Color Plate 3 shows the calendar for four seasonal lines; each seasonal line is represented by a color. An 18-month time span is used to illustrate the overlaps among seasons from design to delivery.

Not all companies produce lines for all six fashion seasons. The number of lines a company will produce depends on both the product category and the target market (the group of customers for whom the line is designed). For example, a company that produces men's tailored suits may create only two lines per year (Fall and Spring), whereas a men's sportswear company may create five lines per year (Fall I, Fall II, Holiday, Spring, and Summer). Some companies produce more than six lines per year. A number of apparel companies produce smaller lines that are shipped to retailers more frequently; the frequent infusion of new merchandise appeals to customers. Many companies that produce store brands (e.g., Victoria's Secret, Ann Taylor, Express) or other forms of private-label merchandise (e.g., Worthington for JCPenney) also ship goods to their retail stores frequently. Chapters 5 and 6 discuss in more detail the development of collections and lines.

As discussed in Chapter 1, the standardization of sizing was necessary for the development of the ready-to-wear industry. Sizes in RTW are based on a combination of standardized body dimensions, company size standards, and wearing and design ease. Clothing sizes were developed by grouping computed average circumference measurements of a large group of people (of average height) into specific size categories. For example, the men's size 42 relates to an "average height" (5 feet 10 inches to 6 feet) male with a chest circumference of 42 inches and waist of 36 inches. These body measurements or dimensions are what are referred to as the standardized size. Standardized tables of body dimensions are available from the American Society for Testing and Materials (ASTM) for various figure types.

The apparel industry does not adhere strictly to the "set" standardized sizes. A company may develop its "company size" based on a target customer with a smaller waist in comparison to the hip circumference, or a larger chest in comparison to the waist circumference. The term *athletic fit* is used to refer to a men's suit built to fit the male body with a larger chest-to-waist ratio than the standardized size (for example, a size 42 athletic fit might be based on a chest circumference of 42 inches and a waist circumference of 35 inches). This is why many consumers find that one brand of apparel fits them better than other brands. "'There's an enormous amount of variation in the population, so if every company has a different fit model with slightly different proportions, then somewhere the consumer will find clothes that fit her,' said sizing researcher Susan Ashdown" (Bond, 2004, p. 53).

As catalog sales of apparel have increased, direct-marketing apparel companies have worked to develop consistent body measurements and related size measurements for all styles that the company produces. A fit that can be determined accurately from a catalog's body measurement chart can reduce returns and thus increase customer satisfaction with the product and the company.

The size chart lists the body measurements for the company's apparel. Wearing ease and design ease allowances are added to the body measurements to create the garment measurements. Each company decides how much wearing ease and design ease to add to create the "look" for the company. Some styles are designed to fit more loosely than other styles. The company sizing will reflect these style aspects. Each company's size range is based on its predetermined body measurements, plus ease. The size measurements increase and decrease in specified increments from the base or sample size to create the size range. The size increments used to create the various sizes will be discussed in more detail in Chapter 9.

A national sizing survey was completed in 2003 using 3D body scanning technology (see Chapter 11). Approved by the U. S. Department of Commerce, the project, called Size USA, set up body scanning sites in more than 12 large cities across the United States and collected body measurement data from thousands of consumers. Part of the funding for this survey was provided by apparel producers, including JCPenney, Sears, Liz Claiborne, VF Corporation, Dillard's, Target, Russell, and Lands' End (for more information, see http://www.sizeusa.com). [TC]^2 provided the scanning equipment. A similar survey was conducted in the United Kingdom. Apparel companies may access the enormous data bank of body dimensions provided by this survey. With the quantity of new data available, the development of new and adapted size ranges, such as those targeted to specific age or ethnic groups, are possible.

The Difference between Ready-to-Wear and Couture

Designer names, such as Coco Chanel, Christian Dior, and Yves Saint Laurent, first became famous in the realm of French **haute couture** (high fashion) and later became associated with expensive ready-to-wear. Because of the continued prominence and importance of these designer labels, it is important to understand the distinction and the relationship between **couture** and ready-to-wear. *Couture* is a French term that literally means "sewing." In general, couture apparel is distinguished by the following characteristics:

- produced in smaller quantities
- utilizes considerable hand-sewing techniques
- sized to fit an individual's body measurements

Generally, more expensive fabrics are used in couture apparel than in RTW.

The term *couture* is derived from *haute couture* (pronounced oat coo-tur), which literally means *high sewing*. As discussed in Chapter 1, the haute couture industry developed in Paris during the nineteenth century. At that time, apparel was produced by dressmakers and tailors who custom-fit each garment to the client. The garment's style and fabric were selected for or by each client, the client's body measurements were taken, and the garment was completed after one or more fittings during the construction process. For persons who did not have personal dressmakers or tailors, apparel was produced in the home by whoever had the necessary skills.

Selecting a fabric and creating a garment prior to an order from a client was a new concept, attributed to Charles Frederick Worth, the founder of the haute couture business during the second half of the nineteenth century. He created several gowns, which were modeled by his wife. Clients came into his shop and selected a style to be copied for them, custom-fit to their body measurements. Soon he had a clientele of wealthy and noble patrons. He used exquisite fabrics and trims and employed a bevy of seamstresses to complete the intricate hand-work. In time, other designers followed Worth's lead, and the haute couture business was formed. These designers "created" new fashions, while the rest of the western fashion world followed their lead.

During the early twentieth century, the *Chambre Syndicale de la Couture* was formed by the French Ministry for Industry to provide an organizational structure and to offer protection for designers against their designs being copied. Currently, the *Chambre Syndicale* does the following:

- arranges the calendar for the showings of the collections twice per year
- organizes accreditation for press and buyers who want to attend the showings
- assists the couture houses so each gains the maximum press coverage possible

In Fall 2007, there were 10 full members of the *Chambre Syndicale* and, therefore, they could be called couture houses: Adeline André, Chanel, Christian Dior, Jean-Paul Gaultier, Givenchy, Christian Lacroix, Jean-Louis Scherrer, Dominique Sirop, Franck Sorbier, and Emanuel Ungaro. Italian designers Versace, Valentino, and Giorgio Armani have also presented couture shows in Paris. To be a member of the Paris haute couture requires specific qualifications, including the following:

- the use of one's own "house" seamstresses
- the presentation of Fall/Winter and Spring/Summer collections each year
- adherence to the dates of showings set by the *Chambre Syndicale*
- registration of the original designs to protect against copying

Each designer's business is called a *house*. Thus, there is the House of Dior, the House of Givenchy, and the House of Chanel. The haute couture designer is called the **couturier** (or **couturière**) or the "head of the house." Whereas some couturiers control their own businesses, many couture houses are owned by corporations that finance them. In recent years, some financial backers have been known to hire and fire head designers frequently. A Paris haute couture designer typically has a *boutique* (store) located on one of several "fashion avenues" in Paris. The boutique sells the designer's licensed products, such as perfume, scarfs, jewelry and other accessories, and home fashions. Some boutiques sell boutique collections of apparel, as well as shoes.

The **salon de couture** is the showroom of the couture designer. The salon is typically located on the second floor of the building that houses the designer's boutique. Entry to the second level, the salon, is limited to those with invitations to a collection show. The **atelier** (pronounced ah-tal´-lee-aye) **de couture**, or workrooms, may be on the floors above the salon or in a separate building.

The twice-per-year Paris haute couture collection openings continue to be huge events in the fashion world and are covered in detail by the fashion press (see Figure 4.1). Fall/Winter fashion season haute couture collections are typically shown in July, and

Figure 4.1 The shows for couture houses, such as John Galliano's Spring 2007 show for Christian Dior, are huge events in the fashion world, and are covered in detail by the media.

Spring/Summer fashion season haute couture collections are typically shown in January. The press, buyers, other designers, celebrities, and wealthy clients are in attendance. While the fashion influence of the couturiers waxes and wanes, the designs presented are considered to represent a laboratory of design creativity.

Paris haute couture houses also produce RTW (*prêt-à-porter*) collections. These RTW collections may be sold in the house boutique, in freestanding boutiques, or in upscale department or specialty stores. Currently, all haute couture houses offer prêt-à-porter collections.

In addition to the couturiers who are members of the *Chambre Syndicale*, there are other designers who consider themselves to be couture designers. Generally, a couture designer is distinguished by the following:

- uses high-quality fabrics
- creates original designs (as opposed to copying another's designs)
- uses high-quality construction and hand-finishing details
- custom-fits the garment to a client's body measurements

Couture designers may produce all custom work (ordered by a specific client), or they may present a seasonal collection and then take custom orders selected from the collection. There are couture designers in New York, Los Angeles, and other cities around the world.

The term *couture* is sometimes used in the apparel industry to impart an elite ambience to an apparel collection. For example, an apparel company might produce a high-priced RTW collection and call it a *couture collection*. Indeed, some stores even have what they call *couture* departments. However, if mass-production techniques are used in producing the apparel, and if garments are not custom-fit to the client, the line should be called RTW and *not* couture.

Types of RTW Apparel Producers

From large corporations to small companies, from those that produce innovative, trendy merchandise to those that produce classics, RTW companies come in all types and sizes and vary tremendously in their organization. Because of the diversity found in RTW apparel company organization, any attempt to classify types of apparel producers is difficult. However, according to industry analysts, the major types of apparel suppliers can be grouped into the following categories: manufacturers, jobbers, contractors, and licensors.

Manufacturers perform all functions of creating, marketing, and distributing an apparel line on a continual basis. These companies may make products in their own plant(s) or factories (e.g., American Apparel LLC), but they typically use outside companies, or contractors, to perform the manufacturing function. Manufacturers include the following:

- multidivision companies that produce several product lines of nationally advertised merchandise (e.g., Levi Strauss & Co., VF Corporation)

- companies that specialize in one or more product categories, such as infants' and children's wear (e.g., Carter's) or fleece wear (e.g., Russell Athletic)

Manufacturers may produce brands of merchandise distributed nationally or regionally, licensed products, or private-label merchandise for a specific store. Retail distribution of products will vary depending on the manufacturer.

Jobber is the traditional term for a company that buys fabrics and acquires styles from independent designers, or that copies or designs lines itself, but uses contractors to make its products. This type of company became popular in the early 1900s, with New York (Seventh Avenue) men's and women's apparel companies serving as intermediaries. They carried huge inventories of merchandise and could make prompt deliveries to retailers. As retailers started sending their own buyers to New York, and as resident buyers became more popular, the need for jobbers declined.

Today, because so many apparel producers contract out the manufacturing functions, the use of the term *jobber* is not as widespread as it used to be. Instead, most apparel producers are referred to as *manufacturers,* regardless of whether or not they use contractors. In fact, this definition of *manufacturer* offered by industry analysts suggests a broader perspective: "Manufacturers in the apparel industry are the main contractors of apparel production. Some have internal production capabilities, but most contract out a substantial portion of actual production to contractors" (Southern California Edison Company, 1995, Appendix A).

Contractors are companies that specialize in the sewing and finishing of goods. Contractors are used by the following:

- manufacturers that lack sufficient capacity in their own plants or choose to contract out the manufacturing function

- retailers for private-label and store brand merchandise

According to the industry definition, "contractors in the apparel industry are the many, usually small factories in which most apparel production actually takes place. Several different types of industry entities source apparel goods from contractors, including manufacturers, retailers, buyers, importers, and trading companies" (Southern California Edison Company, 1995, Appendix A). Most contractors specialize in a product category (e.g., knit tops) or have specialized equipment (e.g., embroidery machines) and skilled workers. The term **item house** is used to describe contractors that specialize in the production of one product. For example, item houses are used in the production of baseball caps. Contractors offer their customers fast turnarounds. **Full-package contractors**, in working with retailers, also offer fabric procurement and apparel design services that were traditionally part of the manufacturers' role.

Some manufacturers and contractors produce goods for the sole use of a particular retailer (or retail corporation) as a private-label brand or **retail store/direct-market brand** merchandise. Some retailers offer a combination of national brands and private-label merchandise (e.g., Nordstrom, Macy's), whereas other retailers offer only store brand merchandise (e.g., Gap, The Limited, Eddie Bauer, Talbot's). Some manufacturers and contractors will produce merchandise for both national brands and private-label or store brands; other manufacturers and contractors will produce merchandise for one national or private-label/store brand only.

Licensors are companies that have developed a well-known designer name (e.g., Calvin Klein, Donna Karan, Ralph Lauren), brand name (e.g., Guess?, Hang Ten), or character (e.g., Mickey Mouse, Barbie, Beauty and the Beast) and sell the use of these names or characters to companies to put onto merchandise. As discussed in Chapter 2, successful licensing depends on a well-known name or image (property). It should be noted that these categories are not mutually exclusive. For example, a manufacturer may use a contractor or may license its brand name to a company that produces product categories different from its own. The details of these various types of apparel production will be discussed in later chapters.

Classifications and Categories of Apparel

Apparel producers are classified in the following ways:

- by the type of merchandise they produce
- by the wholesale prices of the products or brands
- by an industry classification system for governmental tracking

An examination of these classification systems is in order to better understand the diversity of apparel organizations.

The apparel industry is divided into the primary categories of men's, women's, and children's apparel manufacturers. Some companies produce apparel in only one of these categories; others produce apparel for more than one. In some cases, companies began as producers of one category of apparel; then they branched out into one or more other categories as the companies grew. For example, Levi Strauss & Co. began as a producer of men's apparel, and later expanded into women's and children's wear. Liz Claiborne began as a producer of women's apparel, and then developed a men's division.

The separate gender/age categories have their roots in the early history of the U.S. apparel industry. Apparel producers specialized in one category because of a variety of factors. The types of machinery used for producing men's apparel were often different from the types needed for women's apparel. The sizing standards developed differently for men's, women's, and children's apparel. The number of seasonal lines produced per year differs for each category; therefore, the production cycle varies.

The organizational structure of retail stores is related to these categories of apparel, another reason why the apparel industry remains divided into the three primary categories of men's, women's, and children's apparel. Retail buyers are often assigned responsibilities in one of the three categories of apparel. For example, a men's wear buyer buys apparel for the retail store from men's apparel producers. This allows the producers and retailer to establish and maintain profitable working relationships.

Within each of the three primary categories, apparel producers are subdivided into additional categories. Apparel producers generally specialize in one or several subcategories. These subcategories relate to the **classification** of apparel. Apparel classifications are by type of garment produced (product type). Traditional classifications by product type for women's apparel include the following:

  outerwear (coats, jackets, and rainwear)

  dresses

  blouses

  career wear (suits, separates, and career wear dresses)

  sportswear and active sportswear (separates, such as pants, sweaters, and skirts; and active sportswear, such as swimwear and tennis wear)

  evening wear and special occasion

  bridal and bridesmaid dresses

  maternity wear

- uniforms
- furs
- accessories
- intimate apparel, which is further classified into the following categories:
  - foundations (girdles or body shapers, bras, and other shape wear)
  - lingerie (petticoats, slips, panties, camisoles, nightgowns, and pajamas)
  - loungewear (at-home wear, robes, bed jackets, and housecoats)

Foundations and lingerie worn under other clothing are sometimes referred to as *innerwear*. In addition, lingerie and loungewear are sometimes divided into daywear and nightwear.

The various subcategories are organized by size category and clothing classification (see Table 4.1). For example, some apparel companies manufacture apparel only in the missy or the junior-size category. Some companies produce apparel in missy and women's (large) sizes, while other companies manufacture missy, women's, petite, and tall sizes. Figure 4.2 shows how the measurements in several different size categories vary. Within one size range, an apparel producer may manufacture clothing in one or more of the product classifications previously listed.

Table 4.1 Children's, Men's, and Women's Wear Categories and Size Ranges

CHILDREN'S WEAR

Subcategories (organized by gender and size)

Infants	sized by weight/height or sizes 0 to 3 months (or newborn, 3 months), 6 to 9 months (or 6 months, 9 months), 12 months, 18 months, 24 months, or S-M-L-XL
Toddler	sizes 2T, 3T, 4T, 5T
Boys	sizes 4, 5, 6, 7, and 8 to 20 (even numbers only). Also Slim sizes 4S, 5S, 6S, 7S, and 8S to 20S (even numbers only), and Husky sizes 8H to 26H (even numbers only), or S-M-L-XL-XXL
Girls	sizes 4, 5, 6, 6X, and 7, 8, 10, 12, 14, 16, 18. Also Slim sizes 4S, 5S, 6S, 7S, and 8S to 16S (even numbers only), or S-M-L-XL
Girls Plus	sizes 8 ½ to 20 ½ (even numbers only), or 7+, 8+ , 10+, 12+, 14+, 16+, 18+, 20+, or M-L-XL
Preteen (girls)	sizes 6 to 16 or 8 PT to 16 PT (even numbers only)
Young Junior	sizes 3 to 13 (odd numbers only)

Children's, Men's, and Women's Wear Categories and Size Ranges *(continued)*

MEN'S WEAR

Subcategories (organized by classification of apparel)

Tailored clothing	**suits, sport coats, evening wear (tuxedos), overcoats:** sizes: 36, 38, 39, 40, 41, 42, 43, 44, 45, 46, 48, 50, 52, 54, 56, 58, 60 based on chest circumference. Lengths: Regular, Short, Long, Extra Long Regular, Athletic, and Portly fit **separate trousers:** sized by waist (29 to 44)/hemmed at retailer
Sportswear	**sport shirts:** sizes S-M-L-XL-XXL-XXXL **pants:** sized by waist/inseam (29 to 44 waist and 28 to 34 inseam), or sizes S-M-L-XL **casual jackets:** sizes 36 to 50 or S-M-L-XL. Also Tall, Extra Regular, Tall, Big & Tall sizes
Furnishings	**shirts:** sized by neck/sleeve length (e.g., 16/34), or S-M-L-XL-XXL sizes **sweaters:** sizes S-M-L-XL-XXL **underwear:** sized by waist size **robes and pajamas:** sizes S-M-L-XL-XXL **neckwear:** sizes regular, long, and extra long **socks** (based on shoe size)
Active sportswear, swimwear, athletic wear, windbreakers	sizes S-M-L-XL-XXL-XXXL may include Tall and Big & Tall sizes
Uniforms and work wear	**overalls, work pants:** sized by waist/inseam, or S-M-L-XL-XXL-XXXL **work shirts:** sizes S-M-L-XL-XXL-XXXL Regular, Tall, Big & Tall sizes

WOMEN'S WEAR

Classifications include: outerwear, dresses, career wear, blouses, sportswear and active sportswear, evening, bridal, maternity, uniforms, furs, intimate apparel, accessories

Missy	sizes 0 to 18 (even numbers only: 2, 4, 6, 8, 10, 12, 14, 16, 18), or sizes XS-S-M-L-XL
Women's (large size, queen, plus, custom)	sizes 14W to 26W (even numbers only), or Plus sizes 1X, 2X, 3X
Petite (under 5'4")	sizes 0P to 16P, under 5'4" (even numbers only)
Women's Petite	14WP to 20 WP (even sizes only)
Tall (over 5'9")	sizes 10T to 18T (even numbers only)
Junior	sizes 1 to 15 (odd numbers only)
Junior Petite	sizes 1JP to 15JP (odd numbers only)

Note: Not all companies produce the entire size range in the size categories listed.

SWIM BODY SIZES

Misses

Size	6	8	10	12	14	16	18
	S		M		L		XL
Bust	34 ½	35 ½	36 ½	38	39 ½	41	43
Ribcage	28	29	30	31 ½	33	34 ½	36 ½
Waist	25 ½	26 ½	27 ½	29	30 ½	32	34
Hip	36 ½	37 ½	38 ½	40	42	44	46
Torso	59	60 ½	62	63 ½	65	66 ½	68
Long torso	62	63 ½	65	66 ½	68	69 ½	71

Women's

Size	16W	18W	20W	22W	24W	26W	28W
		1X		2X	3X		
Bust	42	44	46	48	50	52	54
Ribcage	35 ½	37 ½	39 ½	41 ½	43 ½	45 ½	47 ½
Waist	34	36	38	40	42	44	46
Hip	45	47	49	51	53	55	57
Torso	65 ½	67	68 ½	70	70	70	70

Juniors

Size	3	5	7	9	11	13
Bust	32 ½	33 ½	34 ½	35 ½	36 ¾	38 ¼
Ribcage	26 ½	27 ½	28 ½	29 ½	30 ¾	32 ¼
Waist	23 ½	24 ½	25 ½	26 ½	27 ¾	29 ¼
Hip	34 ½	35 ½	36 ½	37 ½	38 ¾	40 ¼
Torso	57	58 ½	60	61 ½	63	64 ½

Juniors

Size	XS	S	M	L	XL
Bust	33	34	35 ½	37 ½	39 ½
Ribcage	27	28	29 ½	31 ½	33 ½
Waist	24	25	26 ½	28 ½	30 ½
Hip	35	36	37 ½	39 ½	41 ½
Torso	56 ½	59	61 ½	64	66 ½

Figure 4.2   Women's apparel includes size ranges such as misses (missy), junior, and women's.

In addition to the difference between size categories of missy and junior apparel, there are styling differences as well (see Figure 4.3). The junior size range is designed for a customer who is approximately 16 to 22 years old, whereas the missy size category is designed for a target customer who is approximately 22 years old and upward. The styling, fabrics, and trims of missy apparel have a more mature fashion look than that of junior apparel.

Traditional men's wear classifications include the following:

tailored clothing (structured or semi-structured suits, coats, and separates, such as sport jackets and dress slacks)

sportswear (casual pants, including jeans)

furnishings (dress shirts and casual shirts; sweaters; neckties, handkerchiefs, and other accessory items; underwear and night wear; hosiery; and hats and caps)

Both sizing and styling differences differentiate junior apparel from missy apparel.

active sportswear (athletic clothing, including golf wear, tennis wear, swimwear)

uniforms and work wear (work shirts and pants, overalls)

Table 4.1 (see page 151) lists these classifications and typical sizes offered. The number of seasonal lines produced per year in men's wear varies with the classification of apparel. Tailored-clothing producers tend to develop a large Fall line and a somewhat smaller Spring line, while most sportswear producers develop four to six seasonal lines per year.

In children's wear, the subcategories are organized by age-related size categories and by gender (see Table 4.1, page 150). Many children's wear manufacturers produce apparel in both infant and toddler sizes. In the older-size categories, apparel companies usually specialize in either boys' wear or girls' wear. Seasonal lines produced in children's wear typically include Back-to-School (the largest line), Holiday, Spring, and Summer lines.

Price Zones

Ready-to-wear apparel companies typically specialize in one or more **price zones** or **price points**. These categories are based on either the approximate wholesale price of the merchandise or the suggested retail price of the merchandise. The price zone categories include the following:

Designer: The designer price zone is the most expensive of the price zones. It includes collections of name designers such as Calvin Klein, Donna Karan, Vera Wang, Giorgio Armani, and Chanel, as well as collections of brands such as St. John Knits. Although this category is sometimes referred to as *couture*, it should not be confused with couture apparel that is custom-made to the body measurements of an individual.

Bridge: Bridge lines traditionally fall between designer and better price zones. These may include designers' less expensive lines, sometimes called **diffusion lines** (e.g., Armani Collezioni), or those brands that are situated between designer and better price zones (e.g., Ellen Tracy, Dana Buchman, Adrienne Vittadini).

Better: Lines in the better price zone are generally nationally known brand names, such as Emporio Armani, DKNY in women's wear, or Nautica in men's wear. Many store brands (e.g., Banana Republic) and private-label merchandise (goods that carry the retailer's name) are also in this price zone (e.g., Nordstrom's Caslon and Classiques Entier brands).

Moderate: Lines in the moderate price zone include nationally known sportswear brand names (e.g., Dockers, Guess?, Jones New York Sport) or store brands (e.g., Gap, A/X Armani Exchange) and other reasonably priced lines (e.g., Kasper suits). Moderate lines also include less expensive lines of companies that also produce better merchandise (e.g., Lizwear). Private-label and store brand merchandise may also be in this price zone (e.g., JCPenney's Arizona brand and Macy's I.N.C. brand).

Budget or mass: Found primarily at mass merchandisers and discount stores, budget lines are the least expensive of the price zones. These may include store brands of retailers with low prices as a competitive strategy (e.g., Old Navy—see Figure 4.4). Private-label merchandise for discount stores is also considered to be in the budget price zone category (e.g., Kmart's Jaclyn Smith brand).

It is important to note that the price zones can be considered a continuum for classification purposes. For example, some lines may be considered to be between budget and moderate, while others may be considered between moderate and better. Also, a brand may be offered in the bridge price zone as direct-mail merchandise, while the same brand may be offered in the designer price zone at retail stores. Some companies produce labels in several price zones, or **brand tiers**. Giorgio Armani includes the Giorgio Armani label, the Emporio label, and the A/X Armani Exchange label, each targeted for a different price zone.

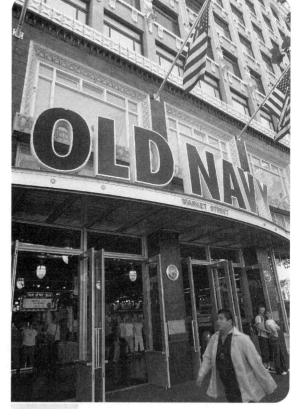

Figure 4.4 Store brand apparel, such as Old Navy, might be priced in the budget price zone.

Apparel companies also vary in the brands they produce. Brand names fall into one of the following categories (Lewis, 1995, p. 3):

National/designer brands: A **national/designer brand** is "a label that is distributed nationally, to which consumers attach a specific meaning. Typically a national brand represents a certain image, quality level and price-point range to consumers" (Lewis, 1995, p. 3). Examples include Hanes, Fruit of the Loom, Calvin Klein, Betsey Johnson, Wrangler, Victoria's Secret, and Nike (see Figure 4.5).

Private-label brands: A private-label brand is "a label that is owned and marketed by a specific retailer for use in their stores" (Lewis, 1995, p. 3). Examples include JCPenney's Worthington label and exclusive licensing agreements, such as Target's Mossimo and Isaac Mizrahi private-label brands.

Retail store/direct market brands: A retail store/direct market brand is "a name of a retail chain that is, in most cases, used as the exclusive label on the

Nike is an example of a national brand.

items in the store" (Lewis, 1995, p. 3). These are sometimes referred to as store brands. Examples include Gap, Eddie Bauer, Banana Republic, The Limited, Victoria's Secret, and L.L.Bean.

Lifestyle brands: A lifestyle brand is a term used to describe brands that are associated with a particular target customer's activities and way of life. Tommy Bahama is a good example of a lifestyle brand as the merchandise is associated with the lifestyle of individuals who live or vacation in tropical locations.

All other brands: In addition to these brands, there are "miscellaneous labels that are not included in the categories above. Includes licensed brands" (Lewis, 1995, p. 3). Examples include Wilson, Mickey & Co., and Looney Tunes/Warner Bros.

Nonbrands: In addition, a product may have "a label to which consumers attach no significant identity, awareness, or meaning" (Lewis, 1995, p. 3).

See Table 4.2 for a listing of the 25 most recognizable brands in men's apparel and accessories.

North American Industry Classification System

The U.S. Department of Commerce categorizes companies based on their chief industrial activity. Industry data is often compiled and reported according to these categories. In the past, Standard Industrial Classification (SIC) numbers were used. With the phasing out of the SIC system, the **North American Industry Classification System (NAICS)** was created. In this classification system, industry sectors in the United States, Mexico, and Canada can be compared. The following are primary NAICS groups for textiles and apparel:

Twenty-five Best-Known Men's Brands in the United States

Rank	Brand	Product	Volume	Owner
	Levi's	Jeanswear, shirts, outerwear, accessories	$2.93 billion	Levi Strauss & Co., San Francisco, CA
	Fruit of the Loom	Underwear, loungewear, T-shirts, hosiery	$1.4 billion	Berkshire Hathaway, Inc., Omaha, NE
	Nike	Activewear, athletic footwear, accessories, sporting goods	$13 billion (Nike brand)	Nike Inc., Beaverton, OR
	Hanes	Underwear, T-shirts, casualwear	approx. $2 billion	Sara Lee Corp., Winston-Salem, NC
	Dockers	Casual pants, shirts, footwear	$780 million	Levi Strauss & Co., San Francisco, CA
	Wrangler	Jeanswear, casualwear	$3 billion (retail)	VF Corp., Greensboro, NC
	Reebok	Activewear, accessories, footwear	$4 billion	adidas Group, Herzogenaurach, Germany
	Lee	Jeanswear	$1 billion	VF Corp., Greensboro, NC
	Gap	Casual apparel, accessories, personal-care products	$6.8 billion	Gap, Inc., San Francisco, CA
	Calvin Klein	Designer and better sportswear, jeanswear, activewear, underwear, fragrance, accessories	$4 billion (retail)	Phillips-Van Heusen, New York, NY
	Old Navy	Sportswear, accessories	$6.9 billion	Gap, Inc., San Francisco, CA
	Adidas	Activewear, athletic footwear, accessories, sporting goods	$5.9 billion (Adidas brand)	Adidas-Salomon AD, Herzogenaurach, Germany
	Jockey	Underwear, sleepwear, loungewear, activewear, hosiery	$600 million (estimated)	Jockey International Inc., Kenosha, WI
	Timex	Watches	$600 million (estimated)	Timex Corp., Middlebury, CT
	Polo by Ralph Lauren	Designer sportswear, jeanswear, activewear, underwear, fragrance, accessories	$3.75 billion	Polo Ralph Lauren Corp., New York, NY

Table 4.2   Twenty-five Best-Known Men's Brands in the United States *(continued)*

Rank	Brand	Product	Volume	Owner
16.	Tommy Hilfiger	Sportswear, jeanswear, activewear, outerwear, underwear, fragrance, accessories, home	$1.7 billion	Apax Partners Worldwide LLP
17.	Haggar	Dress and casual slacks, shorts, sportswear	$470 million	Infinity Associates LLC, Perseus LLC, Symphony Holdings Ltd.
18.	Converse	Athletic apparel, accessories, footwear	$400 million	Nike Inc., Beaverton, OR
19.	Eddie Bauer	Sportswear, accessories, outerwear	$1.1 billion	Sun Capital, Golden Gate Capital
20.	Dickies	Workwear, jeanswear	$1.1 billion	Williamson-Dickie Mfg., Fort Worth, TX
21.	L.L.Bean	Apparel, shoes, outdoor equipment	$1.47 billion	L.L.Bean Inc., Freeport, ME
22.	Arrow	Dress furnishings, sportswear, accessories	undisclosed	Phillips-Van Heusen Corp., New York, NY
23.	New Balance	Footwear, activewear, sportswear, technical outerwear, accessories	$1.5 billion	New Balance, Inc., Boston, MA
24.	Van Heusen	Dress shirts, sportswear, accessories	undisclosed	Phillips-Van Heusen Corp., New York, NY
25.	Nautica	Sportswear, jeanswear, activewear, outerwear, underwear, fragrance, accessories, home	$550 million	VF Corp., Greensboro, NC

SOURCE: (2006, November 27). America's top fifty power brands. *DNR*, pp. 15–24.

- NAICS 313: Textile Mills
- NAICS 314: Textile Product Mills (produce nonapparel textile products)
- NAICS 315: Apparel Manufacturing
- NAICS 316: Leather and Allied Product Manufacturing

Within these major groups, additional numbers are used to designate more specific products (e.g., 31521 refers to cut-and-sew apparel contractors). Table 4.3 lists the NAICS categories for textiles and apparel.

North American Industry Classification System (NAICS)

313 Textile Mills

Industries in the Textile Mills subsector group establishments that transform a basic fiber (natural or synthetic) into a product, such as yarn or fabric, that is further manufactured into usable items, such as apparel, sheets, towels, and textile bags for individual or industrial consumption. The further manufacturing may be performed in the same establishment and classified in this subsector, or it may be performed at a separate establishment and be classified elsewhere in manufacturing.

The main processes in this subsector include preparation and spinning of fiber, knitting or weaving of fabric, and the finishing of the textile. The NAICS structure follows and captures this process flow. Major industries in this flow, such as preparation of fibers, weaving of fabric, knitting of fabric, and fiber and fabric finishing, are uniquely identified. Texturizing, throwing, twisting, and winding of yarn contains aspects of both fiber preparation and fiber finishing, and is classified with preparation of fibers rather than with finishing of fiber.

314 Textile Product Mills

Industries in the Textile Product Mills subsector group establishments that make textile products (except apparel). With a few exceptions, processes used in these industries are generally cut and sew (i.e., purchasing fabric and cutting and sewing to make nonapparel textile products, such as sheets and towels).

315 Apparel Manufacturing

Industries in the Apparel Manufacturing subsector group establishments with two distinct manufacturing processes: (1) cut and sew (i.e., purchasing fabric and cutting and sewing to make a garment); and (2) the manufacture of garments in establishments that first knit fabric, and then cut and sew the fabric into a garment. The Apparel Manufacturing subsector includes a diverse range of establishments manufacturing full lines of ready-to-wear apparel and custom apparel: apparel contractors, performing cutting or sewing operations on materials owned by others; jobbers, performing entrepreneurial functions involved in apparel manufacture; and tailors, manufacturing custom garments for individual clients are all included. Knitting, when done alone, is classified in the Textile Mills subsector, but when knitting is combined with the production of complete garments, the activity is classified in Apparel Manufacturing.

North American Industry Classification System (NAICS) *(continued)*

316 Leather and Allied Product Manufacturing

Establishments in the Leather and Allied Product Manufacturing subsector transform hides into leather by tanning or curing and fabricating the leather into products for final consumption. It also includes the manufacture of similar products from other materials, including products (except apparel) made from "leather substitutes," such as rubber, plastics, or textiles. Rubber footwear, textile luggage, and plastic purses or wallets are examples of "leather substitute" products included in this group. The products made from leather substitutes are included in this subsector because they are made in similar ways leather products are made (e.g., luggage). They are made in the same establishments, so it is not practical to separate them.

The inclusion of leather making in this subsector is partly because leather tanning is a relatively small industry that has few close neighbors as a production process, partly because leather is an input to some of the other products classified in this subsector, and partly for historical reasons.

SOURCE: U.S. Census Bureau (http://www.census.gov/epcd/naics02/naicod02.htm).

Organizational Structure of Apparel Companies

The organizational structure of a typical apparel company is shown in Figure 4.6. Although companies will vary in terms of their exact organizational structure, the following activities are often included:

- research and merchandising
- design and product development
- sales and marketing
- operations
- advertising and sales promotion
- finance and information technology

Very large companies may have separate departments or divisions with dozens of employees who handle each of these activities. On the other hand, in very small companies, a few employees may handle several of these activities.

Research and
Merchandising

Design and   Sales and
Product Development   Marketing

Operations   Advertising and
                                                        Sales Promotion

Finance and
Information Technology

Example of apparel company organization

In reviewing Figure 4.6, it is important to note the connections among all of the areas or divisions. Communication among the various activities is imperative for the success of the company. Merchandisers must communicate with designers; designers must communicate with production management and marketers; those in information technology must understand the computer needs of all areas. This can be a challenge for large companies.

The term **merchandising** generally refers to "a management process of collecting and assimilating information from a variety of sources and drawing conclusions from that information regarding the product offering" (Brown

& Brauth, 1989, p. 78). This process includes conducting necessary trend and market research and developing strategies to get the right merchandise, at the right price, at the right time, in the right amount, to the right locations to meet the wants and needs of the target customer. The merchandising area of apparel companies may include merchandise managers, merchandise coordinators, and fashion directors. These individuals research and forecast fashion trends and trends in consumer purchasing behavior in order to develop color, fabric, and garment silhouette directions for the company's merchandise. When making these forecasts, merchandisers interpret these trends for the company's target market, which is determined by their customer's age, gender, income, and lifestyle. The role of merchandisers in apparel companies can vary. In some companies, they facilitate the creation of lines; in other companies, they oversee the fashion direction of the company. The merchandising function of the apparel company will be discussed in greater detail later in this chapter and in Chapter 5.

Design and Product Development

The merchandisers work closely with those in the **design and product development** area, who will interpret the trend forecasts and create designs to be manufactured by the company. Generally, merchandisers and designers work together on the seasonal and line planning. Those in the design and product development area include designers, assistant designers, product developers, stylists, pattern makers, and sample sewers. For companies that have their own factories, the design and product development area may also include the management and operation of the company-owned factories, including the employment and training of sewing operators. Chapters 5 through 7 focus on the design and product development activities of an apparel company.

Sales and Marketing

The sales and marketing area of the apparel company works to sell the company's merchandise to the retail buyers. The sales and marketing division includes regional sales managers and sales representatives, as well as those who conduct marketing research for the company. The sales and marketing staff show the company's merchandise to retail buyers in the company's showrooms during market weeks and at trade shows (see Figure 4.7). Some companies will employ their own sales staff; others will contract with independent sales representatives to handle their merchandise. Chapter 8 discusses the marketing and sales activities of an apparel company.

Figure 4.7 Designers may meet with merchandisers in their showrooms.

Operations

The operations area includes the preproduction, material management, quality assurance, sourcing, production, distribution, and logistics functions. The preproduction, production, material management, and quality assurance areas of the apparel company include those people involved with the material inspection and buying, production (see Figure 4.8), and quality assurance. (Some companies refer to these activities as product engineering.) It also includes those who identify and monitor domestic and foreign contractors to sew the garments, if the company contracts out these services. Once produced, merchandise is shipped and distributed to retailers. Chapters 9 through 11 focus on production, planning, and control. Chapter 12 focuses on distribution strategies of apparel companies.

Advertising and Sales Promotion

Working with the design and product development staff and the sales and marketing staff, those in the advertising and sales promotion area focus on

Figure 4.8 Operations includes the management of production facilities. Shown is an Eton unit production system (UPS) that transports and ergonomically delivers garment components to the sewing operator.

creating promotional and advertising strategies and tools to sell the merchandise to the retail buyers and to the ultimate consumer (see Figure 4.9). Often these services are contracted to an outside advertising agency that specializes in these activities.

Finance and Information Technology

Because all companies are in business to make a profit, effective financial management of companies is imperative to their success. More than simply "churning out numbers," those in the finance area of an apparel company are responsible for the overall financial health of companies and work closely with all other areas.

With the increased importance of computer systems in the design and production of products and in the product data management of companies, information technology (IT) areas of companies play important roles in overseeing companies' computer operations. Those who work within IT must have technical expertise, and they must understand the operation of the apparel industry. Some companies have chosen to outsource their information technology area.

Merchandising Philosophies of Apparel Companies

According to industry analysts, the overall goal of the merchandising area is to "make a profit by developing an assortment of products that reflects the company's market strategy and that can be delivered and sold on time" (Brauth & Brown, 1989, p. 110). To meet this goal, apparel merchandisers set the overall direction for the merchandise assortment and work closely with the other areas of the apparel company that carry out the design, production, marketing, and distribution of the goods. Effective merchandising and product development depend on the following:

the company's product category (e.g., men's sportswear, women's dresses, children's outerwear)

the price zone(s) of its merchandise

its marketing strategy

Companies can be classified according to their merchandising philosophy, based upon where in the product lifecycle their merchandise belongs:

– design innovators
– design or fashion intepreters
– design or fashion imitators

Design innovators or fashion-forward companies: Design innovators depend upon their innovative designs to attract their target market, which is generally composed of fashion innovators (see Figure 4.10). Because their target market represents a very small number of customers, competition among design innovators is intense. The odds of a company

Advertising and sales promotion departments create strategies and tools to sell the merchandise to retail buyers and to the ultimate customer.

succeeding are probably less than one in one hundred. Designers for such fashion-forward companies often rely on their skill, reputation, and advertising to attract customers. Examples of brands representing design innovator companies include Calvin Klein, Betsey Johnson, Vivienne Westwood, and Anna Sui. Design innovators may also be small companies started by young designers who offer merchandise through boutiques and small specialty stores and who cater to customers who are fashion innovators.

Design or fashion interpreters: Rather than creating their own design innovations, a number of companies interpret successful innovative trends of other companies for their own target market. Although design skills and

Figure 4.10 A company that is considered a design innovator, such as Calvin Klein, depends on its innovative designs to attract its target market.

reputation are often key factors in the success of these interpreters, the risk of creating unsuccessful innovations is reduced.

Design or fashion imitators: Imitators are those who produce affordable knockoffs or similar copies of fashions that have received media attention. Timing is crucial for the imitators, who must react immediately to new trends in the market. Companies that quickly reproduce gowns worn by celebrities at award shows (e.g., Academy Awards) are considered imitators.

Regardless of how innovative a company's merchandise is, all successful companies conduct some type of market research and typically obtain direct feedback from consumers on the product line through processes such as style testing. To be successful in today's global economy, companies must accurately assess consumer preferences, based on style testing and analyses of trends in retail sales. Companies get sales information through their own stores or through partnerships with retailers, and they can produce and ship merchandise quickly, often within weeks. As discussed in Chapter 1, fashion companies such as Zara and H&M offer innovative merchandise very quickly by using a variety of methods to predict and address accurately consumers' preferences.

Trade Associations and Trade Publications in the Apparel Industry

A number of trade associations in the apparel industry promote their industry segments, conduct market research, sponsor trade shows, and develop and distribute educational materials related to various segments of the apparel industry. The largest of these associations is the American Apparel & Footwear

Association (AAFA), which serves as an umbrella trade association for apparel companies. Representatives of member companies and other professionals in the industry are active in many committees. Activities of the AAFA include the following:

compilation of statistical information related to apparel manufacturing, industry forecasts, and trend forecasts

publication of educational materials and information for use by industry analysts and company executives

Other trade associations focus their efforts on specific divisions of the RTW industry, such as intimate apparel, men's sportswear, or knitwear, to name just a few (see Table 4.4).

Selected Trade Associations in the Apparel Industry

American Apparel and Footwear Association (AAFA)
1601 N. Kent Street, Suite 1200
Arlington, VA 22209
Tel: 800-520-2262
Fax: 703-522-6741
http://apparelandfootwear.org

American Apparel Producers' Network (AAPN)
P.O. Box 720693
Atlanta, GA 30358
Tel: 404-843-3171
Fax: 413-702-3226
E-mail: source@aapnetwork.net
http://aapnetwork.net

California Fashion Association
444 South Flower Street, 34th Floor
Los Angeles, CA 90071
Tel: 213-688-6288
Fax: 213-688-6290
E-mail: info@calfashion.org
http://calfashion.org

Canadian Apparel Federation (CAF)
124 O'Connor Street, Suite 504
Ottawa, Ontario K1P 5M9
Canada
Tel: 613-231-3220
Fax: 613-231-2305
E-mail: info@apparel.ca
http://www.apparel.ca

Children's Apparel Manufacturers Association (CAMA)
6900 Decane Blvd.
Montreal, QC 4X3 2T8
Canada
Tel: 613-954-5031
http://www.strategis.ic.gc.ca

Council of Fashion Designers of America
1412 Broadway, Suite 2006
New York, NY 10018
Tel: 212-302-1821
E-mail: info@cfda.com
http://www.cfda.com

Table 4.4   Selected Trade Associations in the Apparel Industry *(continued)*

Fashion Group International, Inc. (FGI)
8 West 40th Street, 7th Floor
New York, NY 10018
Tel: 212-302-5511
Fax: 212-302-5533
E-mail: info@fgi.org
http://fgi.org

The Hosiery Association (THA)
3623 Latrobe Drive, Suite 130
Charlotte, NC 28211
Tel: 704-365-0913
Fax: 704-362-2056
E-mail: info@hosieryassociation.com
http://hosieryassociation.com

International Apparel Federation (IAF)
34 Thornton Ferry Road, #1
Amherst, NH 03031
Tel: 603-672-4065
Fax: 603-672-4064
E-mail: dmschmidea@aol.com

International Association of Clothing Designers and Executives (IACDE)
835 Northwest 36th Terrace
Oklahoma City, OK 73118
Tel: 405-602-8037
Fax: 405-602-8038
http://iacde.com

International Formalwear Association (IFA)
401 N. Michigan Avenue
Chicago, IL 60611
Tel: 312-321-5139
Fax: 312-321-5150
E-mail: IFA@sba.com
http://formalwear.org

International Swimwear and Activewear Market and the Swim Association (ISAM)
13351-D Riverside Dr., #658
Sherman Oaks, CA 91423
Tel: 818-986-2152
Fax: 818-986-2637
E-mail: swim4isam@aol.com
http://isamla.com

Men's Apparel Guild in California (MAGIC International)
6200 Canoga Avenue
2nd Floor
Woodland Hills, CA 91367
Tel: 818-593-5000
Fax: 818-593-5020
E-mail: cs@MAGIConline.com
http://show.magiconline.com

Men's Dress Furnishings Association
151 Lexington Avenue, #2F
New York, NY 10016
Tel: 212-683-8454
http://shirtsandties.org

National Retail Federation
325 7th St NW
1100
Washington DC 20004
Tel: 1-800-NRF-HOW2
Fax: 202-737-2849
http://nrf.com

Professional Apparel Association
994 Old Eagle School Road, Suite 1019
Wayne, PA 19087-1802
Tel: 610-971-4850
Fax: 610-971-4859
E-mail: info@proapparel.com
http://www.proapparel.com

Selected Trade Associations in the Apparel Industry *(continued)*

Sewn Products Equipment Suppliers of the Americas
9650 Strickland Road, Suite 103–324
Raleigh, NC 27615
Tel: 919-872-8909
Fax: 919-872-1915
http://spesa.org

Sporting Goods Manufacturers Association
1150 17th Street NW, Suite 850
Washington DC 20036
Tel: 202-775-1762
E-mail: info@sgma.com
http://sgma.com

Underfashion Club Inc.
326 Field Road
Clinton Corners, NY 12514
Tel : 845-758-6405
Fax : 845-758-2546
E-mail: underfashionclub@aol.com
http://www.underfashionclub.org

A number of trade publications focus on the apparel industry and are of use to professionals in the RTW industry. (See Table 4.5 for a listing of selected trade publications in the apparel industry). These publications range from daily newspapers to monthly magazines (see Figure 4.11).

Selected Trade Publications in the Apparel Industry

Newspapers

California Apparel News (CAN): published weekly, every Friday, by MnM Publishing Corporation. Covers fashion industry news with an emphasis on regional companies and markets on the West Coast. Includes classified advertisements.

DNR (Daily News Record): published weekly by Fairchild Publications. Covers national and international news in men's wear retailing, apparel, fiber, and fabric. Includes classified advertisements.

Women's Wear Daily (WWD): published Monday through Friday by Fairchild Publications. Covers national and international news in the women's and children's fashion industry for retailers and manufacturers. Covers textiles, accessories, and fragrances, in addition to apparel. Includes classified advertisements.

Selected Trade Publications in the Apparel Industry *(continued)*

Magazines

Apparel: published monthly by Edgell Communications. Targeted to apparel and soft goods businesses. Focuses on business and technology.

Canadian Apparel: published six times a year by the Canadian Apparel Federation. Focuses on the entire fashion supply chain.

Children's Business (CB): published monthly by Fairchild Publications. Targeted to retailers. Provides news and fashion coverage of apparel, footwear, toys, entertainment, and juvenile products for infants through preteens.

Earnshaw's Infants, Girls, and Boys Wear Review: published monthly by Symphony Publishing. Targeted to retailers of fashion and accessories for newborns and young children.

Stores (www.stores.org): published monthly by the National Retail Federation. Targeted to retailers. Provides information of general interest, as well as reports on electronic commerce, loss prevention, and computer software and hardware.

International Magazines

Collezioni: published in Italy by Zanfi Editori. Issues with focused content include haute couture, prêt-à-porter, men's wear, children's wear, bridal, shoes, bags and accessories, sport and street, and trends in fabrics and yarns.

Book Moda: published in Italy by Publifashion. Issues with focused content include haute couture, prêt-à-porter, and bridal.

L'Officiel de la Couture et de la Mode de Paris: published in Paris by Les Editions Jalou. Ten issues per year focus on haute couture and prêt-à-porter.

GAP Press: published in Japan by Yoshiaki Yanata. Two issues per year highlight the Paris Fall/Winter and Spring/Summer haute couture collections.

Styling News: published in Germany by mode ... information Heinz Kramer GmbH. Two issues per year focus on color, fabric, and fashion trends.

Moda: published in Barcelona by PrePress. Two issues per year feature the Paris Fall/Winter and Spring/Summer couture collections.

Trade publications provide important information for people employed in the apparel industry.

Summary

Most of the apparel produced and sold today is considered ready-to-wear (RTW); that is, it is completely made and ready to be worn at the time of purchase. RTW apparel is possible because of standardized sizing and mass-production techniques used in the apparel industry. Apparel companies typically produce four to six lines or collections corresponding to the fashion seasons: Spring, Summer, Fall I, Fall II, Holiday, and Resort or Cruise.

It is important to note the distinctions between RTW and couture. In couture, garments are made to the specific body measurements of an individual rather than to standardized sizes found in RTW. In addition, couture garments are generally made with some hand-sewing techniques and from more expensive materials than RTW. Haute couture collections are shown twice per year (in July and January) to the media, others in the fashion industry, and wealthy clients.

Based on their organization and operations, RTW apparel companies fall into the following categories: manufacturers, jobbers, contractors, and licensors. Apparel companies are also classified according to the type of merchandise they produce, the price zones of their products or brands, and by the North American Industry Classification System (NAICS) established by the government.

A typical apparel company includes areas or divisions that focus on the following activities: research and merchandising; design and product development; sales and marketing; operations including production, planning, control, and distribution; advertising and sales promotion; and finance and information technology. Apparel merchandisers set the overall direction for the merchandise assortment and work closely with the other divisions of the company that carry out the design, production, marketing, and distribution of the goods. Companies vary in their merchandising philosophies and may be innovators, interpreters, or imitators. All successful companies rely on consumer and market research, as well as sales data, for setting their fashion direction.

A number of trade associations in the apparel industry promote, conduct market research, sponsor trade shows, and develop and distribute educational materials related to various segments of the apparel industry. Examples include the American Apparel and Footwear Association (AAFA), the Men's Apparel Guild in California (MAGIC International), and the Underfashion Club Inc. A number of trade publications focus on the apparel industry and are used by professionals in the RTW industry. Examples include *Women's Wear Daily*, *DNR*, and *Apparel*.

Careers within apparel companies include positions in merchandising; product/ fashion development; sales and marketing; preproduction; production, control, and quality assurance; and advertising and promotion.

Women's Merchandise Manager
Better Men's and Women's Apparel Company

Position Description

Manage and control the development of merchandise from color, fabric, and style selection to presentation and sales marketing. Work with the development team, which consists of a designer, pattern maker, sample sewer, and product engineer. The merchandise manager is ultimately responsible for the line.

Typical Tasks and Responsibilities

Analyze wholesale and retail performance of the product.

Read trade and fashion publications to keep current on market direction.

Communicate with retail accounts to gain sales information.

Estimate units per style/color for the designated season (design development team produces patterns; merchandising decides in which fabrics each style will be available).

Write and deliver presentations to sales representatives; attend sales meetings held throughout the year.

Travel domestically to meet with sales representatives and retail accounts three to four times per year.

Travel to New York twice per year for major development trips.

Work with the fabric design department to develop fabrics and patterns for future seasons.

Work with contractors to develop garments not produced by the company's factories.

Work with quality control on production problems.

Work with design to develop a style plan; design follows up with prototype development.

Attend fitting sessions; sign off on all pieces to be included in the line.

Key Terms

atelier de couture
brand tier
classification
collection
contractor
couture
couturier, couturière
design and product development
diffusion line
fashion season
full-package contractor
haute couture
item house

jobber
licensor
line
manufacturer
merchandising
national/designer brand
North American Industry
    Classification System (NAICS)
price point
price zone
retail store/direct market brand
salon de couture

Discussion Questions

1. Name your three favorite apparel brands. What companies manufacture these brands? How would you classify these brands in terms of product category, wholesale price zone, and type of brand name?

2. Examine copies of trade publications in the apparel industry. To whom does each of the trade publications cater (i.e., what are the publications' target markets)? What types of information are included in the trade publications? How might this information be used by professionals in the industry?

3. Discuss the advantages and disadvantage of producing four seasonal lines per year versus six seasonal lines per year. What are some examples of merchandise that is well suited to four seasonal lines versus examples of merchandise that is well suited to six seasonal lines per year? Why?

4. Discuss the advantages and disadvantages to the consumer if all apparel companies were to use the same size standards (e.g., if all companies that produce size 6 missy pants used the same waist, hip, crotch depth, and inseam measurements).

American Society for Testing and Materials (2007). American Society for Testing and Materials Home Page [online]. Available: http://www.astm.org/cgi-bin/SoftCart.exe/STORE/filtrexx40.cgi?U+mystore+niox8210+-P+DESIGNATIO+D5586+/usr6/htdocs/astm.org/DATABASE.CART/allversionspick.frm [January 10, 2007].

Bond, Patti. (2004, March). Sizing it up. *Women's Wear Daily Los Angeles*, pp. 50–53.

Brauth, Bonnie, and Brown, Peter. (1989, June). Merchandising malpractice. *Apparel Industry Magazine*, pp. 108–110.

Brown, Peter, and Brauth, Bonnie. (1989, August). Merchandising methods. *Apparel Industry Magazine*, pp. 78–82.

Fédération Française de la Couture du Prêt-à-Porter des Couturiers et des Créatures de Mode (2007). Fédération Francaise de la Couture du Prêt-à-Porter des Couturiers et des Créatures de Mode Home Page [online]. Available: http://www.modeaparis.com/va/collections/2007ephc/ index.html [April 18, 2007].

Lewis, Robin. (1995, November). What's in a Name? *DNR Infotracs: Supplement to Daily News Record*. New York: Fairchild Publications.

North American Industry Classification System (2002). Definitions: 313 Textile Mills [online]. Available: http://www.census.gov/epcd/naics02/def/NDEF313.HTM#N313 [January 14, 2007]; http://www.census.gov/epcd/naics02/def/NDEF314.HTM#N314 [January 14, 2007]; http://www.census.gov/epcd/naics02/def/NDEF315.HTM#N315 [January 14, 2007]; http://www.census.gov/epcd/naics02/def/NDEF316.HTM#N316 [January 14, 2007].

Size USA (2007). Size USA Home Page [online]. Available: http://www.sizeusa.com [January 10, 2007].

Southern California Edison Company. (1995, February). *Southern California's Apparel Industry: Building a Path to Prosperity*. Rosemead, CA: Author.

Eight Steps in the Design Process

Research and Merchandising

Market Research:	**Fashion Research:**
Consumer Research	Fashion Trend Research
Product Research	Color Research
Market Analysis	Fabric and Trim Research
Target Customer Profile	

Seasonal and Line Planning

Design

Design Inspiration

Plan the Line

Sketch Design and Obtain Vendor Samples

Select or Develop Fabrics and Trims

Review and Select Styles to Develop for Line

Write Garment Specifications Sheet and Quick Cost

Design Development and Style Selection

Make First Pattern

Cut and Sew Prototype

Approve Prototype Fit, Revise Style, or Drop Style

Estimate Cost (initial cost estimate)

Present and Review Line

Select Styles for Final Line (line adoption)

Determine the Final Cost

Order Fabric, Trims, and Findings for Sales Samples

Order Sales Samples Cut and Sewn

Marketing the Apparel Line

Designer and National Brands:
Sales Representatives Show Line at Market and
through Other Promotion Strategies
Retail Buyers Place Orders

Private-Label Brands:
Design Team Shows Line to Merchandisers/Buyers
Buyers Place Orders

Preproduction

Order Production of Fabrics, Trims, and Findings

Finalize Production Pattern and Written Documents

Grade Production Pattern into Size Range

Make Production Marker

Inspect Fabric

Spread, Cut, Bundle, and Manage Dye Lots
for Production

Sourcing

Select Production Facility

Apparel Production Processes, Material Management, and Quality Assurance

Sew Production Order (may include approval
of first size run by contractor)

Finish, Inspect, Press, Tag, and Bag Order

Distribution and Retailing

Send Retailer's Order to Manufacturer's
Distribution Center

Pick Orders (may include Quality Assurance Check)

Send to Retail Store Distribution Center
or Directly to Retailer

Review Season's Sales Figures

Creating and Marketing an Apparel Line

CHAPTER 5

Creating a Line:
Research

In this chapter, you will learn the following:

- the concept of an apparel line

- the various types of market research used to understand target customers' characteristics and preferences

- the scope of the job responsibilities of the apparel designer and merchandiser in conducting and interpreting market research

- resources for fashion trend, color trend, and fabric trend forecasting

Step 1: Research and Merchandising

Research and Merchandising

Market Research:	Fashion Research:
Consumer Research	Fashion Trend Research
Product Research	Color Research
Market Analysis	Fabric and Trim Research
Target Customer Profile	

Seasonal and Line Planning

Design

Design Development and Style Selection

Marketing the Apparel Line

Preproduction

Sourcing

Apparel Production Processes, Material Management, and Quality Assurance

Distribution and Retailing

*T*he creation of a group of apparel items into a collection or a line involves a series of steps. Each step is closely related to and influenced by all the other steps in the process. The next several chapters will discuss these steps sequentially. The Eight Steps in the Design Process flowchart at the beginning of Part 2 will help acquaint you with the "big picture." Each stage in the design process will be explored in greater detail in Parts 2 and 3. Step 1, Research and Merchandising, is discussed in Chapter 5. The Step 1 flowchart at the beginning of this chapter shows the research and merchandising step in detail. It is important to keep in mind that this flowchart is a generic one. Some apparel companies deviate from this sequence for a variety of reasons. The industry is constantly changing in areas such as computer integration, speed of production, geographic location for production, regulations on goods manufactured outside the United States, number of new lines introduced each year, and distribution channels. These changes affect the sequence of steps in the design process. A company may also follow one sequence for some lines and use a modified sequence for other lines. In addition, several activities may occur simultaneously during the progress of a line's development.

The terms *line, group,* and *collection* are used to designate a combination of apparel items presented together to the buying public for a particular season. The term *collection* is used generally to refer to the apparel presented through runway shows each fall and spring by the high-fashion designers in Paris, Milan, New York, London, Tokyo, and other locations. The runway shows of designer collections often include a wide range of apparel, including swimwear, dresses, suits, sportswear, evening wear, and, of course, bridal wear as the finale. The designer collections may include approximately 100 to 150 apparel items. Collections are typically inspired by a theme.

An apparel *line* consists of one large group or several small groups of apparel items, or *styles*, developed around a theme that may be based on such factors as color, fabric, design details, or a purpose (such as golf or tennis) that links the items together (see Figure 5.1). For example, Nike develops a line for each of a variety of sports, including men's cycling, men's running, men's tennis, women's

Pendleton Refined • Pearl District Fall 2007

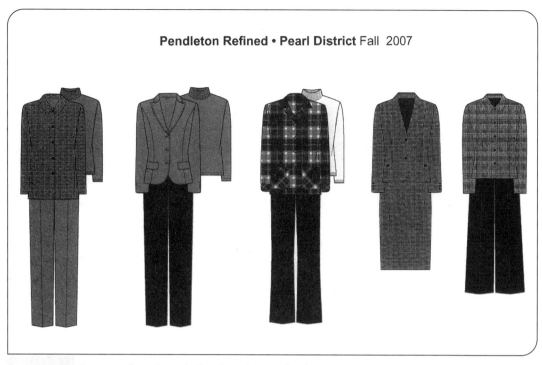

A group of products is developed around a theme.

aerobics, women's tennis, and women's running. A line is composed of a variety of items or styles, such as shirts, pants, jackets, vests, and sweaters. Each line is developed for a specific target customer and could consist of as many as 50 or 60 apparel items. A designer, often with a team of several others, such as a design assistant and a product developer, will be assigned responsibilities for the creation of the line. Some designers will have responsibility for several lines. Sometimes, several small groups will be developed within a line, each with its own theme. A **group** might use three to five fabrics in varying combinations and include approximately a dozen apparel items, all carefully coordinated.

Whereas many apparel companies focus on developing seasonal lines (typically four to six seasons per year), some apparel companies develop new groups to ship every four to six weeks throughout the year. This merchandising strategy places new merchandise in retail stores at frequent intervals, an enticement for many customers to shop often. Liz Claiborne is a company known for providing new style groups approximately every six weeks. Another merchandising strategy focuses on providing new merchandise on a continual basis. Zara, based in Spain, exemplifies fast fashion, a quick-cycle approach to design-produce-distribute discussed in Chapter 1. Zara designs the product as well as owns its retail stores; therefore, it can quickly design, produce, and distribute new merchandise. New styles arrive in Zara's retail stores weekly (read about Zara's *Success Story* at the end of Chapter 11).

Just as fashion, in general, follows an evolutionary pattern, apparel designers who work for companies generally create new seasonal lines in an ongoing, evolutionary manner. New lines tend to develop from previous lines, with some repetition or modification of successful styles. Styles repeated from one seasonal line to the next are called **carryovers**. The target customer, general market trends, fashion trends, color trends, fabric trends, and retailers' needs are all taken into careful consideration in the planning and development of an apparel line.

The stereotypical image of a fashion **designer** is that he or she sits at a drawing table, sketching garment idea after garment idea. The sketches are handed to other employees who turn them into garments. Is this what really happens in the apparel industry? In actuality, the creation of an apparel line is a carefully orchestrated series of processes—a team effort, involving many people. The designer's job includes a variety of responsibilities, such as the following:

- researching the market
- selecting the colors, fabrics, and garment styling for the line based on fashion direction from merchandisers
- consulting with product engineers on costing factors
- preparing the preliminary specification sheets
- presenting technical drawings or sketches of new garment styles
- providing suggestions for linings, interfacings, trims, buttons, and other components
- releasing the approved styles for pattern making
- responding to inquiries about the styles during preproduction and production

A designer typically works with a **merchandiser** to plan the overall look of an apparel line, the color story, the fabrics, the price, and the number of styles for each line (see Chapter 6 for this discussion). The merchandiser's role is to see that all the company's needs for the line are met. This might include seasonal as well as line planning, and coordinating several lines presented by the company. The merchandiser is also responsible for the following:

- conducting market research
- developing and maintaining the line estimate and price targets to meet budget objectives

reviewing the designer's proposed line

approving the line

Years of experience in design or retailing provide the perspective needed for the apparel company's merchandiser.

The creation and design development stage of one line overlaps with the production stage of the previous line and the selling stage of the line presented prior to that one (see Color Plate 3). Thus, at any given time, designers and merchandisers are handling at least three lines, each in a different stage of the product cycle. Developing a line would be much easier if one had the final sales statistics from the previous line before beginning to work on the creation stage of the new line. Unfortunately, this is not possible in the fast-paced world of fashion. Ever-increasing numbers of shopping malls, factory outlet malls and direct mail and electronic shopping options have provided increased opportunities for purchasing apparel and accessories. To help meet consumers' wishes, the timeline in today's apparel industry calls for creating more lines, more quickly than even five years ago.

The most important concept for success in the apparel industry is that the company needs to know its target market and provide the merchandise assortment desired by its customers—when they want it, and where they will purchase it. In other words, consumer demand is the driving force in the apparel industry. The industry expression "You can make it only if it sells" relates to the concept of the consumer-driven market. Thus, the success of any apparel, textile, or home fashions company depends on determining the needs and wants of the consumer. To determine what customers will need and want, and when and where they will want it, a variety of types of research must be conducted. This process is called **market research**.

Market research can be defined as "the systematic and objective approach to the development and provision of information for the marketing management decision-making process" (Kinnear & Taylor, 1983, p. 16). Market research is divided into two general categories (Kinnear & Taylor, p. 17):

1. basic research that deals with extending knowledge about the marketing system

2. applied research that helps managers make better decisions

Company executives, merchandisers, and designers conduct applied market research as a part of the planning process.

Applied market research includes the following three types of research:

consumer research, which provides information about consumer characteristics and consumer behavior

product research, which provides information about preferred product design and characteristics

market analysis, which provides information about general market trends

All three types of market research will be discussed in this chapter.

Each form of applied market research provides valuable information to company executives, merchandisers, and designers about the wants and needs of their target market customers. Some forms of market research take considerable time to conduct, analyze, and interpret. Because of the fast-paced nature of the fashion business, fashion products require a short research-and-development stage. Timing is crucial to the fashion item's successful sale in the marketplace. Therefore, companies generally conduct market research on an ongoing basis.

Trade associations, such as the American Apparel and Footwear Association and Cotton Incorporated, also conduct market research, providing information that can be very beneficial to apparel manufacturers and retailers. (Selected trade associations are discussed in Chapters 3 and 4.) Examples of other sources of information to assist with conducting research will be discussed in this chapter.

Consumer Research

Consumer research provides information about consumer characteristics and consumer behavior. Some forms of consumer research study broad trends in the marketplace. Research on **demographics** focuses on understanding the following characteristics of consumer groups:

age

gender

marital status

income

occupation

ethnicity

geographic location

Consumer research may also focus on **psychographics**. Psychographic characteristics of consumer groups include the following:

- buying habits
- attitudes
- values
- motives
- preferences
- personality
- leisure activities

Demographic information helps describe who the customer is, while psychographic information helps explain why the customer makes the choices he or she makes. Some of these demographic and psychographic characteristics will be discussed further in the market analysis section of this chapter.

Consumer research is conducted and interpreted in a variety of ways. To understand broad consumer trends, companies may review various sources of information available in print form and online. Examples include the following:

SRC's DemographicsNow, an online market demographic analysis Web site (www.demographicsnow.com)

Spectra, a Chicago-based company that provides consumer segmentation and targeting for the consumer goods industry (http://www.spectramarketing.com)

Market research companies also conduct general consumer research, such as the following:

Teenage Research Unlimited is a market research company that tracks teenage trends.

John D. Morris is "a retail analyst who holds focus groups with teenagers in malls around the country" (Rozhon, 2004, p. A13).

Some market research companies include a fashion division. For example, NPDFashionworld is the apparel division of the market research firm NPD Group of Port Washington, New York.

Apparel companies may also conduct and interpret their own consumer research. This often happens when a company is considering expanding into a new target market (see Color Plate 7). For example, Mackey McDonald, chairman and CEO of VF Corporation, "noticed that the Lee Brand did not have a strong franchise among 12- to 14-year-old boys. After extensive consumer research, Lee introduced its Lee Pipes and Lee BMX brands, with styles inspired by board sports and mountain biking" ("Execution is the key to selling," 1999, p. 4).

Similarly, Jerell, a moderately priced women's wear manufacturer based in Dallas, Texas, conducted consumer research when it ventured into a new demographic market, the Hispanic customer. "Marketing to different demographic groups is another path along Jerell's road of diversification. Interested in exploring the possibility, Jerell set to work conducting focus groups and identifying the needs of the Hispanic consumer" (Rabon, 1998, p. 44). Focus groups are composed of potential customers of the new market. A small group of these potential consumers is interviewed to learn more about their needs, wants, and whether they anticipate a market for a new product.

Consumer research is also conducted by companies expanding their markets beyond U.S. consumers to better understand the preferences of these new consumer groups. For example, some women's activewear companies in the United States are expanding into the European market. To market a U.S. company's activewear apparel in France, it is important to research the French activewear consumer if the product is to succeed in that marketplace. It is essential to learn, among other things, that the styles of activewear preferred by French women are not the same as those currently most popular in the United States.

Color preferences vary among countries and cultures. These preferences might be related to the country's climate, personal skin tones of the residents, or cultural heritage. When expanding into a new market, consumer research dealing with color preferences of the intended new market would be important for the success of the line.

Conducting consumer research related to fashion items can be a challenge. Apparel purchase decisions are based on a number of factors (including psychological, social, and financial considerations) of which consumers are often not consciously aware. Therefore, results of market research indicate that consumers often do not actually purchase what they indicate they would purchase when queried in advance.

Product Research

Product research provides information about preferred product design and product characteristics. When new products are developed, or existing products are modified, it is advantageous to assess how well a new or revised product will fare in the marketplace. To try to determine customer preferences, one could conduct product research such as the following:

- survey potential consumers orally
- send a questionnaire
- offer a free trial of a product in exchange for feedback

Sometimes an apparel company will conduct substantial market research before introducing a new line, especially if the company is interested in developing a new product type. For example, Sears conducted focus group research before it ventured into a new suit market. Some large apparel manufacturers, such as JCPenney (for their private-label merchandise) and VF Corporation, have been testing style preferences for years.

Is it possible to predict how apparel consumers will react to a style? Style testing techniques, refined by some of the most respected names in apparel manufacturing, show that one can predict what consumers will want to buy. Some companies use outlet store sales to gather data on how consumers react to various styles and prices. JCPenney surveys mall shoppers and uses in-house video testing to guide the decisions of its buyers, as well as its manufacturing operations. Focus groups guide VF Corporation's style decisions (Henricks, 1991).

Some companies survey a target group to determine potential improvements in their products. "Quiksilver CEO Robert McKnight said his firm keeps close tabs on some 300 avid surfers, snowboarders, and skateboarders to tweak designs that will be more appealing to their consumers. For example, by talking to surfers in Hawaii, McKnight developed board shorts with a special pocket for a bottle of sunscreen" ("Execution is the key to selling," 1999, p. 4).

VF Corporation's Lee brand has established Lee's Trend Leaders Panel, a group "comprised of 35 young men and women who are peer-group fashion leaders who share their views with the product development staff" (Hill, 1998, p. AS-6). The Internet is another source for consumer product input. Lee's Web site receives product input from about 1,000 kids per day.

Listening to comments from sales representatives, retailers, and customers about the success of a line provides another part of the feedback necessary for continued success. Designer John Galliano stated that "he plans to communicate regularly with Bergdorf [Goodman] sales staff to find out what's happening on the floor, including reactions to the cut, fit, and finishing of the clothes, right down to the durability of a button. That kind of information is a gold mine for the designer" (Socha, 1997, p. 12).

Market Analysis

Market analysis provides information about general market trends. Planning ahead to meet the future needs of the consumer is a critical part of continued success in the apparel industry. Market analysis in the apparel, accessories, and home fashions industries can be subdivided into long-range forecasting (or research) and short-range forecasting. **Long-range forecasting** projects market trends one to five years in advance, while **short-range forecasting** focuses on market trends one year or less in advance. Both long-range forecasting and short-range forecasting strategies are used for market analysis. Long-range forecasting includes researching economic trends related to consumer spending patterns and the business climate that affects the apparel industry. Sample research questions include the following:

- Will interest rates be increasing on money borrowed by an apparel manufacturer to purchase fabric?
- Will corporate taxes for the apparel company be increasing?
- Will cost-of-living expenses rise because of inflation, resulting in fewer apparel purchases by consumers?
- Will rising labor costs result in noticeable increases in the purchase price for apparel?

All of these trends can influence the company's plans and the consumer's future purchases.

Long-range forecasting also includes sociological, psychological, political, and global trends. For example, changes in international trade policies will affect long-range forecasting. Political fluctuations among countries can affect sourcing options when planning offshore production. Currency devaluation, economic downturn, and financial turmoil around the world have an impact on the U.S. apparel industry.

Other aspects of long-range forecasting deal with ongoing changes in the apparel industry. Sources of information on these changes include the following:

- *The Apparel Strategist* (www.apparelstrategist.com) is a publication that is directed specifically toward market analysis in the apparel industry.
- NPD Group (www.npd.com), mentioned earlier in the section on Consumer Research, publishes online market research for the apparel and footwear industries.
- Kurt Salmon Associates (KSA) is an example of a company that specializes in conducting and publishing soft-goods business expertise and market analysis.
- Cotton Incorporated, a textile trade organization discussed in Chapter 3, conducts product trend analysis and consumer marketing. *Lifestyle Monitor* is published monthly by Cotton Incorporated (see www.cottoninc.com). Cotton Incorporated also publishes *Lifestyle Monitor Trend Magazine* semi-annually.

The apparel marketplace is in a constant state of flux. Changes in a company's target market, market shifts, or new markets all need to be considered. As a result of market analysis indicating an increased interest in the Big & Tall business in men's sportswear, Polo Ralph Lauren, Tommy Hilfiger, and Nautica expanded their apparel lines and entered the Big & Tall market in 1999 (see Figure 5.2).

Another target market receiving increased interest is the teen market. Market analysis indicated that demographic changes will affect the youth market: "The U.S. population of teen boys, aged 13–19, is projected to grow from 14.2 million in 2000 to 15.4 million by 2010, or an 8.3 percent increase over the decade. The Hispanic and Asian markets will experience the most increases of any ethnic markets" (Schneiderman, 1999, p. 42).

Another market currently of interest to the apparel industry is the aging boomers market. Market research on apparel spending patterns suggests consumers over age 55 will spend less on apparel than this group spent before reaching age 55. As the fashion conscious baby boomers reached age 55, their apparel spending patterns changed. "The aging of America is slowly sneaking up on the apparel industry, and the purse strings are beginning to tighten as the boomers age" (Behling, 1999, p. 53). Table 5.1 lists average annual expenditures on apparel and apparel services by age group between the years 2000 and 2005.

Environmental concerns and quality-of-life factors are other examples of long-range trends that affect apparel companies. Some companies have made the commitment to use fabrics made from recycled products, such as aluminum cans or plastic bottles. For example, Patagonia uses postconsumer recycled (PCR)

Figure 5.2 Market analysis provides the data needed for apparel companies to expand their markets by offering new size ranges, such as Big & Tall sizes.

materials in some of its product line (see Figure 5.3). These fabrics are made using recycled polyester garments and by utilizing other recycled plastics. The use of PCR material in its product line reflects Patagonia's decision to offer products consistent with its company's and customers' values. Patagonia's environmental assessment coordinator Eric Wilmanns stated, "From a lifecycle analysis approach, we look not only at the materials and energy we use, but also what goes into sustaining our products, how they are used, and what eventually happens to them when consumers are finished using them" (Welling, 1999,

Year	Under 25 Years	25–34	35–44	45–54	55–64	65–74	75 and over
2000	1,420	2,059	2,323	2,371	1,694	1,130	701
2001	1,197	1,922	2,110	2,337	1,575	1,151	611
2002	1,365	1,989	2,101	2,029	1,791	1,252	674
2003	1,117	1,849	2,091	1,953	1,562	1,190	611
2004	1,371	2,134	2,142	2,217	1,863	1,200	604
2005	1,577	2,082	2,365	2,318	1,784	1,313	584

Table 5.1 Average Annual Apparel and Apparel Services Expenditures by Age Group (in U.S. Dollars)

SOURCE: Retrieved January 4 and April 23, 2007, from U. S. Department of Labor, Bureau of Labor Statistics, Consumer Expenditure Survey Web site: http://bls.gov.cex/home.htm.

p. AS26). In 2007, Patagonia introduced a major expansion of its garment recycling program. Customers may return used Polartec fleece garments, Patagonia fleece, Patagonia cotton tees, and Capilene baselayers to Patagonia via mail or to any Patagonia retail store ("Patagonia announces ...," 2007). The fabrics from these used garments are then used to produce new PCR material.

Consistent with Patagonia's environmental philosophy, in 1996, the company switched to using 100 percent organic cotton in their apparel products. Earth-friendly choices often cost more to the company, and sometimes a part of this cost must be absorbed by the customer. Each company makes a philosophical choice about whether these decisions will gain customers who respect the company philosophy and are willing to pay more for a product, or whether price is so important that customers might be lost if the product's price is increased. Patagonia's company philosophy regarding environmental concerns extends to all aspects of its business.

Jantzen, a major swimwear manufacturer, developed and introduced the "Clean Water" campaign in 1928, one of the first environmental awareness efforts by an apparel company. Updated in 1992, this campaign highlights the company's commitment to social responsibility by sponsoring beach cleanups and joining forces with environmental groups to effect change. Jantzen linked forces with retailers to bring the message to customers through a donation-with-purchase program.

Another type of environmental concern focuses on waste products resulting from the manufacture of textiles and apparel. Wrangler advertised its EarthWash

Patagonia's Synchilla vest is made from fabric containing postconsumer recycled (PCR) fiber.

process as an alternative to dyes and finishing processes that pollute the water supply. Advertising campaigns are structured to let the retailer and consumer know about the company's activist stance on environmental issues.

What about forecasting long-range fashion trends? Is it possible to forecast fashion trends several years in advance of a season? Long-range forecasting can reap benefits. For example, *The Popcorn Report* (Popcorn, 1991) predicted a trend toward "cocooning," in which people would want to stay home more in the evenings, enjoying leisure time spent in a quiet environment rather than in restaurants, movies, or sports events surrounded by others. Evenings spent at home could signal increased consumer interest in loungewear. Thus, the loungewear industry was wise to prepare for this trend.

Short-range forecasting is critical to an apparel company's success. Planning meetings are held with designers, merchandisers, planners, and sales personnel to discuss the company's short-range forecasts and strategic planning. This planning includes such components as determining the desired percentage of increased sales growth for a company. For example, perhaps the company managers have determined that a 5 percent growth in sales should be planned. The designer for each apparel line that the company produces may be asked to increase the line with a 5 percent sales growth factor in mind. Using sales figures from the current selling season, the designer (and merchandiser) may select one or several styles that are selling particularly well, and add one or several similar styles to the upcoming line. Seasonal and line planning will be discussed in more detail in Chapter 6.

Short-range forecasting also includes the careful study of what the competition is doing. If a competitor seems to be expanding one of its lines, for example, the water sports category of apparel, then perhaps it would be wise to study whether this growth area would be feasible for your company. Apparel, accessories, and home fashions companies constantly observe the marketplace competition.

Short-range forecasting also includes predicting changes in retailing. A retailer may be in the process of expansion, with a number of new stores ready to open in the forthcoming year. If this retailer has been a strong client of an apparel manufacturer in the past, the expansion can signal increased orders for the apparel company. As retailers file for bankruptcy, merge, and divide, it is important for the apparel company to be wary of shipping goods to retailers who may be in the process of disruption.

Target Customer

Each apparel company's goal is to position its apparel lines to be different from the competition and to be enticing to potential customers. The merchandising and design staff's objective is to develop the right product for the company's **target customer** at the right time in the marketplace. This is called its **brand position**. Eddie Bauer, headquartered in Seattle, describes its brand position as follows:

> Innovation, quality and an appreciation of the outdoors: The passions of our founder, Eddie Bauer, remain the cornerstone of the Eddie Bauer business today. In conjunction with innovative design and exceptional customer service, Eddie Bauer offers premium-quality clothing, accessories and gear for men and women that complement today's modern lifestyle. (Eddie Bauer, 2007)

Within a company's position in the marketplace, each apparel line produced by the apparel company requires a clearly defined target customer (see Figure 5.4).

The profile, or description, of the target customer usually includes the following demographic and psychographic characteristics determined for the majority of customers:

- gender
- age range
- average income
- lifestyle
- buying habits
- geographic location
- price zone

A swimwear company may produce several lines, each based on a specific target customer profile. One line may be designed for very conservative missy customers, while other lines may range from appealing to conservative customers to appealing to updated missy customers and to fashion-forward junior customers. Developing a well-defined target customer profile for each line helps the designers and merchandisers focus the line to the specific audience, or market niche. For example, Eddie Bauer outlines its target customer for its classic Eddie Bauer line as follows:

- 42 to 46 years old
- college educated
- average income $70,000
- young families and empty nesters, currently working
- quality and value are a priority
- prefer an active, casual lifestyle

Some companies develop a very detailed target customer profile. A photograph of the "typical" customer might be included with the target customer profile statement to help merchandisers, designers, product developers, and sales representatives visualize the customer. The models used for product advertisements are also selected to portray the image of the target customer. The design team relies on the target customer profile for the following:

- to identify market trends, especially those related to its target customer
- to develop the initial direction for the line
- to develop style sketches (concept sketches) and color concepts

Figure 5.4 The target customer for Donna Karan's DKNY lines (left) is similar to the target customer for the more expensive Donna Karan designer lines for men (center) and women (right). The main difference between the two markets is the price zone.

VF Corporation, parent company to Wrangler, Lee, The North Face, and Jansport, has used a variety of strategies to develop the products that consumers want and need. According to VF Corporation's president and CEO, a company must recognize that it will constantly be changing its business to respond to the continuous changes going on with consumers. VF's Consumer Response System (CRS), introduced in the 1990s, created an active, continuous link between consumer research and new product development. "We focus on specific target consumer segments, defined by differences in key attitudes, lifestyles, and needs. The discovery part is learning everything we can about each brand's specific target consumer—who she is, how she thinks, how her life is changing, and what she really needs" (Hill, 1998, p. AS-5).

GENDER

Whereas some companies produce lines of unisex clothing (for example, a T-shirt company), most lines are focused on men's, women's, or children's apparel. Many companies produce both men's and women's apparel, but they will have separate lines specifically designed for each gender. Other apparel companies produce only men's apparel or only women's apparel.

In the children's wear industry, many companies produce infants' and toddlers' apparel for both boys and girls. While some companies produce children's apparel for both girls and boys, many companies produce only girls' apparel or only boys' apparel.

AGE RANGE

Companies tend to focus on a specific age range, as defined in their target customer profile statement for each of their lines. For a line of junior apparel, a company might profile its customers as ages 15 to 25. This does not mean that a woman over the age of 25 would not wear the apparel in this line. Rather, the design team visualizes the majority of customers as falling within the age range of 15 to 25, and keeps this age range firmly in mind while creating the line. A company may decide to adjust the targeted age of its customer. Raising the upper age of the age range of the target customer might be a logical adjustment as the average age of the population increases. Perhaps the company wants to retain an established customer by broadening the age range at the older end yet continue to include the established target customer in its target market. After acquiring a loyal customer who likes a company's brand, it could be very cost effective to adjust the styling slightly over time to continue to appeal to this customer as he or she ages.

LIFESTYLE AND GEOGRAPHIC LOCATION

A study of the target customer's lifestyle might include information such as the following:

- type of career
- stage in career
- geographic location and its population size
- social or political direction
- education
- attitudes
- values
- interest in fashion (for example, prefers classic looks or is a fashion trendsetter)
- price consciousness

Lifestyle preference descriptions could suggest that the target customer is focused on entertainment or is comfortable with technology. Lifestyle research is conducted to help define the various target groups.

The term **lifestyle merchandising** was coined to recognize the importance of appealing to the target customer's lifestyle choices. The proliferation of popular lifestyle magazines, direct-mail catalogs, and Web sites indicates the importance of appealing to customers' lifestyles. For example, the fitness market has a myriad of lifestyle magazines. Some apparel companies design clothing to appeal to a specific lifestyle preference.

Tommy Bahama is an apparel, accessories, and home fashions company that exemplifies lifestyle merchandising. The brand is a "purveyor of island lifestyles" (Tommy Bahama, 2007). Relaxed fashions, some in tropical prints, as well as island-inspired accessories, home fashions, and store decor all contribute to promoting the island lifestyle.

Some companies may focus a line on a specific geographic location. For example, the resort market in Florida might be a location for a targeted customer. There is a special fashion "look" to resort apparel in Florida that may not sell well in other geographic locations. The garment style characteristics, fabric design motifs, and colorations of apparel for Florida resort wear are easily recognized if you are familiar with that market.

PRICE ZONE

The target customer profile also typically includes a targeted price zone, such as moderate, better, or bridge price, as discussed in Chapter 4. Each line will be planned to fall within the specified price zone, based on the target customer profile. Within the line, not every style of shirt will sell for the same price. There will be a range of prices, based on differences in styling and fabric variations. However, the overall prices for the line will fall within expected ranges for the determined price zone. If a company is known to produce goods in the moderate price zone, a jacket style in its line priced in a better price zone will look overpriced in comparison to the rest of the line. A customer would question why the price is higher than expected and might not purchase the jacket due only to its price.

The design team always keeps the target customer profile in mind in order to create a line that will appeal to the customer. It is important for a company to review and update its target customer profile from time to time. The target customer profile is an important component of an apparel line's marketing campaign, both to the retailer and to the ultimate customer.

Fashion Research

In addition to market research, fashion research is also conducted. Fashion research focuses on trends in silhouettes, design details, colors, fabrics, and trims.

Similar to market research, fashion research may be conducted and interpreted by fashion research or forecasting firms, or by apparel companies themselves.

Fashion trend research tends to be a daily activity for the designer and the merchandiser. **Trend research** activities include reading or scanning appropriate **trade publications**. Each segment of the apparel industry has specific trade newspapers and magazines directed toward fashion trends in that industry segment. Examples include the following:

- *Children's Business* and *Earnshaw's Infant, Girls, and Boys Wear Review*, focusing on children's wear industry fashion trends
- *Footwear News* for the footwear industry
- *Sportswear International* for the men's wear, women's wear, and children's wear apparel and accessories industries

These trade publications require subscriptions, so they are not available for individual purchase at specialty magazine stores.

Trade newspapers include *Women's Wear Daily, California Apparel News*, and *DNR* (men's wear and textiles). *Women's Wear Daily* covers fabrics, fashion ready-to-wear, sportswear, furs, and financial news daily. In addition, each day of the week is targeted to specific market segments (for example, accessories, innerwear, and legwear are covered on Mondays). A few newspaper and magazine retailers offer these publications over the counter, but, for the most part, they are available by subscription only. Several trade publications are available online; for example, *Women's Wear Daily* is available at www.wwd.com.

European **fashion magazines**—such as *French Vogue, Italian Vogue, Elegance,* and *Book Moda Alta Moda* (women's wear); *Book Moda Uomo* and *Vogue Homme* (men's wear); and *Vogue Bambini* (children's wear)—are important sources for fashion trends. Many of the specific fashion magazines are provided to the design team by the apparel company. Some of these fashion magazines are available for purchase at specialty magazine stores in larger cities. Other specialized publications are available only by subscription from fashion publication subscription services in New York and Los Angeles.

Popular fashion magazines, read by the target customer, are sources for fashion trend information and provide an insight into the preferences of the customer. Designers and merchandisers peruse the appropriate publications, depending on their target market. Examples of popular fashion magazines include *Vogue, Elle, Jane, Harper's Bazaar, W, Glamour, Allure, Cosmopolitan,*

Self, Vanity Fair, Town & Country, Essence, InStyle, Lucky, Savvy, YM, Seventeen, Jump, Men's Vogue, Details, Maxim, and *GQ* (see Figure 5.5). These magazines are readily available to the public at news and magazine stands and bookstores. Some of these magazines, such as *Elle, Glamour, Harper's Bazaar, Jane, Seventeen, Teen,* and *Teen People,* have editorial Web sites on the Internet or have previews of the current issue's contents on the Internet. A convenient and fast way for designers and merchandisers to search for fashion trend information related to a specific target customer is by using online access.

Apparel companies and retailers often subscribe to **fashion forecasting services**. Some of these forecasting services cover a broad range of fashion trends. Some specialize in color trends, while others provide both fashion trend and color trend analysis. Examples of fashion trend forecasting services based in the United States include the following:

- The Doneger Group, based in New York, provides merchandising consulting and fashion trend and color forecasts for the apparel and accessories markets. The Doneger Group publishes the *Tobe Report,* a fashion consulting publication for retailers.

- Margit Publications, a division of the Doneger Group, publishes a variety of trend and color forecasts.

- Here & There provides trend and color forecasts as well as collections reports, retail reports, and textile reports.

Publications such as these help merchandisers and designers analyze upcoming fashion trends. An annual subscription to a fashion trend newsletter might cost several hundred dollars.

- Trend Union is a fashion trend, fabric, and color trend forecasting service based in Paris that conducts fashion and fabric trend seminars in locations such as New York, Seattle, San Francisco, and Los Angeles several times a year in addition to its forecasting publications.

- Promostyl provides trend books focusing on men's wear, women's wear, sportswear, streetwear, youth, and accessories. The company produces style trends, color trends, and fabric trend books. Based in Paris, Promostyl sponsors conferences in many major cities throughout the world on a continuous schedule.

- Worth Global Style Network (WGSN) is an example of an online subscription fashion resource. WGSN provides research, trend analysis, and news service daily to its online subscribers. (See Chapter 3 for more examples of trend forecasting companies.)

Popular fashion magazines are a source of fashion trend information.

Fashion DVDs of recent runway shows are another source of fashion trend information. Several resources provide runway images of recent designs shown in Milan, Paris, London, and New York. Fashion information is available online as well. There are many Web sites that show the latest styles as seen on the runways of Milan, Paris, London, and New York. These sources provide examples of current fashions, rather than forecasting future trends. However, many of the new styles shown are those that set new trends and provide a sense of fashion direction for many moderate- and mass-priced manufacturers. Some sources are accessible without a fee, whereas other sources require an online subscription. Often a free introductory preview is available to assess their usefulness before subscribing. A big advantage of these online sources, like online magazines, is their ease of accessibility.

The design team often attends textile and apparel trade shows geared to a specific segment of the market. Trade shows are held in various locations around the world, from Las Vegas to Beijing. Attendance at trade shows might be for a variety of purposes. Often the attendee's company is represented at the trade show. Some designers and merchandisers attend trade shows specifically to view the latest trends. An added benefit for those attending trade shows is that fashion trend and color forecasting seminars geared to a specific product market are presented. Some of these trade shows, such as the Men's Apparel Guild in California (MAGIC) and The Super Show, sponsored by Sporting Goods Manufacturers Association (SGMA), are discussed in Chapter 8.

Computer software programs have been developed to assist with consumer-driven fashion forecasting. Some software programs provide more than total sales figures. The software enables an apparel company to determine specifically who is buying what, and where, taking into account factors such as weather, special events in the area, and store promotions.

Fashion trend research also involves **shopping the market**. Although this sounds like fun, it actually requires considerable concentration and constant vigilance. Merchandisers and designers look for new trends that may influence the direction of an upcoming line. Bodice design details in evening wear may inspire a design detail in a swimsuit, for example. One aspect of shopping the market involves visiting retail stores that carry the company's line. Talking with retailers about how the line is selling at retail provides helpful information for predicting fashion trends. Watching retail store customers' reactions to the line provides helpful feedback. Studying the competitors' lines in retail stores is also important for predicting trends.

The "fantasy" aspect of trend research involves viewing the high-fashion couture and ready-to-wear collections in Paris, Milan, London, Tokyo, and New

York. Designers and merchandisers for some apparel companies are given the assignment to view these twice-yearly collections. The high-fashion collections are often filled with avant-garde styles, probably not worn by the target customer. However, important fashion trends can be extracted and then modified for a line in the moderate price zone.

Some designers and merchandisers also study customers "on the street," or, if the line is an active sportswear line, they watch potential customers on the ski slopes or at the beach participating in the specific sport. Fashion is a reflection of the time and the lifestyle of the society from which and for which it is created. Therefore, trend research involves the collection of information from multiple sources on a continuing basis. The design team does not create in a vacuum; instead, it is influenced by everything on a daily basis. It is important to visit art museums, concerts, and movies, and to participate in other activities that expose the design team to fashion-related trends.

Color Research and Resources

When color trends in apparel, accessories, or home fashions are reviewed over time, it becomes clear that certain **staple colors** appear frequently in the fashion cycle. In apparel, black, navy, white, and beige are considered staple colors and are seen almost continuously season after season. One or more staple colors is included in each line. Pendleton Woolen Mills is known for maintaining a group of staple colors in its classic apparel lines. Pendleton's tartan navy and tartan green are examples of colors that are color matched season after season. If a customer had purchased a navy Pendleton jacket from its classic line, a pair of navy slacks purchased several years later will match the color of the jacket (unless it had faded because of improper care or excessive wear). Pendleton tracks the sales, ranked by dollar volume and color, to ensure that long-term, high-selling colors are represented in each line. Talbots is another company that provides color-matched apparel season after season. The Talbots true red, # 25, and cherry red, #26, are examples of colors that are continued season after season.

Some companies vary a staple color slightly from season to season to reflect fashion influences. One season, a navy may be a violet-navy, while another season, the navy may be a black-navy. This lends an updated fashion look to staple colors. If a print fabric in the line contains navy, then it is necessary to match the navy in the print fabric to the solid navy.

Other colors, called **fashion colors**, appear less frequently over time than do staple colors. Fashion colors often follow cycles, reappearing in a different shade, value, or intensity from one fashion season to the next. For example, an orange-red may evolve into a blue-red, which may evolve into a blue-magenta. It is interesting to follow the trend of a fashion color over a period of years. A color such as aubergine (eggplant) will recur every few years. It may be slightly redder one season, slightly bluer another. For those who have tried to match the color of an item purchased in a previous season or year, it becomes painfully obvious that the lifecycle of some fashion colors is very short. Some customers have learned to purchase all color-matched pieces of a line at one time to avoid disappointment later, when they might be unable to match the color of a shirt they would like to purchase to wear with the pants purchased a year earlier.

Some fashion colors sell more readily, and, therefore, tend to reappear more frequently than others. In the United States, dark reds and wine tones tend to recur often. Orange is a color that flatters fewer people's personal coloring than some other colors, such as blue. Thus, orange does not occur as frequently in the color cycle as some other colors. Apparel designers and merchandisers keep in mind color preferences of their target customers as they look at color trends.

The color forecasting services used by textile producers (see Chapter 3) are also used by apparel companies. These services study color trends in textiles, apparel, home fashions, and related fields. Some color forecasting services predict color trends 18 months in advance of when the product is available to consumers, while others, for a higher subscription fee, predict farther ahead. An apparel company subscribes to the color forecasting service based on the category, such as men's apparel, as well as the length in advance for which forecasts are provided. Most services publish color forecasts twice a year for men's, women's, and children's apparel (see Figure 5.6 and Color Plate 2). Some color forecasting services include forecasts for the home fashions industry.

Resources for color forecasting services based in the United States include the following:

- Color Association of the United States (CAUS) produces seasonal predictions with fabric swatches twice a year. The annual subscription for two seasonal forecasts for men's, women's, or youth costs about $850.

- Pantone, based in Carlstadt, New Jersey, publishes the Pantone View Color Planner twice a year, providing seasonal color direction 24 months in advance (see Chapter 6 for more information about color), and offers color consulting services. Pantone View Home is targeted to the home fashions industry.

- Here & There, mentioned earlier in this chapter, provides both fashion trend and color forecasting services.

- Huepoint Color, based in New York City, is another color forecast service, presenting its color forecasts in small glass test tubes filled with dyed cotton yarns.

The Color Box, also based in New York City and mentioned in Chapter 3, provides four reports per year.

These are a few of the many color resources available. Most apparel, accessories, and home fashions companies subscribe to several color forecasting services to provide a broader view of color trends.

Many people wonder how color trends are determined. Does "someone" predict that ruby red will be *the* color of the fall season, and that all designers will then include ruby red in their lines? Although this is not the case, color forecasting services do conduct color research to assist the fashion industry in the assessment of the color trends. Some U.S. forecast-ers rely on the color directions of fabric producers in Europe. They might watch to see whether these colors are adopted by fashion-forward designers and con-sumer fashion innovators in the United States. Other color forecasting services will focus on analyzing trends in consumer color preferences through sales data.

From the wide variety of possible colors, a palette of certain hues, values, and intensities that reflect upcoming color trends will be identified by the color forecasting service. Many apparel companies subscribe to several color forecast-ing services. It is interesting and informative to compare the similarities and differences of several color forecasting services' predictions for the same season.

The color trends presented by the color forecasting services are represented by a grouping of paint chips, fabric swatches, or yarn pompons, arranged attractively in a spiral-bound notebook or magazine format. These color palette charts may include up to several dozen colors. The colors selected tend to span a range of darks and lights, neutrals and fashion colors. Thus, one color serv-ice will not predict all dark colors while another service shows all light colors. Designers and merchandisers will be able to identify certain overall trends recurring among the various color forecasting services.

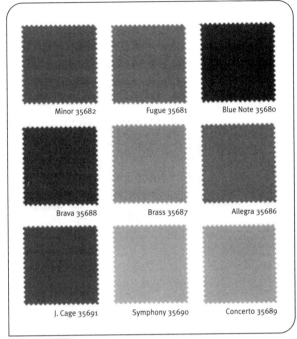

Minor 35682   Fugue 35681   Blue Note 35680

Brava 35688   Brass 35687   Allegra 35686

J. Cage 35691   Symphony 35690   Concerto 35689

Figure 5.6 Color trend reports are issued by color forecasting services.

After studying the color trends, designers and merchandisers will select a **color palette**, or color story, for the upcoming season, taking into consideration the many factors important to the success of their line. A designer may note that varying shades of purple have appeared in many of the color forecasts, indicating a purple trend. Some services provide fashion names for the color chips. The various shades of purple might be named *violet, plum, dahlia, wisteria, African violet,* and *lavender*. The specific name may be transferred to the color name used by the apparel company for that color, or a new name may be created by the apparel company to identify their company's seasonal color. The theme of a line might be linked to the color names used. For example, color names such as *adobe, cactus, sage,* and *sandstone* might be selected to correlate with a southwestern theme for a line.

Fabric and Trim Research and Resources

The designer and merchandiser research the fabric and trim market, in addition to studying fashion and color trends. The designer undertakes fabric research, beginning with such broad fabric trends as the trend toward the use of spandex blended with wool for career apparel, or the use of microfibers for men's suits and raincoats. This research might include such trends as the use of metallic fibers in fabrics, or the use of chenille yarns in suitings. Resources for this type of fabric research include the same trade publications that designers and merchandisers use for fashion trends, as well as textile trade publications.

For more specific fabric trends, textile mills, textile trade associations, and textile manufacturers are eager to acquaint designers with the latest fibers, fabrics, and textures. Fabric manufacturers employ sales representatives who supply designers with fabric swatch cards, usually in response to a phone call by the design team member to the textile sales representative. Sample yardage can also be ordered from the sales representative. Many fabric manufacturers have showrooms in New York and other cities that display the latest fabrics. The textile trade associations' headquarters are excellent resources as well. For example, a designer might visit the New York office of Cotton Incorporated to research a wide range of woven and knit cotton fabrications.

A very effective way to research fabric resources is to visit one of the textile trade shows (see Chapter 3 for a discussion of these trade shows). The shows are usually held twice a year, in the fall and the spring. American fabric manufacturers hold their textile trade shows in New York and Los Angeles. Here, many fabric manufacturers have booths displaying the latest and most enticing fabrics. In addition, smaller shows are held in cities such as Chicago and Seattle.

Some of the international fabric manufacturers bring their fabric lines to New York and Los Angeles to show to the American designers who are not able to travel to Europe. For example, Première Vision Preview New York features Italian, French, Spanish, Austrian, and Portuguese fabrics. The Los Angeles International Textile Show features both imported and domestic fabrics, trims, and findings.

Some designers travel to the European textile trade shows held twice a year to see the latest goods produced by fabric manufacturers in Europe (see Chapter 3 for detailed information). European textile trade shows include the following:

- Première Vision, showcasing Europe's fabric manufacturers, is held in Paris (see Figure 5.7).
- Texworld is also held in Paris twice a year, showcasing fabrics from 42 countries.
- Italian fabrics are featured along with those of many other countries at Ideacomo and Ideabiella near Milan.
- Prato Expo in Florence, Italy, hosts textile companies from Europe, North America, and Asia.
- Interstoff Asia, held in Hong Kong, provides an opportunity to feature Asian-produced textiles.

Designers can place orders for **sample cuts** from the textile producers. Each cut is usually three to five yards long, enough yardage to produce a prototype garment in order to evaluate the possible use of the fabric. The sample cuts are sent to the apparel company after the order is placed at a trade show. Sample cuts can also be ordered directly from the sales representative after the trade show. For many designers, though, these textile shows serve a similar purpose as the couture design shows—as an inspiration and a means to sift through the multitude of ideas for trends appropriate to their company's target customers.

Some types of apparel are especially suited to the use of specialty trims and fasteners. Outdoor activewear is one example. A new design idea might be sparked by a novelty trim or fastener. Trims, as a source of design inspiration, will be discussed in Chapter 6. Research regarding new products is an important aspect for designers and merchandisers. Product trade shows, trade publications, and specialty trim sales representatives are sources of information about such new products.

Armed with information from market research—fashion and color trend research, and fabric and trim research—the designer is ready to bring everything together in the creation of a new line.

Figure 5.7 Designers attend textile trade shows for fabric research and inspiration.

Summary

Creating an apparel line begins with research. Sales figures from the current selling season are taken into consideration as the designer and merchandiser plan the upcoming line. However, a fashion apparel company cannot survive long if it only repeats what has sold well in the past. Market research is often conducted to help predict what specific items or general trends will appeal to customers in the upcoming season. The merchandiser's and designer's job responsibilities include long-range forecasting of major social, economic, retail, apparel manufacturing, and customer trends. Short-range forecasting is also tied to the economy, political climate, availability of resources, and customer needs. The target customer profile, describing such aspects as the target customer's age, lifestyle, and intended price zone, requires constant updating and careful consideration in the creation of an apparel line.

The merchandiser and designer conduct fashion trend research on a daily basis by reading fashion publications, attending fashion events, and developing the ability to sense the fashion mood of the times. They translate this information into styles for the target customer. Color forecasting services provide information for color trend research, another important component of the creation stage. The apparel company may subscribe to one or more of these services. Fabric trend research is another aspect of the designer's responsibility. This may include scrutinizing fashion and textile industry publications and attending textile trade shows in New York and European and Asian fashion centers. While research is being conducted on the upcoming line, it is important to remember that the designer may also be working on fabric and style development for a subsequent line, is involved with production of the current line, and is watching the sales figures on the line currently selling in retail stores.

If you are particularly interested in fashion-related research or the analysis of market trends, color, or fashion trends, additional coursework in consumer behavior, market analysis, statistics, and some related job experience may be helpful.

Fashion Trend Forecaster
Publisher of Trend Forecasting Report

Position Description
Scan stores in trendsetting locales to identify key fashion trends, analyze shopping behavior, advise retail store buyers, and write trend forecasts.

Typical Tasks and Responsibilities

Travel extensively to determine trends.

Gauge shifting trend patterns and public interest in product innovation.

Scan merchandise in trendsetting stores.

Talk with sales associates to discuss trends.

Confer with retail store buyers about significant trends affecting their businesses.

Observe and analyze shopping behavior.

Write trend forecasts for trend reports.

Key Terms

brand position	market research
carryover	merchandiser
color palette	popular fashion magazine
consumer research	product research
demographics	psychographics
designer	sample cut
fashion color	shopping the market
fashion forecasting service	short-range forecasting
fashion magazine	staple color
group	target customer
lifestyle merchandising	trade publication
long-range forecasting	trend research
market analysis	

Discussion Questions

1. What are some examples of trends that can be predicted by long-range forecasting (perhaps five years from now)? How might these trends affect the apparel industry?

2. What are some examples of short-range trend forecasting (perhaps six months from now) in men's apparel, women's apparel, and children's apparel? How might these trends be reflected in an apparel line?

3. Describe what you perceive as the target customer profile for the following national brands: Roxy, 7 for All Mankind, Polo Ralph Lauren, DKNY, and Tommy Hilfiger.

4. What are some current color trends in women's wear? In men's wear? What color or colors do you predict will be popular next season in women's wear? In men's wear? Why do you think these colors will be popular?

5. What are some fabric trends that are on the upswing in the fashion cycle?

6. What are some examples of specific sources of research information for designers and merchandisers? How would you locate examples of these?

Behling, Dorothy U. (1999, January). Aging boomers may shift the apparel empire. *Bobbin*, pp. 53–54.

Eddie Bauer (2007). About Eddie Bauer [online]. Available: http://investors.eddiebauer. com/about [April 28, 2007].

Execution is the key to selling. (1999, May 24). *DNR*, p. 4.

Henricks, Mark. (1991, February). Testing consumer tastes. *Apparel Industry Magazine*, pp. 50–54.

Hill, Suzette. (1998, December). VF's consumerization: a "right stuff" strategy. *Apparel Industry Magazine*, pp. AS-4–12.

Kinnear, Thomas C., and Taylor, James R. (1983). *Marketing Research: An Applied Approach*. New York: McGraw-Hill Book Company, pp. 16–17.

Patagonia announces major expansion of garment recycling program. (2007, January 28). Patagonia.com [online]. Available: http://www.patagonia.com/pdf/en_US/ common_threads_pr_expansion.pdf [February 21, 2007].

Popcorn, Faith. (1991). *The Popcorn Report*. New York: Doubleday.

Rabon, Lisa C. (1998, December). Master of the mix. *Bobbin*, pp. 42–46.

Rozhon, Tracie. (2004, August 16). Student chic is remaking itself, trading grunge for cable knot. *New York Times*, pp. A1, A13.

Schneiderman, Ira P. (1999, September 27). Target marketing to teens should increase in next decade. *DNR*, p. 42.

Socha, Mike. (1997, December 7). Romancing the store. *Women's Wear Daily*, p. 12.

Tommy Bahama (2007). Tommy Bahama Home Page [online]. Available: http:// tommybahama.com/index.jsp [April 27, 2007].

Welling, Holly. (1999, December). Patagonia: Small world view of big business. *Apparel Industry Magazine*, pp. AS-26–32.

Creating a Line:
Design

The discussion of the creation, marketing, production, and distribution of a line in the following seven chapters provides an overview of the processes that occur from the inception of a line until the product reaches the ultimate customer. There are many variations of the specific sequence of processes used by apparel companies. For the most part, a traditional design-and-manufacturing sequence of processes will be used to avoid confusion. Alternative possible sequences will be discussed where appropriate.

In this chapter, you will learn the following:

- the various sources of design inspiration

- the market forces that direct a company's design focus

- the scope of the job responsibilities of the design and merchandising team in designing a line

- the interrelationship between design and merchandising in developing a new season's line

- the ways computer-aided design and graphic design software systems are used in the design process

- the use of product lifecycle management systems to track each style as it progresses through the design, style selection, marketing, preproduction, production, and distribution processes

Step 2: Design

Research and Merchandising

Design

Design Inspiration

Plan the Line

Sketch Design and Obtain Vendor Samples

Select or Develop Fabrics and Trims

Review and Select Styles to Develop for Line

Write Garment Specifications Sheet and Quick Cost

Design Development and Style Selection

Marketing the Apparel Line

Preproduction

Sourcing

**Apparel Production Processes,
Material Management, and Quality Assurance**

Distribution and Retailing

Design Inspiration

*T*he design stage of creating a line combines the designer's and merchandiser's interpretations of market and fashion trends, their understanding of the target customer, and new design inspirations appropriately interpreted for the target customer. Where do designers come up with the multitude of new designs each season? Designers' inspirations for a new line can come from a variety of sources that may have been part of the market and fashion research conducted. All the research information discussed in the previous chapter sifts through the designer's mind during this phase of the design process. For example, designers may be inspired by studying pictures of design ideas from fashion trend sources, collecting swatches of interesting fabric textures and trims, developing some innovative design details, conducting research about a historical period or another culture, or searching the marketplace for a "lightning bolt" idea. Designers may visit historical costume and textile collections, such as the Fashion Institute of Technology's collection or the Metropolitan Museum of Art's Costume Institute, both in New York City. Apparel companies located close to such extensive costume and/or textile resources may pay an annual fee so that their designers can have continual access to the collections. These sources of design inspirations are then interpreted for the specific company's target customer. The interrelationships of various types of information needed to create a new line are shown in Figure 6.1.

A Theme for the New Line

Based on market research, design inspirations, and discussions among the designers and merchandisers who are coordinating the various lines for a company, a theme for the line might be developed. Not every group or line will have a theme, but a theme can help sell a group or a line to retailers and consumers. In some cases, an advertising campaign may be developed around a chosen theme. For example, a company producing an outdoor fishing group might use the theme of a popular sport fish (see Figure 6.2). The theme might be carried through in the graphic art used on items in the group.

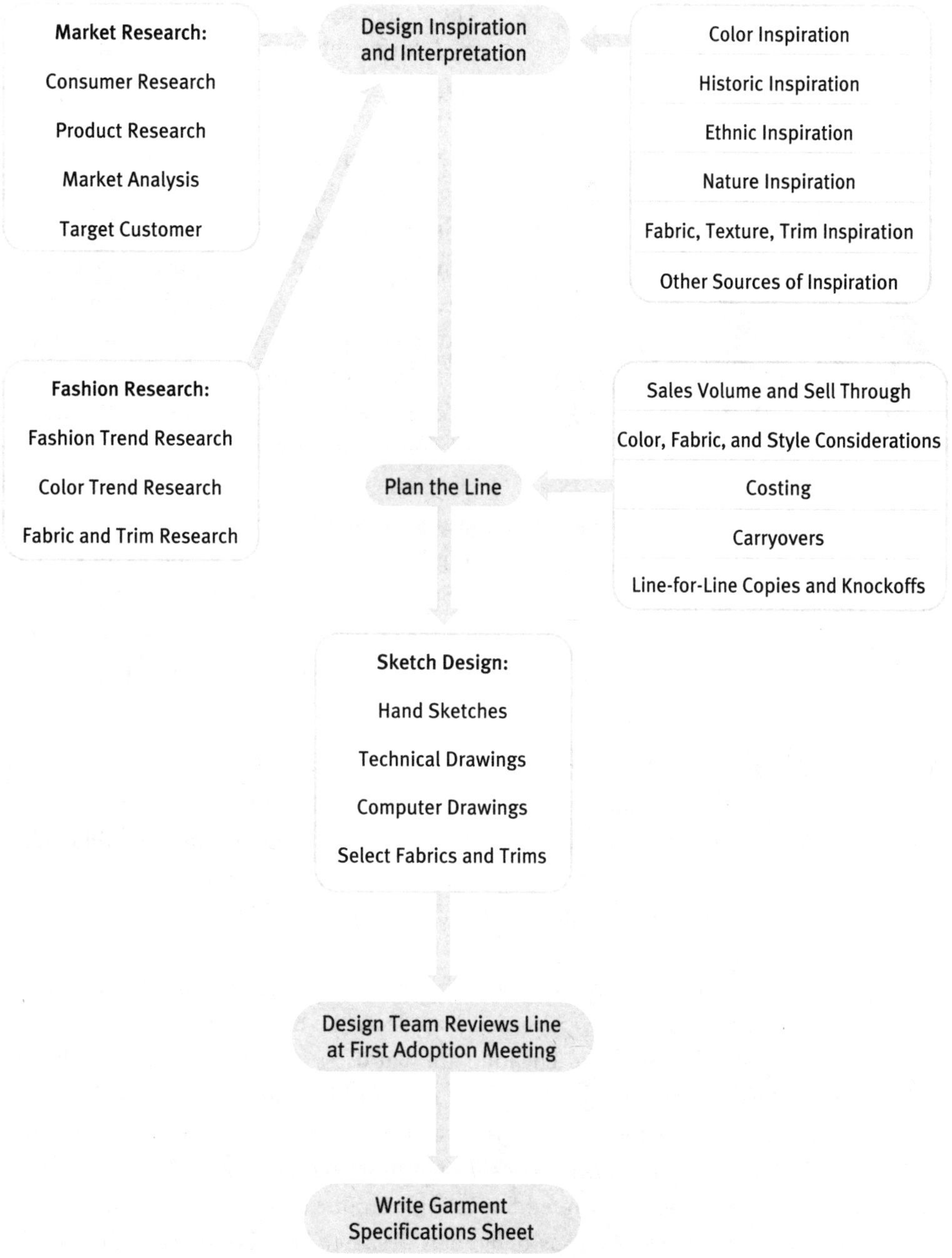

Market Research:

Consumer Research

Product Research

Market Analysis

Target Customer

Design Inspiration and Interpretation

Color Inspiration

Historic Inspiration

Ethnic Inspiration

Nature Inspiration

Fabric, Texture, Trim Inspiration

Other Sources of Inspiration

Fashion Research:

Fashion Trend Research

Color Trend Research

Fabric and Trim Research

Plan the Line

Sales Volume and Sell Through

Color, Fabric, and Style Considerations

Costing

Carryovers

Line-for-Line Copies and Knockoffs

Sketch Design:

Hand Sketches

Technical Drawings

Computer Drawings

Select Fabrics and Trims

Design Team Reviews Line at First Adoption Meeting

Write Garment Specifications Sheet

Figure 6.1   Step 2 Expanded: Design

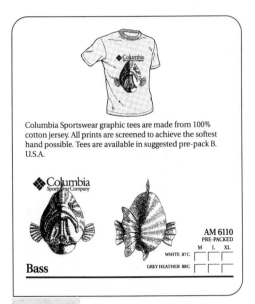

Columbia Sportswear graphic tees are made from 100% cotton jersey. All prints are screened to achieve the softest hand possible. Tees are available in suggested pre-pack B. U.S.A.

Columbia
Sportswear Company

Bass

AM 6110
PRE-PACKED

	M	L	XL
WHITE 87C			
GREY HEATHER 88C			

Figure 6.2 A group within a line might be designed around a theme, such as the colorations of a species of fish.

Color Inspiration

The design team studies color trend reports gathered during the research phase and discusses possible groups of colors, also referred to as color stories, for the new line while thinking about a color theme. The theme might be reflected in the colors chosen for some of the new styles. For example, the colorations seen on a golden trout might be an inspiration for a group of fishing apparel. Colors for fabrics used in the group might include various hues, tones, and values of the fish species' colorations. A graphic design of a golden trout leaping up to catch a fishing fly could be created for a T-shirt in the line. A small version of the leaping trout could be used as an embroidered or printed motif on other pieces in the group. As another example, an Americana theme might be chosen for a group of missy pieces in a Spring collection with a "country flavor" that features fabrics in ruby red, navy blue, and bisque colors in solids, small prints, and plaids.

Historic Inspiration

The high-fashion name designers typically develop a theme for a collection and invest heavily in marketing that theme to retailers and the public. Often the designer's theme is based on historical or ethnic inspiration. Fashion silhouettes or garment details popular during historical periods provide a source of design inspiration.

For example, the **Empire** silhouette was fashionable during the early 1800s. Named for France's Emperor Napoleon, the Empire style was worn by his wife, Empress Josephine. The long, tubular dress included a raised waistline located just under the bustline. Some fashion historians believe that Napoleon was inspired by the ancient Greek silhouette for this new fashion look. This style, known as *neoclassical*, became a fashion trend that spread throughout Western Europe and the United States. The Empire silhouette reappeared in the early 1900s in the fashions of French designer Paul Poiret, seen in his *Directoire* Revival dress (Mackrell, 1990). Once again, other designers copied this style as the fashion look spread throughout Europe and the United States. In the 1960s, the raised waistline of the Empire silhouette appeared again, this time in an above-the-knee minidress version, as well as a long version. In the early 1990s, and again in the first decade of the twenty-first century, the Empire style made fashion headlines. Figure 6.3 shows how the Empire style was adapted for different eras.

As another example of historical inspiration, both American designer Adrian and French designer Balenciaga were inspired by the bustle silhouette of the 1870s and 1880s for their designs created in the 1940s and 1950s. Designers continue to interpret the bustle silhouette, as seen in Richard Tyler's gown from 2000 and the 2007 Givenchy haute couture gown (see Figure 6.4).

Garment details of historic eras serve as another source of inspiration for designers. French designer Karl Lagerfeld used Renaissance fashion details as inspiration for a Chanel design in the 1988–1989 collection (Martin & Koda, 1989). Figure 6.5 shows how Lagerfeld incorporated period details in an imaginative way. The ruff collar popular on Renaissance clothing may inspire a group, a line, or a collection. A sleeve detail from the Renaissance period could be an inspiration for a young girl's party dress. Other examples of often-used sources of historically inspired fashions include the following:

- ancient Greek and Roman costume
- medieval costume
- eighteenth-century fashions
- the unique fashions of the French Revolution
- Victorian fashions

Retro Fashion

A return to the fashion look of more recent decades is called a **Retro** fashion or *Retro look*. During the 1990s, fashion looks reminiscent of the decades of the 1930s, 1940s, 1950s, 1960s, and 1970s were evident in all price zones. Retro fashions continue in the twenty-first century, with fashion looks reminiscent of the 1980s added to the mix of Retro looks from the 1960s and 1970s. Retro fashions tend not to be exact replicas of the previous fashion look; instead, they include a "new" fashion twist, such as the following examples:

A Retro look design may have style details of the earlier fashion but be made from a currently popular fabric rather than a fabric similar to that used in the earlier fashion.

The Retro look might include updated style details that are different from the original, while the fabric might resemble the fabric used for the earlier fashion.

Figure 6.3 The Empire style recurred periodically throughout fashion history. Shown here are examples from (top left) early nineteenth century (neoclassical), (top right) early twentieth century (Directoire Revival), (bottom left) the 1960s, and (bottom right) 2007.

Figure 6.4 Historical fashion silhouettes often serve as a source of inspiration: (left) the bustle silhouette of the 1880s, (center) by Richard Tyler in 2000, and (right) by Givenchy Haute Couture in 2007.

Figure 6.5 Karl Lagerfeld was inspired by a sixteenth-century fashion look (left) for an outfit in his 1988–1989 collection (right).

Ethnic Inspiration

Designers may be inspired by the clothing styles of other cultures. The global environment has increased interest in products from the far reaches of the world. Consumers who purchase and wear fashions inspired by other cultures may derive a sense of adventure and vicarious enjoyment of that culture. Designers seek inspiration from exotic cultures with clothing styles, fabrics, and accessories that are unique. Some designers travel to other locales to seek inspiration for a new line.

Asian clothing styles have been a source of inspiration historically, as well as for current fashions. *Chinoiserie* is a French term for a style that incorporates Chinese motifs. The fabrics of China were used to create Western high-fashion apparel during the 1850s. The Chinese influence on Western fashion grew during the last decades of the 1800s. In the United States, Chinese motifs became fashionable in home fashions, chinaware, house style details, and such clothing styles as the kimono sleeve, Mandarin collar, and frog closures. Chinese clothing and fabrics continue to inspire apparel designers today.

In 1995, the Costume Institute of the Metropolitan Museum of Art in New York presented *Orientalism: Visions of the East in Western Dress*. This exhibition and the catalog (Martin & Koda, 1994) featured apparel inspired by Asian cultures from various decades. Included in the exhibit were several examples of Asian-inspired garments from recent collections of American designers Ralph Lauren, Oscar de la Renta, and Todd Oldham. For French designer Karl Lagerfeld's Fall 2006 Chanel collection, he "was inspired by the tour de force exhibit at London's Royal Academy, 'China: The Three Emperors, 1662–1795.' This show revealed that the emperors Kangxi, Yongzheng, and Qianlong, conquering Manchu warriors from the north, were also highly refined artistic patrons and poets. Lagerfeld took the exquisite pale-jade objects that the emperors commissioned and used them as the starting point for his dazzling evening embroideries…" (Bowles, 2006, p. 142).

Dior's Spring 2007 collection by John Galliano included a number of Japanese geisha-inspired fashions. Perhaps the 2005 release of the film *Memoirs of a Geisha* inspired his designs (see Figure 6.6).

Yves Saint Laurent, a former French couture designer, is renowned for his use of various national and ethnic groups and cultures as inspirations for his collections. He created collections inspired by such regions as Russia, Africa, China, and Spain (Saint Laurent, Vreeland, et al., 1983). Carnivale in Brazil inspired the Spring 2003 collection for Narciso Rodriguez. "Inspired by a trip to Brazil during Carnivale, photos from which adorn a large wall in his studio, Rodriguez has built a spring palette that combines his usual restraint with

The release of the film *Memoirs of a Geisha* may have inspired some of John Galliano's designs for Dior's Spring 2007 couture show.

flashes of exuberant color: 'from natural burlap to fuchsia to gold to glitter,' he says" (MacSweeney, 2003, pp. 214, 216).

American designer Geoffrey Beene provides another example of ethnic inspiration. "The islands of Polynesia also beckoned Beene, its inspiration seen mainly in the subtle draping of the native *pareu*. By changing the fabric from a tropical print to checked gingham, he gave the sarong and its wrap-and-tie successors a new life in the new world" (Wolcott, Luther and Parmal, 2005, p. 178).

Design inspiration is anywhere and everywhere. Nature is another example of a source of inspiration, from flora to fauna, from sky to wind to water. For New York designer Zac Posen's Spring 2004 collection, "he was inspired by images of the Sargasso Sea (out in the blue Atlantic, a vast bed of floating seaweed where mysterious sea creatures swim), and long walks along the sultry beach at sunset. From Botticelli's famous Venus on the half-shell, and from an illustrated science book about seashells, Posen borrowed his soft hues, his muted palette of sea foam and lavender (with jolts of vibrant reds and yellows)" (Talley, 2003, pp. 94, 122).

New York designer Gene Meyer's visit to St. Petersburg, Russia, "sparked the theme for his Fall 1999 collection called 'In the Shadow of the Winter Palace.' '… St. Petersburg was just amazing. It was a combination of the way the city basked in sunlight, the bright pearly sky, and the snow everywhere that inspired me'" (Knight, 1999, p. 16). The inspiration might be the designer's impetus for developing the color story for a group or collection, or the designer might be inspired by the shape or texture of the inspirational source.

Fabric, Texture, and Trim Inspiration

Whereas some designers who create apparel for the higher price zones research a specific period or culture for inspiration, many designers often rely on studying new fabric and texture trends. Sources of information and inspiration used for fabric research were discussed in Chapters 3 and 5. An intriguing fabric texture or interesting print might serve as the design inspiration and become the foundation for a group. Several fabrics in prints, plaids, and solid colors, and with smooth as well as textured surfaces, might be combined to create an interesting group. During this design stage of creation, some designers work with specific fabric ideas gathered at textile shows or obtained directly from textile manufacturers as they begin to sketch garment design ideas (see Chapters 3 and 5). Less frequently, designers might develop a design sketch and then seek the perfect fabric for it. Another option for designers at some companies is to develop, or work with others to develop, a new textile fabrication or a textile print for the new line.

Special trims and **findings** (also known as notions or sundries), such as buttons or fasteners, can be important features of some garment designs. A unique trim can transform an ordinary or classic garment into a new look. Trims inspired by other cultures were a popular design addition to denim jeans, vests, and jackets for the junior market in the late 1990s. For children's apparel, special ribbons, trims, and appliqués frequently "make" the design. A unique clasp or closure on a swimsuit design can increase its appeal (see Figure 6.7), or a special button on a classic jacket may create a fresh look. Designers constantly seek interesting trims and findings as sources of inspiration.

Other Sources of Inspiration

The inspiration for a garment within a line or for an entire line can come from an infinite variety of sources. Sources of inspiration are often linked to the social "spirit of the times," also called the **zeitgeist**. Events and the general spirit of the popular culture might be reflected in new apparel lines. "Tommy Hilfiger, who travels extensively, said he's most inspired by the younger generations in cities across the globe. The most influential factor in every major city is the kids on the streets who set the trends" (Knight, 1999, p. 16).

Ask designers what inspired them to create a particular line, and you may be surprised to learn that Japanese kites were the inspiration for a line of swimsuits or that graffiti was the inspiration for a line of sportswear.

The Market Niche

Successful designers and merchandisers are able to interpret their design inspirations appropriately for their target customer. As noted in Chapters 4 and 5, many apparel companies specialize in a certain type of product, such as casual clothes, swimwear, or evening wear. The apparel company's **product type**, or product line,

Findings, such as the large rings on this swimsuit, provide innovative design details.

is the basis for the development of its line. For example, Lacoste is known for the company's polo-style knit shirts. If you are familiar with this company, a certain type of product comes to mind when the name of the company is mentioned (see Figure 6.8). Consistency in a company's product type helps the customer develop company brand recognition, build product loyalty, and encourage repeat customers. Thus, the design team, which consists of designers, product developers, and merchandisers, will develop the line for the new season with the product type as its foundation.

The importance of keeping the target customer profile in mind when creating a line was discussed in Chapter 5. A strong connection exists between the type of product included in the line and the company's target customer. The blend of product type with target customer is referred to as the **market niche**. Developing and maintaining a line based on the market niche is important to

LACOSTE

New
stretch
polo

a touch of air

www.lacoste.com

Figure 6.8 Consumers associate the name of a company, such as Lacoste, with a specific fashion image.

the success of the apparel line. The line for the new season will include some variation of styles to appeal to the variety of customers' needs and tastes within the market niche. For example, a missy swimwear manufacturer will include some very conservative swimsuit styles as well as some styles that have an updated look (see Figure 6.9). The missy swimwear line might be divided into several groups to appeal to a variety of missy customers.

Based on the changing needs and preferences of the target customer, a company's product line may change over time. If the product line does not change at all, customers might become bored with the same look and decide that they do not need to purchase another item so similar to items they already own. Examples of product line changes include the following:

A company might decide to change the direction of its product from a focus on career suits to a focus on coordinated separates after sensing that women are no longer interested in the look of a matched suit.

A sportswear company may decide to add a golf apparel group to its product line because of the growth in popularity of golf among its target customers.

Sometimes new designers and/or merchandisers are hired by a company to help revamp the product type. However, if a new look for a product is too radical, or if the product type is changed too quickly, it can cause problems for the retailer and the customer. Retaining the loyal customer is important, just as it is important to attract new customers for company growth. The customer who is familiar with and enjoys wearing the company's product may not understand the new look. Balancing the relationships among the current product look, changes that need to occur in the product to maintain interest and provide fashion change, and keeping the target customer happy is one of the responsibilities of the design team.

The Laura Soares missy swimwear line includes styles ranging from conservative (left) to updated (right) looks.

Planning the Line

Although the research and design inspiration stages of the design process—consisting of market research, as well as trend, color, and fabric-and-trim research—continues throughout the year, at a specified time in the year, the design team must begin to develop concrete ideas for the new season's line. Based on the number of lines a company produces each year, each apparel company maintains a master calendar with target due dates for completion of the stages of the creation and production of each line (see the Eight Steps in the Design Process flowchart at the beginning of Part 2 and Color Plate 3). The design team looks at the due date for the finalization of a line, and then works backward to determine when to move from the research stage to the design stage.

The Design Team's Role

The creation of each line relies on a team of people. Designers typically work with merchandisers and product developers on the creation of each new style in the line (see Figure 6.10, an example of an apparel company's design team organizational chart). As discussed in Chapter 5, many larger apparel companies employ a merchandiser whose responsibility it is to oversee and guide the designer or design team to determine what, when, at what price, and how much apparel to produce. A merchandiser often works with designers of several lines to oversee the coordination among the lines. In some companies, especially smaller ones, the designer also performs the job responsibilities of the merchandiser. Some companies employ both designers and product developers. A product developer takes the designer's idea and is responsible for developing the product. The product developer does the following:

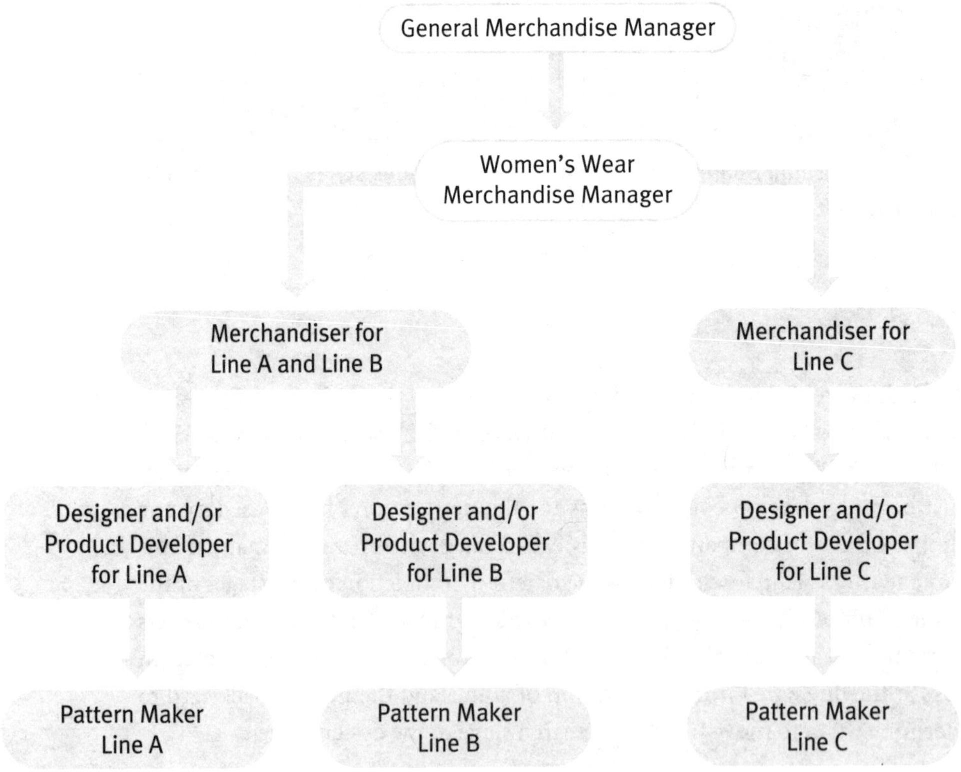

General Merchandise Manager

Women's Wear
Merchandise Manager

Merchandiser for
Line A and Line B

Merchandiser for
Line C

Designer and/or
Product Developer
for Line A

Designer and/or
Product Developer
for Line B

Designer and/or
Product Developer
for Line C

Pattern Maker
Line A

Pattern Maker
Line B

Pattern Maker
Line C

Apparel company organization chart

researches possible fabrics and trims

works with vendors in securing all components for the style

coordinates all aspects of style creation

At some smaller companies, the designer also handles the product development responsibilities.

The designer(s) and merchandiser(s) attend planning meetings during the research and design stages. At planning meetings, the sales figures (including sales volume and sell through) for the previous season are reviewed, the sales projections for the new season are considered, and the overall plan and schedule for the upcoming season's line are discussed. This might include the following:

decisions about the target number of styles to include in the line

the ratio of jackets compared to vests or the ratio of skirts compared to pants

the styles that will be repeated from the previous season (carryovers)

the types of silhouettes for various styles

the decision to try something new to be added to the line

the colors and fabrics that will be used

the costs of all components for the line

There is an expression in the fashion business—"you're only as good as your last line"—that means a company's success is measured by how well the previous season's line sold. Success of a line is measured by sales volume and also by sell through at the retail level. **Sales volume** is the actual level of sales in terms of either the total number of units of each style sold or the total number of dollars consumers spent on the style (dollar volume). Manufacturers tend to measure the success of a line by the total number of units sold, while retailers tend to measure the success of a line by the dollar volume.

The designer and merchandiser have to hit the targeted sales volume with a mix of repeated styles, revised styles, and new styles. Because of the number of lines typically produced per year, the sales volume figures are not usually available in time to rely on the number of units sold during the previous season in order to predict accurately the strategy for the line under development. Therefore, one's intuition also becomes a part of planning the line.

A line may sell well at market to the retailer (see Chapter 8), but a delay in delivery to the retailer could reduce the dollar volume at the retail store. This is one reason why another measurement tool, the line's sell through, is considered a good indicator of the line's success. **Sell through** denotes the percentage of items sold at retail compared to the number of items in the line that the retailer purchased from the manufacturer. For example, if 300 items in a line were delivered by the apparel manufacturer to the retail store and 250 of the items were sold, the sell through would be 83 percent. Keep in mind that mark downs—that is, items that were put on sale—enter into the overall success of the line as well. A strong sell through is the goal for both the manufacturer and the retailer. The sales figures from the current and previous selling seasons are important guidelines in planning how many and what types of apparel items to include in the new line.

Color, Fabric, and Style Considerations

During planning meetings, colors and fabrics for the new season's line are discussed. A color story will be developed based on the color research conducted before the planning meetings. Lines need a balance between some staple colors and some fashion colors (see Chapter 5). The line needs to have a cohesive look, so a great deal of time is spent deciding on the correct balance of colors. The group of colors selected for the line may need to include a color that the design team does not expect to sell well because they know that buyers expect to see a balance of colors in the color group (for example, a light color may be needed to balance the color story of a group of medium and dark colors).

Most garment styles will be produced in more than one color. A specific style may be available in three or four different solid colors, or in three or four color variations of the same print. The varieties of colors available for a style are called **colorways**. Producing the same style in several colorways is efficient in terms of development cost since fewer patterns, spec sheets, prototypes, and cost estimates need to be prepared than if each style were produced in only one colorway. This variety also offers more options to retailers that might want to buy part of a line but not duplicate the same colorways as competing local retailers will offer in their stores. It also allows a retailer to select the colorway choices that the retailer thinks are best suited for its customers.

As discussed in Chapter 5, designers typically attend textile trade shows and are aware of the new colors and fabrics available. Fabric vendors will provide samples of fabrics that the design team is considering for use in the upcoming line. Therefore, decisions regarding the colors and fabrics are frequently made before the garment styles are determined. The new line needs to provide a balance among the colors, styles, and prices offered.

The production cost of each style in a line is an important factor for designers to consider throughout the design stage. Thus, many companies include cost personnel as a part of the team during the planning meetings for a new line. Their role is to provide cost estimates on the new styles in the line as the styles develop.

There are many factors to keep in mind related to costing. Even prior to providing an initial cost estimate, each company has pricing strategies that guide costing. Examples of pricing strategies include the following:

It is important that two garments in the same line do not compete against each other for sales. Some apparel manufacturers follow a pricing strategy that specifies that the prices of two different shirt styles should not be the same—and style differences in the two styles need to support the price difference. A shirt made from a more expensive fabric might have fewer garment details, while a shirt made from a less expensive fabric could have more details to be sold at similar (but not identical) price.

Pricing strategies need to make sense to the customer. Comparing two shirts in a line with different prices, it needs to be apparent to the customer that the higher-priced shirt is made from the more expensive fabric or that the higher-priced shirt has more complex style details to justify the price.

With the pricing strategy called **price averaging**, a shirt manufactured from a more expensive fabric is priced to equalize a shirt manufactured from a less expensive fabric. The manufacturer averages the costs of the two shirts to keep the price of both styles similar. Thus, the shirt made from the more expensive fabric is priced slightly low, while the shirt made from the less expensive fabric is priced slightly high. If both styles sell equally, the company breaks even. If more shirts are sold that are made from the less expensive fabric, the company comes out ahead; if more shirts are sold that are made from the more expensive fabric, the company loses some profit.

Target costing is a pricing strategy that developed as a result of a significant change made by the apparel industry in the design-produce-sell cycle. The process had been to create a new style, and then calculate its cost based on materials and labor. Now, price tends to drive the style decisions, especially in the moderate and budget/mass price zones, as well as in private-label and store brand merchandise. The style and fabric components are manipulated by setting a cost first, and then determining how many yards of fabric and at what price, estimating the cost of other components such as zipper or buttons, and estimating how many minutes of labor are needed to produce the design, based on a per-hour labor price. For example, the design team might determine that they want to produce a jacket to sell at $75 retail ($37.50 wholesale). The team knows from previous seasons' costs that it takes 30 minutes to sew a basic jacket, and that one and one-half yards of fabric are required for a typical style. After estimating a cost per yard of a typical fabric and other components, the design team can calculate the cost. If the estimated total is less than the target cost, more design details (adding labor and materials cost) or more expensive fabrics or trims can be added to enhance the style and still meet the target cost.

The target costing process has been used for some time for certain types of goods, such as styles produced for a specific retail chain (sometimes called *special makeups*) and private-label goods. The design of private-label goods and store brand merchandise will be discussed in more detail later. One of the driving forces behind target costing is that in today's market (with the exception of the couture and some designer price zones), the upper limit of price is based on what the target customer is willing to pay.

Carryovers

A line of apparel typically does not consist of only new styles. In a new line, some styles will be carryovers, some styles will be modifications of good sellers, and some styles will be new designs. A carryover will repeat the same garment style as a successful garment style from a previous season, but often in a new fabric and color. Thus, carryovers provide a less expensive route to add a fresh look to a line. If the new fabric has identical textile characteristics as the previous fabric, the development cost will be minimal because the production patterns made for this style can be reused. However, if the new fabric is different—for example, it has a different shrinkage factor—a new pattern and prototype will need to be made.

Companies vary regarding the number of new items compared with the number of carryovers for each line. For an idea of the approximate ratio for a company that produces apparel in the moderate wholesale price zone, some companies target about one-third of the line to be carryovers, one-third as revisions of previous styles, and one-third as new designs. The percentage of new styles could be as low as 10 percent at some mass to moderate price zone companies, whereas a bridge or designer label might produce mostly new styles. Some styles in a new line might be revisions of a style from a previous season. One or more design details, such as a different collar or pocket, might be changed for the new season to revise a style. This process cuts down on the development time, saves some cost, and also provides some degree of confidence that the revised style will sell well in the marketplace.

Rather than starting with a designer's sketch for a new design, a "new" style might be added to a line in another way. Sometimes while shopping the market or looking through fashion magazines, a designer or merchandiser will find a garment that seems ideal for the company's upcoming line. Thus, the designer and merchandiser may decide to create a copy of an existing garment. Copying a garment may be done in several ways. For example, a unique design, such as a shirt with innovative design details, may seem perfect for the upcoming line. The designer might request that a **line-for-line copy** of the shirt be made by the pattern development department and produced in a similar fabric. The new shirt would be an exact replica of the original; thus the term *line-for-line copy* is used.

Another example is taking a garment that exists in a higher price zone and copying it to be sold at a lower price. This can be done by selecting a less expensive fabric, or by eliminating or modifying some of the design details. These methods are used to create **knockoffs**, designs that are similar to the original, but not exact replicas.

The evening gowns worn by celebrities to the Academy Awards ceremony in Los Angeles every spring are featured heavily in the press. Within days, knockoffs of some of the favorite gowns are available in the moderate price zone. Designer Eletra Casadei had not planned to produce knockoffs from the 2003 gowns. However, when she saw what Renée [Zellweger] and the stars were wearing, she called her design team and said, "'Turn on your TV sets, the dresses are looking good.' In two years, Casadei has turned her awards re-creations into a $1 million business … Casadei chose six looks but tinkered with the styles to make them more salable" (Sarkisian-Miller, 2003, p. 11).

Another well-known manufacturer of Academy Awards gown knockoffs is Allen Schwartz, president of A.B.S. Schwartz. He "… shipped out samples to his showroom Tuesday [following Sunday evening's event] with plans to hit retail stores in four to eight weeks. The dresses will retail from $250 to $300" (Sarkisian-Miller, 2003, p. 11).

Is it legal to copy an existing garment design? The United States has laws to protect against copyright and trademark infringement (see Chapter 2). A specific "invention" in a garment (for example, a unique molding process to create a seamless panty) can be patented in the United States. However, in some countries (including the United States), the actual garment design is considered to be in the public domain. Therefore, it is quite common to see line-for-line copies and knockoffs in the U.S. apparel business. An article in *Women's Wear Daily* stated that creating knockoffs "is a practice so commonplace, and one not clearly prohibited by law, that most designers who have been copied have felt helpless to stop it" (Wilson, 1999, p. 8). Design laws are more strict in some European countries, as evidenced by the 1994 case, in which French designer Yves Saint Laurent took Ralph Lauren to court in France in a dispute over the design copy of a tuxedo dress (see Figure 6.11) ("Tuxedo Junction," 1994).

Several court cases in the United States regarding trade dress law, a part of trademark law (see Chapter 2), have brought the issue of copying into the headlines. As reported by *Women's Wear Daily*, "there have been several recent legal challenges, and now that the Supreme Court has taken up a case with the potential to define what constitutes a violation of existing trade dress law, the practice of knockoffs is under the spotlight, raising questions among manufacturers of what the ramifications of such a decision could be" (Wilson, 1999, p. 8).

In summary, many factors need to be considered during the planning of a line. Among them is the overall number of styles to be included in the line. Some of these styles will be carryover styles from the previous line, some styles

Figure 6.11 The tuxedo dress as presented by Yves Saint Laurent (left), and the tuxedo dress as presented by Ralph Lauren (right)

will be revisions of previous styles, and some styles will be new designs. Decisions are also made about the following:

the number of top styles in relation to the number of bottom styles

styling variety (such as single-breasted and double-breasted jackets)

color and fabric offerings for each style

cost to produce each style

overall pricing balance of the line

Selection of Fabrics and Trims

Sourcing for the right fabrics and trims must often be accomplished at the planning stage of the design process. The fabrics and trims are usually selected before a design is approved for inclusion in a line. Each design sketch or tech drawing includes a small sample of the intended fabric, called a **swatch**, which is attached to the sketch or drawing. It is essential that the fabric be chosen before a design is reviewed by the merchandiser, designer, and cost personnel for possible inclusion in the final line. The design sketch or tech drawing will also include any trim swatches that will be used and may indicate specific findings as well. Sometimes the actual fabric intended for the design is not yet available from the textile manufacturer. In these cases, a facsimile fabric will be used temporarily for the design development stage.

Textile mills produce a large quantity of printed textiles each season. Many apparel companies purchase printed fabrics directly from textile mills for their lines. However, sometimes an apparel company prefers to work with a textile converter (see Chapter 3) to develop a printed textile. A new textile design can be created from the following:

an existing print that is revised into a new colorway

a new textile print developed by the designers, assistant designers, or product developers (for example, if they cannot find the right print on the market)

a textile design that is purchased from a company or a freelance textile designer who creates and sells original artwork for the printed textile industry

When an apparel company purchases a piece of textile design artwork, it owns the rights to copy or change the print as it wishes. Thus, the apparel company's staff can reconfigure a textile design's scale, motif, colors, or repeat to suit their needs.

The Design Sketch

At some point in the design stage (usually determined by the master calendar due date), the designer will begin to transform interpretations of design inspirations into garment idea sketches. A designer might develop some garment sketches early in this stage, and then face a pressing deadline for sketching the remaining pieces. Is it difficult to create 20 new sweater or swimsuit designs each season? By constantly seeking inspiration from a variety of sources, most designers have plenty of new ideas.

Hand Sketches

Some designers rely on hand sketches of their garment ideas. The designer's sketches do not look like the finished artwork of a fashion illustration. In fact, some designers state that they are not good at drawing. Partially because of time constraints, some designers use a body silhouette called a **croquis**, or **lay figure**, as a base from which to develop their garment design sketches. A swimwear designer may have numerous copies of a croquis available, onto which the swimsuit design idea will be drawn in pencil or marker. Some designers place lightweight paper over the croquis and create their garment sketches on an overlay sheet. Other designers begin with a sheet of drawing paper and sketch the garment idea portrayed on a body silhouette (see Figure 6.12). Some designers add color to their sketches by using colored pencils or markers. Often a back view sketch is shown as well as the front view.

Figure 6.12   Some designers sketch their garment design ideas on a body silhouette.

Technical Drawing

Some garment design sketches do not include the body silhouette. If only the garment design is drawn, without an indication of the body, the sketch is sometimes called a *technical drawing*, or **tech drawing**. The garment is drawn as it would appear lying flat, as on a table, so sometimes the term **flat**, or **flat sketch**, is used to indicate this type of drawing. Tech drawings are used by some companies in place of design sketches, especially in the active-sportswear industry. Activewear garments might have many details. Tech drawings might include a close-up sketch of a detail, such as a pocket, cuff, or collar, as well as the back view. Tech drawings are especially useful and often necessary for pattern making and production needs. Sometimes specific dimensions, such as the size and/or placement of a patch pocket, are indicated on the tech drawing.

Computer-Aided Design and Graphics Software

Computer-aided design (**CAD**) software was in use by the 1970s. CAD software developed specifically for the apparel industry was introduced in the early 1980s. Since then, software upgrades have dramatically improved apparel CAD software. Current CAD software used for pattern making (and also for pre-production and production) is much easier to learn than the software used in the 1980s. Graphics software is especially useful for drawing and textile design. Software upgrades have also improved the "user friendliness" of these programs. In the past, the cost of CAD and graphics systems was a hurdle for some companies. The price for computer systems has dropped substantially, making CAD and graphics systems affordable to even small apparel companies.

APPAREL DESIGN

Some designers prefer to draw flats or tech drawings by hand. However, many, if not most, apparel companies expect their designers to create tech drawings using CAD or graphics software programs (see Figure 6.13). Trade shows provide an opportunity to compare CAD and graphics software and to learn about upgrades and new technology. They are an excellent resource for assisting in the selection of CAD and graphics software and hardware for the apparel industry. CAD systems used for pattern making, pattern grading (sizing), and marker making (developing the master cutting plan) will be discussed in other chapters.

Two major advantages of using a CAD or graphics system to create design sketches are the time-saving potential and the capability to try out numerous design ideas quickly. The designer may select a garment sketch from the previous season's line as a starting point and simply modify design details for the new design for the upcoming line. This procedure greatly speeds up this phase of the design process.

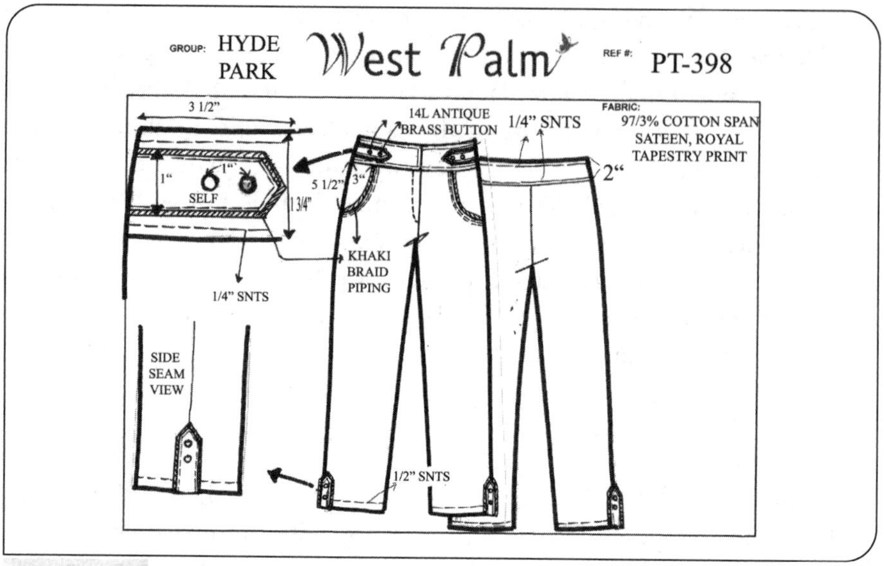

Tech drawings can be used to show design details.

Some designers may think it stifles their creativity to sketch on a computer. They prefer to "think" with pencil in hand. To assist the artist, there are graphics computer programs that allow the designer to use a pencil-like stylus to simulate the act of drawing. After becoming familiar with the process of sketching by CAD or graphics software, most designers find that the speed with which a design can be modified is such an advantage that they have no desire to revert to drawing by hand. However, for the high-end designer price zones, hand sketching design ideas may still be the preferred process. This is due, in part, to the differences in the creation process involved, which will be discussed later.

Designs can be created using the following approaches:

- The computer can store a croquis (see Figure 6.14), or a series of croquis in various poses. The designer selects a desired pose, which then appears on the computer screen. The desired garment sketch can be drawn onto the croquis.

- Some software programs provide a style library of basic garment silhouettes, such as shirts and pants, as well as garment components, such as collar and pocket styles. The designer creates the new style by bringing the desired components together (see Figure 6.15).

- New garment designs are drawn by using true proportions from a croquis stored in the system.

- New garment designs are drawn by specifying exact measurements.

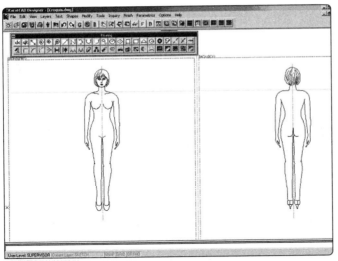

A body image called a croquis can be used as the lay figure for drawing the new garment style.

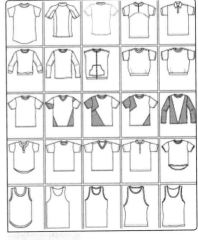

A library of garment components stored in the computer can be selected and imported into a tech drawing to develop a new style.

To visualize what the garment style might look like in a specific color or print, the computer-generated garment drawing can be colored in several possible ways. For example, computer graphics programs can be used to simulate the color of a specific fabric swatch by blending colors on the computer monitor to create an accurate color match. The drawing of the new garment style can then be printed to compare the printed color on paper to the actual color of the fabric swatch. The computer industry is hard at work perfecting the ink technology to match the color on paper to the color as seen on the computer screen. One system includes a calibration tool that "enables designers to create color standards for different fabrics and ink sets to help ensure that the desired color is printed" ("ITMA unveils advances," 1999, p. 10).

Some of the graphics software programs are integrated with the same color system used by textile producers so an exact match can be produced very quickly by keying in the color number. The Pantone color system is supported by a number of graphics software programs and is used by textile producers to match the printed visual version of the garment with the actual fabrics. These integrated systems can be used to produce accurate color matching of the line sheet used later to sell the line at market.

A scanner can be used to input an existing fabric print into the computer system. A facsimile of the fabric will appear on the computer screen. The scale of

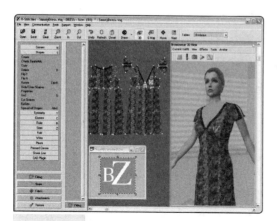

Virtual draping software creates a visual image of the scanned fabric shown on the 3D image of the garment style.

the print or plaid fabric motif can be adjusted to approximate the correct size of the motif for the scale of the drawing. This is much faster than hand drawing and coloring fabric motifs. Some of the more complex software programs can simulate the drape of the fabric on the designer's computer drawing (see Figure 6.16). The computer technology of simulating the three-dimensional drape of fabric is called **virtual draping**.

Using CAD or graphics software at the design stage helps to integrate later steps in the design process. The designer's CAD drawing will be the basis for garment technical drawings used in design development and production. The integration of computers in the entire design process will be discussed later in this chapter and at each step in the design process.

It has become increasingly important for designers to be proficient with CAD and graphics software systems, and design students will increase their opportunities for future employment by developing the ability to use a computer system to sketch their design ideas. If the advantages of using a CAD system are many, why are not all apparel companies currently using CAD? Of course, expense is a factor, but perhaps even more daunting is the time required to train designers, developers, pattern makers, and other personnel and to implement the use of a CAD system. As computer software programs become more user friendly, the length of training and cost to the companies may be greatly reduced.

TEXTILE DESIGN

Computer-aided design and graphics software programs are also important tools for textile design. Since textile design is such an integral part of the garment design, it is important for apparel designers and merchandisers to know as much as possible about the textile design process. More frequently today than in the past, apparel designers find textile design and/or graphic design assignments a part of their responsibilities. For example, an apparel designer may need to design a graphics logo for a T-shirt to coordinate with a print fabric used in a line, or perhaps the apparel designer will need to redesign or recolor an existing textile print.

At some companies, textile designers work side by side with the apparel design team. For example, at Pendleton Woolen Mills in Portland, Oregon, the design of the woven plaid fabric is integrated with the garment design. The textile designers calculate the spacing of the plaid repeat to coincide with the pleat widths of the skirt pattern, or vice versa, depending on the requirements for the specific style. This is not an easy task, as the designer must keep in mind the size range in which the style will be produced.

The Anne Klein textiles department "defines the color trends, the materials, and the prints for each of the three annual collections …. One of the major strengths of our company is that we have our own textiles department. We are independent and the fabrics we design are a reflection of our image" ("Anne Klein," 1999, p. 5). The Anne Klein textiles department uses CAD software to design its prints. The head of the textiles office stated, "we can combine several ideas or go back to previous collections. We have also considerably improved our organization as we keep all our styles in our computer database" ("Anne Klein," 1999, p. 5).

Computer software systems provide numerous advantages for textile design. Some of the computer textile design systems can print the newly created print design directly onto fabric. Several repeats of the print design can be joined together to simulate a large piece of the printed textile. Viewing a large section of the print design helps the textile designer visualize the scale, repeat, and color combination (see Figure 6.17). Changes can be made immediately. This is much

Figure 6.17 Textile designers experiment with various color combinations while designing prints.

faster and less expensive than sending a printed paper sample to a textile mill to make a length of sample yardage of the print, called a **strike off** (see Chapter 9).

It took years to develop processes to print directly onto fabric without backing the fabric with paper to stabilize it. Now, fabric can be printed digitally in sufficient yardage to create entire garments. This technology opens the field to cost savings, time savings, and totally new customization possibilities. With digital printing, the textile design moves from the designer's computer screen to fabric without the textile producer having to make a strike off and perfect the sample fabric ("ITMA unveils advances," 1999). Not only is there a cost savings, but there is a time savings as well. Sometimes it takes weeks for a textile print developed by traditional processes to reach final approval. The ability to perfect the print design quickly and inexpensively using digital printing adds flexibility to the design process. According to the J. Crew director of CAD, "more work can be shown, in a shorter time, than was possible before. This helps everyone in getting a real sense of what something's going to really look like before we ever get involved with the mill" (Weldon, 1999, p. 40). Additional benefits of digital printing are the capability to produce very small runs for limited production or to create custom prints.

Some companies use computer software programs to develop textile prints that can be electronically communicated to textile mills. The textile print computer file can be delivered electronically to the textile mill. According to Craig Crawford, director of design technology at Liz Claiborne:

> Liz Claiborne also has found that CAD shortens the process of translating a design into a printed piece of fabric. Now that we're giving them a digital file, the mill doesn't have to scan it, they don't have to produce the colors, and they don't have to clean it up. All they have to do is adjust it for production. It used to [take] four to eight weeks for a strike off to come back. Now that we can make all our adjustments with them before we ever let the ink hit the fabric, it's more like two weeks to a month. (Swedberg, 2004, p. 40)

Networking of computer systems allows "direct communication with textile mills— or direct printing on greige goods. Eliminating the labor spent recreating these designs in strike offs and samples shortens production cycles and significantly reduces miscommunication and simple human errors" (Weldon, 1999, p. 40).

Where will digital printing technology lead the industry next? A designer specializing in digital printing at [TC]^2 "is breaking industry paradigms by creating and applying custom prints to individual pattern pieces and producing them on a digital printer" (Weldon, 1999, p. 40). This technology merges the textile print and the fit-and-style options of the pattern to exact customization for the customer. Customization will be discussed in more detail in Chapter 11.

Some designers create a design idea three-dimensionally using actual fabric as a starting point, instead of beginning with a sketch of a garment (see Figure 6.18). For this design process, a mannequin or dress form in the sample size is used. Fabrics vary in their **hand** (tactile qualities) and ability to drape around the body. Working with the actual fabric can be a source of design inspiration, especially for fabrics with special draping qualities, such as charmeuse or permanently pleated fabric. Fabrics that are plaid or striped or that have a large print motif are suited to creating the initial design by the **draping** process. Couture designers and some ready-to-wear designers creating lines in the designer price zone frequently use draping to create the initial design.

Some ready-to-wear designers and some couture designers develop the design from the designer's sketch by draping in **muslin**. Muslin is an inexpensive trial fabric, similar to cotton broadcloth. It helps the designer determine silhouette, proportion, and design details, but it does not have the drape of many fashion fabrics. For many fabric types and garment styles, muslin serves the purpose adequately. The muslin trial garment is sometimes referred to as the **toile**, the French word for *cloth*.

French designer Madeleine Vionnet created innovative bias cut garments during the 1920s and 1930s. She always draped, rather than sketched, her design ideas. She worked out the design in fabric on a small-size wooden mannequin (see Figure 6.19). Her design team then draped a full-size replica in muslin. A prototype in fashion fabric was then cut using the pattern pieces developed from the muslin toile. Donna Karan is an example of a contemporary designer who creates designs by draping.

Figure 6.18 Some designers, such as the late Jacques Fath, create three-dimensionally by draping designs in fashion fabric on a live model.

Figure 6.19 French designer Madeleine Vionnet developed her design ideas by draping fabric on a small-scale wooden mannequin, and later perfecting the designs on a full-size mannequin.

There are advantages to developing the design idea by draping, especially if fashion fabric is used. Seeing the design develop, sensing the drape of the fabric, molding the fabric into a three-dimensional shape, and evolving the design during the process bring a great deal of creativity to the design process. However, draping a design may take more time than preparing a design sketch or tech drawing, and draping requires more fabric than if one first makes a pattern and then cuts fabric from the pattern. Therefore, many designers rely on drawings for the design phase of the process.

Product Management Systems

There are increasing demands on apparel, accessories, and home fashions manufacturers to produce new styles quickly. The traditional methods of designing, marketing to retail buyers, producing, and distributing to retailers are no longer effective for many companies. Many forces have affected the need to accelerate the pace of these industries. Several of the most critical factors include the following:

- the length of time a style is in process

- the international scope of sourcing and production

- the need for all partners in the pipeline to communicate accurately and quickly

Following is a typical scenario in today's fashion industry: "Imagine that you are a New York-based apparel designer, carefully formulating the next season's color palette, while meticulously developing the Summer line to which it will apply. Here's the catch. Your design partner is based in Los Angeles, your patternmaker and sample maker are 8,000 miles away in India, and your dyeing mill is in China" (Speer, 2005, p. 40). How do companies handle all the necessary data, in the shortest time possible, across thousands of miles?

Computer technology has provided the means to help meet these requirements. Beginning in the early 1990s, product data management, also known as product information management or product development management systems, were developed to provide a means to track via computer the style's technical information package needed by the preproduction and production facilities. Generally, this management approach began once the new style had been adopted. Often the design team worked through the initial stages of creating a new style using their computer systems or using hand-drawn garment sketches (or tech drawings), along with handwritten or computer-generated style information sheets (spec sheets). Once the style moved to the preproduction department, style information might then be input into that department's computer system. Thus, time delays, errors, and miscommunication of style information between the various departments were constant concerns.

By the late 1990s, it became increasingly important to begin electronic management of product information related to the style at its inception. This led to expanding the style-information tracking process to include the style information from its design inception through to its delivery at the retail store. The two technologies that provide electronic management of files are as follows:

1. **product data management (PDM),** also referred to as **product development management (PDM)**

2. **product lifecycle management (PLM)**

These technologies differ somewhat. PDM solutions "take a product-centric focus to information management. Unlike image- or document-focused management systems, PDM centers on the product, or style at hand, grouping together everything related to that product, including specifications, sketches, and other information, which can then be reviewed and updated by other parties without the need for cumbersome faxes and e-mails that eat up time and create multiple versions of the 'same' style" (Speer, 2005, p. 40). Gerber Technology introduced its WebPDM system in 2005, connecting design, engineering, costing, and manufacturing information through a centralized database of product-related information. Clients use a Web browser and a password-protected login to access the data.

PDM is a part of PLM's broad technology for style management. *Apparel* magazine writer Jordan Speer explained: "PDM is just one component of the much larger task of managing that product's lifecycle. PLM solutions take that set of product data and manage it all the way through the supply chain. PLM's footprint extends to direct materials sourcing, collaborative product design and customer needs management" (Speer, 2005, p. 40).

Sometimes referred to as **PDM/PLM** when combining product data (development) management and product lifecycle management, this approach requires all computer systems in the pipeline to be compatible in order to share product data. The designer's sketch is created in a software program that interfaces with the garment spec sheet software, and on down the pipeline. All partners have online access to the style information. Lectra, a leading software and hardware provider for the industry, developed software that integrates the entire product development process. It works with a simple-to-use graphical interface that allows all users to access the full range of data and to visualize each step in the development of a collection: design, technical specifications, bills of materials, size charts and measurements, sewing instructions, costing, planning control, pattern making, marker making, and packaging ("Gallery revolutionizes business for Russell," 2001, p. 7).

Since all partners have instantaneous access to any change made for a style, the person responsible for inputting the data accurately carries a heavy responsibility. One of the product developers at Nike commented on how nervous she was the first time she logged into the PDM system. She knew that if she input data incorrectly, the error would be transmitted to everyone in the system. In spite of this concern, the advantages of using a PDM/PLM system are tremendous for total work flow management. In summary, product lifecycle management "ties together the whole process from concept development to production" (Kusterbeck, 2005, p. 44).

As mentioned earlier in this chapter, the Liz Claiborne company often designs its own textiles using a CAD system. The company has expanded its computer network to include its offshore partners. According to Craig Crawford, director of design technology at Liz Claiborne, "networking products allow Liz Claiborne to send textile designs to its offshore offices and mills via an internal network. All the company's CAD designers have access to the network, and they can drag-and-drop their production-ready artwork into a file folder for pickup in Asia" (Swedberg, 2004, p. 42).

Design Team Reviews Line

Typically, many more design ideas are sketched than will appear in the final line. At a line review meeting (also called a **first adoption meeting**), the designer presents the design sketches to the review team (for example, the merchandiser, fit or production engineer, and head of sample sewing) according to the time-line on the master calendar (see Figure 6.20). Some designers present the new line as a formal presentation with beautifully rendered drawings, fabric swatches, and perhaps an indication of the design theme or inspiration shown on presentation boards or storyboards (see Color Plate 1). The designer might make an oral presentation to the design team, upper management, or private-label managers to "sell" the line. This first adoption meeting is the first of several review processes that the line must undergo. There will be several subsequent line reviews before the final adoption. The review team discusses and evaluates each of the designs. The team will have determined during previous planning meetings how many of each type of apparel item it will be possible to include in the line. Out of 60 design ideas presented for review, perhaps only 30 or 40 sketches will be selected to continue into the design development stage. Some of these designs will be dropped at later stages as well. At other companies, the merchandisers may request that all or most of the designs be developed as prototypes to better visualize the product.

Guided by the total number of pieces previously determined for the line, other factors enter into the decision to accept or drop designs from the line. The balance

Figure 6.20 At review meetings, the designer, merchandiser, and production engineer discuss the feasibility of each style in the line.

of the line is an important factor in deciding which designs should be included. For a missy career line, jacket style variations are considered so that there will be a range of styles to suit a variety of customers. For example, it is important to include a balance of the number of short versus long, boxy versus fitted, single- versus double-breasted jackets, and jackets with collars versus collarless jackets. The ratio of solid to plaid or print fabrics is another consideration. Skirt style variations must be balanced—short versus long, fitted versus flared, full versus pleated. The skirts need to coordinate with as many of the jacket styles as possible. The mix of classic and fashion-forward styles needs to be considered.

Anticipated cost is an important factor in the review process. The antici- pated prices need to be similar to the previous season's prices, unless a new market niche is sought. Some cost considerations were discussed in the section on planning the line earlier in this chapter. It is important that style features match price. For example, a customer expects to pay less for a short, single- breasted style than for a longer, double-breasted jacket. The team discusses cost estimates and possible style, design details, findings, and fabric changes that might reduce cost.

Other factors to consider include ease of adjusting the style to fit varied body types. For example, elastic added at the sides of the skirt waistband can enhance the adaptability of a garment to fit more figure shapes, especially in the missy and larger-size markets. However, for the junior market, elastic in the waist- band may be considered a negative feature and could adversely affect sales. Ease in alterations is another consideration. A wrap skirt with a curved, faced hem- line is not easily shortened and cannot be lengthened.

There is a constant struggle among the following personnel:

- production personnel who want new styles to be similar to previous styles and as simple to construct as possible

- merchandisers who want the line to "sell itself" in the marketplace with great prices and high quality

- designers who want highly creative, complex styles

This may explain why some companies call the conference room where design reviews are conducted the *war room*. It is important for the designer to be pro- lific with design ideas and to develop an impersonal attitude about the designs that need to be modified or are dropped from the line.

In summary, the merits of each style as it fits in the big picture of the overall line will be discussed at the design review meeting. Sometimes design details will need to be modified to lower the expected cost or to coordinate better with other styles. The team is guided in their review process by the following aims:

to create a cohesive theme

to include an appropriate number of items and a balance of styles

to fit the overall merchandising orientation of the company for the season (e.g., fit the price and lifestyle of the target customer)

Using the Garment Specification Sheet

The designer often has some specific design details in mind that need to be conveyed to the pattern maker and sample sewer in order to create the sample or prototype garment at the next stage of the design process. These details, as well as other vital information, are conveyed on a **garment specification sheet**, also called a *garment spec sheet*, or shortened still more to *spec sheet*. Examples of types of design details that need to be specified include the following:

the placement and spacing of buttons

any edge stitching or top stitching

the spacing between pleats or tucks

findings, such as the number, size, and style of buttons; zipper length, color, and style; snaps and buckles

pocketing, lining fabric, and interfacings

Any information not specified will be decided by the pattern maker. Thus, it is the designer's responsibility to specify all garment aspects that are important to the look of the design. A drawing of the garment design is included on the spec sheet along with fabric swatches. The spec sheet may also include the measurement specifications and construction specifications (see Chapter 9).

A **style number** is assigned to each new style in the line. This number (which might include a letter code as well) is coded to indicate the season and year in which the line will be presented to buyers, plus other information desired by the apparel company. The style number may include a category indicator, such as swimwear or sportswear, and the size category of junior, missy, petite, or tall. The style number is used as the style's reference throughout development, marketing, and production.

Summary

In creating an apparel line, the design process follows the research process. The design team works with planning and production personnel to plan the calendar of due dates in order to provide garments to the retailer at the season's outset. The line is planned to provide the right product type for the target customer at the right time and at the right price. The sales volume and sell through of a line at the retail level are important indicators used to plan the upcoming line. Striking the right balance between carryover styles, revisions of popular styles from the previous season, and new styles is critical to the success of the line.

The merchandiser may work with the designer to develop a theme for a new line. A theme for a line can help sell the products. An example of a color theme for a sport fishing group is one based on the colors of a sport fish. This theme can be enhanced by the use of the fish image as a graphic design on a T-shirt in the collection. Historical and ethnic clothing are sources of design inspiration, as are new fabrics, textures, trims, and fasteners.

Some designers hand sketch their garment design ideas, some use a computer-aided design or graphics program, some prepare technical drawings, and some create the design idea three-dimensionally in fabric by draping. The designer is responsible for creating far more design ideas than will be selected for the line. The designer is also responsible for selecting fabrics, trims, and linings for each design and specifying details, such as buttons and top stitching. The garment specification sheet includes all the pertinent information required to complete a pattern and prototype of the design.

Increasing demands for the fast development, production, and delivery of goods has put pressure on the textile and apparel industries. These demands are coupled with the physical distance between various partners in the global marketplace that rely on one another for sourcing. Electronic technologies have provided the means for instant communication and accurate tracking of each style. Product data management and product lifecycle management systems provide electronic connectivity for instantaneous communication among all parties in the creation, design development, style selection, pre-production, marketing, production, and distribution of goods.

If you are considering a career as a designer or merchandiser for an apparel company, you need to have a creative flair, good technical knowledge, and confidence.

Assistant Designer
Privately Owned Sportswear Company

Position Description
Assist the design director and merchandise manager.

Typical Tasks and Responsibilities
- Create a catalog of the season's prototype garments, including computer illustrations and colorways of all garments.
- Create and weave yarn dyes on the computer and scan in prints.
- Prepare all of the information necessary for the textile mills to do strike offs and handlooms.
- Update and change data when changes in colors are made.
- Design garments from initial sketches through fit sessions.
- Prepare special computer projects for sales reps—drawing and coloring garments and creating mini catalogs.
- Work with all fit models.
- Work with overseas correspondence in the absence of the designer.

Designer
Privately Held Moderate Missy Line

Position Description
Work with merchandisers and marketers to design lines. Work with the graphic designer and textile designer in creating the line.

Typical Tasks and Responsibilities
- Provide ideas, direction, images, and concept(s) for the season's line.
- Research fabric vendor resources.
- Select fabrics for the garments in the line.
- Work with pattern makers in creating patterns for the garments in the line.
- Provide follow-through to production of all garments in the line.
- Give presentations of the line to various groups for feedback.

Key Terms

colorway	PDM/PLM
computer-aided design (CAD)	product data management (PDM)
croquis	product development management
draping	(PDM)
Empire	product lifecycle management (PLM)
findings	product type
first adoption meeting	Retro
flat	sales volume
flat sketch	sell through
garment specification sheet	strike off
hand	style number
knockoff	swatch
lay figure	target costing
line-for-line copy	tech drawing
market niche	toile
muslin	virtual draping
price averaging	zeitgeist

Discussion Questions

1. What are some possible themes for a junior sportswear line? Why did you select these themes?

2. What are some current societal trends (zeitgeist) that might provide an inspiration for a group or line of apparel?

3. What might be an example of an *unconventional* source of design inspiration? Why might it be considered unconventional?

4. What are some of the job responsibilities of a merchandiser and a designer in the design stage of the design process? What are some activities that might be helpful for you to complete as students to help prepare you for these job responsibilities? Examples include a target customer collage for a specific company, a trend board for a jacket line for a year in advance, or an inspiration board for a children's wear beach group.

Anne Klein. (1999, Vol. 1). *Lectra Mag*, p. 5.

Bowles, Hammish. (2006, May). Show business. *Vogue*, pp. 142, 144, 146.

Gallery revolutionizes business for Russell. (2001, number 2). *Lectra Mag*, pp. 6–7.

Knight, Molly. (1999, September 24). Globetrotting for inspiration. *DNR*, pp. 14–16.

Kusterbeck, Staci. (2005, December). Jones Apparel Group. *Apparel*, p. 44.

ITMA unveils advances in digital printing. (1999, September). *Bobbin*, pp. 8–11.

Mackrell, Alice. (1990). *Paul Poiret*. New York: Holmes & Meier.

MacSweeney, Eve. (2003, November). Me and my soul mate. *Vogue*, pp. 214, 216.

Martin, Richard, and Koda, Harold. (1989). *The Historical Mode*. New York: Rizzoli International Publications.

Martin, Richard, and Koda, Harold. (1994). *Orientalism: Visions of the East in Western Dress*. New York: Metropolitan Museum of Art. Distributed by Harry N. Abrams, Inc.

Saint Laurent, Yves, Vreeland, Diana, et al. (1983). *Yves Saint Laurent*. New York: Metropolitan Museum of Art.

Sarkisian-Miller, Nola. (2003, March 27). Oscar's Quick-turn artists. *Women's Wear Daily*, p. 11.

Speer, Jordan K. (2005, September). Design development and pre-production. *Apparel*, p. 40.

Swedberg, Jamie. (2004, May). Designers embrace CAD differently. *Apparel*, pp. 38–42.

Talley, André Leon. (2003, November). Remembrance of things past. *Vogue*, pp. 94, 98, 122.

Tuxedo Junction: YSL, Ralph square off. (1994, April 28). *Women's Wear Daily*, pp. 1, 15.

Weldon, Kristi. Identifying expert CAD users. (1999, October). *Apparel Industry Magazine*, pp. 38–44.

Wilson, Eric. (1999, November 2). The culture of copycats. *Women's Wear Daily*, pp. 8–9.

Wolcott, James, Luther, Marylou, and Parmal, Pamela. (2005). *Beene by Beene/Geoffrey Beene*. New York: The Vendome Press.

Design Development and Style Selection

In this chapter, you will learn the following:

- the steps required to develop a sketch into a prototype garment and to prepare the garment for design team review

- the advantages and disadvantages of using a computer pattern design system for pattern making

- reasons why a style might be eliminated from the line during the review process

- style factors that influence the estimated cost of a new garment style

- the relationships among traditional design development processes and private-label and store brand product development

Step 3: Design Development and Style Selection

Research and Merchandising

Design

Design Development and Style Selection

Make First Pattern

Cut and Sew Prototype

Approve Prototype Fit, Revise Style, or Drop Style

Estimate Cost (initial cost estimate)

Present and Review Line

Select Styles for Final Line (line adoption)

Determine the Final Cost

Order Fabric, Trims, and Findings for Sales Samples

Order Sales Samples Cut and Sewn

Marketing the Apparel Line

Preproduction

Sourcing

Apparel Production Processes, Material Management, and Quality Assurance

Distribution and Retailing

*A*t this point in the design process, the line for the new season consists of a group of sketches with fabric swatches that have made it through the design team's preliminary selection process. This chapter discusses how the first pattern is developed from the designer's sketch, swatch, and garment specification sheet, and how the prototype garment is cut and sewn from the first pattern (see Step 3: Design Development and Style Selection flowchart, at the beginning of this chapter, and Figure 7.1, an expanded view of Step 3, on the next page). The prototype is then tried on a fit model whose body measurements match the company's size standard. The designer, merchandiser, pattern maker, and production engineer analyze the fit and design, and discuss cost factors. An initial cost estimate is calculated. This is an important factor in deciding the feasibility of producing the style. Changes may be made to the prototype, or perhaps the pattern will be modified and a new prototype will be cut and sewn. This process continues with all the styles for the line. The styles in the line are reviewed, and final decisions are made to determine which styles will be adopted for the final line. Participating in the development of a new style from its sketch (or the first drape) to a finished prototype is an exciting part of the design process. On the other hand, it can be a difficult decision to cut some styles from the line after seeing the prototypes and liking all of them. After the final styles have been approved and final cost has been determined, sales samples are cut and sewn.

This chapter focuses on the development process typically used by apparel companies that manufacture **brand merchandise**. This is apparel whose brand labels are well recognized by the public, including Levi Strauss & Co., Liz Claiborne, Calvin Klein, Nike, and Jantzen. Later in the chapter, private-label and store brand product development processes are discussed. Increased vertical integration and changes in the design–retail relationship during the 1980s led to the growth and expansion of this alternative product development process. With private-label and store brand product development, retailers are a part of the design team and/or are in charge of the manufacturing process. Such changing roles and relationships among design, production, and retail will continue in our complex economic market.

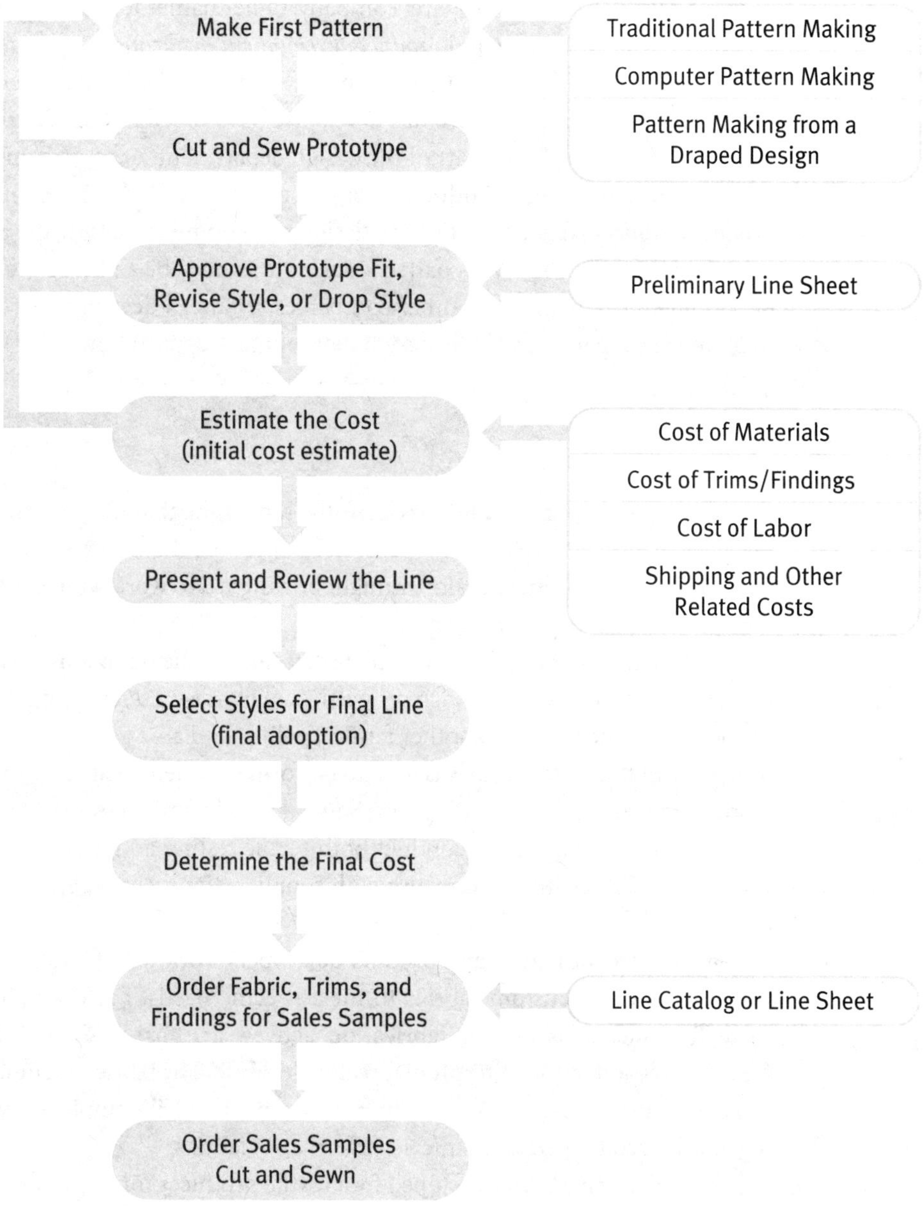

Make First Pattern ← Traditional Pattern Making
Computer Pattern Making
Pattern Making from a Draped Design

Cut and Sew Prototype

Approve Prototype Fit, Revise Style, or Drop Style ← Preliminary Line Sheet

Estimate the Cost (initial cost estimate) ← Cost of Materials
Cost of Trims/Findings
Cost of Labor
Shipping and Other Related Costs

Present and Review the Line

Select Styles for Final Line (final adoption)

Determine the Final Cost

Order Fabric, Trims, and Findings for Sales Samples ← Line Catalog or Line Sheet

Order Sales Samples Cut and Sewn

Figure 7.1   Step 3 Expanded: Design Development and Style Selection

Design Development

The design development stage of creating a line occurs within the **design development department** of an apparel company. Other names for this department include *design department* and *product development department*. Design development teams in this department include designers, assistant designers (also called *design assistants*), and *product developers* (also called *technical designers*). Merchandisers may also be part of the design department. At some companies, the pattern makers and production engineers (also called *cost engineers* or *product technicians*) are a part of the design development team. If the apparel company also has production pattern makers, they may be a part of the design development department. At other companies, a pattern development department may be separate from the design development department.

Fabric Development

Fabric is a key element of a new style. At the same time that the pattern for the new style is under development, potential fabrics for the new style are under consideration. A product developer might be assigned to work with textile mills to develop a new fabric or finish.

New fabrics under consideration are tested early in the design process (prior to making the prototype) for such properties as colorfastness, crocking (transfer of color from one fabric to another fabric), pilling, and abrasion. Sometimes an independent testing laboratory is used to perform specified textile tests on a new fabric being considered for adoption. Some apparel companies maintain their own testing labs that might conduct both textile testing and garment testing. Product developers might also work with suppliers to procure specific findings or trims for the new style.

Some apparel designers and product developers work with fabric manufacturers to produce custom fabrics to meet specific needs. For example, after Gore-Tex's success as a woven fabrication, activewear apparel designers longed for a knit version of the waterproof, breathable fabric. The fabric's manufacturer was able to meet this need. W. L. Gore & Associates and Nike employees worked together to create special technical-performance fabrics.

Fabrics that have been developed by a textile producer for a specific apparel company can be restricted for use solely by that apparel company for a specified period. This adds exclusivity to the product, which in turn can enhance sales. Such a fabric is **proprietary**; that is, it is the property of the private owner (the apparel company).

Couture and high-end designers frequently work with textile mills to develop fabrics for a collection. Balenciaga was one of the great French couture designers of the 1940s, 1950s, and 1960s. Nicolas Ghesquière was hired as the head designer for the House of Balenciaga in 1997. For Ghesquière's Fall 2006 collection, "the fabrics were inspired by research into mid-sixties Balenciaga couture; the wool bouclé tweeds in particular had extraordinary elegance. 'We found people to remake the famous fabrics Balenciaga used,' Nicolas said" (Talley, 2006, p. 78).

As discussed in Chapter 6, textile prints are sometimes developed for the new line by the apparel company. At the same time that the new styles are under development, the designer, assistant designer, or product developer will work with the textile converter to ensure that the prints will be approved and ready for production on schedule (see Color Plate 6).

The designer responsible for the line will have selected a color story, or palette, for the line (see Chapter 6). The colors for the line might be represented by color chips or fabric swatches. **Color management** deals with handling the technical aspects of matching the colors of the fabrics, trims, and findings to ensure that the colors of the finished product match the designer's color swatches. Much work goes into selecting the specific hue, value, and intensity for each color in the color palette. Therefore, it is essential that the fabrics and trim colors of the finished product match the intended color swatch. Color management begins during design development, as the product developer, assistant designer, or designer work with textile mills to procure the exact color match.

For prints, the colors used need to match any solid-colored fabrics intended to coordinate with them. Color matching is challenging, especially when the various fabrics used in a line are composed of a variety of fibers. Different fibers require different types of dyes, so color matching the wide variety of fibers, fabrics, thread, buttons, zippers, and other findings requires constant attention during the design development and preproduction steps. Color management continues in production processes.

Preparation for Pattern Development

As discussed in Chapter 6, the designer sketches—by hand or by using a CAD or graphics system—an idea for a new style as the preliminary design step (see Figure 7.2). After the design team has approved the style for development, the designer's sketch, fabric swatch, and garment specification sheet are delivered to the design development department to begin the pattern making process. In the case of apparel manufacturers that use contractors, the first pattern

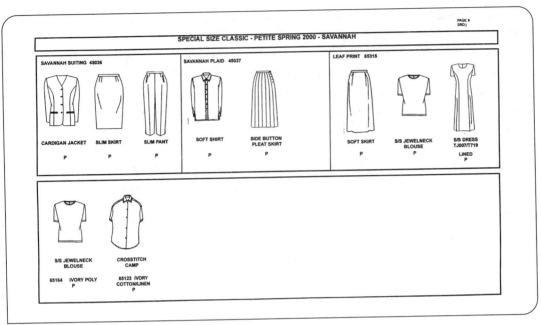

The designer's CAD sketches are prepared for the first adoption meeting.

may be developed by the contractor, or the pattern may be developed by the apparel manufacturer. The responsibility for developing the first pattern is fairly common for contractors who provide full-package (FP) contractor services.

Other designers prefer to drape the preliminary design idea using either muslin or a fashion fabric on a mannequin or dress form (see Chapter 6). After careful markings have been made, the fabric pieces of the draped design are removed from the mannequin. The "drape" is then ready for pattern making.

Making the First Pattern

As noted earlier, some apparel manufacturers develop the line, create the design sketches with accompanying fabric swatches, and write the garment specification sheet. Then, they use either domestic or offshore contractors to manufacture the garments. (These firms are called *CMT contractors* because they cut, make, and trim the garments.) The steps between those involving making the pattern and cutting and sewing the **prototype**, or sample, may be performed by either the apparel company or the contractor.

It may be advantageous for those apparel companies that use contractors to retain the capability to develop the pattern and prototype in-house because schedule delays and communication and visual interpretation problems are possible when a contractor develops the pattern and prototype. A number of factors must be considered by each apparel manufacturer regarding the pattern making, grading, and marker making responsibilities. One of the potential problem areas when using contractors for pattern making has to do with the base pattern used. (A pattern base is a non-stylized basic pattern in the sample size from which the stylized pattern is derived.) Two contractors producing different styles for the same line might not use identical base patterns for pattern making. This can cause differences in the fit of the finished stylized garments between a style produced by one contractor and another style produced by another contractor. More offshore contractors now have computer pattern making systems that eliminate many of the problems that apparel companies previously encountered when they had contractors perform the pattern making functions.

At some companies, the designer is also the first pattern maker. This tends to be the case in very small companies or in some specialty areas, such as children's wear. Some designers enjoy being involved in the development of their design ideas from sketches into patterns and then prototypes. For designers who also are responsible for making the first pattern and prototype, their design ideas or the construction procedure might evolve during the development process. Thus, they might modify the design during the process of making the pattern and/or sewing the prototype. From the designer's sketch, the assistant designer or pattern maker begins the pattern making process, called **flat pattern** design. The pattern maker's role is critical to the accurate translation of the designer's idea. It is important that the pattern maker accurately assesses from the sketch the following information:

- the overall silhouette desired
- the amount of ease (from very snug to very oversized)
- the designer's desired proportions for the design details

An existing pattern is used to begin the new design. This pattern could be a **base pattern** (also called a **block** or a **sloper**) in the company's sample size. For example, a basic shirt block might be used as the base pattern for a new shirt style. The pattern maker creates the new pattern by adding pattern design details such as a collar, pocket, button band, back yoke, and sleeve pleats to the base pattern, as indicated in the designer's sketch or tech drawing.

Another process frequently used by the pattern maker is to select a similar style from a previous season. For example, a shirt style for a new season might be similar to a pattern that has already been made for the previous season.

Modifying an existing pattern can be the fastest way to create the pattern for the new style. Selecting the most appropriate previous style for the starting point of a new style may require some discussion between pattern maker (or assistant designer) and the designer. Alternatively, the designer might make a note to the pattern maker on the design sketch or tech drawing suggesting a previous style from which to begin.

The intended fabric for the final garment is an important consideration during pattern making. For example, the amount of gathers to incorporate into a sleeve depends on the hand, or tactile qualities, of the fabric specified by the designer. The pattern maker may experiment by gathering a section of the intended fabric or a facsimile fabric to better determine the ideal quantity of gathers. To develop patterns for garments made from stretch fabrics, it is necessary to know the exact amount of stretch of the fabric in all directions. The pattern maker selects the base pattern or previous style pattern to correspond to the specific stretch factor of the intended fabric for the new style.

Fabric shrinkage is another pattern making consideration. After the fabric sample has been wash tested to determine accurately its shrinkage in all directions, the pattern is made sufficiently larger to account for the shrinkage factor. All pattern pieces are expanded, based on accurate length and width shrinkage ratios.

The pattern maker needs expertise/knowledge in the following areas:

- pattern making, so that a garment illustration can be translated into a pattern

- production aspects, such as the sequence of sewing operations used by a production facility that affect how the pattern is built, so the style can be made easily and cost effectively in the factory

- the types of equipment at the production facility, in order to produce a pattern that can be sewn satisfactorily by the factory

The pattern maker may work with traditional paper patterns, or the pattern might be created using a computer-aided design system. There are similarities and differences between these pattern making methods; both methods will be discussed.

TRADITIONAL PATTERN MAKING

The base patterns, as well as stylized patterns, are often made of a heavy paper called **tagboard**, *oaktag*, or *hard paper* (see Figure 7.3). Tagboard is similar in weight to the paper used for file folders. This heavy paper is sturdy, and the edges can be traced rapidly to copy a pattern as the beginning point for the new

Figure 7.3 Tagboard patterns from previous seasons are used as reference for making patterns for new styles.

pattern. Traditional pattern making procedures require either that the pattern maker trace the base pattern onto pattern paper, called *soft paper*, or that new patterns be made directly onto new tagboard. Style details are developed, collars can be created, new sleeves designed, and pleats or gathers added in order to create the pattern pieces for the new style.

COMPUTER PATTERN MAKING

Computer pattern making was developed for use in the apparel industry in the early 1980s. Currently, many apparel companies use **pattern design systems (PDS)** for some or all of the pattern making functions (see Figure 7.4). The computer pattern making process is similar to the flat-pattern process previously discussed. The base patterns and all previous style patterns are stored in the computer's files or on a server. To begin a new style, either a base pattern or the pattern pieces for a similar style from a previous season is pulled from the computer's file and appears on the screen. The pattern maker uses a mouse, or stylus (which looks similar to a pen) to select specific areas to change on the pattern. Pattern making commands are either selected from a menu shown on the screen or typed on a keyboard. Once the pattern making is completed, the pattern can be plotted (drawn) in full size (see Figure 7.5).

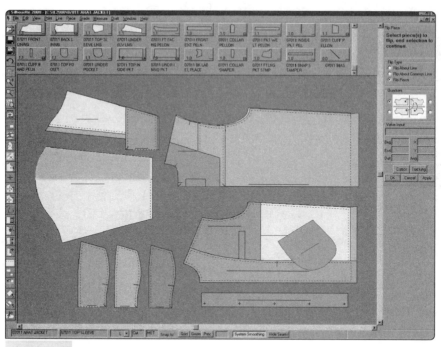

Figure 7.4   Pattern design systems, such as Gerber Technology's AccuMark, provides speed and accuracy for pattern making.

Figure 7.5   After a pattern is completed on a pattern design system, the pattern pieces are drawn full size on a plotter.

Advantages of PDS

Computer technology continues to bring remarkable advances in ease of use, adaptability, and cost effectiveness of PDS. Some of the advantages of PDS include the following:

Speed Since the base patterns and patterns from previous styles are stored in the computer system and used to begin the pattern for a new style, no time is spent tracing an existing pattern to begin pattern making. To add seam and hem allowances, the pattern maker specifies the amount of seam and hem allowances to add to selected edges, and the cutting lines are added in an instant. The lengths of two seam lines that need to match can be compared for accuracy with a computer command. Markings and labels, such as grainlines and notches, are stored in a library and can be quickly added to the pattern pieces. To add gathers, the pattern maker indicates where and how much the pattern should be enlarged, and the pattern piece is spread to insert gathers instantly. A paper pattern, on the other hand, must be slashed in several places, and then spread in order to insert additional width or length for gathers. If the design is modified later in the design process, changes in the pattern can be made more quickly by PDS than they usually can with a paper pattern. Another advantage of using a PDS that enhances the speed of pattern making is its capability to adjust other pattern pieces automatically. For example, a change made by the pattern maker on the jacket front pattern would generate the same change to be reflected on the facing and lining pattern pieces.

Accuracy Using PDS eliminates the incremental growth that can occur when hand tracing a pattern due to the thickness of the pencil lead. Seam lengths and seam allowance widths are more exact than is possible by hand. By always using a stored pattern for the base pattern, consistency in pattern design across all styles is assured. When the pattern maker makes a modification in one pattern piece that affects other pattern pieces, some PDS software programs make an automatic change in the corresponding pattern piece(s). For example, if a change is made in the front side seam length, the back side seam length is automatically corrected. This can greatly reduce potential errors, as well as increase the speed of pattern making.

Improved Ergonomics Sitting or standing at a computer workstation can be easier on the body than bending over a pattern table. It is usually not necessary for the pattern maker to cut out soft- or hard-paper patterns when making a pattern by computer, saving wear and tear on the hands. For anyone who has spent time cutting out hard patterns by hand with scissors, it is a pleasure to be relieved of this task.

Integration with Spec Sheets Some computer software programs provide an interface between the pattern making process and the garment specification sheet (spec sheet). Some PDS programs allow the pattern maker to write parts of the spec sheet as the pattern is being made on PDS. A file of potential sewing steps is retrieved and edited on one screen, while the pattern is being made and viewed on another screen. The measurement specifications can also be written during the pattern making process. With some PDS software programs, the widths and lengths of the pattern being made in the sample size can be requested at any time during the pattern making process. This information is the basis for the completion of the measurement specifications (which are discussed in more detail in Chapter 9). The possibility of an error in the spec sheet is reduced when the pattern maker writes the spec sheet simultaneously with making the pattern.

Integration with Production Later in the product development process, production is faster if the pattern pieces have been stored in the computer than if it is necessary to input the pattern pieces for computerized grading and marker making. These processes will be discussed in Chapter 9.

Product Lifecycle Management (PLM) By using computer pattern design software, the pattern can be communicated electronically among all departments to integrate the business and manufacturing systems seamlessly (Hill, 1999). This, in turn, speeds the product through production and reduces the possibility of errors (see Chapter 9 for additional discussion). A Woolrich executive stated, "We utilize zip files to send the pattern pieces back and forth. But in other cases, we work with an actual physical set of pattern papers, which obviously adds considerable delay as well as additional expense" (DesMarteau, 2003, p. 34).

Disadvantages of PDS

Although the advantages of PDS are many, some pattern makers and company executives note that there are disadvantages. Possible disadvantages of using PDS include the following:

Cost The initial cost of PDS is high, although some of the new technology systems cost less than earlier versions. Some apparel manufacturers, especially smaller companies, may not see a substantial return on their investment for some years. If a company produces only a limited number of new styles per season, PDS will not be utilized to its maximum. Another aspect of cost has to do with training pattern makers. Typically, pattern makers are sent to the computer software company's headquarters for a week or two of intensive training on the system. In addition to the dollar cost of the training, there is the cost of lost time while training occurs and the greater time required to make patterns while the new system is being mastered. During the transition time, some pattern styles may still be made on the table from existing patterns, while some new styles will be made on PDS and stored in the computer. Thus, both PDS and paper patterns will be used for a while, which can create complications.

Visualization Difficulties For pattern makers who are used to working with full-size patterns, the use of PDS requires an adjustment because they are looking at reduced-size pattern pieces on the computer screen. When working by hand, the pattern maker slashes the pattern for gathers and spreads the pattern the desired amount. These decisions often are based on what *looks* correct. When pattern makers use PDS, they select the quantity of gathers to add. The new pattern piece, with the selected quantity of gathers, then appears on the screen. In other words, the pattern maker must choose the quantity before seeing how the pattern looks. However, if the quantity of gathers seems too great or too small, it takes very little time with PDS to undo the maneuver and request a different quantity of gathers. With experience, it becomes easier for pattern makers to visualize scale using PDS.

User Friendliness One of the hurdles with learning a computer software system is learning the operating system and memorizing the commands and the various steps needed to complete a process. Some of the early PDS programs were not user friendly. Recently, great strides have been made in the language used for commands and in the use of "real size" pattern tables, instead of smaller sensitized screen areas for pattern making. Some PDS programs allow pattern makers to work from full-scale patterns on a special sensitized pattern table. This system can reduce the time it may take pattern makers to feel comfortable with PDS. (Most current PDS programs use PCs and the latest operating environment, maintaining the familiarity for the user with other computer applications.)

"Down" Time If the system "goes down," the delay can cause great problems and affect the subsequent production steps. Any delays can be extremely costly to the manufacturer and retailer. Fortunately, most PDS companies have excellent technical support by phone and online, easing the time loss and stress.

Ergonomic Challenges There are a number of ergonomic challenges with computers. Repetitive strain injuries (RSIs), such as the wrist injury known as carpal tunnel syndrome, may result from long hours at the computer, certain wrist and body positions while using a keyboard or a mouse, and other factors. It is important that the keyboard, monitor, and mouse be at the correct heights for the individual and that he or she have an ergonomically designed, easily adjustable chair and good light. Frequent, short breaks can also help prevent injuries.

In the future, an increasing number of apparel companies will use PDS. Costs of PDS programs have been reduced as more price competition among CAD companies has developed and technology costs have decreased. Many CAD systems operate with standard computer industry PCs, providing additional price competition in the huge PC market. Most large apparel manufacturers already rely completely on computer-generated pattern making. An increasing number of small apparel companies use CAD systems in order to be fully integrated with their manufacturers.

PATTERN MAKING BY DRAFTING

Rather than beginning the pattern making process with a base pattern, some companies prefer to draft the pattern by using body measurements. The pattern shapes are drawn based on the body dimensions plus ease allowances. Pattern drafting can be done using paper and pencil, or using a CAD program. Pattern drafting to create stylized patterns is used more frequently in Asia than in North America.

PATTERN MAKING FROM A DRAPED DESIGN

As discussed in Chapter 6, some designers, especially in the designer and bridge price zones, create the initial garment by draping the design on a mannequin. The fabric, either fashion fabric or muslin, is draped onto the sample size mannequin. The design is developed by cutting into the fabric, molding the fabric to the desired shape, and then pinning the fabric in place. After finalizing all aspects of the design, the style lines and construction details of the drape are very carefully marked in preparation for removal from the mannequin. The fabric pieces are removed and laid flat over pattern paper. The shapes of the pattern pieces are traced onto paper; then the pattern is perfected, and markings such as grainlines, notches, buttonholes, seam and hem allowances, and facings are added.

Some companies digitize the paper pattern into a computer pattern design system. This allows the remaining stages of the design development process, preproduction, and production processes for the new style to be handled electronically.

Regardless of the procedure by which the pattern is made—by using flat pattern design with paper, by using PDS, by drafting, or from a draped design —the full-scale final pattern of the style is now ready to be cut and sewn into a prototype for style review.

The next step in the design development process is to cut and sew the prototype or sample garment.

As mentioned in Chapter 6, some apparel companies use computer software systems to create three-dimensional replicas of the styles in the line that show simulated fabrics draped on the mannequin viewed on the computer screen. Rather than continuing the development process by cutting and sewing the sample, some companies use these computer-generated images to sell the styles to the retail buyers. This marketing process will be discussed later as well.

Most companies produce a sewn prototype. This provides the opportunity for the following:

- to test the design in the selected fabric(s)

- to evaluate the style on a live fit model

- to test the construction sequence

- to use a physical sample to perform a cost analysis for materials and labor costs

- to see all the styles in the line as a whole

The prototype made from the first pattern for the new style may be cut and sewn by an in-house sample sewing department, or it might be made by a contractor. If the pattern was completed by the apparel company on a PDS and will be sewn by a contractor, then the pattern is traced and sent to the contractor. Or, if the contractor has a compatible computer system, the pattern can be sent electronically to the contractor. Many contractors, especially those located in Asia, realize that their business opportunities expand greatly if they invest in computer systems.

The completed pattern is delivered to the **sample sewing department**, accompanied by a swatch of the intended fabric for the actual garment and the garment specification sheet. If the intended fabric is available (sometimes as a sample cut ordered from the textile mill), it will be used to make the prototype garment. Sometimes the intended fabric is not yet available, so a substitute or facsimile fabric, as similar as possible to the intended fabric, will be used (see Figure 7.6).

The garment spec sheet will indicate any special cutting instructions. For example, a shirt with back yoke may require that the shirt's striped fabric be cut on the lengthwise grain for the body, sleeves, and collar, and on the crosswise grain for the yoke. Stretch fabrics for swimwear and bodywear may require some

Figure 7.6 A new style may be developed using a substitute fabric before a prototype is made in fashion fabric.

pattern pieces to be cut with the greatest stretch in the horizontal direction and other pattern pieces to be cut with the greatest stretch in the vertical direction. The sample cutter will match plaids where specified and make other decisions about how the pattern pieces are laid on the fabric (*layout*). The sample cutter will cut all pieces needed for the prototype, including pocketing, interfacings, and linings (see Figure 7.7). The pattern is removed from the fabric after cutting; then the pattern is usually returned to the design development department rather than accompanying the fabric pieces of the prototype through the sample sewing process.

The **sample sewer** is highly skilled in the use of a variety of sewing machines as well as in the production processes used in factories. Without an instruction sheet and rarely consulting the pattern pieces, the sample sewer sews the entire prototype garment. The sample sewer moves from one piece of equipment to the next, until the garment is finished. The sample sewer may need to send a section of a prototype to another area for work. For example, it may be necessary to embroider a logo onto a shirt front after it is cut out and before the shirt is sewn. Keeping the work flowing smoothly is also part of the process. Generally, for companies that produce prototypes in-house, the prototype is completed within a few days after cutting.

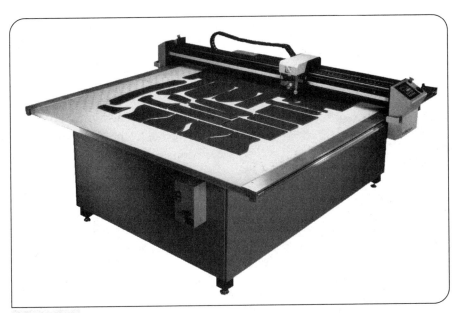

The sample cutter is used to cut the garment pieces for the sample or prototype.

If the design development department is located near the sample sewing room, the sample sewer might consult with the pattern maker regarding a specific sewing process or technique, or they may discuss possible alternative solutions to a pattern or construction problem (see Figure 7.8). A team approach among pattern maker, cutter, and sample sewer is an advantage. After the sample sewer finishes making the prototype, it is sent back to the design development department for evaluation. Often the pattern maker reviews the prototype first to assess whether any changes need to be made before the style is reviewed by the designer and merchandiser.

APPROVING THE PROTOTYPE

The fit of the company's products is important in achieving a competitive advantage through product differentiation. Therefore, an assessment of how each style fits can be very important to a company. A **fit model** is used to assess the fit, styling, and overall look of the new prototype. The fit model is a person selected to represent the body proportions that the apparel company feels are ideal for its target customer and that correspond to the base pattern size used to make the prototype. Some fit models, called *in-house models*, may work for the company in another capacity and are asked to try on prototypes as needed as a

Figure 7.8   The pattern maker and the sample sewer discuss possible alternatives for a pocket detail.

part of their job duties. Other companies hire a professional fit model who may work for a number of apparel companies. With professional fit models, specific appointments will be made for fit sessions, requiring both lead time to book the appointment and on-time delivery of prototypes for the fit session. Fit models can provide valuable information about the comfort and ease of the garment.

Men's wear fit models tend to have well-proportioned bodies and usually are about 5 feet, 10 inches to 6 feet tall. In missy apparel, fit models differ from runway models and photographic models. A missy fit model has body proportions that are "average," with a height of 5 feet, 5 inches to 5 feet, 8 inches, as compared to the tall and svelte runway models. Large-size, tall, and petite fit models are used for their respective size categories. In children's wear, the fit model outgrows the sample size very quickly, requiring the apparel company to search for a new fit model every few months.

In junior and missy apparel, there are wide variations among apparel companies in the body dimensions for one size (Workman, 1991). For a pant created to fit an individual with a 25-inch waist, one company may use a 36-inch hip measurement for its size standard, and another company may use a 37-inch hip measurement. The pattern's crotch depth measurement may also differ among companies. Finding the "perfect" fit model for an apparel company can be a challenge, especially for swimwear and inner wear companies that make garments that fit closely to the body. The model's cup size and bust contour are factors in selecting the fit model. Some fit models are in very high demand, especially in the more populous market centers.

Body forms (such as dress forms, torso forms, and pant forms) can be a valuable tool for assessing the fit and design of a prototype. Body forms based on specified body dimensions are used by many apparel companies. Customized body forms, made to a company's measurement specifications, are also available from a variety of body form companies. New developments in 3D body scanning allow an apparel company to have their fit model's individual shape duplicated as a body form. Thus, assessing the fit on a true-to-life body form can provide great accuracy when the fit model is not available. Other developments in body forms include the use of more pliable materials that better replicate the malleable characteristics of flesh. Body forms made from these materials are especially valuable for swimwear, underwear, and lingerie companies.

When several prototypes are ready for assessment, a fit session is scheduled with the fit model. While the garment fit is a part of the assessment, much of the discussion among designer, assistant designer, and pattern maker may focus on the prototype's overall style and garment details. Sometimes production engineers are asked to provide feedback about potential difficulties in factory production of the style. If any of these aspects need revision, either the existing prototype will be redone or the pattern will be revised and a new prototype will be cut and sewn. The final design will be approved by the designer and/or the merchandiser. The style might be eliminated from the line at this point if reworking the design does not seem feasible.

After the prototype has been completed, a wash test might be performed on the finished garment using a typical washer and dryer used for home launder- ing. The wash test performed on garments to be sold in other countries would use the type of laundering equipment used by the customer in those countries to simulate the conditions under which the garment will be laundered. Occasionally, problems that were not evident when the individual fabrics or trims were tested arise after laundering a garment.

Three-Dimensional Tools

Three-dimensional technology provides the ability to move from the two-dimen- sional pattern to a three-dimensional image of a garment draped onto a body form. "When using 3-D for patternmaking, a designer can drape garments over a digital image, rotate them, zoom in, and visualize how the piece will look" (McAllister, 2004, p. 1). Originally developed as a "virtual dressing" tool at the retail level, the customer could envision how a garment might look on them. Lands' End was one of the first retailers to introduce online shoppers to the soft- ware *My Virtual Model*™. The customer inputs personal data such as personal coloring, body build, and favorite colors. The program shows the virtual model on the computer screen wearing suggested styles in colors from the catalog.

The three-dimensional tools have been revamped for use in the design and product development arenas. "The shift toward 3-D product development has

brought a whole new arsenal of tools to the fingertips of product designers …
that allow 2-D patterns to be draped over a 3-D virtual avatar" (DesMarteau and
Speer, 2004, p. 28). The rapidly developing technology has introduced plug-in
tools that replicate "how fabrics twist and turn during movement, giving the
3-D form a more lifelike appearance and giving designers a better picture of
how clothing will actually look and move" (McAllister, 2004, p. 10).

Three-dimensional technology has many applications in the apparel industry in addition to allowing designers and product developers to view a design
three-dimensionally before the pattern is made, sample cut, and sewn. The concept of designing entirely on the computer may seem far off, but the reality is
that not only can we create the three-dimensional image of the garment style
with replica fabric on the computer screen, but retail buyers can write their
orders from the garments viewed on the screen. No prototype samples need to
be sewn. The cost savings related to design development are substantial. Some
companies, such as Liz Claiborne, use CAD to create a virtual collection.
The "style and design teams create simulated fabric and knit swatches for
each apparel line directly on screen. They can show all their collections in virtual
form. They 'map' sketches and even photos of models with the different materials,
including aspects such as shadow and fabric distortion" ("U4ia contributing to
creativity," 1999, p. 9).

Advances in computer technology will allow the three-dimensional virtual
garment to be transferred into a two-dimensional pattern. Other advances
include the technology to compute the cost difference (in material usage and
time to sew) between slightly different versions of a design.

Preliminary Line Sheet

A sketch or a tech drawing of each new style in the group or line will be used
to develop a **preliminary line sheet** showing all the styles in the line (see
Figure 7.9). Fabric swatches and other pertinent details might also be listed.
The line sheet is used within the department to help all the team members
keep track of the styles in the group as they are developed. The preliminary
line sheet will become the basis for the development of the final line sheet, or
line catalog, used later to market the line.

Determining the Initial Cost Estimate

The cost to mass-produce the style is an important consideration in the selection
of styles for the final line. Thus, preliminary costing needs to be done prior to the
decision to adopt or reject a style. An **initial cost estimate** (also called *precosting*)

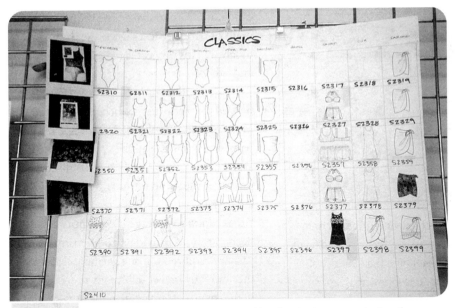

Figure 7.9 The preliminary line sheet is used by the design team during the development process of the line.

for the style is based primarily on material cost and labor cost. A "quick cost" may have been calculated during the design stage; however, until the prototype is constructed, the quick cost serves only as a preliminary estimate. To calculate the cost more accurately, an initial cost estimate is determined based on the components of materials, trims and findings, labor, and other related costs.

MATERIAL COST

The cost of the materials is estimated based on the number of yards of fabric required to make the prototype. Included in the cost of materials are such items as interfacing, pocketing, and lining needed for the prototype. To calculate the quantity of yardage required to make a new style, a layout plan of the pattern pieces, called a **marker**, needs to be made. The term **costing marker** refers to the layout plan for the pattern pieces that are used to determine the yardage (called **usage**) to produce one garment of the new style (see Figure 7.10). If the pattern for the new style was made using PDS, the pattern pieces for this style have been stored in the computer and can be brought into a computer program that is used to develop the costing marker. The pattern pieces are arranged by using the mouse or stylus and are viewed on the computer screen within a rectangular space representing the width and length of the intended fabric. Various layouts

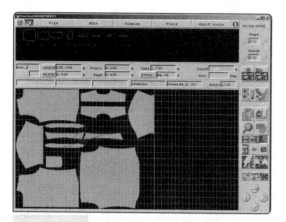

Figure 7.10   A costing marker created from the pattern pieces stored in the pattern design system is used to determine the quantity of material required for one garment.

can be analyzed to determine the best arrangement of pattern pieces using the least quantity of fabric. This process is repeated for the lining and other materials required for the new style.

In theory, the quantity of the various fabrics needed to produce one medium-size garment in the new style multiplied by the apparel company's cost for the fabrics would be used to arrive at a total materials cost. If the company produces the same number of small sizes and large sizes as medium sizes, then using the size *medium* to average the quantity of fabrics needed should provide a good estimate of the yardage required for one garment. However, if the company in fact sells many more size *small* items than size *large* items, the average cost of materials would be higher than the actual cost.

Conversely, if many more size *large* items were sold than size *small* items, then the average cost of materials would be too low. Therefore, some companies may use a size other than size *medium* to calculate their average usage.

TRIM AND FINDINGS COST

The quantity of all trims and findings used for the new style must be included in the initial cost estimate. Examples of trim items include braid or lace, and findings include items such as elastic, zipper, and buttons. For the initial cost estimate for the cotton pants shown in Table 7.1, one button and one zipper are needed to make this style. Note that the cost of one button is based on the cost when a gross of buttons is purchased. The cost per item is based on a large quantity purchase for other trims and findings as well.

LABOR COST

The other major component of the initial cost estimate is the cost of labor to cut and sew the new style. The labor cost is determined by estimating the number of minutes required to cut (and fuse interfacing), sew, and finish the garment multiplied by the cost per minute of labor for a specific sewing factory. To estimate the number of minutes required to cut, sew, and finish a new style, sewing time data from similar styles produced in the previous season can be very useful. For an accurate labor cost estimate, it is necessary to select a possible site for production since labor costs vary considerably around the world.

Cost to Manufacture a Pair of Cotton Pants in the United States

Style #8074	Quantity	Price/Yard	Amount	Subtotal
Materials				
fabric	1.7 yd.	$2.90	$4.93	
interfacing	0.2 yd.	$0.55	$0.11	
ship fabric to company		$0.20	$0.34	
			($0.20 x 1.7)	
Total Materials Cost				$5.38
Trim/Findings				
buttons	1	$2.00/gross	$0.02	
zipper (7")	1	$0.13	$0.13	
Total Trim/Findings Cost				$0.15
Labor				
marking ($45/order)		$0.23		
grading ($70/order)		$0.35		
cutting ($75/order)		$0.38		
sewing labor (0.5 hour @$15.00)		$7.50		
Total Labor Cost				$8.46
Other				
packaging/hanger, hangtag, labels		$0.15		
freight		$0.35		
duty (none, U.S. production)		$0.00		
shipping agent, consolidator fees (none)		$0.00		
Total Other Costs				$0.50
Cost to Manufacture				**$14.49**

WHOLESALE PRICE: The manufacturer determines the wholesale price to include overhead and profit. If keystone markup is used, then the wholesale price paid by the retailer to the manufacturer will be **$28.98**.

In some countries, the labor cost varies month by month. One approach to estimating the labor cost for a new style is to use the known cost of labor to sew a similar garment from the previous season. However, due to economic and political conditions, it may not be feasible to use the same factory that produced a similar style for the previous season. At this point in the development process, the estimate is just an estimate. An exact cost will be calculated later. As production time nears, costs might be researched in several countries to select the source country for the best production cost (see Chapter 10).

OTHER COSTS

When establishing the initial cost estimate, it is necessary to include other items that affect the cost. Table 7.1 details some of these items: packaging and/or hanger, hangtags, labels, and freight charges. If a style is produced offshore, other costs might include duty charges and fees to shipping agents and freight consolidators.

TARGET COSTING

Designing a product based on target costing (also discussed in Chapter 6) works a little differently from the product development sequence discussed previously. Jantzen uses target costing to develop some of its missy and junior swimwear lines. The designer's sketch is reviewed by the *cost engineer,* also called a *product technician.* The cost is carefully estimated from the designer's sketch. The design team works out fabric choices, garment details, and construction factors to bring the design within the required cost for each style in the line. The design sketch may need to be reworked to meet the target cost and to be approved; then a prototype garment is cut, sewn, and given final approval after a careful cost estimate has been made. Each style that is approved is added to the line. At Jantzen, the line might be composed of five groups, with three to four styles in each group.

Target costing is frequently used by retailers as they develop private-label goods. The retailer's design department sets a specific cost for each item that will be produced. During the design development process, style features and fabrics are adjusted in order to meet the target cost.

Style Selection

Each style in the new line goes through a similar process of development and costing. When all the styles have received the approval of the designer (and merchandiser), the line is ready for design review. Because of the lag time in receiving some fabrics, the review garments may have simulated textile elements in order to visualize the style in the intended fabric. For example, sometimes a print or stripe is painted onto a fabric to simulate the final textile design. Occasionally, these simulated prototypes are even used for promotional photos, since the difference between the mock-up and the actual garment will not be apparent in the photograph.

On the scheduled master calendar date, the new line is presented for review. The merchandiser, designer, assistant designer, production engineer, and any other review team members (such as a selected sales representative) assemble for the line review meeting (see Figure 7.11). Upper management may also be included in the review session. The individual garment styles may be displayed on walls in the conference room (sometimes referred to as the war room), or fit models may try on the garments to present the styles to the review team.

Sometimes the designer or merchandiser begins the review session with a presentation. Design presentation boards or concept boards may be included as a part of the presentation, showing fabrics, various colorways, inspirational pictures, and garment sketches. The presentation might include information about the following:

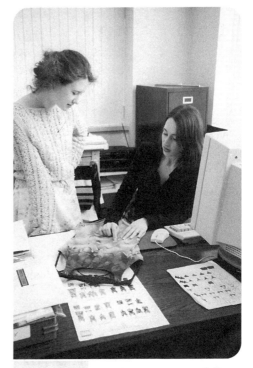

The design team carefully reviews each style in the line.

  the concept or inspiration for the line

  how the styles coordinate or work together

  the target customer profiles for various styles within the line

It may be to the designer's advantage to "sell" the styles in the line to the company review team.

Each style in the line is reviewed, and questions are asked by the review team to determine how well the style works in the areas of cost, production, styling, relationship to the rest of the line, and fabric and trims.

  Cost: Will the estimated cost result in a retail price that is within the range of the target customer's expectation? Is its cost in proportion to that of other similar styles? Are there changes in design that might reduce the cost? Could less expensive buttons be substituted? For companies that do cost averaging among several similar items (see Chapter 6), is this approach feasible?

  Production: Are there any potential difficulties in production? Are there changes in design that could make production easier or less expensive? Could a seam be eliminated?

- *Styling:* Does the style fit the "look" of the target customer? Does the styling look too fashion forward or too conservative when compared with the rest of the line? Could pockets be added if this is important to the target customer? Does the style look sufficiently different from competitors' styles?

- *Relationship to the Rest of the Line:* Does the style work well with other styles in the line? Is there another style so similar that the two will compete with each other? Is the style so different from others that it looks out of place in the line?

- *Fabric and Trims:* Are there potential problems with the fabric? If the fabric is new to the line, will it snag, pill, or wrinkle? Has the fabric been adequately tested? Are there potential problems with lengthy lead time required for a fabric or high minimum yardage requirements by the textile mill?

Each of these points, as well as others, is discussed by the review team for each of the styles in the line.

Selecting the Styles for the Line at the Final Adoption Meeting

At the conclusion of the line review meeting, some styles will be eliminated, and some changes may be required in a few styles. For styles in which changes are required, patterns are modified and new prototypes are sewn and approved. The line is thus honed to develop a tight group, line, or collection of styles with the hope that all styles will sell well at market.

Occasionally, one or more styles are included in a line that the review team speculates may not sell well to the retail buyers. A company may want to experiment with a slightly more fashion-forward look. The line may include one or two jackets with more updated styling than has been shown in the past to see how the retail buyers react to these styles.

Thus, the styles that have been approved join to become the new line. It is reviewed and finalized at the final adoption meeting.

Determining the Cost to Manufacture

The cost to manufacture each of the styles to be shown in the new line must be determined before showing the line at market. Establishing as accurate a cost as possible is important to the successful financial outcome of the line. A design that sells well but is underpriced can be a disaster for the apparel company. The amount that the company calculates will be spent to make the garment is called the **cost to manufacture**.

Calculating the cost requires knowledge about production techniques and facilities. Production engineers, or cost engineers, use known costs as well as estimated costs for unknown factors to arrive at the cost to manufacture each of the styles. There is always the possibility that a style will actually cost more than was calculated, or perhaps less. However, it is critical that the cost to manufacture be as accurate a figure as possible. Forgetting to include the cost of a hanger or plastic bag can affect the overall profit when multiplied by thousands of items produced in that style.

If an apparel company uses contractors for production, they can be asked to do one of the following:

examine a prototype garment of the style to provide a cost figure

sew a sample garment, and thus provide a cost figure

review a complete and detailed spec sheet and provide a firm cost

The **wholesale price** is the price quoted to the buyers at market and is the amount the retail store will pay the apparel company for the goods. The wholesale price is the cost to manufacture the style plus the manufacturer's overhead and profit. Some apparel companies double the cost to manufacture (sometimes referred to as "keystone") to arrive at the wholesale price (see Table 7.1 on page 273).

Preline

Some apparel companies invite their key retail accounts (those retail buyers who place large orders with them) to preview the line prior to its introduction at market. The preview is sometimes referred to as **preline**. The line might be composed of actual samples, or virtual samples shown on the computer. These retail buyers provide their opinion to the apparel company about the potential success of the styles they are shown. Retailers might place orders at this time. Advantages to the apparel company of holding a preline showing include the following:

knowing in advance which styles will sell well, allowing the apparel company to plan production needs accordingly so it has adequate quantities of anticipated successful products and avoids producing poor-selling styles

maintaining a strong working relationship with key retail accounts

receiving feedback from retailers about styles that might sell better if changes were made

A disadvantage is that, since the styles have not yet been produced in the factory, unknown factors may still emerge that will require later changes in a style that buyers have already ordered.

Some companies forecast sales without actual written orders from retailers. For example, black ski pants tend to be constant sellers at market. In advance of orders being placed, the skiwear company may begin production of a certain number of black ski pants to avoid the pressure on production during that industry's very short production season.

Preparation for Market

Now that the new line is ready to be shown to retail buyers, additional **samples** or **duplicates** need to be made (see Chapter 9) so that sales representatives throughout the country or world can sell the line by showing samples to retail store buyers. The marketing process involved in selling the line will be discussed in detail in Chapter 8.

Ordering and Making Sales Samples

Each sales representative and/or each market center showroom will require a representative group of styles from the new line to show to the retail store buyers. Because of cost limitations, not every style in every colorway will be made for sales representatives' samples, or duplicates. However, line catalogs, or line sheets, will show all colorways. As soon as the line is final, the styles that will be made as samples to sell the line at market are selected. The quantity of fabric, as well as linings, buttons, zippers, and other supplies required for the samples, is calculated and ordered. If the textile producer is late in delivering the ordered fabrics, complications in producing the samples on time may occur. Late arrival of fabric could result in the samples not arriving in time for the sales representatives to show at market.

Contractors or the apparel company's sewing factories cut and sew the sample garments. If any production difficulties arise during this small production run, there is an opportunity to make an adjustment to ensure a smooth run later during production of the retailer's goods. Late delivery of samples from the sewing facility could also cause complications at market.

The apparel company may also produce a fashion show and visual presentation of all the company's lines at a special event for the company's sales representatives. This line presentation creates enthusiasm for the new season's goods and helps the sales force sell the line at market. The line's designer (and merchandiser) may be responsible for producing the line presentation. Social events might also be held when the representatives gather for the line presentation. Events such as golf or tennis tournaments, that involve friendly competition among the sales representatives, build company spirit.

Line Catalog or Line Sheet

As soon as the new line has been finalized, a **line catalog** (also called a **line sheet** *or line style book*) is prepared. This is a catalog, usually with color illustrations, of all the styles available in the line in the various colorways available for each style. Color photographs of featured styles may also be included. Charts show the sizes and colors available for each style and can serve as order sheets as well. Wholesale prices and sometimes suggested retail prices for each style are included. Figure 7.12 shows a typical line catalog page. The line catalog is used by sales representatives and buyers to augment the sample garments shown during presentations. More information about the selling process is presented in Chapter 8.

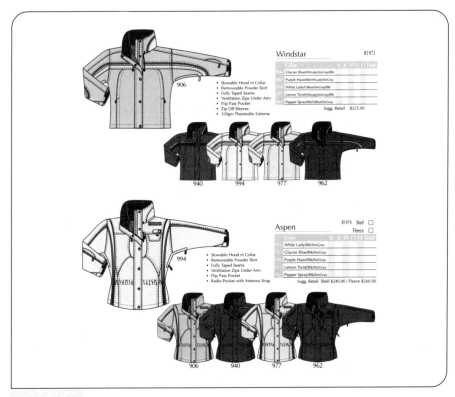

Sales representatives use line catalogs in their presentations.

Most companies use specialized CAD or graphics software to produce the color illustrations of the garments for the line catalog. The technical details about scanning the actual fabric prints into these computer systems for the line catalog are discussed in Chapter 6. Typically, if the first sketch used in the design stage is produced using a computer system, this sketch is revised as needed and then used for the line catalog (see Color Plate 8).

It is important that the line catalog accurately represent the colors of the actual fabrics for each style. Retail buyers expect the finished goods to match the colors depicted in the line catalog. In the early years of computer technology, color printers often made accurate color rendition difficult to achieve. Color printing technology has now improved greatly, as discussed in Chapter 6. Some apparel companies show actual fabric swatches in their line catalogs, or they send a set of fabric swatches with the line catalogs. Seeing the actual fabric texture, plaid repeat, or variety of print colorways helps sell the line to the retail buyers.

Private-Label and Store Brand Product Development

In today's marketplace, there are a variety of ways in which the creation and development of an apparel line occurs. Possible design–retail relationships include the following:

1. traditional design development in which the garment carries the brand name or designer brand of the apparel company

2. **private-label product development** or **store brand product development** through one of the following arrangements:
   - The retailer provides the garment specifications, and the manufacturer or contractor sources the goods (**specification buying**).
   - The retailer and the manufacturer collaborate in the creation of the retailer's line.
   - The manufacturer or contractor designs the entire program for the retailer ("Regional Brands," 1996).

It is important to understand the differences between traditional design development and private-label or store brand development as they affect the design, production, and pricing strategies for apparel, accessories, and home fashions.

We have traced the progress of a style from its creation through its development stages, using a model based on a conventional marketing channel used for brand merchandise in the apparel industry. The apparel company conceives the design, controls manufacturing (using their own factories or contractors they select), and then markets the product to the retailer. The retail buyer evaluates the sample garment and decides whether or not to purchase the style in anticipation of the retailer's target customer desiring the product. A profit is expected at each step of the marketing channel. Conventional design development, marketing, and production involves several profit making steps, including sewing by a contractor and selling by a sales representative. The final price of the product to the ultimate consumer usually reflects the number of profit making steps.

As the price of apparel at the retail level has escalated in recent years, retailers and apparel companies have sought ways to reduce costs and increase their share of the profit. Using offshore production in countries with lower labor costs is one solution. Another approach is to reduce the number of steps involved in the marketing channel. By reducing the number of profit making steps, either the cost of the product can be reduced, or the profit to the remaining companies can be increased (or both). If a retailer works directly with an apparel company to cocreate a product or a line, the sales representative's position is no longer needed. If a retailer decides to create a product to sell in its retail stores and goes directly to a sewing contractor, the apparel company's services are not needed. These are examples of private-label product development or store brand product development.

Private-Label and Store Brand Product Development Processes

Creating private-label or store brand merchandise can be achieved in several ways. One method for developing private-label or store brand goods is for the retailer to work directly with the manufacturer, sewing contractor, or their agents, providing them with garment specifications. Or, retailers such as Target, JCPenney, and Nordstrom have their own product development departments for developing their store brand merchandise. These companies work directly with contractors to source and produce the goods to their very detailed specifications. Target, JCPenney, and Wal-Mart, among others, have sourcing offices in Asia. Thus, the retailer assumes the responsibility of designing the product as well as overseeing its production. One advantage to the retailer in dealing directly with the contractor for production is that the retailer has no intermediaries to deal with, thus avoiding communication pitfalls and eliminating the need to share the profits. From the contractor's viewpoint, working directly with the retailer has certain risks. The contractor usually carries the financing for the materials during the production process. After delivery of the goods to the retailer, the contractor is paid for both labor and materials. This is different from the conventional market channel discussed earlier, in which the apparel company often carries the financing of the materials. As these new marketing channels expand and are modified, the advantages, disadvantages, and risks to contractor and retailer may vary as well. Some retailers own their production facilities, carrying all the risk, while reducing the number of intermediaries in the marketing channel.

Another of the private-label or store brand development processes uses an apparel company's design and development staff to create the entire program for the retailer. Nike, an apparel company that produces lines of apparel under its own label, also develops special lines for other sports specialty retail stores, carrying the retailer's label. This type of collaborative business is very common in the apparel industry. One advantage to the retailer is that the apparel company handles all the production processes. Often the apparel company has a strong working relationship with vendors, relieving the retailer of developing systems to oversee the production.

The third type of the private-label or store brand development process teams a retail partner with a manufacturer in the creation of the retailer's line. In a new development for the retailer, Bloomingdale's has a joint venture with Tahari, a fashion-forward apparel company. This type of venture is called **co-branded apparel**. The company offers complete collections of jackets, skirts, pants, dresses, sweaters, T-shirts, and outerwear ("Private label's new identity," 1999, p. 8) in place of more traditional private-label merchandise based on single items.

Early Development of Private-Label and Store Brand Products

The British retailer Marks & Spencer has been a leader in private-label apparel since its merchandise development department was established. "The company's low prices were the result of trading direct with manufacturers for cash, a principle which remains unchanged to this day. Marks & Spencer's goods are immediately recognized by their 'St. Michael' trademark, which first appeared on 'pajamas and knitted articles of clothing' back in 1928" (Bressler, Newman & Proctor, 1997, p. 68). Rather than purchasing lingerie items from apparel companies to sell in their retail stores, Marks & Spencer determined the goods they wanted to produce, and then went directly to contractors who produced the goods. By eliminating the apparel company's role (and its profit) in the design and manufacturing process, Marks & Spencer could produce and sell its goods at very appealing prices.

Soon, other retailers began to realize the advantages of private-label product development. In the 1950s, Hong Kong was well known for its knitwear manufacturing, especially sweaters. The quality was good, production was dependable, and prices were low. Retailers such as Frederick and Nelson (no longer in business) contracted with knitwear companies in Hong Kong to produce exclusive products such as sweaters for their retail stores. The sweater label read "Made Exclusively for Frederick and Nelson in Hong Kong." This private-label product development remained a small part of the specialty and department store retail picture in the United States until the 1980s.

Growth of Private-Label and Store Brand Product Development

The growth of off-price stores and factory outlet mall stores in the 1980s added pressure on department and specialty store retailers to offer products at competitive prices. Added to retailers' pressures was the fact that apparel companies such as Liz Claiborne, Tommy Hilfiger, Polo Ralph Lauren, and Nike opened retail stores of their own. One remedy for department store retailers was to increase the percent of private-label merchandise they carried. Thus, the private-label business continues to expand, both within department store retailers and with specialty retailers.

With private-label goods, all the risk in selling is in the retailer's hands. The risk to retailers is lessened by the fact that basic goods (as compared to fashion goods) have a long-term sales potential. Thus, as department store retailers built and expanded their private-label business in the early 1990s, most chose to produce basic garment styles such as polo shirts, shorts, casual pants, and jeans, well suited for private-label manufacturing. Another advantage of producing these types of private-label goods is that it makes differentiation between a national brand and a private-label item difficult to discern. A customer could purchase a private-label polo shirt for several dollars less than the national brand shirt that looked nearly identical. The price-conscious customer would eagerly select the private-label polo shirt and be well satisfied with its quality.

Most department stores strive toward a balance between national brands and their private-label merchandise. For example, Macy's offers a variety of private-label lines, such as Charter Club and INC International, in addition to the national brands, such as Levi Strauss & Co., Quiksilver, Koret, and Pendleton.

Some retailers link their private-label lines to celebrities to enhance the stature of the label and the retail store. Kmart offers Kathy Ireland and Jaclyn Smith

Figure 7.13 Private-label products linked to celebrities can enhance the status of the label and the retailer.

labels (see Figure 7.13 and Table 7.2). Target has expanded from its private labels of Cherokee and Merona to include its "high-profile brand partnerships, such as Mossimo, Stephen Sprouse, and Todd Oldham" (Ryan, 2003, p. 38). In an interesting twist, some retailers have signed licensing deals with Seventh Avenue fashion designers. Target signed an exclusive licensing deal with designers Gene Meyer, Issac Mizrahi, and Cynthia Rowley in 2003. For these fashion designers, the financial risk of designing under their own business has been transferred to the retailer.

As sales volume of private-label merchandise increased, retailers developed more fashion-forward private-label merchandise in addition to the basic items that were "safe" choices to begin their private-label businesses. To do so, retailers organized product design teams similar to the design teams at apparel companies. Mass retailers such as Target and JCPenney were some of the first retailers to have private-label product development departments.

Chain stores, on the other hand, have been heavily stocked in private-label goods for a long time. In 1998, more than 40 percent of women's products were private-label goods at chain stores (D'Innocenzio, 1998). In 2003, about 40 to 45 percent of apparel sales at JCPenney were in private label. JCPenney "is renowned for private-label innovation, such as the development of the latest in wrinkle-free private-brand shirts and the successful establishment of brands such as Arizona, delicates, Stafford and JCPenney Home" (Ryan, 2003, p. 37). For comparison, Federated stated in 2003 that its long-term goal is to have private labels reach about 20 percent of sales. Nordstrom's private labels represented 17 to 18 percent of sales in 2003, and that could grow to represent 20 to 22 percent (Ryan, 2003).

Selected Apparel Private Labels

Store	Labels
Dillard's	Allison Daley, Bechamel, Investments, Westbound, Copper Key, Aigle, Caribbean, Daniel Cremieux, Murano, Roundtree & Yorke, Trailer, Turnbury, Class Club, First Wave, Starting Out
Macy's, Inc.	Charter Club, Morgan Taylor, INC International, Alfani, Greendog, Club Room, John Ashford, Style & Co.
JCPenney	Worthington, St. John's Bay, Arizona/Arizona Kids, Stafford, delicates, Okie Dokie
Kmart	Joe Boxer, Jaclyn Smith, Kathy Ireland, Basic Editions, Route 66, Knightsbridge, Hunter's Glen, Small Wonders
Kohl's	Croft & Barrow, Sonoma, Urban Pipeline
Mervyn's	Ellemenno, High Sierra, Sprockets, Cambridge Classics, Hillard & Hanson, Partners
Nordstrom	Caslon, Classiques Entier, Halogen, Baby N, Façonnable
Saks Incorporated	The Works, Real Clothes
Sears	Canyon River Blues, Covington, Classic Elements, Personal Identity, Stacy Adams
Target	Greatland, Merona, xhilaration
Wal-Mart	Starter, No Boundaries

During the 1980s and early 1990s, a number of specialty retailers opened businesses that sell 100 percent private-label merchandise or store brands (see Chapter 4). This strategy, known as **store-is-brand**, results in the retail outlet (i.e., store, catalog, Web site) and the apparel brand being one and the same in the consumer's mind. Examples of companies that employ this strategy include The Limited, Victoria's Secret, Express, Gap, Banana Republic, Old Navy, Casual Corner, Eddie Bauer, Talbots, and Benetton. As with other retailers that offer private-label merchandise, companies that offer only store brands either employ their own designers and/or product developers who turn their designs over to contractors for production, or their buyers seek out full-package contractors who design, develop, and produce specified merchandise exclusively for the store. Exceptions include Benetton and Zara, both vertically integrated companies that control production from fabric to finished garment.

With the store brand merchandising strategy, the appropriateness of the design, quality, and price of the merchandise for the target customer is imperative to the success of the retailer. Trends indicate that the private-label and store brand business will continue to expand. Thus, individuals with expertise in both merchandising management and design have additional career options in the design and merchandising sectors.

Advantages and Disadvantages of Private-Label and Store Brand Product Development

Retailers may decide to offer private-label merchandise, expand their private-label business, or offer only store brands. As noted earlier, one of the major advantages to private-label and store brand product development is the reduction in the number of intermediaries involved, providing an increased profit (gross margin) to the retailer and/or a reduced price for the consumer.

Another advantage of private-label and store brand business is that the retailer can fill in voids in some product categories (D'Innocenzio, 1998, p. 14). Also, the customer is looking for value, and private-label merchandise can provide that value. Quality private-label products offered at a good price can build and maintain store loyalty, as well as private-label loyalty among customers. One of the goals for retailers is to make the private label into a well-defined brand in the customer's mind. "More private-brand managers are charged with making sure the brand's message is consistent across categories and seasons, with the goal of creating destination brands" (Ryan, 2003, p. 32).

Store differentiation is another advantage. National-brand merchandise is available at many retail and specialty stores, creating a sameness to these stores' merchandise. Once customers become familiar with retailers' private-label brands or store brands, they may choose to shop at that retailer's location because the store merchandise has an appeal and is different from what other stores offer. James Coggin, president of Saks stated, "Our private-label initiative is extremely important to Saks Inc. because it provides a way to differentiate ourselves from our competitors and allows us to provide quality merchandise for our customer at a greater gross margin return than normal brands" (Hye, 1999, p. 17). Presenting exclusive merchandise to the customer who wants to associate with the retailer's image is an increasingly important retail trend.

Further, "retailers want increasing control over more aspects of the product than branded manufacturers offer them. That includes at least colors, tailoring, and fabrics" (Henricks, 1997, p. 40). Finally, retailers have the closest tie to the customer. They have a finger on the pulse of what the customer really is buying and what she or he wants.

The major drawback to private-label and store brand business has been mentioned. The retailer takes all the risk. Since the retailer usually owns the merchandise, if it does not sell well, the retailer loses profit.

Summary

The design development stage in the progress of a new line begins with the delivery of the designer's approved sketch. Development of the new style includes making the first pattern using either traditional paper pattern making techniques or computerized PDS. An alternative to relying on a designer's sketch is a draped design, in which the designer creates the new style using fabric pinned directly to a mannequin. This drape is then transferred onto a paper pattern.

A prototype is cut from the pattern and sewn by a sample sewer, using the intended fabric (or a substitute facsimile if the actual fabric is not yet available). The new prototype is tried on a fit model for review of the design and fit by a design team, and revised if necessary. Sometimes, several prototypes of a new style are sewn in order to perfect the design. The cost for the final design is estimated. The line is reviewed again, at which time each style is scrutinized carefully by the design team. The final line consists of styles that have been approved at this stage. Additional samples of styles in the line are sewn for sales representatives, and a line catalog and other types of promotional materials are prepared for marketing purposes.

Computer applications in design development continue to expand. Each year, more apparel companies realize the need to utilize this technology in order to survive in today's marketplace. The computer integration of design, pattern making, and production is another critical step for continued survival in the ever-increasing pace of the apparel industry.

The changing structure of apparel marketing channels will continue to bring changes in the relationship between the apparel company, contractor, sales representative, and retailer. Trends in the apparel industry include continued expansion of private-label and store brand product development, the use of product lifecycle management systems, and 3D tool development.

Career opportunities in the development area include assistant designer/ pattern maker, cutter, sample sewer, supervisor, or specification technician.

Pattern Engineer
Publicly Held Sportswear and Athletic Shoe Company

Position Description

Create fit-approved and manufacturable patterns from design sketches through CAD patterns and flat patterns, ensuring design concepts are correctly interpreted and production capabilities are considered. Manage approximately 90 to 150 styles annually, from inception through distribution. Provide construction, specification, and fabric utilization expertise for the design and development of the line.

Typical Tasks and Responsibilities

- Draft prototype patterns on CAD.

- Develop preliminary specifications and construction details for sewers and engineers.

- Collaborate with design, development, and engineering departments to interpret sketches into cost-effective production styles.

- Monitor fit sessions, review garments for accuracy of measurements and construction details, and revise patterns.

- Calculate and provide fabric-utilization information throughout the development process.

- Oversee the sample making process on assigned styles.

- Prepare traced patterns, specifications, construction details, usage, and special grading requirements for contractors' samples.

Specification Buyer
Sportswear Manufacturer and Retailer

Position Description

Responsible for assisting the product engineer in the documentation of all sample reviews and the follow-up communication to vendors relating to specification development, product evaluation, and control of specification files.

Typical Tasks and Responsibilities

- Be responsible for fit reviews.
- Create specification packages (bill of materials, construction, size specifications).
- Sketch front and back details of garments.
- Read electronic mail from product engineer and domestic and overseas vendors.
- Tag, log, and track all incoming samples.
- Perform engineer's tasks when needed.
- Complete counter sample reviews and preproduction reviews.

Key Terms

base pattern	preliminary line sheet
block	preline
brand merchandise	private-label product development
co-branded apparel	proprietary
color management	prototype
cost to manufacture	sample
costing marker	sample sewer
design development department	sample sewing department
duplicate	sloper
fit model	specification buying
flat pattern	store brand product development
initial cost estimate	store-is-brand
line catalog	tagboard
line sheet	usage
marker	wholesale price
pattern design system (PDS)	

Discussion Questions

1. Discuss how an apparel company interested in converting from paper pattern making to a pattern design system (PDS) might decide what system to purchase.

2. As a merchandiser for an apparel company, what reasons might you have for recommending that a style be dropped from the line during a line review session?

3. As a retail buyer, what are advantages to viewing an apparel line as virtual samples as compared with a market showroom?

4. As a retailer, what are some advantages in producing private-label merchandise?

5. As an apparel company, what are some advantages in producing a special private-label apparel line for a retailer?

6. As a retailer, what are some potential problems in producing private-label merchandise?

References

Bressler, Karen, Newman, Karoline, and Proctor, Gillian. (1997). *A Century of Lingerie.* Edison, NJ: Chartwell Books.

D'Innocenzio, Anne. (1998, October 7). Punching up private label. *Women's Wear Daily,* pp. 14–15.

DesMarteau, Kathleen. (2003, April). PLM the Potential for 3-D & e-Collaboration. *Apparel,* pp. 33–36.

DesMarteau, Kathleen and Speer, Jordan K. (2004, January). Entering the third dimension. *Apparel,* pp. 28–33.

Henricks, Mark. (1997, October). Convergence 2: Vertical retail. *Apparel Industry Magazine,* pp. 38–46.

Hill, Suzette. (1999, February). Product development: The next QR initiative? *Apparel Industry Magazine,* pp. 48–54, 71.

Hye, Jeanette. (1999, November 17). Saks sources technology for private label. *Women's Wear Daily,* p. 17.

McAllister, Robert. (2004, February 13–19). 3-D Tools speed up production for apparel companies. *California Apparel News*, pp. 1, 10.

Private label's new identity. (1999, March 11). *Women's Wear Daily*, pp. 1, 8, 20.

Regional Brands. (1996). Kurt Salmon Associates Branding Report.

Ryan, Thomas J. (2003, June). Private labels: Strong, strategic & growing. *Apparel*, pp. 32–37.

Talley, André Leon. (2006, May). Tsar Nicolas. *Vogue*, pp. 72, 78.

U4ia contributing to creativity. (1999, Vol. 2). *Lectra Mag*, pp. 8–9.

Workman, Jane. (1991). Body measurement specifications for fit models as a factor in clothing size variation. *Clothing and Textiles Research Journal*, 10 (1), pp. 31–36.

CHAPTER 8

Marketing a Line of Apparel or Home Fashions

In this chapter, you will learn the following:

- the marketing process within apparel and home fashions companies

- the histories, functions, and activities of U.S. apparel, accessory, and home fashions market centers, marts, market weeks, and trade shows

- the nature of the selling function of apparel and home fashions companies, specifically the roles of sales representatives and showrooms

- the distribution and sales promotion strategies used by apparel and home fashions companies

Step 4: Marketing the Apparel Line

Research and Merchandising

Design

Design Development and Style Selection

Marketing the Apparel Line

Designer and National Brands
Sales Representatives Show Line at Market and
through Other Promotion Strategies

Retail Buyers Place Orders

Private-Label Brands
Design Team Shows Line to Merchandisers/Buyers

Buyers Place Orders

Preproduction

Sourcing

**Apparel Production Processes,
Material Management, and Quality Assurance**

Distribution and Retailing

The Role of Marketing

A s discussed in Chapters 4 and 5, the term marketing *is used to describe a process that includes identifying and describing the target customer and developing the marketing mix. This includes the products and/or services offered, the pricing strategy, the promotion strategy, and the place strategy (where the products are to be sold). Because most apparel and home fashions companies approach their business from this marketing orientation, the marketing process is a part of all stages of line development—from research through production. Using this marketing approach, successful apparel and home fashions companies have accurately identified and assessed the wants and needs of their target customer and have designed goods and services that meet the needs of consumers at a price that is consistent with what the target customer has the capacity to spend. Now the manufacturer must make sure the product gets to the target customer at the appropriate time and place.*

Within the organizational structure of an apparel or home fashions company, the area called *research and merchandising* typically focuses on market research and developing sales, promotion, and distribution strategies (see Chapter 4). Marketing divisions or departments in apparel or home fashions companies are organized in a number of ways, depending on the size and goals of the company. Figure 8.1 shows a variety of organizational structures for marketing divisions of apparel companies. Although the marketing area of an apparel or home fashions company is most often associated with the promotion and sales of the products, it should be noted that without an accurate understanding of the target customer attained through market research, and without designing and producing goods and services that meet the needs of the target customer, even the best of promotion strategies will undoubtedly fail. Thus, the marketing of apparel and home fashions products connects the research conducted previously with the appropriate strategies for getting the product to the right consumers at the right price and in the right place.

The term **market** can be used in the following ways:

- One may say that a particular product has a *market*, meaning that there is consumer demand for the product. Chapter 5 discussed research used in assessing the consumer demand or market for a product.

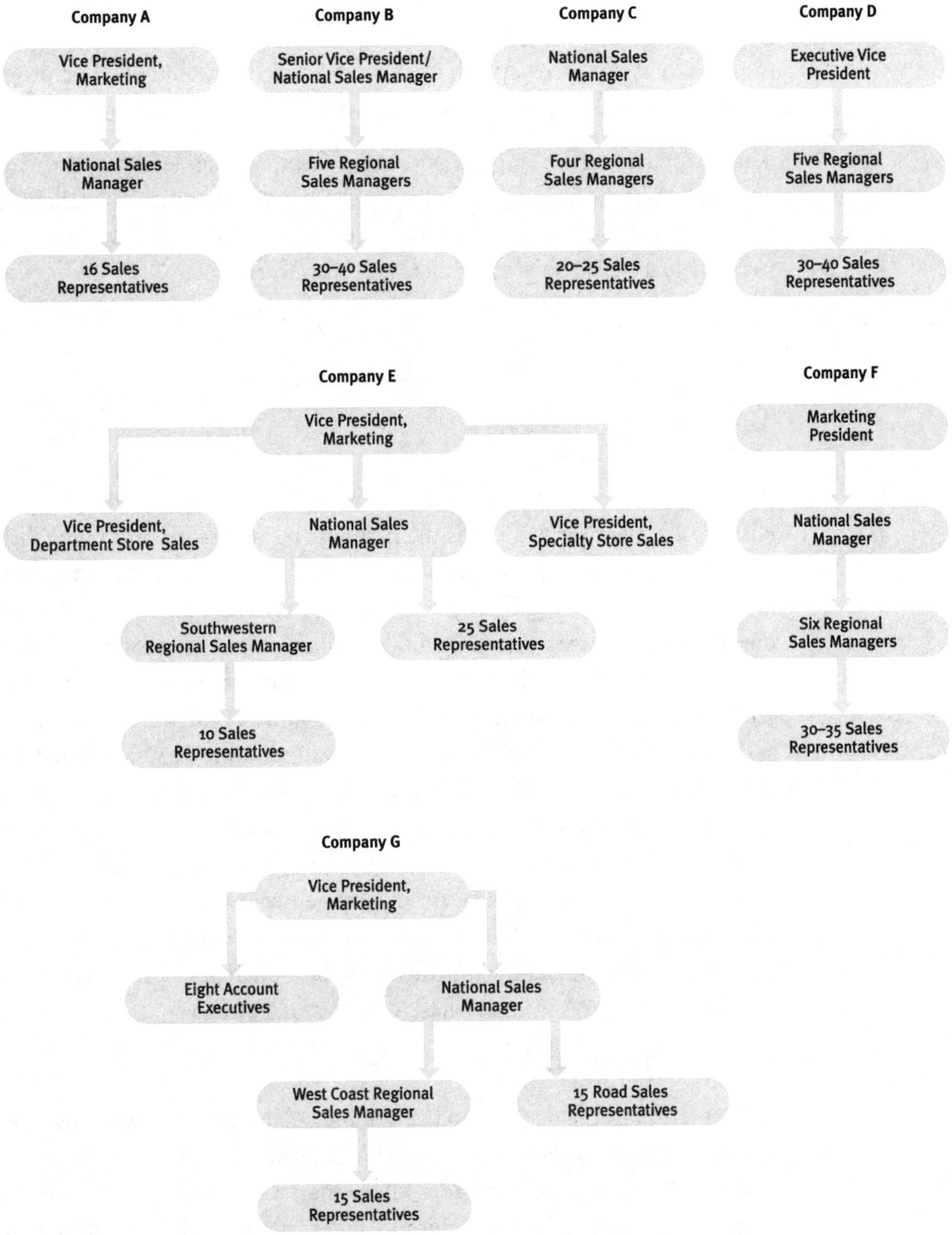

Company A

Vice President, Marketing
↓
National Sales Manager
↓
16 Sales Representatives

Company B

Senior Vice President/ National Sales Manager
↓
Five Regional Sales Managers
↓
30–40 Sales Representatives

Company C

National Sales Manager
↓
Four Regional Sales Managers
↓
20–25 Sales Representatives

Company D

Executive Vice President
↓
Five Regional Sales Managers
↓
30–40 Sales Representatives

Company E

Vice President, Marketing
↓
Vice President, Department Store Sales | National Sales Manager | Vice President, Specialty Store Sales

National Sales Manager
↓
Southwestern Regional Sales Manager | 25 Sales Representatives
↓
10 Sales Representatives

Company F

Marketing President
↓
National Sales Manager
↓
Six Regional Sales Managers
↓
30–35 Sales Representatives

Company G

Vice President, Marketing
↓
Eight Account Executives | National Sales Manager
↓
West Coast Regional Sales Manager | 15 Road Sales Representatives
↓
15 Sales Representatives

Figure 8.1 Examples of Marketing Division organizational structures

• The term *market* can also be used to refer to a location where the buying and selling of merchandise takes place. For example, retail buyers often talk about going to market to purchase merchandise for their stores.

• One can also *market* a product, meaning that the product will be promoted through advertising in the media and public relations efforts.

This chapter examines apparel and home fashions markets as locations where apparel and home fashions companies sell their merchandise to retailers. It also explores the distribution and promotion strategies that apparel companies use in marketing their goods to retailers and consumers.

Market Centers, Marts, Market Weeks, and Trade Shows

Growth of Market Centers and Marts

Historically, New York City was the first apparel, accessory, and home fashions market center in the United States. Buyers from large, upscale stores would travel to New York City once or twice a year to view the new lines and purchase merchandise for their stores. In addition, manufacturers' salespeople would travel from town to town within a specific region, inviting buyers from local stores to see the lines in a hotel room or in the retailers' stores. With the growth of apparel and home fashions manufacturing and retailing in the 1950s, regional market centers began to be established. In the early 1960s, the first regional apparel and merchandise marts were built. Currently, any city where apparel and merchandise marts and showrooms are located can be viewed as a market for apparel and home fashions lines. The term **market center** is sometimes used to refer to those cities that not only house marts and showrooms, but also have important manufacturing and retailing industries. In the United States, these cities include New York City, Los Angeles, Dallas, Atlanta, and Chicago.

Marts

A **mart** is a building or a group of buildings that houses showrooms in which sales representatives show apparel and home fashions lines to retail buyers. Most major cities (except for New York) have marts; some are devoted entirely to apparel, accessories, home fashions, and related goods (e.g., Los Angeles' California Market Center); some also house showrooms for a variety of types of products (e.g., Chicago's Merchandise Mart). Figure 8.2 shows the locations and names of the major market centers and regional marts in the United States.

All marts also include exhibition halls that are used during **market weeks** (primary times during the year in which seasonal lines are shown to retail buyers) as temporary showrooms for apparel or home fashions companies or sales representatives without permanent showrooms at that mart. Exhibition halls are also used for trade shows. To facilitate the buyers' trips to market, apparel and merchandise marts publish directories for market weeks that list the apparel and home fashions lines being offered, sales representatives, and services available at the mart.

1. **Atlanta**
AmericasMart
http://www.americasmart.com

2. **Boston**
Bayside Expo Center
http://www.baysideexpo.com/index.php

Boston Design Center
http://www.bostondesign.com

3. **Charlotte**
Charlotte Merchandise Mart
http://www.carolinasmart.com

4. **Chicago**
The Merchandise Mart
http://www.merchandisemart.com/mmart

5. **Dallas**
Dallas Market Center
http://www.dallasmarketcenter.com

6. **Denver**
Denver Merchandise Mart
http://www.denvermart.com

7. **Kansas City**
Kansas City Market Center
http://www.kcgiftmart.com

8. **Los Angeles**
California Market Center
http://www.californiamarketcenter.com

L.A. Mart
http://www.merchandisemart.com/lamart

9. **Miami**
Miami International Merchandise Mart
http://www.miamimart.net

10. **Minneapolis**
Hyatt Merchandise Mart
Northstar Fashion Exhibitors
http://www.northstarfashion.com

11. **New York City**
Fashion Center
http://www.fashioncenter.com

12. **Pittsburgh**
The Pittsburgh Expo Mart
http://www.pghexpomart.com

13. **Portland, OR**
Oregon Convention Center
http://www.oregoncc.org

14. **Seattle**
Pacific Northwest Apparel Association
http://www.seattletrendshow.com

Qwest Field
http://www.qwestfield.com

15. **San Francisco**
Golden Gate Apparel Association
Fashion Market of San Francisco
http://www.fashionsanfrancisco.com

U.S. apparel and home fashions markets and marts

RETAIL RELATIONS PROGRAMS

After experiencing growth throughout the 1980s, some apparel and home fashions marts saw a decline in the 1990s. This decline led marts to increase efforts to attract buyers through various services designed to make the buyer's job easier. For example, in response to shorter turnaround times and faster delivery of apparel and because buyers are purchasing less merchandise more often, the larger marts are open year round, typically five days a week, 52 weeks a year. This allows buyers to come at any time during the year, not just during market weeks.

Most marts currently have ongoing retail relations programs, including a number of services designed to assist retail buyers. These services include the following:

- educational seminars (e.g., trend reports, visual merchandising, new merchandising strategies)
- fashion shows
- credit and financing assistance
- discounts on travel expenses
- entertainment (e.g., concerts, food fairs)

A number of marts offer seminars focusing on international markets and sourcing (purchasing goods and services) in other countries. Topics include how to do business in Mexico or China, labeling requirements for exporting goods, and other issues surrounding exporting.

Although the growth of apparel and merchandise marts outside of New York City was primarily due to the need for regional market centers, the larger apparel and merchandise marts (e.g., California Market Center in Los Angeles, International Apparel Mart in Dallas) have become more than regional centers that cater to store buyers in the local area and from surrounding states. Because of their expanded services, they are now considered national and international resources; many marts are working to attract international buyers from Mexico, Canada, Central and South America, Asia, and Europe. Many marts offer translation services for international buyers.

Marts are sometimes viewed as self-contained in that they generally house consultants' offices, restaurants, banks, hotels, auditoriums, health clubs, dry cleaners, business centers, and other services for retail buyers. Marts may also be involved in many aspects of the apparel and home fashions industries. For example, the California Market Center includes offices of fixture and display companies, employment agencies, buying offices, trade associations, and private-label manufacturers. Thus, when buyers come to market, the mart serves as a one-stop location for all of their needs.

Market Weeks and Trade Shows

MARKET WEEKS

Market weeks are the times of the year when retail buyers come to showrooms or exhibit halls to see the seasonal fashion lines. During market weeks, retail buyers do the following:

- set appointments with manufacturers' sales representatives
- discover new lines
- attend fashion shows
- attend trend seminars and other educational sessions
- review manufacturers' lines
- place orders for merchandise for their stores

They typically come to market weeks with a specific amount that they can spend (referred to as their *open-to-buy*) for specific categories of merchandise. Marts generally sponsor a variety of market weeks throughout the year, each focusing on a particular product category (e.g., women's, juniors', men's, children's, bridal, swimwear, and so on) and fashion season (e.g., Fall, Holiday, Resort, Spring, Summer). Market week dates are set years in advance during meetings with representatives from the various marts and New York City fashion councils. In general, market weeks for Fall fashion season are held in March and April, and market weeks for Spring fashion season are held in October and November. Market weeks may also be sponsored in conjunction with an industry trade association. Through these joint efforts, buyers are exposed to a greater variety of apparel manufacturers at a single location than they would be otherwise. Table 8.1 outlines the typical months in which U.S. women's and children's ready-to-wear market weeks are held for each fashion season. Table 8.2 gives an annual calendar of selected market weeks and trade show dates.

Market weeks provide advantages for both the apparel and home fashions manufacturer and the retailer. The advantages of market weeks for apparel and home fashions manufacturers include the following:

- Sales representatives can show the new lines to a large number of retail buyers in a very short time. Retailers may also place orders during market week shows.

Table 8.1   Women's and Children's RTW Market Weeks

Fashion Season	Market Weeks
Summer	NYC market: October All other markets: January
Fall I	NYC market: January All other markets: March–April
Fall II	NYC market: February All other markets: June
Holiday and Resort	NYC market: June All other markets: August
Spring	NYC market: August All other markets: October–November

Table 8.2   Selected Market Week and Trade Show Calendar

January

United States

New York RTW Market (Fall I)	NYC
RTW markets (Summer)	LA, Dallas, Chicago, Atlanta, etc.
Bridal Markets (and February)	NY, LA, Atlanta, etc.
FAME (Fashion Avenue Market Expo)	NYC
NY Accessories Market Week	NYC
AccessoriesTheShow	NYC
Accessorie Circuit	NYC
Gift and Home Furnishings Market	LA
Texworld USA	NYC
Interior Lifestyle USA	Las Vegas

International

Haute Couture Collections (Spring)	Paris
Paris Men's Collections	Paris
Alta Moda Roma (couture) Collections (Spring)	Rome
Milano Moda Uomo (men's wear)	Milan
Hong Kong Fashion Week	Hong Kong
Heimtextil (home textiles)	Frankfurt

Selected Market Week and Trade Show Calendar *(continued)*

February

United States

New York RTW market (Fall II) into March	NYC
Mercedes-Benz Fashion Week—NY	NYC
New York Men's Collections	NYC
NY Intimate Apparel Market weeks	NYC
Fashion Coterie	NYC
MAGIC	Las Vegas
WWDMAGIC	Las Vegas
MAGICKids	Las Vegas
ISAM (swimwear and activewear)	Las Vegas
Sourcing at MAGIC	Las Vegas

International

London Fashion Week	London
Global Fashion—Igedo	Düsseldorf
Première Vision (fabrics)	Paris
Ideacomo (fabrics)	Milan

March

United States

RTW markets (Fall I) into April	LA, Dallas, Chicago, Atlanta, etc.
NY Accessory Market Week	NYC
NY Intimate Apparel Market Week	NYC
Mercedes-Benz Fashion Week—LA	LA
National Bridal Market	Chicago
Children's Club	NYC
Gift and Home Furnishing Market	LA
High Point Market (home textiles)	High Point, NC

International

Interstoff Asia (fabrics)	Hong Kong

April

United States

Bridal Market Weeks	NYC, Chicago, Atlanta
NY Home Textile Show	NYC

Selected Market Week and Trade Show Calendar *(continued)*

NY Tabletop Show	NYC
LA International Textile Show	LA

May

United States

NY Accessory Market Week	NYC
NY Intimate Apparel Market Week	NYC
FAME	NYC
AccessoriesTheShow	NYC
Accessorie Circuit	NYC
Global Home Textiles	Orlando

June

United States

NY RTW Market (Resort)	NYC
RTW markets (Fall II)	LA, Dallas, Chicago, Atlanta, etc.
FFANY (shoes)	NYC
NeoCon World's Trade Fair	Chicago

International

Paris Men's Collections	Paris
Milano Modo Uomo	Milan

July

United States

NY Menswear Show	NYC
Mercedes-Benz Fashion Week—Miami	Miami
Chidren's Club	NYC
Gift and Home Furnishings Market	LA
Texworld USA (fabrics)	NYC

International

Haute Couture (Fall/Winter) Collections	Paris
Alta Moda Roma (couture) Collections	Rome
Global Fashion—Igedo	Düsseldorf
Hong Kong Fashion Week	Hong Kong

Selected Market Week and Trade Show Calendar *(continued)*

August

United States

NY RTW market (Spring)	NYC
RTW markets (Resort)	LA, Dallas, Chicago, Atlanta, etc.
NY Accessory Market Week	NYC
NY Intimate Apparel Market Week	NYC
FAME	NYC
Accessorie Circuit (accessories)	NYC
AccessoriesTheShow	NYC
MAGIC	Las Vegas
WWDMAGIC	Las Vegas
ISAM (swimwear and activewear)	Las Vegas
MAGICkids	Las Vegas
KID Show—Las Vegas	Las Vegas
Sourcing at MAGIC	Las Vegas
NeoCon Xpress	LA

September

United States

Fashion Coterie	NYC
National Bridal Market	Chicago
Gift and Home Furnishings Market	LA
High Point Market	High Point, NC

International

London Fashion Week	London
Ideacomo (fabrics, Fall/Winter)	Milan

October

United States

NY RTW market (Summer) into November	NYC
Mercedes-Benz Fashion Week	NYC, LA
NY Menswear Shows	NYC
RTW markets (Spring) into November	LA, Dallas, Chicago, Atlanta, etc.
Children's Club	NYC
NY Tabletop Show	NYC
LA International Textile Show	LA

Selected Market Week and Trade Show Calendar *(continued)*

International	
Interstoff/Asia	Hong Kong
November	
United States	
NY Intimate Apparel Market Week	NYC
NY Accessory Market Week	NYC
NY Home Textile Show	NYC
December	
United States	
FFANY (shoes)	NYC

NOTE: Months may vary slightly from year to year.

- Sales representatives can talk with the buyers and acquire information regarding consumer and retail trends.

- Based on buyer interest, sales representatives also can determine which pieces in the line will most likely be put into production.

- Through such market week activities as fashion shows and displays, apparel and home fashions companies can receive publicity for their lines with the potential for securing new retail accounts.

- Manufacturers can often view the lines of competing companies (although many exclusive lines are available for viewing to retail buyers only).

For retail buyers, the advantages of market weeks include the following:

- Market weeks allow them to review a large number of lines of merchandise in a very short time.

- By attending seminars held during market weeks, they are also able to acquire information about fashion trends, advertising, visual merchandising, and a number of other topics.

- Buyers can also become aware of new lines that they may want to purchase for their stores.

Individuals involved with product development often attend market weeks to identify manufacturers that may be able to produce private-label merchandise. Thus, market weeks are important times for the apparel and home fashions companies in determining the success of their lines.

TRADE SHOWS

Some trade associations or trade show producers sponsor their own shows for the purpose of promoting lines of apparel, accessories, and home fashions (see Figures 8.3 and 8.4). These trade shows, lasting anywhere from three to eight days, are typically located at large hotels or convention centers. Below are selected examples of trade shows for several categories of merchandise.

Shoes and Accessories

  AccessoriesTheShow, Jacob Javits Center, New York City

  WSA (World. Shoes. Accessories) Show, Las Vegas

  Fashion Footwear Association of New York (FFANY) New York Shoe Expo, Pier 94 Convention Center and Hilton Hotel, New York City

Active Sportswear and Sporting Goods

  Sporting Goods Manufacturers Association (SGMA) Fall and Spring Markets, Las Vegas

  Action Sports Retailer (ASR) Trade Expo, San Diego, CA

Apparel Fashions and Accessories

  Atelier, creative international fashions, New York City

  Fashion Avenue Market Expo (FAME), Jacob Javits Convention Center, New York City

  Fashion Coterie, Show Piers on the Hudson, New York City

  KID Show, Las Vegas

  Men's Apparel Guild in California (MAGIC) Marketplace, Las Vegas
    – MAGIC—men's wear
    – WWDMAGIC—women's wear
    – International Swimwear/Activewear Market (ISAM)
    – MAGIC kids—children's wear
    – Sourcing at MAGIC—global sourcing resources

Figure 8.3   Retail buyers attend trade shows such as FAME to review lines from a number of companies.

- Mezzanine, Los Angeles
- STYLEMAX, Chicago Merchandise Mart, Chicago

Home Fashions

- International Home Fashion Fair, Tokyo
- NeoCon World's Trade Fair (design for the built environment), Chicago Merchandise Mart, Chicago
- NeoCon West, L.A. Mart, Los Angeles
- New York Home Textile Show, Metropolitan Pavilion, New York City
- New York International Gift Fair, Jacob Javits Convention Center, New York City

Figure 8.4   The Men's Apparel Guild in California (MAGIC) is a cosponsor of WWDMAGIC, a trade show of women's apparel and accessories.

Some companies rely heavily on trade shows for presenting their lines; others display their lines primarily during market weeks in New York City and/or at apparel and merchandise marts and may attend only one or two trade shows. Retail buyers, product developers, and sourcing agents may attend both market weeks and trade shows to review lines and services for their stores. Web sites for trade shows include show information and registration, appointment scheduling, and show evaluations.

Trade shows have utilized virtual trade shows through online exhibits of lines and expanding buyers' opportunities to purchase goods over the Internet. Virtual trade shows for textiles, home fashions, and specialized apparel (e.g., protective clothing, uniforms) are quite common. However, because of the desire to touch and examine textile, home fashions, and apparel products, face-to-face trade shows will still remain popular for these product categories. According to one retail buyer, "There's something about seeing a line in person. You can judge the quality, color, and texture. I might use the Web to check out T-shirt graphics. For most clothes, I would still want to see it in person" (Feitelberg, 1999, p. 15).

New York City (NYC) is considered the preeminent U.S. market center for apparel, accessories, and home fashions. As noted in Chapter 1, NYC has a long history and tradition of being the heart of apparel manufacturing and marketing in the United States. Interestingly, NYC is the only U.S. market center that does not have an apparel or merchandise mart. Instead, showrooms are located throughout a portion of Manhattan known as the *garment district*, the *garment center*, or what NYC refers to as the *fashion center*. NYC's fashion center is an area in midtown Manhattan located between Fifth Avenue and Ninth Avenue and between 35th Street and 41st Street (see Figure 8.5). The central area is between Seventh Avenue (designated *Fashion Avenue* in 1972) and Broadway. The fashion center started as a manufacturing center, but the cost of space in the city has turned it into a design, marketing, and sales center. Of the manufacturing that remains in the NYC area, much occurs in nearby locations outside Manhattan where costs are lower.

Currently, the fashion center includes approximately 450 buildings with more than 5,000 fashion industry tenants, including showrooms and factories. It is estimated that more than 20,000 out-of-town buyers visit the fashion center every year. For companies that also have their design headquarters in NYC, showrooms

Figure 8.5 New York City's fashion center, located in midtown Manhattan, is the home of thousands of showrooms.

are often in the same building—if not on the same floor—as the design area. Although NYC is the home of marketing efforts for a wide variety of companies, the NYC market is best known for women's apparel and for designer and bridge price zones.

Virtually all name designers (e.g., Calvin Klein, Donna Karan, Ralph Lauren, Vivienne Tam, and so forth) have offices in New York and sponsor extravagant runway shows during NYC market weeks. In recent years, many designers, such as Betsey Johnson, BCBG Max Azria, Ralph Lauren, and Badgley Mischka, have held their runway shows in tents in Bryant Park as part of the Mercedes-Benz Fashion Week (see Figure 8.6). In addition to being the home of marketing efforts for a number of companies, New York City is also the home of corporate headquarters for companies such as Danskin, Nautica Enterprises (owned by VF Corporation), Phillips-Van Heusen, Polo Ralph Lauren, Donna Karan International, Liz Claiborne, and the Warnaco Group.

In an effort to facilitate buyers' trips to NYC, certain buildings have tried to specialize in specific apparel categories. However, despite some attempts to specialize buildings, NYC, in general, is not very convenient for retail buyers, who must go from building to building to visit showrooms during their buying trips. Resources for accessories, for example, are spread throughout the garment district, adding to the inconvenience. Thus, in comparing the NYC market with the "regional" apparel marts, NYC is often viewed as less personal and more overwhelming.

To add greater convenience for retail buyers, the Fashion Center Business Improvement District (FCBID), funded by owners of property devoted to the garment industry, was created to provide additional services and capital improvements to enhance the fashion center. FCBID activities include the following:

The Mercedes-Benz Fashion Week is a highlight in New York City.

administering an information kiosk on the corner of Seventh Avenue and 39th Street

maintaining a Web site (www.fashioncenter.com) with an NYC industry database

distributing maps with buildings color coded according to primary industry use

hiring sanitation and security crews to maintain a safe environment

Given the fact that the city is expensive, crowded, and inconvenient, why does NYC continue to serve as an important market center? In addition to its historic foundation as a fashion center, NYC offers companies access to buying offices, textile wholesalers, findings and trim wholesalers, consultants, advertising agencies, offices of major trade associations, and publishing companies located in the city. As a cultural center, designers can draw inspiration from the continuous influx of art, theater, dance, opera, and other cultural events. They can also view historic costume and textile collections at the Metropolitan Museum of Art and the Fashion Institute of Technology. In addition, because so many companies have showrooms in NYC, the NYC market remains a "must attend" for many buyers, regardless of whether they attend market weeks elsewhere.

Los Angeles

Whereas NYC is considered the primary market center on the East Coast, Los Angeles is considered the primary market center on the West Coast. Los Angeles is home to the California Market Center (CMC), which opened in 1964 with 700 permanent showrooms. Its 13 floors currently house more than 1,000 show-rooms representing 10,000 lines of women's wear, men's wear, children's wear, accessories, textiles, and gifts and home furnishings (see Figure 8.7). The New Mart, across the street from the California Market Center, provides additional space and has showrooms for many designers and brand name apparel manufac-turers (currently 95 showrooms). In addition to the major markets, the CMC offers a number of category-specific specialty markets, such as the following:

- Technology-by-Design show during the L.A. International Textile Show
- TRANSIT/LA Shoe Show during fashion markets
- the Garden District during gift markets

The California Market Center has become one of the most technologically advanced of the market centers. This market center caters to retail buyers

Figure 8.7   Los Angeles is the site of the California Market Center, the largest apparel mart on the West Coast.

primarily in the western and southwestern states (e.g., California, Arizona, New Mexico, Nevada, Utah, Oregon, Washington, and Idaho), but it also attracts buyers from across the United States and internationally.

The L.A. Mart® is home to the Design Center and L.A. Gift and Home Furnishing Market. The L.A. Mart has approximately 200 showrooms for furnishings, lighting, gifts, and services for interior designers. The Design Center houses trendsetting furniture and home fashions showrooms for both residential and commercial design projects. The L.A. Mart is also the venue for NeoCon West, one of the largest trade shows for design in the built environment.

Once one of the nation's largest garment manufacturing centers, Los Angeles has shifted its emphasis to design and marketing. Indeed, in the late 1990s, the Los Angeles garment district was renamed the L.A. Fashion District to reflect the evolution from being a production center to a design and marketing center. With the passage of the North American Free Trade Agreement (NAFTA) in 1994 and California's proximity to Mexico, much of the production has moved south. However, despite job losses on the production side, in 2003, the Los Angeles fashion industry was a $24.3 billion industry, employing nearly 68,000 people, according to the L.A. County Economic Development Corporation.

When we think of California, casual apparel and sportswear come to mind; Los Angeles is best known for sportswear, swimwear, and the "L.A. Style" of casual chic. Companies with headquarters in the Los Angeles area include Ocean Pacific Apparel Corp., Guess? Inc., Quiksilver, American Apparel, Tarrant Apparel Group (maker of JCPenney's Arizona jeans and other private labels), Lucky Brand Jeans, and Pacific Sunwear of California (PacSun), to name a few. Los Angeles and San Francisco areas also include a number of contractors for branded and private-label merchandise. California is also home to the headquarters of a number of other large apparel/retailing companies including Levi Strauss & Co., Charlotte Russe, Koret, Patagonia, and Wet Seal.

Chicago

The Chicago Merchandise Mart and the Chicago Apparel Center cater to industry customers from around the world. For apparel and accessories, their clientele comes primarily from the northern and midwestern regions of the United States. The Chicago Merchandise Mart was opened in 1930 by Marshall Field & Company as the largest wholesale center in the United States. Since that time, the Merchandise Mart has remained one of the largest trade centers in the world. As a design center, the Merchandise Mart is the venue for the gift and home markets, as well as for NeoCon.

Figure 8.8 Chicago Merchandise Mart

Built in 1977, the Apparel Center is located next to the Chicago Merchandise Mart. During market weeks, the Apparel Center's 140,000-square-foot Expo Center can accommodate 500 booths from temporary vendors (see Figure 8.8). Some consider the Apparel Center's bridal market (which now consists of an entire floor with more than 60 manufacturers' showrooms) to be second only to New York's. Chicago is also home to the headquarters of Hartmarx, a prominent manufacturer of men's and women's wear, and Sears, Roebuck & Co.

Dallas

In the south, Dallas has become the key apparel market center. The Dallas Market Center (DMC) includes the International Apparel Mart, the International Menswear Mart, the Trade Mart, and the World Trade Center. It claims to be the largest wholesale merchandise resource in the world. DMC offers more than 50 markets a year for merchandise including textiles; women's, men's, and children's apparel and accessories; and home furnishings and gifts. Currently, the International Apparel Mart (opened as the Dallas Apparel Mart in 1964) and International Menswear Mart (opened as the Menswear Mart in 1982) house approximately 1,100 permanent showrooms (1.8 million square feet in the apparel mart and 400,000 square feet in the adjacent men's apparel mart). Both permanent and temporary showrooms offer retail buyers more than 14,000 manufacturers' lines. The International Apparel Mart and International Menswear Mart cater not only to retail buyers from Texas, Arkansas, Oklahoma, and Louisiana, but they also attract buyers from Mexico and Central America.

Dallas is sometimes viewed as a fashion barometer in that what sells at the International Apparel Mart and International Menswear Mart is typically what is going to sell across the country. In fact, some New York companies use Dallas as a test market for new lines. As with California, the passage of the North American Free Trade Agreement and Texas' proximity to Mexico have resulted in decreased employment in the apparel production industry in Texas. However, increased

China Blue

Plate 1 The design process often begins with trend analysis and fabric research resulting in a storyboard.

Textile trade associations such as the Color Association of the United States provide color forecasts to member companies for the upcoming 12 to 24 months.

MASTER CALENDAR FOR FOUR DEVELOPMENT SEASONS

	January	February	March	April	May	June	July	August	September	October	November	December
WEEK 1				-NYC Dev. Trip	-Prints in repeat	-Issue sale samples	-Final Forecast -1st Forecast	-Counter Samples approved	-Style Boards -Yarn Dye Dev. -NY line Release	-Sales Samples to DC	-NY line Release	-Yarn Dye Dev.
WEEK 2	-Concept Mtg	-Prints in repeat			-Sales samples fabric exit mills -Style Boards -Yarn Dye Dev.	-Concept Mtg	-Sales Samples to DC -Import packages exit merch. office			-Concept Mtg	-Sales samples fabric exit mills	-Issue sale samples -Prints in repeat
WEEK 3				-Import packages exit merch. office			-Issue sale samples -NYC Dev. Trip		-Final Forecast	-NYC Dev. Trip		
WEEK 4	-NYC Dev. Trip	-Style Boards -Yarn dye dev.	-Concept Mtg.	-1st Forecast			-Sales samples fabric exit mills	-Final Forecast -Prints in repeat	-1st Forecast	-Import packages exit merch. office	-Counter Samples approved -Style Boards	

■ = SPRING
■ = SUMMER
■ = FALL
■ = HOLIDAY

Concept mtg = season plan by color & style
Prints in rpt = artwork in final form from printer
Forecasts = overall unit plan to style/color level
Sales sample fabric = shipped to garment factories

Sales samples to DC = salesmen's samples arrive for salesmeeting showing
NY Line Release = sales associates show line to buyers at NY market
Ship = Final production shipped to stores

This 24-month master calendar shows design development for a prominent apparel company that creates for four fashion seasons.

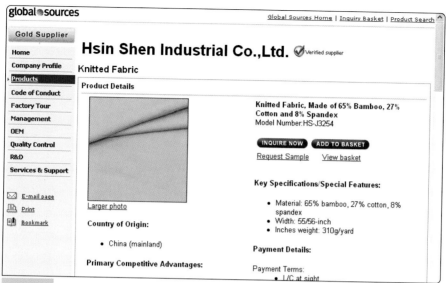

Plate 4 Web sites such as the Global Sources site act as online marketplaces to facilitate sourcing of fabrics, yarns, and other textile goods.

MASTER CALENDAR FOR FOUR DEVELOPMENT SEASONS (CONT'D)

	January	February	March	April	May	June	July	August	September	October	November	December
WEEK 1	Ship Spring 1		-NY line Release Ship Final Spring	Ship Summer 1		Ship Fall 1 -NY line Release Ship Final Summer		Ship Final Fall	Ship Holiday 1		Ship Final Holiday	
WEEK 2		-Sales Samples to DC	-Sales samples fabric exit mills		-Sales Samples to DC							
WEEK 3	-Final Forecast -1st Forecast		-Counter Samples approved -Issue sale samples									
WEEK 4	-Import packages exit merch. office			-Final Forecast								

= SPRING
= SUMMER
= FALL
= HOLIDAY

Concept mtg = season plan by color & style
Prints in rpt = artwork in final form from printer
Forecasts = overall unit plan to style/color level
Sales sample fabric = shipped to garment factories

Sales samples to DC = salesmen's samples arrive for salesmeeting showing
NY Line Release = sales associates show line to buyers at NY market
Ship = Final production shipped to stores

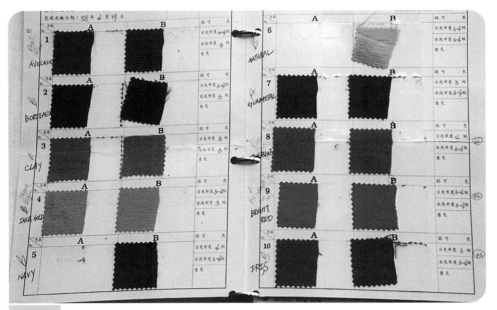

Plate 5 A lab dip includes two attempts by the vendor to match the paint chip or fabric sample provided by the apparel company. One of these two lab dips is selected, or another lab dip is requested.

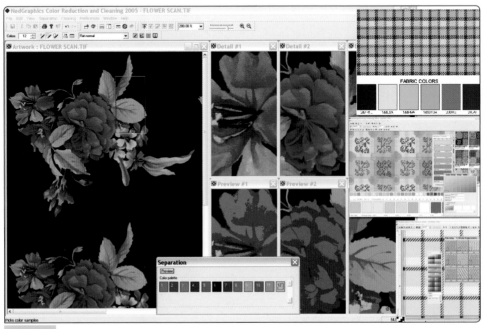

Plate 6 Textile design software is used to create the fabric design images on-screen and to print the design digitally onto fabric.

Plate 7 Consumer research includes an analysis of the wants and needs of targeted market segments. Old Navy markets a women's plus line to a targeted market segment.

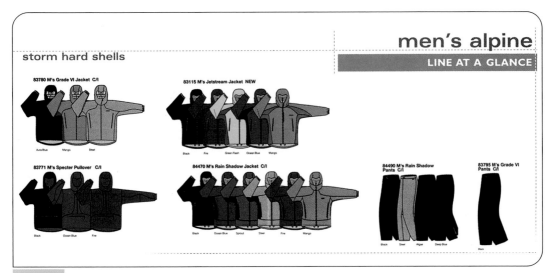

Plate 8 Patagonia's line catalog is used to market a new line to retailers. Color technical drawings illustrate the colorways for each style in a new line.

Plate 9 Sample garments are used to present Pendleton's new line to sales representatives at Pendleton's showroom.

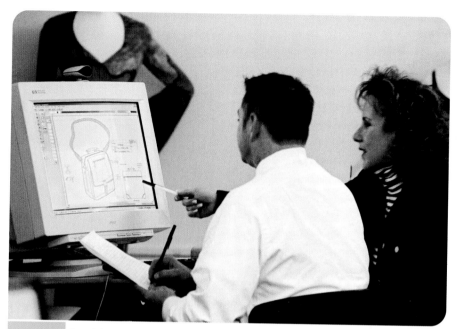

Plate 10 Graphics and CAD programs are used to create product spec drawings.

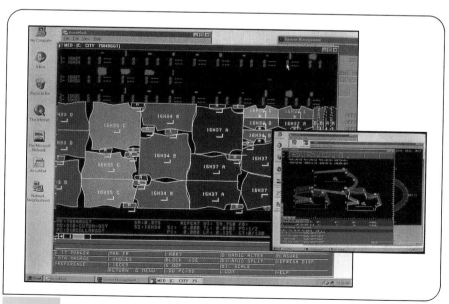

Plate 11 Computer grading and marker making software can be integrated with a computerized cutting system to speed production.

Plate 12 Coldwater Creek uses a multichannel retailing strategy, offering merchandise through bricks-and-mortar stores, catalogs, and its Web site.

trade with Mexico has increased employment in sectors of the industry other than production as companies have located operations along the Mexican border. For example, VF, the world's largest manufacturer of jeans, has operations in Texas. Dallas is also home to the corporate headquarters of Haggar, a men's wear manufacturer. JCPenney Corporation is headquartered in Plano, Texas, near Dallas.

Atlanta

AmericasMart in Atlanta includes the Apparel Mart (opened in 1979 as the Atlanta Apparel Mart), the Merchandise Mart (opened in 1961), and the Gift Mart (opened in 1992). AmericasMart hosts more than 25 markets per year. The Apparel Mart consists of 15 floors, including a large fashion theater (see Figure 8.9), and it has the capacity to house 2,000 showrooms and 11,000 apparel and accessory lines, including more than 800 children's wear lines. Because NYC does not have a mart, the Atlanta Apparel Mart is the largest mart on the East Coast, catering primarily to states in the East and Southeast (e.g., Georgia, South Carolina, North Carolina, Florida, Alabama, Mississippi, Tennessee, Kentucky, and Virginia), as well as Mexico, Central America, and South America. Corporate headquarters for Russell Corporation and Oxford Industries are also located in Atlanta.

Other Regional Markets

In addition to these market centers, smaller regional marts also exist in many U.S. cities. Although these marts cater to a more localized clientele, with the increase in fast turnaround and the fact that retail buyers are buying less merchandise more often, they have grown in importance. The most prominent of these regional marts are in Miami, San Francisco, and Seattle.

MIAMI

The Miami International Merchandise Mart contains more than 300 showrooms. Known for swimwear, sportswear, and

Figure 8.9 The Apparel Mart's fashion theater in Atlanta is used for promotion events.

children's wear, Miami's apparel industry grew as a result of Cuban immigration in the 1960s. During the 1980s, Miami saw change and increased growth in its apparel industry because of the arrival of offshore production, particularly in Caribbean Basin countries. The United States had trade initiatives with countries in the Caribbean Basin (e.g., Honduras, Guatemala, Dominican Republic), which allowed goods cut in the United States and sewn in one of these countries to be imported into the United States with tariff (taxes on imports) benefits. With the passage of the Central America–Dominican Republic–United States Free Trade Agreement (CAFTA-DR) in 2005, Miami has attracted a number of apparel manufacturers that produce in these areas of the world, and it has served as a U.S. hub for imports from these areas.

SAN FRANCISCO

In 1981, the San Francisco Apparel Mart was built to cater to northern California retailers. Although San Francisco had a thriving fashion industry, the San Francisco Apparel Mart failed because of a lack of marketing support for its tenants. Then, in 1990, the Fashion Center was built in San Francisco. It catered to northern California and the Pacific Northwest, as well as to Nevada and Utah. The Fashion Center was sold in 1996. Now the Golden Gate Apparel Association presents its Fashion Market of San Francisco at the Concourse Exhibition Center in downtown San Francisco. The Fashion Market of San Francisco offers five markets per year. San Francisco is the third-largest apparel manufacturing center in the United States, after New York and Los Angeles. Many large companies have headquarters in San Francisco, including Levi Strauss & Co., Gap, Inc., Jessica McClintock, and Byer California, as well as retailers such as Williams Sonoma and Macy's West.

SEATTLE

Since the closure of the Seattle Trade Center apparel mart in 1999, the Pacific Northwest Apparel Association offers Seattle Trend Shows for five fashion seasons each year at the Qwest Event Center near downtown Seattle. These shows are an important regional format for buyers and exhibitors from Washington, Oregon, Idaho, Montana, Alaska, and British Columbia. As with other regional shows, exhibitors tend to be independent sales representatives who offer lines from a number of companies.

Seattle is famous for its men's and young men's sportswear and outerwear manufacturers. In the late 1970s, Seattle was the home to Brittania Sportswear, then the largest privately owned sportswear manufacturer in the United States.

In Brittania's wake came a second generation of sportswear companies that achieved success in the 1980s, including the following:

- Seattle Pacific Industries (Unionbay, Reunion)
- Generra (no longer headquartered in the Seattle area)
- BUM Equipment (no longer headquartered in Seattle)
- Shah Safari

Proximity to Asian contractors is an advantage for Seattle companies that source in that region of the world. With the inclusion of established sport and outdoor wear companies, such as Cutter and Buck, Helly Hansen, Eddie Bauer, and Recreational Equipment Incorporated (R.E.I.), successful bricks-and-mortar retailers headquartered in Seattle, such as Nordstrom, and e-retailers such as Amazon.com, Seattle has gained prominence in the fashion industry.

OTHER MARTS

Marts can be found in a number of other cities, including Boston, Charlotte, Denver, Kansas City, and Minneapolis. These general merchandise marts typically house permanent showrooms for a variety of merchandise, only some of which may be devoted to apparel, home fashions, and accessories. These marts sponsor apparel market weeks relying on traveling sales representatives who set up temporary showrooms or booths. These markets cater to buyers within a fairly small region (primarily within a 250-mile radius of the mart). For these buyers, attending a regional market is much less costly and time consuming than traveling to a larger apparel mart or to NYC. In addition, even buyers who attend other markets may attend these regional markets to supplement their stock between major market weeks.

The Selling Function

The selling function of apparel and home fashions companies is handled in one of the following ways:

- internal selling for private-label merchandise and store brands
- corporate selling
- sales representatives and showrooms

Most apparel companies rely on sales representatives to perform the selling function, but a few rely on internal selling and corporate selling.

With private-label merchandise (e.g., JCPenney's Arizona brand) and store brands (e.g., Gap, Eddie Bauer, The Limited), the selling of merchandise to the retail buyers is handled internally. This is because merchandise is designed and produced for a particular retailer (see Chapter 7 for a description of private-label and store brand product development). With **internal selling**, the design team will present seasonal lines to merchandisers within the company who will select specific pieces of the line for production. Merchandisers also determine which items of the line will be sold at specific stores.

Corporate selling is typically used by some companies that manufacture designer price zone merchandise and sell to a limited number of retailers. For example, the designer Zoran sells to only a few high-end retailers. Corporate selling is also used by very large companies that sell moderately priced merchandise to large corporate retailers. In these cases, selling is often done through their corporate headquarters without the use of sales representatives or showrooms.

The **sales representative** or *sales rep* is the individual who serves as the intermediary between the apparel manufacturer and the retailer, selling the apparel line to retail buyers (see Figure 8.10). Other names for sales representatives are *vendor representative*, *account executive*, and *manufacturer's representative*. **Showrooms** are the rooms used by sales representatives to show samples of an apparel line to retail buyers. Depending on the size of the company, showrooms can be elaborately decorated or very simple in decor. They always include display racks for the apparel samples, and tables and chairs for the retail buyers.

Showrooms can be either permanent or temporary. Permanent showrooms are located in buildings in NYC's fashion center, in apparel marts, in buildings adjacent to marts, or within a company's headquarters or production facilities. During market weeks, sales representatives for companies that do not have permanent showrooms in that area use temporary showrooms or booths. Booths are set up and staffed by either the company's sales representative or a multiline representative. Some sales reps always use temporary showroom or booth space during market weeks. Some companies will use temporary showroom or booth space to "test the water" in a new region during a market week without having to commit to a sales rep or the mart on a permanent basis. Although using temporary space can provide companies with a feel for the mart and the sales opportunities, there are also disadvantages. Because buyers are looking for long-term customer service from sales reps, they may seek assurance of continued service from reps who do not have a permanent showroom.

TYPES OF SALES REPS AND SHOWROOMS

One of the most important decisions made by apparel and home fashions marketers is whether to open an exclusive corporate showroom with company sales representatives or to use established independent **multiline sales representatives**. The primary difference between the two is that company sales reps work for a particular

Figure 8.10 Sales representatives show seasonal lines to retail buyers.

company and are housed in corporate showrooms owned by the company; independent multiline sales reps work for themselves and typically represent lines from several different, noncompeting but related, companies. For example, a multiline sales rep may offer a variety of noncompeting children's wear lines from several companies. In addition, this sales rep may also represent lines of children's toys and nursery accessories. Both company and multiline sales reps are assigned and work in a geographic territory (**regional sales territory**), which may be quite large (e.g., the West) or quite small (e.g., northern California), depending on the company and product line.

The main criteria used by an apparel company in deciding whether to use a corporate showroom or multiline sales rep are the type of product line and the amount of business the company expects to do. The **corporate showroom** is appropriate for a company with a large sales volume in a particular region of the country. For some marts, it is recommended that the company be capable of producing at least $1 million in sales at the mart in order to support a corporate showroom. Corporate showrooms are managed by company sales representatives who represent the lines of only that company. (It should be noted that because company sales reps generally represent large companies, most are based in a showroom.) Company sales reps may work on salary plus commission or on a straight commission basis, depending on the sales philosophy of the company. If the company pays the sales reps' expenses, which is often the case for company sales reps, then commission is lower than if expenses are not paid.

In addition to managing the showroom, company sales reps may travel to other marts' market weeks and trade shows. They may also visit retail accounts. Road travel is most typical for lines in the moderate price zone. For this type of merchandise, apparel manufacturers can often get sample lines (discussed in Chapter 7) to the sales rep prior to market weeks. This allows the sales reps to travel to accounts and sell outside of market weeks. Because of the costs associated with producing samples of designer and bridge lines, companies that produce these lines may only have one or two sets of sample lines per season. Thus, the sample line may travel from one city to another for their market weeks.

Corporate showrooms have advantages and disadvantages. With a corporate showroom, the staff can devote 100 percent of their time to the company's line(s) and the company's customers. In addition, the showroom can better portray the company's image and style of merchandise to retail buyers. However, a corporate showroom is an expensive investment. Space is leased from the mart; lease contracts should be evaluated in terms of services offered (e.g., janitorial services, utilities, mart-sponsored promotion activities, directory listings), as they can vary from mart to mart.

Rather than opening a corporate showroom, many companies choose to go with an independent multiline sales representative. Multiline sales representatives typically work for small manufacturers that cannot afford or do not want to hire their own sales representatives. The multiline sales rep works on straight commission, typically 5 to 10 percent of the wholesale price of goods that are shipped by the company. This means that if the company ships $100,000 (wholesale) in goods that are, in turn, sold by the sales rep, the sales rep would receive 5 to 10 percent of this amount ($5,000 to $10,000) as payment.

Independent multiline sales reps must pay all their own expenses, including the following:

- cost of leasing and furnishing showrooms (if they have them)
- travel expenses to market weeks or to visit retailers
- in some cases, the purchase of manufacturers' sample lines

For smaller companies, using an independent multiline sales representative can have several advantages. The main advantage is that no initial capital investment in the showroom is needed. In addition, established sales reps are familiar with local accounts and can promote the line with buyers. Although the initial costs of using an independent rep are less than with opening a corporate showroom, additional expenses to be expected include the following:

- fees for market week activities
- cooperative advertising expenses
- costs for hospitality service
- fashion shows

Some companies will begin with an independent multiline rep and then, as they grow, they will move into their own corporate showroom.

Finding the right fit between the product line and the sales representative is important to both the apparel company and the sales rep. Companies want to find a rep who has access to the types of retailers appropriate for the product line. Independent multiline sales reps should not represent competing lines. The company must be assured that the sales rep will spend the appropriate amount of time in promoting its line(s). Another consideration is whether the sales rep needs to travel to different retail accounts prior to market weeks. Table 8.3 compares the advantages and disadvantages of corporate showrooms and multiline sales representatives.

SAMPLE LINES

The manufacturer provides the sales representatives with a set of samples for the line(s) being presented to retail buyers. The samples include an example of each style included in the line in one colorway. The line catalog or brochure is used in conjunction with the samples to provide information about the line to the retail buyer. Some companies require the sales rep (usually independent multiline sales reps) to purchase the samples. In these cases, the sales reps are generally allowed to sell the samples at the end of the selling season. Other companies provide the samples to the sales rep (usually company sales reps). In these cases, the sales rep generally returns the samples at the end of the season. These companies may then allow employees to purchase samples at wholesale prices. Computer technology has made it possible for sales reps to use alternatives such as virtual samples and computer-generated buying instead of actually showing sample lines.

Virtual Samples

As was mentioned in Chapter 6, the technology is in place to show a line with **virtual samples**, which are viewed on a computer screen. The intended fabric color and print of the style will be shown, including fabric folds and shadows, so that it looks like a photograph of an actual prototype. "The fabric is draped over the form, automatically simulating an image so real that it can be used

Table 8.3   Comparisons between Corporate Showrooms and Multiline Sales Representatives

Type of Selling	Advantages for the Manufacturer	Disadvantages for the Manufacturer
Corporate showroom	Control over image of showroom possible	Capital investment necessary
	Staff can devote 100 percent of time to line	Lease agreements may vary from mart to mart
		In addition to commission, there may be other promotion expenses
Multiline sales representative	No initial capital investments needed	Determining right fit between sales rep and line may be difficult
	Established reps know local accounts	Rep may not devote adequate time to the line
	Buyers are exposed to related but noncompeting lines in the same showroom	Lack of control over image of the showroom

for storyboards, advertisements, and catalogs. Designers and manufacturers dramatically reduce sample making costs" (Freedman, 1990, p. 12). However, nothing duplicates a buyer's ability to touch and feel samples of merchandise.

Computer-Generated Buying

Retail buyers and sales representatives can view the line and place orders without the manufacturer producing actual prototypes. Pieces of the line can be combined in a video presentation to show a variety of coordinating combinations. Video presentations can be customized for a specific customer. A photograph of the customer's site can be "dubbed" in the background. For example, "One uniform manufacturer uses its CAD system to create presentations for buyers that visualize what the uniforms actually will look like in a particular environment" (Gilbert, 1995, p. 49).

An advantage of computer-generated buying is that key buyers can "forecast" the hot-selling styles. As more aspects of design, development, and production are computerized and software programs are fully integrated, the time savings increase exponentially. The new style can be created by the designer on a three-dimensional CAD system, revised by the design team, shown to buyers (even in remote locations), and orders placed without the cost of developing a prototype.

Computer-generated buying systems that are part of an integrated computer-generated garment design, pattern, and material utilization system enhance the entire process of creating and marketing a new line. Linking the computer-aided design system to the computer-integrated manufacturing system provides the maximum cost efficiency, speed, accuracy, and quality. For example, it is possible to predict the efficiency of the fabric usage for a style and to revise the garment design for a more efficient fabric utilization without going through the pattern making process. Chapters 9 and 11 discuss computer applications in the pre-production and production processes.

JOB FUNCTIONS OF THE SALES REPRESENTATIVE

The sales representative (whether a company sales rep or an independent multiline sales rep) performs a number of job functions, including selling activities, selling support activities, and nonselling activities (Howerton & Summers, 1988). The most obvious of the functions that sales representatives perform are the selling functions (see Color Plate 9). These include the following:

  showing lines to retail buyers and demonstrating product features

  negotiating terms of sale

  writing orders for merchandise

In negotiating the terms of sale, the sales representative and retail buyer will focus on several areas, including delivery date, cooperative advertising, and discounts (see Terms of Sale section, later in the chapter).

Order writing software has reduced the amount of time that manufacturers' sales representatives spend on writing orders. Sales representatives will use software systems whereby they can do the following:

  access up-to-date inventory information

  enter orders for next-day shipment

  analyze information from the order database

Sales representatives also perform a number of activities that support and expand the selling function, including the following:

  advising retail buyers regarding trends related to the target customer

  providing retailers with product and merchandising information

  training buyers and/or salespeople to promote and advertise the merchandise

  ordering and reordering merchandise for retailers to guarantee sufficient inventory

- dealing with complaints from retail customers regarding merchandise orders
- promoting customer relations

In addition, sales representatives perform many nonselling activities, including the following:

- making travel arrangements
- writing reports for the company
- keeping books of account
- attending sales meetings
- participating in market week activities, such as fashion shows
- managing and maintaining the showroom or trade booth (see Figure 8.11)

Although their career paths vary greatly, many sales representatives have retail buying experience before they become sales representatives. With this background, they understand the retail buying process and can address the needs of retail buyers.

Orders and Canceled Orders

The sales reps work with the retail buyers in placing orders for merchandise to be produced and delivered to the retailer. It is important to keep in mind that not every style in the line that is presented to buyers will be produced. Usually, only those styles that have a sufficient number of orders from retail buyers will be produced. Therefore, at the time the buyer places the order for a specific style, in specified colors and sizes, the order is tentative. Whether a specific style in a specific color will be produced is based on the cumulative orders from other retail buyers. The style will be produced only if the minimum number of orders for the style and color is achieved. The minimum number of items required to put a style into production is based on any of a number of factors. Sometimes a minimum order is based on the fabric manufacturer's minimum yardage requirement. Or the minimum order might be determined by the contractor who will sew the style. In some cases, a minimum of 300 units might be required, whereas with another company, the minimum order might be 3,000 units.

Thus, retail buyers place orders without knowing for certain whether every style they order in the preferred color will be produced. Orders can be canceled due to the following reasons:

- There are insufficient orders for a particular style or color.

In addition to selling merchandise to retail buyers, sales representatives also manage showrooms or trade booths (top). Temporary showrooms or booths are often set up during market weeks to show lines to retail buyers (bottom).

The fabric is not available from the textile manufacturer. The textile company will produce the fabric only if a sufficient number of yards has been ordered by various apparel companies to meet the textile manufacturer's minimum order. This creates a domino effect in these interrelated industries.

- A variety of production problems can occur, both with the textile manufacturer and with the apparel production facilities.

- Natural disasters and political crises in countries where the merchandise is being produced can make it impossible to meet retailers' orders.

When a retailer's order for a style cannot be filled by the apparel or home fashions manufacturer, the retailer may be willing to accept a substitute style or color. Or, the retailer may cancel the order, filling in any gaps in apparel style choices on the retail floor with merchandise from other companies.

Terms of Sale

A number of **terms of sale** are negotiated between the sales representative and retail buyer, including the following:

- delivery time for the goods to be delivered

- guarantees related to whether styles ordered will, in fact, be produced

- reorder capabilities and timing of the reorders (especially important for basic merchandise, such as jeans or hosiery, for which continuous inventory is essential to optimum sales)

- cooperative advertising allowances (will the manufacturer or retailer help pay for advertising?)

- discounts if bills are paid within a certain time period

- discounts if a certain quantity is purchased

- markdown allowances (is any credit given on goods that had to be marked down?)

- availability of promotion tools such as gift-with-purchase promotions or displays

As orders are placed by the retailer for styles in the new line, delivery dates and payment terms are arranged between the manufacturer and the retailer. If the manufacturer does not meet the delivery date, the manufacturer may be required to take a reduced payment for the shipment, or the retailer may be allowed to cancel the order. Late delivery may be the result of fabric arriving late from the textile mill, production delays with the contractor, or delays in transportation. With offshore production and the resulting time needed for communication and transportation, delays can be a problem. A manufacturer may have to pay the much greater cost of air shipment, instead of using sea transportation, to avoid a late penalty and the risk of losing the retailer's business.

The manufacturer needs to be aware of financial problems facing the retailer, especially in today's business environment of mergers, takeovers, and bankruptcies. For example, on the eve of a predicted announcement of bankruptcy by a major retailer, the management of a large apparel company faced the decision of whether to ship a large order to the retailer. If the retailer remained in business, the late shipment penalty would cost the apparel company substantially. However, if bankruptcy occurred, the apparel company would lose far more money by shipping the goods. These are difficult management decisions.

The primary goal of a company's distribution policies is to make sure the merchandise is sold to stores that cater to the customers for whom the merchandise was designed and manufactured (the target customers). Thus, it is important for apparel and home fashions marketers to identify store characteristics and geographic areas that will optimize the availability of the merchandise to the target customers. For example, a manufacturer of designer price zone men's suits may identify specialty stores in areas where residents have above-average incomes as its primary retail customers. A manufacturer of moderate-priced women's sportswear, on the other hand, may identify department stores as its primary retail customer. Once these basic criteria are established, apparel marketers must next decide on the company's policy regarding merchandise distribution. In general, there are two basic distribution policies: **open-distribution policy** and **selected-distribution policy**.

With open-distribution policy, the manufacturer will sell to any retailer that meets the basic characteristics.

With selected-distribution policy, manufacturers establish detailed criteria that stores must meet in order for them to carry the manufacturer's merchandise. Typically, the criteria focus on the following:

expected sales volume

geographic area

store image

For example, some manufacturers will sell their merchandise to only one or two retailers within a certain geographic region; others will sell only to retailers that portray an image that is consistent with the merchandise; others will sell only to retail accounts that can purchase a specified amount of merchandise.

Based on these decisions, apparel and home fashions marketers focus on retail accounts that are consistent with their distribution policy. Distribution strategies will be discussed further in Chapter 12.

International Marketing

As U.S. apparel and home fashions companies expand their businesses to include foreign markets, it is important to review the ways in which apparel is marketed internationally. There are four basic ways apparel and home fashions are marketed internationally (Ellis, 1995, p. 10):

1. *Direct Sales:* In some cases, U.S. manufacturers sell directly to foreign retailers through independent or company sales representatives.

2. *Selling through Agents:* In some cases, U.S. manufacturers prefer to use international agents to handle the selling function in other countries. These agents have expertise in market demand, import/export issues, and international currency issues. Therefore, they can facilitate the establishment and processing of international accounts.

3. *Selling through Exclusive Distribution Agreements:* In some cases, U.S. manufacturing companies have established agreements with specific international retailers for the exclusive distribution of their merchandise.

4. *Marketing through Foreign Licensees in a Specific Country or Region:* In some cases, U.S. manufacturers license their lines to foreign companies. These licensing arrangements with foreign companies facilitate the marketing of the goods internationally.

Sales Promotion Strategies

Apparel and home fashions companies have essentially two groups of customers that need to know about their lines: retailers and consumers. Thus, sales promotion strategies developed by apparel and home fashions companies will focus on both of these groups. Apparel and home fashions companies use a number of promotion strategies to let retailers and consumers know about their merchandise. Decisions regarding promotion strategies are based on the following:

- company's advertising budget
- characteristics of its target customer
- characteristics of the product line
- area of distribution

Promotion strategies include advertising, publicity, and other promotion tools made available to retailers.

ADVERTISING

Through paid **advertising**, apparel and home fashions companies buy space or time in the print or broadcast media to promote their lines to retailers and consumers. Although some large companies may have in-house advertising departments, most companies hire advertising agencies to develop campaigns for them. Large companies that manufacture a brand name or designer merchandise (e.g., Nike, Ralph Lauren, Calvin Klein) can spend millions of dollars per year on advertising. Companies can also share the cost of the advertisement with a retailer, trade association, or another manufacturer through **cooperative advertising**, or **co-op advertising**. For example, a company and a retailer may share the cost of an advertisement that features both the merchandise and the retailer (see Figure 8.12).

The specific print, broadcast, or electronic media used in advertising campaigns depends upon the following:

- advertising budget
- target audience
- product line
- company image

For example, a company may rely on advertisements in trade publications, such as *Women's Wear Daily* or *DNR*, when targeting retailers. When targeting consumers, designers such as Donna Karan or Calvin Klein may focus on slick print advertisements in fashion magazines; companies that

Figure 8.12 Cooperative advertisements are often used to connect a brand name with a retailer in the consumer's mind.

manufacture national brand name merchandise (e.g., Russell, Levi's, Fruit of the Loom, or Nike) or store brands (e.g., Gap, Victoria's Secret) may use television ads to reach a wide audience.

PUBLICITY

Although the effect of positive **publicity** is the same as advertising (to promote lines to retailers and to consumers), unlike advertising, publicity is not controlled by the marketer. With publicity, the company or the company's line is viewed as "newsworthy" and thus receives coverage in print or electronic media or on television or radio. For example, media coverage of designers' runway shows often results in news stories and photographs or videos of the designers' collections in trade (e.g., *Women's Wear Daily*, *DNR*) or consumer newspapers, magazines, on television, or on the Internet. Sometimes, the company will create news by sending out news releases about its company or lines. The primary advantage of publicity to the apparel or home fashions company is that the company does not have to pay the media source for communicating information about the company. In addition, consumers may respond positively to publicity that includes a third-party endorsement, since the endorsement may be perceived as more credible than a marketer-controlled advertisement. The primary disadvantage of publicity is that the company has little control over how the company or its merchandise will be portrayed.

OTHER PROMOTION TOOLS

A number of other tools are provided by apparel companies to promote their lines to retailers and to consumers:

- line catalogs or brochures
- media kits
- DVDs
- electronic communications
- direct mail inserts
- visual merchandising tools
- trunk shows
- merchandise representatives
- style testing and participation promotions

Line Catalogs or Line Brochures
Line catalogs or line brochures provide important information about the line to retail buyers (see Figure 8.13 and Color Plate 8). They include photographs

or drawings of the items in the line, along with style numbers, sizing information, colors (some may even include fabric swatches), and information regarding ordering procedures and guidelines.

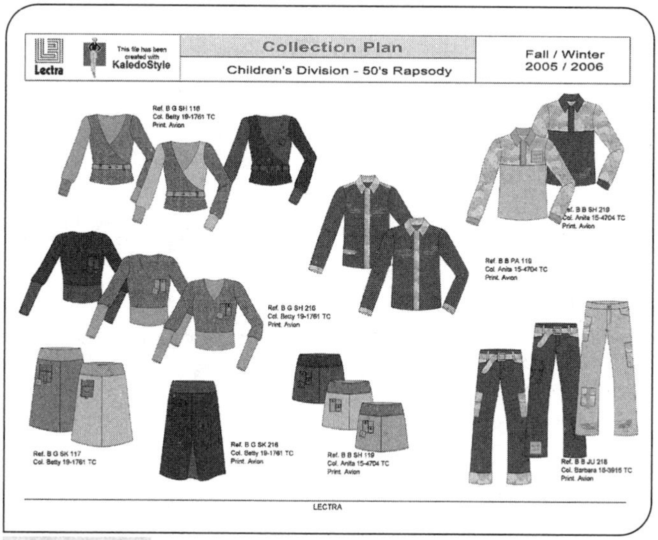

Media Kits

Photographs, media releases, television or radio spots, and other information are sometimes provided by manufacturers for publicity purposes or for retailers to use in advertisements.

Figure 8.13 The line catalog or line brochure shows all of the styles, sizes, and colors available for a line. Sales representatives and retail buyers use the line brochure to place orders.

DVDs

Manufacturers may provide DVDs for use by retailers in training their sales associates about the line or in promoting the line to consumers. For example, DVDs may be used to demonstrate visual displays, to demonstrate product usage, or to give fashion or styling information.

Electronic Communications

Communications technology is being used by apparel and home fashions manufacturers to promote goods to retailers, as well as to the ultimate consumer. Some companies, such as New Jersey-based Burlington Coat Factory, use Web sites with virtual showrooms where retail buyers can "walk" through the showroom to view new seasonal lines. Other companies, such as Liz Claiborne, use private networks called *extranets* to communicate with their manufacturing and retail partners. Benefits include the ease of communication and simplification of order tracking. Liz Claiborne also has a Web-based system that allows retail buyers to place orders for merchandise online. Manufacturers and retailers have found the following advantages of business-to-business (B2B) Web technology (see Figure 8.14):

- No appointments are necessary.

- Paperwork is reduced.

- Because buyers need an ID and password to log on, security issues are resolved.

Figure 8.14   Apparel industry manufacturers and retailers find it advantageous to use B2B Web technology.

Many companies also have Web sites designed as online stores for consumers to purchase goods (see additional discussion of e-commerce in Chapter 12). In addition, these sites assist manufacturers in gathering information about their target customers.

Direct Mail Inserts

As a form of cooperative advertising, manufacturers may provide promotion inserts to be included with retail store mailings (e.g., credit card bills).

Visual Merchandising Tools

A variety of visual merchandising tools may be provided by apparel companies. These can range from providing posters and signs to setting up actual in-store shops and supplying all the necessary fixtures (e.g., Ralph Lauren's in-store shops).

Trunk Shows

Typically, a retail buyer will not purchase a company's entire line for the store. Through the use of **trunk shows**, a representative from the company (or the designer himself or herself) will bring the entire line (or part of a line) to a store. Customers invited to attend the showing can purchase or order any piece in the line, whether or not it will be carried by the store (see Figure 8.15). Designers often make appearances at their trunk shows to promote their collections.

Trunk shows can benefit manufacturers, retailers, and consumers in the following ways:

- Manufacturers use trunk shows not only to promote their lines, but also to get consumers' reactions to their merchandise.

- For retailers, trunk shows provide an opportunity to offer an exclusive service to their customers. They also provide feedback from their customers about their tastes and preferences.

- Customers benefit because they have access to the full line of merchandise. "For shoppers who love fashion and want the luxury of reviewing and trying on a designer's entire collection in an uncrowded setting, but don't mind waiting a couple of months for their goods to arrive, trunk shows are a good bet" (Agins, 2001, p. B1).

Trunk shows are used to promote apparel lines to prospective customers.

Merchandise Representatives

A growing trend is the use of *specialists*, *merchandisers*, or *sales executives*, who are paid either partly by the apparel company and partly by the retailer or entirely by the apparel company, but who work in the retail store(s). These individuals may be based in one store or may travel to various stores within a region. Their role is to do the following:

- educate the retail sales staff and consumers about the merchandise

- demonstrate display procedures

- assist retailers in maintaining appropriate stock

- get feedback from the retailers and consumers for the apparel company

Style Testing and Participation Promotions

Active sportswear companies often ask retail executives and athletes to test styles in a line or participate in sports activities as a way of promoting the line to retailers and ultimate consumers. For example, Columbia Sportswear invited selected retailers, sales reps, and skiers to test a new performance-oriented outerwear line on the slopes of Oregon's Mount Hood. The retailers could learn about the product, and Columbia Sportswear could hear suggestions from both retailers and ultimate consumers. Nike has invited retailers to go golfing, Patagonia has sponsored kayaking trips for retailers, and Fila has taken retail executives sailing to promote its sailing apparel (Feitelberg, 1999).

Summary

The marketing of apparel and home fashions products connects market research with the appropriate strategies for getting the right product to the target consumers at the right time, at the right price, and in the right place. Markets for apparel lines can be any city where apparel marts and showrooms are located. Market centers (New York City, Los Angeles, Dallas, Chicago, and Atlanta) are large markets with important manufacturing and retailing industries. All U.S. market centers, except New York City, have an apparel or merchandise mart that houses showrooms and exhibition halls used during market weeks. Marts can also be found in a number of other cities throughout the United States. In New York City, showrooms are located in buildings throughout the fashion center in midtown Manhattan. During specific times of the year, known as *market weeks*, buyers come to apparel markets to purchase merchandise for their stores. They may also attend trade shows sponsored by apparel marts or trade associations.

The selling function of apparel and home fashions companies is handled either through corporate selling or through sales representatives who work out of permanent or temporary showrooms. Sales representatives serve as liaisons between manufacturers and retailers. Some sales representatives work from a corporate showroom and focus on the line(s) of one company; others are multiline sales reps, representing a number of related but noncompeting lines. The job of sales representatives includes both selling and nonselling functions.

Apparel and home fashions marketers develop distribution and promotion strategies for their company. In general, there are two basic distribution policies: open distribution and selected distribution. These policies help determine which retail customers will be the focus of selling efforts. Sales promotion strategies of apparel and home fashions companies are directed to both retail customers and consumers. Strategies may include advertising, publicity, and other promotion tools.

The marketing of apparel and home fashions has career opportunities for individuals who manage apparel or merchandise marts, organize market weeks and trade shows, and serve as sales representatives, as well as those who perform promotion work such as advertising and public relations. For these careers, an understanding of the marketing process, product knowledge, creativity, organizational skills, analytical skills, and negotiation skills are important.

Field Sales Representative
Privately Owned Designer Hosiery Company

Position Description
Sell basic stock and seasonal merchandise to the hosiery buyers for major department stores and specialty stores within a specific region; service the accounts that carry the merchandise within the sales territory.

Typical Tasks and Responsibilities

- Prepare six-month merchandise plans in retail and cost dollars.

- Write orders.

- Obtain buyers' approvals for orders.

- Visit store accounts.

- Talk to sales associates about the merchandise.

- Entertain buyers and divisional merchandise managers.

- Make sure goods are shipped as planned.

- Keep in close contact with buyers and report on the status of orders.

- Plan and help with store promotions.

- Analyze sales using spreadsheets with sell-through and stock-to-sales ratios and stock turns for each stockkeeping unit by store.

- Plan model stocks (13-week supply) based on sales analysis (basic stock fill-in orders or automatic reorders are based on model stock plans).

- Hire and supervise merchandisers who also visit store accounts and conduct inventories.

Key Terms

advertising
co-op advertising
cooperative advertising
corporate selling
corporate showroom
internal selling
market
market center
market week
mart

multiline sales representative
open-distribution policy
publicity
regional sales territory
sales representative
selected-distribution policy
showroom
terms of sale
trunk show
virtual sample

Discussion Questions

1. Interview a retail buyer in your community. Document the type of retailer (e.g., specialty store, department store) and the type of merchandise offered (e.g., children's wear, men's wear). Ask which markets or trade shows the buyer attends and why. Compare your findings with those of your classmates. Are there any patterns in market attendance related to geographic area, type of retailer, or type of merchandise?

2. Find two examples of co-op print advertisements in either a trade publication or a consumer publication. What companies and/or associations joined forces for each advertisement? What are the advantages and disadvantages for the companies in using co-op ads as part of their promotion strategy?

3. Locate the Web site of an apparel manufacturer. What type of information is provided on the site? Would this information be useful to retailers, to the target customer, or to both? Evaluate the site as to its effectiveness.

References

Agins, Teri. (2001, February 5). Trunk show chic. *The Wall Street Journal*, pp. B1, B4.

AmericasMart (2006). AmericasMart—Atlanta [online]. Available: http://www.americasmart.com [September 5, 2006].

California Market Center (2006). California Market Center [online]. Available: http://www.californiamarketcenter.com [September 5, 2006].

Cedrone, Lisa. (1991, December). Moving in on the marts. *Bobbin*, pp. 75–80.

Corwin, J. Blade. (1989, March). What it takes (& pays) to sell. *Bobbin*, pp. 76–82.

Dallas Market Center (2006). Dallas Market Center [online]. Available: http://www.dallasmarketcenter.com [September 10, 2006].

Daniels, Linda. (1996, March). Getting orders faster. *Apparel Industry Magazine*, pp. 46–48.

Ellis, Kristi. (1995, October). U.S. firms look overseas. *Women's Wear Daily*, p. 10.

Feitelberg, Rosemary. (1999, April 29). Retailers get a real workout. *Women's Wear Daily*, p. 12.

Feitelberg, Rosemary. (1999, December 15). Stores sticking to trade shows. *Women's Wear Daily*, p. 15.

Foxenberger, Barbara. (1994, April). West Coast harbors apparel niches. *Apparel Industry Magazine*, pp. 18–26.

Freedman, Linda. (1990, April). New developments in computer-aided draping. *Apparel Manufacturer*, pp. 12–14.

Friedman, Arthur. (1994, August 3). FCBID building a better SA. *Women's Wear Daily*, pp. 20–21.

Gilbert, Laurel. (1995, July). CAD comes of age. *Bobbin*, pp. 48–52.

Howerton, Renee, and Summers, Teresa A. (1988, Spring). Apparel sales representatives: Perceptions of their roles and functions. *FIT Review*, 4 (2), pp. 10–18.

Lee, Georgia. (1999, December 15). Timing is everything. *Women's Wear Daily*, pp. 4–5.

Los Angeles County Economic Development Corporation (2003, February 10). Fashion 2003 [online]. Available: http://www.laedc.org/reports/fashion-2003.pdf [September 15, 2006].

Lytle, Lisa. (1990, October). The west side story. *Earnshaw's Review*, pp. 99–106.

Mart to mart. (1993, March 8). *California Apparel News*, pp. 28–34.

Rabon, Lisa C., and Abend, Jules. (1999, May). VF takes e-commerce plunge. *Bobbin*, pp. 49–52.

Smarr, Susan L. (1988, April). Seattle: Supersonic sportswear star. *Bobbin*, pp. 75–78.

Williamson, Rusty. (1999, December 15). Big plans in Big D. *Women's Wear Daily*, p. 13.

Part 3

Apparel Production and Distribution

CHAPTER 9

Preproduction Processes

In this chapter, you will learn the following:

- the role of financial agencies, called factors, in the apparel industry

- the process and timing used by apparel companies to order production fabrics and trims

- scheduling and management considerations in ordering production fabrics and trims

- the processes used to finalize a production pattern, grade the pattern, create a production marker, and to cut, spread, and bundle the fabric pieces

- ways in which grade rules, size range, styling, cost considerations, and grading processes influence pattern grading

- the advantages to the apparel company of computer grading and marker making over other grading and marker making methods

- uses of company Web sites, e-mail communication, and related technologies in preproduction

Step 5: Preproduction

Research and Merchandising

Design

Design Development and Style Selection

Marketing the Apparel Line

Preproduction

Order Production Fabrics, Trims, and Findings

Finalize Production Pattern and Written Documents

Grade Production Pattern into Size Range

Make Production Marker

Inspect Fabric

Spread, Cut, Bundle, and Manage Dye Lots for Production

Sourcing

Apparel Production Processes,
Material Management, and Quality Assurance

Distribution and Retailing

Production Orders

he sales force has shown the new line to retailers during market week, and the retail buyers have placed their orders with the apparel or home fashions company. As discussed in Chapters 7 and 8, those styles in specific colors and sizes that meet the company's required minimum order will continue in the development process. Usually, styles that do not attain the minimum number of orders will be dropped from the line. Sometimes after a week or two of selling the line, a manufacturer will decide to drop a style that is not selling well. Let us imagine that, for the style we are following through the development process, a sufficient number of orders has been placed to warrant a production run (see Step 5 of the flowchart on the previous page).

Factoring

A company's financial credit line is an important consideration prior to the approval of any business transactions or approval of work orders. Therefore, apparel manufacturers, contractors, and retailers need to establish a credit line or cash advance so they can buy materials in advance of the season in which payment will be received.

Because of the nature of retailing fashion products, there is a high level of financial risk in the textile and apparel industries. Commercial banks are used by some textile and apparel businesses for their financial backing. However, their interest rates may be high, and some commercial banks are not willing to accept the degree of risk involved with fashion-related companies. Therefore, another type of financial agency called a **factor** is often used. **Factoring** is "the business of purchasing and collecting accounts receivable or of advancing cash on the basis of accounts receivable" (Young, 1996, p. 1). As an example, the factoring agency advances (loans) money to the apparel company so that the apparel company can pay the textile mill for the fabric that has been delivered. The loan allows the apparel company to pay for fabrics well in advance of the date that the apparel company receives its payment for the new styles that the retailer has purchased from the apparel company.

Factoring agencies are the companies that provide protection against bad debt losses, manage accounts receivable, and provide credit analysis in the apparel industry. The factor's procedures include the following:

running a credit check on the company

approving a credit line to the company

approving the orders for shipping to the company

receiving the invoices from the company's suppliers

advancing the cash needed to pay the invoices to the company

The company pays interest on the money advanced until the company can repay the factor. Usually, a 60-day or 90-day payment period has been arranged between the factor and the company. The length of the time period is determined by the length of time the company usually waits to be paid by its customers. For example, based on the terms of agreement, the textile producer might need to wait 90 days after shipping the fabric to the apparel manufacturer to receive payment for the fabric. The factor's fees are similar to the interest paid on credit card debt. For example, a large apparel manufacturer might be charged the prime rate plus 1 percent of the value of each invoice.

Small apparel companies often do not qualify for financial backing by a factor because their sales volume is lower than the factor's minimum. Therefore, such companies go to refactor agencies that take smaller accounts—those apparel companies "with sales as low as $250,000 and ranging up to $5 million or more" (Rutberg, 1997, p. 12).

Before production can begin, the financial arrangements must be approved by the company's factoring firm or other lending institution. Examples of the credit checks that are done include the following:

The textile producer checks the credit of the apparel manufacturer before shipping fabric to the manufacturer.

The manufacturer checks the credit of the contractor before shipping fabric or cut goods to the contractor.

The contractor may check the credit of the manufacturer before deciding to accept the order.

The manufacturer checks the credit of the retailer before shipping finished goods to the retailer.

The retailer may check the credit of the manufacturer before deciding to place an order.

Keep in mind that the apparel manufacturer has paid the textile producer for the fabric and the contractor for the labor many months before the manufacturer is paid for the goods by the retailer. Some type of lending institution is used by all of these participants. After approval of credit, production can proceed. Some manufacturers will decide to take an account on their own, without the factor's approval. For example, a manufacturer may decide to sell to a new retail account, such as a specialty store that has just opened and has not yet established credit. In this situation, the manufacturer carries the financial risk that the specialty store will pay the manufacturer for the merchandise delivered to the store.

Now that sufficient orders have been placed and the retailers' credit standings have been approved, the style is ready for the next step in development: preproduction.

Product Data (or Development) Management and Product Lifecycle Management

Some of the advantages of using computer systems such as PDM/PLM throughout the development process or throughout the lifecycle of a new style were discussed in previous chapters. Software provides seamless integration among all of these segments of a new style's development process (see Figure 9.1). A drawing created by the designer on a graphics program can be integrated into the garment specification sheet *(spec sheet)* used by design development, preproduction, and production personnel. Data from the garment specification sheet can be integrated with the bill of materials and other forms needed for production. The first pattern created by the pattern maker using a pattern design system (PDS) is used for the production pattern. The PDS base pattern used for the new style can include the measurement dimensions and sizing standards (grade rules) coded into the base pattern, providing integration between design development and preproduction. In addition, some software programs are integrated so that a change on one form triggers that change to be made on all other forms in the database system. For example, changing the zipper length on a garment spec sheet will trigger a change on the bill of materials, the form used to order the zippers. While this system has many advantages, it can also mean that a mistake will be transmitted throughout the system, too.

Companies rely more and more on computer system integration, both internally (within the company) and externally (outside the company). Maintaining accurate and up-to-the-minute information about each style (and every change in each style during design development) in the line will increase the speed of work flow and increase accuracy within the system for all company personnel who need access to the data.

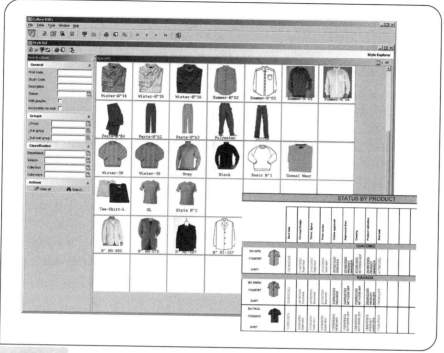

Figure 9.1 A PLM system, such as GalleryWeb software, enables a system server to provide authorized access to style information anywhere in the world by means of electronic communication.

Providing electronic access to style information to external contacts, such as vendors and contractors, speeds information exchange and increases accuracy as well. Garment specifications can be shared instantly with contractors who intend to bid on production jobs. Web technology provides global exchange of product specifications and other pertinent information within companies and throughout contractor networks.

GFT Donna is the women's wear division of Italy's largest apparel company. This company provides an example of the benefits of using CAD and product lifecycle management systems:

> GFT Donna has made each product easily accessible to the circle of those who style, cost, order, supply, and buy. Connected to that circle, a multinational network of high-end contractors does the actual cutting and sewing in Italy, Portugal, Romania, Hungary, and the Far East. The new system allows complex sourcing decisions to be made at lightning speed, without losing sight of the creative function of the enterprise. (Conrad, 1999, p. 38)

With Web access to style information by vendors and contractors, the speed of receiving price quotes is greatly enhanced, and the possibility for errors is greatly reduced. Sears was one of the early users of PDM/PLM, adapting the software to meet its specific needs. The director of product development stated:

> Between reducing errors by as much as 30 percent because of clear, detailed specs and increasing productivity by as much as 50 percent, the application has more than paid for itself. We've also eliminated faxes and overnight packages, which is quite a savings. And because vendors have quicker access and get digital photos and scanned documents with specs, it lessens their work as well. (Hill, 1999, p. 71)

Another advantage of PDM/PLM software is enhanced work flow management. Some of the PDM/PLM systems include calendar functions that set the dates when each phase of the new style's development needs to be completed. "As individuals complete a form or their sections of it, the application generates the next activity and sends it to the next person" (Hill, 1999, p. 54).

Cut Orders

A production **cut order** is issued in either of the following two situations:

- when a targeted number of orders for a style has been placed by retailers and received by the manufacturer
- when the apparel manufacturer decides to produce a style prior to receiving orders

The cut order specifies the number of items in each color and each size that will be included in the production run. A cut order for a specific style might include cutting fewer small sizes and more large sizes, and may contain a mix of colors for each size. For example, a cut order for Style XXYY might include 80 items of size 6, divided into 24 of color A, 24 of color B, 16 of color C, and 16 of color D; 160 items of size 8 of the same style, divided into 40 of color A, 60 of color B, 40 of color C, and 20 of color D; and so forth. The cut order includes the date when the goods must be delivered to each retailer. Thus, the production schedule is calculated from end to beginning—that is, from the retailer's delivery date backward, to the date when production of the goods must be finished, to the date production must begin, to the date when the fabrics, trims, and findings must be ordered.

In an ideal situation, the apparel company would be able to wait until the majority of retail buyers had placed their orders before ordering the needed quantity of fabrics from the textile producers (a production run of one style might require 6,000 yards of fabric), as well as ordering the trims and findings for each style in the new line. Such a situation would eliminate any financial risk that would result from ordering fabric that might turn out not to be needed. If apparel companies were to wait to order fabrics until they knew exactly how much of each fabric in their lines would be needed, they would have to wait weeks for the fabrics to arrive from the textile producers. If textile producers, not wanting to risk manufacturing excess fabric, were also to wait until the apparel companies had ordered fabric before beginning to produce the yardage to fill the manufacturers' orders, the apparel company would have to wait even longer, perhaps months, for the production yardage to be manufactured and delivered to the sewing facility. Producing the apparel goods would probably take several more weeks. As you can imagine, these cumulative delays would be so lengthy that the retailers would not receive the goods at the peak selling time. Thus, the apparel company is positioned between the textile producer and the retailer, with pressures from both sides. As one observer described it:

> In the middle of the supply chain, set against conflicting priorities, are apparel manufacturers. On one side are the retailers who ask for a variety of garments by size and color variation, delivered frequently in small lots, just in time for merchandising. On the other side, there are fabric mills that want to produce long runs and require advance commitments from manufacturers. (Gaffney, 1999, pp. 74–75)

In reality, few apparel companies can afford to wait until all, or nearly all, of the buyers' orders are placed before ordering production fabric for the line. Therefore, apparel companies use a variety of means to determine how much yardage to order and when to order the yardage from the textile producers. Furthermore, some companies begin production on some styles before the buyers' orders have been received. This helps maintain an even work flow during production. These methods include the following:

- early production of proven sellers in basic colors
- the use of preline selling
- the use of early-season lines to predict sales
- the use of test markets
- the use of past sales figures

Some companies will project production estimates of some of the more "staple" styles and colors, especially if these are carryovers from a previous season. Some colors are known to sell especially well. For example, skiwear manufacturers know that black ski pants tend to sell well every year. Therefore, they may decide to begin early production on several styles of "proven sellers" in this basic color. Early production also allows the company to maintain a constant production flow in order to avoid times when the factories are overcommitted.

Preline selling was discussed in Chapter 7. Some apparel companies invite key retail accounts to place orders prior to market weeks. Early production of these styles can be advantageous to both retailers and apparel companies. Swimwear companies might use an early-season line to help predict which styles will sell well. An early January line of swimsuits sold at resorts in Florida could be used to help forecast production of the Spring line to be introduced to northern climates in April. Some of the hot-selling styles from Florida retail sales could be put into production for the main selling season before the line is sold at market to retailers in the rest of the country.

Sometimes a specific region is targeted as a *test market*, in which a small production run of the new line will be placed in key stores. Occasionally, an apparel company has its own test store(s), in which early sales help forecast production quantities. Levi Strauss & Co. also uses some of its stores as test markets for new styles. This "provides some sort of sell-through background [in order to give the retailers] some sort of data on whether it's a valuable new style" (DesMarteau, 2003, p. 35).

Past sales figures and the opinions of leading sales representatives and leading retail buyers might be used to determine which styles and colors might go into early production. For styles that are carryovers, production might be started prior to buyers' orders since management is fairly certain these styles will sell well.

Selection of Vendors

Using as much information as possible as early as possible, production yardage, trims, and findings are ordered from the various **vendors** (or **sources** or **suppliers**) of textiles, trims, and findings. Many variables influence the selection of vendors, including the following:

- lead time needed to secure the goods
- past history of on-time delivery
- the quality of goods
- whether the vendor uses supply chain management strategies
- the minimum yardage (or quantity) requirement for an order
- the financial stability of the vendor

Some manufacturers will ask for bids from several vendors as part of the decision making process. There are software programs that provide cost comparisons based on inputting variables such as material costs from different vendors. Clearly, the selection of fabric and trim vendors is based on many important considerations. Sourcing will be discussed in more detail in Chapter 10.

Production Fabric Considerations

During the process of planning production fabric orders, constant communication occurs between the apparel company and the fabric vendors. Vigilance is required to ensure that the production fabric matches the fabric used for the samples. Some of the fabric considerations include color control, lab dips, and strike offs. Various requirements are also important considerations when ordering printed fabrics, staple fabrics, and trims and findings.

PREPRODUCTION COLOR MANAGEMENT

During preproduction processes, the apparel company needs to finalize a number of aspects regarding the fabrics that will be ordered for the new line. Chapter 7 discussed some of the aspects of color management; for example, one requirement was that all components of the prototype accurately match the intended color for the new style (see Figure 9.2).

As discussed in Chapter 7, staff in the design development department might be responsible for working with the textile, trims, and findings vendors to develop and maintain exact color matching of all components of each style and to ensure that all products in the entire production run maintain the specified color match. Color management may begin at the prototype stage if a textile is to be dyed to match a color chip or swatch provided by the apparel company. If available, the specially dyed sample goods are used to make the prototype. Trim, findings, sample yardage, and production yardage will be ordered to match the prototype color.

It is important to the consumer, and thus to the retailer and the apparel company, that colors remain consistent throughout all the components that are used to make a garment style. First, the color of the garment style needs to match the

Figure 9.2 Color management software programs enhance the ability to manage all the color data for a line.

color intended by the design team. This could require that the fabric vendor submit test samples until the "perfect" color is achieved. The trims and findings, such as buttons, zippers, and thread, must also match the garment color. If the color of the rib knit used for the sleeve band of a rugby shirt is not the same shade as the body of the shirt, the consumer will quite likely decide not to purchase the garment. Thus, when contractors supply the trims and findings for the products they make, it is important that they receive approval of the color match from the apparel company. An acceptable color match for contractor-provided matched goods is referred to as a **commercial match**.

When producing coordinated items in a line, color management can be a challenge. A fabric composed of one fiber might be selected for pants, and a fabric composed of another fiber or blend of fibers might be selected for the top. For example, rayon crepe pants might be planned to match a silk jersey tank. However, the color of the pants may not look like an exact color match to the tank because of the different reflective qualities of the fibers and fabrics. As another example of color management concerns, adjacent colors in plaid and print fabrics tend to affect their neighboring colors' hue, value, and intensity. Because of this optical effect, a color in a print or plaid may not look like it matches its solid-colored coordinate, even though when viewed by itself, the color in the plaid or print does match the color standard. Thus, much time can be spent on perfecting the colors in a line.

To ensure that color matching will be as perfect as possible, the vendor will supply a sample of the product (such as fabric, rib knit trim, or button) in the color requested (the apparel company might supply a fabric swatch or paint chip to the vendor that needs to be color matched). The sample the vendor supplies to the apparel company is called a **lab dip** because, in most cases, the fabric swatch (or trim or finding) was dipped in a specifically prepared dye bath in the "lab" to dye the sample (see Color Plate 5). Vendors submit lab dips (called **submits**) for all the individual components required in a line. Since various blends of fabrics and other materials absorb dyestuffs differently, accurate color matching of all components may require multiple attempts by vendors.

The Lilly Pulitzer company is known for its easily identified colors and fabric prints. As explained by its vice president of production:

> Color matching is so important to us, but the sewing, as well as the fabric and trim dyeing processes take place in so many countries—including Peru, Columbia, Hong Kong, China, the Philippines, Turkey, Portugal, the United States, and Vietnam—that it requires a long timetable to ensure the lab dips from all these locations can be approved in one place and then compared. (Speer, 2004, p. 23)

Apparel companies usually have equipment to view colors to assess their match accuracy under controlled lighting conditions. Various lighting conditions can be simulated, such as daylight, fluorescent lighting, and incandescent lighting. The fabrics under consideration are placed into a cabinet and observed under controlled lighting conditions to assess the color accuracy.

The manufacturer may require that the vendor submit results of textile tests, such as color fastness and light fastness, performed by approved textile testing laboratories, for each sample. These testing procedures are especially important for certain fabrics, such as nylon fabrics in neon bright colors. Each fabric, trim, and finding that is to match the line's color choice will require approval on a form supplied by the apparel company.

The approval process requires time and accurate record keeping. According to the vice president of production for Lilly Pulitzer, "it takes four to six weeks to complete two rounds of lab dip evaluations, and it requires two to four rounds to achieve approval. At the high end, that can mean an eight-to-twelve week color approval cycle" (Speer, 2004, p. 23). Therefore, if time can be saved in the lab dip approval process, the cycle time for style development can be shortened, thus resulting in a cost savings to the apparel company.

Enhanced computer software programs have decreased the time devoted to the color development and management processes. Datacolor's ENVISION software is one example. It includes "on-screen product simulations to eliminate the transportation of physical samples" (Cole, 2005, p. 22). Some of the software programs provide digital color communication via e-mail or the Web. Users can communicate digital color standards (for example, using the Pantone color system), send and receive color submissions, and keep records of color approvals. New computer technology can "see" beyond the human eye's color vision. The science of numeral spectral curves can be used for color management. The use of uniform digital standards allows global partners to communicate color standards electronically.

PRINTED FABRIC CONSIDERATIONS

Not all printed fabrics are printed by the textile mills that produce the fabrics. Sometimes the fabric is printed by a textile converter to the specific textile design requested by the apparel manufacturer (see Chapters 3, 6, and 7). Thus, many apparel companies work with textile converters as well as textile mills. The fabric might be purchased from the textile mill and then sent to a textile converter to print before it arrives at the cutting facility. For apparel companies that use textile converters, careful scheduling is required to ensure that the printed fabric is ready on time. Custom print fabrics require substantial lead time for orders; therefore, decisions about custom prints occur early in the design/ production process. As mentioned in Chapter 6, some apparel companies create some or all of their textile designs in-house. This also requires careful planning for lead time, as well as the considerations discussed above.

STRIKE OFF

A *strike off* is a fabric sample that is printed by the textile converter (the company printing the fabric) (see Figure 9.3). Chapter 6 discussed strike offs in relation to samples of textile prints submitted by textile converters. Usually, a strike off consists of no more than a few yards of fabric. It shows the rendition of the textile print made from the artwork submitted to the textile converter by the apparel company (or textile company that develops the print). The strike off is examined carefully by the apparel company before approval is given to print production yardage. For screen prints composed of more than one color, each color requires a separate screen. The placement of each of the screens must be exact, or the print will appear blurred. The accuracy of placement, or **registration**, of each of the color screens is checked (see Figure 9.4). The color match of each screened color is compared to color chips or fabric swatches submitted to the textile converter. The accuracy of the pattern repeat match is checked. Sometimes it is necessary for several strike offs to be made by the textile converter before approval is given.

STRIKE OFF/LAB DIP APPROVAL FORM

TO: CARA HOHENSTEIN

CC: CAITLIN THOMAS, MARIAH PAUL-BRYANT

PATTERN NAME	SUMMER EXPLOSION	COLOR CODE	CR25 RED
PATTERN NUMBER	35632-C	STYLES	S2019, S2020
VENDOR	APS	SEASON	CRUISE 2008
PRINTED ON	COTTON SHEETING	SECTION	ANN ALLEY INC.
APPROVAL	MARIAH PAUL-BRYANT		

COMMENTS APPROVED PENDING PSO. RED NEEDS MORE ORANGE-
MATCH TO SWATCH ATTACHED

A strike off is a sample of the fabric provided by the textile vendor and sent to the apparel company for approval before the textile print is produced in large quantity.

Figure 9.4   The strike off is sent from the textile mill or converter to the apparel manufacturer for approval. Sometimes it takes several attempts to gain approval. At left, the strike off has poor registration—the screen printing of the two colors was not properly aligned. At right, the approved strike off has perfect registration.

STAPLE FABRIC ORDERS

Some staple fabrics, such as linings and interfacings, and some fashion goods, such as cotton poplin and cotton broadcloth, and wool crepe and wool jersey in staple colors or piece dyed textiles, can be purchased closer to production (late-cycle ordering). These types of staple fabrics might be very suitable for online sourcing. Textile producers incorporate online technology using several automated sourcing services. The apparel manufacturer can view and order textiles using custom searches (Greco, 1996). For goods already produced and awaiting shipment at the textile producer, online sourcing is a viable option because it allows late-cycle ordering, which has advantages for the apparel manufacturer.

TRIMS AND FINDINGS

It may be necessary to order special trims very early in the planning process. For example, elastic for a waistband might be ordered in a three-color stripe to match the print colors used for pants. On the other hand, elastic in a standard width and color might be ordered just in time for production. Findings such as snaps, hooks, zippers, and thread tend to be kept in stock in large quantities at the production facility. Sometimes a new fashion color requires ordering thread or other findings that are not in stock. Thus, careful planning needs to take place to ensure that all the needed trims and findings are available for production at the appropriate time.

Decisions about findings, such as specifying the type of thread, may be more complex than one might imagine. For example, "in denim production, making the right thread choice is crucial because the garments typically are exposed to wash processes with harsh chemicals, enzymes and/or beds of stone" ("Thread selection made simple," 1999, p. 46). Some of the issues to consider for thread selection for washed jeans include the following:

- the weight of the denim being sewn

- the desired seam appearance or boldness of stitch

- the wash procedures to be used

- the desired after-wash color

- the degradation that will occur during washing ("Thread selection made simple," 1999, p. 46)

Thus, the selection process for findings may involve research and testing of some products in order to ensure a quality finished garment.

Pattern Finalization and Written Documents

The pattern for the style that has been approved for production needs to be finalized. Every detail needs to be perfect for production to run smoothly. Sometimes, minor pattern adjustments need to be made to improve ease of production. The production pattern, which has been made in the company's sample size, is then ready for **grading**; that is, each individual piece of the pattern in the sample size is remade in each of the sizes specified. Next, all the pattern pieces in all the sizes are arranged into a master cutting plan, called a **production marker**. The style is ready to move to the next stage, the production cutting and sewing operations. Each of these steps will be discussed in more detail.

Finalizing the Production Pattern

A specialist called a **production engineer** or *pattern engineer* may be part of the team that is responsible for preparing the pattern for production. Production engineers are familiar with factory production processes and types of equipment. The pattern may need some minor changes to facilitate production. The production engineer is responsible for suggesting such changes in the pattern.

He or she might also be responsible for suggesting the specific factory where production could best be accomplished.

All markings for factory production must be perfect, including the following:

- notches to ensure accurate matching of one piece to its mate
- drill holes to indicate dart tips (actually, the drill holes are marked at a specified distance from the dart tip to avoid creating a weakness in the fabric at the dart tip)
- placement for pockets or other details

One forgotten notch marking can cause production problems, especially since this notch marking would be missing on the pattern piece for the entire size range after the pattern has been graded. If the first pattern has been made on a computer pattern design system, any changes in the pattern needed at the preproduction stage can be accomplished very quickly because the pattern is already in the computer system (see Chapter 7).

Finalizing the Garment Specification Sheet

At the time the designer's sketch or drape of the style is delivered to design development, a garment specification sheet accompanies the design (see Chapter 7). The spec sheet lists all fabrics, trims, findings, and important construction details, such as placement of any logo, label type and placement, and color and weight of top-stitching thread (see Figure 9.5). Any changes that may have occurred during the development of the style must be transferred to the garment spec sheet. Any requested change not transferred to the spec sheet can cause difficulties in production. If a PDM/PLM software system is used to create and maintain the spec sheet, all changes can be made very easily as soon as they have been approved and will automatically be changed on any other necessary documents. Some computer systems include bilingual and multilingual flexibility, which is especially helpful when working with offshore sources.

Another component of the garment specifications is the bill of materials (see Figure 9.6). It lists the fabrics, trims, and findings requirements for each color of a style in the line.

Construction Specifications

Included with the written documentation that accompanies the style will be additional construction specifications related to the production sequence (see Figure 9.7). The production engineer or product technician often determines the

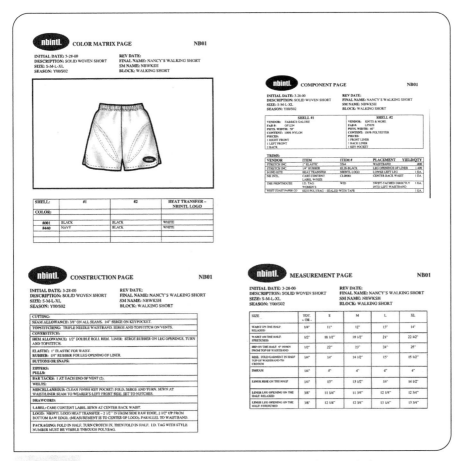

(Top left) The garment specification or spec sheet includes important information for producing the style, including the color matrix. (Top right) Fabric, trim, and findings are specified on the component page of the garment spec sheet. (Bottom left) This page of the garment spec sheet details construction-related instructions. (Bottom right) The measurement page details finished garment dimensions and allowable tolerances.

sequence of steps (what will be sewn first, second, third, and so forth) required for factory production of the style. When the style is made in a factory owned by the apparel company, the production engineer is an employee of the apparel company. When the style is made by a contractor, the contractor's production engineer determines the production sequence. The sequence of production is related to the cost to manufacture the goods. Thus, the production sequence may have been determined at the time the final cost was calculated, as discussed in Chapter 7.

```
* C O M P O N E N T *        **** O P T I O N S ****          ******** C U R R E N T / S T A N D A R D ********
S C                    Style **** ** MANUF. ***                CURR/STD    CURR/STD    CURR/STD          STD COST OWN
SEA T NUMBER    Clr    SX Clr   Dim SIZE PR Opt PL PA          PRICE UM    CONU FACT   QUANTITY UM    COST      VARIANCE DIV $

                       1  FOR DEMONSTRATION PURPOSES ONLY - DATA IS FICTITIOUS

D  A LF567B    001                                            2.5000 YD   1.0000      .3000 YD      .7500               01
   LINER FABRIC $567B                                         2.5000 YD               .3000 YD      .7500
   BLACK                                                                              STD 3/28/00 LMT 0/00/00

D  A 0F1234    001                                            2.8000 YD   1.0000      .4000 YD      1.1200              01
   OUTER FABRIC $1234      001                                3.0000 YD               .4000 YD      1.2000    .0800
   BLACK                                                                              STD 3/28/00 LMT 3/28/00

D  A 0F1234    440                                            2.9000 YD   1.0000      .4000 YD      1.1600              01
   OUTER FABRIC $1234      440                                3.0000 YD               .4000 YD      1.2000    .0400
   NAVY                                                                               STD 3/28/00 LMT 3/28/00

D  E 1/4"ELASTC 001                                           2.0000 YD   1.0000      1.4000 YD     2.8000              01
   1/4" ELASTIC FOR LINER                                     2.0000 YD               1.4000 YD     2.8000
   BLACK                                                                              STD 3/28/00 LMT 0/00/00

D  E 1"ELASTIC  100                                           2.0000 YD   1.0000      .8000 YD      1.6000              01
   1" ELASTIC FOR WAIST                                       2.0000 YD               .8000 YD      1.6000
   WHITE                                                                              STD 3/28/00 LMT 3/28/00

D  H HTNBINTL   100                                           .0500 EA    1.0000      1.0000 EA     .0500               01
   HEAT TRANSFER NBINTL                                       .0500 EA                1.0000 EA     .0500
   WHITE                                                                              STD 3/28/00 LMT 0/00/00

D  T 8X10PB                                                   .0300 EA    1.0000      1.0000 EA     .0300               01
   8 X 10 POLYBAG                                             .0300 EA                1.0000 EA     .0300
                                                                                     STD 3/28/00 LMT 3/28/00

D  W CL00001                                                  .0500 EA    1.0000      1.0000 EA     .0500               01
   CARE LABEL $1                                              .0500 EA                1.0000 EA     .0500
                                                                                     STD 3/28/00 LMT 3/28/00

D  X WOMENSID                                                 .1000 EA    1.0000      1.0000 EA     .1000               01
   WOMEN'S ID TAG WID                                         .1000 EA                1.0000 EA     .1000
                                                                                     STD 3/28/00 LMT 0/00/00


GL# C DESCRIPTION ******   PART PROC PLNT  Opt    ***** VARIABLE *******  ******* FIXED ********
                                    PCT        AMOUNT         PCT    AMOUNT
00050 NFLAM LABOR COST CMT                     2.5000                        -CUR-        3/28/00
                                               2.5000                        -STD-        3/28/00
00051 MODT OTHER INVENTORY                      .2000                        -CUR-        3/28/00
      502 CUT/MAKE/TRIM DEVD QUICK COST         .2000                        -STD-        3/28/00
      OVERHEAD ALLOWANCE

Style Clr        * * * * * * * * *  Style BILL-OF-MATERIAL COST SUMMARY * * * * * * * * * * * * * *
```

Figure 9.6 The bill of materials is used to order and track all components. Some garment styles require an extensive number of fabrics and trims.

A GUIDE TO SEWING BLUE JEANS

Union Special

Sequence Of Operations For Traditional Blue Jeans

	OPERATION NUMBER	OPERATION	RECOMMENDED MACHINE STYLE	STITCH & SEAM TYPE	
PRELIMINARY					
✔	1	Hem top of hip and watch pockets	56500R18 or FS311L51-2H72	401 EFb-2(inv.)	
✔	2	Decorative stitch hip pockets	56500R18 or FS311L51-2H72	401 OSa-2	
	3	Precrease hip and watch pockets	Pocket Creaser		
✔	4	Make belt loops	FS321J01-2A60Z	406 EFh-1	
✔	5	Attach facings to front pockets	FS311L41-2H64CC1Z3	602 LSbj-1(mod.)	
	6	Set watch pocket to right front facing	Juki LH2178	301 LSd-2	
	7	Bag pockets	Juki MO3716	516 SSa-2	
✔	8	Serge left and right fly pieces	39500CRU	504 EFd-1	
✔	9	Attach zipper tape (continuous) to left fly piece	56400PZ16	401 SSa-2	
✔	10	Attach zipper tape to right fly piece	56300G or FS311S01-1M	401 SSa-1	
FRONTS & BACKS					
	11	Set left fly piece and edgestitch	Juki DLN5410	301 SSe-2	
	12	Topstitch left fly	Juki LH2178	301 EFa-2 (inv.)	
	13	Set right fly piece and cord fly	Juki DLN5410	301 LSq-2b	
	14	Hang front pockets	Juki LH2178	301 LSd-2	
✔	15	Attach risers to backs	FS315L63-3H36CC2PA1	401 LSc-3	
	16	Set hip pockets to backs	Juki LH2178	301 LSd-2	
✔	17	Join backs (seat seam)	FS315L63-3H36CC2PA1	401 LSc-3	

✔ (Union Special machine available)

Union Special, an industrial sewing machine producer, distributes this guide, which illustrates a typical production sequence to manufacture jeans.

Experienced production engineers can examine a finished sample garment and quickly provide a reliable estimate of the number of minutes (and thus, the actual labor cost) required to sew a specific style. One of the reasons why production engineers are often included in the development design team (see Chapter 7) is that their engineering and costing experience is highly valuable as a factor in style decisions. Computer software programs can be used to help analyze cost in comparing various production sequence options.

Measurement Specifications

The actual measurements at specific locations on the finished goods for each size specified for the style will be listed on the **measurement specification** chart. Measurement specs are part of the garment specifications. For example, for a jacket style, measurement specifications for each size to be produced would be recorded in chart form and might include the following:

- chest circumference
- waist circumference
- jacket hem circumference
- back length from neck to hem
- neck circumference
- sleeve length
- sleeve lower edge circumference

Since garments are measured flat, sometimes the circumferences are measured across just the front width or just the back width. These half-circumference measurements are listed as the *sweep*. This dimensional information is important to maintain accurate sizes, especially if several factories will be used to produce the same style for a large production order. Two jackets in the same style and size may fit differently if one factory is less accurate in sewing than another.

Some computer pattern design systems include a feature that allows the pattern maker to request the dimensions at specific points on the pattern. When this is the case, the pattern maker completes the measurement specifications on a separate computer screen during the pattern making process. This saves considerable time in comparison to measuring each of the specified locations on the pattern pieces by hand. The software can provide the measurement specs in metric measurements as well as imperial (inches), since many offshore contractors use the metric system.

The measurement specifications also include a **tolerance**, usually listed as "+/−" a certain fraction of an inch that indicates a narrow range of acceptable dimension variations (see Figure 9.8). This means that a stated dimension on the measurement specifications may vary by the stated tolerance amount. The tolerance amount might be ½ inch (1.3 cm) for larger circumferences (such as the chest) or lengths (such as back length), and ¼ inch (6 mm) for smaller circumferences (such as the neck). The stated dimensions, with allowable tolerance, serve as a contract between the apparel company and the sewing facility. If dimensional accuracy is not maintained within the tolerance range, the goods can be rejected by the apparel company.

The apparel company's quality assurance department is usually responsible for checking the finished dimensions of the delivered goods. Since it would be too time consuming to measure the specified dimensions of every garment in a production order, a sampling technique is used to measure a specified number of garments in specific sizes. If goods sewn by a contractor must be rejected due to size inaccuracy, the apparel company may miss the deadline for delivery of goods to the retailer. Therefore, it is important for apparel companies to select carefully the contractors with whom they do business, and it is critical for contractors to carefully adhere to the garment specifications.

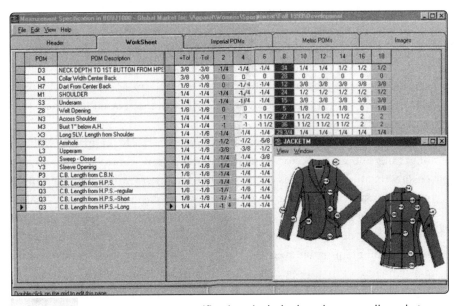

The measurement specifications include the tolerances allowed at each specified garment location.

Grading the Production Pattern

Pattern grading involves taking the production pattern pieces that have been made in the sample size for the new style and creating a set of pattern pieces for each of the sizes listed on the garment spec sheet. The written documents and production pattern are delivered to the pattern grading and marker making department, if the apparel company is responsible for the grading and marker making operations. As mentioned in Chapter 7, when contractors are used for production, they will be responsible for one of the following scenarios:

- making the first pattern and production pattern, grading and making the marker, cutting and sewing (full-package contractor)

- making the production pattern (based on a first pattern developed by the apparel company), grading and making the marker, cutting and sewing

- grading and making the marker (based on a production pattern developed by the apparel company), cutting and sewing

- cutting and sewing (termed "CMT" for cut, make, and trim) only (based on a marker delivered by the apparel company). The fabric may be supplied by the apparel company, or it may be supplied by the contractor.

Chapter 10 discusses sourcing options in detail.

Some apparel companies that use contractors prefer to take responsibility for grading and marker making. For example, there are incentives in the U.S. trade laws for apparel companies that use offshore contractors located in specific countries. The trade laws require that U.S.-produced fabrics be used, and that the garment pieces be cut in the United States. The cut pieces are then sent offshore for production.

Sending cut goods to the contractor minimizes the risk to the apparel company of grading and marker errors that could develop at the contractor's facility, and ensures that the contractor is not responsible for any errors in pattern grading or marker making. However, if anything is not correct on the pattern or marker that the apparel company has provided, the contractor can blame the manufacturer for a late delivery or other problem. For the manufacturer who provides the marker, maintaining an even work flow in the grading and marker making department is difficult, especially when the time frame for producing a season's line—determining that a style will be produced and having the marker ready for cutting—is very tight. Some contractors that have well-established partnerships with apparel companies communicate data such as patterns, markers, and garment specifications electronically. Although the contractor's initial investment in technology is high, the speed and accuracy provided may pay off quickly.

Grading requires different amounts of growth (for a larger size) or reduction (for a smaller size) at various points on each pattern piece. Thus, it is not possible to place a pattern piece into a photocopy machine and enlarge or reduce the pattern piece uniformly. The amounts and locations of growth/reduction are called the **grade rules**. There is no industry standard for these grade rules, and some companies guard their grade rule standards carefully. The grade rule itself is the combination of a specific length and width that the pattern pieces need to increase or decrease at a specified point on the pattern. For example, the shoulder-neck point may need to change (increase for each subsequent larger size or decrease for each subsequent smaller size) by ⅛ inch in height and 1/16 inch in width for each pattern size.

Pattern grading is more complex than it may appear. There are different grade rules for garments with set-in sleeves, raglan sleeves, kimono sleeves, and shirt sleeves. Style variations magnify the complexity of the different grade rules. For example, a raglan sleeve shirt could also include a front panel, so the grade rules would need to be modified for the extra style line added to the shirt front. Also, some companies use different grade rules for various sizes: for sizes 4, 6, and 8, a 1-inch width change increment per size may be used for the waist and hip dimensions; for sizes 10, 12, and 14, a 1½-inch width change increment per size may be used for the waist and hip dimensions; and for sizes 16, 18, and 20, a 2-inch width change increment per size may be used for the waist and hip dimensions.

Depending on the style and the apparel company's policy, the size range might include a large number of sizes—for example, from size 4 to size 18 for a missy dress. Another apparel company might produce garments in a size range of small, medium, large, and extra large (designated S-M-L-XL). The cost to grade a pattern with many pattern pieces into a wide range of sizes may be more than the cost to grade a pattern with only a few pattern pieces in just four sizes. These cost differences are considered from the design stage onward. Another cost variation related to styling concerns designs that are asymmetrical—that is, different pattern pieces are required for the left and right halves of the body. An asymmetrical design might also require different left and right facing and interfacing patterns. Each separate pattern piece needs to be graded, multiplied by the number of sizes in the size range. Thus, asymmetrical designs can be more costly to grade if using noncomputer grading technology (for computerized grading, one can very quickly apply the same grade rules to a front facing pattern as was used for the front pattern).

The fabric selected may influence the size range in which the style will be produced. Some fabrics will look best in a narrow size range. Based on the scale of a plaid size and repeat, a plaid pleated skirt in missy sizes may look attractive only in certain mid-sizes—for example, sizes 8 through 16. It would be ideal to select a fabric that looks good in a wide size range, but this is not always possible. Some styles look best in certain sizes. Thus, the style may be offered in a limited size range.

Grading Processes

The pattern grading process can be accomplished by a variety of methods, and there are several approaches to these methods. Computer grading, combined with computer marker making, has gained widespread acceptance. It is the method of choice for apparel companies and contractors that can invest in a computer grading and marker making system. Other processes include hand grading and machine grading.

HAND GRADING

The hand grading process requires a ruler, pencil, and paper as the minimum tools. Using the production pattern pieces for the new style, the pattern grader (person grading the pattern) traces a copy of the pattern piece by moving the pattern piece the distance designated by the grade rules at specific points throughout the tracing process. Some hand graders use special grading rulers or graph paper as aids to grading.

MACHINE GRADING

Pattern grading machines are used by some companies to speed the grading process (see Figure 9.9). The grading machine is equipped with two dials—one for width increase/decrease, and the other for length increase/decrease. The pattern piece to be graded is clamped into or taped to the grading machine, and paper is laid beneath. The pattern is traced in sequence by moving the dials on the grading machine to correspond to the grade rules at designated points on the pattern piece.

COMPUTER GRADING

Whereas machine grading is faster than hand grading, computer grading is much faster than either of these methods. Computer programs for pattern grading and marker making have been in use since the 1970s. The combined process is called **computer grading and marker making (CGMM)**. Companies that

Figure 9.1 Some pattern graders use a grading machine to grade patterns into the entire size range.

utilize computer systems to grade and make markers may refer to the department as the *computer grading and marker making department.* Many large apparel companies began their shift to computerization and formed CGMM departments early on. Computer use in pattern making and design areas developed more recently. Although the investment in hardware, software, and employee training is substantial, the cost savings are quickly evident for companies that have a substantial quantity of work. For example, Jantzen helped pay for its investment in computer equipment by running two shifts per day and serving as a CGMM facility for other apparel companies in the area that paid for grading and marker making services provided by Jantzen.

For companies that use a computer pattern design system for the production pattern, the pattern is ready for computer grading. Some companies, however, converted to computer grading before they began to use computers to make the patterns. For these companies, it is necessary to input the production pattern pieces into the computer before grading can be done. The process of inputting a pattern piece into the computer can be done by tracing the pattern piece or by scanning the piece. To trace a pattern piece, a table called a **digitizer** (also called a *digitizing table*) is used. The digitizer is sensitized at very small increments in both vertical and horizontal directions. These correspond to the *x* and *y* coordinates displayed on the computer monitor. The pattern piece is laid in place on the digitizer and traced using a hand-held cursor (see Figure 9.10). The traced pattern piece appears on the computer monitor. During the tracing process, the pattern grader uses a keypad on the cursor to input the specific grade points and grade rules at the desired locations. The pattern grader must plan the grade rules to be used, which may require a great deal of thought and pattern grading experience for some complicated styles.

Scanning equipment can be used to input the pattern piece information, including piece perimeters, grade points, and notches. Stripe lines, used to match pattern motifs on the fabric, and grainlines can be read from the pattern. The scanner will reorient a pattern piece as it is scanned if the pattern piece enters the scanner askew. Patterns can be scanned from a traced drawing, from a tagboard pattern, or from a plastic pattern piece.

The computer grading system not only calculates the graded dimensions for the entire size range, but it also develops smooth necklines, armholes,

Figure 9.10   A digitizer is used to input pattern pieces directly into a CAD system if the pattern was not made using a computer system.

waistlines, and other curves. Each pattern piece can be viewed on the monitor as a "nest," with all of its sizes nested together (see Figure 9.11). This helps the grader decide if a grade rule is incorrect or a curve is not adequately smoothed. By using the horizontal and vertical coordinates for a specific point, corrections can be made quickly without starting over. To check the grade, a full-size or miniature version of the graded nest can be printed or plotted.

Some PDS programs include the option to select a grading function as the pattern is being made. These systems are integrated so that the pattern blocks used to begin making the style have specific grade rules "embedded" in them. Once the pattern has been completed, the grading is completed automatically. A major developer of PDS, Lectra Systems, offers a grading package that

> enables the operator to distribute the new measurements to all affected pieces automatically, without having to manually choose each pattern piece to be graded. For example, when a measurement change is made on the front shirt piece, the program automatically modifies the measurements of the opposite front, side and back pieces, which will save pattern makers substantial time and effort. ("Lectra demonstrates," 1995, p. 62)

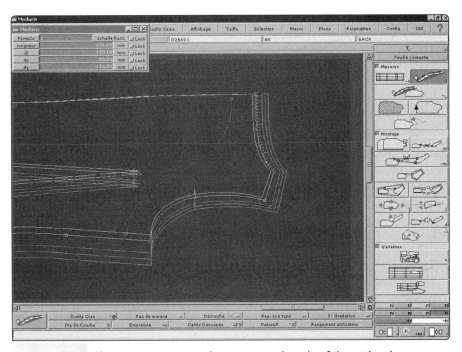

The computer screen shows a nested grade of the entire size range for this dress pattern piece.

Figure 9.12 Some computer programs provide tools to allow faster grading processes, measurements of pattern dimensions, and electronic sharing of graded patterns with production facilities.

Other improvements to increase speed and ease of use while reducing the possibility of grading errors are being developed (see Figure 9.12).

Making the Production Marker

A costing marker, used to calculate the usage (yardage) required for one garment, was discussed in Chapter 7. At the preproduction stage, another type of marker is required. The production marker is the full-size cutting layout of all the pattern pieces for all the sizes specified for the style. The marker is drawn on paper, showing the outline of all the pattern pieces. Arranging all the pattern pieces into an efficient layout can be a challenge. A tightly arranged layout is the goal for the marker, so that very little fabric is wasted. The waste, called **fallout**, represents fabric that cannot be used, and thus money lost to the apparel company. The efficiency of a marker's layout plan (*marker efficiency*) is measured in the percentage of fabric utilized. Thus, a high-utilization percentage represents a cost-effective marker. Highly efficient markers attain utilization with percentile figures in the high 80s and into the 90s (90 percent utilization means that there is about 10 percent fallout, or fabric waste).

If a pattern for a style requires 10 pattern pieces, and 7 sizes are produced, the marker will include 70 pattern pieces. Sometimes, a marker is planned so that the layout will have two sets of pattern pieces in the most frequently purchased sizes—often those in the mid-size range. Therefore, the marker for a missy style could have two sets of sizes 10 and 12, for a total of 90 pattern pieces for the marker with 10 pattern pieces. For styles offered in the S-M-L-XL size range, it is fairly common to cut one set each of size S and size XL pattern pieces, and two sets each of size M and size L pattern pieces (or, one set of size S and two sets each of size M, L, and XL, especially in men's athletic wear). The cut order specifies the sizes and number of size sets in each of these sizes needed for the marker (as well as the colorway by size if various colors of fabrics will be stacked up for the cut order).

Marker Making by Hand

Prior to the development of computerized marker making, markers were typically made by hand. The layout is planned on a long sheet of paper (for example, 30 feet long), that is the width of the fabric to be cut. The tagboard pattern pieces are shifted into the tightest arrangement possible. The outlines of all the pattern pieces are traced by hand onto the paper beneath. Typically, the marker paper is of double thickness. The paper can be carbonless or have carbon between the layers, so that a copy of the original marker is made at the same time. Thus, after the original marker has been cut up, a reference copy remains. This copy can be traced again if another production order for the same style is received. If a similar style is produced later, the marker maker can refer to the file of markers to help guide the layout plan for the new style. After the pattern pieces have been traced, they are removed. The marker is laid onto the stacked layers of fabric. The cutter, using an industrial cutting knife, follows the drawn outlines of the pattern piece on the marker.

Other Marker Making Methods

Some apparel companies and contractors continue to make markers by hand. Other methods were developed years ago to increase the speed and efficiency of marker making. These methods include the following:

- the use of miniaturization of pattern pieces to create the marker in small scale, combined with enlargement photography to produce a full-size marker
- the use of light-sensitive paper in which the paper areas covered by the tagboard pattern pieces remain white, while exposed areas of the light-sensitive paper darken to show the silhouette of pattern pieces
- the use of water-soluble dye sprayed over the pattern pieces while they lis on the fabric, leaving the fabric uncolored in the areas covered by the pattern pieces

Computer Marker Making

While various marker making methods are in use in today's industry, computer marker making is the most efficient and effective method. With CGMM, the marker making function is tied to the pattern grading function. Thus, a company that grades by computer also makes markers by computer. The CGMM system is purchased as a package, including the plotter that draws the marker. Once the pattern pieces have been graded by computer and stored in the computer's memory, the marker maker can retrieve all of the pattern pieces needed in the size range. The fabric width is displayed on the monitor, along with markings for stripes, plaids, or prints that need to be matched, if applicable. With the use of the mouse, each pattern piece is moved one by one into the fabric area designated on the computer monitor, creating the layout plan. The computer is programmed to keep all pattern pieces aligned "on grain," to avoid skewing pattern pieces. Accidental overlapping of pattern pieces is avoided, because the pattern piece blinks as a signal to the marker maker if one piece overlaps another, or the pattern piece cannot be set down if it would overlap another pattern piece. The marker making software calculates the usage, or fabric utilization, so the marker maker can continue to arrange pattern pieces until the utilization goal has been reached. After the marker is completed, the system generates a letter-size printout of the layout. The small-scale marker can be analyzed for utilization and accuracy. It can also be used for reference during preproduction and production.

ADVANTAGES OF COMPUTER MARKER MAKING

As discussed earlier, the marker program calculates the fabric utilization, and this figure appears as a percentage on the monitor (see Figure 9.13 and Color Plate 11). This helps the marker maker attain the highest utilization. An article in *Apparel Industry Magazine* discussed the complexity of marker making variables:

> Your greatest single cost is cloth. The management of cloth is unconditionally crucial to the successful management of your business and your profits. As you can see, finding the ideal approach to the many variables requires elaborate mathematical calculations using sophisticated computer programs. There is just no other practical way to arrive at an optimal solution. The variety of factors make the standard approach (based on human experience) far too unreliable. (Dennison, 1993, pp. 82–84)

Some manufacturers have estimated that the cost savings in better fabric utilization have paid for the computer equipment in less than two years. According to a study conducted at Clemson Apparel Research (Hill, 1994), a computer system used for grading and marking will result in a 2 percent fabric savings per year, quickly paying for the cost of the system for large manufacturers.

To save time, a marker from a previous similar style stored in the computer system might be studied by the marker maker to provide some guidance for creating a high-utilization marker on the first attempt. Some of the current marker software includes functions that will generate several possible marker layouts. Constraints such as plaid or stripe repeats can be accommodated by the software.

Multiple copies of the marker can be plotted whenever they are needed. Accuracy is extremely high with CGMM, as each copy is exactly the same as the

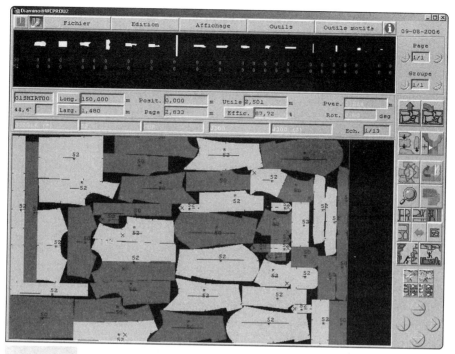

Figure 9.13 A production marker is displayed on the computer screen, showing the tight layout on the left and the utilization percentage on the right.

original. No accidental growth occurs as can happen when hand tracing markers.

Some companies that began their computerization with CGMM systems have integrated CGMM with other stages in design, development, and production using PDM/PLM software, as discussed earlier. Production integration will be covered in Chapter 11. Complete integration of computer systems throughout the entire process provides advantages to all parties in the fiber-textile-apparel-retail supply chain.

As the cost of some CGMM systems decreases and their user friendliness increases, more companies are purchasing these systems. Some systems are in a price range affordable to small apparel companies. Other small companies might use the CGMM service of a larger company. Many contractors in foreign production centers as well as in the United States have CGMM equipment. As discussed in Chapter 7, the apparel company's PDS can be linked electronically to the contractor's CGMM system. This saves time and increases accuracy.

Some apparel companies may not have the funds to invest in, and continually upgrade, computer hardware and software for pattern design, grading, and marker making. An alternative is available in some of the large metropolitan areas around the world. Centers have been established that rent or lease time on their computer systems, as well as provide training for use of computer pattern design, grading, and marker making. However, the apparel company's staff needs to be trained on the center's software, requiring the apparel company's investment in time and money. The alternative is to pay a staff member of the center to perform the work. These centers are open 24 hours a day.

Fabric Inspection

The preproduction steps include ordering production fabrics and trims. A part of this process involves approving fabric and trim colors and the quality of components (discussed earlier in this chapter). Samples are submitted by suppliers and approved by the apparel company. It is assumed by the apparel company that the production fabrics and trims will accurately match the samples submitted and used for the production of the sample garments. As noted earlier, this is called a *commercial match*. The production fabrics are inspected to ensure that they match the samples.

The retailer's orders are written based on the materials, trims, and construction quality seen in the sample garment. If the quality or color match of any part of the production goods is inferior, the retailer may reject an entire order. Fabric inspection can be the responsibility of the apparel company or the textile producer.

Fabric Inspection by the Apparel Company

To avoid problems arising from inferior fabric quality, some apparel companies inspect fabrics on their arrival from the textile producers. Various types of machinery are used to speed this process, including computerized equipment that scans across the fabric along the entire length to note any shade variation from beginning to end of the fabric roll. Other equipment checks the density of the weave or knit. Some companies rely on visual inspection.

On occasion, it may be necessary to reject fabric orders because of color or quality problems. Ordering replacement fabric can delay production by weeks. At times, a textile producer may be unable to replace rejected goods. The production schedule for the contracted arrival date of the goods at the retailer can be jeopardized because of fabric problems. Therefore, every effort is made to ensure the arrival of satisfactory, on-time production fabrics.

If the apparel company is responsible for inspecting fabrics, the fabric goods must arrive at the cutting facility in time to allow for inspection before cutting begins. This requires a crew of workers paid by the apparel facility to inspect the goods. In addition, costs of production increase any time the fabric is in storage or in inventory and not being processed, such as when the fabric is waiting to be cut and sewn. As the apparel industry moved toward faster turnaround time, it became obvious that several processes would need to change. Among them is fabric inspection by the textile producer.

Through Quick Response and supply chain management strategies, partnerships have been formed between the textile producer and the apparel manufacturer, ensuring that the textile producer inspected the goods and they were of the quality shown by the sample; and that the goods would arrive at the production facility just in time to cut and sew, as set forth by the apparel company's schedule. Therefore, the apparel company would not need to inspect fabric routinely. Instead, textile producers inspect the goods before they leave the textile facility. At the textile facility, any flaws in weaving or knitting are marked along the selvage edge of the fabric, so that the apparel producer knows where the flaws are and can cut around them. Printed fabrics are inspected for color match and registration of motif placement when more than one color is printed. Once inspected, the fabric ordered for production is sent in large rolls from the textile producer, converter, or fabric wholesaler to the cutting facility.

Currently, many small apparel companies do not have the production volume to participate in this aspect of supply chain management. They continue to inspect the fabric and trims prior to sending them to cutting. Even with supply chain management participants, fabric flaws can occur. It is important for all workers to be alert to flaws, such as off-grain stripes, that could lead to the rejection of an order by the retailer.

For apparel companies that own their own factories, the fabric and trims are usually sent from the supplier either directly to the company's production plant or to the apparel company's warehouse (where inspection may occur), and then on to the production facility. For companies that use contractors for the cutting and sewing operations, the fabric might be ordered, received, and inspected by the apparel company, which then sends the fabric rolls to the cutting facility. Another option is that the fabric might be ordered by the contractor and sent directly to the production facility, in which case, the contractor assumes the responsibility for the quality of the fabrics and trims. This is typically done when the fabric is manufactured offshore, and the cutting and sewing also occur offshore.

Production Spreading, Cutting, Fallout Disposal, Bundling, and Dye Lot Control

Several steps are involved in preparing the fabric for garment production. These steps include the following:

- spreading the fabric onto cutting tables
- cutting the fabric
- disposing of the excess fabric
- preparing the cut fabric pieces for production

These steps might be done at the production facility, such as at the contractor's facility. If the apparel company owns its production plants, then these steps might be done at one or more of the apparel company's facilities. Sometimes the apparel company is responsible for cutting and bundling. Then it ships the bundled pieces to a production facility. This might be done if the production facility is located in a country with trade incentives, as mentioned earlier in this chapter, or if the apparel company wants to control the cutting of the goods, or if the selected contractor only makes and trims garments.

Spreading

Spreading (or *laying up*) is the process of unwinding the large rolls of fabric onto long, wide cutting tables. The fabric is stacked, layer upon layer, depending on the size of the cut order. For **production cutting**, the fabric is laid flat across its entire width from selvage to selvage (nothing is cut on a fold, as is frequently done in the home sewing industry). The length of each layer of fabric is determined by the specific style's marker length. For large cuts, thin sheets of paper may be laid between every 12 layers of fabric, in order to count quickly the stacked layers of pieces by dozens. This saves a great deal of time after cutting, when the stacks of cut pieces need to be assembled into different groups (bundles) for sewing. When a style will be produced in several colors, the fabric layers will reflect the correct number of layers for each color needed.

Fabrics that have a directional print, or napped fabrics such as corduroy and velvet, need to be laid so that all layers face the same direction (called *face-up*). This is a more time-consuming process than face-to-face spreading (two-directional), and is reflected in the labor cost for cutting. Fabrics such as stripes and plaids require matching, so they also take more time to lay up; therefore, these fabrics cost more to cut. Stretch fabrics, such as fabrics used for swimwear or intimate apparel, require great care during lay-up to avoid distorting the fabric. Stretch fabrics also require time to relax on the table after laying up and before cutting.

A variety of equipment speeds the fabric laying process. **Spreading machines** guided on tracks along the side edges of the cutting table carry the large rolls of fabric, spreading the fabric smoothly (see Figure 9.14). For face-up cutting, a cutting knife is sent across the fabric at the desired length (that corresponds to the length of the marker), the spreading machine is returned to its origin, and another layer is spread on top of the previous layer. This process allows each layer to be laid face up. This process is also used if a print fabric is one directional, that is, if the motifs on the print all need to face in the same direction. For plaids and stripes, each layer is stacked so that the plaids or stripes match the layer beneath.

Figure 9.14 Fabric is spread carefully and stacked layer upon layer in preparation for production cutting. A spreading machine is used to roll the fabric onto the cutting table.

Other systems utilize spreading machines that roll along the floor beside the cutting table. Some spreading machines require operators, but automatic and robotic spreaders are an option. In 1995, Saber Industries introduced the first robotic, digitally controlled spreader in the apparel business ("Saber introduces," 1995).

Cutting

Either the apparel company or the contractor is responsible for making the production marker. The marker, whether drawn by hand or plotted by computer, is sent to the cutting facility or contractor for the cutting process. The marker made during preproduction is laid onto the top layer of fabric, serving as a cutting guide if the fabric will be cut by one of several hand processes. There are several types of specialized hand-guided electric knives and rotary cutters used for cutting the multiple thicknesses of fabric. Most electric knives look similar to a band saw, with a reciprocating blade that oscillates vertically to "saw" through the fabric layers.

Die cutting is another type of cutting process used for specific purposes. For very small pieces that will be cut repeatedly, season after season, it is more precise and more economical in the long run to use a die. The die is similar to a cookie cutter—a piece of metal with a sharp edge, tooled to the exact dimensions of the shape of the pattern piece. The die is positioned over several layers of fabric. Then, a pressurized plate is applied to the die to cut through the thicknesses of fabric. A fabric appliqué that might be used season after season is an example of a pattern piece that would be economical to cut using a die. The original cost of the die is expensive, but its continued use amortizes the initial cost and increases the cutting accuracy compared to hand cutting the same piece.

For facilities that have computerized cutting, special tables are required to accommodate the cutting equipment (see Figure 9.15). The table surface is covered with bristles that allow the cutting blade to slide between them. The fabric layers are compressed with air to provide a more compact cutting height, thereby increasing the accuracy of the cut. The table surface is designed to accommodate the required suction. The computer-generated marker is laid onto the top layer of fabric. The cutting equipment is guided by computer coordinates, not by "seeing" the pattern piece outlines on the marker. The plotted marker is used for the following two purposes: (1) to ensure that the marker is laid properly onto the fabric, especially when plaids or stripe notations must be aligned; and (2) to indicate the sizes of the pattern pieces and styles for the workers who will bundle the pieces after cutting. Computerized cutting is much faster and generally more accurate than hand cutting or even die cutting. Either a reciprocating knife blade or a rotary cutting blade is used for computerized cutting. The rotary cutting blade is effective for cutting very stretchy fabrics, such as swimwear fabrics. The rolling action of the blade minimizes fabric stretching and, thus, distortion of the fabric during cutting. However, notch marking with a rotary cutter is more limited.

Laser cutting is also driven by computer. It offers many of the same advantages as knife-blade computer cutting, including high speed and accuracy. Laser cutting can be done economically with one or several layers of fabric (called *single-ply cutting* and *low-ply cutting*), compared to the many stacked layers used with computer cutting. Several low-ply cutters can be purchased for about the same cost as one high-ply computerized cutting system. Since low-ply cutters offer the flexibility to produce small runs very quickly, there are additional benefits to consider as well. Several low-ply cutters can be working on different orders at the same time. They lend themselves well to the short-cycle manufacturing environment. Single-ply cutting systems are needed for individually customized cuts for the mass-customization manufacturing environment (see Chapter 11).

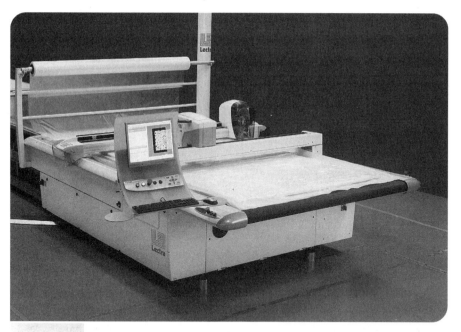

Figure 9.15 A computerized cutter requires a special table surface to accommodate the knife blade requirements. This Lectra cutter automatically conveys material from a spreading table to the cutting area, and then directly onto the bundling area.

On the other hand, if a production facility handles primarily large orders for mass production, a large-scale computerized cutter that cuts up to 300 dozen pieces per hour may be more efficient.

Computerized cutting and sewing facilities may be linked electronically to the apparel company's computer, so that the marker file can be downloaded electronically. This increases the speed of delivery of the marker to the cutting facility or contractor. Often sewing contractors have CGMM equipment and may be responsible for making the marker. As mentioned earlier, the style's pattern file might be sent electronically from the apparel company to the sewing contractor, which will use CGMM equipment to grade the pattern, make the marker, and cut the style.

Fallout Disposal

Although the marker's layout utilizes the fabric in the most efficient plan possible, there is still a substantial quantity of fallout, or waste material. In the past, the waste goods commonly were delivered to landfills. This procedure has become more expensive, in part because of the reduction in available landfill space and the increase in transportation costs to disposal sites. Furthermore, today's society expects responsible recycling. Textile and apparel waste recyclers provide a market for some of this waste. The payback varies among categories. For example, cotton fabric by-products are very marketable, especially if they are white.

There are trade associations that promote the international trade of secondary and scrap textiles. These include Secondary Materials and Recycled Textiles (SMART), the Council for Textile Recycling, and the Textile Recycling Association (based in the U.K.). These associations help divert tons of textile waste from the solid waste stream.

Bundling

After cutting, the component pieces for each size and in each color must be grouped together in some way. **Bundling** is the process of disassembling the stacked and cut pieces and reassembling them, grouped by garment size, color dye lot, and number of units in which they will proceed through production. Bundling is done by hand, with one or more workers picking the required garment parts from the stacks and grouping them in bundles that are ready for production. The type of production process determines the number of garments to be included in each bundle. This varies from the cut fabric pieces for an individual unit (one garment) bundled together, to bundles of a dozen units (or sometimes specified parts of a dozen garments), usually in the same size and color (including same color dye lot) for all 12 garments. For some types of production, up to three dozen units might be bundled together.

Dye Lot Color Management

All coordinating pieces of an outfit, and those styles that are to coordinate in a line, need to be color matched exactly. Mismatching can occur if strict color management is not maintained. Even with adherence to color management, slight variations in shading can occur in the same dye lot of a production order. Therefore, it is important to code all fabric bolts with the dye lot number and to maintain accuracy in matching dye lots throughout spreading, bundling, production, and distribution processes.

Often an apparel company uses one sewing contractor for the suit pants production and another contractor for the suit jacket production. Each contractor receives a shipment of "matching" fabric from the textile producer. If dye lots are not matched, the suit pants might be a slightly different shade from the suit jacket. This discrepancy may not be noticed until the goods arrive at the apparel company's distribution center, the retailer's distribution center, or the retail selling floor, where the sale may be lost when the customer is trying on the jacket and pants and notices that the colors do not match exactly. The importance of maintaining dye lot consistency for pieces that are intended to match in color is critical to the success of the line.

Retail buyers' written orders in sufficient quantity to warrant production signal the chain of events that begins the process of producing a new style. The preproduction steps include ordering production fabrics, trims, and findings; maintaining color management, including the use of lab dips and strike offs; and finalizing the production pattern and written documents. To ensure quality production, the documents that accompany the pattern are as important as the pattern itself. These documents comprise the garment specification package. They include a tech drawing of the garment style; a list of all fabrics (with fabric swatches), trims, and findings in all colorways; construction specifications (construction details and sewing steps in sequence); and measurement specifications with stated tolerances. Accurate documentation is essential.

In company-owned production facilities, the production pattern is graded into the specified size range, and a production marker is made by the apparel company. For contracted production, either the apparel company or the contractor is responsible for the grading and marking procedures. Computer grading and marker making systems have gained widespread use in the apparel industry. The advantages of CGMM include increased speed and improved accuracy. Integrated computer systems provide product information management, including instantaneous electronic linkage between PDS (pattern design system) and CGMM, whether the two systems are separated by miles within a city (such as the design development department located at company offices, and the grading and marking department located at the company's factory) or by an ocean (such as the design development department located in the United States, and the contractor's grading and marking department located at the factory in South Korea).

Fabric inspection may be the responsibility of the textile producer, the apparel company, or the contractor. Spreading can be done by laying the fabric layers onto cutting tables by hand or by using spreading machines. Cutting can be done by hand-held cutting equipment, by computer knife blade, or by laser. After cutting, the fabric pieces are bundled into units ready for production.

The future promises continued developments in a "seamless" integration of all aspects of design, development, marketing, production, and distribution.

Possible career opportunities in preproduction processes include specification writing, production pattern making, pattern and marker making, and materials management.

Purchasing Manager or Raw Materials Control Manager
Publicly Held Sportswear and Athletic Shoe Company

Position Description

Manage raw materials buyers to ensure department goals are met. Manage the sales sample materials buyer to ensure timelines are met and all needed materials are ordered. Develop partnerships with vendors for the supply of necessary raw materials to ensure company needs are met. Develop partnerships with contractors to be sure the best possible services are provided for the company. Develop, monitor, and update systems to ensure efficiency in the department and to provide necessary information exchanges with other departments and liaison offices.

Typical Tasks and Responsibilities

- Prepare annual department budget and action plans.

- Determine greige goods commitments and/or forecast company-developed styles. Have contracts issued. Work with offshore liaison offices to provide accurate and timely reports, updates, and information as requested to make ongoing greige goods commitments with vendors.

- Color assort and preorder raw materials as needed, keeping excess to a minimum and maintaining a program to dispose of excess raw materials.

- Monitor lab dip and first production. Submit information from the apparel lab to ensure materials will meet production timelines. Monitor deliveries to contractors. Troubleshoot quality problems.

- Generate computer reports using a variety of systems.

- Use telephone, fax, and electronic communications to communicate with vendors, contractors, other company departments, and offshore liaison offices.

- Perform constant ongoing "coaching" of buyers to meet department goals.

Trim Buyer
Publicly Held Suit and Dress Company

Position Description

Write garment specifications, and source vendors. Order trims, buttons, zippers, cording, snaps, interfacings, and lining fabrics. Work with designers and the production team on trim selection. Organize shipments to contractors in the United States and abroad.

Typical Tasks and Responsibilities

- Make phone calls and send e-mails to vendors.
- Meet with sales representatives to review lines of trim, buttons, zippers, interfacings, and linings.
- Price and order trims and findings.
- Organize and oversee shipments of fabrics and trims to contractors.
- Meet with designers and the production team to select trims.
- Write the garment specifications for all styles in the line.

Key Terms

bundling	measurement specification
commercial match	pattern grading
computer grading and marker making (CGMM)	production cutting
	production engineer
cut order	production marker
die cutting	registration
digitizer	source
factor	spreading
factoring	spreading machine
fallout	submit
grade rules	supplier
grading	tolerance
lab dip	vendor

Discussion Questions

1. Describe orally or bring to class a product that provides an example of lack of color management, with one or more components not matching. How would you suggest that this mistake could have been avoided?

2. Give several examples of problems that may occur with fabric quality. Discuss options available to the apparel manufacturer to correct the problem, and explain how such problems—and their correction—affect production and delivery to the retailer.

3. Computer grading and marker making systems are an expensive investment. What are some ways in which a CGMM system can quickly pay for itself?

Cole, Michael D. (2005, November). Technology's next frontier on display at Tech Conference. *Apparel*, pp. 20–22.

Conrad, Andrée. (1999, January). The industrialization of "couture" in Italy. *Apparel Industry Magazine*, pp. 36–40.

Dennison, Roger. (1993, September). Optimize cloth consumption with CAD marker making. *Apparel Industry Magazine*, pp. 82–86.

DesMarteau, Kathleen. (2003, April). The Potential for 3-D & e-Collaboration. *Apparel*, pp. 33–36.

Gaffney, Gary. (1999, May). SCM: In reach for $5M to $25M firms? *Bobbin*, pp. 74–78.

Greco, Monica. (1996, February). Is on-line fabric sourcing next? *Apparel Industry Magazine*, pp. 32–34.

Hill, Suzette. (1999, February). Product development: The next QR initiative? *Apparel Industry Magazine*, pp. 48–54, 71.

Hill, Thomas. (1994, March). CAR Study: UPS, CAD provide 300%+ return on investment. *Apparel Industry Magazine*, pp. 34–40.

Lectra demonstrates its new CAD grading package. (1995, August). *Apparel Industry Magazine*, p. 62.

Rutberg, Sidney. (1997, October 17). Re-Factors racking up strong sales gains. *DNR*, pp. 12–13.

Saber introduces first truly robotic spreader. (1995, August). *Apparel Industry Magazine*, pp. 46–48.

Speer, Jordan K. (2004, June). Color profile: Examining Processes. *Apparel*, pp. 22–26.

Thread selection made simple. (1999, April). *Bobbin*, pp. 46–50.

Young, Kristin. (1996, February 2–February 8). The F word. *California Apparel News*, pp. 1, 8–9.

Sourcing Decisions and Production Centers

In this chapter, you will learn the following:

- the criteria used by apparel, accessories, and home fashions manufacturers and retailers in their sourcing decisions

- the various sourcing options available to manufacturers and retailers

- the advantages and disadvantages of these sourcing options

- current issues related to sourcing decisions

- the locations of the primary domestic and international production centers

Step 6: Sourcing

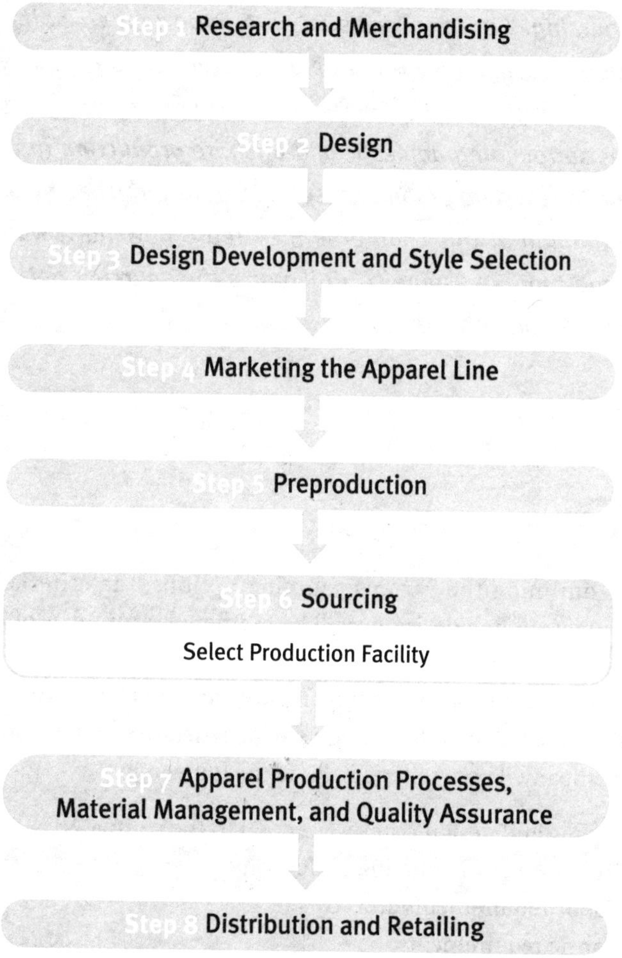

Step 1 Research and Merchandising

Step 2 Design

Step 3 Design Development and Style Selection

Step 4 Marketing the Apparel Line

Step 5 Preproduction

Step 6 Sourcing

Select Production Facility

Step 7 Apparel Production Processes,
Material Management, and Quality Assurance

Step 8 Distribution and Retailing

S ome of the most important decisions made by a company are how, when, and where to manufacture goods. This decision making process is called **sourcing**. Sourcing decisions are important to both manufacturers and retailers because they often help to determine a company's competitive advantage. This section outlines decision criteria, production options for companies, and issues surrounding domestic and **offshore production** (producing outside the United States using production specifications furnished by U.S. companies). At the beginning of this chapter is the Step 6 flowchart, which summarizes the sourcing process. Figure 10.1 diagrams the **sourcing options** available to manufacturers and retailers.

Before outlining the various sourcing options, the criteria companies use in making sourcing decisions will be examined. A number of criteria are considered when companies decide what sources will manufacture their products and where their products will be manufactured. The answers to a number of questions related to each criterion will help determine the best sourcing option for a company. These criteria include the following:

company and design criteria (internal to the company)
- the company's sourcing philosophy
- labor requirements and costs
- fabric requirements
- quality control standards
- equipment requirements
- required plant/factory capacities

political and geographical criteria (external to the company)
- trade barriers and government regulations
- shipping distance and expected turnaround time
- infrastructure of the country; availability of materials and supplies
- political and economic conditions of the country

Fabric Procurement	Domestic				Foreign
Apparel Production	**Company-Owned Production Facility**			**Contract Production**	

Company-Owned Domestic Plant	Company-Owned Foreign Plant	807 or 9802 Production (MT)	Domestic Contractor	Foreign Contractor
			MT	
			CMT	
			FP	
			Grade pattern, make marker, CMT	
			Make pattern, grade pattern, make marker, CMT	

Apparel Categories		Brand Name Apparel	Private Label and Store Brand Apparel

Apparel Marketing	Sales Reps Apparel Marts

Retail Level	Retailer

Consumer Level	Consumer

Sourcing options

Because of the labor-intensive nature of the textile, apparel, and home fashions industries, labor costs have been a primary criterion for companies in their sourcing decisions. However, other factors must come into play when companies make sourcing decisions. These criteria are continually assessed to meet the philisophical and production needs of a company. Because of the complexity of sourcing decisions, computer software programs have been developed that simulate the implications of various sourcing decisions for a company. Through these simulations, companies can assess the outcomes of varying sourcing decisions before the decisions are implemented.

In small companies, sourcing decisions are generally the responsibility of merchandisers. In larger companies, merchandisers may work with sourcing agents or sourcing managers in making these decisions. Some very large companies have a staff of individuals who make the sourcing decisions for a particular product category. Those who work in design and product development, fabric procurement, and production sourcing must coordinate their efforts so that the product line will be successfully produced and distributed to the retailers on time.

THE COMPANY'S SOURCING PHILOSOPHY

Often companies have a general philosophy toward sourcing that serves as a guideline or framework for sourcing decisions. For example, some companies are very committed to domestic production and want to be able to put "Made in the U.S.A." labels on their products (see Figure 10.2). Other companies have strong ties and positive working relations with contractors in other countries and, therefore, generally prefer offshore production.

In recent years, many companies have adopted a sourcing philosophy that incorporates **corporate responsibility**, or **social responsibility**. For these companies, sourcing decisions must take the following into account:

- human rights
- labor conditions
- environmental implications of the decisions

This is often referred to as a *triple bottom line* for sourcing decisions; that is, people, planet, and profit factors are all considered. These philosophies are implemented in the selection of countries and factories, and in the monitoring of factory conditions. Questions companies might ask include the following:

- How do we design, produce, and distribute the highest quality merchandise under the best factory and business conditions?

- How do we design, produce, and distribute products and services that are sustainable and still provide consumers with what they want and need?

Figure 10.2 For some companies, the ability to put the "Made in the U.S.A." logo on their products contributes to their sourcing decisions.

These topics will be discussed in greater detail later in the chapter.

Apparel and accessory production is very labor intensive, even though techno-logical advances are increasingly automating the processes. Therefore, labor costs are an important issue in sourcing decisions. Questions companies might ask include the following:

How many workers will be required to produce the goods efficiently?

What is the labor cost of domestic workers compared to workers in another country?

How are the workers treated?

If the company owns the factories, what investments in technology and personnel training need to be made?

As discussed in Chapter 1, the U.S. and international textile and apparel indus-tries have always been in search of cheaper labor—first within England; then within the United States; then in Japan, South Korea, and Hong Kong in the 1950s; in the Caribbean Basin from the 1960s to the 1980s; in Mexico, Canada, and the Caribbean Basin in the 1990s; and in China and Southeast Asia after quotas were phased out for most World Trade Organization members in the first decade of the twenty-first century. Over the past 50 years, U.S. textiles, apparel, accessory, and home fashions companies and retailers have moved a great deal of production offshore where labor costs are considerably lower than in the United States. For example, in 2002, the average hourly compensation cost (in U.S. dollars, including fringe benefits) for apparel production workers in the United States was $15.05, compared to $2.70 in Costa Rica, $2.45 in Mexico, $0.88 in China, and $.038 in India. Obviously, the labor costs in these other countries are much lower than in the United States. This is the primary reason why many manufacturers produce goods offshore (see Table 10.1).

To compare sourcing options according to labor cost, many companies have relied on comparisons of minimum wages. However, according to industry ana-lysts, "direct labor comparative analyses, based on minimum wage, prove to be misleading for the following four reasons: (1) no one can sustain productive manufacturing operations on minimum wage; (2) not many significant manu-facturers pay minimum wage; (3) not many employees will be attracted to work for minimum wage pay; and (4) employees typically cannot be persuaded to stay at a company when receiving minimum wage pay" (Cruz, 1995, p. 80). Instead, industry-specific minimums, area-specific minimums, and factory minimums

Comparisons of Hourly Compensation (including wages and fringe benefits) for Apparel Production Workers (in 2002 U.S. dollars)

NAFTA		South Asia	
United States	15.05	India	0.38
Canada	9.04*	Pakistan	0.41
Mexico	2.45	Sri Lanka	0.48
European Union		**ASEAN Countries**	
France	11.60*	Indonesia	0.27
Germany	15.97*	Philippines	0.76
Italy	11.68*	Vietnam	0.32
United Kingdom	12.24*	Thailand	2.45
Middle East and Africa		**Central and South America**	
Egypt	0.77	Costa Rica	2.70
Israel	6.38*	Dominican Republic	1.65
South Africa	1.38	Guatemala	1.49
Kenya	0.38	Honduras	1.48
East Asia		Colombia	0.98
China	0.88		
Taiwan	4.14*		
Korea	4.08*		

* Does not include fringe benefits.

SOURCE: U.S. Department of Labor Statistics and Jassin-O'Rourke Group (2002).

have been used for comparative purposes. When comparing labor costs, fringe benefits for workers (e.g., health benefits, retirement benefits, day care) must also be taken into account. Industry analysts suggest that the term *labor costs* refer to earned wages and the term *fringe benefits* refer to all other labor costs.

It is important to note that simply because the labor costs are lower in a particular country, one cannot assume that overall production costs will also be lower. Costs associated with support services and infrastructure, transportation, and shipping will vary across sourcing options and must also be taken into account when comparing costs of one option with another. Companies must examine both fixed and variable costs associated with manufacturing in the various options in order to assess accurately the financial benefits of any one option (Brooks, 1992).

Table 10.2 compares the costs of manufacturing a sports jacket using offshore contract production (e.g., Mexico) with domestic production in a company-owned factory. Note that although the cost to purchase the jacket from an off-shore contractor is less than the total manufacturing costs using domestic production, transportation, credit, and administrative costs substantially raise the total buying costs. In addition, costs might not be the most important criterion for a company. Indeed, quality of the merchandise and delivery schedules may be more important criteria to a company than simply cost of labor.

FABRIC REQUIREMENTS

Whether the fabric will be procured in the United States or from a foreign supplier is also an important sourcing decision. If fabric is procured in the United States, companies may also want to manufacture the goods in the United States to possibly reduce shipping costs. If foreign fabric is used, typically the products are also produced offshore at a location relatively close to where the fabric was

Domestic-Owned Facility and Offshore Contract Production per Jacket Cost for a Sports Jacket

Cost Element	Production Site	
	Domestic	Offshore
Materials, including fabric, lining, and trim	$ 18.50	
Direct labor, including cut, make, trim, taxes, and fringe benefits	$ 13.40	
Factory expenses		
Supervision/indirect	$ 2.50	
Facilities	$ 2.00	$ 2.00
Insurance	$ 2.50	$ 2.50
Depreciation	$ 3.00	$ 3.00
Total cost to manufacture	$ 41.90	$ 7.50
Cost to purchase		$ 31.00
Other assignable costs		
Letters of credit (2 percent)		$ .62
Interest on higher inventory		$ .26
Transportation (5 percent)		$ 1.55
Procurement and administration		$ .31
Total transaction cost	$ 41.90	$ 41.24

produced, thus keeping fabric shipping costs to a minumum. Another important question regarding the fabric is whether the fabric will be cut in the United States. With certain trade agreements, if fabric manufactured in the United States is also cut in the United States, companies can take advantage of certain tariff allowances if the goods are then sewn offshore in the countries covered in the trade agreement. This and other trade issues will be discussed later in the chapter.

QUALITY ASSURANCE/CONTROL STANDARDS

The importance of maintaining specific quality assurance/control standards is one criterion in a company's sourcing decision. Because quality is most effectively controlled in company-owned facilities, a company's response to the importance of quality control may be the primary reason for using company-owned factories for production or for selecting a contractor that the company knows produces high-quality products (although they may be at a higher cost). When using either a domestic or offshore contractor, companies will articulate (specify) quality standards that the contractor must meet and will also expect to see sample merchandise (see Figure 10.3).

EQUIPMENT AND SKILL REQUIREMENTS

Depending on the product line, equipment and skills needed to produce the product line will vary. Some products require specific types of equipment or sewing skills. Therefore, companies will ask the following questions:

Figure 10.3   The ability to ensure that garments meet quality specifications is often a criterion in sourcing decisions.

- What equipment is needed to produce the goods efficiently?
- How specialized are these equipment needs?
- What specific skills are required to produce the product line?
- Will different equipment be needed next season or next year to produce goods for the company?

Companies will analyze the factory's equipment and the skills of sewing operators in terms of their production needs in their sourcing decisions (see Figure 10.4).

PLANT/FACTORY CAPACITIES

Another criterion for sourcing decisions is what the factory capacities are relative to production needs. Companies will want to know the production capabilities of company-owned factories, as well as contractors, and whether these are sufficient to meet expected production needs. If they are found to be insufficient, the company may decide to hire (additional) contractors, expand current factories, or build new factories. Financial capacities to invest in new equipment will need to be analyzed. If factory capacities are found to be greater than needed, then downsizing strategies are in order, or subleasing their facilities may be considered. Facility costs will vary across countries, as will the terms of leasing. Some factories also require minimum orders. It is important for companies to read the fine print of lease contracts to determine what is included.

TRADE BARRIERS AND GOVERNMENT REGULATIONS

Under current international trade policies, textile and apparel goods imported into the United States from many countries are subject to trade barriers, such as

Figure 10.4   When specialized production equipment is required, companies work with contractors that have the needed equipment.

tariffs, and, in some cases, quotas. **Tariffs** are taxes assessed by governments on imports; **quotas** are limits on the number of units, kilograms, or square meters equivalent (SME) in specific categories that can be imported from specific countries. (The metric system for measurement is generally used for these numerical limits because of the predominant use of this system outside the United States). If offshore production is an option, the company must decide if and how these trade barriers may affect importing the goods they produce into the United States (or other countries). Because both tariffs and quotas add to the cost of production, companies that produce offshore must weigh these additional costs against the lower costs of labor in these countries.

For example, the North American Free Trade Agreement (NAFTA) reduced trade barriers among the United States, Mexico, and Canada. Therefore, a number of U.S. companies moved their production to Mexico to take advantage of the lower labor costs there. The term **maquiladora** operations is used to describe "assembly plants, mostly along the U.S.–Mexico border, in which garments are assembled from U.S.-cut parts and shipped back to the United States" (Dickerson, 1995, p. 189).

Other government regulations that companies consider when making sourcing decisions include country-specific laws associated with government intervention regarding the following:

- industrial pollution
- the monitoring of air and water quality
- minimum wage requirements
- child labor laws

When laws in other countries are less strict than U.S. companies believe is appropriate, or when enforcement of the laws is problematic, companies may establish their own **codes of conduct** that they require their offshore contractors to follow. These codes of conduct will be discussed later in the chapter. Tax laws are also a consideration for companies.

SHIPPING DISTANCE AND EXPECTED TURNAROUND TIME

In an era when getting products to the consumer as quickly as possible is important to the success of a company, production, shipping, and distribution times need to be determined and compared. Questions asked by companies include the following:

How fast can goods be produced, shipped, and distributed to retailers?

Would turnaround time be faster if production location changed?

Would shipping costs be reduced if production location changed?

Companies should consider the distance and shipping time between the sewing factory and the company's distribution center. For example, a company with a distribution center in New York may choose a contractor in Mexico over a contractor in Thailand because of shipping time and costs.

Strategies associated with Quick Response are designed to shorten the time between fiber and finished product through increased use of technology. In addition, with improved supply chain management strategies such as enhanced communication and transaction technologies (e.g., e-mail, business-to-business Web technologies), information, business forms, and even money can be sent electronically and, therefore, reduce the time involved.

Turnaround time is particularly important for time-sensitive products such as swimwear. It is estimated that two-thirds of all swimwear is sold from May through July. Therefore, for reorders, swimwear companies need the fastest turnaround possible. Because of this, many swimwear companies manufacture their goods in locations close to where the goods will be distributed.

INFRASTRUCTURE OF THE COUNTRY—AVAILABILITY OF MATERIALS AND SUPPLIES

When making sourcing decisions, companies must also analyze the availability and reliability of each country's infrastructure and support areas. Questions asked by companies include the following:

- Are quality trims and threads readily available?
- Are sewing machine technicians and parts available?
- Are power sources, transportation methods, and shipping options reliable?

These questions are particularly important when exploring production in less developed countries.

POLITICAL AND ECONOMIC CONDITIONS

Companies that source offshore continually monitor the political and economic conditions of countries where production is taking place. Political instability or economic problems can dramatically affect the availability of materials and the reliability of transportation and shipping alternatives. Safety of employees must also be taken into consideration when violence or terrorism may pose threats to employees.

Sourcing Options

Based on these factors, a number of sourcing options are available to manufacturers and retailers. In general, major sourcing decisions focus on the following:

1. whether production will be
   - domestic
   - offshore
   - a combination of both
2. whether production will be
   - in a company-owned facility
   - contracted to others
   - a combination of both

When using contractors, the decision must also be made about which of the following options to employ:

- **Cut, Make, and Trim Services:** With the **cut, make, and trim (CMT)** option, the company provides the patterns, fabrics, and trims, and the contractor provides labor and supplies. The contractor cuts, makes, and trims.

- **Full-Package Services:** With the **full-package (FP)** option, the contractor provides preproduction services, fabrics, trims, supplies, and labor.

- **Other Options:** For example, the apparel company provides the fabric, and cuts and bundles the fabric; the contractor sews and trims.

Advantages and disadvantages of each option must be weighed by companies in light of their product line, operation strategies, and organization philosophy. For some companies, the flexibility afforded by using contractors is necessary; other companies believe they have greater quality control by producing products in their own factories. Some companies produce offshore to take advantage of lower labor costs. However, just because labor costs are lower in another country does not necessarily mean that overall production costs are lower or that producing offshore is the right decision for a company. What follows are the basic sourcing alternatives available to manufacturers and retailers. Tables 10.3 and 10.4 outline the primary advantages and disadvantages of these sourcing options.

Advantages and Disadvantages of Domestic and Offshore Production

	Advantages	Disadvantages
Domestic production	Trade barriers not a concern Shipping time and costs may be lower Known infrastructure Known culture Supported by consumers who prefer products "made in the U.S.A."	Labor costs may be higher than in other countries Some types of fabrics may not be readily available
Offshore production	Labor costs may be lower than in the United States Can take advantage of trade agreement incentives Some types of fabrics are more readily available	Differences in cultural norms Monetary/currency differences Language barriers Possible trade barriers

Advantages and Disadvantages of Company-Owned Facility Production and Contractor Production

	Advantages	Disadvantages
Company-owned facility production	Greater quality control Greater control over production timing Communication with textile suppliers and retailers optimized	Financial requirements associated with equipment and personnel Need to ensure continuous production Higher labor costs Foreign ownership creates additional financial risks
Contractor production	Greater flexibility to changing equipment or production needs No investment in factories, equipment, or training needed	Less control over quality or production timing

Domestic Fabric—Domestic Production in Company-Owned Facility

In this case, fabric produced in the United States is shipped to a company-owned factory in the United States for production. With vertically integrated companies, garment production facilities are in the same general location as where the fabric is produced. This option allows for the greatest control over quality and timing of production. Communication with textile suppliers and retailers is also optimized. To be competitive, companies that own their own facilities need to (and have the control to) invest in technology to increase productivity and reduce sewing costs. Companies that choose this option typically produce similar types of goods each year so that equipment requirements do not change drastically. Companies must also invest in training personnel and plan to maintain consistent and continuous production so that personnel are not continually laid off during slow periods and then rehired during busy periods. To maintain continuous production, these companies will sometimes serve as contractors for other companies during times of slow production. Labor costs are generally higher for companies that own their own factories, but many companies are dedicated to making domestic production competitive through increased productivity.

Generally, companies that have chosen this option are proud to put the "Made in the U.S.A." label on their products and are committed to domestic production. American Apparel is an example of a vertically integrated company that produces merchandise in its own facility in Los Angeles. American Apparel manufactures and retails men's, women's, and children's knitwear. Their seven-story factory and 3,100 employees (4,000 worldwide) make them the largest garment factory in the United States. The factory houses the following:

- 75 knitting machines
- cutting operations that have the capacity to cut eight T-shirts every 9.2 seconds
- sewing facilities that can produce 210,000 T-shirts per day

In addition, if someone orders 1,000 T-shirts at 2 p.m., they can be shipped by 5:30 that evening. This vertical integration allows American Apparel to control all aspects of production, thereby increasing the speed and quality control of the operations.

Domestic or Foreign Fabric—Domestic Contractor Production

Under this option, fabric is procured either domestically or from a foreign vendor, and production is contracted to a domestic company (contractor) that specializes in the type of production and services (CMT or FP) required.

By using a contractor, the company may lose some control over quality and timing of production. However, with contractor production, the company does not have to invest in factories, equipment, or training personnel. This is important for small companies that may not have the financial resources to build or buy a production facility. By using contractors, companies have increased flexibility in production methods. This is important for companies with product lines—and, therefore, equipment needs—that vary from year to year. Sometimes manufacturers that typically produce in their own factories choose this option when orders outpace their production capacity. For those that believe producing in the United States is important, companies can still put "Made in the U.S.A." on their labels when they use domestic contractors. If the fabric is procured from another country, certain trade barriers (e.g., tariffs) would need to be handled. Otherwise, trade barriers are not a concern, and shipping costs and production time may be advantageous.

An example of a successful domestic contractor is Koos Manufacturing, a Los Angeles-area high-end jeans manufacturer. Although in recent years, Koos has lost business from customers in the moderate price zone to offshore contractors, the company has managed to maintain a market for designer price denim. It finds its competitive advantages to include the following:

- its responsiveness to customers' needs (e.g., a sample can be turned out in 24 hours) and fast turnaround for orders

- the specialty sewing and quality production expected in the designer price zone

- its proximity to denim laundry facilities (where denim is given its faded or distressed appearance)

How do companies find the right contractor to produce their merchandise? Contractors can be located in the following ways:

Sourcing Fairs: These are trade shows that bring contractors and companies together. At these fairs, contractors have booths with samples of their merchandise and information regarding their expertise and capacities. Sourcing fairs are also held in conjunction with other trade shows, such as MAGIC. Both domestic and foreign contractors use sourcing fairs to connect with companies, and companies use them to find appropriate domestic and foreign contractors.

Classified Advertisements: Contractors and companies also use classified advertisements in trade papers, such as *Women's Wear Daily* or *DNR,* to advertise their needs or availability.

Business-to-Business (B2B) Electronic Commerce: This is used for sourcing raw materials (fabric, trims) as well as production. Growth is expected to continue in B2B electronic commerce in enhancing supply chain management, including sourcing.

Headquartered in Atlanta, Georgia, the American Apparel Producers' Network is the primary trade association for contractors worldwide who produce apparel for the U.S. consumer market. The association provides educational forums, research and data on sourcing effectiveness and on supply chain management technologies, and opportunities to build relationships among companies.

Domestic or Foreign Fabric with 807 (9802) Production

Using fabric produced either in the United States or elsewhere, companies choosing this option combine domestic production (i.e., design and cut) with a special type of offshore production known as **807 (9802) production**. Under the Harmonized Tariff Schedule number 9802 (formerly number 807) of the U.S. tariff regulations, when garment pieces are cut in the United States and shipped to contractors in specified countries for assembly, tariffs are only on the "value added" (typically, the cost of assembly) to the garment. For example, suppose the value of the cut garment pieces was $50,000 when they were shipped to Costa Rica for assembly. After assembly, the garments were worth $150,000 when they were shipped back to the United States. Under this tariff regulation, the import tax would be calculated on $100,000, the value added to the garment pieces.

The passage of the North American Free Trade Agreement in 1994 and the Central America–Dominican Republic–United States Free Trade Agreement (CAFTA-DR) in 2005 further solidified reciprocal reductions in tariffs among the United States and countries within North America and the Central America/Caribbean Basin region and, thus, fostered the use of contractors in these areas of the world. Miami has grown as a hub for numerous cutting operations for companies taking advantage of lower labor costs outside the United States and these various trade incentives.

This sourcing option allows the manufacturer to control the design and cut of the garments, while taking advantage of lower labor costs in other countries. Contractors that participate in this type of production offer a variation of CMT services—that is, the MT (make and trim) without the C (cut). With this option, however, companies must be able to handle possible language and cultural differences when working with contractors in other countries.

Domestic or Foreign Fabric—Foreign Contractor Production

This option is similar to the previous option, except that garments are not cut in the United States. Foreign contractors can provide both CMT and FP services to companies (see Figure 10.5). The primary advantage is the lower labor costs found in other countries. Disadvantages are similar to those for the previous option: possible trade barriers, and language and cultural differences in other countries. When using domestic fabric, shipping time and costs may be higher than if fabrics were produced and procured closer to the production facilities.

Foreign Fabric—Foreign Production in Company-Owned Foreign Facility

In some cases, companies may own production facilities in other countries. For example, since the passage of NAFTA, there have been increased investments in production facilities by U.S. companies in Mexico. Although this option allows companies to have control over quality and timing of production while taking advantage of lower labor costs in other countries, the financial risks associated with building and running a production facility outside of the United States are great. Government policies, personnel expectations, and cultural norms regarding business operations in another country may be very different from those in the United States. In fact, under some countries' policies, foreign ownership of factories is prohibited. Companies that own their production facilities must abide by the laws governing international trade regarding tariffs and quotas, just as companies that contract offshore do.

Combination of Alternatives

Many companies are diversifying their sourcing; that is, they use a combination of options depending on their production requirements at any point in time. Using a variety of sourcing options provides companies with the flexibility needed to change production in response to consumer demand, production requirements, and international relations. Diversification of sourcing options also safeguards companies against natural disasters and political or economic crises that may occur within a country or region of the world.

Companies often combine domestic and offshore production. A company that has successfully combined domestic and offshore contractor production is Karen Kane, a manufacturer of women's better sportswear and separates. With corporate and design headquarters and distribution center located in Los Angeles,

Nike's Contract Factory Footprint

Chart 43
Nike's Contract Factory Footprint
As of Feb. 28, 2007

COUNTRY	FACTORIES
ARGENTINA	7
AUSTRALIA	5
BANGLADESH	6
BELGIUM	1
BOSNIA	1
BRAZIL	26
BULGARIA	1
CAMBODIA	3
CANADA	7
CHILE	1
CHINA	132
COLOMBIA	1
ECUADOR	1
EGYPT	3
EL SALVADOR	2
FIJI	1
GREECE	1
GUATEMALA	1
HONDURAS	9
HONG KONG	12
INDIA	21
INDONESIA	38
ISRAEL	4
ITALY	6
JAPAN	28
JORDAN	3
KOREA	29
LITHUANIA	2
MACAU	4
MALAYSIA	34
MEXICO	20
MOLDOVA	2
MOROCCO	3
PAKISTAN	2
PHILIPPINES	1
PORTUGAL	8
SINGAPORE	3
SOUTH AFRICA	4
SPAIN	4
SRI LANKA	18
TAIWAN	24
THAILAND	63
TUNISIA	4
TURKEY	22
UK	2
USA	47
VIETNAM	35
GRAND TOTAL	652

0-20   20-50   50+

Americas*
19%

Europe,
Middle East,
Africa
11%

North Asia
41%

South Asia
29%

* Includes the United States

Figure 10.5 Nike produces goods through contractors around the world.

most of the cutting and all of its sewing operations are sourced to both domestic and foreign contractors that provide both CMT and FP services. The company believes these sourcing decisions allow for the greatest flexibility in meeting its production needs (Winger, 1999).

Another company that successfully combines U.S. and offshore contract production is Patagonia, headquartered in Ventura Beach, California. Patagonia uses contractors located in the United States, Asia, Mexico and other countries where 807 (9802) production occurs, and Europe. To ensure product quality and that the contractors abide by environmental requirements, minimum wage, and minimum age standards set by Patagonia, company representatives visit each contractor. When working with a new contractor, Patagonia orders 1,000 practice items made by the contractor, which may be sold later at one of its outlet stores (Welling, 1999).

One of the most diverse contracting systems is that of Nike, Inc., the world's largest apparel and footwear company, headquartered near Beaverton, Oregon. In 2007, Nike contracted with 652 factories in more than 45 countries, including 132 factories in China, 63 in Thailand, 47 in the United States, 38 in Indonesia, and 35 in Vietnam (see Figure 10.5 on page 400). The company also requires contractors to abide by a code of conduct.

Sourcing decisions are complex, and companies continually assess sourcing options to best meet their needs. In order to be competitive, production facilities—both domestic and offshore—must be responsive, flexible, efficient, and cost-effective. In the U.S. textile, apparel, and home fashions industries, a trend toward offshore production continues. According to industry analysts, much of the offshore movement has been—and is expected to continue—to Asia (particularly China and southeast Asia) and to Mexico and countries in the Caribbean Basin and Central America.

Movement of production to China and other countries in Asia has been spurred by the following:

the elimination of quotas for members of the World Trade Organization in 2005 (some quotas still exist for certain products being imported from China, Russia, Ukraine, and Vietnam)

the low labor costs

specialization in certain types of fabrics and/or production processes that cannot be found elsewhere

relatively fast production

The move south has been fueled largely by the following:

- favorable trade legislation (e.g., NAFTA and CAFTA-DR)
- competitive labor costs
- the advantages of proximity to the U.S. market, which include the following:
  - the ability to manage what are essentially nearby operations
  - lower shipping and transportation costs (compared to Asia)
  - the convenience of doing business in the same or close time zones

Reasons for the increase in offshore contract production include the following:

- the number of offshore contractors that have design and/or production capabilities (full-package services)
- the progress that has been made in computer compatibility, which has led to an increased use in electronic transmission of information, such as garment specification sheets or patterns

Such shifts in production have contributed to declines in employment in domestic apparel production. In fact, according to the Bureau of Labor Statistics (Department of Labor), the number of jobs in textile and apparel manufacturing in the United States has declined steadily since 1990.

Production Centers

U.S. Production Centers

U.S. production facilities pride themselves in offering flexibility, innovation, speedy turnaround time, and efficient delivery to retailers. Employment in apparel production can be found in almost every state, although the states with the largest employment in apparel production are California, New York, Texas, and Florida (see Table 10.5). This distribution reflects the historical concentration of apparel manufacturing in the New York City and Los Angeles areas and the lower wages found in the southern states in comparison to other states.

The domestic apparel industry has experienced decreasing employment over the past 15 years. According to the Bureau of Labor Statistics, in 2004, employment in apparel manufacturing nationwide was estimated at 285,000, down from 929,000 in 1990. Within the United States, California, New York, North Carolina, and Texas continue to have small but viable apparel production industries. Southern California has a pool of skilled labor, primarily from the Latino and Asian populations in the area. Southern states have benefited from trade

Top 10 States for Employment in Apparel Manufacturing

State	Number of Employees in Apparel Manufacturing
California	95,523
New York	44,011
North Carolina	35,384
Pennsylvania	19,978
Texas	17,154
Alabama	13,373
New Jersey	12,221
Tennessee	11,355
Florida	9,163
Georgia	8,843

SOURCE: U.S. Census Bureau. 2002 Economic Census.

agreements (NAFTA, CAFTA-DR), which have enhanced production activities such as garment cutting in these states, as well as from vertically integrated manufacturing facilities (see Figure 10.6).

From a global perspective, apparel production facilities can be found in the following:

developed countries (industrialized countries) such as the United States, Canada, Japan, and countries in Western Europe

newly industrialized countries (NICs) such as Hong Kong, South Korea, and Taiwan

developing countries such as China, India, Bangladesh, Costa Rica, and Guatemala

Historically, production within developed countries focused on domestic consumer markets, and production within newly industrialized and developing countries focused on exports. As consumer markets have grown in countries such as Japan, Hong Kong, Taiwan, Korea, and China, greater attention is being paid to both domestic and export production.

Figure 10.6 Headquartered in Los Angeles, American Apparel is one of the largest vertically integrated apparel manufacturers in the United States.

Many of the newly industrialized countries have large textile and apparel industries. For example, textile and apparel exports account for 52 percent of Hong Kong's total exports of manufactured goods. In the 1980s, Hong Kong, Taiwan, and South Korea were referred to as the "Big Three" Asian producers of textiles and apparel because of their importance in global trade of textiles and apparel. In the 1990s, China, India, Pakistan, Indonesia, and other Asian countries emerged as important worldwide producers.

Trade arrangements also spurred growth in apparel production in the following world regions:

- central and eastern Europe, where the European Union has production sharing arrangements
- Central America, where the United States has similar production sharing arrangements

Asia continues to be the largest producer of textiles and apparel. It is expected to remain so for many years as investments in infrastructure, technology, and equipment over the past 15 years have resulted in efficient high-quality production processes.

Worldwide, according to the United Nations, the largest textile exporters are European Union, China, Korea, United States, Taiwan, and Japan; the largest apparel and accessory exporters are China, European Union, Hong Kong, Turkey, India, and Mexico (see Table 10.6). The largest textile importers are European Union, United States, China, and Hong Kong; the largest apparel importers are the United States, European Union, Japan, Hong Kong, and Canada. According to the Department of Commerce Office of Textiles and Apparel, in 2005, the United States imported the most textiles and apparel (as measured in value in U.S. dollars) from the following countries/trade regions (in order): China, Caribbean Basin, Mexico, India, Hong Kong, Indonesia, Pakistan, Vietnam, and Canada.

As with the newly industrialized countries, many developing countries rely on textile and apparel manufacturing for their economic development and compete worldwide as low-wage production centers (See Table 10.7). Indeed, a significant proportion of these countries' exports are in textiles and apparel, as can be seen by the following statistics:

Largest Exporters of Apparel and Clothing Accessories (in billions of U.S. dollars, 2005)

Country	$Billion
China	74.283
Hong Kong	27.404
Italy	18.683
Germany	12.449
Turkey	11.833
India	9.228
France	8.431
Mexico	7.306
Belgium	6.709
Indonesia	5.167
United States	5.009
United Kingdom	4.930

SOURCE: United Nations (2006). Commodity Trade Statistics Database.

Textile and Apparel Exporters to the United States (percent share)

Country	Percent Share
China	28.24
Mexico	6.96
India	5.40
Indonesia	4.13
Pakistan	3.49
Hong Kong	3.29
Bangladesh	3.21
Canada	2.83
Honduras	2.66
Thailand	2.30
Italy	2.22
Sri Lanka	1.84
Dominican Republic	1.70
Taiwan	1.63
Turkey	1.42

SOURCE: U.S. Department of Commerce (2006). Office of Textiles and Apparel.

- 86 percent of Bangladesh's exports
- 61 percent of Sri Lanka's exports
- 63 percent of Mauritius' exports
- 63 percent of Honduras' exports
- 60 percent of El Salvador's exports
- 20 percent of China's exports

Several characteristics of textile and apparel manufacturing account for this. Because textile and apparel production is highly labor intensive, the industry provides work for many people. Compared with other manufacturing industries, apparel production is fairly inexpensive to establish. Essentially, all that is needed are industrial sewing machines, pressing equipment, and a building. In addition, because of continuously changing fashion trends, there is a constant demand for textile and apparel products. Therefore, developing countries in Southeast Asia, Africa, the Caribbean Basin, and South America greatly contribute to the global production of textiles and apparel (see Figure 10.7).

Current Issues in Domestic and Foreign Production

International Trade Laws and Free Trade Agreements

International trade laws are constantly changing, and it is important for apparel companies and retailers to stay on top of trade issues. Trade restrictions, including tariffs and quotas, must be taken into account in sourcing decisions. Several developments in international trade laws have affected apparel manufacturers' and retailers' decisions regarding offshore production.

WORLD TRADE ORGANIZATION

Established in 1995, the World Trade Organization (WTO) is a global trade organization that deals with the "rules of trade" among member countries. As of 2007, 150 countries were members. The WTO's Agreement on Textiles and Clothing phased out quotas established by the Multi-Fiber Arrangement (MFA) and reduced tariffs on textiles and apparel over a 10-year period between 1995 and 2005. The quota phaseout (quotas still exist for certain product categories for China, Russia, Ukraine, and Vietnam) provided countries with more open access to consumer markets. This has been advantageous for the textile

Figure 10.7 Production facilities for apparel and accessories can be found worldwide. The plant at left produces apparel for Gap in Lesotho. The facility at right is in Honduras.

and apparel industries in some countries (e.g., China, India, Indonesia) that continue to have low wages and increased investments, and less advantageous for other countries (e.g., Costa Rica, Mauritius) that have relatively high wages.

FREE TRADE AGREEMENTS

The United States has a number of Free Trade Agreements (FTA) negotiated with specific countries or world regions. The goals of these FTAs have been to accomplish the following:

- reduce trade barriers between/among the countries
- encourage economic development
- foster business relationships

Two of these FTAs (see Table 10.8 for a complete listing of U.S. FTAs) have had the most impact on the textile and apparel industries of the countries involved: the North American Free Trade Agreement (NAFTA) and the Central America–Dominican Republic–United States Free Trade Agreement (CAFTA-DR).

NAFTA, which took effect on January 1, 1994, phased in duty-free trade between Canada, Mexico, and the United States. It is estimated that trade among the three countries has increased more than 200 percent since NAFTA's implementation. Prior to NAFTA, most of the U.S.-imported apparel from Mexico had been cut in the United States and imported under 807 (9802) trade regulations. In addition, at that time, quality and communications issues kept many U.S. companies from sourcing in Mexico. Since the implementation of NAFTA, the countries have done the following:

Table 10.8   U.S Free Trade Agreements and Dates of Implementation

North American Free Trade Agreement (NAFTA, 1994): United States, Canada, and Mexico

Central America–Dominican Republic–United States Free Trade Agreement (CAFTA-DR, 2005): Costa Rica, El Salvador, Guatemala, Honduras, Nicaragua, the Dominican Republic, and the United States

U.S.–Australia (2005)

U.S.–Bahrain (2006)

U.S.–Chile (2004)

U.S.–Columbia (2006)

U.S.–Israel (1985)

U.S.–Jordan (2001)

U.S.–Morocco (2006)

U.S.–Singapore (2004)

developed specializations within the supply chain (with the United States and Canada focusing more on technology, design, and marketing, and Mexico focusing on production)

improved communication and supply chain management strategies among the countries

Production in Mexico has become more technologically advanced, quality has improved, production has increased (particularly full-package contract production), and U.S. apparel companies are making more long-term financial commitments in Mexico (Kessler, 1999).

CAFTA-DR was signed into law in 2005. Although most of the countries included in CAFTA-DR benefited from earlier trade initiatives implemented to boost economic development in Central America, CAFTA-DR further strengthened these relationships. Because developing countries in Central America, such as Honduras and El Salvador, compete with countries such as China and India as low-wage production centers, CAFTA-DR offered additional incentives (e.g., reduced tariffs on selected items) for U.S. companies to source in Central American countries.

TRADE ACTS

The United States has also implemented several trade acts that have enhanced opportunities for trade and economic development with specific regions of the world. The Trade and Development Act of 2000 included the African Growth and Opportunity Act (AGOA) to support nations in sub-Saharan Africa. The Trade Act of 2002 included the Andean Trade Preference initiative to support nations in western South America. Both acts provide incentives for companies to source in these regions of the world through investments and infrastructure enhancements.

Sweatshops in Domestic and Offshore Production

WHAT IS A SWEATSHOP?

Definitions of sweatshops vary depending upon the source of the definition. Three different sources provide the following definitions of sweatshops:

- According to the U.S. General Accounting Office, a **sweatshop** is an employer that violates two or more federal or state labor, occupational safety and health, workers' compensation, or other laws regulating an industry.

- The International Labor Rights Fund defines sweatshops as "work environments that include some of the following characteristics: pay is less than a living wage; excessively long hours of work are required often without overtime pay; work is done in unsafe or inhumane conditions; and workers are systematically abused by the employer or suffer from sexual harassment, and/or workers have no ability to organize to negotiate better terms of work" (International Labor Rights Fund, 2000).

- As reported in the *New York Times* (Finder, 1995, p. B4), sweatshops "generally employ 20 to 50 workers, many of them illegal immigrants, willing to suffer long hours, low pay, and miserable working conditions, just to have a job … [Owners] pay their workers in cash and often deny them the minimum wage, overtime, holidays, or any other benefits."

Because of the highly decentralized nature of the industry, it is difficult to estimate the number of sweatshops in the United States and abroad. However, in the United States, the New York City and Los Angeles areas, where there are large concentrations of immigrants, are often cited as meccas for such establishments (Malone, 2001).

HISTORY OF THE SWEATSHOP ISSUE

Although sweatshops have been around since the turn of the twentieth century, after the Triangle Shirtwaist Co. factory fire of 1911, increased attention was paid to sweatshop conditions in the United States. Until the 1960s, a majority of U.S. apparel companies owned large factories where workers were usually unionized. Federal and state agencies could easily inspect the facilities and enforce labor, health, and environmental laws. However, in a highly competitive environment, many companies moved away from owning their own facilities to using contractors for the assembly phase of production. This resulted in a shift in apparel production from large, company-owned factories to a vast array of small, specialized contractors and subcontractors both within the United States and in other countries. Along with this shift, in the 1980s and 1990s, the industry saw a growth in and proliferation of sweatshops (Bonacich & Appelbaum, 2000). At the same time, there was a decrease in government agencies' ability to regulate working conditions. See Table 10.9 for a timeline of the sweatshop issue.

Table 10.9 A Timeline of the Sweatshop Issue

1851	Isaac Singer patents the sewing machine for factory use.
1900	International Ladies' Garment Workers Union (ILGWU) is formed to improve working conditions in the U.S. garment industry.
1911	146 garment workers die in a fire at the Triangle Shirtwaist Co. factory in New York's garment district. The tragedy stimulates a movement to end "sweatshop" conditions.
1917	The Amalgamated Clothing Workers of America union is formed as the primary union for the men's wear industry.
1951	Employment in the apparel and knitwear industries in New York City peaks at 380,000.
1968	Minimum wage increases to $1.60 per hour.
1976	The Amalgamated Clothing Workers of America merges with the Textile Workers of America and the United Shoe Workers of America unions to form the Amalgamated Clothing and Textile Workers Union.
1984	Crafted With Pride in U.S.A. Council is formed.
1992	Levi Strauss & Co. becomes one of the first companies to establish a code of conduct for its hired contractors.
1995	The Amalgamated Clothing and Textile Workers Union and the International Ladies' Garment Workers Union merge to become the Union of Needletrades, Industrial, and Textile Employees (UNITE).

A Timeline of the Sweatshop Issue *(continued)*

1996–April	The Kathie Lee Gifford sweatshop scandal: merchandise she endorsed is found to have been made in sweatshops in El Salvadoran maquiladoras.
1996–August	The White House forms the Apparel Industry Partnership (AIP), a voluntary partnership of apparel and shoe manufacturers, trade unions, and consumer and human rights organizations. The Partnership's task is to develop a plan of action to end sweatshops.
1997–April	The AIP releases a code of conduct for apparel producers.
1997–Fall	University of Notre Dame becomes the first college or university in the country to adopt a code of conduct for companies producing licensed merchandise.
1998–March	Duke University releases its code of conduct with student input.
1998–July	Activists found the United Students Against Sweatshops (USAS).
1998–August	The first National Labor Committee–USAS delegation goes to Central America to speak with workers and local nongovernmental organizations (NGOs). They spend one week in El Salvador, Honduras, and Nicaragua collecting data.
1998–November	The AIP creates the Fair Labor Association (FLA), backed by the U.S. Labor Department, UNITE, and the Interfaith Center for Corporate Responsibility; other NGOs drop out of the association. (www.fairlabor.org)
1999 Winter–Spring	Student activists conduct sit-ins at Duke, Georgetown, UW-Madison, Michigan, Arizona, and UNC-Chapel Hill. By March, 17 universities had signed with the FLA.
1999–July	The USAS National Organizing Conference is held in Washington, D.C. Some 200 students protest the FLA at the Labor Department.
1999–Fall	Anti-sweatshop activists create an alternative system to the FLA: The Workers Rights Consortium (WRC). The WRC is "a nonprofit organization that supports and verifies licensee compliance with production codes of conduct." (www.workersrights.org)
1999 Fall– 2000 Winter	Citing student demand, Nike names 41 factory locations in 11 countries making its merchandise. Gear for Sports, Champion, Russell Athletic, Jansport, and Eastpak follow suit.
2000–Spring	A second wave of sit-ins rocks the country (U. Penn., Michigan, UW-Madison, Johns Hopkins, and Toronto). The WRC grows from 2 members to 13 (in March). U. Penn and UW-Madison are the first two schools to leave the FLA.

Table 10.9 A Timeline of the Sweatshop Issue *(continued)*

2000–March	Duke University sends termination letters to 28 companies that do not meet its code of conduct (out of 409 companies that had licensing agreements).
2000–April	Founding conference of the WRC.
2000–July	The WRC successfully completes its first board meeting.
2000–November	To date, 66 colleges and universities have affiliated with the WRC.
2001–January	The FLA approves seven companies for participation in their monitoring program and accredits its first independent external monitor (Verité).
2005	Quotas on textiles and apparel imported from World Trade Organization members are phased out; quotas on some imports from China are imposed until 2008.
2007	To date, 194 colleges and universities have affiliated with the FLA; 170 have affiliated with the WRC.

Reminiscent of the early 1900s, stories emerged of lurid working conditions (see Figure 10.8), piecework pay below minimum wage, and children working and playing alongside their mothers in factories (Lii, 1995), and of the notorious sweatshop in El Monte, California, where Thai immigrants were held in conditions of semi-enslavement (Bonacich & Appelbaum, 2000). In the 1990s, many apparel manufacturers and retailers were admonished for using contractors in both the United States and abroad that violated human and labor rights by using child labor, tolerating poor working conditions, and accepting violence against union groups.

Initially, the government, as well as labor, human rights, and religious groups, put pressure on apparel manufacturers and retailers to refrain from using foreign suppliers that violated human and labor rights, and hiring contractors in countries with political policies that violated human and labor rights. However, companies and organizations soon realized that simply boycotting such contractors or countries was not necessarily the answer to this complex problem. In many developing countries, apparel production was found to provide much-needed jobs for thousands of workers. In many cases, the wages of working children were essential for providing basic necessities for themselves and their families. Therefore, rather than punishing these individuals by boycotting the country or contractor and leaving them without

Figure 10.8 Sweatshop conditions in apparel manufacturing still exist despite government and industry pressure to maintain safe and healthful working conditions.

needed jobs, apparel companies responded by attempting to reform working conditions and making sure that workers were not abused.

COMPANY RESPONSES—CODES OF CONDUCT AND FACTORY MONITORING

Manufacturers and retailers have taken greater responsibility for monitoring the working conditions of their contractors and subcontractors. Many large retailers and mass manufacturers have adopted sourcing guidelines and regularly inspect contractors' facilities to ensure that workers are not being exploited.

One of the first companies to implement such guidelines was Levi Strauss & Co. In 1992, it established guidelines for its hired contractors, covering issues such as the treatment of workers and the environmental impact of production (Zachary, 1994; see Tables 10.10 and 10.11). Levi Strauss & Co., which works with contractors throughout the world, regularly inspects factories and will cancel contracts with companies that breach these rules.

In 1996, President Clinton established the Apparel Industry Partnership, a task force of apparel companies, unions, and human rights groups to focus on sweatshop and human rights issues within the global apparel industry. Member companies and groups included the following:

- Nike
- Liz Claiborne
- Nicole Miller
- L.L.Bean
- Reebok
- Phillips-Van Heusen
- Patagonia
- Union of Needletrades, Industrial, and Textile Employees (UNITE)
- National Consumers League
- Retail Wholesale Department Store Union
- International Labor Rights Fund
- Business for Social Responsibility

Table 10.10   Levi Strauss & Co. Country Assessment Guidelines

The numerous countries where Levi Strauss & Co. has existing or future business interests present a variety of cultural, political, social, and economic circumstances.

The Country Assessment Guidelines help us assess any issues that might present concern in light of the ethical principles we have set for ourselves. The Guidelines assist us in making practical and principled business decisions as we balance the potential risks and opportunities associated with conducting business in specific countries.

- Health and Safety Conditions—must meet the expectations we have for employees and their families or our company representatives;
- Human Rights Environment—must allow us to conduct business activities in a manner that is consistent with our Global Sourcing and Operating Guidelines and other company policies;
- Legal System—must provide the necessary support to adequately protect our trademarks, investments, or other commercial interests, or to implement the Global Sourcing and Operating Guidelines and other company policies; and
- Political, Economic, and Social Environment—must protect the company's commercial interests and brand/corporate image. We will not conduct business in countries prohibited by U.S. laws.

SOURCE: Levi Strauss & Co.

Levi Strauss & Co. Terms of Engagement

Our Terms of Engagement (TOE) help us to select business partners who follow workplace standards and business practices that are consistent with Levi Strauss & Co.'s values and policies. These requirements are applied to every contractor who manufactures or finishes products for Levi Strauss & Co. Trained assessors closely monitor compliance among our manufacturing and finishing contractors in approximately 50 countries. The TOE are as follows:

Ethical Standards

We will seek to identify and utilize business partners who aspire as individuals and in the conduct of all their businesses to a set of ethical standards not incompatible with our own.

Legal Requirements

We expect our business partners to be law abiding as individuals and to comply with legal requirements relevant to the conduct of all their businesses.

Environmental Requirements

We will only do business with partners who share our commitment to the environment and who conduct their business in a way that is consistent with Levi Strauss & Co.'s Environmental Philosophy and Guiding Principles.

Community Involvement

We will favor business partners who share our commitment to improving community conditions.

Employment Standards

We will only do business with partners who adhere to the following guidelines:

Child Labor

Use of child labor is not permissible. Workers can be no less than 15 years of age and not younger than the compulsory age to be in school. We will not utilize partners who use child labor in any of their facilities. We support the development of legitimate workplace apprenticeship programs for the educational benefit of younger people.

Prison Labor/Forced Labor

We will not utilize prison or forced labor in contracting relationships in the manufacture and finishing of our products. We will not utilize or purchase materials from a business partner utilizing prison or forced labor.

Disciplinary Practices

We will not utilize business partners who use corporal punishment or other forms of mental or physical coercion.

Table 10.11   Levi Strauss & Co. Terms of Engagement *(continued)*

Working Hours
While permitting flexibility in scheduling, we will identify local legal limits on work hours and seek business partners who do not exceed them except for appropriately compensated overtime. While we favor partners who utilize less than sixty-hour work weeks, we will not use contractors who, on a regular basis, require in excess of a sixty-hour week. Employees should be allowed at least one day off in seven.

Wages and Benefits
We will only do business with partners who provide wages and benefits that comply with any applicable law and match the prevailing local manufacturing or finishing industry practices.

Freedom of Association
We respect workers' rights to form and join organizations of their choice and to bargain collectively. We expect our suppliers to respect the right to free association and the right to organize and bargain collectively without unlawful interference. Business partners should ensure that workers who make such decisions or participate in such organizations are not the object of discrimination or punitive disciplinary actions and that the representatives of such organizations have access to their members under conditions established either by local laws or mutual agreement between the employer and the worker organizations.

Discrimination
While we recognize and respect cultural differences, we believe that workers should be employed on the basis of their ability to do the job, rather than on the basis of personal characteristics or beliefs. We will favor business partners who share this value.

Health and Safety
We will only utilize business partners who provide workers with a safe and healthy work environment. Business partners who provide residential facilities for their workers must provide safe and healthy facilities.

Evaluation and Compliance
All new and existing factories involved in the manufacturing or finishing of products for LS&CO. are regularly evaluated to ensure compliance with our TOE. Our goal is to achieve positive results and effect change by working with our business partners to find long-term solutions that will benefit the individuals who make our products and will improve the quality of life in local communities. We work on-site with our contractors to develop strong alliances dedicated to responsible business practices and continuous improvement. If LS&CO. determines that a contractor is not complying with our TOE, we require that the contractor implement a corrective action plan within a specified time period. If a contractor fails to meet the corrective action plan commitment, Levi Strauss & Co. will terminate the business relationship.

SOURCE: Levi Strauss & Co.

In 1997, the Apparel Industry Partnership presented its agreement and plan of action to end sweatshops. The agreement outlined a Workplace Code of Conduct and Principles of Monitoring that companies would voluntarily adopt and would require their contractors to adopt. The Workplace Code of Conduct includes the following:

prohibitions against child labor, discrimination, and worker abuse or harassment

recognition of workers' rights of freedom of association and collective bargaining

a minimum or prevailing industry wage, a maximum 60-hour work week, and a cap on mandatory overtime

a safe and healthful working environment

A number of companies, including Nike, Liz Claiborne, Gap, Kellwood, Columbia Sportswear, Reebok, JCPenney, Wal-Mart, Nordstrom, and others, have established their own guidelines and codes of conduct (see Table 10.12 for an example of these guidelines).

Even as companies adopted guidelines, improvement of working conditions in factories was difficult, particularly if companies did not inspect factories and enforce their codes and if governments did not enforce certain standards. In many cases, countries resisted adopting certain guidelines, which they viewed as "Western standards" of business. Large companies that may contract in more than 50 countries and work with hundreds of different contractors also found it difficult to inspect and regulate working conditions in every factory. In addition, according to some critics, some companies were interested only in the public relations appeal of sourcing guidelines, but did very little to enforce the rules (Ortega, 1995).

Increased public attention was drawn to the sweatshop issue when, in 1996, merchandise endorsed by Kathie Lee Gifford for Wal-Mart was found to have been made in sweatshops in El Salvador and the United States. The negative publicity surrounding this scandal led many manufacturers and retailers to take human rights issues more seriously. At this same time, student activists were waging protests and sit-ins on campuses throughout the United States, asking that colleges and universities provide assurances about how merchandise bearing the college or university name and/or logo was made. In 1998, student activists founded the United Students Against Sweatshops (USAS) as a vehicle for sharing information and organizing activities ("Colleges join effort," 1999; Manning, 1999).

Table 10.12   JCPenney Foreign Sourcing Requirements

Supplier Selection

In selecting suppliers, JCPenney attempts to identify reputable companies that are committed to compliance with legal requirements relevant to the conduct of their business.

Legal Requirements

JCPenney requires of its suppliers strict compliance with all contract provisions, as well as all applicable laws and regulations, including those of the United States and those of the countries of manufacture and exportation.

Country-of-Origin Labeling

JCPenney will not knowingly allow the importation into the United States of merchandise that does not have accurate country-of-origin labeling.

Factory Working Conditions

JCPenney will not knowingly allow the importation into the United States of merchandise manufactured

- with convict labor, forced labor, or illegally indentured labor
- with illegal child labor
- in violation of any other applicable labor or workplace safety law or regulation

Manufacturer's Certificate

JCPenney requires that its foreign suppliers and its U.S. suppliers of imported merchandise, for each shipment of foreign-produced merchandise, obtain a manufacturer's certificate that the merchandise was manufactured at a specified factory, identified by name, location and country; that neither convict labor, forced labor, or illegally indentured labor, nor illegal child labor, was employed in the manufacture of the merchandise; and that the merchandise was manufactured in compliance with all other applicable labor and workplace safety laws and regulations.

Factory Visits

On visits to foreign factories, for any purpose, JCPenney associates and buying agents have been asked to be watchful for the apparent use of prison or forced labor, or illegal child labor, or apparent violations of other applicable labor or workplace safety laws or regulations, or indications of inaccurate country-of-origin labeling, to take immediate responsive action when necessary and to report questionable conduct in these areas to their management for follow-up and, when appropriate, corrective action.

Corrective Action

If it is determined that a foreign factory utilized by a supplier for the manufacture of merchandise for JCPenney is in violation of these foreign sourcing requirements, JCPenney will take appropriate corrective actions, which may include cancellation of the affected order, prohibiting the supplier's subsequent use of the factory, or terminating JCPenney's relationship with the supplier.

SOURCE: JCPenny.

As an outgrowth of the Apparel Industry Partnership, in 1998, the Fair Labor Association (FLA) was established as a factory monitoring association. Members of the FLA must ensure that their factories and contractors comply with an established code of conduct. In 2001, the FLA began approving company factory monitoring programs and accrediting independent external factory monitors for use by its member companies. Critics of the FLA voiced concerns over the organization's apparent industry focus. Therefore, in 1999, anti-sweatshop activists created an alternative system to the FLA, the Worker Rights Consortium, a "nonprofit organization that supports and verifies licensee compliance with production codes of conduct" (Worker Rights Consortium, 2001).

In 2000, the American Apparel and Footwear Association and counterpart manufacturers' associations from Mexico, South Africa, the Philippines, El Salvador, Honduras, the Dominican Republic, Nicaragua, Jamaica, and Sri Lanka endorsed their own core production principles of the Worldwide Responsible Apparel Production (WRAP) program. These production principles form the basis of WRAP's factory-based certification program dedicated to the promotion of "lawful, humane, and ethical manufacturing throughout the world" (American Apparel and Footwear Association, 2001). The principles address labor practices, workers' compensation, freedom of association, factory and environmental conditions, and customs compliance.

The need for effective enforcement of company codes of conduct resulted in the development of factory monitoring programs by companies and organizations. Many companies conduct their own factory monitoring or contract with an independent factory monitor to conduct periodic reviews of factories. The overall goal of these factory monitoring programs and organizations is to improve the working conditions in apparel factories in the United States and abroad.

Some apparel companies require that contractors pay the cost of any necessary improvements required to meet their codes of conduct; others help pay some of the costs. For example, Timberland has provided money for educational purposes and water treatment systems in communities in China, where its products are manufactured. When Levi Strauss & Co. discovered a group of underage workers at two contractor factories in Bangladesh, the company convinced the contractors to take the children off the production lines so they could attend school. Levi Strauss & Co. paid for the children's school fees, books, and uniforms, while the contractors agreed to continue their wages while they attended school. The contractors also agreed to stop employing child labor.

Increased media attention and customer interest has led many companies and trade associations to enhance their efforts to improve workers' conditions.

However, according to former Labor Secretary Robert Reich, even though these efforts are making the situation "a bit better," sweatshops continue to exist here and abroad (Malone, 2001, p. 4).

Summary

The term *sourcing* refers to the decision making process companies use to determine how and where the textile and apparel products or their components will be produced. In making sourcing decisions, companies take into consideration factors that are internal to the company: their general sourcing philosophy, labor requirements and costs, fabric requirements, quality control standards, equipment and skill requirements, and plant/factory capacities; as well as factors external to the company: trade barriers and government regulations, geographic location and expected turnaround time, country infrastructure and availability of materials and supplies, and political and economic conditions. Based on these criteria, a number of sourcing options are available to apparel companies and retailers. Major sourcing decisions focus on whether production will be domestic or offshore, and whether production will take place in a company-owned facility or will be contracted to others. When contracting, companies also must decide whether cut, make, and trim (CMT), full-package (FP) services, or other options will be used.

Apparel production within the United States has decreased dramatically over the past 15 years. Small but viable production centers are found in many states, but they are concentrated in New York, California, Texas, and Florida. With regard to global production, Asia is the largest producer of textiles and apparel. China, the European Union, Hong Kong, Mexico, Turkey, India, and Bangladesh are the world's largest exporters of apparel; the United States, the European Union, Japan, Hong Kong, and Canada are the world's largest importers of apparel.

One of the current issues surrounding apparel production is international trade laws that have reduced trade barriers among countries. These include the World Trade Organization agreements, Free Trade Agreements implemented by the United States with other countries, and trade acts that provide incentives for economic development within certain world regions. Another current issue affecting the apparel industry is that of sweatshops in the United States and abroad. Companies have addressed this issue through the adoption and implementation of codes of conduct and factory monitoring.

Sourcing Success Story: Saks

QRS Sourcing is integrated with Saks' design applications, its purchase order management systems, and inventory control systems, all of which reside at the Saks control data center in Jackson, Mississippi.

As an item is created and a pricing decision is made, all information flows through Sourcing and populates all systems so no data is rekeyed or duplicated. The first step in the sourcing process requires the private brand group to create its seasonal plan, followed by the design team's preview of all designs. Approved designs are then passed on to potential manufacturers through a secure portal via the Saks intranet. The retailer next receives bids from the manufacturers regarding their charge to create the merchandise, based on thread count, seam specifications, and other requirements necessary to construct the garment.

Once Saks selects the manufacturer that will create the merchandise, QRS Sourcing takes over. The system creates a purchase order for the merchandise, and sends the document electronically to the chosen supplier. As the manufacturer accepts the purchase order and completes the order, the manufacturer electronically sends an advance ship notice when the merchandise is ready for transport. The sourcing tool also creates all invoices and letters of credit and payments, keeping all documentation electronic and available in real time.

The end-to-end solution also provides Saks with visibility into all logistics and customs, brokers fees, and duty costs that accumulate as goods enter the country.

EXCERPTS FROM: Amato-McCoy, Deena M. (2004, March). Saks overcomes the global sourcing challenge. *Stores*, p. 96.

Companies that produce goods within the United States as well as offshore will have positions related to sourcing. An excellent knowledge of company goals, trade laws, production requirements, and available sourcing options, as well as negotiation skills, are important for success in these areas.

Sourcing Analyst
Publicly Held Sportswear Company

Position Description
Develop sourcing plans and costing worksheets, taking into consideration quotas, capacities, pricing, competitiveness, and quality of goods.

Typical Tasks and Responsibilities
- Determine the source for garment production, and negotiate the terms of production with resources.
- Determine the effect of quotas, tariffs, freight, and other miscellaneous charges on the landed cost of garments.
- Conducts margins analyses.
- If needed, examine sample goods submitted by a source.
- Communicate with other departments (marketing, product development, forecasting and scheduling, customs, and cost accounting).
- Travel to inspect production facilities, examine samples, and negotiate terms.

Key Terms

code of conduct

corporate responsibility

cut, make, and trim (CMT)

807 (9802) production

full-package (FP)

maquiladora

offshore production

quota

social responsibility

sourcing

sourcing option

sweatshop

tariff

Discussion Questions

1. What does a sourcing philosophy of social responsibility mean for a company? How might a company implement this sourcing philosophy?

2. Over the past 15 years, many U.S. apparel companies have shifted from domestic production to offshore production. Why has this shift occurred? What are the advantages and disadvantages for a U.S. company to produce offshore?

3. Explore the Web site of a large apparel and/or footwear manufacturer. What is included in the company's code of conduct? How are these codes of conduct implemented? How are these codes of conduct beneficial to consumers?

References

Amato-McCoy, Deena M. (2004, March). Saks overcomes the global sourcing challenge. *Stores*, p. 96.

American Apparel and Footwear Association (2001). Industry social responsibility statement [online]. Available: http://www.apparelandfootwear.org/LegislativeTrade News/SocialResponsibility.asp [June 7, 2007].

American Apparel and Footwear Association (2004). Trends: An Annual Compilation of Statistics on the U.S. Apparel and Footwear Industry [online]. Available: http://www.apparelandfootwear.org/Statistics.asp [October 8, 2006].

Bassuk, David, and Skatoff, Ashley. (2001, February). Guidance for choosing B2B exchanges, partners. *Bobbin*, pp. 48–53.

Bonacich, Edna, and Appelbaum, Richard P. (2000). *Behind the Label: Inequality in the Los Angeles Apparel Industry.* Berkeley: University of California Press.

Brooks, Gary. (1992, September). Make domestically or import: How to avoid costly mistakes. *Apparel Industry Magazine*, pp. 180–184.

Brown, Christie. (1995, September). The body-bending business. *Forbes*, pp. 196–204.

Bureau of Labor Statistics, U.S. Department of Labor (2006). Career Guide to Industries, 2006–07 Edition, Textile, Textile Product, and Apparel Manufacturing [online]. Available: http://www.bls.gov/oco/cg/cgs015.htm [October 08, 2006].

Colleges join effort to fight sweatshops. (1999, March 17). *The Oregonian*, p. B3.

Cruz, Sergio. (1995, November). Site selection: Straight talk about costs. *Bobbin*, pp. 80–84.

Dickerson, K.G. (1995). *Textiles and Apparel in the Global Economy* (2nd ed.). Englewood Cliffs, NJ: Prentice-Hall.

Finder, Alan. (1995, February 6). Despite tough laws, sweatshops flourish. *New York Times*, pp. A1, B4.

Friedman, Arthur. (1996, March 26). Sourcing now: The proximity factor. *Women's Wear Daily*, p. 6.

Haas, Robert D. (1994, May). Ethics in the trenches. *Across the Board*, 31, pp. 12–13.

Henricks, Mark. (1998, January). Koos Manufacturing's success is "Made in USA." *Apparel Industry Magazine*, pp. 48–50.

International Labor Rights Fund (2000). *Definition: sweatshop* [online]. Available: http://www.laborrights.org [July 7, 2000].

Jacobs, Brenda A. (1999, November). Regional pacts produce new trade patterns. *Bobbin*, pp. 65–68.

Kessler, Judi A. (1999, November). New NAFTA alliances reshape sourcing. *Bobbin*, pp. 54–62.

Lii, Jane H. (1995, March 12). Week in sweatshop reveals grim conspiracy of the poor. *New York Times*, pp. 1, 40.

Malone, Scott. (2001, March 22). The Triangle legacy: 90 years after fire, sweatshops persist. *Women's Wear Daily*, pp. 1, 4–5.

Malone, Scott. (2004, September 28). Winners and losers. *Women's Wear Daily*, pp. 10–11.

Manning, Jeff. (1999, March 7). Students, Nike fighting war against sweatshops. *The Oregonian*, pp. C1, C6.

Mexico tax reform exposes U.S. apparel firms to "Double Income Tax." (1999, November). *Bobbin*, pp. 56–57.

Moore, Lila. (1995, September). Home is where you sew it. *Apparel Industry Magazine*, pp. 38–54.

O'Rourke, Mary T. (1992, September). Labor costs—From Pakistan to Portugal. *Bobbin*, pp. 116–122.

Ortega, Bob. (1995, July 3). Broken rules: Conduct codes garner goodwill for retailers, but violations go on. *Wall Street Journal*, pp. 1, A4.

Ostroff, Jim. (1995, December 12). Mexico's fast trip to the top. *Women's Wear Daily*, pp. 7, 11.

Ostroff, Jim. (1996, April 23). Third world sourcing: Prices are enticing, perils are numerous. *Women's Wear Daily*, pp. 1, 6–7.

Raney, Joanna. (1995, October 10). Reich: Inside the sweatshop war. *Women's Wear Daily*, p. 32.

Ratoff, Paul. (1994, May 27–June 2). To manufacture in-house—Yes or no? *California Apparel News*, p. 7.

Seideman, Tony. (2001, March). Reebok develops information system to monitor supplier human rights issues. *Stores*, pp. 102–103.

Survival of the fittest. (1998, May). *Apparel Industry Magazine*, pp. 34–36.

United Nations (2006). United Nations Commodity Trade Database [online]. Available: http://comtrade.un.org [May 13, 2007].

U.S. Census Bureau (2002). 2002 Economic Census [online]. Available: http://www.census.gov/econ/census02/guide/geosumm.htm [May 13, 2007].

U.S. Department of Commerce (2006). Office of Textiles and Apparel. Total textile and apparel importers [online]. Available: http://www.otexa.ita.doc.gov/MSRCTRY.htm [June 7, 2007].

Welling, Holly. (1999, December). Patagonia: Small world view of big business. *Apparel Industry Magazine*, pp. AS26–AS32.

Winger, Rocio Maria. (1999, April). A marriage of style and efficiency. *Apparel Industry Magazine*, pp. 20–24.

Worker Rights Consortium (2001). WRC Home Page [online]. Available: http://www.workerrights.org [March 28, 2001].

Zachary, G. Pascal. (1994, July 28). Levi tries to make sure contract plants in Asia treat workers well. *The Wall Street Journal*, pp. A1, A9.

CHAPTER 11

Production Processes and Quality Assurance

In this chapter, you will learn the following:

- The different types of environments used for production
- The production processes used in manufacturing
- The definition of quality assurance and the importance of quality assurance in delivering quality, acceptable merchandise to the retailer
- The product agents who assist manufacturers in bringing products produced overseas into the United States

Step 7: Apparel Production Processes, Material Management, and Quality Assurance

Research and Merchandising

↓

Design

↓

Design Development and Style Selection

↓

Marketing the Apparel Line

↓

Preproduction

↓

Sourcing

↓

Apparel Production Processes, Material Management, and Quality Assurance

Sew Production Order (may include approval of first size run by contractor)

Finish, Inspect, Press, Tag, and Bag Order

↓

Distribution and Retailing

Production Considerations

*T*he previous chapters discussed the development of a product line from market research, creation, design development, pattern development, and preproduction through sourcing options. The product line is now ready for production. **Production** is the construction process by which the cut fabric pieces, findings, and trims are incorporated into a finished apparel, accessory, or home fashions product (see Step 7 of the flowchart on the previous page). The cost to produce the product is affected by the product design and pattern, as well as by the production process used. Therefore, it is essential to the success of the company that the designer, product developer, and pattern maker be well versed in the production processes used to manufacture the product. Some of the decisions regarding the relationship among the design, pattern, and production processes occur during the planning and review meetings. Other production decisions take place as the new style proceeds through preproduction. However, if difficulties arise during the production of a new style, the designer, product developer, and pattern maker are typically consulted, along with the production engineer.

Production processes and **manufacturing environments** (the production facility, location of production, choice of production process, and cycle time) vary greatly, depending on factors such as the following:

- available technology
- price zone
- geographic location of production

Chapter 10 discussed some of these aspects of manufacturing environments. Computer technology has had a great impact on manufacturing environments. In turn, changes continue to occur in the entire soft-goods pipeline from the fiber producer to the consumer. Continual new developments in supply chain management and product lifecycle management (PLM) create great flexibility in production processes and manufacturing environments. This chapter will provide an overview of the methods of producing, assuring product quality, and importing goods within three manufacturing environments.

The three manufacturing environments, or strategies, as described by Peter Butenhoff, president of [TC]² (1999), include mass production, short-cycle production, and mass customization. The product type as well as the strategy used for replenishment of the product will determine which of these three environments will be used for production. Each of these three manufacturing environments is discussed below.

Mass Production

The mass production manufacturing environment is suitable for cutting and sewing very large quantities of each product, using one of several possible mass production processes that will be discussed later in this chapter. Mass production capitalizes on economies of scale. Basic staple products such as T-shirts, jeans, underwear, socks, and hosiery fit this manufacturing environment. These products have a low fashion risk, in part because they can remain on the retail floor longer than many fashion goods. The focus of mass production is on in-store replenishment of products (see Chapter 12). Seasonal goods include some staple products, such as turtlenecks, produced in seasonal colors. The selling time for seasonal goods falls between the selling time for staple goods and for fashion goods. Thus, some seasonal goods are manufactured in the mass-production environment, while other seasonal goods are manufactured in the short-cycle manufacturing environment, which is discussed in the next section.

The demand for staple goods and some seasonal goods tends to be easier to forecast than for fashion goods. This provides an opportunity for a slightly longer lead time for the mass-production manufacturing environment than the other manufacturing environments offer. Longer lead time means that production can be sourced globally, providing an opportunity for lower labor costs. With the relatively high labor costs for U.S. production, production of high-volume basic products is more cost efficient at vertically integrated factories or in factories in areas of the world where labor costs are lower. Because of its longer production time and retail selling time, the cost of carrying this inventory (both to the manufacturer and to the retailer) is greater than for goods that are manufactured closer to the time of their market demand. However, as long as interest rates remain fairly low, the carrying cost is offset by the lower manufacturing costs (Butenhoff, 1999).

Short-Cycle Production

A second manufacturing environment is **short-cycle production**. As the name implies, this manufacturing environment is well suited to products that are produced closer to the time of their market demand than mass-produced products. Short-cycle production is well suited to "very high-fashion products, which are placed into the market for short selling seasons (six to eight weeks), with no intention of in-store replenishment" (Butenhoff, 1999, p. SCM-4). According to Butenhoff, these high-fashion products will be manufactured predominantly in Asia because of the fabric availability and the well-established skill base there. In time, short-cycle production may migrate to other parts of the world as manufacturing capabilities become more developed worldwide.

Due to the ever-increasing speed of the product development cycle (in part, a result of the application of computer technology to supply chain management, PDM/PLM, and the monitoring of consumer sales), seasonal products, such as men's slacks in seasonal colors, with a slightly longer selling season (6 to 12 weeks) are strong candidates for short-cycle production as well (Butenhoff, 1999).

Mass Customization

A short-cycle manufacturing environment that is applied to an individual customer is called the mass-customization manufacturing environment. **Mass customization** involves the ultimate consumer in the customization of fit, design, or personalization of the product. Because the ultimate consumer is involved with design and/or fit choices, it may appear that mass customization can best be categorized as a design variation. However, mass customization deals with products that are already designed; the customer is simply customizing the product. Thus, the topic of mass customization is well suited to a discussion of manufacturing environments (Conrad, 1999).

The emergence of new technology has provided a means to link the customer at the retail store to the apparel factory, resulting in mass customization. The cost efficiency of mass production is maintained. One key point in mass customization is that the customer selects and pays for the product before it is produced. Thus, the phrase *sell one, make one* is appropriate.

Mass customization requires electronically linked, seamless integration of components throughout the entire supply chain in order to operate. It requires a manufacturing environment suited to individualization, yet with a fast turnaround time and at a low cost. Custom tailors and dressmakers are not producing these goods; within the mass-customization manufacturing environment, agile manufacturing is required. This production process will be discussed along with other production processes later in this chapter. The mass-customization manufacturing environment utilizes all the newest computer technologies, supply chain management, PDM/PLM, and some level of customization of the product for the individual customer (see Figure 11.1). The key technologies include body scanning, pattern alteration software, virtual try-on, and ink-jet printing. Each of these technologies will be discussed.

As previously mentioned, there are three types of mass customization: fit, design, and personalization. Each of these will be discussed.

FIT CUSTOMIZATION

The more traditional approaches to developing a design for a target market have been discussed in previous chapters. The pattern is developed based on

A sales clerk measures the customer using instructions from a computer as an aid.

The clerk enters the measurements, and adjusts the data based on the customer's reaction to samples.

The final measurements are relayed to a computerized fabric-cutting machine at the factory.

Bar codes are attached to the clothing to track it as it is assembled, washed, and prepared for shipment.

Mass customization is made possible by computer technology.

a company's target customer size standard. The "standard" size apparel fits some bodies better than others. With the development of new computer technology, PDM/PLM, and supply chain management, a type of custom apparel different from the custom-made apparel produced by personal tailors or dressmakers of the past is possible. "It is a consumer-driven strategy that allows limited customization of a standard style, such as size, color, or trim choices" ("Made to measure," 1998, p. 3). On the other hand, **made-to-measure** apparel "is a fully customized process where a garment is made specifically for one individual based on his/her measurements and preferences" ("Made to measure," 1998, p. 3). The difference between made-to-measure and mass customization is the degree of customization offered. However, the difference is blurring as technology provides tools to blend made-to-measure with mass customization.

Brooks Brothers, a retailer and manufacturer of men's and women's classic professional clothing, provides an example of mass customization with which customers can build their own dress shirt. "Ordering shirts from the catalog is a simple process that gives customers basic choices, such as: neck size, sleeve length, choice of three body styles, choice of three cuff styles, and 17 top-end fabric selections. It should come as no surprise that customers love this process" ("Made to measure," 1998, p. 6). Pattern making software provides the capability to adapt the standard pattern to specific measurements, such as making one sleeve longer than the other to fit the customer's different arm lengths. Delivery takes two to three weeks.

Early ventures in made-to-measure using mass production at the factory included men's tailored suits. The customer was measured at the tailor's retail store. With some systems, front, back, and side-view photographs of the customer standing in front of a measurement grid were also sent to the factory. The customer's measurements were input into the computer system that was linked electronically to the apparel factory's computer. The body dimensions were translated into specific differences between the "standard" pattern and the customer's needed adjustments. The pattern changes were made by computer calculations, and a customized pattern was plotted. Laser cutters allowed fast, single-ply computerized cutting of the garment pieces. With careful tracking through production, the cut pieces for each customized suit were sent through the mass-manufacturing process. The customer returned to the retail store for a final "fitting" for pant hemming and other minor adjustments handled by the retailer before the customer received the finished goods.

Brooks Brothers formed a partnership with suit manufacturer Pietrafesa Corp. of Liverpool, New York. The Brooks Brothers/Pietrafesa partnership is the culmination of four years of research and development, which began with the introduction of a manual made-to-measure process that required stores to fill out and mail to Pietrafesa order forms with alteration information. Today, eMeasure has evolved into a touch-screen kiosk system that allows customers to create and visualize 25 different made-to-measure suit silhouettes in 300 to 500 fabrics, which can be referenced through swatch books in the stores. (Rabon, 2000, p. 40)

After the selection process is complete, a sales associate enters the order into the system along with the customer's measurement information taken at the retail store. One of the challenges of made-to-measure apparel is the assessment of customer fit preferences, since some customers prefer a looser fit, while others prefer a more snug fit to their suits. The system "suggests a try-on size from the store's inventory, which is an integral part of the process" (Rabon, 2000, p. 40). Mass-customization options that include customizing the fit have expanded greatly with the continued development of electronically linked body measuring, pattern making, cutting, and production technology.

Body Scanning Technology

The development of **body scanning** technology has greatly enhanced the capabilities of mass customization. At the retail store, the customer is provided with a close-fitting garment to wear while standing in a scanning chamber or on a platform. In just a few seconds, the scanner captures the body dimensional data of the customer (see Figure 11.2). Software later translates the data into body dimensional measurements to be used by pattern making software.

Brooks Brothers has invested heavily in digital tailoring. Body scanners located at their retail stores are used to gather the measurement data for each customer. "The sales associate confirms the order by sending it to Brooks Brothers' manufacturing facility in North Carolina, the same facility that makes custom garments for the firm based on traditionally collected measurements" (Haisley, 2002, p. 29).

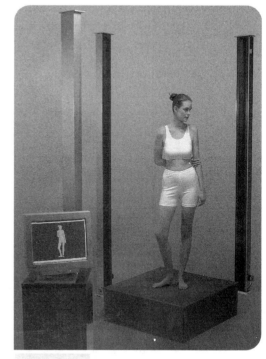

Body scanners capture precise body measurement data into a computer system.

Pattern Alteration Software

Body measurement data are sent electronically to an integrated computer pattern making system used for adapting the pattern. At the factory, patterns and markers are made automatically using a computer pattern alteration program. Currently, the mass-customized turnaround time is approximately 10 business days for shirts and 15 business days for suits.

Advances in computer pattern design systems have aided the implementation of mass customization. In some cases, once the customer's measurements have been input, the software analyzes the measurements and compares them to standard profiles to recommend a best size. Some made-to-measure software systems have built-in posture adjustments that can be requested, such as for round shoulders.

Reorders

The body measurement data can be saved on a **Smart Card** (about the size of a credit card) that contains the customer's body measurements. This data can be used again and updated by rescanning the customer if the body size changes. One of the benefits of using a made-to-measure pattern system is that the customer's data are saved, ensuring accuracy and consistency for reorders. The use of the manufacturer's or retailer's Internet site for reorders becomes a fast and easy option. The selection of other colors and fabrics for a style that the customer wants to reorder through the Internet is also an option.

For the manufacturer and retailer, the advantages to mass customization include the following:

- reducing large inventories that eat up profits and floor space
- minimizing returns
- reducing distribution costs
- building strong customer relationships
- solidifying brand loyalty
- identifying customer preferences and buying habits ("Made to measure," 1998, p. 3)

Another product well suited to mass customization is footwear. Each person's left foot is somewhat different in size from the right foot. By scanning each foot, the shoes can be customized to fit each foot precisely. The huge inventories of shoes stocked in varying lengths and widths, styles, and colors can be greatly reduced by mass customization, while the customer's shoe fit can be enhanced by scanning technology.

CAESAR Project

Compiling the body scanning data of many individuals creates a large bank of information about current customer sizes. An international project termed CAESAR (Civilian American and European Surface Anthropometry Resource) was launched in the late 1990s by the U.S. Air Force. This project was seeking better-fitting uniforms and gear. It is a partnership among the following:

- military

- several apparel companies such as Lee, Levi Strauss & Co., Vanity Fair, and Jantzen

- companies such as Boeing, Nissan Motor Co., and Caterpillar that build products (such as airplanes, automobiles, farm equipment) that people need to fit into (Silverman, 1998)

The bodies of thousands of men and women in the United States and Europe were scanned to build a database of body dimensions of the current population. From this accumulated data, manufacturers may determine new size standards for their target customers. The project partners have exclusive rights to the database of body measurements for one year before being released to the public ("The shape of clothes to come," 2000). The CAESAR project was implemented prior to the Size USA study discussed in Chapter 4. CAESAR included subjects from Europe, but it included fewer subjects than did the Size USA study. Some manufacturers have utilized the data gathered from Size USA in their pattern grading specifications.

In England, a national sizing survey to body scan thousands of men, women, and children has been funded by leading British retailers in partnership with technology vendors and universities. The intention is to use the data to manufacture made-to-measure clothing and for three-dimensional virtual shopping (Fallon, 1999).

DESIGN CUSTOMIZATION

Another approach to mass customization is design customization. Style preferences, as well as color and print choices available for each style offered, can be viewed by the customer at an interactive kiosk, or even at home through e-commerce. A customer selects a style that is shown in a video catalog; then he or she selects a preferred color, fabric print, and perhaps a choice of style features (see Figure 11.3). The customer can view his or her selection as a three-dimensional computer image.

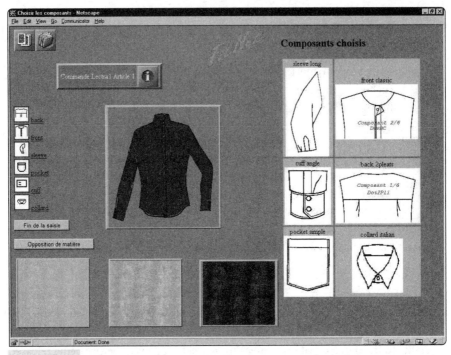

Figure 11.3   Mass customization links the customer's style preferences selected at the retail store or through the Internet to the production site.

College students were asked about their preferences for types of apparel that they would be most likely to customize. Researchers reported that both male and female students were most likely to customize jeans (Lee et al., 2002). Several companies offer customized jeans (e.g., JCPenney, Pittsburgh Jeans Company, makeyourownjeans.com).

Levi Strauss & Co. offers customized jeans at some retail stores. Various styling options are selected by the customer at an interactive kiosk. The customer selects from the following:

- several choices of leg styles
- several choices of fly styles
- several choices of waist styles
- several fabric options

Individualization also includes a customized inseam length selected by the customer. Levi's customized jeans arrive at the customer's home about two weeks later.

Currently, the customized product costs more, but many customers are willing to pay an additional amount for it. A survey by Kurt Salmon Associates indicated that "more than one third (36 percent) of consumers said that they would be willing to pay up to 12 percent to 15 percent more for custom-made apparel and footwear" ("Doing it their way," 1998, p. 42). The customer is provided with what he or she wants, when he or she wants it.

As mass customization is used more frequently as a manufacturing environment, the cost of the product to the consumer may well meet or fall below the cost to manufacture a similar style using mass production or short-cycle manufacturing environments. There is the potential for a substantial savings to manufacturers and retailers by maintaining a reduced inventory and by not producing the product until a customer's prepaid order has been submitted.

Combining design customization with scanned body dimensions provides additional options. When a customer inserts a Smart Card into the system, a three-dimensional replica of his or her body is shown on a computer screen. Thus, the customer can view the appearance of the garment style he or she has selected draped on his or her own body image, as a virtual try-on, before the garment is ordered. The color, fabric print, as well as style preferences can be changed on screen, and the customer can view a range of choices before making the final selection.

The future will include additional adaptations. Perhaps the pattern will be customized, the garment cut, a fabric printed with a customized print, and the garment sewn while the customer shops at one of the megamalls, returning a few hours later to collect the finished product.

PERSONALIZATION

One example of customizing a finished product, called *personalization*, is currently available at Levi's San Francisco retail store. A designated area at the retail store offers embroidery, laser etching, and fabric ornamentation while customers wait. Customers can add these personalized details to just-purchased items or to previously purchased items. This option appeals greatly to customers by satisfying their desire for individuality within our mass society—with a minimum of expense and waiting time. NIKEiD (http://nikeid.nike.com/) offers customers the opportunity to personalize sports apparel and footwear.

The three options for manufacturing environments—mass production, short-cycle production, and mass customization—provide the framework for examining the steps in production, from production sewing systems through delivery of finished goods. The first phase of production focuses on a discussion of the types of production sewing systems.

Production Sewing Systems

Although new production systems have been developed, older, traditional mass-manufacturing systems are still used in some facilities. It is important to understand the variety of production systems in order to make informed decisions about the production system most suitable for the garment style, price range, and sourcing option.

Single-Hand System

As discussed in Chapter 7, the prototype product is produced by a single individual. The sample maker (also called a *sample hand*) completes all the steps required in production, moving from one type of specialized equipment to another as needed, based on the garment or product style's requirements. Some apparel and accessory goods are produced in limited quantities using a system similar to that used to sew the prototype. In a single-hand system, one individual is responsible for sewing an entire garment. The bundle for this production system would include all the garment or product parts for one style in one size. In today's market, the **single-hand system** is used for couture and for some very high-priced apparel produced in a limited quantity. This system is slower than mass-production systems, and it may include considerable detail or handwork during production.

While some apparel is still sewn one at a time in a single-hand system, most apparel is manufactured using one of several production systems of large-quantity or *mass manufacturing*. The most common categories of these production systems are progressive bundle systems and flexible manufacturing systems.

Progressive Bundle System

Before the implementation of Quick Response and supply chain management strategies, the **progressive bundle system** was the most common production system used by apparel manufacturers. With the progressive bundle system, garment parts for a specified number of garments (for example, a dozen garments) are bundled together and put in carts that are rolled from one sewing machine operator to another. Each machine operator is responsible for the following:

  opening the bundle of the garment parts

  performing one or two construction steps on each garment in the bundle

  rebundling the garment parts for transport to the next operator

The operator's pay is calculated based on the number of pieces completed per day (*piece-rate wage*) (see Figure 11.4).

The progressive bundle system is especially well suited to large bundles of work, usually from one dozen to three dozen units per bundle. At each operator's work station, there is one bundle in process and one or several more bundles waiting. Sometimes referred to as a *batch* or *push* system, the progressive bundle system tends to generate high levels of **work-in-process (WIP)** and often creates bottlenecks in the production line as some operators outperform others (Hill, 1992). Also, a considerable investment of inventory is tied up with the WIP.

With the progressive bundle system, equipment is selected and sometimes customized to perform one or several functions needed for the production of the specific style. Each piece of equipment is positioned on the floor in relation to the equipment and sewing sequence required before and after each step in the production sequence. The machine operator is highly trained

With the bundle system, a sewing operator performs one or several sewing steps on each garment in the bundle.

to perform one or several steps on specific equipment. Each sewing facility tends to specialize in certain types of products, such as backpacks or swimwear. This specialization is due in part to the fact that different types of equipment are needed for producing different categories of products.

Sometimes the facility is arranged so that the body of the jacket is assembled in one part of the facility, and the lining is assembled in another part of the facility. The two parts of each garment are united at the final assembly stage. This requires careful tagging to ensure that sizes and dye lots are matched correctly at the final assembly stage. Due to the nature of the progressive bundle system, it can be difficult to pinpoint where a quality problem originates.

A new style ready for production may differ from previous styles in its production sequence or equipment needs. Machine operators may need additional training, so it may take time to develop the expertise to run at full capacity. Equipment may have to be moved within the facility to prepare for a different production sequence.

Flexible Manufacturing Systems

For mass-manufactured products, the bottom line is cost containment. This is affected by the following:

- the length of time that is required to prepare the product for production
- the length of time that the product is in process (work-in-process or WIP)

Reduction in one or both of these will result in a lower production cost. In the late 1980s, managers at manufacturing facilities began to explore ways to improve productivity and reduce production costs. Some companies focused on developing more **flexible manufacturing systems** involving one or all of the following:

- reorganization of existing equipment on the floor into a new systems approach
- development of new equipment
- reorganization of the way garments are routed through production
- reorganization of workers into teams who are cross-trained to handle a variety of operations using an assortment of equipment

Flexible manufacturing (FM) is defined as "any departure from traditional mass-production systems of apparel toward faster, smaller, more flexible production units that depend upon the coordinated efforts of minimally supervised teams of workers" (AAMA, Technical Advisory Committee, 1988, as cited in Hill, 1992). FM systems are known by many names, including the following:

- **modular manufacturing**
- self-directed work teams
- compact production teams
- flexible work groups

The emphasis of the strategy is on group effort, employee involvement, and employee empowerment.

In FM systems, manufacturing management makes a shift away from high individual productivity and low cost to short manufacturing cycles, small quantity of work-in-process, and quick delivery of the finished product. Flexible manufacturing is well suited to smaller production runs compared to large production runs that are efficient with the progressive bundle system. The term *modular manufacturing* is most often used in the U.S. apparel industry to describe flexible manufacturing (Hill, 1992).

With modular manufacturing, which is often referred to as a *pull system*, the sewing facility is organized into teams of seven to ten operators each. Operators are cross-trained in all areas of garment construction. Each operator might work on two or three machines. Operators might perform several tasks at each machine, or one machine might be used for a series of assembly operations. Every team is responsible for the production of entire garments, instead of one operator being assigned a single operation, such as setting in a sleeve or a zipper (as is done with the progressive bundle system). Equipment is arranged in modules so that work can be passed from one team member to another, who may work in either a standing or sitting position. The number of units within each operation may vary from only one to as many as ten.

Within a module, operators work as a team and solve problems, thus creating a more productive environment. Flaws in production are handled as a team; if a mistake is found, the entire garment is returned to the team, where the operators decide how best to fix it. Therefore, the traditional piece-rate wage is not applicable. The team is paid not only according to the quantity it produces, but also by the quality of its work. Pay is based on a collective effort. In theory, if an apparel factory was completely "modular," it would be redesigned into modular units, with each module producing complete garments in a few hours.

The following factors must be taken into consideration before a company decides to change to this system of manufacturing:

- Downtime is particularly critical with modular methods. With modular manufacturing, each minute a machine is down costs money, as it can slow down the entire team's work progress. A worker's absence can also slow down production.

- Converting to a modular manufacturing system requires the involvement of all employees, an investment in education and training, a shift of management responsibilities from a few people to the team as a whole, and support from management (Bennett, 1988).

- The shift to modular manufacturing requires a cultural change within a company. To create effective teams, the way employees think and perform has to change (Abend, 1999).

Some manufacturing facilities shifted to modular manufacturing in hopes of reducing manufacturing costs. For some companies, however, costs rose at first. Not only is there the cost involved if new equipment is purchased, cross-training employees costs money, and reduced productivity during training is an additional start-up cost. It may take months before a cost savings is realized (Abend, 1999).

For companies that commit to modular manufacturing, its cost benefits have been realized by containing costs through inventory reduction, a reduction in work-in-process, and for some facilities, an improvement in product quality. In one plant, "it has been possible to reduce a 5 percent to 10 percent level of irregulars production to less than 1 percent in one year ..." (Abend, 1999, p. 51).

Productivity has increased dramatically at some facilities that shifted to modular manufacturing. Production capacity at Nygård International's "Winnipeg manufacturing headquarters jumped from 20,000 to approximately 75,000 units per week under the modular arrangement" (Winger, 1998, p. AS-16).

Another advantage of modular manufacturing is that production facilities can shift quickly from manufacturing one type of product category to another. For example, a manufacturer can change its production facilities to accommodate producing intimate apparel, backpacks, and swimwear. At one facility, "engineers swap out the equipment as the last items in one product go through the line. Overnight the facility is ready for the new line, and then it's a matter of training operators, which can take one to three weeks to reach full capacity" (Hill, 1998, p. AS-8).

At Seams Reasonable, a contractor located in Red Boiling Springs, Tennessee, modules are composed of flexible eight-person sewing teams. Owner Toby Russell stated, "I couldn't sew the ladies' sleepwear line any other way because the production runs on certain styles are so small. We might sew four different styles out of three different fabrics in one day" (Abend, 1999, p. 51). Russell commented that the greatest benefit of modular manufacturing is fast turnaround time on small production runs of selected goods.

Some companies that have tried modular manufacturing found it was not successful for them. Although Levi Strauss & Co. no longer has production facilities in the United States, its trial with modular manufacturing is worth reviewing. The company opened a new modular manufacturing facility in 1995. At the end of the first year, excess costs were astronomically high, attributed to exceptional start-up costs. By the end of the second year, the capacity had increased about 53 percent, but excess costs were over 31 percent. Halfway into the third year, capacity had increased 6 percent over the second year. However, the excess costs had increased to 49 percent over standard (Dunagan, 1999). In an article about Levi's modular manufacturing attempt, consulting engineer Charles Gilbert stated, "Thirty-four months after start-up in modules, we converted the plant to the 'old' progressive bundle system" (Dunagan, 1999). Management at Levi Strauss & Co. did not have the answer regarding what went wrong with its attempt at modular manufacturing. A number of factors may have contributed to its lack of success. In some cases, companies do not completely convert all aspects of employee training, equipment needs, and management commitment to modular manufacturing. It is clear that the choice of manufacturing method is dependent on many variables.

UNIT PRODUCTION SYSTEMS

To achieve efficient and effective short-cycle manufacturing, some companies have invested in new technology. One form of technology investment is a computerized overhead transport system such as the **unit production system (UPS)**. With UPS, garment parts are fed on overhead conveyors, usually one garment at a time, to sewing machine operators (see Figure 11.5). Garment parts are delivered directly to the operators' ergonomically designed workstations. This dramatically reduces operator handling time during production. Workstations can be moved easily to accommodate different equipment needs for various garments. Operators are cross-trained in a number of procedures in the manufacturing cycle, similar to the way they are for modular manufacturing. The transport system is designed to include bar codes to track WIP.

Figure 11.5   With a unit production system, the pieces of each garment are delivered to the sewing operator. The operator may not need to remove the garment from the conveyor while performing the sewing operation.

A study by Clemson Apparel Research (Hill, 1994) determined that UPS would provide the hypothetical apparel manufacturing plant a 329 percent return on its investment and would pay for itself in 11 months. The primary savings to the company would be in the areas of reduced direct labor costs (shorter waiting periods, less overtime, improved ergonomics) and reduced work-in-process inventory levels. Figure 11.6 shows computerized tracking of WIP. Many production facilities have shown substantial increases in production with UPS. Other companies have found UPS to be less successful. As with modular manufacturing, many variables enter into the success of UPS.

AGILE MANUFACTURING

Agile manufacturing combines a variety of technologies that together form a totally integrated, seamless exchange of information linking retailers and suppliers to the manufacturing facility ([TC]^2, 1993). An example is mass customization. This manufacturing environment allows for individual changes in style, color, and fit, using a customer's body measurements and modifications of a pattern based on a style developed by the apparel company. The manufacturing

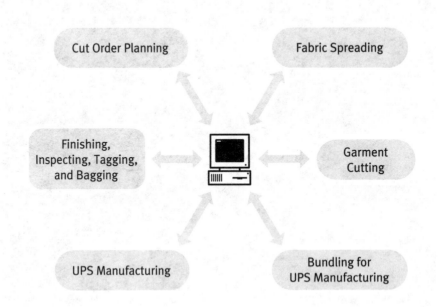

Cut Order Planning

Fabric Spreading

Finishing, Inspecting, Tagging, and Bagging

Garment Cutting

UPS Manufacturing

Bundling for UPS Manufacturing

Figure 11.6 Computerized production systems permit computer tracking of work-in-process, as well as increased efficiency compared with the bundle system.

facility cuts an individual customized style from a PDS and marker making system linked electronically to a single-ply cutter. White fabric prepared for digital printing might be printed before or after cutting (see Chapter 6) to the customer's color and print specifications. After printing and cutting, the garment is manufactured using a production system that is designed to accommodate units of one (see Figure 11.7).

Rabon and Deaton (1999) contended that an overhead conveyor system for unit production (UPS) is a key to success of companies in the mass-customization arena. Modular manufacturing teams of cross-trained operators sew the customized orders. Computer-based learning materials and interactive programs help provide the training that sewing operators need. After completion, the order is packaged and sent directly to the customer, eliminating warehouse inventories ([TC]^2, 1993). It is the integration of these technologies that creates agile manufacturing.

Figure 11.7 Digital printing integrates design, pattern making, and production.

Combination of Systems

Some production facilities utilize more than one type of production system. For example, a contractor may use UPS for certain garment styles that suit this production system, while using a progressive bundle system for other styles. As discussed earlier, the number of units to be made influences the production system. For example, modular manufacturing may be more economical for small production runs than the progressive bundle system.

Production Workers' Wage Rates

The progressive bundle system of production frequently uses a **piece-rate wage** system. Each operator's pay is based on individual productivity. The number of units the operator has completed at the end of each workday or week is the basis for the operator's pay for that time period. New developments in software provide a means to set accurate piece rates in a manufacturing environment that is constantly changing (Hill, 1998).

With modular manufacturing, some companies use a team wage calculation rate. Bonus incentives might be provided for exemplary productivity and/or a very low rate of errors or irregulars.

Some companies have decided that an hourly rate is most equitable. An hourly rate gives the flexibility to change production runs during the day, especially if a priority order has just been cut and needs to be produced immediately. Also, an hourly rate is fairer if production includes diverse products.

Developments in Production Equipment and Technology

The industrial machines used in production facilities are designed to sew much faster than home sewing machines. While home sewing machines are driven by motors, industrial machines have engines, with a clutch, a brake, and continuous oil feed. Home sewing machines can perform many different functions (sew straight stitch seams, zigzag, overcast, blind hem, and make buttonholes), whereas industrial machines perform very specialized functions (sew buttonholes or sew straight stitch (lockstitch) seams or blind stitch hems). The specialized equipment may be fitted with additional devices or guides to customize an operation further. For example, a metal plate can be added to the sewing bed to guide elastic evenly under the needle.

While many machines for production were developed so that operators sit during operation, standup sewing is another option (see Figure 11.8). It costs about $1,000 to convert a sewing machine to standup operation. Ergonomic analysis indicates that there are substantial advantages to standup sewing.

An example of a development in production technology is one that focused on reducing the puckering encountered when assembling wrinkle-resistant cotton and cotton/polyester-blend dress shirts, lightweight slacks, uniforms, and other casual wear. TAL Apparel of Hong Kong, one of the world's largest shirt makers, spent four years developing its TAL Pucker Free process. A bonding tape is inserted into the seam between two layers of fabric. The tape, which contains a thermal adhesive component, is melted during the manufacturing process. "The result is a strong, permanent bond along the seam that eliminates differential shrinkage between the thread and fabric, the primary cause of seam puckering" (DesMarteau, 1998). The company patented a seam sealing process in the United States and has licensed the technology to U.S. manufacturers. Licensees pay a royalty fee, a percent of the retail price of the garment, to TAL.

Figure 11.8 Sewing equipment has been developed to facilitate operation by workers who stand rather than sit while sewing.

Equipment maintenance is a critical concern for production sewing. Any breakdown of equipment can stall production, which can be of great concern to an entire team on a production line. Maintenance personnel must be ready to troubleshoot, repair, or replace equipment rapidly. New developments have alleviated some of the maintenance concerns. For example, computerized systems have been developed to distribute power and electrical information to all sewing stations. In some countries, machine parts or technicians are not immediately available, causing delays in the production schedule.

The noise level and airborne fiber particles in sewing facilities are concerns, especially in some offshore facilities. In the United States, workers wear protective clothing, air filtration systems are used in factories, and other environmental controls have been implemented.

High-technology systems will continue to play an increasingly important role in cost reduction efforts. Regardless of the production system used, new equipment will be developed to enhance production. These developments include new types of computerized, programmable sewing machines; robotic sewing equipment; and continued improvements in cutting equipment. Just as the cost of personal computers has declined over time, high-tech equipment costs have also declined, making it more affordable to apparel manufacturers.

Production Sequence

Different categories of products may require very different processes and types of equipment. For example, men's tailored suits require many more steps in production than men's casual sportswear. In addition, the types of sewing and pressing equipment are quite different for tailored apparel as compared to sportswear. In Chapter 4, it was mentioned that different sewing processes and types of equipment are required for various classifications of apparel. Boys' and girls' clothing requires similar sewing processes and equipment and could be manufactured at the same facility, whereas men's tailored clothing and men's sportswear production need to be handled by different production facilities.

An important aspect of preproduction and production is planning the sequence of operations required to produce the garment style. Production includes the sewing sequence, as well as other tasks performed at the sewing facility that relate to completing the product. These tasks might include the following:

- fusing interfacing
- applying embroidery
- applying labels
- pressing
- attaching hangtags
- folding and packaging (or hanging and bagging) the finished product

These production steps and the time required for each step need to be determined for each garment style. This information is referred to as the *construction specifications* (see Chapter 9).

As discussed in Chapter 9, the sequence of sewing operations may have been determined at the time that the style's cost was calculated. The production sequence used to sew the sales representatives' samples, made to market the style to retail buyers, is frequently the same as the sequence used to sew the production orders. Any problems in production might be corrected during the production of the sales samples.

Determining the most efficient production sequence depends on many factors, such as the following:

- the equipment capabilities of the specific production facility (e.g., the availability of a pocket setting machine can greatly speed production of a style with a welt pocket)
- the labor cost of the operators (in some factories where labor is very inexpensive, more work may be done by hand than with expensive equipment)

whether certain steps should be subcontracted (e.g., a shirt with a pleated front inset might be less expensive to produce if the fabric for the front inset were sent to a pleating contractor, and then returned to the production facility for cutting and sewing into the shirt)

Some operations may be performed prior to the sewing process, such as the following:

- Interfacing may be fused to garment sections prior to sewing. The pieces to be fused are laid on conveyor belts and moved through large fusing "ovens" to adhere the interfacing.

- Patch pockets, such as those sewn to the back of jeans, are prepared for sewing by prepressing the raw edges to the inside. By folding the edges over a metal template of the exact size of the finished pocket, accurate dimensions can be maintained. A fusing agent might be applied to help the seam allowances adhere to the inside of the pocket. Hundreds of pockets are prepared; then they are delivered to the site where they will be attached to the pants. Since garment pieces may be cut from dye lots with varying color, care must be taken to match pocket pieces to garment sections from an identical dye lot. If the pockets were made in small, medium, and large sizes, care must be taken to attach the prepared pockets to the correct size pant.

- Belt loops might be made from very long strips prepared for the entire production run. Yards of the strips are wound onto holders attached to the sewing station. The belt loops are cut to length one at a time and sewn sequentially around the pant waistband.

Many processes are streamlined to provide the most labor-effective production.

Sometimes several different factories are used to produce a large order. In such cases, the production sequences may not be exactly the same at the different factories producing the same style. Each contractor submits a sample sewn at its factory to the apparel manufacturer for approval. For the samples sewn for sales representatives by contractors, the same process of submitting a sewn sample is used. The contractor's sample is called a **sew by** or a **counter sample**. After approval, this sample is used as the benchmark against which to check the sewn production goods.

Although great effort is expended to plan a smooth production run, many problems can stall production. Some problems that involve the procurement of materials have already been discussed. Production problems include complications due to delays in receiving a shipment of zippers or late arrival of subcontracted work. Troubleshooting is an integral part of production. When sourcing offshore, unexpected problems can be difficult to solve.

A flood in Bangladesh, a hurricane in the Dominican Republic, or a rail workers' strike in France can cause production or delivery delays that could not be planned for or avoided. Management personnel of apparel manufacturers often travel to production facilities (whether company-owned or contractor-owned) to check on production or help solve production problems.

Finishing

At the end of the production line, the goods await various finishing steps. Pressing may occur only at this stage in production. Edge stitching or topstitching may be used to reduce the need to press during production, thereby reducing labor costs. Specialized pressing equipment produces excellent results on finished goods very quickly. For tailored jackets, a steam mannequin might be used to press the entire jacket while on a three-dimensional form. Other types of specialized equipment perform other functions, such as turning pant legs right side out (pants come off the production line inside out). Finishing operations include thread trimming, button and snap attachment, shoulder pad and lining tacking, pressing, and buttoning the garment.

Some labels are sewn in during production. These might include care labels, brand labels, and size labels. Printed care, fiber content, and size information can also be heat sealed directly onto the product. This method eliminates the potential for skin irritation from a woven label, as well as the bulk produced by one or more sew-in labels applied to a product. Called **tagless labels**, they debuted first on T-shirts, then underwear, performance wear, and children's wear, products where labels can be particularly annoying (Speer, 2004). The market trend is toward increased use of tagless labels (see Figure 11.9).

Other labels, as well as hangtags, might be attached during finishing operations. Hangtags can be used to provide additional product marketing information. For example, the water resistance or UV protective properties of a jacket's fabric might be explained on the hangtag. Providing goods with floor-ready labels and hangtags takes place at this stage in production. Preparing floor-ready merchandise will be discussed later in this chapter, as well as in Chapter 12. Labels might include

Figure 11.9 Finishing processes include the use of machinery to apply tagless labels.

identifying characteristics hidden to the eye. A bar code "fingerprint" visible to a scanning device can be included in the sew-in label to identify the product's production facility or retail destination. This technology can reduce the possibility of counterfeit goods and can also be used by the retailer to verify the origin of goods returned by customers. One system uses a silicon chip tagging system. Called Radio Frequency Identification (RFID), the silicon chip is attached to an antenna made of thin, flexible silver ink that utilizes radio frequency identification technology. In addition to deterring hijacking and shoplifting, the tag can be used to sort laundry and to log the number of times a uniform has been laundered. The tag is about the size of a garment label and is coated with a plastic laminate to protect it from dry-cleaning chemicals. The tag can be sewn into a seam, hidden from view to deter removal by shoplifters or counterfeiters. (See also Chapter 1.) Another technology used to verify authenticity of products is the use of "metallic strips (similar to those in U.S. currency) that are woven into labels and covert yarns that are visible under certain wavelengths of light. Companies are also weaving serial numbers into labels, providing each garment with a unique identifier" (Speer, 2004, p. 29).

Other types of finishing operations include a variety of fabric treatments. Special finishes might be incorporated during finishing of the garments, rather than to the textile goods at the textile mill. For example, a wrinkle-resistant finish might be applied to apparel goods, such as 100 percent cotton trousers, after they are sewn. Technological developments will continue to improve garment-applied finishes.

Garments might be laundered before shipping. Laundering might be performed to enhance the hand or visual appeal of the fabric. For example, stone washing is used to soften denim fabric. Other treatments are used to "age" or distress denim. Another reason for laundering is to shrink a product prior to shipping. While we are familiar with purchasing some products large enough to "shrink to fit," many consumers find it advantageous to know that the garment has been preshrunk. They know that the way the garment fits when it is tried on at the retail store is the way it will fit after washing at home. For garments that will be laundered after production and before shipping, the pattern pieces for the garment have to be created very carefully with the exact shrinkage factor incorporated into each pattern piece. Koos Manufacturing, located in the Los Angeles area, produces "nearly 100,000 pairs of denim and twill pants a week for Calvin Klein and the ubiquitous Gap chain, and produces another 80,000 garments with the help of four subcontractors" ("A showroom of high-tech sewing," 1998, p. 54). These pants are laundered before shipping. The laundry section operates 24 hours a day in three shifts, processing about 200,000 units weekly.

Many apparel manufacturers produce dyed products in color allotments based on the quantity of orders for each color. Other manufacturers produce "colorless" garments, and then dye the garments during finishing. Such goods are referred to as **garment dyed**. Dyeing finished goods has several advantages. It can provide quick delivery of the goods to the retailer because production can begin on the colorless garments while the sales force is accumulating the sales totals by color. For the same reason, it represents a reduced risk to the manufacturer. Garment dyeing can be considered one of the Quick Response strategies. Care must be taken to select buttons and other findings and trims that can accommodate the dyeing operation.

Finishing operations can produce air pollutants or waste products that must be discarded. Since concern was first raised about the environmental consequences of some finishing operations, much has been done to minimize their negative environmental impact. New developments will continue to improve environmental protection.

Goods are prepared for shipping by being folded or hung. At some facilities, folding might be accomplished by hand, with cardboard, tissue, straight pins, and plastic bags. At other facilities, machines are used to fold the goods. For garments placed on hangers, overhead conveyors bring the garments to equipment that covers each item with a plastic bag. Some hanger and bagged garments are moved from a conveyor belt at the factory directly onto an overhead track on the truck that delivers the bagged garments to the manufacturer's distribution center, to the retailer's distribution center, or directly to the retail store (see Chapter 12).

Floor-Ready Merchandise

Floor-ready merchandise (FRM) is an aspect of Quick Response and supply chain management that results from an alliance between the apparel manufacturer and the retailer. FRM shifts certain steps from the retailer to the manufacturer, where they become part of the finishing process. The FRM policies generally require that the apparel manufacturer ship the goods to the retailer's distribution center or retail store with bar coded price tickets, carton labels, shipping documents, and hanger applications. "If FRM can only remove two days of delay associated with a retailer's distribution center, and if the DC [distribution center] is typically receiving goods every two weeks, then it is possible to get 52 additional selling days per year" (Swank, 1995, p. 106). The use of floor-ready merchandise from the retailer's perspective will be discussed in Chapter 12.

As discussed in Chapter 3, **quality assurance** involves making sure the product meets the standards of acceptance set forth by the contracting party. The contracting party might be the apparel manufacturer for goods produced by a contractor. The contracting party might be a retailer for private-label or store brand goods. Many of the fabrics and trims and sewing operations are specified in detail on the garment specification sheet and are an important part of quality assurance. Visual inspection after completion of production—for loose threads, for example—forms another important part of quality assurance.

The fabric inspection component of quality assurance was discussed in Chapters 3 and 9. The spreading and cutting operations include considerations such as on-grain garment parts and dye lot color matching. Quality assurance also takes place during the sewing and finishing operations. Garments are inspected during production to assure the specified quality standard. Inspectors can include machine operators, team quality auditors, plant supervisors, or quality auditors sent by the contracting party (apparel manufacturer or retailer).

Quality assurance includes the use of quality thread, buttons, zippers, snaps, elastic, hem tape, and other products; and the quality and accuracy of sewing operations such as stitch type and length, stitch tension, seam type, edge finish, top stitching, turned edges, buttonhole stitching, hem stitching, and plaid matching. Quality assurance personnel are well versed in evaluating all aspects of production quality and accuracy.

Another component of quality assurance is the consistency of the size specifications for all products produced in each size. All the finished products must conform to the specified tolerances (the amount the product can deviate, plus or minus, from the garment dimension) stated on the measurement spec sheet (see Chapter 9). Many apparel manufacturers check a specified number of garments in each shipment received from the contractor to determine whether the measurement specs have been met.

The difficulty lies in deciding what to do with any products that do not meet the quality standards. It may not be possible to cut and sew a replacement order of garments if a group of finished goods does not meet the specifications. The textile manufacturer may not have replacement fabric, or the time necessary to produce replacement garments may exceed the deadline established by the retailer. Some garments end up as seconds at company employee stores and outlet malls, may be purchased by jobbers, or are given to charities. In addition to the loss to the apparel manufacturer and contractor, the retailer expecting the goods may suffer if an order cannot be filled. Therefore, it is to everyone's benefit to assure quality production.

In developing quality assurance programs, companies are relying less on after-the-fact inspection and more on building quality into the products during production. Through modular manufacturing methods, operators are responsible for the quality of the product throughout production.

Current emphasis in quality assurance focuses on actively monitoring the manufacturing methods, materials, work environment, and equipment to achieve the expected specifications on a continual basis. One such method is called statistical process control (SPC). SPC "requires the in-line measurement of quality in a statistical sampling of consecutive garments—usually in small batches—as they come off a particular operation hour by hour. This is opposed to other commonly used methods, which tend to involve in-line and end-of-line inspections of large random samples" (DesMarteau, 1999, p. 35). By in-process measurement and quality inspection, anomalies can be identified at a time when it is more likely that a correction can be made. Thus, quality assurance is a proactive rather than reactive approach to quality.

Export Agents, Freight Forwarders, and Customs Brokers

A substantial portion of the apparel and accessories industries relies on offshore factory production. Thus, it is important to discuss some of the aspects related to shipping goods out of the country where they were produced and into the United States. Many foreign countries have export regulations for shipping goods out of the country. It can be helpful for the U.S. apparel manufacturer that contracted the goods (the *importer*) to appoint an **export agent** in the exporting country to assist with exporting the products.

A **freight forwarding company** arranges to move a shipment of goods from the country where the goods were produced to the United States. In Figure 11.10, a shipment of goods is off-loaded at its port of entry in the United States. Tariffs and quotas (regulations affecting apparel manufacturers that import apparel and textile products into the United States) were discussed in Chapters 2 and 10. The Office of U.S. Customs and Border Protection, a part of the federal government, is the regulatory agency. A **customs broker** (licensed by the Office of U.S. Customs and Border Protection) in the United States is an agent hired by the U.S. apparel manufacturer to assist the company in importing the products produced for the company in another country. The customs broker is familiar with the complex U.S. customs regulations concerning importing textiles and apparel, and will assist the apparel manufacturer

Figure 11.10   Container ships at the Port of Long Beach, California, unload their cargoes.

to gain customs clearance. The manufacturer is charged a fee by the customs broker on a transaction basis, not by the number of items in a transaction. While using a customs broker is optional, it can be very helpful to the apparel manufacturer. Sometimes, a shipment of goods is stalled by customs or sent back to the country of origin to correct the documentation. Not only does the apparel manufacturer face losing the retailer's business, but it may also face a fine by the shipping company that cannot unload the shipment. Of course, additional transportation costs are also involved. A consolidator might also be hired by the apparel manufacturer to serve as an intermediary for the freight forwarder and the customs broker.

Summary

This chapter examined some of the important aspects of production. With the background of the previous chapters, the interrelationship among research, design, pattern development, marketing, preproduction, sourcing, and production should be clear. All systems must work together for production to flow smoothly. Any problem along a style's path may slow production. Delays to the contracted delivery date may cost the manufacturer not only the style's profits, but future business from retailers.

A significant portion of the cost to produce apparel is consumed by the labor required to cut and sew the goods. Reducing labor costs can help retain reasonable prices for finished goods. Specialized equipment has been developed to speed production and improve accuracy. New technology in equipment and manufacturing systems has dramatically changed apparel production and provided a more efficient use of the labor team. Workers are more actively involved in providing an efficient production system and in team responsibility for the quality of the goods produced. Even with the high cost of new, technologically advanced equipment, the increase in production efficiency can rapidly pay for the cash outlay to purchase new equipment.

Changes in production sewing systems have required changes in the manner in which employee compensation is determined. Pay based on the team's performance, group incentives for high performance and quality, and straight hourly wages have replaced traditional piece rates at many facilities. Workers are cross-trained on various types of equipment and in a variety of skills to provide greater flexibility to the workforce.

The number of different garment styles produced per season has increased for many production facilities. This makes it more difficult for production to flow smoothly. Flexibility in production systems will continue to be an important cornerstone of increased efficiency and decreased labor costs. Concern for workers' ergonomic needs is another trend that has changed the look of production facilities. We no longer see banks of seated sewers bent over sewing machines. Workers stand, walk from point to point, and sit on stools to provide better body positioning, circulation, and muscle relaxation.

Finishing operations performed at the end of production include laundering and applying garment finishes and garment dyeing, as well as packaging products ready for distribution. Providing floor-ready merchandise for the retailer with bar coded hangtags improves the efficiency of the entire flow of goods.

Quality assurance is an integral part of the product, from its inception to arrival in the customer's hands. Quality assurance includes meeting quality standards for all aspects of the product: the textile goods, component parts such as buttons and zippers, sewing, measurement specifications, and finishing.

With the growth in offshore apparel manufacturing, it is increasingly important to understand the various processes, agencies, and personnel involved in these complex business transactions. Changes in regulations, as well as in political and economic conditions and environmental considerations, can affect the production of goods.

Product Lifecycle Management Success Story: Zara

In the world of fashion sourcing, Zara's achievements are legendary. The specialty apparel chain has figured out how to cut the lead time for sourcing apparel from six months or more to just 15 days. In fact, Spain-based Zara delivers new products to all of its 600-plus stores twice a week, and designs and produces more than 11,000 new products each year.

The secret to Zara's speed to market, inventory efficiency, and customer responsiveness is its vertically integrated supply chain. The company makes about 40 percent of its own fabric and produces around 60 percent of the merchandise it sells.

Zara keeps the process close to its vest. Fabrics are cut and dyed on demand in the retailer's automated factories in Spain, and the company relies on a network of 300 to 400 small workshops throughout Spain and Portugal to piece together finished goods. Products are typically produced in small lots, a strategy that translates into fewer risks and markdowns.

The genius of the Zara model is that they ask their customers what they want, and then they give it to them. Using hand-held electronic devices, store managers communicate customer feedback on what shoppers like, what they don't like, and what they're looking for. That data is instantly funneled back to Zara's designers who begin sketching on the spot.

EXCERPTS FROM: Reda, Susan. (2004, March). Retail's Great Race. *Stores*, p. 38.

Careers in production include positions as production cutters, sewing operators, production supervisors, plant managers, and quality assurance coordinators. If you are considering a career in the production area, what would your position description entail, and what would some of your typical tasks and responsibilities be?

Production Manager
Private-Label Manufacturer of Intimate Apparel

Position Description

Manage the production of in-house sampling requirements (market, first fit, sew by, and photo samples); technical development; standards; quality control; price negotiations; place orders with suppliers and subcontractors; develop and implement production procedures and controls; and oversee production personnel. Manage contracted production in countries where the garments are produced.

Typical Tasks and Responsibilities

- Serve as a liaison with design, sales, and the sample room, as well as with factories.
- Visit factories for a preproduction review of new styles and to check production in process, as well as approve production for shipment.
- Review samples from factories to check for specifications, and approve fabric, trims, and color.
- Organize labels and packaging.
- Prepare cost sheets.

Apparel Quality Analyst
Publicly Held Athletic Sportswear Company

Position Description

Investigate and prepare reports on all apparel quality issues working toward a resolution. Recommend action and follow up with affected parties (development, marketing, sales, promotion). Develop and maintain a strong working relationship with related departments. Conduct meetings with departments to inform and reach a joint decision. Arrange for components, fabric, and finished product tests and inspections as necessary. Communicate with quality assurance managers in the United States and throughout the world. The apparel quality analyst position functions as a global position.

Typical Tasks and Responsibilities

- Communicate daily by e-mail and telephone with related departments throughout the life of the quality issue.

- Prepare weekly quality logs for the QA department.

- Investigate the scope, nature, probable cause, and resolution of quality issues. Samples from the field and distribution center come to this position.

- Prepare reports and submit samples to the textile testing lab when the quality issue involves fabric development.

- Perform inspection/audits at factories once a month. Being a field auditor is a small part of the apparel quality analyst's responsibility as there are other field auditors who inspect/audit factories.

Key Terms

agile manufacturing
body scanning
counter sample
customs broker
export agent
flexible manufacturing (FM)
flexible manufacturing system
floor-ready merchandise (FRM)
freight forwarding company
garment dyed
made-to-measure
manufacturing environment
mass customization

modular manufacturing
piece-rate wage
production
progressive bundle system
quality assurance
sew by
short-cycle production
single-hand system
Smart Card
tagless label
unit production system (UPS)
work-in-process (WIP)

Discussion Questions

1. The quality assurance department finds that the contracted goods do not meet the stated size specifications within the allowed tolerance. What are some of the problems faced by the apparel company if the shipment (or part of it) is rejected?

2. Compare and contrast the advantages and disadvantages of the progressive bundle and flexible manufacturing systems of apparel production.

3. Describe a quality defect that you have encountered with an apparel/home fashions product or accessory. How might quality assurance have prevented this problem?

References

Abend, Jules. (1999, January). Modular manufacturing: The line between success and failure. *Bobbin*, pp. 48–52.

Bennett, Billy. (1988, October). It's a mod, mod, mod environment. *Bobbin*, pp. 50–55.

Butenhoff, Peter. (1999, May). Mass production, short-cyle, and mass customization: SCM's manufacturing trio. *Apparel Industry Magazine*, p. SCM-4.

Conrad, Andrée. (1999, May). Designing for demand: SCM dream or reality? *Apparel Industry Magazine*, pp. SCM-6–SCM-11.

DesMarteau, Kathleen. (1998, August). Wrinkle free now carefree. *Bobbin*, p. 188.

DesMarteau, Kathleen. (1999, July). Liz launches global quality coup. *Bobbin*, pp. 34–38.

Doing it their way. (1998, May). *Apparel Industry Magazine*, pp. 42–44.

Dunagan, Evelyn. (1999, January). Another perspective on modular manufacturing: Levi's was right. *Apparel Industry Magazine*, pp. 96–98.

Fallon, James. (1999, February 10). British retailers kick off body-scanning project. *DNR*, p. 13.

Haisley, Tracy. (2002, February). Brooks Brothers digital tailors measure up. *Bobbin*, pp. 26–30.

Hill, Ed. (1992, February). Flexible manufacturing systems, Part 1. *Bobbin*, pp. 34–38.

Hill, Suzette. (1998, December). VF's consumerization: A "right stuff" strategy. *Apparel Industry Magazine*, pp. AS-4–AS-12.

Hill, Thomas. (1994, March). CAR study: UPS, CAD provide 300 percent return on investment. *Apparel Industry Magazine*, pp. 34–40.

Lee, Seung-Eun, Kunz, Grace I., Fiore, Ann Marie, and Campbell, J.R. (2002, 20:3). Acceptance of mass customization of apparel: Merchandising issues associated with preference for product, process, and place. *Clothing & Textiles Research Journal*, pp. 138–146.

Made to measure or mass customization: Is it for you? (1998, vol. 18, no. 1). *Cuttings*, pp. 2–6.

Rabon, Lisa. (2000, January). Mixing the elements of mass customization. *Bobbin*, pp. 38–41.

Rabon, Lisa, and Deaton, Claudia. (1999, December). Pre-production: Laying the cornerstones of mass customization. *Bobbin*, pp. 35–37.

Reda, Susan. (2004, March). Retail's great race. *Stores*, p. 38.

The shape of clothes to come. (2000, January). *Consumer Reports*, p. 8.

A showroom of high-tech sewing: Koos Manufacturing Inc. (1998, May). *Apparel Industry Magazine*, p. 54.

Silverman, Dick. (1998, November 11). A better fit through body scanning. *Women's Wear Daily*, p. 8.

Speer, Jordan K. (2004, April). A label-conscious world. *Apparel*, pp. 24–29.

Swank, Gary. (1995, January). QR requires floor-ready goods. *Apparel Industry Magazine*, p. 106.

[TC][2] (Producer). (1993). [Video]. Agile Manufacturing: "The Vision."

Winger, Rocio Maria. (1998, December). The Nygård vanguard: The way to chargebacks. *Apparel Industry Magazine*, pp. AS-14–AS-18.

CHAPTER 12

Distribution
and Retailing

In this chapter, you will learn the following:

- the strategies and processes for distributing apparel, accessory, and home fashions products to the ultimate consumer

- the nature of the alliances between manufacturers and retailers in carrying out supply chain management and product lifecycle management activities related to distribution

- the definitions and characteristics of the various categories of retailers

- the primary trade publications and trade associations involved in the distribution of apparel, accessory, and home fashions products

Step 8: Distribution and Retailing

Research and Merchandising

Design

Design Development and Style Selection

Marketing the Apparel Line

Preproduction

Sourcing

Apparel Production Processes,
Material Management, and Quality Assurance

Distribution and Retailing

Send Retailer's Order to Manufacturer's Distribution Center

Pick Orders (may include quality assurance check)

Send to Retail Store Distribution Center or Directly to Retailer

Review Season's Sales Figures

Distribution Strategies

W*e have followed apparel, accessory, and home fashions products from their design through their production. The next stage is distribution to retailers and, finally, to the ultimate consumer (see Step 8 of the flowchart on the previous page). Companies must decide on the strategies they will use to distribute merchandise. Decisions regarding distribution strategies are based on a number of factors, which will be examined in detail in this chapter.*

Factors Affecting Distribution Strategies

Decisions regarding distribution strategies are based on a number of factors:

- *Type of marketing channel to which the company belongs:* Companies using direct marketing channels will sell directly to the ultimate consumer. Companies using limited marketing channels will sell merchandise through store or nonstore retailing venues. Companies using extended marketing channels will sell merchandise through a wholesaler, who then sells the merchandise to a retailer. (These channels—direct, limited, and extended—were described in Chapter 2.)

- *Buying characteristics of the target customer:* Certain target market customers will prefer certain distribution strategies. For example, a manufacturer of women's career apparel may focus on retail venues that are convenient to large office complexes and are service oriented.

- *Product type:* Categories of merchandise may lend themselves to certain retail distribution strategies. For example, socks, underwear, and other packaged merchandise lend themselves to retailers who include self-service fixtures in the retail venues.

- *National, private-label, or store brand product?:* National brands are generally found in many different retail stores, whereas private-label merchandise and store brands are unique to particular stores or groups of stores.

- *Price zone of merchandise:* Budget-priced merchandise will more often be distributed through discount stores than through other types of retailers, whereas designer-priced merchandise will more often be distributed through boutiques or specialty stores than through other types of retailers.

Classifications of Distribution Strategies

Distribution strategies can be classified as mass distribution, selective distribution, or exclusive distribution.

- *Mass distribution:* With **mass distribution** (also called **intensive distribution**), products are made available to as many consumers as possible through a variety of retail outlets, including supermarkets, convenience stores, and mass merchandisers or discount stores. The L'eggs and Hanes hosiery brands use this distribution strategy, as do activewear brands, such as Champion and Russell.

- *Selective distribution:* With **selective distribution**, manufacturers allow their merchandise to be distributed only through certain stores. Some manufacturers require a minimum quantity to be purchased; others limit their products' distribution to retailers in noncompeting geographic areas. Some manufacturers also set criteria as to the image and location of stores in which their merchandise can be sold. Most national brands use this type of distribution strategy. For example, 7 for All Mankind premium denim is distributed through selected specialty and department stores based on criteria set by the manufacturer.

- *Exclusive distribution:* With **exclusive distribution**, manufacturers limit the stores in which their merchandise is distributed in order to create an image of exclusiveness. Companies that produce merchandise in the designer price zone (e.g., Chanel, Armani, Vera Wang) often use an exclusive distribution strategy by selling goods only through a few stores or boutiques. The distribution of private-label merchandise (e.g., JCPenney's Arizona brand, Kmart's Jaclyn Smith brand, Target's xhilaration brand, Macy's INC International brand), exclusive licensing brands (e.g., Target's Mossimo and Isaac Mizrahi brands), and store brands (e.g., Gap, The Limited, Ann Taylor) that are specific to a particular retailer is also considered to be exclusive because the brands are available only at specific stores.

Distribution Territories

Retailers must also determine how broad their distribution territories will be. Some retailers will focus on a local target customer with retail establishments in a single community; others will distribute more broadly, either regionally or nationally; and still others will be global retailers, distributing merchandise in more than one country. With the retail saturation of the U.S. market, many companies have expanded their retail operations to other countries. Examples include the following:

- Wal-Mart, the world's largest retailer, has retail operations in the United States, Canada, South America, and Asia.
- JCPenney has retail operations in Brazil and Puerto Rico, in addition to the United States.
- Gap has retail operations in Canada, France, Germany, the United Kingdom, Japan, and the United States.

In addition, with nonstore retailing, such as e-retailing and television shopping, companies have expanded their distribution beyond local or even national markets. Before retailers expand their operations into other countries, it is imperative that they understand the demographics, decision making orientation, and cultural norms of the consumers in the country.

Distribution Centers

For some apparel and home fashions companies, shipments of finished merchandise to their retail accounts are made directly from the production facility. For other apparel and home fashions companies, the flow of goods from production facilities to retailers involves the use of **distribution centers (DCs)**. Both manufacturers and retailers may utilize distribution centers as part of their distribution processes. Their decision to use distribution centers in their distribution processes is based on the following:

- the size of the company
- the number of products being distributed
- the number of retail stores being serviced
- the distance between where the merchandise was produced and where the retail accounts are located

The larger the company and the more products and retailers involved, the more likely distribution centers will be used.

Manufacturers' Distribution Centers

Apparel and home fashions manufacturers will use distribution centers when shipments to retailers consist of goods produced in more than one location (especially when contractors are used). In these cases, merchandise from the various locations is brought to a central location for quality assurance, *picking* (selecting the appropriate assortment of goods to fill a specific retailer's order), packing the merchandise, and distributing to the retail store accounts (see Figure 12.1). Technology has become important in increasing the efficiencies of distribution centers. Robotics that pick orders and conveyor systems that move orders from one area to the next have been incorporated into distribution center processes.

To speed up the process, some companies have reduced the use of distribution centers and are shipping to retailers directly from the production facility (Moore, 1994). Other companies are changing the purpose of their distribution centers from warehousing inventory to storing it for only short periods. Such *flow-through* facilities move merchandise from receiving to shipping with little, if any, time in storage (Nannery, 1995). For example, Nike, Inc.'s 1.2 million-square-foot distribution center in Memphis, Tennessee, which opened in 1997, promotes a 12-hour turnaround from the time the product is received at the DC to the time it is shipped to the retailer.

There is also a trend among apparel companies to use DCs for *adding value* (doing something to a product to make it worth more to the manufacturer, retailer, or consumer) to the merchandise by affixing hangtags, labels, and price information in order to make the goods floor ready (Moore, 1994). When manufacturers preticket merchandise, retailers do not have to spend extra time

The distribution process includes packing and shipping merchandise to retail accounts.

ticketing the items before the apparel hits the selling floor. This process, known as **vendor marking**, results in *floor-ready merchandise* (see also Chapter 11).

Whereas modular methods have been used primarily at production facilities (see Chapter 11), some companies have introduced systems based on the same philosophies to improve the efficiency of their distribution centers. One such company is Columbia Sportswear, headquartered in Portland, Oregon (Gilbert & Carlson, 1995). Columbia Sportswear has introduced modular methods in the customer returns and quality assurance areas of the distribution center. Similar to modular (or flexible) manufacturing practices, teams of workers move products from one operation to the next rather than one person performing the same function continually. Pay for the employees depends on overall facility performance rather than on individual performance. Columbia has found that the implementation of these systems has increased the speed for the processes and improved the quality of the work performed.

Retailers' Distribution Centers

Retailers also use distribution centers to facilitate distribution of merchandise from a variety of apparel companies (vendors) to a number of stores. Goods are shipped from the manufacturers to a centralized retail distribution center, where merchandise for the retailer's stores is picked, combined, and shipped to the individual stores. If merchandise has not been vendor marked, then hangtags, including stockkeeping unit (SKU) codes and price information, are affixed to the merchandise at the retailer's DC.

Retail distribution centers are often at geographical locations chosen to speed delivery to stores. For example, as of 2006, Target had 31 distribution centers located throughout the United States; Wal-Mart had 99 distribution centers. According to Wal-Mart's Web site (2006):

> A typical Wal-Mart distribution center is more than one million square feet, or the equivalent of ten Wal-Mart retail stores. More than two hundred and fifty dock doors serve the fleet of Wal-Mart distribution center trucks that wait in the vast parking lots surrounding the buildings. The aforementioned LaGrange distribution center, which serves stores in Georgia and Alabama, loads and ships over five hundred tractor-trailers of merchandise a day from the one Wal-Mart distribution center alone.

In recent years, the productivity of distribution centers has been enhanced through warehouse management system (WMS) computer software programs, along with the use of bar coding and RFID tagging of pallets and cartons. These software programs and tracking devices assist retailers in the following:

- maximizing the space within the DC
- automating warehouse operations
- integrating data throughout the supply chain
- improving communication with vendors (manufacturers)
- improving shipping accuracy (Hill, 1999b)

Alliances between Manufacturers and Retailers: QR, PLM, and SCM

The primary goals of Quick Response (QR), product lifecycle management (PLM), and supply chain management (SCM) strategies are to increase the speed with which merchandise gets to the consumer, and to lower the costs of manufacturing and distributing merchandise through the sharing of data among companies throughout the production and distribution of the product. The establishment of alliances between manufacturers and retailers is imperative for these goals to be achieved.

The Foundations: UPC Bar Coding, Vendor Marking, EDI, and RFID

Alliances between manufacturers and retailers depend on several basic operation strategies that have been adopted by manufacturers and retailers. These include the use of the following:

- UPC bar coding on products and shipping containers
- vendor marking of merchandise
- electronic data interchange (EDI)
- the use of RFID tagging

UPC BAR CODING AND VENDOR MARKING

The **Universal Product Code (UPC)** system is one of several bar code symbologies used for the electronic identification of merchandise. The use of UPC bar coding is often seen as the foundation of many QR and SCM strategies because it is considered necessary for electronic communications between the manufacturer and retailer. A UPC is a 12-digit number that identifies manufacturer and merchandise items by stockkeeping unit: vendor, style, color, and size. It is represented by a bar code made up of a pattern of dark bars and white spaces of varying widths. A group of bars and spaces represents one character or digit.

UPC bar codes are electronically scanned and "read" by scanning equipment. The scanning equipment provides a source of intense light that illuminates the symbol. The dark bars absorb the light. The scanner collects the reflected pattern of light and dark, and converts it into an electrical signal that is sent to a decoder. The decoder, which may be part of the scanner unit or may be a separate device, translates the electrical signal to binary numbers for use by the point-of-sale terminal or computer. Scanners can be categorized as one of the following:

1. contact readers that must touch or come in close proximity to the symbol

2. noncontact readers that can read the bar code when it is moved past a fixed beam or moving beam of light (see Figure 12.2)

UPC bar codes are attached to the merchandise by the manufacturer/vendor (vendor marking) or the retailer. Both vendor-marked merchandise and retailer-prepared bar codes are used to increase the speed of checkout and the accuracy of inventories. There are a number of benefits of UPC bar coding and point-of-sale (POS) scanning:

- maximizing the efficiency of store personnel
- speeding up the checkout process
- improving the accuracy of pricing
- providing accurate sales information
- providing accurate ongoing inventory counts

One of the most obvious benefits of using bar codes is the reduction in time needed to complete a transaction at the point of sale. An even more important

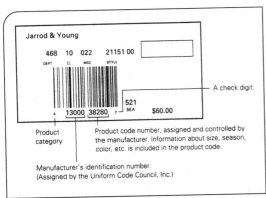

Figure 12.2   The Universal Product Code (UPC) or bar code (left) contains product information in electronic form. UPC bar codes on apparel hangtags (right) facilitate the collection of point-of-sale information.

benefit of scanning bar codes is that accurate SKU information is retrieved at the point of sale. This means that product sales and retail inventory are automatically tracked. With this accurate and timely sales information, retailers and manufacturers can plan inventory needs to match more closely sales or projected consumer demand. For example, with accurate sales data, retailers are able to track sales trends. This helps retailers avoid overstocking merchandise and, thus, reduce markdowns.

Correct point-of-sale information can also be used to reorder merchandise more efficiently and, thereby, reduce the possibility of a retailer being out of stock in a particular style, size, or color of merchandise. In addition, automatic reordering of merchandise (*replenishment*) is dependent upon the use of point-of-sale information provided by UPC bar codes. Replenishment strategies will be discussed later in this chapter.

In addition to using bar codes for these point-of-sale (POS) benefits, retailers also use them to scan inventory in their distribution centers and to facilitate the movement of shipping cartons in distribution centers. The bar codes identify each shipping container's contents and are used for tracking and sorting merchandise at the DCs. While the UPC bar code is made up of only numbers, two other bar code formats—code 39 or code 128—can include both numbers and letters, and are often used on shipping cartons.

ELECTRONIC DATA INTERCHANGE

Electronic data interchange (EDI) makes possible computer-to-computer communications between the manufacturer and retailer (see Figure 12.3). In the past, purchase orders, invoices, and any other type of written communication generated by one company were sent to another company by mail or fax. The receiving company would then enter the data into its computer. With EDI technology, business data is transmitted electronically. In other words, computers from one company "talk" directly to computers from other companies or through a third party's computer system called a *value-added network* (VAN). This eliminates the processing of much of the paperwork and, in effect, creates a paperless office. Not only are paper documents replaced by electronic documents, but the time delays associated with using mail services and paper handling are eliminated. Currently, the most common EDI transactions in the apparel industry include the following:

- purchase orders, invoices, packing slips, and advance shipping notices (ASN)
- reports of inventory counts and changes in inventory, such as sales and returns data
- price/sales catalogs

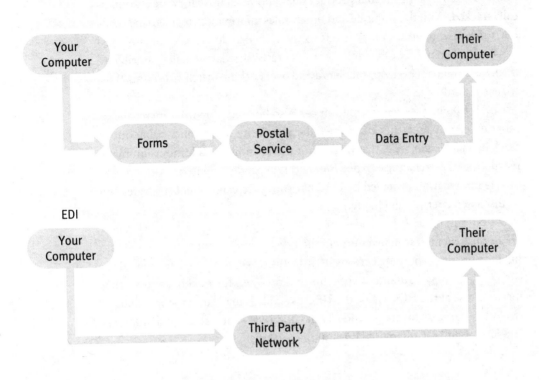

Figure 12.3 Electronic data interchange (EDI) improves efficiency by making possible computer-to-computer communications between manufacturers and retailers.

In addition, through EDI, retail distribution centers can accommodate cross-dockable shipments. This means that goods are received from the manufacturer as floor-ready merchandise, so they can be sorted for store distribution without the need for additional processing (Robins, 1994). For cross-docking to happen, the retailer must request and receive advance shipping notices from the manufacturer, and the goods must arrive floor ready. This would not be possible without EDI technology.

In the age of supply chain management, the EDI capabilities of the manufacturer have become increasingly important to both manufacturers and retailers. In many cases, EDI is the backbone of supply chain management, through which retailer POS data feeds directly into apparel companies' manufacturing systems and by which manufacturers are directly linked to the suppliers of fabric, trims, and findings. However, as Alan Brooks, president of New Generation Computing, stated, "EDI is not a technical issue as much as it is an area for management to control. We can have all the numbers and standards, but those will never bring good business judgment to the table. In the garment industry, you have to keep a feel for what is going on everywhere—especially in this electronic age" (DeWitt, 1993, p. 41).

With the onset of business-to-business (B2B) Internet, communities of companies, known as **eMarkets**, have moved to conducting business primarily through B2B Web sites. Fundamentally, eMarkets change the relationship dynamics between buyers and sellers from one-to-one to many-to-many. They have enabled trading partners to conduct business over the Internet, eliminating the need for more costly paper and custom EDI methods ("eMarkets," 2001, p. P4). In effect, eMarkets have built on the relationships established through EDI technologies and simplify the process so that each vendor and each buyer have to make only one connection—to the eMarket—rather than to each of their vendors and each of their buyers. As such, eMarkets improve buying efficiency, lower costs, and improve access to markets ("eMarkets," 2001).

Replenishment Strategies

In the traditional manufacturer–retailer relationship, the retail buyer would order goods from the manufacturer, and the entire order for the season would then be delivered to the retailer at the beginning of the fashion season. The retailer would hope that the correct number of each style, color, and size had been ordered and delivered. However, with this arrangement, it was not uncommon for a customer to walk into a store knowing the style and size of a product he or she wanted, only to find that the store did not have the size in stock. Out-of-stock merchandise may have been a result of the desired product not being delivered on time, or it may be that the desired product had been purchased by another customer and a replacement product had not arrived at the store. Either way, a sale was lost. To help alleviate situations such as this, the retailer must be able to replenish merchandise in an accurate and timely manner. There are several replenishment methods used by manufacturers and retailers, including the following:

- The retailer initiates a paper order when it determines that the stock level warrants a reorder.

- The retailer initiates an electronic (EDI) order when it determines that the stock level warrants a reorder.

- Information about stock levels is automatically communicated to the manufacturer through EDI, and the manufacturer (vendor) automatically ships reorders when the merchandise stock at the retail store reaches a certain level.

- A specified percent of the retail buyer's order is delivered before the start of the fashion season, with the remainder of the order delivered either throughout the fashion season or as a single reorder. The mix of styles, colors, and sizes in the reorder(s) is based on POS data from the retail stores.

Replenishment strategies vary with the type of merchandise and size of retailer. For basic (staple) items, such as hosiery and jeans, replenishment may be an ongoing activity. For seasonal goods, such as turtleneck sweaters and outerwear, replenishment may occur only within a particular fashion season. For fashion goods, merchandise may not be replenished during the fashion season. In addition, large retailers will utilize electronic replenishment strategies more often than will small retailers.

Manufacturers may use a variety of replenishment strategies depending upon their retail customers, and retailers may use a variety of replenishment strategies depending upon the capabilities of their vendors (manufacturers). Apparel, accessory, and home fashions companies often rely on electronic orders from retailers to get merchandise to the retailers in a timely manner. For example, Nygård International, a Canadian apparel manufacturer and retailer, has tied its electronic orders from retail accounts to their PDM/PLM systems. When an electronic order is received, it sets the manufacturing process in motion, resulting in a 72-hour produce-and-ship time from when the electronic order was placed.

One of the strategies most beneficial to improving the efficiency in the apparel supply pipeline between the manufacturer and retailer has been to establish programs whereby sales and *stockout data* (data on out-of-stock goods) are reviewed by the manufacturer, and replenishments are ordered as often as required. The strategy of having the manufacturer (vendor) automatically ship merchandise to the retail store based on POS data from the retailer is known as **vendor-managed inventory (VMI)** or *vendor-managed replenishment*. In some cases, data are reviewed daily rather than monthly or bimonthly, as was done in the past (Robins, 1993). Obviously, this type of strategy would not be possible without the retailer sending POS data to the manufacturer. "While retailers early in the QR movement showed some apprehension about sharing POS data, this apprehension has all but disappeared, and the sharing of POS data is now an accepted cornerstone of QR partnerships" (Robins, 1993, p. 22).

Vendor-managed inventory strategies are most commonly used with merchandise such as lingerie, hosiery, T-shirts, and basic jeans where style changes from season to season are minimal and it is important for retailers to have desired sizes and colors in stock (see Figure 12.4). Wrangler, a subsidiary of VF Corporation that manufactures men's and women's jeans, is another example of a company that has been very successful in managing retailer inventories (Hasty, 1994). Wrangler salespeople work closely with retail buyers in determining product mix and appropriate stock levels for specific stores. Wrangler sends new orders whenever the store's stock falls below a specified minimum. Wrangler receives POS information from more than 5,000 stores either daily or weekly, and each order is customized for a specific store depending upon the store's stock levels of various SKUs. Wrangler's goal is to receive POS information in the morning and ship jeans the same day.

Going the next step in vendor-managed inventory, some apparel producers are incorporating **data mining technology** to examine sales of products by style, size, and color. Data mining technology analyzes data information, searching for selling patterns or trends in the data and identifying correlations among data characteristics. For example, one company discovered that the selling season for shorts was longer in locations with higher median incomes. According to a representative of Kurt Salmon and Associates, New York:

Figure 12.4   Manufacturers of lingerie typically deliver preticketed, floor-ready merchandise as part of their vendor-managed retail inventory strategies.

A number of apparel producers are taking the data, using it to see what sizes, colors, and styles are selling in a particular retail chain, and then going back to the retailer, either in the next season or in replenishment, and tailoring the assortment a lot more closely to the individual outlets. It's the first level of micro-marketing, and it presents huge opportunities for improved performance. (Hill, 1998, p. 18)

The technology is also being used to justify and manage retail floor space so that the correct amount of space is being allocated to the right products. Although the technology is currently expensive, database and data mining services will allow even small companies to take advantage of it (Hill, 1998).

Implementing Quick Response, Product Lifecycle Management, and Supply Chain Management

This book has focused on Quick Response (QR), product lifecycle management (PLM), and supply chain management (SCM) strategies implemented throughout the design, manufacturing, and retailing of apparel, accessory, and home fashions products. The implementation of QR, PLM, and SCM strategies requires a shift in a company's management style, in addition to an increased investment of a company's resources in technology, training, and evaluation. Therefore, a company typically phases in strategies that are most consistent with its strategic plans. The following four steps are common:

1. Initially, a company will use bar coding and EDI, which provide accurate sales data and speed communications.

2. Next, as it grows, the company will add replenishment strategies, whereby retailers and suppliers jointly review sales data, develop plans and forecasts for future demand, and reduce inventory while keeping stores fully stocked. Replenishment strategies will start with basic (staple) goods and seasonal goods.

3. Going one step further in replenishment, the manufacturer customizes assortments and replenishment, not only for each retailer, but for each store unit in a retail chain. Fashion goods may be added to the replenishment mix.

4. In some cases, new products are created jointly by the manufacturer and retailer, bypassing the traditional buyer–salesperson process and shortening the time from concept to new product on the shelf. In-store testing of new products is part of this stage.

With SCM and PLM, either an order from a retailer or a retail sale electronically triggers the manufacturing process. Orders or sales data are tied to the apparel company's PDM/PLM systems and fabric and findings suppliers. At the retail level, the retailer's financial and merchandise plans are integrated. That is, the retailer's assortment plan is integrated with how much space each retail department will be allocated at each store, thus optimizing the store's merchandise mix (Hill, 1999a). These processes are also phased in over time. Integrated processes include the following:

- integration of an apparel company's pattern making systems (PDS) with other product information through product information management (PIM) software (see Chapter 9)

- integration of an apparel company's various CAD/CAM systems, resulting in PDM/PLM (see Chapter 11)

- alliances between apparel companies and retailers, resulting in vendor-managed retail inventory

- integration of a retailer's merchandise assortment planning, financial planning, distribution processes, and store layout

Retailing and Categories of Retailers

By definition, **retailing** is the "business activity of selling goods or services to the final consumer," and a **retailer** is "any business establishment that directs its marketing efforts toward the final consumer for the purpose of selling goods and services" (Lewison, 1994, p. 5). Retailers range in size from small sole proprietorships that cater to a local market to large corporate store ownership groups. Table 12.1 lists some of the primary retail corporations and the stores owned and operated by these corporations.

Retailers can be classified according to many of their characteristics, including their ownership, merchandise mix, size, location, and organizational and operational characteristics (see Figure 12.5). One typical way of classifying retailers is on the basis of their merchandising and operating strategies, which results in the following categories:

- department stores
- specialty stores
- chain stores
- discount retailers
- off-price retailers
- supermarkets and hypermarkets
- warehouse retailers

- convenience stores
- contractual retailers
- nonstore retailers

Because of the diversity found among retailers, these categories are not mutually exclusive. For example, a specialty store retailer may also be a chain store operation; a department store may also engage in nonstore retailing by sending

Table 12.1   Selected Major Retail Corporations

Abercrombie & Fitch
(www.abercrombie.com)
Abercrombie & Fitch
abercrombie
Hollister Co.
Ruehl 925

Bed Bath & Beyond Inc.
(www.bedbathandbeyond.com)
Bed Bath & Beyond
Christmas Tree Shops
Harmon Stores
buybuy BABY

Burlington Coat Factory Warehouse
Corporation (www.coat.com)
Burlington Coat Factory Stores
Luxury Linens
Baby Depot
Cohoes Fashions
MJM Designer Shoes

Charming Shoppes, Inc.
(www.charmingshoppes.com)
Lane Bryant
Fashion Bug
Catherines
Petite Sophisticate
Crosstown Traders, Inc.

Dillard's (www.dillards.com)

Foot Locker Inc. (www.footlocker-inc.com)
Foot Locker
Lady Foot Locker
Kids Foot Locker
Champs Sports
Footaction
Eastbay

Gap Inc. (www.gap.com)
Gap
GapKids
babyGap
GapMaternity
gapbody
Banana Republic
Old Navy
Forth & Towne
Piperlime

JCPenney Company, Inc.
(www.jcpenney.com)

Kohl's Corporation (www.kohls.com)
Kohl's Department Stores

Limited Brands (www.limitedbrands.com)
The Limited
Express
Victoria's Secret
Henri Bendel
Bath & Body Works
The White Barn Candle Co.

Table 12.1   Selected Major Retail Corporations *(continued)*

C.O. Bigelow
La Senza
Diva London

Macy's (www.macys.com)
Bloomingdale's
Macy's East
Macy's Florida
Macy's Midwest
Macy's North
Macy's Northwest
Macy's South
Macy's West

**Neiman Marcus Group
(www.neimanmarcus.com)**
Neiman Marcus
Bergdorf Goodman
Horchow

Nordstrom (www.nordstrom.com)
Nordstrom
Nordstom Rack
Last Chance

**Saks Incorporated
(www.saksincorporated.com)**
Saks Fifth Avenue
Off 5th
Club Libby Lu

**Sears Holdings Corporation
(www.searsholdings.com)**
Sears, Roebuck & Co.
(www.sears.com)
  Sears
  Sears Grand
  Sears Essentials
Kmart (www.kmart.com)
  Kmart
  Big Kmart
  Kmart Super Centers
The Great Indoors
Orchard Supply Hardware

Spiegel Brands, Inc. (www.spiegel.com)
Spiegel
Newport News
Carabella
A.B. Lambdin

Target Corporation (www.targetcorp.com)
Target
Super Target

The TJX Companies, Inc. (www.tjx.com)
T.J. Maxx
Marshalls
Winners
A.J. Wright
HomeGoods
T.K. Maxx
HomeSense
Bob's Stores

**Urban Outfitters Inc.
(www.urbanoutfittersinc.com)**
Urban Outfitters
Anthropologie
Free People

**Wal-Mart Stores, Inc.
(www.wal-mart.com)**
Wal-Mart Discount Stores
Wal-Mart Supercenters
Wal-Mart Neighborhood Markets
SAM's Club
Wal-Mart International

**Williams-Sonoma, Inc.
(www.williams-sonoma.com)**
Williams-Sonoma
Pottery Barn
Pottery Barn Kids
PB Teen
Williams-Sonoma Home
West Elm

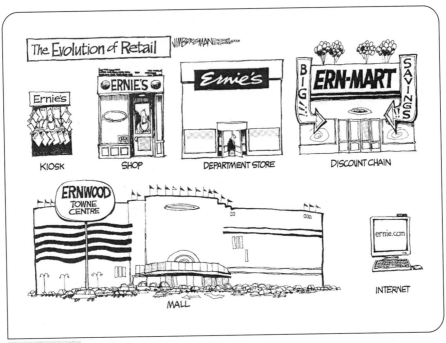

Figure 12.5 This illustration shows the evolution of retail.

mail order catalogs or selling through a Web site. Indeed, **multichannel retailing** strategies involve offering merchandise through several types of retailers. Most common is for companies to have bricks-and-mortar stores along with catalogs and/or Web sites. Examples of companies that focus on multichannel retailing strategy include Coldwater Creek, J.Jill, Talbots, Pottery Barn, and Crate and Barrel (see Color Plate 12). Table 12.2 lists the number of retail establishments in the United States by category of retailer. It is important to note the number of retailers that are small businesses with no paid employees.

Department Stores

Department stores are large retailers that divide their functions and their merchandise into sections or departments. Department stores have the following features:

- a fashion-oriented merchandise assortment

- a variety of services for customers (e.g., credit cards, wedding registry)

- merchandise offered at full markup price with seasonal sales

Number of Retail Establishments by Category

	Establishments with Employees	Establishments without Employees
General Merchandise Stores	40,723	29,763
Department stores	3,705	NA
Discount department stores	5,650	NA
Warehouse clubs and supercenters	2,912	NA
Specialty Stores		
Clothing	90,954	62,123
Shoes	28,499	3,862
Jewelry, luggage, and leather goods	30,357	30,312
Furniture and home furnishings	65,204	40,711

SOURCE: U.S. Census Bureau. 2002 Economic Census, Retail Trade in the U.S.

at least 50 employees

operate in stores large enough to be shopping center anchors (see Figure 12.6).

The category includes traditional department stores such as Macy's, Bloomingdales, JCPenney, Sears, and Dillard's, as well as limited-line department stores such as Nordstrom, Saks Fifth Avenue, and Neiman Marcus (which were once classified as specialty stores). Multiunit department stores generally have a flagship or primary store. For example, the 34th Street Manhattan Macy's store is considered the flagship store for Macy's East division; the downtown San Francisco Macy's store is considered the flagship store for Macy's West division. Table 12.3 is a list of the top 10 department stores based on sales volume.

With the goal of catering to a broad range of consumers, department stores carry a wide variety of merchandise lines with a reasonably wide selection within each category. Department stores usually carry national brands and private-label

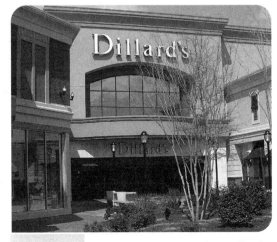

Figure 12.6 Department stores such as Dillard's often serve as shopping center anchors.

Table 12.3   Top Department Stores by Revenues

Company	2005 Revenues (000)
Sears Holdings (includes Sears and Kmart)	$53,962,000
Federated Dept. Stores (now Macy's)	22,390,000
JCPenney	18,781,000
Kohl's	13,402,200
Dillard's	7,798,000
Nordstrom	7,722,860
Saks	5,953,352
Neiman Marcus Group	3,821,924
Mervyn's	3,000,000
Belk	2,970,000

SOURCE: *Stores*. (2006, July). Top 100 Retailers.

merchandise, typically in the moderate and better price zones. Depending on their price assortment, they may also carry merchandise in the bridge and designer price zones.

Although department stores have been criticized for being boring, confusing, and "dinosaurs" of retailing, they continue to have a large share of the apparel market (Schneiderman, 1995). However, faced with increased competition, department stores are refocusing, with a new emphasis on presentation, customer service, and having the right products for their target market—products that are different from the products carried by other stores. This merchandising strategy, known as **relationship merchandising**, addresses the needs of individual customers. Nordstrom has been cited as the prototype of this merchandising strategy.

Many department stores also have **in-store shops** of designers and major brands. These in-store shops are merchandised according to the manufacturer's specifications and carry only the merchandise of the apparel company. Companies/brands such as Ralph Lauren, Nautica, Tommy Hilfiger, Calvin Klein, Liz Claiborne, BCBG Max Azria, and Dockers have all had successful in-store shops. In-store shops benefit both the manufacturer and the retailer. For the manufacturer, they create brand awareness and make shopping easy for their customers. For the department stores, the in-store shops create a specialty store "feel" within the department store environment. Companies are expanding the in-store shop concept to their nonstore retailing venues. For example,

Bloomingdales.com offers **concept shops** for a number of brands, including Ralph Lauren, DKNY, and Carolee.

Specialty Stores

A **specialty store** focuses on a specific type of merchandise in one of the following ways:

- by carrying one category of merchandise or a few closely related categories of merchandise (e.g., jewelry, shoes, eyeglasses, intimate apparel, housewares)
- by focusing on merchandise for a well-defined target market (e.g., men, women, bicyclists, large-size consumers, individuals with small children)
- by carrying the merchandise of one manufacturer or brand (e.g., Nine West, Ralph Lauren, Baby Guess/Guess Kids)

Specialty stores carry a limited but deep assortment (i.e., excellent selection of brands, styles, sizes) of merchandise. They may carry national brands or have their own store brand (e.g., The Limited, Talbots, Crate and Barrel). Most specialty stores will carry merchandise in only one or two price zones. Two of the largest apparel specialty store chains in the United States are The Limited and Gap (see Figure 12.7). See Table 12.4 for a listing of specialty chains. Specialty stores that concentrate on designer price zone merchandise or unique merchandise distributed exclusively to only a few stores are sometimes referred to as **boutiques**.

Chain Stores

Chain store organizations own and operate several retail store units that sell similar lines of merchandise with a standard method and function under a centralized organizational structure. Chain stores are characterized by the following features:

- centralized buying
- no single main or flagship store (which multiunit department stores with branches typically have)
- centralized distribution
- standardized store decor and layout

Figure 12.7 Gap is an example of a specialty store chain that focuses on a limited number of apparel and accessory categories.

Table 12.4   Top Apparel Specialty Chains by Revenues

Apparel Chain	2005 Revenues (000)
Gap	$16,023,000
MarMaxx (T.J.Maxx and Marshall's)	10,956,788
The Limited	9,668,559
Ross Stores	4,944,179
Burlington Coat Factory Warehouse	3,199,840
Abercrombie & Fitch	2,784,711
Charming Shoppes	2,755,725
American Eagle	2,309,371
Ann Taylor	2,073,146

SOURCE: *Stores*. (2006, July). Top 100 Retailers.

All management and merchandising decisions and policies are made by managers at a central headquarters or home office. Chain store operations include large chains (defined as 11 or more units), which may be national or international in scope, such as JCPenney, Sears, Wal-Mart, Target, and The Limited; or they can be small chains (two to ten retail units) within a local or regional area. Although chain stores benefit from the economies of scale that come with purchasing merchandise for a number of stores, they also carry merchandise that caters to the wants and needs of the local target markets. Private-label merchandise is an important part of the merchandise mix for chain store retailers (e.g., JCPenney's Arizona, Worthington, and Stafford labels).

Discount Retailers

A **discount store** sells brand name merchandise at less than traditional retail prices and includes apparel merchandise at the mass or budget price zone. Examples of discount chain department stores are Target, Kmart, and Wal-Mart. An example of a discount chain specialty store is Bed, Bath & Beyond. In addition to national brands, discounters also carry private-label merchandise (e.g., Kmart's Jaclyn Smith brand), and exclusively licensed brands (e.g., Isaac Mizrahi for Target brand).

Through mass merchandising and supply chain management strategies, discounters are able to keep prices lower than other retailers. These strategies include the following:

- quantity discounts from manufacturers
- effective replenishment strategies to ensure that the merchandise customers want is in stock
- high turnover rates on products
- limiting brands and styles to only the most popular items
- self-service
- lower overhead costs
- promotions that cater to a broad target market

Figure 12.8 Wal-Mart, a national discount chain, sells a variety of merchandise, including family apparel and accessories.

National and international discount chains such as Wal-Mart (Figure 12.8), Kmart, and Target buy huge quantities of merchandise from manufacturers and can operate on smaller profit margins than can traditional department stores. Stores such as Target are sometimes referred to as *upscale discounters* because they have a department store feel, and apparel accounts for 45 percent or more of total sales. Table 12.5 lists the top discount stores.

Table 12.5 Top Discount/Value/Warehouse Retailers by Revenues

Company	2005 Revenues (000)
Wal-Mart	$315,427,000
Sears Holdings (includes Sears and Kmart)	53,962,000
Costco	52,935,228
Target	52,620,000
Meijer	12,500,000
Dollar General	8,582,237
BJ's Wholesale Club	7,949,934
Family Dollar	5,824,808
Dollar Tree Stores	3,393,924
ShopKo/Pamida	3,200,000

SOURCE: *Stores*. (2006, July). Top 100 Retailers.

Off-Price Retailers

Off-price retailers specialize in selling national brands, designer collections, or promotional goods at discount prices. Off-price retailers are characterized by their buying of merchandise at low prices, carrying well-established (including designer) brands, and having merchandise assortments that change quickly with inconsistent sizes and styles (sometimes referred to as broken assortments). The following are types of off-price retailers: factory outlet stores, independent off-price retailers, retailer-owned off-price retailers, closeout stores, and sample stores.

FACTORY OUTLET STORES

Manufacturers' outlets sell their own seconds, irregulars, or overruns (merchandise produced in excess of their orders), as well as merchandise produced specifically for the outlet stores. In some cases, manufacturers will use their outlet stores as test markets for styles, colors, or sizes of merchandise. Once located primarily near production or distribution centers, factory outlet stores comprising entire shopping centers are now common throughout the United States. They are typically located at a distance from full-price retailers that carry their goods (based on agreements with local full-price retailers).

Figure 12.9 Independent off-price retailers, such as Ross, sell national brands and promotional goods at discount prices.

INDEPENDENT OFF-PRICE RETAILERS

These stores buy irregulars, seconds, overruns, or leftovers from manufacturers or other retailers. Ross (Figure 12.9), T.J. Maxx, and Burlington Coat Factory are examples of independent off-price retailers.

RETAILER-OWNED OFF-PRICE RETAILERS

Some retailers operate their own off-price stores (e.g., Off 5th, Nordstrom Rack). In these off-price stores, retailers sell merchandise from their regular stores that had not sold within a specified time period, private-label merchandise, or special orders purchased specifically for the off-price store.

CLOSEOUT STORES

Closeout stores specialize in buying a variety of merchandise through retail liquidations, bankruptcies, and closeouts. Then they sell this merchandise at bargain prices.

SAMPLE STORES

Sample stores specialize in selling apparel companies' sample merchandise at the end of the market selling period. These stores are located near major apparel marts, such as the California Market Center.

Supermarkets and Hypermarkets

Conventional **supermarkets** are large self-service grocery stores that carry a full line of foods and related products. Some supermarkets have broadened their merchandise and service offerings. **Superstores**, or **hypermarkets**, are upgraded supermarkets that combine the elements of a supermarket and a department store by offering a wide range of merchandise, including food, electronics, clothing and accessories, furniture, and garden items. These "big box" stores can be as large as 150,000 to 250,000 square feet.

At one time, only a limited number of apparel products (e.g., hosiery, packaged undergarments) or home fashions (e.g., kitchen towels) were distributed through supermarkets. However, with the growth of large discount retailer superstores/hypermarkets in the United States (e.g., Wal-Mart Super Store, Super Kmart, SuperTarget) and internationally (e.g., Carrefour), more apparel, home fashions, and accessories are being sold through these types of stores.

Items sold through supermarkets and superstores must accommodate a self-service merchandising strategy, so visual displays that assist consumers in selecting the right style and size are common. These items are also most likely to use an extended marketing channel that facilitates the supermarkets' buying of these goods.

Warehouse Retailers

Warehouse retailers offer goods at discount prices by reducing operating expenses and combining their warehouse and retail operations. In some cases, merchandise is obtained through an extended marketing channel. This category of retailers includes stores such as "big box" home improvement centers (e.g., The Home Depot, Lowe's) and warehouse clubs (e.g., Costco, Sam's Club).

Traditionally, apparel and home fashions products were not the primary merchandise sold through warehouse retailers. However, home improvement centers are now offering a larger array of home fashions goods (e.g., towels, bedding, carpets, rugs), and warehouse clubs are offering more styles and types of apparel and home fashions products. Indeed, Costco has offered fashion brands including Prada sunglasses, Hugo Boss men's suits, Laura Ashley girls' dresses, and Nautica women's sweaters; and home fashions brands such as Kirkland Signature sheets and Laura Ashley blankets. Generally, at warehouse retailers, apparel and home fashions are sold through self-service strategies with limited services (e.g., there are generally no fitting rooms).

Convenience Stores

Convenience stores are small stores that offer fast service at a convenient location (on a busy street or combined with a gas station), but they carry only a limited assortment of food and related items. 7-Eleven is one of the most famous and largest international convenience store chains, with over 25,000 stores in over 20 countries. The most typical apparel and accessory products carried by convenience stores are basic items such as mass-merchandised hosiery (e.g., L'eggs, Hanes), inexpensive novelty T-shirts or baseball caps, and inexpensive sunglasses, as well as fashion magazines.

Contractual Retailers

Retailers may enter into contractual agreements with manufacturers, wholesalers, or other retailers in order to integrate operations and increase market impact. Such contractual agreements include the following:

- retailer-sponsored cooperatives that take the form of an organization of small independent retailers
- wholesaler-sponsored voluntary chains, in which a wholesaler develops a program for small independent retailers
- franchises
- leased departments

The term **contractual retailers** covers all such arrangements. Franchises and leased departments are the most typical of the contractual retailers for the distribution of apparel.

FRANCHISES

In a **franchise** agreement, the parent company gives the franchisee the exclusive right to distribute a well-recognized brand name in a specific market area, as well as assistance with organization, visual merchandising, training, and management. In return, the franchisee pays the parent company a franchise payment. The franchisee agrees to adhere to standards regarding in-store design, visual presentation, pricing, and promotions specified by the parent company. Examples of franchises include Ralph Lauren's Polo shops and Yves Saint Laurent's Rive Gauche boutiques.

LEASED DEPARTMENTS

Some retailers will lease space within a larger retail store to a company that operates a specialty department. The larger retail store provides space, utilities, and basic in-store services. The specialty department operator provides the stock and expertise to run the department, and adds to the service or product mix of the larger store. Their lease or commission is typically based on square footage and sales.

Typical **leased departments** include beauty salons and spas; vision care and eyewear; florists and garden shops; books; restaurants; ticket offices; and fine jewelry, fur, and shoe shops. In each of these cases, specific expertise and investment in stock are needed. With this arrangement, the primary advantage for the larger retailer is that it can offer its customers products and services that it might not be able to offer otherwise. The primary advantage for the specialty department is its association with the larger retailer and a convenient location for consumers to purchase their goods or services.

Nonstore Retailers

A **nonstore retailer** distributes products to consumers through means other than traditional bricks-and-mortar retail stores. For apparel, accessories, and home fashions, the three most prevalent forms of nonstore retailing include mail order/catalog, electronic/Internet, and television selling. Other forms of nonstore retailing include at-home selling and vending machines. In the past 20 years, nonstore retailing, particularly mail order/catalog, electronic/Internet, and television selling, has grown tremendously. This trend is due to a number of social, economic, and lifestyle changes, including the following:

- the increased demand by consumers for convenience, product quality, and selection

- a highly fragmented market that demands products to fulfill special needs and interests

- the continued growth in the number of women in the workforce and dual-income families, which creates increased time pressures for shopping among household members

- the expanding use and promotion of credit cards, such as those offered by Visa, Mastercard, American Express, and Discover, and store cards (e.g., Nordstrom)

- increased speed of delivery by package carriers (e.g., Federal Express, UPS, Priority Mail)

- technological advances in e-commerce, including improved security for sending credit card numbers electronically

In addition to selling merchandise, nonstore retailing, particularly mail order/catalog, electronic/Internet, and television retailing venues, are used by companies for a number of other purposes, such as the following:

- educating customers about the company and its product lines
- providing customers with fashion direction and style advice
- obtaining information from customers regarding product preferences
- building more traffic in their retail stores
- providing customers with a more convenient and/or more recreational form of shopping
- building relationships with customers through personalized customer service

Retailers selling apparel through mail order/catalog, electronic/Internet, and television retailing methods are faced with a unique set of challenges. Because the customer cannot physically evaluate the product, feel the fabric, or try on the merchandise, customer service and information about sizing, fabric, styling details, and color are important. J. Crew now uses color matching software to assist customers visiting the company's www.jcrew.com Web site in viewing garments in their actual colors. Lands' End will send customers fabric swatches. In addition, the Pantone color specification system has been adapted for electronic color communication (Karas, 2001). Many nonstore retailers offer means for customers to connect with customer service representatives through the phone or online "chat rooms." Customers also have questions and concerns about shipping costs, timeliness of shipping, and returns. Because customers use nonstore retailing for its convenience, the ease in selecting styles, ordering, and returning merchandise is important.

Will nonstore retailing eventually put bricks-and-mortar stores out of business? Most analysts believe that many consumers still want to touch and try on garments and accessories before purchasing them, and will still want the social experience of shopping in bricks-and-mortar stores. However, the growth in nonstore retailing has forced retailers to think about their retail environments in terms of better meeting customer needs. Retailers are merging technologies so that consumers reap the benefits of each of the retail formats. For example, many malls and bricks-and-mortar stores provide kiosks whereby consumers can search products and stores online.

MAIL ORDER/CATALOG RETAILERS

Mail order/catalog retailers sell to the consumer through catalogs, brochures, or advertisements, and deliver merchandise by mail or other carriers. Apparel is one of the top-selling items bought through catalogs, with nearly one in five Americans buying apparel through catalogs. Customers can order by mail, phone, Internet, or fax. All types of retailers may operate mail order/catalog businesses.

Some companies focus almost entirely on the use of catalogs (e.g., L.L.Bean, Lands' End, Spiegel). In 1975, Lands' End began its catalog. By 1985 it was distributing monthly catalogs, and by 1990, it had introduced three new catalogs targeted to the home, children's wear, and men's wear markets. Some companies offer merchandise through their catalogs that is not available in their stores (e.g., J. Crew, Victoria's Secret, Nordstrom). Other companies, such as Talbots, offer the same merchandise assortment in their catalogs as in their stores. In addition to paper catalogs, electronic catalogs (available to the consumer as CD-ROM disks or as online catalogs) provide consumers with a range of alternatives for browsing, evaluating, and purchasing merchandise (see Figure 12.10).

ELECTRONIC/INTERNET RETAILERS

Electronic/Internet retailers use **e-commerce**, the selling of goods over the Internet, to reach customers. Since the mid-1990s, e-commerce has grown consistently each year as more consumers have access to the Internet and as security issues related to sending credit card numbers electronically are being addressed by Internet retailers. Many apparel retailers and manufacturers have included e-commerce in their distribution strategy, offering goods only over the Internet or using the Internet as an addition to their stores and/or catalog retailing business as another aspect of their multidistribution strategy.

Figure 12.10 Mail order retailers, such as L.L.Bean, provide their customers with electronic catalogs and Internet online ordering services.

Although online apparel sales are a relatively small percentage of overall apparel retail sales, the number of "dot-com" Web sites devoted to apparel and accessories continues to grow. E-retailers generally fall into one or more of the following categories:

- exclusive e-retailers
- catalog retailers who added Web sites
- department and specialty stores who added Web sites
- apparel, accessory, and home fashions manufacturers' Web sites
- online fashion malls
- online auction/trade Web sites

Exclusive E-retailers

Some companies sell exclusively on the Web. These include merchants for specialized or niche products, such as organic cotton merchandise, and small retailers who may not be able to afford other forms of retail distribution. Web sites such as ebay.com also provide opportunities for businesses to sell merchandise through these Web sites.

Catalog Retailers Who Added Web Sites

Companies that had been successful selling apparel through catalogs found they could make the transition to the Web fairly easily. In 1995, Lands' End offered fewer than 100 products online as an experiment. It is now one of the largest Internet apparel sites, offering customers services such as the following:

- My Virtual Model ™, whereby a customer can select body characteristics and sizes to create a 3D model that is similar to himself or herself
- custom-fit apparel
- opportunities to "chat" with customer service representatives
- assistance with comparing swimwear styles for particular body types
- assistance with comparing jacket styles for weather conditions

Department Stores and Stores Who Added Web Sites

By the late 1990s, a number of department stores and specialty stores had moved to multichannel distribution strategies by adding catalogs and e-commerce to their businesses. Online customers gravitated to Web sites of well-known and trusted retailers such as Gap, Wal-Mart, Target, Nordstrom, Sears, Macy's, and JCPenney.

Store retailers have found that access to new customers can be enhanced with online services. For example, whereas 90 percent of Victoria's Secret's store customers are women, approximately 35 percent of their online customers are men.

The success of traditional store and catalog retailers in their online operations will be based to some extent on their ability to integrate their various retail methods. For example, consumers will expect to return merchandise they purchased online to the same retailer's store (Reda, 1999).

Apparel, Accessory, and Home Fashions Manufacturers' Web Sites

These Web sites may or may not include direct sales of merchandise to the ultimate consumer. Examples include the following:

- Liz Claiborne's Web site, www.lizclaiborne.com, offers customers store information, advice, and links to Liz Claiborne lines.

- The North Face uses its thenorthface.com Web site as a vehicle to promote products, provide information about The North Face athletes and expeditions, and highlight The North Face stores and other dealers.

- Nike uses its nike.com Web site as a way of educating the consumer about Nike products. Nike also uses its site to solicit information from its customers regarding product characteristics and performance, in addition to selling merchandise directly to the consumer. See Table 12.6 for a listing of the top apparel Internet retailers.

Table 12.6 Top 10 Apparel/Beauty Internet Retailers by Number of Unique Visitors

Company	Number of Unique Visitors/Month[1]
eBay Clothing, Shoes & Accessories	11.142
eBay Jewelry & Watches	5.30
victoriassecret.com	4.45
eBay Health & Beauty	4.37
AVON	3.88
Old Navy	3.19
Lands' End	3.08
Zappos	3.03
Gap	2.54
L.L.Bean	2.47

[1] In millions for April 2007
SOURCE: *Internet Retailer* (2007, May 18).

Online Fashion Mall

One of the first Internet sites where apparel could be purchased online was Fashionmall.com, which was started in 1994. It provided a central location for a number of retailers, manufacturers, and magazines to offer fashion goods and services directly to customers (see Figure 12.11). Since that time, online fashion malls have served as destination Web sites that offer merchandise from a number of online stores. As such, consumers can go to a single Web site for products from multiple companies. Examples of online fashion malls and the companies/retailers that feature products for online purchase include the following:

- Currently, fashionmall.com offers merchandise from approximately 50 companies/retailers, including Gap, Coldwater Creek, dELiAs.cOm, J.Crew.com, International Male, PacSun.com, and REI.

- Amazon.com, another portal for fashion goods from multiple companies, has featured merchandise from Polo.com, Macy's, Eddie Bauer, Foot Locker,

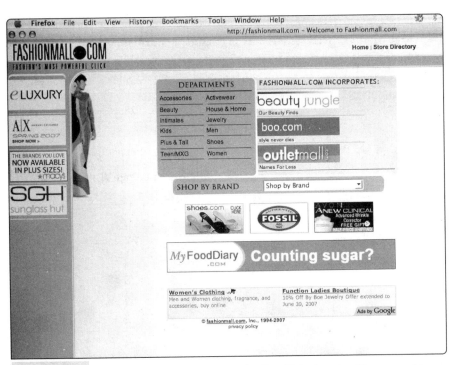

Figure 12.11 Fashionmall.com was one of the first Web sites to offer apparel to consumers over the Internet.

Guess, Lands' End, and Nordstrom. Featured sellers on Amazon.com for bed and bath products have included The Company Store, JCPenney, Macy's, Domestications, and Bombay.

- Yahoo.com also offers "one-stop shopping" for name brand merchandise including Nike, Juicy Couture, adidas, Sean John, and Phat Farm, to name only a few.

Online Auction/Trade Web Sites

Web sites such as ebay.com offer opportunities for anyone worldwide to sell apparel, accessories, and home fashions online. Started in 1995 as an online auction Web site, ebay.com has grown into one of the largest Web sites, selling over 45,000 categories of merchandise, with millions of items bought and sold daily. Multitudes of new and previously worn apparel and accessories are offered for sale by individuals and companies throughout the world.

TELEVISION RETAILERS

Some retailers use television shopping channels to sell apparel, accessories, and home fashions products. With these formats, merchandise is presented on the television (and on accompanying Web sites), and customers order it over the telephone (usually using a toll-free number) or on the Web. Payment is by credit card, cash on delivery (C.O.D.), or check. Merchandise is delivered through the mail or by another carrier.

Home shopping has become big business. QVC (see Figure 12.12), Home Shopping Network (HSN), and Shop at Home are three of the largest of these television shopping channels. TV shopping has expanded its merchandise assortment to include designer lines and a variety of product categories.

As with other retailers, the movement to multichannel strategies has also been found to be successful for those who started as nonstore retailers. For example, QVC has a very successful Web site and recently opened a flagship bricks-and-mortar store (QVC@The Mall) at Minnesota's Mall of America. The company also has five outlet stores throughout the United States. QVC (which stands for quality, value, and convenience) was founded in 1986. In 2004, QVC shipped over 137 million units, with sales of over $5.7 million. QVC has a buying staff of over 100 individuals, and it has 16 distribution centers worldwide. Another television shopping powerhouse, Home Shopping Network (HSN), had sales of over $3 billion in 2005, delivering more than 60 million products worldwide.

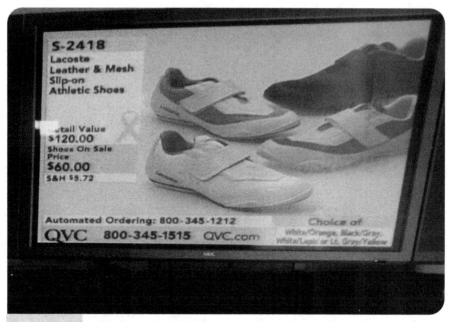

Figure 12.12   Television shopping channels, such as QVC, continue to grow in importance for apparel retailing.

AT-HOME RETAILERS

At-home retailers (e.g., Doncaster, Bella Handbag Purse Parties) use the marketing strategy of making personal contacts and sales in consumers' homes. At-home retailing includes door-to-door sales or party plan selling methods. The party plan method involves a salesperson giving a presentation of merchandise at the home of a host or hostess who has invited potential customers to a "party."

The at-home retailer Doncaster also makes provision for customization of products for the customer. He or she can select style, fabric, and size, and the product is made according to his or her specifications. Accessories and lingerie are typical apparel products sold using this retail method.

VENDING MACHINES

Vending machines are coin-operated machines used to meet the needs of consumers when other retailing formats are unavailable or when space is limited for selling merchandise. Although vending machines are seldom used for the distribution of apparel products, they have been used to sell hosiery, T-shirts, and even men's dress shirts. One would most likely find such vending machines in locations such as airports or train stations.

Trade Associations and Trade Publications

As with other areas of textile and apparel industries, a number of trade associations and trade publications serve those involved in the distribution of apparel. Table 12.7 lists some of the primary retail trade associations. The National Retail Federation (NRF) is the largest trade association for retailers in the United States. It represents 27 national retail associations, all 50 state associations, and stores from 50 different nations. The NRF Annual Convention and Expo is held in New York each January.

The NRF has four divisions that focus on specific aspects of retailing: technology standards, chain restaurants, advertising and marketing, and Internet retailing (see Table 12.8).

The NRF publishes *Stores* magazine, a monthly trade publication that addresses the interests of those in the retailing industry. A number of other trade publications cater to those involved with distribution and retailing. Table 12.9 lists some of these publications.

Table 12.7 Selected Retail Trade Associations

Electronic Retailing Association
2000 N. 14th Street
Suite 300
Arlington, VA 22201
Tel: 703-841-1751
Fax: 703-841-1860
www.retailing.org

International Council of Shopping Centers
1221 Avenue of the Americas, 41st Fl.
New York, NY 10020-1099
Tel: 646-728-3800
Fax: 732-694-1755
www.icsc.org

National Retail Federation
325 7th St. NW, Suite 1000
Washington, DC 20006
Tel: 202-783–7971
Fax: 202-737-2849
www.nrf.com

National Shoe Retailers Association
7150 Columbia Gateway Drive
Suite G
Columbia, MD 21046-1151
Tel: 410-381–8282
Fax: 410-381-1167
www.nsra.org

Retail Industry Leaders Association
1700 N. Moore Street
Suite 2250
Arlington, VA 22209
Tel: 703-841-2300
Fax: 703-841-1184
www.retail-leaders.org

Shop.org of the NRF
325 7th Street, NW, Suite 1100
Washington, DC 20004
Tel: 202-626-8192
Fax: 202-737-2849
www.shop.org

Table 12.8   Divisions of the National Retail Federation

Association for Retail Technology Standards (ARTS)
ARTS is an international membership organization dedicated to reducing the costs of technology through application standards exclusively to the retail industry. ARTS has four standards: The Standard Relational Data Model, UnifiedPOS, IXRetail and the Standard RFPs.

National Council of Chain Restaurants (NCCR)
NCCR is the leading trade association exclusively representing chain restaurant companies.

Retail Advertising & Marketing Association (RAMA)
RAMA is a trade association of retail marketing and advertising professionals, plus their counterparts on the agency, media, and service-provider sides of the business.

Shop.org
Shop.org is the association for retailers online focusing on the evolving world of the Internet and multichannel retailing.

SOURCE: National Retail Federation (2007).

A Look to the Future

Change has become the norm in the textile, apparel, accessories, home fashions, and retailing industries. Faced with increased global competition, textile, apparel, accessories, home fashions, and retailing companies have made rapid changes in order to survive. The belief has been that the strongest advantage the U.S. industries could offer in this new, global marketplace was speed. If we could produce the goods faster, we could have them at market sooner. If we could produce goods closer to the delivery date, we could predict more accurately what would sell, and we would pay less interest on borrowed money needed for inventory and business operations. If we could automatically replenish goods sold by the retailer, then consumers would be more likely to find the goods they want when they want them.

How could we increase speed without decreasing product quality? The answer has been technology. It has become our most valuable competitive edge. Though the initial cost of computer technology was high, management pushed forward. Computers invaded every aspect of the industry. It was clear that the investment paid for itself, both in speed and in accuracy. In time,

Selected Trade Publications Related to Business, Distribution, and Retailing

Advertising Age (www.adage.com): weekly newspaper that focuses on advertising, marketing, and media news and information.

Business Week (businessweek.com): weekly magazine that focuses on business news on Wall Street, media and advertising, international business, banking, interest rates, the stock market, and currencies and funds.

Chain Store Age (www.chainstoreage.com): monthly news magazine that focuses on information of interest to retail headquarters management, including trends and strategies in areas such as retail technology, store construction, marketing, physical support systems, finance, security, store design and visual merchandising, electronic retailing, payment systems, human resources, and supply chain.

Multichannel Merchant (multichannelmerchant.com): monthy news magazine for catalog companies and online merchants, as well as retailers, manufacturers, and wholesale/distributors, who sell goods through print catalogs and/or transactional Web sites.

Retail Merchandiser (www.retail-merchandiser.com): monthly magazine for executives and managers in the mass-merchandise, drug, club, and specialty retailing industries. Topics focus on merchandising and marketing issues, providing ideas and concepts that work within a retail environment.

Retailing Today (www.retailingtoday.com): newspaper that focuses on mass-market retailing business news, trends, and research analysis.

Stores (www.stores.org): monthly publication/magazine of the National Retail Federation with a focus on information of interest to retailers in general. Topics include supply chain, logistics, electronic data interchange, e-marketing, customer service, loss prevention, human resources, B2B, and international trends.

Supermarket News (www.supermarketnews.com): weekly trade magazine for the food distribution industry. Executives use it as their information source for industry news, trends, and product features. Many large food retailers sell selected apparel, accessory, and home fashions products.

VM+SD (Visual Merchandising and Store Design) (www.visualstore.com): monthly magazine for retail designers and store display professionals with information on trends in store design and visual presentations, new products, merchandising strategies, and industry news.

integrated computer systems arrived. Now, every phase of the textile/apparel/accessory/home fashions/retail complex can be linked with data interchange and data management. Ordering can be transacted online. Both intranet and Internet computer networks form the basis for communication of images and data. A computer screen has replaced most of the paper trail. Such dramatic changes in ways of doing business have been dependent on increased alliances among companies within the textile/apparel/accessory/home fashions/retailing marketing channel.

Some said that computer technology was only for the big companies. While many large companies were the first to use computer technology, small companies began to embrace technology as well. Costs have decreased, and technology has improved to the point where very small apparel companies and retailers cannot afford *not* to use computers.

At the same time as the industry increased its emphasis on technology, the traditional assembly line approach to production was reexamined. A trend developed that centered on a team approach rather than workers functioning as individual units. Teams became responsible for work flow and were given group responsibility for the quality of the product.

Although segments of the manufacturing process continued to make advances in technology, many companies chose to manufacture offshore. For a while, labor was cheap in certain countries. Then, as these developing countries advanced economically, labor costs increased. New countries were selected for less expensive labor. Many of the offshore contractors realized that they also needed computer technology for the same reasons that the U.S. companies needed it a decade earlier. Contractors in the more developed countries began to utilize computers, not only for increased speed and accuracy in their facilities, but also to integrate their operations with companies in the United States. Such global communication is now the norm.

A number of issues will shape the future of the U.S. textile, apparel, accessory, home fashions, and retailing industries: changes in international trade laws, global competitiveness, concerns for human rights and the environment in the production and distribution of products, changes in the way consumers buy goods, and changes in the way companies conduct their business. Emanuel Weintraub, president and CEO of Emanuel Weintraub Associates, and longtime apparel industry consultant, offers "10 tips for excellence in the new era":

1. Stay in constant touch with your target consumers—know their lifestyles, their wants, their needs, the limitations of their pocketbooks. Your knowledge of the marketplace is a major competitive advantage.

2. Make a desirable product. While execution of service to the customer is increasingly critical, there's no getting around the time-tested truth: "The price of admission is a merchantable product."

3. Think strategically. The industry's top manufacturers and retailers have been doing it for years, and a solid, consistent marketing strategy is a must for doing business with them. Latch on to the large retailers, as they will continue to call the shots and reel in the big sales via both traditional and non-traditional selling methods in the future.

4. Build trust with your clients by demonstrating fiscal stability. Strive to establish excellent bonding relationships to strengthen your ability to finance large orders, purchase piece goods, and hold inventory as needed.

5. Be the low-cost value supplier in whatever you produce, whichever market you supply. "Consumers expect value for every dollar they spend, whether it's a $300 blouse or a $10 blouse."

6. Pursue excellence in product execution, from sourcing to quality assurance to logistics, warehousing, and delivery. Focus on making it easy to do business with your firm. "There's no room for anything less."

7. Focus on your core competencies. For instance, if you are a private-label producer, stay focused clearly on price, quality, and service. If you elect to enter a new distribution channel or product category, recognize that you will need top talent and deep pockets to fuel the venture until it becomes a financial success.

8. Speed your products to market. The first garments to the selling floor have the best chance of selling at full margin price, leaving your firm at less risk for margin dilution by retailers. Continually review all internal processes that can inhibit speed.

9. Stake your claim with suppliers that are prepared to assume critical responsibilities essential to effective supply chain management. As more processes are passed from retailer to manufacturer to contractor, remember: "You may be logistically and technologically in the new millennium, but your vendors may be living in the '60s or '70s."

10. Hire the best talent your money can buy, bearing in mind that "big league" hitters—whether in information systems, marketing, or other fields—often will require not only competitively high salaries, but also sizeable budgets to execute their action plans.

SOURCE: DesMarteau, Kathleen. (2000, January). 10 tips for excellence in the new era. *Bobbin*, pp. 60–62.

Thus, in the twenty-first century, the strength of the textile, apparel, accessory, home fashions, and retailing industries depends on our ability to change and respond to the wants and needs of consumers.

Summary

Apparel, accessory, and home fashions companies have a number of options with regard to the distribution of their merchandise to the ultimate consumer. Companies must decide how widely their merchandise will be distributed; some will choose mass distribution, whereas others will decide on a selective or exclusive distribution strategy. Many companies now have multichannel distribution strategies whereby merchandise is sold through a variety of retail formats. Apparel, accessory, and home fashions companies will distribute their goods either directly to their retail accounts or through distribution centers. Retailers with many stores may also use distribution centers as central locations for merchandise, from which it is then shipped to the various stores.

Quick Response, product lifecycle management, and supply chain management strategies are important in the distribution process, and alliances between apparel companies and retailers contribute greatly to the success of these strategies. The foundations for these strategies are to use Universal Product Code bar coding on product labels and shipping cartons; RFID tagging on shipping cartons; to have vendors (manufacturers) assuming responsibility for affixing labels and price information on products; and to use electronic data interchange for the electronic transmission of invoices, advance shipping notices, and other information. Replenishment of goods at the retail level is built on the foundation of these operations. In some cases, programs have been established whereby the vendor (manufacturer) manages retail inventory and automatically replenishes the retailer's stock when needed. Data mining technology makes possible even more sophisticated systems for making sure that the retailer has the right stock at the right time.

The retailing level of the marketing involves the selling of merchandise to the final consumer. Retailers are often classified according to merchandising and operating strategies into the following categories, which are not mutually exclusive: department stores, specialty stores, chain stores, discount retailers, off-price retailers, supermarkets and hypermarkets, convenience stores, contractual retailers, warehouse retailers, and nonstore retailing. Apparel, accessory, and home fashions manufacturers use a variety of retailers in the final distribution of their products to the ultimate consumer, although they use some (e.g., department stores, specialty stores, discount stores) more than others. Nonstore retailing, including mail order/catalog and electronic/Internet retailing, has experienced greater growth than traditional forms of retailing in recent years. Many companies are now focusing on multichannel retailing strategies whereby they distribute merchandise through both bricks-and-mortar stores and nonstore retailing venues.

Supply Chain Efficiency Story: JCPenney

JCPenney has raised the bar for the retail industry when it comes to supply chain collaboration. Its direct-ship initiative is a prime example. The suppliers produce the goods in response to incoming orders in a few days, instead of producing apparel far in advance and storing it in warehouses. The concept-to-consumer cycle used to take two years. That has been chiseled down to 45 days in some cases, thanks to close ties with vendors established through the direct-ship program.

Here's how the concept works, using Hong Kong-based manufacturer TAL Apparel Group as an example. JCPenney outsources responsibility for sales forecasting and inventory management to TAL, which decides how many shirts to make, and in what styles, colors, and sizes. TAL sends the shirts earmarked for individual JCPenney stores, bypassing any requirement to store the product in the retailer's warehouses.

TAL began working with JCPenney on this initiative about a decade ago. This early collaboration gave TAL a long history of visibility into the retailer's demand, which allowed TAL to synchronize with JCPenney at the warehouse level in the initial phases of the direct-ship program rollout. Weekly orders were communicated to TAL from JCPenney via EDI. TAL then shipped the merchandise within a week of order receipt, cutting cycle time from four to six months down to 30 days.

Now, TAL has better visibility into demand at the store level from POS data, and determines its inventory according to each store's requirements. It then packs, barcodes, and consolidates shipping orders for delivery directly to the stores, eliminating warehouse inventory. This has led to savings of 15 percent of cost free on board (FOB).

EXCERPTS FROM: Atkinson, William. (2006, April). JCPenney: Pioneer of supply chain efficiency. *Apparel*, pp. 15–17.

SUCCESS STORIES

Careers in retailing are as varied as the stores themselves. Some of the career possibilities include store management, merchandise buying, private-label product development, catalog and nonstore retailing, and promotion and advertising, just to name a few.

Retail Store Manager
Women's Specialty Store Chain

Position Description
Lead a management team of three to five assistant managers and oversee the performance of 25,000 to 30,000 square feet of store space. Identify key opportunities to increase sales, and manage payroll and expenses, as well as supervise and develop assistant managers.

Typical Tasks and Responsibilities
- Ensure adherence to customer service policies and procedures.
- Oversee merchandise presentation activities on an ongoing basis.
- Motivate people to reach the store's goals.
- Manage payroll and operations.
- Oversee the development of assistant managers.

Merchandising Manager/Head Buyer
International Specialty Store

Position Description
Ensure merchandise mix, availability, distribution to all stores, inventory management, pricing, market development, and trends for the future, and purchase target allocation for all stores.

Typical Tasks and Responsibilities
- Select the merchandise mix to be carried throughout the stores.
- Work with local suppliers, and negotiate terms and conditions for each line of merchandise.
- Control inventory levels of merchandise (maximum three months inventory levels).
- Keep informed about the latest trends and developments (competitors, etc.).
- Set up a target purchase budget on a yearly basis.

Key Terms

boutique

chain store

concept shop

contractual retailer

convenience store

data mining technology

department store

discount store

distribution center (DC)

e-commerce

electronic data interchange (EDI)

electronic/Internet retailer

eMarket

exclusive distribution

franchise

hypermarket

in-store shop

intensive distribution

leased department

mail order/catalog retailer

mass distribution

multichannel retailing

nonstore retailer

off-price retailer

relationship merchandising

retailer

retailing

selective distribution

specialty store

supermarket

superstore

Universal Product Code (UPC)

vendor-managed inventory (VMI)

vendor marking

warehouse retailer

Discussion Questions

1. Describe the roles of distribution centers for apparel/home fashions manu-facturers and retailers. How and why have the roles changed?

2. Bring to class several apparel or home fashions merchandise hangtags or packages that have UPC bar codes. What information does the bar code provide to the manufacturer? To the retailer? To the consumer? What other information is on the ticket or package that is helpful to the consumer?

3. Name and describe your three favorite stores. What type of retail store is each? What are the characteristics of the types of retail stores you named?

4. Explore three Web sites that sell apparel or home fashions online. What are the common features of the sites? What strategies do these retailers use to inform customers about product characteristics?

References

Abend, Jules. (1998, September). In-store shops: Up the ante for apparel brands. *Bobbin*, pp. 32–40.

Aron, Laurie Joan. (1998, January). Duck head: The process is the product. *Apparel Industry Magazine*, pp. 16–19.

Atkinson, William. (2006, April). JCPenney: Pioneer of supply chain efficiency. *Apparel*, pp. 15–17.

Bailey, Thomas. (1993, August). *The Spread of Quick Response and Human Resource Innovation in the Apparel Industry*. New York: Institute on Education and the Economy, Teachers College, Columbia University.

Barnes, Mike. (1996, January). Technology's role in the '90's. *Apparel Industry Magazine*, p. 78.

Bert, Jim. (1989, March). The EDI link. Connections. Supplement to *Apparel Industry Magazine*, pp. 4–5.

DesMarteau, Kathleen. (2000, January). 10 tips for excellence in the new era. *Bobbin*, pp. 60–62.

DeWitt, John W. (1993, June). EDI's new role: Electronic commerce. *Apparel Industry Magazine*, pp. 36–41.

Drori, Neil. (1992, February). Taking the bull out of bar codes. *Bobbin*, pp. 14–18.

eMarkets. (2001, January). *Stores*, pp. 4–8.

Gilbert, Charles, and Carlson, Dave. (1995, October). Making the modular pay in the DC. *Bobbin*, pp. 84–88.

Hasty, Susan E. (ed.). (1994, March). *The Quick Response Handbook*. Supplement to *Apparel Industry Magazine*.

Hill, Suzette. (1998, May). Crystal ball gazing becomes a science. *Apparel Industry Magazine*, pp. 18–23.

Hill, Suzette. (1999a, May). Sell: Demand chain tools that watch the store. *Apparel Industry Magazine*, pp. SCM-30–SCM-32.

Hill, Suzette. (1999b, May). Store: A warehouse is not just a storehouse anymore. *Apparel Industry Magazine*, pp. SCM-23–SCM-26.

Home Shopping Network (2006). Home Shopping Network Home Page [online]. Available: www.hsn.com [October 29, 2006].

Internet Retailer (2007, May 18). eBay clothing tops the apparel & beauty April rankings [online]. Available: www.internetretailer.com/dailyNews.asp?id=22450 [May 19, 2007].

Karas, Jennifer. (2001, April). NRF/Pantone Partnership offers electronic color-coding system for retailers, consumers. *Stores*, pp. 124–125.

Lewison, Dale M. (1994). *Retailing.* (5th ed.). New York: Macmillan.

Mastercard International. (1996, February). Internet shopping: New competitor or new frontier? Supplement to *Stores*, MC1–MC24.

Moore, Lila. (1994, September). DCs face uncertain future. *Apparel Industry Magazine*, pp. 58–62.

Nannery, Matt. (1995, March 15). Fred Meyer bets the warehouse on QR. *Women's Wear Daily*, p. 25.

National Retail Federation (2007). NRF Divisions [online]. Available: http://www. nrf.com/modules.php?name=Pages&sp_id=172 [May 19, 2007].

Olive, Robert. (1988, February). L.L.Bean: Rapid receiving. *Apparel Industry Magazine*, pp. 56–60.

QVC (2006). QVC Home Page [online]. Available: http://www.qvc.com [October 29, 2006].

Reda, Susan. (1999, September). Top 100 Internet retailers. Special supplement to *Stores*, pp. V–V18.

Robins, Gary. (1993, March). Quick response. *Stores*, pp. 21–22.

Robins, Gary. (1994, March). Less work, more speed. *Stores*, pp. 24–26.

Schneiderman, I. P. (1995, October 5). Lost in a maze. *Women's Wear Daily*, pp. 1, 8–10.

U.S. Census (2002). 2002 Economic Census, Retail Trade United States [online]. Available: http://www.census.gov/econ/census02/data/us/US000_44.HTM#N448 [May 20, 2007].

Wal-Mart (2006). Wal-Mart Distribution Centers [online]. Available: http://www. walmartfacts.com/wal-mart-distribution-centers.aspx [October 1, 2006].

Welling, Holly. (2000, February). Unveiling AIM's store of the future, part I. *Apparel Industry Magazine*, pp. 24–31.

Winger, Rocio Maria. (1998, December). The Nygård vanguard: The way to no charge-backs. *Apparel Industry Magazine*, pp. AS-14–AS-18.

PART 4

Organization
and Operation of
the Accessories and
Home Fashions
Industries

CHAPTER 13

Accessories

In this chapter, you will learn the following:

- the relationship between fashion apparel and accessories

- the similarities and differences between the design and manufacturing of accessories and that of fashion apparel products

- the marketing and distribution strategies for fashion accessories

W *hat would a men's suit be without the right necktie? What would a new fashion look be without the right shoe style, belt, or jewelry? The accessories industries comprise a vital component of the total fashion industry and are integral to the success of the apparel industry. Primary accessory categories include footwear; hosiery and leg wear; hats and head wear; scarfs and neckwear; belts, handbags, and small leather goods; gloves; and jewelry. Other accessories not discussed in this chapter include sunglasses, handkerchiefs, hair accessories, and umbrellas. Each season, changes occur in accessories that relate directly to the changes occurring in fashion apparel. For example, the styling, colors, textures, and scale of jewelry will correspond to the type of apparel with which it will be worn (see Figure 13.1). Fashion trends in apparel and accessories are so closely linked that one can purchase a sweater, belt, and shoes in the same hot new fashion color at the same time in the market. It is clear that these industries work together.*

Yet fashion apparel products and accessories are distinctly different in some respects. Some accessories such as simple scarfs can be manufactured very quickly when a new trend in apparel develops. According to the national sales manager for a hosiery company, "In developing a product mix, the hosiery industry really has to follow other market segments. We can't set the trends, but we can accessorize them" (Rabon, 1995b, p. 66). In other cases, the accessories themselves are the fashion statement that can update classic apparel styles.

Other accessories take much longer to produce. The footwear industry needs time to design and produce the product, including time to procure materials. The design phase for shoes may begin before the design phase for an apparel product, especially if specialty leather materials are required. Therefore, forecasters in the shoe industry must be keenly aware of market and fashion trends in order to predict accurately appropriate shoe fashions that complement and coordinate with fashion apparel.

Accessories Categories

Accessories manufacturers are grouped into categories, including the following:

- footwear
- hosiery and leg wear

Figure 13.1 Fashion trends in apparel and accessories are closely linked.

- hats and head wear
- scarfs and neckwear
- belts, handbags, and small leather goods
- gloves
- jewelry

Many accessory companies specialize in manufacturing only one type of product; that is, some companies manufacture only shoes, and other companies produce only neckwear. Some companies prefer to diversify into more than one accessory category (see Figure 13.2). Dooney & Bourke and Coach, both traditionally handbag and small leather goods manufacturers, have diversified into footwear. Coach further diversified with a licensed apparel line.

The term **cross-merchandising** refers to the strategy used by both apparel companies and retailers to combine apparel and accessories in their product offerings. Some apparel manufacturers create their own accessories to coordinate with their apparel lines (e.g., Timberland, Eddie Bauer). Nike produces a line of backpacks and sports equipment bags in conjunction with its footwear and apparel lines. Other companies form agreements to produce coordinating apparel and accessories. In skiwear, for example, one apparel company may produce the outerwear apparel products, while another company produces the coordinating knit sweaters, head wear, and hand wear. Thus, the responsibility for manufacturing each type of product rests in the hands of the company with the required expertise and the best qualifications to produce it. Retailers employ cross-merchandising through displays that create a total fashion image and demonstrate to consumers how accessories might be worn with the apparel.

Licensing is a very important cross-merchandising strategy for coordinating apparel and accessory looks. In the typical licensing agreements, accessory manufacturers pay a royalty to the licensor company for the use of the brand, logo, or trademark on the merchandise. As discussed in Chapter 2, licensing agreements can be beneficial to both the accessory manufacturer and the designer. For the accessory manufacturer, the designer name provides immediate brand recognition among consumers. For the designer, he or she can expand into a variety of product lines bearing his or her name and become a total lifestyle brand by taking advantage of the manufacturer's product and market expertise ("The spell is in the name," 1999).

Some accessories companies have licensed their names for apparel lines (e.g., Hush Puppies, Kenneth Cole). Many name designers of apparel use licensing agreements with accessory manufacturers to produce the specific styles of accessories that complete the total fashion looks they desire. Designers such as Tommy Hilfiger, Ralph Lauren, Liz Claiborne, Donna Karan, and Calvin Klein have their names linked to belts, hosiery, shoes, and eyewear. Kenneth Cole has successfully licensed a broad range of merchandise, including all of the company's nonfootwear products except handbags. Depending on the licensing agreement, designers vary in their involvement and

Figure 13.2 Some companies, such as Kenneth Cole, produce goods in more than one accessory category.

approval requirements with the licensee. Some designers, such as Kenneth Cole, are involved with design and approval. Others turn over design decisions to the licensee.

Athletic footwear companies often have unique licensing agreements with professional and collegiate sports leagues (e.g., Major League Baseball) or individual teams. In these agreements, footwear companies pay the leagues or teams for the right to sell merchandise with the league or team logo. In addition, they may also purchase the right to outfit the team with athletic footwear and/or uniforms bearing the company's logo.

Consumers' purchases of accessories are often impulse buying decisions; that is, the purchases are not planned. Therefore, to facilitate these impulse purchases, accessories are often sold on the main floor of department stores, included in displays throughout stores, and positioned near the checkout locations in stores. In general, consumers favor discount stores (e.g., Wal-Mart, Kmart, Target) for their accessories purchases, with nonstore (e.g., catalog, television, online) purchasing of accessories growing fast (Accessories Council, 2000).

As with other segments of the fashion industry, the accessories industries rely on trade associations for research, education efforts, marketing, public relations, and advertising. These trade associations may focus on several categories of accessories (e.g., Accessories Council) or on a single category of accessories (e.g., Neckwear Association of America). For example, the mission statement of the Accessories Council, founded in 1995, is

> to stimulate consumer awareness and demand for fashion accessory products, and to serve as the advocate of the $30 billion accessory business in the United States. (Accessories Council, 2007)

Table 13.1 lists selected trade associations for accessories (see Chapter 4 for additional information). Trade publications are also essential to the dissemination of industry news and advertising to individuals in the accessories industry. Table 13.2 lists selected trade publications related to accessories.

Table 13.1   Selected Trade Associations for Accessories

Accessories Council
Athletic Footwear Association
Fashion Footwear Association of New York (FFANY)
Footwear Industries of America (part of American Apparel and Footwear Association)
Independent Footwear Retailers' Association
International Fashion Jewelry and Accessory Group
Jewelers of America (JA)
Men's Dress Furnishings Association
National Association of Fashion and Accessory Designers
National Association of Milliners, Dressmakers, and Tailors
National Fashion Accessories Association (NFAA)
National Shoe Retailers Association (NSRA)
Neckwear Association of America
Sporting Goods Manufacturers Association (SGMS)
Sunglass Association of America (SAA)
The Hosiery Association (THA)
Two Ten Footwear Foundation
Western Canadian Shoe Association (WCSA)
Western Shoe Retailers Association (WSRA)

Selected Trade Publications for Accessories

Accessories Magazine: published monthly by Diamond Publications; information for manufacturers and retailers of accessories including fashion trends, industry statistics, merchandising, and promotion.

California Apparel News: published every Friday by MnM Publishing Corporation; covers fashion industry news with an emphasis on regional companies and markets on the West Coast.

DNR: published weekly by Fairchild Publications; covers national and international news in men's wear apparel, retail, and textiles.

FN—Footwear News: published weekly by Fairchild Publications; includes footwear news, fashion trends, and business strategies targeted especially to manufacturers and retailers.

Women's Wear Daily: published weekdays by Fairchild Publications; includes special accessories supplements; Monday issues feature accessories, innerwear, and leg wear industry news.

Although there are differences in production processes within the accessories industries, most accessory lines are produced following procedures similar to the steps in the research, design, production, and distribution of apparel. These steps include the following:

research, including color, material, trend, and market research

design, including sketching and the use of CAD or graphics software

pattern making (or creating molds in the jewelry industry)

developing prototypes

costing and sourcing

marketing, including presenting a minimum of two lines per year during market weeks and at trade shows (see Table 13.3)

production

distribution and retailing

Important aspects of research, design, production, marketing, distribution, and retailing of accessories for each of the major categories will be discussed in the following sections.

Table 13.3   Selected Trade Shows for Accessories

Accessorie Circuit, held in New York

Accessories The Show, held in New York and Las Vegas

China International Clothing and Accessories Fair, held in Beijing, China

China International Footwear Fair, held in Hong Kong

Fashion Accessory Exposition, held in New York

Fashion Footwear Association of New York (FFANY) trade shows, held in New York

International Fashion Jewelry and Accessories Fair, held in Dubai

International Fashion c and Accessories Show, held in New York

International Footwear Fashion Fair (Aymod), held in Istanbul, Turkey

International Hosiery Exposition (IHE), held in Charlotte, North Carolina

International Manufacturers of Fashion Jewelry and Accessories Fair, held in
    Madrid, Spain

International Shoe Fair (GDS), held in Dusseldorf, Germany

International Shoes, Sportsgoods, and Leathergoods Fair, held in São Paulo, Brazil

JA International Jewelry Show, held in New York

JCK Fine Jewelry Show, held in New York and Las Vegas

Los Angeles Shoe Show, held in Los Angeles

Midec International Footwear Fashion Fair, held in Paris, France

Moda Accessories, held in Birmingham, UK

Moda Footwear, held in Birmingham, UK

Mode Accessories Show, held in Toronto and Calgary, Canada

New York Accessories Market (Fall, Holiday, Spring, Summer, Transitional), held in
    New York

New York Shoe Expo, held in New York

Peru Moda (textiles, apparel, footwear, jewelry), held in Lima, Peru

Shoe Fair, held in Bologna, Italy

TMC Fashion Square (textiles, clothing, footwear, accessories), held in Zurich,
    Switzerland

World Shoe Association, held in Las Vegas

NOTE: Many apparel trade shows listed in Chapter 8 also include accessories.

Footwear categories include the following:

- athletic footwear
- dress shoes and boots
- casual shoes
- sandals
- work shoes and boots
- western/casual boots
- hiking, hunting, and fishing boots

During the past few decades, the footwear industry has changed in a number of ways. First, as with apparel, footwear sold by U.S. manufacturers has shifted from domestic to global production. This is primarily because of the availability of raw materials and of rising labor costs in the United States; shoe production can be very labor intensive. Second, the production of leather footwear has been augmented by the production of footwear using a variety of manufactured materials. The types of shoes most frequently purchased have shifted as well. Athletic footwear has gained a tremendous market share of the footwear industry, with more athletic shoes sold than any of the other footwear categories. In recent years, the "brown shoe" type of footwear (i.e., rugged-looking footwear exemplified by Timberland and Wolverine) has seen market growth. Another trend is the crossover between athletic shoe styling and fashion shoe styling. Style components of each type of shoe are combined (see Figure 13.3).

The footwear industry in the United States is sometimes referred to as an *oligopoly* (see Chapter 2), in that several large shoe

Figure 13.3 Crossover styling between athletic shoe styling and fashion shoe styling is seen in these shoes.

manufacturers produce the vast majority of shoes. The largest shoe manufacturers in the United States are no longer fashion shoe companies. Currently, Nike controls approximately one-third of the U.S. athletic shoe market. Both Nike and the adidas Group have diversified their footwear lines, with Nike acquiring Cole Haan and Converse, and the adidas Group acquiring Reebok. Several large companies also dominate the fashion footwear business. Among them are the United States Shoe Corporation and Brown Shoe Company.

From an international perspective, Nike and the adidas Group are two of the world's largest footwear companies. Italy, however, has a reputation for leading trends in fashion footwear. In addition to its design reputation, Italy has produced fine leathers for apparel as well as for footwear for centuries. The handcrafting of Italian leather products has maintained a worldwide reputation for centuries as well. Salvatore Ferragamo shoes and handbags, Bruno Magli shoes, and Gucci shoes and handbags epitomize quality Italian leather materials and workmanship.

Some of the high-end footwear producers continue to utilize handstitching and other handwork. Hermès (France), Manolo Blahnik (England), and Ferragamo (Italy) are examples of companies that feature handwork. There still exists a market for handmade shoes and boots, perhaps most evident on Savile Row in London, where custom shoemakers such as Lobb are neighbors to custom shirtmakers and tailors.

Research, Design, and Production

The first steps in creating a footwear line and an apparel line are similar. Many footwear companies produce two lines per year: Fall/Winter and Spring/Summer. Footwear companies begin their lines by conducting market research, including consumer research, product research, and market analysis. They examine demographic and consumer buying trends of their target customer, explore innovations in footwear styles and technology, and analyze trends in the footwear market in general. They develop a target customer profile describing the typical customer for their various lines of footwear.

Athletic shoe giants Nike and the adidas Group invest heavily in footwear research. One of Nike's early developments was the Nike air cushioning technology that debuted in 1979. Nike's Sports Research Lab employs a dozen researchers who "study how feet and shoes function—from the way pressure dissipates each time a runner's foot strikes the ground to how women's toes flex and grip better than men's" (Jung, 2004, p. E1). In 2004, Nike introduced its Nike Free, based on creating a shoe that simulates how the foot performs while running barefoot. Nike is not alone in investing heavily in footwear research. For three years, the adidas Group worked to develop a computer-chip-embedded running shoe.

Fashion shoe designers research fashion trends in much the same way as do apparel designers. Many shoe designers throughout the world attend the Italian leather shows, as well as various shoe trade shows, to view the latest developments in leather and shoe design. Shoe designers work in conjunction with the company's merchandisers and production team to develop the shoe line each season. Designers work with the following shoe design components each season: materials, trims, style features, and heel height and shape. It is remarkable that shoe designers create such a variety of innovative styles each season, given the small surface area of footwear. The fabrication of prototype shoe styles and patterns is performed using steps similar to those discussed for apparel products.

Shoes are made by forming the raw materials around a **last**. The last is a wood, plastic, or metal mold, shaped like a foot. In the United States, lasts are sized in widths as well as lengths. Historically, the width of the last for European sizes has been different from that for U.S. sizes. Some U.S. footwear manufacturers produce shoes in Italy in order to take advantage of the Italian raw materials and craftsmanship. The shoes made in Italy for U.S. manufacturers are produced using U.S. lasts in order to fit the target customer's foot.

CAD technology has become an important part of the footwear industry. Computer software allows the shoe design to be viewed three-dimensionally on the screen. Some merchandisers for shoe companies consider computer images of the styles to be sufficient when selecting the shoes for the line. Thus, prototypes would be made only for those styles selected for production.

The sizes of pattern pieces for shoes are small compared to the sizes of most apparel pattern pieces. Accurate cutting is vitally important to the fit and craftsmanship of shoes. Therefore, cutting footwear often utilizes a die cutting process (see Chapter 9) because of its accuracy. A metal die similar to a cookie cutter is made to duplicate the shape of each of the pattern pieces. Its very sharp edge cuts through the layer or multiple layers of materials. Computerized cutting and laser cutting are other options (see Chapter 9) that provide extremely accurate cut pieces.

Leather hides are used for much of the fashion footwear produced worldwide (see Chapter 3). The hides are irregular in shape, and they often have blemishes and thin areas, as is to be expected of this natural product. Thus, cutting hides for the production of shoes, handbags, belts, and other leather goods requires additional time and expertise, creates some waste of material due to the irregular shape of hides, and often necessitates single-ply cutting to avoid blemished areas. Another factor to consider is that leather hides are a commodity traded on a market with a price that varies according to the supply.

Figure 13.4 Shoe manufacturing involves a large number of steps that must be performed by skilled workers.

In this respect, the shoe industry is similar to the fur industry. Not only do prices vary based on supply, but since some of the hide sources are in other countries, the monetary exchange rate can affect the price of the raw materials.

Because shoe manufacturing involves a large number of steps that demand skilled workers, labor costs tend to be high (see Figure 13.4). Adding to the production time, and thus to the labor cost, is the difficulty of manipulating an awkwardly shaped product composed of many small pieces. Examine the tiny material sections of a pair of toddler's athletic or hiking shoes to imagine what it would be like to assemble the shoe sections. The development of specialized machinery has helped to keep labor costs down for those manufacturers that can afford to invest in the equipment. Most of the domestic shoe production occurs in Pennsylvania, Maine, and Missouri. As labor costs have risen in the United States, more shoes are being produced offshore. South America (especially Brazil) and Asia produce large quantities of the shoes sold in the United States. China has become the leading producer of shoes.

Marketing and Distribution

New York City serves as the marketing center for footwear, with most companies having showrooms there. Domestic and international shoe trade shows, or markets, similar to the apparel market shows, are held two to four times a year. Fall/Winter shoe lines are typically shown in January or February, and Spring/Summer shoe lines are typically shown in August. The Fashion Footwear Association of New York (FFANY) sponsors footwear trade shows in New York City. Retail buyers, as well as manufacturers and footwear producers, attend these shows, just as the apparel trade shows are attended by people representing all aspects of the apparel industry.

The footwear industry utilizes similar promotional tools as the apparel industry in selling their lines to retail buyers. Sales representatives for footwear companies provide line catalogs to their retail customers. Some companies are currently using digital images of footwear in their presentations to retail buyers, thus creating a "virtual showroom" (Thilmany, 1998). DVDs, Web sites, trunk shows, and participation promotions are all used by footwear companies.

Footwear is sold in many department stores, specialty stores that offer footwear in addition to other products, specialty shoe stores, sporting goods and athletic footwear stores, discounters, and by nonstore retailing venues (catalog, television, and Internet/Web). Some specialty shoe stores carry products from a range of manufacturers. Foot Locker and Lady Foot Locker stores, an athletic footwear chain, carry a variety of athletic footwear brands. In addition, the strategy of vertical integration is also common in the footwear industry; that is, some manufacturers own the shoe stores in which only their products are sold. Examples are Thom McAn, Redwing, and Stride Rite. Footwear companies such as Nine West and Etienne Aigner have stores in outlet malls. Companies engaged in nonstore retailing of footwear include Lands' End, L.L.Bean, and Eddie Bauer, which offer shoes in addition to apparel products. The Nike.com Web site allows mass-customization, whereby customers may select colors and separate shoe sizes for left and right feet. In addition, sensors can be added to the shoes to provide instant performance feedback through the wearer's iPod (see Figure 13.5). Another type of mass-customization uses three-dimensional body scanning equipment to individualize the size and shape of shoes to fit the customer more accurately (see Chapter 11).

Figure 13.5   Nike.com offers customers customization options.

Private-label and store brand apparel strategies were discussed in Chapter 7. In the footwear industry, store brand and private-label business is also an important component. In 2005, Nike bought the Starter footwear brand and began to produce Starter sneakers for over 400 Wal-Mart stores. This partnership provided an opportunity for Nike to enter a new channel of distribution. The Nike-engineered shoes cost more than the older Starter footwear, but they sport a sleeker design and have been endorsed by an NFL quarterback. The discount retailers represent a very strong market segment, since "consumers purchased about $1.5 billion worth of athletic shoes at discount stores" in 2004 (Callimachi, 2005, April 2, p. B9).

Footwear retailing requires an immense inventory because of the large combination of shoe widths and lengths. When the range of seasonal colors is added to the size inventory, it is clear that shoe retailers have a challenging task to meet the consumer's need for the right product in the specific color and size. The footwear retailer must make a significant capital outlay and have large inventory space. This is one reason why some retailers lease their shoe departments to companies that specialize in shoe retailing (see Chapter 12).

The shift in location of footwear production from predominantly domestic, with some Western European production, to Asia and South America was discussed earlier in this chapter. The footwear industry has also shifted its customer market from domestic consumption to a global marketplace. Canadian, Mexican, and Japanese consumers have become major markets for U.S. footwear. American athletic shoe brands are sought worldwide. The reputation for quality of the casual footwear produced by U.S. manufacturers, such as Timberland, has opened European markets for these products. For survival and expansion, footwear manufacturers must continue to seek a global market for their products.

Disposal of used athletic shoes has become a concern, as landfill issues are brought to light. At the same time, some populations are in desperate need of shoes, and many of the discarded athletic shoes have much wearing life left in them. In response to these issues, several athletic footwear companies have sponsored events to encourage the public to donate their used athletic shoes to charity.

Hosiery and Leg Wear

The hosiery/leg wear industry comprises companies that produce men's, women's, and children's socks, stockings, pantyhose, and tights. This industry has a long and notable history in the United States. There is evidence that stocking knitting machines were in operation in New England as early as 1775. By 1875, the U.S. hosiery industry focused on the production of silk stockings, with an estimated worth of $6,000. By 1900, the industry had grown to a value of $186,413.

For centuries, stockings were knit by hand, using a circular knitting procedure so that no center back seam was required. The foot and leg shapes were produced by adding or subtracting stitches to increase or decrease the circumference of the stocking. The development of framework knitting machines (see Figure 13.6) in England at the end of the sixteenth century provided a way to produce stocking blanks ("The history of hosiery," 1974). However, the material was knit flat, or **flatknit**. This meant that a seam had to be sewn along the center back to create the tubular stocking. The **full-fashioned** technique provided the shaping of the knit goods to conform to the foot and leg shapes along the seam edges. The first full-fashioned hosiery factory in the United States was established by E. E. Kilbourn in the late 1860s.

The development of circular knitting machines in the nineteenth century provided a means to produce seamless (except for the seam used to close the toe) stockings, socks,

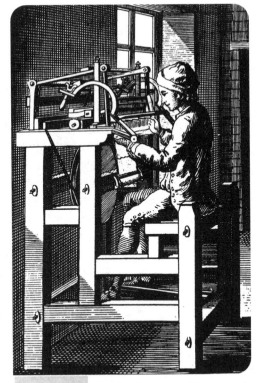

Figure 13.6 The development of framework knitting machines provided a faster way to produce hosiery.

and, later, tights and pantyhose. Early seamless stockings did not fit as well as full-fashioned seamed stockings. When women's hemlines were shortened during the 1920s, the better fit of seamed stockings was preferred. This is reflected in the increase in production of full-fashioned stockings from 26 percent of the market in 1919 to 60 percent of production in 1929 and more than 80 percent in the 1950s ("The history of hosiery," 1974).

The hosiery/leg wear industry underwent major developments during the twentieth century. At the beginning of the twentieth century, hosiery consisted of primarily white, "nude," and black socks and stockings in cotton, wool, and silk (and later, rayon) knits. By 1928, technological advances in knitting allowed for the production of full-fashioned men's hosiery in argyle patterns, English ribs, and cable stitches. In 1939, stockings made of DuPont's nylon fiber were introduced. Women loved their sheerness. Just as the demand for "nylons" soared, they were removed from the market. Nylon was needed for the war effort during World War II, and women wore socks that coordinated creatively with their suits. An amusing anecdote survives regarding women's sense of loss during the war. Sixty women in Tulsa, Oklahoma, were asked what they missed most during the war. Twenty said they missed men the most; 40 said they missed nylons the most! In 1946, when nylon stockings became available again, the crowds waiting to purchase them created a legendary sight.

Pantyhose were developed during the 1960s when very short hemline lengths required a product to replace stockings. As the name implies, the hose, or stocking, is joined to a panty, creating an all-in-one product. This eliminated the need for garters that are used to connect the stockings to a girdle or a garter belt. Nylon is the most prevalent fiber for pantyhose. Some pantyhose include a cotton-knit crotch piece. The pantyhose may include spandex fiber to provide some figure control. Since the 1980s, blending a small percentage of spandex with nylon in the leg portion of pantyhose has gained popularity. In the 1990s, *microfiber* (smaller-than-standard fiber diameter) nylon became popular, especially for opaque pantyhose or tights. Tights are similar to pantyhose, but they are made of a heavier material. Tights, as well as pantyhose, are either seamless or seamed along the center back.

Because pantyhose are made of manufactured fibers that are heat sensitive, the foot and leg shape can be built into the product during the finishing process. A heat setting process is used to mold the foot and leg shape by placing the hosiery over a leg-shaped board. Terms used for the application of heat to create the final shape in the finishing process are **blocking** or **boarding**.

Like textile production, hosiery production developed primarily in the Northeast. As with textile mills, however, production shifted to the South as labor costs increased in the Northeast. Hosiery/leg wear is a dynamic, high-fashion industry for men's, women's, and children's products. Staple hosiery goods have been augmented with "fashion" socks, stockings, and pantyhose suitable for every holiday, to express one's personality, or to add extra punch to an outfit. As with apparel, hosiery/leg wear can be found in all price zones, from mass/budget to designer. However, this product category has strong price appeal. The consumer can update an outfit inexpensively with accessories such as hosiery. The popularity of hosiery in today's marketplace is evidenced by the specialty sock shops that have proliferated in retail and outlet malls.

Hosiery and Leg Wear Producers

The hosiery/leg wear industry is dominated by large firms that are often part of vertically integrated companies that produce knitted fabrics as well as the finished hosiery and leg wear products. Most of the domestic hosiery/leg wear producers are located in the Southeast, concentrated primarily in North Carolina, Alabama, Tennessee, and in Pennsylvania. Some of the largest U.S. hosiery manufacturers include Kayser-Roth (No nonsense, HUE, Calvin Klein), Gold Toe Brands, Inc. (Gold Toe, Silver Toe, Auro), and Hanesbrands, Inc. (Hanes, L'eggs, Just My Size) (see Figure 13.7).

Research, Design, and Production

Companies that produce hosiery and leg wear analyze apparel style trends and consumer buying trends to make design decisions. In addition, color forecasting plays a very important role in determining the various colors in which the hosiery and leg wear will be produced. Designers also focus on new developments in textiles and knitting technology. For example, microfiber technology has provided consumers with softer and more sheer hosiery alternatives.

Socks are produced in varying lengths, including anklets, crew, mid-calf, and calf lengths. The most popular fibers for socks are cotton, wool, silk, acrylic, nylon, polypropylene, or blends of these fibers. Cotton and acrylic fibers are used frequently for ankle-length socks, while calf-length socks are often made of nylon, wool, silk, acrylic, or blends of two of these fibers. A small percentage of spandex might be added to provide some elasticity. Sport socks or athletic socks continue to be a market growth area. These include casual sport socks, as well as sport-specific socks that are designed with appropriate cushioning for various sports (Feitelberg, 1999) (see Figure 13.8).

The size range of hosiery varies according to the type of product. Sock and stocking sizes for men, women, and children are indicated with size numbers that correlate to shoe size. The consumer refers to a chart that shows the correct sock or stocking size based on the wearer's shoe size. There are fewer sock and stocking sizes than shoe sizes; each hosiery size fits a range of shoe sizes. For some products, the sock or stocking is available in only one size, which fits the

Figure 13.7   Some of the most recognized brands are in hosiery.

Figure 13.8 Sports socks or athletic socks continue to be a market growth area.

majority of shoe sizes. Pantyhose generally are sized to fit women who fall within categories based on their height and weight. Typical pantyhose sizes are *short, average,* and *tall. Queen size* and *Plus size* are size categories for the larger or taller size market. Some pantyhose producers provide a petite size as well.

One of the strengths of the hosiery industry is the impressive variety of innovative textures, colors, and patterns available for hosiery and leg wear products. New technology continues to bring an ever-increasing array of materials for hosiery. Much of the machinery required to produce hosiery is automated or computerized, and some of it operates 24 hours a day. Computer software designed for hosiery includes a library of design components, including sock pattern templates, and a wide variety of knit stitch effects. Courtaulds Socks, a part of Sara Lee Courtaulds, is a leading sock supplier to British retail giant Marks & Spencer, as well as other department stores and supermarkets in the United Kingdom. At Courtaulds Socks, the design team is constantly creating new designs, as many as 30 per week. They rely on CAD:

Images can be imported from other media such as sketches, photos, prints, and other CAD systems, or the designer may choose to draw the design directly on the system with the mouse or pressure-sensitive stylus; either way, the design is quickly converted into stitch format, and visualized on the sock template at the correct finished stitch tension. ("At Courtaulds socks, knitting is created on screen," 2001, p. 18)

Equipment innovations include the development of machinery to knit a one-piece pantyhose unit ("Hosiery automation," 1995). Labor costs can be kept down by advanced technology. Thus, the hosiery industry is not threatened as much by inexpensive imports as some other industries. A strength of the hosiery industry is that many manufacturers are vertically integrated and, therefore, have enhanced supply chain management opportunities.

Although the hosiery industry will face challenges in the future, it is positioning itself for continued success. Whereas the North American Free Trade Agreement has prompted more imports of hosiery into the United States, the trade balance still favors the United States. The hosiery industry relies on a close working partnership among the fiber producers, hosiery manufacturers, and retailers. By working together, the hosiery industry in the United States may be able to remain competitive with imported goods.

Marketing and Distribution

Market weeks for hosiery typically coincide with those for ready-to-wear apparel, although many hosiery and leg wear products are marketed and distributed through extended distribution channels. The hosiery industry is a low-margin business. This means that the dollar amount of profit per item sold that the producer earns from the sale to the retailer is small. Similarly, the dollar amount of profit that the retailer garners from the sale to the customer is also small. Thus, the manufacturer and the retailer need high sales volume to compensate for the low margin. A number of strategies are used to create high sales volume. These strategies include vendor-managed inventory systems, distribution through discount stores, enhancing ease of shopping, and licensing.

VENDOR-MANAGED INVENTORY

To produce a large sales volume, it is important to maintain a complete stock of hosiery in the appropriate sizes, styles, and colors. Therefore, many large hosiery manufacturers use Quick Response and supply chain management strategies, including vendor marking and vendor-managed inventory. Through the sharing of sales data, stock is automatically replenished at the retail store to ensure a complete selection of products for the customer. The director of a hosiery association stated the following:

> Retailers are requiring new benchmarks for product development and delivery. Just-in-time and quick turnaround are realities, and it is becoming more and more pressure driven every day. The new benchmarks are for deliveries to be shipped within 48 hours of receipt of order. (Rabon, 1995a, p. 60)

> A casual and athletic sock manufacturer specializing in the private-label business, Clayson Knitting Co., is totally computerized with full EDI capabilities, and all major customers send orders electronically. These orders are processed and shipped within 48 hours to 72 hours using back stocks that are maintained for these large customers. (Rabon, 1995b, p. 66)

DISTRIBUTION THROUGH DISCOUNT STORES

Most hosiery and leg wear is sold through large discount chain stores (e.g., Wal-Mart, Target, Kmart). Brands such as L'eggs, Hanes, and No nonsense are sold in this manner. Sid Smith, the president and CEO of the former National Association of Hosiery Manufacturers (NAHM), now the Hosiery Association, pointed out that the domination of discount store sales "means that it is extremely price competitive both at retail and at wholesale. Hosiery manufacturers have to compete very aggressively on price" (Rabon, 1995a, p. 60).

To allow for a self-service retailing strategy, package marketing is used by companies that sell hosiery in supermarkets, convenience stores, and discount retailers. This includes large-format sizing charts mounted on display racks, packaging that is color coded by style and size, and samples of the product available for consumers to touch and evaluate.

EASE OF SHOPPING

Because of the number of styles, colors, and sizes, selecting hosiery can be confusing for consumers. Therefore, retail stores have adopted a number of strategies to assist the consumer in selecting the right product. Because of the self-service approach to selling hosiery and leg wear, companies have simplified packaging, improved signs, and enhanced display fixtures in an effort to assist the consumer (Feitelberg, 1998).

Fashion trends also affect the sales volume of hosiery. In the 1990s, the trend toward more casual dressing at the office may have been a stimulus for the increase seen in the sales volume of socks. Promoting hosiery as a fashion accessory rather than a staple commodity can enhance sales volume. Hosiery departments in retail stores may feature body wear in addition to the hosiery products. Many retailers have added cross-merchandising displays, whereby hosiery (as well as other accessories) is displayed with coordinating apparel.

Some retailers have narrowed the number of brands or have focused on private-label hosiery to simplify options for consumers. In addition, private-label hosiery can provide for greater markups for the retailer. Retailers such as JCPenney, Nordstrom, and Talbots, to name just a few, distribute private-label hosiery. Services for the ultimate consumer, such as automatic replenishment programs, can also increase sales volume. Both Saks Fifth Avenue and Nordstrom will send consumers a designated supply of hosiery on a regular basis (Feitelberg, 1998).

LICENSING

Licensing products is another marketing strategy that has proved successful in the hosiery industry. As with footwear and other accessories, many name designers license their names for hosiery. Givenchy, Ralph Lauren, Calvin Klein, and Donna Karan are examples of designers who have licensing agreements with large hosiery companies for hosiery products.

Hats, Head Wear, Scarfs, and Neckwear

Accessories such as hats, head wear, scarfs, and neckwear typically are manufactured by a company that specializes in the specific accessory item. These accessory categories are integrally connected with apparel fashions and social norms.

Hats and Head Wear

Men's, women's, and children's dress hats comprise a much smaller segment of the accessories category than they did several decades ago. For women, the bouffant hairstyles of the 1960s did not lend themselves to wearing most hat styles. The pillbox hat made famous by then First Lady Jacqueline Kennedy in 1961 marked the end of the hat-wearing social requirement. The custom of businessmen wearing hats began to decline during the 1960s as well. The press coverage regarding the fashion apparel and head wear of the British royal family during the 1980s renewed interest in fashion hats, but sales remain a small percent of the accessories category.

The Paris designer runway shows provide a striking contrast, though, to the lack of emphasis on fashion head wear by the masses. The hats and head wear worn during the shows to complement the designer's fashion look are highly imaginative creations, providing strong visual interest to support the impact of the apparel collections (see Figure 13.9).

Whereas the popularity of wearing dress hats has waned, the popularity of wearing casual hats, sport hats, and sport caps (especially baseball caps) has increased, providing a growth area for the industry. For sports,

Figure 13.9 Millinery created for couture shows, such as Gaultier's Spring 2007 show, can be highly imaginative.

such as skiing, that require head covering for functional purposes, the demand for head wear has remained at the same level as the demand for apparel in these categories.

Many hat and head wear producers specialize in one type of product. For example, a manufacturer (sometimes referred to as an **item house**) will specialize in producing only baseball caps. Soft-fabric hats and caps are usually sewn using construction techniques similar to those used for apparel. Handwork might be required for the more expensive hats, while less expensive hats and head wear are machine made. Traditionally styled wool felt hats and straw hats are usually formed over a hat block, using steam to mold the hat into shape (see Figure 13.10).

Men's hats are produced in sizes, from 6¾ to 7¾ (in ⅛-inch intervals), that correspond to head circumference, or, for less structured hats, in sizes *small, medium, large,* and *extra large.* Caps may be produced in one size. Most women's hats are made in one size; however, some designer hats are produced in several sizes. Small children's caps and hats may be sized by age, while older children's hats may be produced in sizes *extra small, small, medium,* and *large.*

Baseball caps are used extensively as promotional items for many businesses. They can be manufactured quickly with technologically advanced equipment. A large number of baseball caps with a company logo might be ordered for a special event. Quick delivery of the product is a necessity to meet this need.

The New Era Cap Co. of Buffalo, New York, is a business built on speedy production in large quantities through flexible manufacturing. It is a licensed official supplier of caps to Major League Baseball, the National Basketball Association, and the National Hockey League, as well as a supplier to many colleges and universities and hundreds of Little League teams.

Millinery is a term that refers specifically to women's hats and usually denotes that handwork is involved in the hat making process. Until the late 1960s to early 1970s, most large department stores had millinery departments with millinery specialists. However, very few retailers have retained millinery departments. The hats sold in most retail stores are machine made

Figure 13.10 Felt hats, such as this dress hat, are molded into shape over hat blocks.

and moderately priced. Only a small market for fine millinery continues to exist. Most of the fine milliners are located in New York City, although milliners can also be found in Los Angeles and other major metropolitan areas.

Scarfs and Neckwear

Scarfs (preferred industry spelling) represent another product for which styles follow fashion cycles, and sales rise and fall with fashion trends. At times, large square scarfs, perhaps even in shawl sizes, are popular; at other times, small square scarfs or oblong scarfs might be fashionable. The scarf business is very specialized. A scarf manufacturer may specialize in only silk scarfs or only woolen (or wool-blend, acrylic, or cotton) scarfs. The printing processes used to apply the fabric design to silk are different from those used for woolen materials; thus, it is common for companies to specialize in one of these materials to ensure a quality product.

The cost of producing scarfs is tied to the fabrics, designs, and printing methods used. The Italian design house of Emilio Pucci is well known for scarfs in the designer price zone. Pucci's silk scarfs in brightly colored prints became famous in the 1960s and have been instantly recognizable ever since. The scarf prints are very carefully silk screened, so that the narrow black outlines around each motif are perfectly aligned (registered).

Many item houses in the United States produce scarfs in a wide variety of materials, from silk chiffon to cashmere, in an array of textures, colors, and prints (see Figure 13.11). Echo is one of the best-known U.S. manufacturers in the moderate-to-bridge price zones. Echo produces scarfs, neckties, and bedding under its own label, as well as private-label goods for stores such as Saks Fifth Avenue and Ann Taylor, and licensed scarfs for Ralph Lauren. Echo invested in CAD technology to enhance the speed

Figure 13.11 Many item houses produce scarfs.

and flexibility in designing scarfs and can create as many as 1,000 design patterns annually (Grudier, 1998). Many name designers, such as Ralph Lauren, Liz Claiborne, Oscar de la Renta, and Bill Blass, license their names for scarfs and neckties.

Many scarf manufacturers use fabric manufactured in Asia, and use Asian contractors for the printing as well. The material cost and labor cost related to printing may be less in Asia, thereby making it more profitable to source offshore. The actual construction process for scarfs can be very rapid, with machine-rolled hemming for moderate- and mass-priced goods, or time consuming, with hand-rolled hemming for some scarfs in the designer price zone.

Necktie manufacturers are usually specialists that produce only neckties. Finer-quality neckties are made of silk, while lower-priced neckties are polyester. Wool, linen, cotton, leather, and other specialty materials comprise a small segment of production. Most necktie materials are woven; a small percentage of neckties are made of knit fabric. For neckties made of woven fabrics, the material is usually cut on the **bias**, or diagonal, to provide a more attractive knot and contour around the curve of the neck. Because a large amount of fabric is required to cut neckties on the bias, this practice increases the cost. The bias cut also produces the diagonal angle of the stripe seen on neckties as they are worn (see Figure 13.12).

The fabric design for neckties is either a print, applied to the surface of the woven fabric, or a stripe, plaid, or motif woven into the fabric. Typical necktie stripes are called **regimental stripes** because they are derived from various historical military regiments. These stripes are spaced with wider widths for the background and narrower widths for the various stripes. Many schools (private secondary schools, military schools, colleges, and universities) have their own regimental stripes with unique combinations of colors

Figure 13.12 Men's ties are usually cut on the bias, producing the diagonal angle of the stripe on the necktie.

and spacing that denotes the specific institution. The regimental stripe tie is considered a classic choice for conservative business attire.

The construction process for neckties involves machine processes; some higher-priced goods require handwork as well. The price reflects the amount of time required to produce the necktie, as well as the cost of the materials. Computer-aided textile design processes and new computer printing technologies provide additional ways to reduce costs for the scarf and necktie industries in the United States.

The market for neckties reflects fashion cycles. The fashion pendulum moves from narrow ties to wide ties, from bow ties to no ties, from bright prints to subtle stripes. With the trend toward casual business dress, neckties are no longer required at some offices that traditionally had required that neckties be worn. This change may have had some impact on the necktie business. On the other hand, specialty tie shops in retail malls provide consumer awareness, interest, and offer shopping convenience. *Conversational* or theme necktie prints have provided an impetus to sales. Whether the necktie displays one's profession or hobby or promotes a seasonal holiday, the consumer can use his necktie to "speak" to observers.

In addition to neckties, other types of neckwear for men include neck scarfs, or **mufflers**, often wool or silk, worn as an accompaniment to a wool overcoat for more formal occasions or worn with a casual jacket or coat to provide neck warmth or a fashion statement. An **ascot**, a long neck scarf worn looped at the neck, is another item of men's neckwear. While neck scarfs and ascots are not purchased as frequently as neckties, retailers such as Brooks Brothers include such items as a necessary component of a well-stocked classic men's retail store.

Scarfs, neckties, and other neckwear are sold to consumers through a variety of retail venues: department stores, specialty stores, discount stores, boutiques, and nonstore retailers (e.g., catalog companies). The merchandising of scarfs and neckwear often requires instruction to consumers on how to tie the scarf or necktie effectively. Retailers often use promotion tools provided by the manufacturer to educate the consumer. These might include point-of-sale videos, booklets, and demonstrations.

Belts, Handbags, and Gloves

Belts, handbags, gloves, and other small leather accessories add elements to project one's personal style. These items, too, reflect fashion trends seen in apparel and other accessories. When pants are cut with a low rise, contour belts that shape to fit the body contour are fashionable. When the waist is a fashion focus, wide belts are an important accessory. Some of the unique aspects of each of the accessories categories of belts, handbags, and gloves will be discussed separately in the following section.

Belts

The belt industry is divided into the following two segments: **cut-up trade** and **rack trade**. The cut-up trade includes manufacturers that produce the belts that apparel companies add to their pants, skirts, and dresses, and supply as a component of the products that apparel companies ship to retailers. The rack trade is made up of manufacturers that design, produce, and market belts to retailers.

Manufacturers in the cut-up trade specialize in low-cost, high-volume items. These garment belts might be made with less expensive materials and processes, such as gluing, rather than stitching the backing material to the belt. Self-belts made from the same fabric as the garment might be produced by a belt contractor or the apparel manufacturer at the same time that the garment is produced.

Belts for the rack trade often provide an important component of a fashion look; therefore, this part of the accessories industry works closely with the apparel segment. U.S. belt production is centered in New York City's fashion district. Typical materials include leather as well as numerous other materials, from cording to beaded fabrics. The type of material used determines the construction techniques and manufacturing processes.

For leather belts, cutting can be performed by hand or by the use of a strap cutting machine that cuts even-width strips. Some leather belts are curved, or contoured, in which case the leather can be die cut for speed and accuracy. A myriad of decorative effects can be used to enhance belts (see Figure 13.13). Belt designers add creativity with the use of buckles, stitching, jewels, chains, metal pieces, plastics, stones, nailheads, and other embellishments. Belt backings are attached by stitching or gluing.

Handbags and Small Leather Goods

Although this category of accessories is referred to as *handbags*, a variety of products is retailed within the classification. Handbags are also called *purses*. Many of the purses produced and sold today are actually shoulder bags rather than handbags. Women's briefcases are included in the *handbag* category, as are wallets, coin purses, eyeglasses cases, and schedule planners. (Men's briefcases are typically sold with luggage.)

Handbags are made from a variety of materials. Many of the handbags sold in the United States are made of leather, reptile (such as snakeskin), or eel skin.

Other materials include a variety of fabrics, plastics (vinyl is the most common), and straw. Judith Leiber creates beaded and metal evening bags, with retail prices beginning at approximately $500.

Structured handbags are supported by a frame that provides a distinctive shape and to which hardware, such as the closure, is attached. Soft handbags, such as pouch styles, may not use a frame. Handles or straps are attached to carry the handbag. **Clutch** bags are designed to be held in the hand (the term is derived from the fact that the bag is *clutched* in the hand) and may have a strap that can be stored inside the bag. Most handbags are lined in materials such as leather, suede, cloth, or vinyl. Structured bags may also have an interlining made from a stiff material to provide a firm shape.

Handbag styles range from large satchels to tiny clutches. While fashion trends play an important role in handbag styling, personal choice plays a role as well. Some women prefer a very functional bag, designed to hold everything,

Figure 13.13 Decorative effects using buckles, stitching, and other enhancements add a lively interest to belts.

either in a roomy tote or a compartmentalized style. Other women prefer a compact style that could range from a wallet-on-a string to a decorative evening bag to hold only a few essentials. Many European men carry bags, and some American men have adopted this practice, particularly to store personal electronic devices.

Designing handbags requires the same steps as many other products. Ideas are sketched, and decorative trims, handles, hardware, and materials are researched. It is interesting to imagine what it would be like to be a designer for a classic handbag company such as Coach or Dooney & Bourke (see Figure 13.14). How, and how much, can a designer modify a handbag? Materials and trims, and size and shape of a bag are some of the design parameters. A myriad of possible design details contributes to the design inspiration. Colored piping is

Figure 13.14   Dooney & Bourke designers use new shapes, colors, textures, and hardware for bags to create new styles each season.

considered "classic" for some handbags, but new color combinations add a fresh look. After ideas and sketches have been generated, prototypes are made, and then the line is finalized (see Color Plate 10).

Leather handbags follow manufacturing procedures similar to other leather products discussed in this chapter. Fabric handbags may use die cutting and other processes similar to garment and shoe production. Computerized cutting equipment is used by the factory in Sainte Florence, France, to produce Louis Vuitton's "Alma" bag made from the famous monogram fabric. Plant director Pascale Tinozzi commented, "There is absolutely no allowance for error in cutting; the maximum permissible tolerance is half a millimeter" ("Louis Vuitton: 15 Vectors meet exacting production demands," 2001, p. 10). Thus, the factory uses computerized cutting equipment.

For all handbags, some of the assembly processes, especially adding the hardware, require handwork. Thus, labor costs are an important part of the costing structure. For leather goods, the price and availability of hides is another cost consideration. There are a number of small companies that produce many of the handbags produced in the United States. Most of these companies are centered in the mid-Manhattan area of New York City. New York City is also the primary market center for handbags and small leather goods. Since most handbags and small leather goods sold in the United States are imported, offshore production sites in Asia, Spain, Italy, and South America are important production centers.

Because many of the production processes are similar for various leather goods, shoe manufacturers might also make handbags and belts. For example, Ferragamo produces coordinated handbags for some of its shoes, and Coach produces belts and other small leather goods as well as handbags. The handbag trade shows, generally four per year, coincide with the apparel markets.

In the 1970s, several designer names became sought after by consumers. The Louis Vuitton vinyl handbags with the "LV" logo appeared everywhere and sold at a premium price. Gucci bags became a status symbol. French fashion designer names, such as Pierre Cardin and Christian Dior, appeared on the outside of handbags. Since then, the licensing of designer and well-known brand names for handbags has become a major component of this business.

Handbags and small leather goods are sold through department stores, specialty stores, discount stores, boutiques, and nonstore venues. Some department stores have established in-store shops to feature the leather products of a specific manufacturer. Coach bags and belts often have a designated retail space, distinctively styled with shelf units and signage that the customer associates with Coach. We also see vertical integration within this industry. For example, Coach also operates its own retail stores (see Figure 13.15).

Gloves

Gone are the days when a well-dressed man, woman, or child did not leave home without both hat and gloves. The popularity of dress gloves rises and falls with fashion trends. Functional gloves and mittens, such as those worn for cold winter weather, remain a steady part of the industry. Sport gloves are a rising segment of the glove industry, with gloves specially designed for skiing, snowboarding, bicycling, weight lifting, golf, and many other sports. Women's dress gloves are produced in a variety of lengths, from wrist-length "shorties" to shoulder-length 16-button gloves for bridal and evening wear. (The term *button* is used to designate each inch of length.)

The two primary categories of the glove industry are leather gloves and fabric gloves. The difference in the handling of these two

Figure 13.15 Coach handbags might be sold through in-store shops in department stores or through Coach specialty stores.

types of materials results in substantial differences in production. The majority of fabric gloves are made of knit fabric. Production is similar to that of other knit items and is located primarily in the Southeast, where many knitting mills are located. Knit gloves and mittens are produced quickly by using a circular knitting machine (see the section in this chapter on hosiery).

The production of leather gloves, however, still requires many hand operations. Automating the processes is difficult, and skilled operators are required. Because of the labor-intensive nature of the industry, many glove manufacturers use offshore contractors, primarily in Asia and the Philippines, to reduce labor costs. In the United States, a large portion of glove manufacturing is located in the state of New York. Two of the glove industry's largest companies, Fownes Brothers and Co. and Grandoe Corporation, are headquartered there.

The types of leather used for gloves need to be strong, yet thin and supple. Leather gloves are produced in a variety of lengths and from many different leathers (see Figure 13.16). Typical glove leathers include kidskin, lambskin (cabretta is a type of lambskin), pigskin, deerskin, and sueded leathers. Among the steps in the production of better-quality gloves is a process to dampen and then stretch the leather in order to improve suppleness. Some leather glove manufacturers specialize in only one part of the production process, such as cutting. This step requires careful assessment of the hide for quality and most efficient utilization. Cutting might be accomplished entirely by hand (**table cutting**) for the top-quality gloves, or by less time-consuming die cutting (**pull-down cutting**) for less expensive gloves.

Higher-quality leather gloves include a number of separate sections that provide flexibility for hand movement. These sections include the following:

- a thumb section
- a **trank** piece for the palm and another piece for the face of the hand
- **fourchettes**, which are rectangular strips between the second/third, third/fourth, and fourth/fifth fingers to provide width
- three **quirks**, tiny triangular gussets at the base of the second, third, and fourth fingers

Each of these pieces requires painstaking care in construction in order to fit the pieces together properly.

Woven-fabric gloves require pattern pieces and steps similar to those for leather gloves. Less expensive gloves may have fewer pattern pieces and, therefore, may not provide as much hand mobility and comfort as gloves made with more pattern pieces. The seams may be stitched so the raw edges are to the inside or may be sewn with raw edges to the outside, depending on the style of glove. Gloves can be made of a combination of leather and fabric. For example, a sport glove might have leather tranks and knit fourchettes. Some leather gloves are lined with knit fabric or fur.

Knit gloves may be manufactured in one size if the fabric stretches sufficiently to fit a wide range of hand sizes. Leather gloves usually are produced in sizes *small, medium, large,* and *extra-large,* or they are sized numerically, in ¼-inch intervals, corresponding to the circumference in inches around the palm and forehand (sizes 7 to 10 for men and sizes 5½ to 8 for women). For children, gloves and mitten sizes (often sized as *small, medium,* and *large*) are related to age.

New York City is the primary market center for gloves, and most glove companies have showrooms

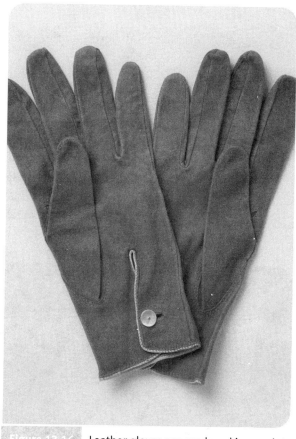

Figure 13.16   Leather gloves are produced in a variety of lengths and from many different leathers.

there. Specialists called glove buyers in retail stores are from a bygone era. Today's gloves are sold in the accessory departments of department or specialty stores, along with belts, scarfs, handbags, and sometimes jewelry. Gloves are also sold by specialty accessory retailers.

The competitiveness of the domestic glove industry will depend upon companies being flexible, offering high quality and fast turnaround, and having the ability to produce small lot runs. Grandoe Corporation exemplifies the type of flexibility needed by successful companies. Grandoe produces dress and casual gloves; sports gloves for skiing, snowboarding, and other outdoor activities; and private-label gloves for retailers such as L.L.Bean, JCPenney, and Bloomingdale's (Rabon, 1998).

Jewelry

Jewelry is divided into three categories: fine jewelry, bridge jewelry, and costume jewelry.

Fine Jewelry

Fine jewelry is the most expensive jewelry category. This category includes pieces made from precious metals, such as silver, gold, and platinum, either alone or with precious and semiprecious gemstones (see Figure 13.17). Because gold is too soft to be used by itself, it is usually combined with other metals for jewelry. The gold content of a piece of jewelry is expressed in *karats*, or k, with 24k referring to solid gold; 18k and 14k gold are most often used in fine jewelry. Any alloy less than 10 karats cannot be labeled *karat gold*. Platinum, which is heavier and more expensive than gold, is often used for rings, particularly diamond rings. Silver is the least expensive of the precious metals. Silver is often combined with other metals (usually copper). To be labeled *sterling silver*, the metal must be at least 925 parts silver to 1000 total parts.

Precious gemstones include diamonds, emeralds, sapphires, and rubies. All are measured in karats, with 1 karat equaling 100 points. Pearls are also included in this category, even though they are not a stone per se. Semiprecious stones include amethyst, garnet, opal, lapis, jade, topaz, and aquamarine. In recent years, semiprecious stones have gained popularity as consumers' preference for colored gemstones has increased.

Fine jewelry companies are often vertically integrated organizations,

Figure 13.17 Fine jewelry often includes precious and semiprecious gemstones.

with the designer, producer, and retailer under one roof. Fine jewelry is sold through specialty jewelry stores and the fine jewelry departments of upscale department stores. Many consumers have turned to nonstore retailers, particularly television retailers such as QVC, to purchase fine jewelry.

Bridge Jewelry

Similar to the bridge price zone for ready-to-wear apparel, which falls between designer and better price zones, **bridge jewelry** falls between fine and costume jewelry. *Bridge jewelry* serves as an umbrella term for several types of jewelry, including ones that involve the use of silver, gold (typically of 14, 12, or 10 karats), and less expensive "stones," such as onyx, ivory, coral, or freshwater pearls. One-of-a-kind jewelry designed by artists using a variety of materials is also considered bridge jewelry. Bridge jewelry is sold in the same stores or departments within stores as fine jewelry and costume jewelry.

Costume Jewelry

Costume jewelry is the least expensive of the jewelry categories. In the 1920s and 1930s, Coco Chanel was the first prominent designer to accessorize her couture garments with costume jewelry, thus legitimizing the wearing of less expensive jewelry by women everywhere. This type of jewelry is mass produced using plastic, wood, brass, glass, lucite, and other less expensive materials. Although there are large companies in the costume jewelry industry, including Monet and Trifari, the industry is dominated by small companies that produce jewelry sold through a variety of retail outlets, including nonstore retailers (see Figure 13.18).

Figure 13.18 Monet produces costume jewelry sold through department and specialty stores.

Summary

Accessories comprise important segments of the fashion industry. Changes in accessories complement changes found in the ready-to-wear apparel industry. Therefore, the apparel and accessories markets work together in creating total fashion looks. Accessories are grouped into the following categories: footwear; hosiery and leg wear; hats and head wear; belts, handbags, and small leather goods; gloves; and jewelry. Although production processes vary, most accessory lines are created according to the following steps: research, designer's sketches, pattern making, development of prototypes, costing, marketing, production, distribution, and retailing. These steps mirror the steps used for the creation of apparel.

The footwear industry produces men's, women's, and children's dress shoes and boots, athletic shoes, casual shoes, and other footwear. The main raw materials used for footwear include leather, fabrics, and plastics. Shoes are produced by forming raw materials around a last or mold shaped like a foot. To reduce labor costs, shoe production has shifted from domestic to primarily offshore venues. New York City serves as the primary market center for footwear.

The hosiery/leg wear industry produces men's, women's, and children's socks, stockings, and hosiery. The hosiery industry is dominated by large firms that are often part of vertically integrated companies. Most of the domestic hosiery producers are currently located in the Southeast. Production of hosiery is highly automated and, therefore, is not threatened by imports as much as are other industries. Hosiery companies are very involved with Quick Response and supply chain management strategies, including vendor-managed retail inventory.

Although hats and head wear companies currently comprise a much smaller segment of the accessories industries than they did decades ago, they are still important. Item houses that produce specialty merchandise, such as baseball caps, have grown as the popularity of this type of accessory has increased. The belt industry includes the rack trade (manufacturers that design, produce, and market belts to retailers) and the cut-up trade (manufacturers that produce belts for apparel companies). The handbag industry produces small leather goods as well as handbags. Leather gloves and fabric gloves are the two primary categories in the glove industry. Jewelry is divided into three categories: fine jewelry, bridge jewelry, and costume jewelry. New York City serves as the market center for virtually all accessories. Trade shows and trade associations play an important role in promoting all components of the accessories industries.

As with the ready-to-wear industry, the accessories industries include a wide variety of career possibilities, from design to production to marketing and distribution.

Color and Paint Coordinator/Assistant Designer
Publicly Held Athletic Shoe Company

Position Description

Create a color palette for each season; decide what colors to use on each shoe, taking into consideration the target customer; decide on the materials to use in the shoe production; paint prototype shoes.

Typical Tasks and Responsibilities

- Create different colorways for shoes.
- Use freehand and streamline applications to create the colorways.
- Attend meetings to communicate with others in the department and in other departments.
- Render drawings for these meetings to communicate the designer's ideas visually.

Accessories Pattern Maker/Sample Maker
Publicly Held Sportswear and Athletic Shoe Company

Position Description

Support the design prototype process for the accessories team, including drafting patterns; interpreting design and constructing prototypes; and creating specifications, technical drawings, and construction details.

Typical Tasks and Responsibilities

- Draft accessories patterns from design sketches.
- Construct, build, and/or sew accessories samples, such as bags, hats, or gloves.
- Create product specifications and ensure accuracy.
- Create product technical drawings, complete with construction details, to facilitate more accurate samples from the field.
- Review accessory samples for accuracy, color matching, durability, and function.
- Review construction details to ensure that specifications are correct.

- Collaborate with accessory designers, developers, and engineers to ensure that the best product is produced, and work out construction problems.
- Calculate fabric utilization data and other costing factors in collaboration with engineers, designers, and developers.
- Evaluate new equipment with the sample room supervisor and technology services manager.
- Cut fabrics and trim.
- Purchase and maintain inventory of materials, supplies, and notions.

Key Terms

ascot
bias
blocking
boarding
bridge jewelry
clutch
costume jewelry
cross-merchandising
cut-up trade
fine jewelry
flatknit
fourchette

full-fashioned
item house
last
millinery
muffler
pull-down cutting
quirk
rack trade
regimental stripe
table cutting
trank

Discussion Questions

1. Think about the accessories you are currently wearing. How do they complement the fashion apparel you are wearing? How are the design, production, and distribution of these accessories similar to and different from the fashion apparel?

2. If you were a shoe designer, before starting your next line of shoes, what sources of information would you turn to for market and trend research? Why would this information be important in your design decisions?

3. Study the ads for accessories in a current fashion magazine. Note how many ads there are for shoes, jewelry, and purses. How do the number of accessories ads compare to the number of apparel advertisements? Can you think of some reasons for the ratio of accessories to apparel ads?

References

Accessories Council. (1999, April 19). Main floor magic. Advertising supplement to *Women's Wear Daily*.

Accessories Council. (2000, November 6). The accessory industry speaks. Advertising supplement to *Women's Wear Daily*.

Accessories Council (2007). Accessories Council Home Page [online]. Available: http://www.accessoriescouncil.org [May 25, 2007].

At Courtaulds socks, knitting is created on screen. (2001). *Lectra Mag* number 2, p. 18.

Callimachi, Rukmini. (2005, April 2). Nike, Wal-Mart meet with new athletic shoes. *Corvallis Gazette Times*, p. B9.

Feitelberg, Rosemary. (1998, April 6). Stores give hosiery a makeover. *Women's Wear Daily*, p. 14.

Feitelberg, Rosemary. (1999, September 13). It's not just a white sock now. *Women's Wear Daily*, p. 34.

Grudier, Alison. (1998, February). Echo on bringing CAD in and sourcing it out. *Bobbin*, pp. 36–42.

The history of hosiery: Early industry developed slowly. (1974, November 8). *Hosiery Newsletter*, pp. 3–9.

Hosiery automation advances at F.A.S.T. show. (1995, August). *Hosiery News*, pp. 32–34.

Jung, Helen. (2004, August 22). Freeing the foot. The *Sunday Oregonian*, pp. E1, E3.

Louis Vuitton: 15 Vectors meet exacting production demands. (2001). *Lectra Mag* number 2, pp. 8–10.

Rabon, Lisa C. (1995a, December). Makers target new benchmarks. *Bobbin*, pp. 60–63.

Rabon, Lisa C. (1995b, December). Survival of the sock. *Bobbin*, pp. 65–66.

Rabon, Lisa C. (1998, January). Gloves grip new markets to keep their hands in the industry. *Bobbin*, pp. 24–29.

The spell is in the name. (1999, April 19). Advertising Supplement to *Women's Wear Daily*.

Thilmany, Jean. (1998, December 9). Footwear digitalization. *Women's Wear Daily*, p. 26.

CHAPTER 14

Home Fashions

In this chapter, you will learn the following:

- the similarities, differences, and relationships between the home fashions and the ready-to-wear apparel and accessories industries

- the design, marketing, production, and distribution processes of textile products, such as upholstery fabrics, window coverings, area floor coverings, towels, and bedding

- the steps the industry has taken to ensure sustainable design in home fashions

*P*revious chapters in this book have primarily examined the design, marketing, and production of ready-to-wear apparel and accessories. Because of the growth and increased relationship between apparel and home fashions, this chapter will focus specifically on the home fashions industry. **Home fashions** are textile products, such as towels, bedding, upholstery fabrics, area floor coverings, draperies, and table linens for home end uses that have styles that change over time in response to evolving fashion trends. Therefore, home fashions include the upholstery; window treatments; soft floor coverings; and bed, bath, and tabletop categories of the broader home furnishings industry. The home fashions industry consists of companies that design, produce, market, and distribute these home fashions products.

This chapter will examine the similarities, differences, and relationships among the design, production, and marketing of home fashions and ready-to-wear apparel and accessories. An understanding of the organization and operation of the home fashions industry in the broader context of apparel fashions is important for several reasons. Home fashions companies are important customers for many companies that also cater to the apparel industry, such as trend forecasting companies, textile mills, and textile converters. Also, the ready-to-wear industry and the home fashions industry have become increasingly interconnected as a growing number of apparel companies are now designing, producing, marketing, and distributing home fashions.

As we examine the home fashions industry, it is important to keep in mind that the average **product turn** (the frequency rate at which a product is sold and replaced at the retail store) in home fashions is less than two per year, compared to the apparel industry where the average turn is four to six times a year. This difference in product turn has implications for the design, manufacture, distribution, and retail sales of home fashions.

Categories for Home Fashions

In general, the home fashions industry is divided into the following four primary end-use categories (Yeager, 1988):

- upholstered furniture coverings and fillings
- window treatments and wall coverings

- soft floor coverings, including area rugs, scatter rugs, runners, and cushions (room and wall-to-wall carpeting are beyond the scope of this chapter)
- bed, bath, tabletop, and other home textile accessories and accents

Later in this chapter, these end-use categories will be discussed in greater detail. First, an overall context for the design, marketing, and production of these end-use products will be provided in the following sections:

- a general discussion of some overarching trends in the home fashions industry
- the organization and operation of the home fashions industry
- the marketing of home fashions

Home Fashions Industry Trends

A number of trends in the home fashions industry affect the design, production, and distribution of home fashions. These trends include the following:

- strong consumer demand for home fashions
- crossover between apparel and home fashions
- growth of private-label and store brand products
- increased social responsibility in the production of home fashions (discussed later in the chapter)

Consumer demand for home fashions has been strong, and analysts predict continued strong demand. This trend can be attributed to a favorable housing industry, a growing remodeling industry, consumers' desire to spend more time at home, and the growing selection of home fashions available to consumers. "Consumers are now trading up to better quality via ensembles, collections, designer names, and fashion, which are the most promising aspects of the business for all channels of distribution, especially the discounters" ("Retailers duel," 1999, p. 20). Even with a slowing housing market, analysts continue to predict a growing demand for home fashions, as evidenced by the increasing number of home fashions centers sprouting up in growing markets such as Phoenix, Las Vegas, and Orlando. Home fashions centers bring together a variety of home improvement and decorating retailers, such as furniture, tile, carpeting, and lighting, in addition to restaurants (Popovec, 2005). With this continued growth, the design, production, marketing, and distribution of home fashions encompasses a large potential market for exciting and rewarding careers for individuals who have expertise in textiles, design, and marketing.

The crossover between apparel and home fashions continues to be a strong trend. Since the early 1980s when Laura Ashley and Ralph Lauren started licensing their brand names to home fashions items, numerous apparel designers and ready-to-wear manufacturers have moved from the apparel arena into the home fashions market, including the following:

- Giorgio Armani
- Tommy Bahama
- Tommy Hilfiger
- Calvin Klein
- Nautica
- Sigrid Olsen
- Pendleton Woolen Mills
- Lilly Pulitzer

Retailers have found that these well-known designer and manufacturer brand names attract customers who purchase home fashions through their various retail venues (see Figure 14.1).

Another trend in home fashions has been the growth of private-label and store brand merchandise. A number of stores have introduced their own lines and collections of home fashions under brand names unique to the stores. Macy's offers private-label brands, including Charter Club and Barbara Berry. Kmart continues to do extremely well with the exclusive line Martha Stewart Everyday. Martha Stewart "credits her brand's number-one status to a massive communication effort, from her retailing program at Kmart, to mail order, radio and television programs, newspaper columns, magazines, books, and a Web site" (Musselman, 1999, p. 25). Target offers private-label brands, such as Isaac Mizrahi Home and Simply Shabby Chic by Rachel Ashwell, through exclusive licensing agreements. Pottery Barn, Crate and Barrel, and Pier 1 offer home fashions as store brands.

Figure 14.1 Tommy Hilfiger entered the home fashions market after attaining strong market penetration in the men's, women's, and children's apparel markets.

Home Fashions and the Textile Industry

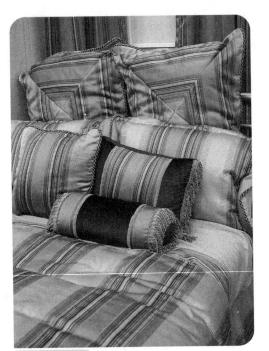

Figure 14.2 Charter Club is one of Macy's private-label store brands.

The textile industry forms the base for the structure of the home fashions industry. The design and performance of the textiles used in home fashions play a very important role in the success of the end-use product. For many home fashions, the design of the fabric is as important as the design of the end-use product itself (see Figure 14.2). As mentioned in Chapter 3, textile companies often focus entirely on home fashions end uses. The general organization and structure of textile companies that produce textiles primarily for the home fashions industry are the same as for those companies that produce textiles for the apparel industry (see Figure 3.1 about the organizational structure of the U.S. textile industry). It should be noted that many textile companies produce fabrics for both apparel and home fashions (e.g., International Textile Group, Milliken, Springs Global, and Dan River Global).

The home fashions industry is dominated by vertically integrated textile companies that produce both fabrics and home fashions end-use products (see Figure 14.3). These include home fashions powerhouses such as WestPoint Stevens, Springs Global, and Dan River Global. This is because production of home fashions is often highly automated and can be accomplished very efficiently within a vertical operation. In many cases, the fabric may not need to be cut and sewn to complete the product (e.g., towels and rugs), or minimal sewing, such as sheet hemming, is performed at the textile facility. For example, a single facility owned by WestPoint Stevens performs all production processes, from cleaning cotton to creating the finished products (e.g., sheets and pillowcases) that are ready for distribution.

Because of this vertical integration and automation of production, many large production facilities still exist in the United States. Home fashions fabric companies have also expanded production internationally. For example, Dan River Global has over 3,500 employees at production facilities in Virginia, North Carolina, and Canada. Springs Global has operations in the United States, South America, Mexico, and Canada.

Figure 14.3 Vertical integration and automation of production are typical characteristics of major producers of home fashions.

Licensing in Home Fashions

Licensing agreements involve the manufacturer purchasing the rights to use an image, design, or name on its products (see Chapter 2 for a complete discussion of licensing). As in the apparel industry, licensing agreements have become an important component of the home fashions industry. Licensing agreements in home fashions are classified in the same categories as apparel, including the following:

- designer name licensing
- character licensing
- corporate licensing
- nostalgia licensing
- sports licensing

Well-known ready-to-wear apparel designers have moved into the world of home fashions through licensing agreements with textile mills and home fashions manufacturers. One of the first apparel designers to license home fashions was Laura Ashley, who now has licensing agreements with Hollander Home Fashions, for bedding and other sleep items; with Kravet, for upholstery and other home fashions fabrics; and Mohawk Home, for area rugs. In 1983, Ralph Lauren became the first fashion designer to establish an entire home fashions licensed collection, including bedding, towels, area rugs, wall coverings, and tabletop accessories (see Figure 14.4). Today, some of the best-known designer brand names with home fashions licensing agreements include Giorgio Armani, Ralph Lauren, Liz Claiborne, Laura Ashley, and Calvin Klein.

In addition to name designers, companies with well-known brand names are also entering into licensing agreements for home fashions. For example, Hollander Home Fashions produces bedding under the J.G. Hook brand name; Springs Global manufactures infant and children's bedding under the Daisy Kingdom brand name; and WestPoint Stevens produces bedding under the Martha Stewart Everyday and Harley-Davidson brand names.

Historic reproductions and historically inspired fabrics have a strong market appeal. The Williamsburg Collection, inspired by eighteenth- and nineteenth-century designs, is produced by Waverly in a licensing agreement with Colonial Williamsburg. The designs for coordinated fabrics for upholstery, pillows, and window coverings are adapted from the eighteenth-century archives of Colonial Williamsburg.

Figure 14.4 Ralph Lauren became the first fashion designer to establish an entire home fashions licensed collection.

Licensing is also big business for home fashions geared to children. As with apparel, licensing has been successful for cartoon and movie characters (e.g., Disney, Warner Brothers), sports teams (e.g., St. Louis Rams), and toys (e.g., Barbie). Beatrix Potter and Winnie the Pooh are timeless and endearing character licenses for juvenile home fashions.

What makes these licensing agreements successful? As discussed in Chapter 2, a successful licensing agreement, whether in ready-to-wear or home fashions, depends on a well-recognized brand name with a distinct image and a licensed product that reflects that image. Successful licensed home fashions collections that follow this strategy include Ralph Lauren Home Collection, Laura Ashley Home, and Tommy Bahama Home Furnishings.

Home Fashions Design

During the design phase of developing home fashions products, textile and trim designers create exciting materials, and product designers determine the form of the final end-use product. As previously discussed, some home fashions products roll out of the textile production facility as finished products. For other types of products, the product designer works with new textiles, trims, and findings to create exciting pillows, comforters, tabletop accents, and accessories for the home. In general, designers in the home fashions industry create designs for two fashion seasons: Spring/Summer and Fall/Winter. Because fashion trends do not change as quickly for home fashions as for apparel, home fashions designs may stay on the market longer than apparel designs.

Research

Designers must take into account many factors (influences and constraints) in order to develop new and exciting products successfully season after season. Inspiration can come from numerous sources when creating new shapes, textures, and color combinations. New fiber and fabric developments are a part of the design inspiration. In addition, there are important functional needs that must be met. Performance criteria are important to the consumer. A towel must be absorbent, soft, easily laundered, and durable, as well as look attractive while displayed in the bathroom. As with apparel, fabrics used for home fashions are designed and tested for performance characteristics. Some home fashions products (e.g., rugs, fabrics for upholstered furniture) must meet specific safety standards (e.g., flammability) set by law.

The designer strives to be aware of emerging social, political, economic, and consumer trends. Anticipating and meeting customer needs are critical components of the design and production aspects of the industry. Two key elements of current home fashions trends are self-expression and individuality. These are evidenced by the increased customization of products to meet a consumer's individual wants and needs. The research conducted on home fashions products and consumer trends is similar to the research for apparel products. For example, Thinsulate, an insulative material manufactured by 3M with an established name in apparel, also has attributes suited to the bedding market. However, the fiber composition needed for bedding differs from Thinsulate's specifications for apparel products. In order to apply this fiber to a new end use in the home fashions market, 3M needed to conduct research and development procedures. "Through independent research, 3M found that consumers would be receptive to Thinsulate in bedding, and 'the consumer told us they would be willing to pay more for it'" (Rush, 1996, p. 6).

Color Forecasting

As in the apparel industry, color forecasting is an important component of home fashions product development. Some of the color forecasting services mentioned in Chapters 3 and 5 provide research and trend forecasting for home fashions, as well as for apparel products.

Historically, changes in the color palette for home fashions were based on a 10-year cycle. Who can forget the following color palettes?

- pink, salmon, cerise, turquoise, and gray of the 1950s
- avocado and orange of the 1960s
- beige, yellow (harvest gold), and brown of the 1970s
- mauve, forest green, slate blue, and gray of the 1980s
- the neutrals and jewel tones of the 1990s
- the oranges, greens, and purples of the early twenty-first century

However, that 10-year color cycle appears to be accelerating as consumers are interested in updating their home **decor** (interior decoration) more frequently, and companies are providing consumers with more alternatives. Designers are often inspired by colors of the past and reintroduce them with a contemporary feel.

Home textile sample books might be used to market home textiles for several years. Therefore, accurate color forecasting is necessary for the fashion colors to appear as up to date as possible. In addition, substantial lead time is needed to produce coordinated home fashions products. Therefore, on-target color forecasting is critical for success. Some of the color forecasting services discussed in Chapters 3 and 5 provide color forecasts specifically for the home fashions industry.

Based in Alexandria, Virginia, the Color Marketing Group (CMG) is an international not-for-profit color forecasting association of over 1,000 color professionals. One of its purposes is to forecast color directions for all industries, manufactured products, and services. CMG sponsors two international conferences each year, during which members meet and come to a consensus on future color trends (12 to 18 months in advance) for a variety of consumer products, including home fashions.

Many interrelated factors and influences are considered during the selection process for the seasonal color palette for a new home fashions line. According to the CMG Web site, "these 'influences' run the gamut from social issues to politics, the environment, the economy, and cultural diversity. It is an understanding of the influences that provides the most useful information, and it is the input of so many Color Designers that gives each Forecast its tremendous validity" (CMG, 2007). The president of CMG discussed color choice as it relates to lifestyle:

> Many retailers often appeal to a specific lifestyle or age group and develop their color palette with that in mind. Target, Pottery Barn, Crate and Barrel, Pier One, and IKEA all sell to a similar demographic.... The colors found in these stores can be very similar, reinforcing the notion that design, style, and price often dictate what will work on those products. (Verlodt, 1999, p. 13)

Textile Processes

TEXTILE DESIGN

Textile design for home fashions includes the design of the fabric structure (e.g., weave pattern) as well as the surface design (e.g., printing, napping, glazing). Although woven fabrics are more common than other fabric structures for home fashions products, the industry has seen an increased use of knits and nonwoven fabrics, primarily for less costly products.

Textile designers for home fashions often work with computer-aided design (CAD) programs to develop their designs. Textile designers also create original painted artwork for fabric prints that are later scanned into a CAD system. Once the textile design is in the CAD system, details of the design are refined. The various colors used in the print design can be separated by computer for the printing process. Each color of the print requires a separate roller for rotary printing or a separate screen if screen printed.

CAD systems greatly speed the work pace in rug design studios (see Figure 14.5). The textile designer creates a new rug design on a CAD system in hours or scans an image into the system in minutes. CAD/CAM technology provides the means to design exclusive patterns for private-label programs rapidly and easily.

TEXTILE PRINTING

Prints with a larger number of colors (13 to 15) are more costly to produce than prints with a few colors (1 to 3). Therefore, some companies set a limit on the number of colors that can be included in their print designs. The cost of developing the new print is more economical if the print can be produced in

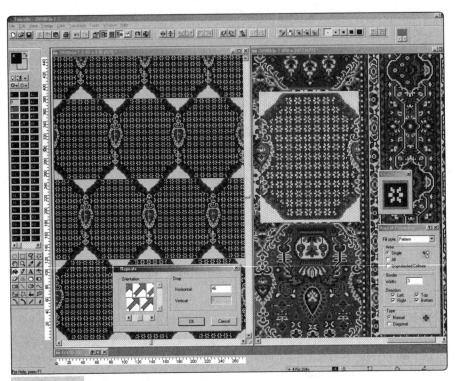

Figure 14.5   CAD/CAM software increases the efficiency of carpet and rug designers.

several color combinations, or colorways. Therefore, several colorways, or color variations, are typically created for each print design. When designing a print, textile designers must take into consideration the repeat of the print so that the design can be printed efficiently (see Chapters 3, 6, and 9 for additional discussion of textile design).

Digital printing used in the apparel industry was discussed in Chapters 3, 6, and 11. This printing technology is in use by some textile producers for home fashions. Seiren Co. is a Japan-based textile converter, dyer, printer, and finisher. The company's digital textile dyeing system "enables direct interactive communication between Seiren's production site and its consumers via the Internet," allowing for product customization (Seiren, 2007).

WEAVING

Weaving looms for products such as rugs are controlled by sophisticated computer-aided manufacturing programs. Computers are used in the production of woven, tufted, and printed rugs. For example, carpets and rugs manufactured by Shaw Industries, one of the largest carpet manufacturers in the world, are produced on state-of-the art computerized looms that are integrated with the CAD system. This allows for immediate communications of designs to the weaving floor where the design is loaded into the computerized loom. Rugs are produced as orders are received, thus greatly reducing inventory.

CONVERTERS

As in the apparel and textile industries, textile converters play an important role in the production of textiles for specific home fashions end uses. These end uses include upholstery fabrics, table linens, and other fabrics that are printed or finished to improve the aesthetics and performance of the end-use product. For example, soil-hiding and soil-resistant finishes are often applied to fabrics used for upholstery or table linens. As with the apparel and textile industries, many home fashions textile print converters—such as Covington Fabrics (a division of Covington Industries), Richloom Fabrics, and F. Schumacher & Co.—are based in New York. The Robert Allen Group, another home textile converter, is headquartered in Foxboro, Massachusetts.

In most cases, converters will provide either original painted fabric print designs or CAD designs to a finishing company that will incorporate the design into a computer system, develop pigments for printing, and print and finish the fabric. The textile converter is also heavily involved in the marketing of the textiles and promotion of the home textile brands. For example, F. Schumacher & Co. designs and markets the following brands: Waverly, Village, Gramercy, Rosecore, Greeff, and Schumacher.

Marketing Home Fashions

Marketing components for home fashions are similar to those used in the apparel industry, including manufacturers' showrooms, company sales representatives, trade shows, and advertising and promotion. However, the home fashions industry relies on textile converters and jobbers to perform marketing and distribution functions more often than does the apparel industry.

As with apparel, the establishment of well-respected brand names is important in the marketing of home fashions. Consumers often rely on brand names in their decisions to purchase goods. WestPoint Stevens is well known for its Martex, Utica, Vellux, Martha Stewart Everyday, Lauren Ralph Lauren, and Patrician brands. Springs Global is known for its Springmaid, Wamsutta, Court of Versailles, and Graber brands. As discussed earlier, retailers have developed private-label brands of home fashions to further distinguish their merchandise (e.g., Macy's Charter Club, Target's Isaac Mizrahi Home).

Manufacturers' Showrooms and Sales Representatives

Marketing headquarters and manufacturers' showrooms for many home fashions companies are located in New York City. Companies use showrooms to provide enticing visual displays of new home textiles as well as finished products for their interior design, manufacturing, and retail customers. Most companies will display new fabrics made into end-use products to show customers how the new fabrics can be used. Coordinated ensembles of products for bed and bath, kitchen, living room, and dining areas are presented. Companies also distribute sample books to interior design and manufacturing customers. These sample books include swatches of home textiles that are available and pictures of finished products using the textiles.

Decorative Fabric Converters and Jobbers

In addition to manufacturers' showrooms, textile decorative fabric converters and jobbers also play an important role in the marketing of home fashions. As mentioned earlier, textile converters in the home fashions industry design and sell finished textiles to jobbers, designers, and manufacturers, who use the textiles in home fashions end-use products. Some converters also produce end-use products such as bed linens and window treatments. Similar to manufacturers, converters also create and distribute sample books. They also have showrooms in New York City or elsewhere where they display and sell their goods to jobbers, as well as to interior design, manufacturing, and retailing customers.

The Robert Allen Group, one of the largest residential woven-fabric converters in the United States, has showrooms in over 60 countries and in more than 30 U.S. states. In each fabric category (e.g., upholstery, drapery), teams of designers work to create new fabrics for their customers under the following four distinct brands: Robert Allen, Beacon Hill, Robert Allen Contract, and Robert Allen@Home. The Robert Allen Group markets its products through showrooms and showroom boutiques, where finished products are shown using exclusive fabrics. In addition to fabrics, these showrooms have displays of wall coverings and finished products, such as bed coverings and draperies. Other well-known converters include Covington Fabrics, Richloom Fabrics, F. Shumacher & Co., and Kravet.

Decorative fabric jobbers are also involved in the marketing and distribution of home textile piece goods, particularly upholstery and drapery fabrics. Traditionally, jobbers have served a warehousing and distribution function within the industry. In the past, regional jobbers would visit New York twice a year, where they would buy large quantities of fabrics from a number of mills and converters. They would then sell smaller quantities to interior designers, furniture manufacturers, and retail customers.

Over the years, the jobber market has evolved into a year-round market, with a number of jobbers providing nationwide distribution. Jobbers continue to select colors, designs, and fabrics that best meet their customers' needs. Similar to manufacturers and converters, jobbers put together sample books for their customers.

In recent years, the jobber market has changed as jobbers have started providing a number of services, such as importing fabrics, creating exclusive in-house fabric designs, converting fabrics, and marketing fabrics through showrooms. Thus, the differences between the functions of textile mills, converters, and jobbers are less distinct than in the past. In fact, as some jobbers have turned to converting, some top converters have begun to perform jobbing/distribution functions.

Marketing Tools

As in the apparel industry, companies in the home fashions industry use a variety of marketing tools to advertise and promote their products to their customers and to the ultimate consumers. These marketing tools include the following:

- sample books (for home textiles)
- catalogs
- print advertisements in trade and popular press publications
- Web sites
- television advertisements

Co-op advertising (see Chapter 8) helps to provide the links in consumers' minds between brand names, end-use products, and retailers. The use of Web technology will continue to expand and open new marketing possibilities for the entire soft-goods pipeline. Business-to-business communication and Web-based commerce have opened new opportunities for marketing home fashions. Textile converters generally have *to the trade* links on corporate Web sites where commercial customers can contact sales representatives and preview and purchase goods.

Trade Associations, Trade Shows, and Trade Publications

TRADE ASSOCIATIONS

In both the ready-to-wear and the home fashions industries, there are trade associations for various textiles, general categories of merchandise, and specific aspects of the industry. Textile trade associations for home fashions are the same as those for fashion apparel. These include the National Council of Textile Organizations, Cotton Incorporated, and the Wool Council (see Chapter 3 for a description of these trade associations). For example, Cotton Incorporated promotes the use of cotton in home fashions products (see Figure 14.6). Cotton Incorporated's research department develops new products that are adopted and produced by textile mills. Cotton Incorporated has also developed cotton fabrics that can be used for upholstery, window treatments, wall coverings, table linens, and area rugs.

Some trade associations promote home furnishings or home fashions in general. Other trade associations focus on specific aspects of the industry, such as the Carpet and Rug Institute (CRI) and the National Home Furnishings Association. These trade associations assist in conducting market research, connecting suppliers with customers, and promoting specific end uses or areas of the industry. Table 14.1 lists selected trade associations in the home fashions industry.

TRADE SHOWS

Trade shows that showcase products from the home fashions industry often cover a variety of other related markets as well. In addition, home fashions may be displayed in trade shows that focus primarily on other industries. For example, textile trade shows such as Fabric at MAGIC may include textiles for home fashions, although the primary focus is on apparel. Gift markets also include home fashions products. For example, the Atlanta International Gift and Home Furnishings Market includes home accents, fine linens, and area rugs, in addition to tabletop accessories, fine home furnishings, and fine gifts. The New York Home Textiles Show runs concurrently with the New York International Gift Fair. Design trade shows are attended by interior designers and architects, as well as some professionals in the home fashions industry. One example is the Fine Design Residential Furnishings Show at NeoCon World Trade Fair, which is geared toward furniture, lighting, kitchen cabinets,

comfort

Sheets. Towels. Jeans. Underwear. When it comes to comfort, consumers everywhere look for cotton. Cotton. The fabric of our lives? www.cottoninc.com

Figure 14.6 Cotton Incorporated, a trade association, promotes the use of cotton fiber for the home fashions industry.

Table 14.1   Selected Trade Associations for the Home Fashions Industry

American Home Furnishings Alliance
317 W. High Avenue, 10th Floor
High Point, NC 27261
Tel: 336-884-5000
www.ahfa.us

Carpet and Rug Institute
730 College Drive
Dalton, GA 30720
Tel: 706-278-3176
Fax: 706-278-8835
www.carpet-rug.com

International Furnishings and Design Association (IFDA)
150 S. Warner Road, Suite 156
King of Prussia, PA 19406
Tel: 610-535-6422
Fax: 610-535-6423
www.ifda.com

International Home Furnishings Representatives Association (IHFRA)
209 South Main
P.O. Box 670
High Point, NC 27261
Tel: 336-889–3920
Fax: 336-883–8245
www.ihfra.org

International Sleep Products Association (ISPA)
501 Wythe Street
Alexandria, VA, 22314-1917
Tel: 703-683-8371
Fax: 703-683-4503
www.sleepproducts.org

National Association of Decorative Fabrics Distributors (NADFD)
One Windsor Cove, Suite 305
Columbia, South Carolina 29223
Tel: 1-800-445-8629
Fax: 1-803-765-0860
www.nadfd.com

National Home Furnishings Association (NHFA)
3910 Tinsley Drive, Suite 101
High Point, NC 27265-3610
Tel: 1-800-888-9590
Fax: 336-801-6102
www.nhfa.org

Upholstered Furniture Action Council (UFAC)
Box 2436
High Point, NC 97261
Tel: 336-885–5065
Fax: 336-885–5072
www.ufac.org

Window Coverings Association of America (WCAA)
2646 Hwy 109
Suite 205
Grover, MO 63040
Tel: 636-273-4090
Fax: 636-273-4439
www.wcaa.org

and wall coverings, as well as textiles, carpets, and bath products. Other trade shows focus on decorator fabrics, such as Heimtextil in Frankfurt, Germany. In addition to housing most manufacturers' showrooms for home fashions,

New York City is also the home of the New York Home Textiles Show. During market weeks, companies show samples of home textiles to jobbers, designers, manufacturers, and retailers (see Figure 14.7).

Some of the home fashions markets are held in the same merchandise marts that house the apparel trade shows, such as the Chicago Merchandise Mart (where the Fine Design Residential Furnishings Show is held), and Dallas Market Center (where the Dallas International Gift and Home Accessories Show is held).

On the other hand, the High Point Market, held in High Point, North Carolina, is the largest home furnishings market in the world. High Point Market shows upholstery fabrics, as well as furniture, with 2,500 exhibitors and 70,000 attendees from over 100 countries. Most of the markets for the home fashions industry are held twice a year. Table 14.2 lists selected trade shows for the home fashions industry.

Figure 14.7   Textiles are marketed to home fashions retailers at trade shows. The New York Home Textiles Market Week, held twice a year, offers access to nearly 500 mid-to-high-end home textiles resources at the New York International Gift Fair, and permanent showrooms at 230 Fifth Avenue and 7 West 34th Street.

Table 14.2 Selected U.S. and International Trade Shows for the Home Fashions Industry

Atlanta International Gift and Home Furnishings Market
AmericasMart, Atlanta
  home accents, fine linens, fine furnishings, tabletop, fine gifts, area rugs

Fine Design Residential Furnishings Show at NeoCon World Trade Fair
Merchandise Mart, Chicago
  high end in homeware products

Dallas International Gift and Home Accessories Show
Dallas Market Center, Dallas
  gifts, tabletop, collectibles, home textiles, Christmas trim, gourmet foods, floral, stationery, toys, and jewelry/ fashion accessories

Decorex International
London, various locations
  decorator fabrics

Decosit International Trade Fair Brussels
Brussels, Belgium
  decorator fabrics

Gift & Home Furnishings Market
L.A. Mart, Los Angeles
  gifts, tabletop, home textiles

Global Home Textiles
Orlando, FL
  offshore manufacturing resources for home fashions, including bed and bath fashions, table linens, kitchen textiles, pillows, area rugs, window treatments, fashion hardware, infant/juvenile merchandise, decorative accessories, decorative fabrics and trims

Heimtextil International Trade Fair for Home and Contract Textiles
Heimtextil, Frankfurt
Heimtextil, India
Heimtextil, Japan
Heimtextil, Russia

High Point Market
High Point, NC
  largest and most comprehensive exhibition of residential home furnishings in the world

Interior Lifestyle, Japan
Interior Lifestyle, USA
Las Vegas
  features high-end bedding, kitchen and bath textiles, decorative and furnishing fabrics, window and tabletop products

Intertextile
Shanghai, China
  home textiles

Maison et Objet
Paris, France
  furniture, rugs, decorative lighting, home textiles

New York Home Textiles Show
New York City
  bed and bath fashions, kitchen textiles, area rugs

TRADE PUBLICATIONS

Trade publications are an important source of information for professionals in the home fashions industry (see Figure 14.8). As with the apparel industry, some trade publications cover the entire industry, whereas others focus on specific aspects of the industry. See Table 14.3 for a listing of selected trade publications in the home fashions industry.

Production of Home Fashions

Price, value, and quality are key features sought by home fashions consumers. These features are related to the production of the product. Fast, efficient production can help to control costs. Chapter 11 discussed how quality must be built into the product throughout the production processes in the apparel industry. This is also true for home fashions. Quality assurance programs are an integral part of home fashions production facilities.

Figure 14.8 Trade publications on home fashions provide important information to industry professionals.

Table 14.3   Selected Trade Publications for the Home Fashions Industry

Bed Times: monthly business journal of the sleep products industry (www.sleepproducts.org/TemplateBedtimes.cfm?Section=BEDtimes)

Floor Covering Weekly: weekly newspaper geared to the flooring and interior surfacing product industry; reports news to floor covering retailers, contract dealers, distributors, and manufacturers (www.floorcoveringweekly.com)

HFN: (previously named *Home Furnishings News*) weekly newspaper featuring in-depth news and analysis of products and retail trends in the home furnishings industry (www.hfnmag.com)

Home Accents Today: monthly magazine on merchandising and fashion news for the home accent industry; aimed at decorative accessory, specialty home accent, and gift buyers (www.homeaccentstoday.com)

Home Textiles Today: weekly newspaper covering the marketing, merchandising, and retailing of home textile products (www.hometextilestoday.com)

Interior Design: monthly magazine for professional interior designers of office, commercial, and residential interiors (www.interiordesign.net)

UDM—Upholstery Manufacturing: monthly magazine with information related to the design trends, fabrics, and manufacturing innovations of upholstery textiles and upholstered seating for the home, office, hospitality, and transportation industries (www.udmonline.com)

As indicated earlier, the home fashions industry includes a number of vertically integrated companies that produce not only the fabric but also the end-use product. To avoid increasing costs, some vertically integrated companies have ceased production of their own yarns. For example, a mill might save money by outsourcing yarn production rather than investing in new yarn facilities. Some domestic apparel manufacturers turned to offshore production as a cost-saving procedure years ago. This trend has repeated itself in the home fashions industry. Many home fashions manufacturers have also elected to cease domestic production, sourcing production in other parts of the world. Increased global competition in home textiles has forced U.S. companies to develop new competitive strategies.

In some cases, factories have been closed. In 2003, Pillowtex Corporation, which produced home textiles under the Fieldcrest, Canon, and Royal Velvet brands, filed for bankruptcy. That action ended 116 years of being one of the largest vertically integrated home textile producers in the United States. The brand names are now licensed to Target, WestPoint Stevens, and Li & Fung.

Quick Response strategies, supply chain management, and product lifecycle management, which were discussed in previous chapters, are applicable to the home fashions industry as well. Home fashions companies continue to upgrade their operations with product information management and computer integrated manufacturing. Whether companies are vertically integrated or focus on specific design, production, or marketing aspects of the home fashions industry, integrating computer design and information systems has been crucial for remaining competitive in the global home fashions industry. Internet communication provides immediate access for fiber, fabric, trim, and findings suppliers; manufacturers and contractors; retailers; and consumers.

As in the apparel industry, fast delivery of raw goods from suppliers and quick turnaround time on production help speed the product to the retailer and ultimate consumer. Continued reduction in the lead time needed to produce goods has provided additional cost savings. Faster delivery of products has also resulted from the following:

- increased vertical integration
- partnerships among segments of the industry
- UPC bar coding
- floor-ready merchandise

For example, Oriental Weavers, a multinational corporation that produces woven carpets and rugs, incorporates companies that integrate all stages of the design and production, from raw material to finished product. As such, they are able to deliver machine-made rugs to retailers quickly and efficiently (Oriental Weavers, 2007). Capel, a vertically integrated rug manufacturer headquartered in Troy, North Carolina, integrates spinning, dyeing, weaving, braiding, sewing, and selling operations to increase speed of delivery (Capel, 2007).

End-Use Categories

As stated earlier, the home fashions industry is divided into the following four general end-use categories:

- upholstered furniture coverings and fillings
- window and wall coverings
- soft floor coverings, including area rugs, scatter rugs, and runners
- bed, bath, tabletop, and other textile accessories and accents

Coordinated ensembles among categories have become popular. The same or coordinated textiles produced by one textile manufacturer might be used for the upholstered furniture, window treatments, bedding, and wall coverings for an entire room. Examples include the following:

- Waverly, a division of F. Schumacher & Co., has been at the forefront of providing consumers with a coordinated, total home look by producing coordinated bed linens, bath rugs, shower curtains, laminated fabrics, lamp shades, and other products.

- Coordinated prints, stripes, plaids, and monochrome cotton fabrics are produced by Laura Ashley, in addition to coordinating wallpaper, lamp shades, ceramic tile, and tableware.

Upholstered Furniture Coverings and Fillings

Upholstery fabrics for home fashions are used primarily for sofas, love seats, chairs, and ottomans (see Figure 14.9). Textiles used for upholstery fabrics are made from many natural and manufactured fibers. Before the development of manufactured fibers, wool, cotton, and linen were the most prevalent fibers used in upholstered home fashions. Silk has been used less frequently for upholstery due to its cost, care requirements, and delicate structure. Manufactured fibers, particularly nylon and polyester, are commonly used in today's market. Fiber companies in the United States known for producing fibers for upholstery fabrics include the following:

- American Fibers and Yarn Co.
- FiberVisions, Inc.
- Honeywell International
- INVISTA
- Solutia, Inc.
- Wellman, Inc.

Advances in olefin (also known as polypropylene or polyolefin) have made it a popular fiber in the upholstery market, and cotton has regained some of its importance. Rayon blends for upholstery fabrics are experiencing growth in sales.

The performance characteristics of wool and cotton fibers are highly valued for some types of upholstered home fashions. The rising cost of these natural fibers lowered their market share in comparison to the less expensive manufactured fibers. Currently, the high-end market uses a higher percentage of natural fibers than the moderate and mass markets.

Figure 14.9   Upholstery fabrics create an important part of the atmosphere for the home.

Fabric structure is another important consideration for upholstery. The durability of a fabric is affected by its fabric structure. For example, twill weaves are very durable, whereas satin weaves are less durable for upholstery. Whereas both pile and nonpile fabrics are used for upholstery, nonpile fabrics are preferred for heavy-use upholstered items, such as family room sofas.

Some upholstery fabrics are coated with a backing substance to enhance end-use properties, such as durability. Protective and soil-resistant or soil-release finishes are often applied to upholstery fabrics. Many of these, such as INVISTA's DuPont Teflon finish, are fluoropolymer resins that protect the fabric against oil and water-based stains, dust, and soil. 3M's Scotchgard upholstery fabric protector can be applied by the manufacturer or by the consumer (see Figure 14.10).

The price range for upholstery fabrics is broad, from budget to designer price zones. Low-cost upholstery fabric made from manufactured fibers or blends is the mainstay for most furniture manufacturers and retailers. Some upholstery fabrics are created and sold to the high-end market segment. The company founded by textile designer Jack Lenor Larsen is known for creating innovative high-end textile designs for upholstery and other home fashions end uses. His company is now part of Colefax and Fowler, a British home fashions company.

Over-the-counter upholstery fabrics (sold at fabric stores) provide a source for individuals who want to create their own home fashions. Consumers enjoy the opportunity to coordinate their home fashions from the broad choice of materials offered over the counter. Textile converter F. Schumacher & Co.'s Waverly brand of decorator fabrics and Robert Allen fabrics are sold over the counter to individuals as well as to manufacturers. Thus, individuals who want to create their own home fashions have access to some of the same fabrics used in manufactured home fashions.

BEAUTY THAT GOES BEYOND THE SURFACE

Signature
PLUS
by Milliken

FOR MORE INFORMATION, CALL US AT
1-800-322-8326

Figure 14.10 Stain-resistant finishes are often applied to fabrics used for table linens or upholstery.

Window and Wall Coverings

Window treatments consist of draperies, curtains, and fabric shades, as well as decorative treatments such as valances, cornices, and swags. Curtains are typically described as "sheer, lightweight coverings that are hung without linings" (Yeager & Teter-Justice, 2000, p. 261), whereas draperies are described as "heavy, often opaque and highly patterned coverings usually hung with linings" (Yeager & Teter-Justice, 2000, p. 261). Curtains might be combined with draperies for home use, providing both decorative and functional purposes. During the day, sheer curtains allow diffused light into a room while providing some privacy. At night, opaque draperies can be drawn for total privacy and increased warmth. Fabric valances, cornices, and swags are popular window treatments.

Customers feel more confident about changing window treatments than about changing more expensive items of home decor. Thus, the category of window treatments is a very popular segment of home fashions. However, the display of window treatments in retail stores is a challenge because window treatments require substantial floor space. Department stores and mass merchants have developed creative ways of displaying window treatments with small-scale versions of the window treatments and the use of photographs that show the items on actual windows.

The fibers and fabrics used for curtains and draperies must withstand more exposure to heat and sunlight than many other textile products. Some manufactured fibers, such as nylon and polyester, withstand environmental exposure better than natural fibers, such as silk and cotton. Linen and wool, at one time quite commonly used for window coverings, are now used only occasionally. Manufactured fibers such as rayon, acrylic, nylon, and polyester fibers are typically used in blends with other fibers for window treatments. The ease of care of manufactured fibers and blends that combine natural with manufactured fibers is another important consideration for many consumers. Figure 14.11 gives a sense of the wide variety of fabrics available for home fashions.

Figure 14.11 A variety of colors and textures adds an inviting fashion appeal to bedding and window coverings.

There are many similarities in the design, development, and production processes of apparel products and home fashions. However, one of the differences is the length of time that the home fashions producers want fabric lines to be available for reorders compared to the time wanted by apparel producers. Home fashions producers want the fabric lines to be available for several seasons, whereas many of the fabric lines used by apparel producers change every season. For those home fashions producers, such as window treatment companies, who use some of the same fabrics used by the apparel industry, this presents a problem. Therefore, selection of fabric lines that will remain in production for several seasons is critical to the window treatment producers.

A variety of textiles is used for **wall coverings** and vertical panels and partitions. Fabric used as a wall covering can provide a room with a cozy ambiance or an elegant distinctiveness. There are various techniques for applying fabrics to wall surfaces. A tightly woven material with a sturdy fabric structure will withstand the tension needed to provide a smooth fabric surface. Cotton is one of the easiest and most versatile fabrics for use as a wall covering. Luxurious visual statements can be made with velvet or moiré fabrics; however, these fabrics are more challenging to mount. Silk fabrics function best as wall coverings if they are first quilted or laminated to a backing fabric to stabilize them.

Soft Floor Coverings

Soft floor coverings include wall-to-wall carpeting, area rugs, runners, and scatter rugs. The discussion of this end-use category will focus on area floor coverings (area rugs, runners, and scatter rugs). Area floor coverings are produced in a wide variety of fibers and blends. For kitchens and bathrooms, cotton, polyester, and nylon fibers are most typical. Ease of cleaning is an important consideration to the consumer for bath and kitchen area rugs. Bedroom area floor coverings might consist of natural fibers, including wool and cotton, manufactured fibers, or blends of fibers.

For other areas of the home, such as the living room, family room, and dining room, a wide variety of fibers is available. Fibers used for area floor coverings include nylon, polyester, olefin, wool, and cotton, as well as sisal, jute, and other natural plant materials. Companies in the United States that produce manufactured fibers used in carpets and rugs include Honeywell Nylon, INVISTA, FiberVisions, Inc., and Solutia.

Area floor coverings might be laid atop a hardwood floor or carpeting. A variety of sizes for area rugs and runners provides many home fashions options (see Figure 14.12). Scatter rugs are usually small, for example, 2 by 3 feet or 3 by 5 feet. Area rugs tend to be larger, in sizes such as 8 by 11 feet or 11 by 14 feet. Runners are long and narrow because they are designed for hallways or entries.

A number of companies in the United States produce area floor coverings, including the following:

- The Dixie Group, headquartered in Chattanooga, Tennessee, produces carpets and rugs through its Fabrica International, Masland Carpets and Rugs, and Dixie Home divisions.

- Mohawk Industries, headquartered in Calhoun, Georgia, produces carpets and rugs under the Aladdin, American Rug Craftsmen, American Weavers, Horizon, Karastan, Lees Carpet, and Mohawk Home brands.

- Shaw Industries, headquartered in Dalton, Georgia, manufactures residential carpets and rugs under the Cabin Crafts Carpets, Philadelphia Carpets,

Figure 14.12   A golf rug includes textured sand traps, serving as a source of entertainment as well as an area floor covering.

Queen Carpets, ShawMark Carpets, Shaw Rugs, Sutton Carpets, TrustMark Carpets, and Tuftex brands.

- Milliken, headquartered in Spartanburg, South Carolina, produces residential carpets and area rugs in addition to commercial applications.

Some area floor coverings are made by machine, in a process similar to that used for carpet manufacturing. The design and texture of an area rug is often determined during the production stage by varying the colors and types of yarns used, or by the weaving or fabrication techniques. Multicolor effects can be achieved by applying the same dye color to a yarn composed of different fibers, producing a heather effect.

Continual improvements in technology for carpet and rug production have increased the variety of patterns and textures available to the consumer. Computerized systems allow companies to create different multilevel surfaces, colors, and textures in rugs ranging from basic bath rugs to high-fashion accent rugs. Several other production methods are used to create handwoven, braided, hooked, crocheted, knotted, or embroidered area floor coverings. Many ethnic floor coverings are produced by hand processes. Both the ethnic design and hand processes add an exotic flavor to home fashions.

As with other types of home textiles, carpets and rugs are often developed or finished to enhance their performance. For example, the INVISTA STAIN-MASTER brand of carpet and area rugs are manufactured with a specified nylon 6.6, which has a unique fiber structure that is stain resistant and crush resistant. INVISTA's DuPont Teflon finish is applied to carpets and rugs. This finish repels most liquids, thus allowing for spills to be removed before stains set in.

Bed, Bath, Table, and Other Home Textile Accessories and Accents

Textile accessories and accents include the following:

- textile bedding products, including sheets and pillowcases, blankets, bedspreads, quilts, comforters, and pillows (see Figure 14.13)

- textile products for the bath, including towels, bath rugs and mats, and shower curtains

- textile accessories for tabletops, including tablecloths, napkins, table runners, and place mats

- textile products for the kitchen, including towels, dishcloths, hot pads, and aprons

- textile accents, such as textile wall hangings, tapestries, quilts, needlework accents, and lace accents

The term **linens** refers to towels, sheets, tablecloths, napkins, and other home textiles once made almost exclusively from linen. Although these products are rarely made from linen anymore, they are commonly still referred to as linens.

BEDDING AND BATH

Cotton fiber has an estimated 60 percent share of the sheet industry. Most sheets are made from a blend of cotton and polyester (often 50 percent of each

Figure 14.13 Bedding includes sheets as well as mattress covers and top-of-the-bed items such as comforters, duvet covers, blankets, bedspreads, dust ruffles, pillow shams, and throws.

fiber). A number of companies also offer 100 percent cotton sheets. Recently, rayon and bamboo rayon have been introduced as fabrics for sheets. Wrinkle-free, all-cotton sheets have also become popular. Several luxury producers offer linen and silk sheets.

Percale and flannel are the most typical fabric structures for sheets. Satin, sateen, and jacquard weaves are available for the specialty market. Knit fabric, especially cotton jersey knit, is another option for sheets. Eyelet trims, contrast piping, and scalloped edging are used as embellishments.

Besides fiber content and fabric structure, woven sheets are distinguished by their thread count and their size. **Thread count** refers to the total number of threads or yarns in one square inch of fabric. Typical thread counts range from 200 to 400. A higher thread count tends to signify a softer fabric. Sheets are available in crib, twin, double, queen, and king sizes, corresponding to standard bed sizes.

The **top-of-the-bed** category includes comforters, duvet covers, blankets, bedspreads, dust ruffles, pillow shams, and throws. This category has been growing in recent years as consumers strive for a coordinated look in bed and bath decoration. Bedspreads are made from a variety of fabrics and in a variety of styles, including quilted fabrics. Quilts and comforters typically are made from multicomponent fabrics and filled with down, feathers, fiberfill, or other materials.

The infant and juvenile bedding category has grown in recent years. Licensed printed goods are spurring the market. Examples include Disney products, featuring characters from recent films (e.g., *Pirates of the Caribbean*) or classic Disney characters (see Figure 14.14), as well as Looney Tunes products, with characters such as Bugs Bunny. There are specialty trade shows and associations for the juvenile market. The International Juvenile Products Manufacturers Show, sponsored by the Juvenile Products Manufacturers Asso-ciation, is the largest U.S. trade event for specialty baby-to-teen retailers. The show includes furniture, bedding, and decorative accessories.

Figure 14.14 Licensed products, such as Disney characters, are a part of the business for home fashions geared to the juvenile market.

In the bath market, cotton is by far the dominant fiber, with an estimated 95 percent share (see Figure 14.15). Terry cloth is by far the most popular fabrication for towels. The yarns forming the loops of terry cloth are generally all cotton to enhance moisture absorbency for drying purposes. The warp and weft yarns that form the base weave structure that holds the loops in place might consist of a blend of cotton with a small percentage of polyester for increased durability. When the loops have been sheared on one side or both sides, the terry cloth fabric is called velour.

Towel size is a product feature that can provide market appeal. For years, towel sizes were standardized. Then, longer towels became popular at luxury hotels and spas. Soon manufacturers began to offer a variety of towel lengths at various price points for the retail market.

Figure 14.15   In the bath market, cotton is by far the dominant fiber.

Market research on customer preferences contributes valuable information to both producers and retailers. What are the factors customers consider to be the most important for their towel purchasing decisions? A survey conducted by Cotton Incorporated's Lifestyle Monitor™ (2006) found that the three most important, desirable features of bath towels were as follows:

- softness (83 percent)
- absorbency (83 percent)
- durability (76 percent)

However, the following features were also important influences for bath towel purchases:

- size (73 percent)
- life of the bath towel (67 percent)
- price (66 percent)
- color (61 percent)

Figure 14.16 Table linens provide visual appeal as well as protection for table surfaces.

More than 25 percent of the women surveyed purchased bath towels more than once per year, and nearly 40 percent purchased new bath towels because their current towels were worn out.

A wide variety of coordinating bath mats contributed to an increase in sales in the bath category. The surge in the bath market coincided with a similar increase in popularity of coordinated kitchen towels, dishcloths, oven mitts, pot holders, and aprons.

TEXTILE ACCESSORIES FOR TABLETOP AND KITCHEN

Textile accessories for the tabletop include tablecloths, napkins, place mats, and table runners. The terms **napery** and **table linens** are both used to refer to tablecloths and napkins. Tabletop accessories can protect the finish of fine wood tables and can enhance the warmth and visual theme of a dining room (see Figure 14.16). Therefore, many fibers and fabrics that provide visual appeal are used in tabletop accessories.

One especially important feature for tabletop accessories is that they be easy to care for. For example, Milliken applies a soil release finish to table linens to increase their performance. Tabletop accessories are available in a variety of sizes to fit a wide range of table shapes and sizes. Labeling laws require that the "cut size" given on labels on tablecloths must be the dimensions of the finished product.

Textile accessories for the kitchen include towels, dishcloths, pot holders, oven mitts, and aprons. As with other textile accessories, both appearance and performance characteristics are important determinants for fiber and fabric choices.

Distribution and Retailing of Home Fashions

Home fashions constitute an important segment of the retail industry. Discount retail stores (e.g., Wal-Mart, Target, and Kmart), which carry budget and moderate-priced floor and window coverings, bed and bath fashions, and products for kitchens and bathrooms, are the dominant players in the retailing of home fashions. Bed and bath accessories, window and wall coverings, floor coverings, and upholstered furniture also provide substantial sales for department stores such as JCPenney, Macy's, and Dillard's. Specialty stores, including Bed, Bath & Beyond, Linens 'n Things, Pottery Barn, Williams Sonoma, and Crate and Barrel, offer a mix of home fashions with other merchandise related to home activities and lifestyles. Direct marketing companies such as Lands' End, Domestications, The Linen Source, and The Company Store fill another market niche. Home improvement stores such as The Home Depot and Lowe's have expanded their home fashions offerings as they strive to take advantage of the growing number of customers involved with do-it-yourself home decorating.

Even apparel and accessory retailers, such as Nordstrom, offer home fashions items. As with other areas of the fashion industry, nonstore and multichannel retailing has created multiple purchasing venues for consumers. QVC and other television shopping networks consistently sell bedding, tabletop accessories, and area rugs.

Consumers are currently updating the decor of their home environments more frequently by changing the decorative fabrics used in their homes. In light of this trend, the retailing of home fabrics has grown in recent years (see Figure 14.17). Some stores, such as Calico Corners, headquartered in Kennett Square, Pennsylvania, focus entirely on home fabrics. For other fabric stores, an increasing percentage of their business comes from home fabrics. In response to this growing demand for over-the-counter home fabrics, a number of home furnishing fabric suppliers have increased their attention to the over-the-counter home textiles business. Jo-Ann Stores, Inc., based in Hudson, Ohio, is the largest fabric and craft retailer in the United States, with 838 stores in 47 states and an online division (joann.com).

Figure 14.17 Reflecting consumer demand, Martha Stewart home decorator fabrics are sold through a variety of retailers.

Social and Environmental Responsibility

The soft-goods industry thrives on change at a fast pace. This can lead to a public perception that it is an industry that encourages waste. As a society, we discard many products long before their full potential for use is exhausted. In recent years, the industry has focused on social and environmental responsibility in all phases of the product use cycle.

The home fashions industry has been a leader in efforts to promote **sustainable design** (also called green design), a term used to designate the "awareness of the full short- and long-term consequences of any transformation of the environment" (DesignTex, 1995, p. 53). Sustainable design encompasses the concept that the creation, use, and discarding of a product should not cause harm to the ecosystem.

Sustainable design efforts include the following examples from the fiber stage through the discard stage:

- naturally grown fibers, such as cotton and ramie
- humanely sheared, free-range sheep
- yarn blended for user comfort and compostability
- environmentally compatible dyes and chemicals
- elimination of pollutants used in textile manufacturing
- use of recycled components (e.g., fibers) in textile manufacturing
- elimination of toxic vapors emitted during production or product use (such as formaldehyde on fabric wall coverings)
- biodegradability or reuse of post-consumer products (see Figure 14.18)

In the early 1990s, DesignTex, based in New York City, created an environmentally responsible line of textiles that met sustainability guidelines (DesignTex,

Figure 14.18 This furniture is made entirely from recycled paper.

1995). William McDonough and Michael Braungart designed a fabric collection for upholstered furniture. Their first collections utilized fabrics made from a blend of wool and ramie, both natural fibers. Working with an independent environmental research institute in Germany and an environmental chemist, DesignTex selected dyes that used no toxins. The textile mill selected to manufacture the fabric improved its manufacturing processes to conform to McDonough's design principles and criteria, referred to as Cradle to Cradle. McDonough calls this "the Second Industrial Revolution. What we're now saying is that environmental quality must be an integral part of the design of every product" (DesignTex, 1995, p. 65). Since that time, DesignTex's commitment to sustainability has continued through their use of nontoxic chemical dyes, organically grown renewable resources, and environmentally responsible polyester and nylon (DesignTex, 2007).

Many other companies in the home fashions industry have adopted a variety of environmentally responsible business practices in the development, production, and marketing of their products (see Figure 14.19). Examples include Shaw Rugs Eco Solution Q nylon fiber, EcoWorx Broadloom sustainable carpet backing, and Milliken's Earthwise Ennovations process to encourage customers to reuse carpet tile.

Another approach is to recycle postconsumer materials into new products, rather than creating a new fabric. In 1993, Wellman, Inc. introduced Fortrel Ecospun® polyester, which is made entirely from postconsumer PET packaging. This fiber is used for carpets and filling for pillows and comforters. Since that time, they have introduced recycled fiberfill,

Figure 14.19 Some companies produce wallcoverings made with environmentally compatible dyes and chemicals.

carpet fiber, and industrial fibers. In 2007, they were the world's largest producer of recycled polyester (Wellman, 2007).

The home fashions industry provides many other examples of sustainable design. Local, regional, and national network directories offer databases of references to locate product manufacturers that utilize recycled materials.

The retailer may play an additional part in a product's lifecycle. Some retailers offer convenient home pickup and recycle options for discarded products for consumers who have purchased a new product. At the time a new mattress is delivered to the consumer, the old mattress might be picked up by the retailer's delivery crew and recycled.

Lifecycle evaluation of products from the producer's, the retailer's, and the consumer's points of view will continue to be an important component in the home fashions industry. It may add complexity and cost to the design-manufacture-market-consume process, but sustainable design is important to future success in business.

Other forms of socially responsible behavior in the industry include community development efforts by local and national companies. Companies such as The Home Depot and Lowe's sponsor community-focused initiatives that assist individuals, nonprofit organizations, and environmental programs throughout the United States. In addition, our global marketplace provides opportunities to support socially responsible practices throughout the world. The RugMark Foundation is an international foundation that certifies manufacturers who agree to do the following:

- produce carpets without illegal child labor
- register all looms with the RugMark Foundation
- allow access to looms for unannounced inspections
- pay associated license fees for use of the RugMark label on their products

Since the RugMark Foundation's formal establishment in 1994, over 4 million carpets and rugs bearing the RugMark label have been sold in Europe and North America (RugMark, 2007).

New York-based Tufenkian Artisan Carpets sells carpets made by weavers using traditional design and weaving techniques. The carpets are produced in partnership with designers and workers in Nepal and Armenia. By providing a marketing outlet for these beautiful products, the company helps ensure that traditional carpets can continue to be produced. The weavers earn a livelihood with satisfactory working and living conditions, and Tufenkian provides a

Montessori school for children at the factory site to ensure that children are not involved in the production. To avoid pollution of the environment, the carpet washing is not done in Nepal, since pollution controls there are inadequate. This collaboration of producer/weaver and marketer provides an example of social, economic, political, and environmental responsibility (Tufenkian, 2007).

Summary

This chapter has focused on the home fashions industry, which includes four end-use categories: upholstered furniture coverings and fillings; window and wall coverings; soft floor coverings; and bed, bath, tabletop, and other home textile accessories and accents. The design and performance of the textiles used for home fashions play a very important role in the success of the end use. That being the case, the textile industry is the base for the home fashions industry, which is dominated by vertically integrated textile companies that produce both fabrics and home fashions products. Production of home fashions is often highly automated and can be accomplished very efficiently within a vertical operation. Some home fashions, such as towels and rugs, come off the production line as finished goods, not needing further cutting and sewing to complete the product.

An understanding of the organization and operation of the home fashions industry in the broader context of apparel fashions is important for several reasons. In recent years, the apparel and home fashions industries have become more interrelated. Many apparel companies have entered the home fashions market, and well-known apparel designers have moved into home fashions through licensing agreements with textile mills and home fashions manufacturers. Other licensing agreements for children's home fashions include ones for cartoon and movie characters, sports teams, and toys.

Consumer demand for home fashions continues to be strong. Home fashions constitute an important segment of the retail industry. Discount retailers such as Wal-Mart, Target, and Kmart are dominant competitors in the retailing of home fashions. Other important home fashions merchants include department stores, specialty stores, direct marketing companies, and home improvement retailers. Sales of over-the-counter fabrics for the home sewing industry are also strong.

Market research and color forecasting are conducted prior to developing the seasonal collections. The textile and trim designers, who create innovative materials, and the product designers, who determine the form of the final end-use product, consider many factors and work within many constraints. Important functional needs and performance criteria must be met. Some products must also meet safety standards set by law. Converters that print or finish fabrics to improve their performance play an important role in the production of textiles for home fashions. Often the converter contracts for specific finishing work with a variety of finishing plants.

The marketing process for home fashions is similar to the process used in the apparel industry that includes the use of manufacturers' showrooms, company sales representatives, trade shows, and advertising and promotion. However, the home fashions industry relies on converters and jobbers to perform marketing and distribution functions more frequently than does the apparel industry. The establishment of well-respected brand names is important in the marketing of home fashions. Trade associations, trade shows, and trade publications form an important network for promoting the home fashions industry.

In recent years, the industry has focused on social and environmental responsibility for all phases of the product use cycle. The home fashions industry has been a leader in efforts to promote sustainable design, encompassing the concept that the creation, use, and discard of a product should not cause harm to any ecosystem. Efforts to practice sustainable design include procedures from the fiber stage through discarding of the product. In addition, some retailers have entered the arena by providing consumers with recycling services when new products are delivered to their homes.

As with the ready-to-wear and accessories industries, the home fashions industry includes a wide variety of career possibilities, from design to production to marketing and distribution.

Design Manager, Woven Bedding
Home Fashions Products Company

Position Description
Supervise the woven bedding design team in product development, color direction, and finished product for all retail channels of distribution.

Typical Tasks and Responsibilities
- Coordinate with design, sales, product development, and outside resources to achieve goals and meet deadlines.
- Be responsible for maintaining a flow of woven and heat transfer prints for use in top-of-the-bed and sheeting products.
- Provide leadership in color direction, design, and product development for top-of-the-bed and sheeting products.

Stylist, Sourced Product Development
Home Fashions Products Company

Position Description
Be responsible for assisting the design manager in the development of concepts, finished art, colorings, concept boards, and vendor specification packages for sourced bed and bath products.

Typical Tasks and Responsibilities
- Assist the design manager to develop concept boards.
- Utilize CAD and graphics software to create finished art for textile prints.
- Be responsible for providing vendor specification packages for bed and bath products.

Key Terms

decor

decorative fabric jobber

home fashions

linens

napery

product turn

soft floor covering

sustainable design

table linens

textile accessory and accent

thread count

top-of-the-bed

upholstery fabric

wall covering

window treatment

Discussion Questions

1. What are three aspects of the home fashions industry that are similar to the ready-to-wear apparel industry? What are three aspects of the home fashions industry that are different from the ready-to-wear apparel industry? Why do these similarities and differences exist?

2. Select a home fashions product (e.g., towel, rug, sheets). Outline the process used in the design, production, marketing, and distribution of the product.

3. Select a home fashions product in your home that will need replacement in the future. Discuss sustainable design criteria that might be used in the selection of the replacement product and the disposal of the used textile product.

References

Blackwood, Francy. (1995, April 10). Name dropping. *HFN*, pp. 25, 74.

Capel (2007). Our Story [online]. Available: http://www.capelrugs.com [April 28, 2007].

Color Marketing Group (2007). About CMG [online]. Available: http://www.colormarketing.org [April 28, 2007].

Cotton, Incorporated (2006, July 6). The bath towel: More than just fluff [online]. Available: http://www.cottoninc.com/lsmarticles/?articleID=498 [April 29, 2007].

DesignTex, Inc. (1995). *Environmentally Intelligent Textiles*. (2nd ed.). (#DT052495). Charlottesville, VA: Author.

DesignTex, Inc. (2007). Sustainability [online]. Available: http://www.dtex.com [April 29, 2007].

Fiberfill that is recycled. (1993, May/June). *What's New in Home Economics*, p. 40.

Frinton, Sandra. (1995, November 20). Strength in baby bedding. *HFN*, pp. 19, 21.

Get back to basics with bath towels. (1999, September 27). *HFN*, pp. 7–10.

Home Depot wins community award. (1995, December 4). *HFN*, p. 8.

The home fashions leader board. (1999, June). *Bobbin*, p. 52.

Musselman, Faye. (1999, September 20). Familiar textile brands provide sense of security. *HFN*, pp. 20–25.

Oriental Weavers (2007). Profile [online]. Available: http://www.orientalweavers.com [April 28, 2007].

Popovec, Jennifer. (2005, August). Feathering the nest: Home fashion centers take off. *Retail Traffic*, pp. 42–45, 62.

Retailers duel for consumer dollars. (1999, January). *Bobbin*, pp. 18–22.

RugMark Foundation (2007). History [online]. Available: http://www.rugmark.org/ home.php [April 29, 2007].

Rush, Amy J. (1996, February 19). 3M's Thinsulate coming to bedding. *HFN*, p. 6.

Seiren Corporation (2007). High fashion [online]. Available: http://www.seiren.com/ english/index.html [April 28, 2007].

Tufenkian Artisan Carpets (2007). Our philosophy [online]. Available: http://www. tufenkiancarpets.com [April 29, 2007].

Verlodt, Patricia. (1999, August 30). Color trends: Technology, nostalgia are equal influences. *HFN*, p. 13.

Wellman, Inc. (2007). The recycling story [online]. Available: http://www.wellmaninc.com [April 29, 2007].

Yeager, Jan. (1988). *Textiles for Residential and Commercial Interiors*. New York: HarperCollins.

Yeager, Jan, and Teter-Justice, Lara. (2000). *Textiles for Residential and Commercial Interiors*. (2nd ed.). New York: Fairchild Publications.

advertising Strategy by which companies buy space or time in print, broadcast, or electronic media to promote their lines to retailers and consumers.

agile manufacturing Use of a combination of technologies that form an integrated, seamless exchange of information linking retailers and suppliers to the manufacturing facility ([TC]^2, 1993; see Chapter 11).

articles of association see **articles of incorporation**.

articles of incorporation or **articles of organization** or **articles of association** Legal document that outlines the nature and scope of ownership and operations of a corporation.

articles of organization see **articles of incorporation**.

ascot A long neck scarf worn looped at the neck.

atelier de couture Workrooms of haute couture designers and staff.

base pattern or **block** or **sloper** Basic pattern in the company's sample size, without any style features, used as the starting point for creating a pattern for a new style.

bias The diagonal cut of fabric, or 45 degrees to the length or width of the fabric, used to produce better shaping of the fabric than a straight-grain cut.

block see **base pattern**.

blocking or **boarding** The application of heat to create the final shape in the finishing process for knit goods.

board of directors Chief governing body of a corporation; elected by the corporation's stockholders.

boarding see **blocking**.

body scanning A three-dimensional computerized body-imaging system that captures body contours. Software is used to translate the image data into body dimensions to be used for fit customization.

boutique Specialty store that concentrates on designer price zone merchandise or unique merchandise distributed to only a few stores.

brand extension Expanding the use of a well-known brand name to a variety of merchandise; e.g., decorative pillows and throw rugs manufactured by WestPoint Stevens with the Harley-Davidson logo.

brand merchandise Apparel, accessories, or home fashions whose brand or label is well recognized by the public.

brand name or **trade name** Distinctive name given to a product or service for the purpose of making the product or service readily identifiable to consumers.

brand position Strategy by which products are developed in alignment with the company's target customer and position in the market.

brand tier Strategy by which a manufacturer or retailer offers brands in two or more price zones, with each brand focusing on a specific price zone.

bridge jewelry Umbrella term for several types of jewelry, including those made from silver, gold (14K, 12K, 10K), and less expensive stones; jewelry designed by artists using a variety of materials.

bundling The process of disassembling stacked cut fabric pieces and reassembling them grouped by garment size, color dye lot, and quantity of units ready for production.

business-to-business (B2B) Business operations that are conducted between companies through Web-based technologies.

C corporation or **regular corporation** Type of corporation whereby profits of the corporation are distributed to shareholders in the form of dividends.

carryover A garment style repeated in a line from one season to the next.

cashmere A soft, luxury fiber that comes from the undercoat wool of the Cashmere or Kashmir goat, mainly from China, Mongolia, and Tibet.

catalog retailer see **mail order/catalog retailer**.

chain store Retail organization that owns and operates several retail outlets that sell similar lines of merchandise in a standardized method, and function under a centralized form of organizational structure.

classification The process by which apparel manufacturers are categorized (classified) by the type of merchandise produced, by the wholesale prices of the products or brands, or by an industry classification system for government tracking.

close corporation see **private corporation**.

closely held corporation see **private corporation**.

clutch Handbag designed to be held (clutched) in the hand, but may have a strap that can be stored inside the bag.

co-branded apparel Product development strategy whereby a retailer partners with an apparel manufacturer in the creation of the retailer's private-label line.

code of conduct Guidelines for contractors and subcontractors regarding workplace environment and operations; generally focus on safeguards for workers' health and rights.

collection A group of apparel items presented together to the buying public, usually by high-fashion designers.

color control Color matching requirement for all like garments in a line and for all their components, such as knit collars and cuffs, buttons, thread, and zippers.

color forecasting Process of predicting consumers' future color preferences for merchandise for a specific fashion season.

Predictions are based on research conducted by color forecasters for companies and trade associations.

color forecasting service A company that predicts consumers' future color and trend preferences in textiles, apparel, accessories, and home fashions.

color management Process of maintaining an acceptable color match for all like garments in a line, including all their components, such as knit collars and cuffs, buttons, thread, and zippers.

color palette A selected group of colors, often represented by color chips. Each new line will be composed of a group of selected colors.

color story Color palette identified for each group's fashion season.

colorway The variety of three or four seasonal color choices for the same solid or print fabric available for each garment style.

commercial match Contractor-provided acceptable match of color for fabric, trim, or finding to a control color chip or fabric provided by the apparel company.

computer-aided design (CAD) Both the hardware and software computer systems use to assist with the design phase of the fabric design or garment design.

computer grading and marker making (CGMM) The computer hardware and software systems that process the pattern grading and marker making segments of the pattern for production.

concept garment End-use garment created by a textile company to promote its new fibers to textile mills.

concept shop A company's in-store shop when applied to a nonstore retail venue, such as the Ralph Lauren concept shop on Bloomingdales.com.

conglomerate Diversified company involved with significantly different lines of business.

consolidation The combining of two companies to form a new company.

consumer research Information gathered about consumer characteristics and consumer behavior, including broad trends in the marketplace as well as more specific information about a target group of consumers.

contractor Company that specializes in the sewing and finishing of goods or that specializes in a specific part of the production process (such as pleating piece goods).

contractual retailer Retailer that has entered into a contractual agreement with a manufacturer, wholesaler, or other retailers in order to integrate operations and increase market impact.

controlled brand name program or **licensed brand name program** Marketing strategy whereby minimum standards of fabric performance for trademarked fibers are determined and promoted.

convenience store Retailer that offers fast service and convenient location.

conventional manufacturer A company that performs all functions of creating, marketing, and distributing an apparel line on a continual basis.

conventional marketing channel Independent companies that separately perform the manufacturing, distribution, and retailing functions.

converted goods or **finished goods** Fabrics that have been dyed, printed, or finished.

converter or **textile converter** Company that specializes in finishing fabrics (including printing).

co-op advertising A type of advertising strategy whereby companies share the cost of the advertisement that features all of the companies.

cooperative advertising see **co-op advertising**.

copyright The exclusive right of the copyright holder to use, perform, or reproduce written, pictorial, and performed work.

corporate responsibility or **social responsibility** A philosophy whereby a company takes into consideration human rights, labor conditions, and environmental implications when making business decisions.

corporate selling Strategy by which apparel companies sell their merchandise directly to retailers without the use of sales representatives.

corporate showroom Showroom owned and operated by a single company to market its lines of merchandise; generally managed by company sales representatives.

corporation Company established by a legal charter that outlines the scope and activity of the company. Corporations are legal entities regardless of who owns stock in the company.

cost or **cost to manufacture** or **wholesale cost** The total cost to manufacture a style, including materials, findings, labor, and auxiliary costs such as freight, duty, and packaging.

cost to manufacture see **cost**.

costing marker The layout of the pattern pieces for the prototype used to determine the yardage required for the new style (yardage is one of the factors required to calculate the cost).

costume jewelry Mass-produced jewelry made from plastic, wood, brass, glass, lucite, and other less expensive materials.

cotton Natural fiber obtained from the fibers surrounding the seeds of the cotton plant.

cotton gin Machine that cleans cotton seed from the cotton fibers; invented in 1794 by Eli Whitney.

counter sample or **sew by** A sample garment sewn by a contractor and submitted to the apparel manufacturer for approval.

This sample is then used as a benchmark to compare the sewn production goods.

counterfeit goods Products that incorporate unauthorized use of registered trade names or trademarks.

couture A French term that literally means sewing, it refers to the highest-priced apparel produced in small quantities, made of high-quality fabrics utilizing considerable hand-sewing techniques, and sized to fit individual clients' bodies.

couturier (couturière) Designer of haute couture (couturier = masculine; couturière = feminine).

Crafted with Pride in U.S.A. Council Trade association formed in 1984 to promote U.S.-made textiles and apparel.

croquis or **lay figure** A French term that refers to a figure outline used as a basis to sketch garment design ideas.

cross-merchandising Strategy by which apparel companies and retailers combine apparel and accessories in their product offerings.

customs broker A person in the United States, licensed by the Office of Customs and Border Protection, to assist manufacturers in gaining customs clearance to import goods produced offshore.

cut, make, and trim (CMT) Apparel contractors who cut, make, and trim the garments for the apparel manufacturer.

cut order Instructions for production cutting that include the specific number of items in each color and each size that will be included in the production run.

cut-up trade Belt manufacturers who produce belts for apparel manufacturers to add to their pants, skirts, and dresses.

data mining technology Technology used by companies to analyze purchasing data to determine selling patterns or trends and identify correlations among data characteristics.

decor The interior decoration that creates a room's ambiance.

decorative fabric converter Company that designs and sells finished textiles to jobbers, designers, and manufacturers who use the textiles in home fashions end-use products.

decorative fabric jobber Company involved in the marketing and distribution of home textile piece goods, particularly upholstery and drapery fabrics.

demographics Information about consumers that focuses on understanding characteristics of consumer groups, such as age, gender, marital status, income, occupation, ethnicity, and geographic location.

department store Large retailer that departmentalizes its functions and merchandise.

design and product development The process by which a new style moves from concept sketch to prototype.

design development department Staff assigned to develop a new style, usually including pattern development, prototype development, color management, line sheet development, initial costing, and line review and adoption decisions, and sometimes including fabric development.

designer Individual who is responsible for the design of a product.

die cutting A piece of metal with a sharp edge similar to a cookie cutter tooled to the exact dimensions of the shape of the pattern piece (the die). The die is positioned over the fabric to be cut; then a pressurized plate is applied to the die to cut through the fabric layers.

diffusion line A designer's less expensive line (e.g., A/X Armani Exchange, DKNY)

digitizer A table embedded with sensors that relate to the X and Y coordinates (horizontal and vertical directions) that allow the shape of the pattern piece to be traced and converted to a drawing of the pattern in the computer.

direct market brand or **store brand** Brand name on merchandise that is also the name of the retailer, e.g., Gap, L.L.Bean.

direct marketing channel Marketing channel by which manufacturers sell directly to the ultimate consumer.

discount store Retailer who sells brand name merchandise at below traditional retail prices, including apparel at the budget/mass wholesale price zone.

distribution center (DC) Centralized location used by manufacturers and retailers for quality assurance, tagging, picking, packing of merchandise, and distribution to retail stores.

distribution strategy Business strategy to assure that merchandise is sold in stores that cater to the target market for whom the merchandise was designed and manufactured.

dividend Corporate profits paid to its stockholders; dividends are taxed as personal income.

double taxation Situation with a C or regular corporation whereby earnings of the corporation are taxed twice—once at the corporate level and again at the individual level.

draping A process of creating the initial garment style by molding, cutting, and pinning fabric to a mannequin.

dual distribution Distribution strategy whereby manufacturers sell their merchandise through their own stores as well as through other retailers.

duplicate or **sample** A copy of the prototype or sample style used by the sales representatives to show and sell styles in the line to retail buyers.

e-commerce Buying and selling of goods and services conducted over the Internet.

e-market Companies that "enable trading partners to conduct business over the Internet eliminating the need for more costly paper and custom EDI methods" (eMarkets, 2001, p. 4; see Chapter 12).

807 (9802) production Under the Harmonized Tariff Schedule number 9802 (formerly number 807) of the U.S. tariff regulations, when garment pieces are cut in the United States and shipped to contractors in specified countries for assembly, tariffs are only applied to the "value added" (typically, the cost of assembly) to the garment.

electronic data interchange (EDI) computer-to-computer communications between companies.

electronic/Internet retailer Company that offers goods and/or services over the Internet or uses the Internet in addition to its stores and/or catalog retailing business.

eMarket Community of companies that conduct business primarily through B2B Web sites.

Empire A dress style with a raised waistline and a tubular silhouette, named for the French empire under Napoleon Bonaparte. Napoleon's wife, Josephine, popularized this dress style.

exclusive distribution Strategy whereby manufacturers limit the stores in which their merchandise is distributed in order to create an image of exclusiveness.

export agent A person located in the country that produced the goods who assists the (U.S.) manufacturer with exportation of the products.

extended marketing channel Marketing channel in which wholesalers acquire products from manufacturers and sell them to retailers, or jobbers buy products from wholesalers and sell them to retailers.

Fabric and Suppliers Linkage Council (FASLINC) Organization formed in 1987 to establish voluntary electronic data interchange standards between textile producers and their suppliers; disbanded in 1991.

fabric construction   Methods used to make fabrics from solutions, directly from fibers, and from yarns; weaving and knitting are the most common methods.

fabrication   see **fabric construction**.

factor   An agency that provides protection against bad debt losses, manages accounts receivable, and provides credit analysis in the apparel industry.

factoring   The business of purchasing and collecting accounts receivable or of advancing cash on the basis of accounts receivable ("The F Word," 1996, p. 1; see Chapter 9).

fallout   The fabric that remains in the spaces between pattern pieces on the marker, representing the amount of fabric that is wasted.

fashion color   Color used in a seasonal line that reflects the current color trends, determined by the apparel company for the target customer.

fashion forecasting service   A company that predicts consumers' future style preferences and trends in textiles and apparel. Predictions are based on research conducted by its staff and other associations.

fashion magazine   Magazine sold over-the-counter as well as by subscription whose primary focus is on the latest fashion trends.

fashion season   Name given to lines or collections that correspond to seasons of the year when consumers would most likely wear the merchandise; e.g., Spring, Summer, Fall, Holiday, and Resort.

fast fashion   Ultra-fast supply chain operations that focus on consumer demand of fashion goods. In some cases, products go from concept to retail store in less than three weeks.

fiber   The basic unit in making textile yarns and fabrics.

filament yarn   Yarn created by spinning together long continuous fibers.

findings   Also called notions or sundries, the garment components other than fabrics, such as fasteners, elastic, stay tape, and hem tape.

fine jewelry   Jewelry made from precious metals alone, and with precious and semi-precious stones.

finish   Application to a fiber, yarn, or fabric that changes the appearance, hand, or performance of the fiber, yarn, or fabric.

finished goods   see **converted goods**.

finishing   "Any process that is done to fiber, yarn, or fabric either before or after fabrication to change the *appearance* (what is seen), the *hand* (what is felt), or the *performance* (what the fabric does)" (Kadolph & Langford, 2002, p. 270, see Chapter 3).

first adoption meeting   Gathering when a new line is presented (often as sketches and fabric swatches), and each style in the line is reviewed by the design team.

fit model   The live model whose body dimensions match the company's sample size and who is used to assess the fit, styling, and overall look of new prototypes.

flat or **flat sketch**   Also called a tech drawing, this technical sketch of a garment style represents how the garment would look lying flat, as on a table. Garment details are clearly depicted.

flatknit   Goods that are knit flat, as compared to goods knit in a tube (tubular knit).

flat pattern   The pattern making process used to make a pattern for a new style from the base pattern (or block or sloper).

flat sketch   see **flat**.

flexible manufacturing (FM)   Production that focuses on optimizing equipment, flow of goods, and teams of workers to produce the product as efficiently as possible.

flexible manufacturing system "Any departure from traditional mass production systems of apparel toward faster, smaller, more flexible production units that depend upon the coordinated efforts of minimally supervised teams of workers" (AAMA Technical Advisory Committee, 1988, as cited in Hill, 1992, p. 34; see Chapter 11).

floor-ready merchandise (FRM) Merchandise shipped by the manufacturer or distribution center affixed with hangtags, labels, and price information so that the retailer can place the goods immediately on the selling floor.

fourchette On gloves, a strip of material located between the second/third, third/fourth, and fourth/baby fingers to provide depth for the thickness of the finger.

franchise A type of contractual retail organization whereby the parent company provides the franchisee with the exclusive distribution of a well-recognized brand name in a specific market area, as well as assistance in running the business in return for a franchise payment.

freight forwarding company A company that moves a shipment of goods from the country where the goods were produced to the United States.

full-fashioned Goods knit with shaping along the edges to conform to the body contour.

full-package (FP) A type of service option whereby the apparel contractor provides pre-production services, fabrics, trims, supplies, and labor.

garment dyed Apparel produced as white or colorless goods, and then dyed during the finishing process.

garment spec sheet see **garment specification sheet**.

garment specification sheet or **garment spec sheet** A listing of vital information for the garment style including garment sketch, fabric swatches and/or specifications, and specifications for findings, sizes, construction, and finished garment measurements.

general partner Co-owner of a company who shares responsibilities with other owners in the running of a company under a partnership agreement.

general partnership Form of ownership in which co-owners of a company share in the liability as well as the profits of the company according to the conditions of the partnership contract.

generic family Classification of fibers according to chemical composition and characteristics.

globalization Process whereby the economies of nation states become integrated.

grade rules The amounts and locations of growth or reduction for pattern pieces to create the various sizes.

grading or **pattern grading** Using the production pattern pieces made in the sample size for a style to develop a set of pattern pieces for each of the sizes listed on the garment spec sheet.

greige goods Fabrics that have not received finishing treatments, such as bleaching, shearing, brushing, embossing, or dyeing; unfinished fabrics.

group Coordinated apparel items using several colors and fabrics within an apparel line.

hand How a fabric feels to the touch.

haute couture Also sometimes referred to as couture, apparel in the highest price zone. This apparel is produced in small quantities, utilizes hand-sewing techniques, is sized to fit an individual's body dimensions, and uses very expensive fabrics and trims.

hide An animal pelt weighing more than 25 pounds when shipped to the tannery.

home fashions Textile products for home end uses such as towels, bedding, upholstery fabrics, area floor coverings, draperies, and table linens.

horizontally integrated Business strategy whereby a company focuses on a single stage of production/distribution but with varying products or services.

hypermarket see **superstore**.

importer/packager Company that develops full lines of apparel with contractors in other countries and sells them to retailers as complete packages for use as private-label merchandise.

information flow Communication among companies within the marketing channel pipeline.

initial cost estimate The preliminary estimate of the cost of a new style based on materials, trims, findings, labor, and other components such as duty and freight.

in-store shop Area within a department store that is merchandised according to manufacturers' specifications and carries only the merchandise of the manufacturer.

intensive distribution or **mass distribution** Strategy whereby products are made available to as many consumers as possible through a variety of retail venues.

internal selling Process used for private-label merchandise whereby a company's design team will present seasonal lines to merchandisers within the company who will select specific pieces of the line for production.

International Ladies' Garment Workers' Union (ILGWU) Formed in 1900, the primary union of garment workers in the women's apparel industry until 1995 when it combined with the Amalgamated Clothing and Textile Workers Union to form the Union of Needletrades, Industrial, and Textile Employees (UNITE).

item house Contractor that specializes in the production of one type of product such as baseball caps.

jobber An intermediary in the apparel industry who carries inventories of apparel for ready shipment to retailers.

kip Animal pelt weighing 15 to 25 pounds when shipped to the tannery.

knockoff A facsimile of an existing garment that sells at a lower price than the original. The copy might be made in a less expensive fabric and might have some design details modified or eliminated.

lab dip The vendor-supplied sample of the dyed-to-match product such as fabric, zipper, button, knit collar or cuff, or thread.

last A wood, plastic, or metal mold, shaped like a foot and used to form shoes.

lay figure see **croquis**.

leased department Contractual retail agreement whereby a retailer leases space within a large department store to run a specialty department. Typical leased departments are fine jewelry, furs, and shoes.

licensed brand name program see **controlled brand name program**.

licensing An agreement whereby the owner (licensor) of a particular image or design sells the right to use the image or design to another party, typically a manufacturer (licensee), for payment of royalties to the licensor.

licensor Company that has developed a well-known image (property) and sells the right to use the image to manufacturers to put on merchandise.

lifestyle merchandising Use of the appeal of the target customer's lifestyle choices, especially in product advertising.

limited liability Arrangement whereby owners of a company are liable only for the amount of capital they invested in the company but are not personally liable beyond that for debts incurred by the business.

Limited Liability Company (LLC) Form of company ownership that provides owners with the tax advantages of a partnership, along with the limited liability of a corporation.

limited marketing channel Marketing channel in which manufacturers sell their merchandise to consumers through retailers.

limited partnership A specialized type of partnership in which a partner is liable only for the amount of capital invested in the business, and any profits are shared according to the conditions of the limited partnership contract.

line One large group or several small groups of apparel items developed with a theme that links the items together.

line catalog or **line sheet** A brochure or catalog of all the styles and colorways available in the line, used to market the line to retail buyers.

line-for-line copy A garment made as an exact replica of an existing garment style, produced in a similar fabric.

line sheet see **line catalog**.

linens Towels, sheets, tablecloths, napkins, and other home textiles once made almost exclusively from linen. The term *linens* continues to be used, even though these products are rarely made from linen anymore.

long-range forecasting Research focusing on general economic and social trends related to consumer spending patterns and the business climate.

made-to-measure "A fully customized process where a garment is made specifically for one individual based on his/her measurements and preferences" (Made to measure or mass customization: Is it for You?," 1998, vol. 18, no. 1 *Cuttings*, p. 3, see Chapter 11).

mail order/catalog retailer Retail company that sells merchandise to consumers through catalogs, brochures, or advertisements, and delivers the merchandise by mail or other carrier.

manufacturer A company that performs all functions of creating, marketing, and distributing an apparel, accessory, or home fashions line on a continual basis. These companies may use outside contractors to perform the manufacturing function.

manufacturing environment Production circumstances including choice of production facility, location of production, production process, and cycle time to produce goods.

maquiladora "Assembly plants, mostly along the U.S.-Mexico border, in which garments are assembled from U.S.-cut parts and shipped back to the United States" (Dickerson, 1995, p. 189; see Chapter 10).

margin The difference between the cost to manufacture a style and the wholesale price the retailer will pay the manufacturer for the style. Margin can also refer to the difference between the cost the retailer paid the manufacturer for the goods and to the selling price for the goods.

marker A master cutting plan for all the pattern pieces in the sizes specified on the cut order to manufacture the style.

market 1) consumer demand for a product or service; 2) location where the buying and selling of merchandise takes place; 3) promote a product or service through media or public relations efforts.

market analysis Information about general market trends.

market center Name given to cities that not only house marts and showrooms, but also have important manufacturing and retailing industries, e.g., New York, Los Angeles, Dallas, Atlanta, Chicago.

market niche Specific segment of the retail trade determined by a combination of product type and target customer.

market research   Process of providing information to determine what the customer will need and want, and when and where the customer will want to make purchases.

market week   Time of the year in which retail buyers come to showrooms or exhibit halls to see the seasonal fashion lines offered by apparel companies.

marketing   Process of identifying a target market and developing appropriate strategies for product development, pricing, promotion, and distribution.

marketing channel or **marketing pipeline**   Sequence of companies that perform the manufacturing, wholesaling, and retailing functions to get merchandise to the ultimate consumer.

marketing channel integration   Process of connecting the various levels of the marketing channel so that they work together in getting the right product to the the right customer at the right price and the right place.

marketing pipeline   see **marketing channel**.

mart   Building or group of buildings that house showrooms in which sales representatives show merchandise lines to retail buyers.

mass customization   The use of computer technology to customize a garment style for the individual customer, by individualizing the fit to the customer's measurements, by offering individualized combinations of fabric, garment style, and size options, or by personalization of a finished product.

mass distribution   see **intensive distribution**.

mass production   Type of production in which identical apparel is made in large quantities using machines.

measurement specification   The actual garment measurements at specific locations on the finished goods for each of the sizes specified for a style.

merchandiser   1) An apparel company employee who is responsible for planning and overseeing to ensure that the company's needs for a line are met. This person often coordinates several lines presented by the company; 2) one who visually displays merchandise within a retail store (visual merchandiser).

merchandising   1) The process of buying and selling goods and services; 2) area of an apparel company that develops strategies to have the right merchandise, at the right price, at the right time, at the right locations to meet the wants and needs of the target customer.

merger   Blending of one company into another company.

millinery   Women's hats, and especially hat making that requires hand work.

modular manufacturing   A term often used in the U.S. apparel industry to describe flexible manufacturing (Hill, 1992, p. 34; see Chapter 11).

mohair   Natural fiber obtained from the wool of the Angora goat.

monopolistic competition   Competitive situation in which many companies compete in terms of product type, but the specific products of any one company are perceived as unique by consumers.

monopoly   Competitive situation in which there is typically one company that dominates the market and can thus price its goods and/or services at whatever scale its management wishes.

muffler   Long oblong scarf, often wool or silk often worn wrapped around the neck to provide added warmth.

multichannel distribution   Distribution strategy whereby a manufacturer offers merchandise through varying retail venues: bricks-and-mortar stores, catalogs, and/or Web sites.

multichannel retailing   Retail strategy whereby merchandise is offered through bricks-and-mortar stores, catalogs, and/or Web sites

multiline sales representative   Individual who sells lines from several non-competing but related companies to retail buyers.

multinational corporation   Private or publicly traded corporation that operates in several countries.

muslin   An inexpensive fabric, usually unbleached cotton, often used to develop the first trial of a new garment style.

napery or **table linens**   Home fashions products that include tablecloths and napkins.

nanotechnology   Technology that functions in the range of nanometers, one-billionth of a meter, with applications in enhanced manufacturing and the development of "smart" fibers.

national/designer brand   Brand name that is distributed nationally and to which consumers attach a specific image, quality level, and price.

nonstore retailer   Distributor of products to consumers through means other than bricks-and-mortar retail stores.

North American Industry Classification System (NAICS)   U.S. Department of Commerce categories and subcategories based on the company's chief industrial activity.

off-price retailer   Retailer who specializes in selling national brands or designer apparel and home fashions lines at discount prices.

offshore production   Production outside the United States using production specifications provided by U.S. companies.

oligopoly   Competitive situation in which a few companies dominate and essentially have control of the market, making it very difficult for other companies to enter.

oligopsony   Competitive situation that involves a large number of sellers offering goods and services to a small number of buyers.

open-distribution policy   Policy by which a company will sell to any retailer who meets basic characteristics.

ownership flow or **title flow**   Transfer of ownership or title of merchandise from one company to the next.

partnership   Company owned by two or more persons; operation of partnerships is outlined in a written contract or "articles of partnership."

patent   "Publicly given, exclusive right to an idea, product, or process" (Fisher & Jennings, 1991, p. 595; see Chapter 2).

pattern design system (PDS)   A computer hardware and software system that is used by the pattern maker to create and store new garment (pattern) styles.

pattern grading   see **grading**.

payment flow   Transfer of monies among companies as payment for merchandise or services rendered.

PDM/PLM   A term used when combining product data management and product life-cycle management. This approach requires all computer systems in the pipeline to be compatible in order to share product data.

pelt   The unshorn skin of an animal used in making leather and fur.

perfect competition   see **pure competition**.

personalization   The process of customizing a product for an individual consumer.

physical flow   Movement of merchandise from the manufacturer to the ultimate consumer.

piece-rate wage   Method of compensation whereby each production operator's pay is based on individual productivity, that is, specified task completed by the operator on the total number of units in a given time period.

popular fashion magazine   Magazine available for individual purchase or by subscription to consumers and typically read by the target customer.

power loom   Automated machine used to weave cloth. Francis Cabot Lowell invented the power loom in 1813.

preliminary line sheet   Page or pages of drawings of styles in a line used internally by a company in the process of line development.

preline   A preview of the line shown to key retail buyers prior to its introduction at market. These accounts may place orders in advance of market.

price averaging   A price strategy whereby one style will be priced to sell for less than the company's typical profit margin while another style in the same line will be priced to sell for more than the typical profit margin. The margin's gain and loss of the two styles are averaged.

price point or **price zone**   A price range that relates to the merchandise available in a given price range; designer, bridge, better, moderate, or mass.

price zone   see **price point**.

private corporation   Type of corporation whereby there is not a public market for the stock in the corporation and stock has not been issued for public purchase.

private-label brand   Brand name that is owned and marketed by a specific retailer for use in its stores. Private-label merchandise bears the retailer's label; the retailer has partial or full control over the manufacture of the product.

private-label product development or **store brand product development**   Development of new styles by retailers to sell in their retail stores under a store brand label or private label.

privately held corporation   See **private corporation**.

product data management (PDM) or product development management (PDM)   The integration of computer systems that link style information among departments within a company, and/or among external contacts such as vendors and contractors.

product development management (PDM)   see **product data management (PDM)**.

product lifecycle management (PLM)   Electronic access to style information throughout the design, development, production, and distribution processes within a company and by external contacts such as vendors and contractors.

product research   Information gathered by a company regarding preferred product design and product characteristics desired by a specific customer group.

product turn   The frequency rate at which a product is sold and replaced at the retail store.

product type   the specific category or categories of apparel the company specializes in producing.

production   The construction process by which the materials, trims, findings, and garment pieces are merged into a finished apparel product, accessory, or home fashion.

production cutting   Process in which the production fabric, laid open across its entire width and many feet in length, is stacked in multiple layers with the marker resting on the top, and cut by computer or by using hand-cutting machines.

production engineer   A specialist who is responsible for the production pattern and/or for planning the production process, facilities, and final costing.

production marker The full-size master cutting layout for all the pattern pieces for a specific style, for all the sizes specified for production.

progressive bundle system Groups of a dozen (usually) garment pieces placed in bundles and moved from one sewing operator to the next. Each operator performs one or several construction steps on each garment in the bundle, then passes the bundle on to the next operator.

promotion flow Flow of communication to promote merchandise either to other companies or to consumers in order to influence sales.

proprietary A contractual agreement between two parties (such as a textile company and an apparel manufacturer) that allows exclusive rights to the use of a product or process for a specified period of time.

prototype The sample garment for a new style in the company's base size made in the intended fashion fabric or a facsimile fabric. If made in muslin, the prototype is usually called a toile.

psychographics Information gathered about a target group's buying habits, attitudes, values, motives, preferences, personality, and leisure activities.

publicly held corporation Type of corporation whereby stock has been issued for public purchase and at least some of the shares of stock are owned by the general public.

publicly traded corporation see **publicly held corporation**.

publicity Promotional strategy whereby the company's activities are viewed as newsworthy and thus are featured or are mentioned in print, television, electronic, or other news media.

pull-down cutting The process of cutting gloves by die cutting the pieces.

pure competition or **perfect competition** Competitive situation in which there are many producers and consumers of similar products, so that price is determined by market demand.

quality assurance Area of a company that focuses on quality control issues but also takes into consideration satisfaction of consumer needs for a specific end use; standards of acceptance set forth by the contracting party (the apparel manufacturer, for example) for the product being produced.

quality control Area of a company that focuses on inspecting finished products and making sure they adhere to specific quality standards.

Quick Response (QR) Comprehensive business strategy that promotes responsiveness to consumer demand, encourages business partnerships, and shortens the business cycle from raw materials to the consumer.

quirk Tiny triangular gusset in gloves at the base of the second, third, and fourth fingers.

quota Limits on the number of units, kilograms, or square meters equivalent in specific categories that can be imported from specific countries.

rack trade Belt manufacturers who design, produce, and market belts to retailers.

radio-frequency identification (RFID) Tagging technology that utilizes a silicon computer chip. The chip is incorporated into containers, pallets, merchandise packaging, or individual items, and is used for purposes of accurate tracking of merchandise through production processes and the supply chain or to deter counterfeiting and shoplifting.

ready-to-wear (RTW) Apparel made with mass production techniques using standardized sizing; sometimes referred to as "off-the-rack."

regimental stripe Fabric used for men's ties with wide and narrow stripes that were used originally to signify the various historical military regiments.

registration For printed textiles with more than one color screen, specified placement for each of the screens to produce the multi-color print.

regional sales territory Geographic area assigned to be covered by a corporate or multiline sales representative.

regular corporation see **C corporation**.

regular tannery or **tannery** Tannery that buys skins and hides, performs tanning methods, and sells finished leather.

relationship merchandising An emphasis of retail stores on presentation, personal customer service, and having the right products for their target market that are different from the merchandise carried by other stores.

retail store/direct market brand A retail store whose merchandise carries the retail store name as its exclusive label.

retailer "Any business establishment that directs its marketing efforts toward the final consumer for the purpose of selling goods and services" (Lewison, 1994, p. 5; see Chapter 12).

retailing The "business activity of selling goods or services to the final consumer," (Lewison, 1994, p. 5, see Chapter 12).

Retro The return to the fashion look of recent decades (abbreviated use of the word *retrospective*).

S corporation Type of corporation that is given special status by the Internal Revenue Service in that earnings of the corporation are taxed only at the individual level.

sales representative Individual who serves as the intermediary between the manufacturer and the retailer, selling the apparel, accessories, or home fashions lines to retail buyers.

sales volume The actual level of sales, expressed as either the total number of units of a style that sold at retail or the total number of dollars consumers spent on the style.

salon de couture Haute couture designer's showroom.

sample see **duplicate**.

sample cut A three- to five-yard length of fabric ordered from a textile mill by the apparel manufacturer to use for making a prototype garment.

sample sewer A highly skilled technician who sews the entire prototype (sample) garment using a variety of sewing equipment and production processes similar to those used in factories.

sample sewing department The team of highly skilled technicians who cut and sew new style samples.

selected-distribution policy Policy by which a company establishes detailed criteria that stores must meet in order to carry the company's merchandise.

selective distribution Strategy whereby manufacturers allow their merchandise to be distributed only through certain stores.

sell through The percentage computed by the number of items sold at retail compared to the number of items in the line the retailer purchased from the manufacturer.

servicemark Trade name, symbol, or design used to identify a service that is offered for sale.

sew by see **counter sample**.

sewing machine Through inventions of Walter Hunt (1832), Elias Howe (1845), and Isaac Singer (1846), this machine made it possible for apparel to be made quickly and in factory settings.

shopping the market   Looking for new fashion trends in the retail markets that may influence the direction of an upcoming line.

short-cycle production   Mass production of goods that can be produced quickly. It is especially suited to high-fashion products that are produced close to their market demand.

short-range forecasting   Researching specific fashion trends and new styles for an upcoming season and determining the level of demand and timing for these styles (also referred to as what, when, and how much to manufacture).

showroom   Facility used by sales representatives to show samples of a line to retail buyers; may be permanent or temporary.

single-hand system   A garment production method in which an individual sewer is responsible for sewing an entire garment. It is used primarily for couture or very high-priced, limited-production apparel and for sewing prototypes.

size standards   Proportional increase or decrease in garment measurements for each size produced by a ready-to-wear apparel company.

skin   Animal pelt weighing 15 pounds or less when shipped to the tannery.

sloper   see **base pattern**.

Smart Card   Personal data, such as a customer's body measurements, stored on a computer-read card, about the size of a credit card, that is used for mass customization orders.

"smart" fiber   Optical fiber with integrated electronics that allow the fiber to sense, process, and store data, and which can be woven into fabric; applications include medical devices, high performance and protective fabrics, and military uniforms.

social responsibility   see **corporate responsibility**.

soft floor covering   Area rugs, runners, and scatter rugs, as well as wall-to-wall carpeting.

sole proprietorship   Company owned by a single individual.

source or **supplier** or **vendor**   Company from which textile producers, apparel manufacturers, or retailers purchase components or products necessary in their production and distribution operations (e.g. fiber sources, fabric sources, apparel product sources).

sourcing   Decision process of determining how and where a company's products or their components will be produced.

sourcing option   Alternative for how and where a company's products or their components will be produced; options include domestic or offshore production and in company-owned facilities and/or contracted to others.

specialty store   Retailer who focuses on a specific type of merchandise.

specification buying   Retailer-initiated design and manufacturing of apparel goods in which the retailer may work directly with the sewing contractors (or their agents) to produce store brand or private-label goods. Sometimes the retailer works with an apparel manufacturer to produce store brand or private-label goods.

spinning mill   Company that specializes in the spinning of yarn. The first spinning mill in the U.S. was opened in 1791 by Samuel Slater.

spreading   The process of unwinding the large rolls of fabric onto long, wide cutting tables, stacked layer-upon-layer, in preparation for cutting.

spreading machine   Equipment designed to carry the large rolls of fabric, guided on tracks along the side edges of the cutting table or rolled along the floor next to one side of the cutting table, to spread the fabric smoothly, and quickly onto the cutting table.

spun yarn Yarn created by the spinning together of short staple fibers.

staple color Color such as black, navy, white, gray, or tan that is used in a line that appears frequently, season after season.

stockholder Owner of stock or shares in a corporation; each share of stock owned by a stockholder represents a percentage of the company.

store brand see **direct market brand**.

store brand product development see **private-label product development**.

store-is-brand The retail outlet (store, catalog, Web site) and the apparel brand are one-and-the-same in the consumer's mind. Examples include Banana Republic, Old Navy, and Victoria's Secret.

strike off A length of sample yardage of a printed fabric, used to proof the colors and quality of the print.

style number A number (usually 4 to 6 digits) assigned to each garment style that is coded to indicate the season/year for the style and other style information.

submit Product submitted by vendor of a sample of the custom-dyed product (lab dip) that would be used if the vendor supplies the product.

Sundries and Apparel Findings Linkage Council (SAFLINC) Formed in 1987 to establish voluntary electronic data interchange standards between apparel manufacturers and their non-textile suppliers. In 1994, it was integrated into the Quick Response Committee of the [then] American Apparel Manufacturers Association.

supermarket Retailer who carries a full line of foods and related products using a self-service strategy.

superstore or **hypermarket** Upgraded large supermarkets that offer a wide range of merchandise including food, electronics, clothing and accessories, furniture, sporting goods, and garden items.

supplier see **source**.

supply chain management (SCM) "Collection of actions required to coordinate and manage all activities necessary to bring a product to market, including procuring raw materials, producing goods, transporting and distributing those goods and managing the selling process" (Abend, 1998, p. 48; see Chapter 1).

sustainable design A term used to designate the "awareness of the full short- and long-term consequences of a transformation of the environment" (DesignTex, 1995, p. 53; see Chapter 14).

swatch A small sample of the fabric intended to be used for a garment style.

sweatshop Company that violates labor, safety and health, and/or worker compensation laws, or that has work environments that are unsafe, inhumane, or abusive without providing opportunities for workers to organize or negotiate better terms of work.

table cutting The process of cutting gloves entirely by hand, on a work table.

table linens see **napery**.

tagboard A heavy-weight paper (also called oaktag or hard paper) used for pattern pieces instead of pattern paper.

tagless label Printed information such as care instructions, fiber content, and size, heat sealed directly onto the product.

takeover The result of one company or individual gaining control of another company by buying a large enough portion of the company's shares; can be either a merger or consolidation.

tannery see **regular tannery**.

tanning The process of finishing leather, making the skins and hides pliable and water resistant.

target costing   A pricing strategy in which the fabric cost and styling features are manipulated in order to provide a new style for a predetermined cost.

target customer   Description of the gender, age range, lifestyle, geographic location, and price zone for the majority of the company's customers for a specific line.

tariff   Tax assessed by governments on imports.

tawning   The process of finishing furs, making the pelts pliable and water resistant.

tech drawing   A drawing of the garment style as viewed flat rather than depicted three-dimensionally on a fashion figure (an abbreviation of the term *technical drawing*). It could include drawings of close-up details of the garment. A tech drawing might also be called a flat or a flat sketch.

terms of sale   Negotiated agreements between the manufacturer and retailer regarding the sale of merchandise; may include discounts, terms of delivery, availability of cooperative advertisements and other promotional tools.

textile   "Any product made from fibers" (Joseph, 1988, p. 347; see Chapter 3).

textile accessory and accent   Includes a wide variety of textile products for bedding, bath, tabletop accessories, kitchen, and textile accents such as wall hangings, tapestries, quilts, needlework, and lace accents.

Textile/Apparel Linkage Council (TALC)   Organization formed in 1986 to establish voluntary electronic data interchange standards between apparel manufacturers and textile companies. In 1994, it was integrated into the Quick Response Committee of the [then] American Apparel Manufacturers Association.

Textile/Clothing Technology Corporation [TC]²   Nonprofit corporation that develops, tests, and teaches advanced apparel technology.

textile converter   see **converter**.

textile jobber   Company that buys fabrics from textile mills, converters, and large manufacturers, and then sells to smaller manufacturers and retailers.

textile mill   Company that specializes in the fabric construction stage of production (e.g., weaving, knitting).

textile stylist   Individual who has expertise in the design and manufacturing of textiles as well as an understanding of the textile market and works directly with manufacturers and retailers in creating textile designs.

textile testing   "Process of inspecting, measuring and evaluating characteristics and properties of textile materials" (Cohen, 1989, p. 165; see Chapter 3).

thread count   Total number of yarns (warp plus weft) in one square inch of fabric.

throwster   Company that modifies filament yarns for specific end uses.

title flow   see **ownership flow**.

toile   A French term whose literal translation means cloth; refers to the muslin trial or sample garment.

tolerance   The stated range of acceptable dimensional measurements as a (+) or (−) in inches (or metric dimensions) of the size specifications.

top-of-the-bed   Home fashions products that includes comforters, duvet covers, blankets, bedspreads, dust ruffles, pillow shams, and throws.

trade association   Nonprofit association made up of member companies designed to research, promote, or provide educational services regarding an industry or a specific aspect of an industry.

trade dress   Subset of trademark law; protects the overall look or image of a product or the packaging of a product.

trade name   see **brand name**.

trade publication A publication such as a newspaper or magazine that is targeted to the trade, such as retailers, manufacturers, or textile producers, and generally is available by subscription or at some specialty book and magazine sellers.

trade show Event sponsored by trade associations, apparel marts, and/or promotional companies, to allow companies to promote their newest products to prospective buyers who have the opportunity of reviewing new products of a number of companies under one roof.

trademark "Distinctive name, word, mark, design, or picture used by a company to identify its product" (Fisher & Jennings, 1991, p. 595; see Chapter 2).

trademark infringement Illegal use of a trademark or servicemark; use without the permission of the owner of the trademark or servicemark.

trank The section of a glove that covers the palm and the face of the hand.

trend research Information on future directions of consumer behavior, color, fabrics, and fashion styling obtained by reading trade publications and/or fashion magazines, making observations, or other data collection methods.

trunk show Marketing strategy by which a company will bring an entire line to a retail store as a special event to show and sell to customers.

unit production system (UPS) Production system whereby the parts for each garment are transported as a unit on a conveyor track, one garment at a time, to the sewing operator who performs one or several sewing operations, and then releases the garment for transport to the next work station.

Universal Product Code (UPC) One of several bar-code symbologies used for electronic identification of merchandise. A UPC is a 12-digit number that identifies the manufacturer and merchandise item by stockkeeping unit.

unlimited liability Situation in which owners of a company are personally liable for debts incurred by the business; often the case in sole proprietorships and in some partnerships.

upholstery fabric Textiles used primarily for covering sofas, love seats, chairs, and ottomans.

usage The number of yards (yardage) of fabric(s) required to make the garment style. It usually denotes the most economical layout to use the least amount of fabric.

vendor see **source**.

vendor-managed inventory (VMI) Programs whereby retail sales/stockout data are reviewed by the manufacturer and replenishments are ordered as often as required.

vendor marking Affixing hangtags, labels, and price information to merchandise by the vendor (manufacturer).

vertical integration or **vertical marketing channel** Business strategy whereby a company handles several steps in production and/or distribution.

vertical marketing channel see **vertical integration**.

vertically integrated see **vertical integration**.

virtual draping Computer-created simulation of a fabric draped three-dimensionally over an image of a garment as shown on a body or mannequin.

virtual sample Digital images of merchandise samples that are viewed on the computer screen.

Voluntary Interindustry Commerce Standards (VICS) Association Formed in 1986 as the Voluntary Interindustry Communications Standards Committee.

It initially focused on voluntary standards for product and shipping container marking. The association has now expanded into standards for floor-ready merchandise and Internet commerce.

Voluntary Interindustry Communications Standards (VICS) Committee see **Voluntary Interindustry Commerce Standards (VICS) Association**.

wall covering Products such as textiles used to cover walls, vertical panels, and partitions.

warehouse retailer Retailer who reduces operating expenses and offers goods at discount prices by combining showroom, warehouse, and retail operations.

wholesale cost see **cost**.

wholesale price The price of the style that the retailer will pay the apparel manufacturer for the goods. The price is based on the manufacturer's cost to produce the style plus the manufacturer's profit.

window treatment Draperies, curtains, and fabric shades as well as decorative treatments such as valances, cornices, and swags.

wool Natural fiber derived from the fleece of sheep, goats, alpacas, and llamas.

work-in-process (WIP) The quantity of goods in the process of assembly in the sewing factory at a given time.

yarn Collection of fibers or filaments laid or twisted together to form a continuous strand strong enough for use in fabrics.

zeitgeist The social spirit of the time of a popular culture during a specific time frame.

Photo and Text Credits

Chapter 1

1.1: © Bettmann/Corbis.

1.2: © Bettmann/Corbis.

1.3: © Bettmann/Corbis.

1.4: © Bettmann/Corbis.

1.5: © Bettmann/Corbis.

1.6: © Bettmann/Corbis.

1.7: © Bettmann/Corbis.

1.8: © Bettmann/Corbis.

1.9: © Bettmann/Corbis.

1.10: © Bettmann/Corbis.

1.11: © Bettmann/Corbis.

1.12: © Reuters/Corbis.

1.13: © 2007 E. I. du Pont de Nemours and Company.

1.14: Images courtesy of [TC]^2, Gary, NC, USA (www.tc2.com).

1.16: Crafted with Pride in USA Council.

1.17: © A3508 Rolf Vennenbernd/dpa/Corbis.

1.18: © Ashley Cooper/Corbis.

Chapter 2

2.1: (left, top) Courtesy of Wellman, Inc.; (left, bottom) The Levi's Tab Device® is a Registered Trademark of Levi Strauss & Co.; (right, top) The Nike and Swoosh Design are Registered Trademarks of Nike, Inc.; (right, center) Courtesy of Crate and Barrel; (right, bottom) Courtesy of Invista.

2.2: Courtesy of Hanna Andersson.

2.3: Mark Mainz/Getty Images for IMG.

2.4: (left) Getty Images; (right) Nicholas Roberts/Reuters/Landov.

2.5: (left) TENCEL® Lyocell is a registered trademark of Lenzing Fibers; (center) The Nike and Swoosh Design are Registered Trademarks of Nike; (right) Courtesy of Guess?, Inc.

2.6: © Levi Strauss & Co.

2.8: © Theodore Scott/istockphoto.

Chapter 3

3.1: *Apparel Manufacturing* by Gluck/Kunz © 2000, reprinted by permission of Pearson Education, Inc., Upper Saddle River, NJ 07458.

3.2: Ryan McVay/Stone/Getty Images.

3.3: AP Photo/Elliott Minor.

3.4: Harry Sheridan/Photonica/Getty Images.

3.5: Reprinted by permission of Cotton Incorporated.

3.6: Reproduced with the kind permission of the Woolmark Company.

3.7: Courtesy of The Mohair Council of America.

3.8: Reprinted by permission of Cotton Incorporated.

3.10: Courtesy of The Color Association of the United States.

3.11: (all) Courtesy Pendleton Woolen Mills.

3.12: © 2006 Photo Researchers.

3.14: Courtesy of Leslie Burns.

3.15: American Textile Manufacturers Institute.

3.16: © Lectra (www.lectra.com).

3.17: *Spring 2005 Saks Fifth Avenue Catalog*, page 63, provided courtesy of Saks Fifth Avenue.

3.18: Courtesy of Foss Manufacturing LLC. Foss Manufacturing LLC has the exclusive right to use the Ecospun® trademark and logo. They are the only licensed manufacturer of Ecospun® fiber.

Chapter 4

4.1: Chris Moore/Catwalking/Getty Images.

4.3: © Levi Strauss & Co.

4.4: Justin Sullivan/Getty Images.

4.5: © Cathrine Wessel/Corbis.

4.7: Courtesy of Nancy Bryant.

4.8: Courtesy of Eton Systems Inc. (www.eton.se).

4.9: Courtesy of Diesel S.p.A. Reproduced with permission of Diesel S.p.A.

4.10: © Peter Foley/epa/Corbis.

4.11: (top, left and right; bottom, right) Courtesy of Fairchild Publications, Inc.; (bottom, left) Copyright 2007, NRF Enterprises, Inc. Used with permission.

Chapter 5

5.1: Courtesy Pendleton Woolen Mills.

5.2: © Kim Kennedy

5.3: Courtesy of Patagonia, Inc.

5.4: (left) Courtesy of Fairchild Publications, Inc., © J. Acquino; (center) Courtesy of Fairchild Publications, Inc., © George Chinsee; (right) Courtesy of Fairchild Publications, Inc., © Tom Iannaccone.

5.5: (all) Courtesy of Condé Nast Publications.

5.6: Courtesy of The Color Association of the United States.

6.2: Courtesy of Columbia Sportswear Company.

6.3: (top, left) National Museum of American History/Smithsonian Institution/Behring Center; (top, right) The private collection of Joanne Bergen at www.artophile.com; (bottom, left & right) Getty Images.

6.4: (left) Courtesy of the Staten Island Historical Society; (center) Courtesy of Fairchild Publications, Inc. © Robert Mitra; (right) Getty Images.

6.5: (left) The Royal Collection © 2000, Her Majesty Queen Elizabeth II; (right) Courtesy of Fairchild Publications, Inc.

6.6: Chris Moore/Catwalking/Getty Images.

6.7: Bill Ivy/Ivy Images.

6.8: Courtesy of Lacoste.

6.9: (all) Laura Soares Signature line 2007 (www.LauraSoares.com).

6.11: (all) Courtesy of Fairchild Publications.

6.12: © Marianne Egan/College of Health and Human Sciences, Oregon State University.

6.13: Courtesy of SML Sport.

6.14: © Freeboarders.

6.15: Courtesy of SnapFashun®.

6.16: © Gerber Technology, Inc. (www.gerbertechnology.com).

6.17: © Lectra (www.lectra.com).

6.18: © 2001 By Cornell Capa/Magnum Photos.

6.19: © Bettman/Corbis.

6.20: © Krystal Ng.

7.2: Courtesy Pendleton Woolen Mills.

7.3: Courtesy of Nancy Bryant.

7.4: © Gerber Technology, Inc. (www.gerbertechnology.com).

7.5: © Gerber Technology, Inc. (www.gerbertechnology.com).

7.6: © Chuck Savage/Corbis.

7.7: © Gerber Technology, Inc. (www.gerbertechnology.com).

7.8: © Attal Serge/Corbis Sygma.

7.9: Courtesy of Nancy Bryant.

7.10: © Lectra (www.lectra.com).

7.11: Courtesy of Nancy Bryant.

7.13: John M. Miller/Getty Images.

Chapter 8

8.1: Courtesy of the Bobbin Group.

8.3: Courtesy of Fairchild Publications, Inc.

8.4: Courtesy of Fairchild Publications, Inc.

8.5: © studio55/maxximages.com.

8.6: Bryan Bedder/Getty Images for IMG.

8.7: (all) Courtesy of Fairchild Publications, Inc., © Tyler Boye.

8.8: Courtesy of Photo Ops, Inc.

8.9: © Vince LaMonica/vjlphoto.com.

8.10: © Kristina Bowman/Courtesy of Fairchild Publications, Inc.

8.11: (all) Courtesy of Photo Ops, Inc.

8.12: Scott Olson/Getty Images.

8.13: © Lectra (www.lectra.com).

8.14: © Lectra (www.lectra.com).

8.15: Steve Eichner/Courtesy of Fairchild Publications, Inc.

Chapter 9

9.1: © Lectra (www.lectra.com).

9.2: © Lectra (www.lectra.com).

9.4: Courtesy of Nancy Bryant/Fairchild Publications, Inc.

9.5: Courtesy of Kristen Sandberg.

9.6: Courtesy of Kristen Sandberg.

9.7: Courtesy of Union Special Technical Training Centre.

9.8: © Gerber Technology, Inc. (www.gerbertechnology.com).

9.9: Courtesy of Nancy Bryant.

9.10: © Gerber Technology, Inc. (www.gerbertechnology.com).

9.11: © Lectra (www.lectra.com).

9.12: © Lectra (www.lectra.com).

9.13: © Lectra (www.lectra.com).

9.14: © Lectra (www.lectra.com).

9.15: © Lectra (www.lectra.com).

Chapter 10

10.3: Maurizio Pracella.

10.4: Robert Nickelsberg/Time & Life Pictures/Getty Images.

10.5: Courtesy of Nike, Inc.

10.6: AP Photo/Ric Francis.

10.7: (left) CP/© Rex Features (2005) all rights reserved; (right) © Tomas Bravo/ Reuters/Corbis.

10.8: © Alison Wright/Corbis.

Chapter 11

11.1: © 1994 by The New York Times Company.

11.2: Human Solutions GmbH.

11.3: © Lectra (www.lectra.com).

11.4: Miguel Alvarez/AFP/Getty Images.

11.5: Courtesy of Eton Systems Inc. (www.eton.se).

11.7: © Lectra (www.lectra.com).

11.8: Images courtesy of [TC]^2, Gary, NC, USA (www.tc2.com).

11.9: Courtesy of Insta Graphic Systems (www.instagraph.com).

11.10: AP Photo/Reed Saxon.

Chapter 12

12.1: © William Taufic/Corbis.

12.2: (all) Courtesy of Fairchild Publications Inc.

12.4: © James Leynse/Corbis.

12.5: Borgman © 1999 The Cincinnati Enquirer. Reprinted by permission of Universal Press Syndicate. All rights reserved.

12.6: Photo courtesy of Dillard's, Inc.

12.7: CP/AP Photo/Ted S. Warren.

12.8: Courtesy of Fairchild Publications Inc.

12.9: Courtesy of Ross Stores.

12.10: Joe Raedle/Getty Images.

12.11: Redux.

12.12: Getty Images for QVC.

Chapter 13

13.1: Ernest Washington/DK Stock/Getty Images.

13.2: Courtesy of Fairchild Publications, Inc., © George Chinsee & David Turner.

13.3: © Gail Mooney/Corbis.

13.4: © Stephanie Maze/Corbis.

13.5: Courtesy of Nike, Inc.

13.6: Bettmann/Corbis.

13.7: Scott Wintrow/Getty Images for the Miami Group.

13.8: Bill Ivy.

13.9: Chris Moore/Catwalking/Getty Images.

13.10: Dave King/Dorling Kindersley/Getty Images.

13.11: Brad Barket/Getty Images for IMG.

13.12: Lukas Creter/Stone/Getty Images.

13.13: Pascal Le Segretain/Getty Images.

13.14: Trish Lease/Getty Images.

13.15: Robert Mora/Getty Images.

13.16: Dorling Kindersley/Getty Images.

13.17: Jamie Grill/Stone/Getty Images.

13.18: Courtesy of Fairchild Publications, Inc.

Chapter 14

14.1: Nancy Ostertag/Getty Images.

14.2: Bill Ivy.

14.3: Virgil Smithers/Fieldcrest Cannon.

14.4: Kazuhiro Nogi/AFP/Getty Images.

14.5: Image from Vision Carpet Studio™ by NedGraphics BV.

14.6: Reprinted by permission of Cotton Incorporated.

14.7: Courtesy of George Little Management, LLC photo library, photographed by The Photo Group.

14.8: Courtesy of Fairchild Publications, Inc.

14.9: Bill Ivy.

14.10: Courtesy of Milliken & Company.

14.11: D. Trask/Ivy Images.

14.13: Bill Ivy.

14.14: Bill Ivy.

14.15: Bill Ivy.

14.16: Bill Ivy.

14.17: John Kalil/Bloomberg News/Landov.

14.18: © Pitchal Frederic/Corbis Sygma.

14.19: Ellis Lucia/Newhouse News Service/Landov.

Color Plates

1: Courtesy of SML Sport.

2: Courtesy of The Color Association of the United States.

3: Courtesy of Chris Jackson.

4: Courtesy of Global Sources (www.globalsources.com).

5: Courtesy of Nancy Bryant.

6: © Gerber Technology, Inc. (www.gerbertechnology.com).

7: Tim Boyle/Getty Images.

8: Courtesy of Patagonia, Inc.

9: Courtesy Pendleton Woolen Mills.

10: © Lectra (www.lectra.com).

11: © Gerber Technology, Inc. (www.gerbertechnology.com).

12: (all) Courtesy Coldwater Creek, Inc. (www.coldwatercreek.com).

TEXT CREDITS

Table 10.6

The United Nations is the author of the original material. Used with permission.

Table 10.10

Levi Strauss & Co.

Table 10.11

Levi Strauss & Co.

Table 10.12

JCPenny: from "Supplier Programs/Legal Compliance" at www.jcpenney.net/company/supplier/legal/index.htm [July 21, 2007].

Chapter 10, page 421, Success Story

Copyright 2007, NRF Enterprises, Inc. Used with permission.

Chapter 11, page 457, Success Story

Copyright 2007, NRF Enterprises, Inc. Used with permission.